THE
THOMPSON
CHAIN-REFERENCE

BIBLE
SURVEY

THE
THOMPSON
CHAIN-REFERENCE®
BIBLE
SURVEY

HOWARD A. HANKE

WORD BOOKS
PUBLISHER
4800 WEST WACO DRIVE
WACO, TEXAS
76703

Dedicated to my wife,
Hazel K. Hanke,
and to our children,
George, Katherine, Ilka, and *Raymond*

Abbreviations

ABC—*Abingdon Bible Commentary.* New York: Abingdon-Cokesbury, 1929.

Ant.—William Whiston, trans. *Josephus Complete Works.* Grand Rapids: Kregel Publications, 1963.

Arch.—Archaeology.

ASV—American Standard Version

CBC—Adam Clarke. *Clarke's Bible Commentary.* New York: Abingdon-Cokesbury, n.d.

Ch.—Chapter, refers to another chapter in this book.

DDB—John D. Davis. *Davis Dictionary of the Bible.* Grand Rapids: Baker Book House, 1973.

EA—*Encyclopedia Americana.* New York: Americana Corporation, 1957.

EHB—*Eerdmans' Handbook of the Bible.* Ed. David Alexander and Pat Alexander. Grand Rapids: Wm. B. Eerdmans Co., 1973.

ER—*Encyclopedia of Religion.* Ed. Vergilius Ferm. New York: The Philosophical Library, 1945.

HBD—Madeleine S. Miller and J. Lane Miller. *Harper's Bible Dictionary.* New York: Harper and Brothers, 1954.

HBH—Henry H. Halley. *Halley's Bible Handbook.* Grand Rapids: Zondervan Publishing House, 1962.

ISBE—*International Standard Bible Encyclopedia.* Grand Rapids: Wm. B. Eerdmans Co., 1959.

JEDP—See Ch. 7, I, p. 73f.

KJV—King James Version

NBC—*New Bible Commentary.* Ed. F. Davidson, A. M. Stibbs, and E. F. Kevan. Grand Rapids: Wm. B. Eerdmans Co., 1953.

NIV—New International Version

NT—New Testament

OT—Old Testament

RSV—Revised Standard Version

SBD—William Smith. *Smith's Bible Dictionary.* Old Tappan, N.J.: Fleming H. Revell, 1977.

TCRB—*Thompson Chain-Reference Bible.* 4th ed. Indianapolis: B. B. Kirkbride Bible Co., 1964.

TMC—*The Modern Commentary.* New York: Grosset and Dunlop, 1935.

TSB—*The Story of the Bible.* New York: Wm. H. Wise and Co., 1952.

TWBC—*The Wesleyan Bible Commentary.* Grand Rapids: Wm. B. Eerdmans Co., 1967; reprinted Grand Rapids: Baker Book House, 1978.

TWBE—*The World Book Encyclopedia,* 1975.

WBC—*Wycliff Bible Commentary.* Chicago: Moody Press, 1962.

WBE—*Wycliff Bible Encyclopedia.* Ed. Charles F. Pfeiffer and Everett F. Harrison. Chicago: Moody Press, 1975.

ZPEB—*The Zondervan Pictorial Encyclopedia of the Bible.* Grand Rapids: Zondervan Publishing House, 1975.

Scripture references in this study are all based on the fourth edition of the *Thompson Chain-Reference Bible.*

Contents

Illustrations

Note: Unless otherwise indicated in
text, all photos are by author.

Acknowledgments

The author owes a debt of gratitude to:
1. Ruth Lashbrook, Professor of English at Asbury College, for checking grammatical construction, sources, and biblical references.
2. Hazel K. Hanke, for typing this manuscript.
3. George A. Turner, Professor of English Bible at Asbury Theological Seminary, for checking the sections dealing with Theology and Archaeology.
4. Dr. Kenneth L. Swank and David J. Metzger for pictures of Nineveh.
5. The following publishers for permission to quote from copyrighted materials:

Abingdon-Cokesbury Press.
   Abingdon Bible Commentary.
Augsburg Press:
   Alvin N. Rogness: *The Land of Jesus.*
Baker Book House:
   Gleason L. Archer: *Jerome's Commentary on Daniel.*
   John D. Davis, Ed. *Davis Dictionary of the Bible.*
   Robert Gromacki, *New Testament Survey.*
   Thea B. van Halsema, *Safari for Seven.*
   Twentieth Century Encyclopedia of Religious Knowledge
   Charles W. Carter, Gen.Ed. *The Wesleyan Bible Commentary.*
Beacon Hill Press (Nazarene Publishing Co.)
   W. T. Purkiser, *Exploring Our Christian Faith.*
   _____, *Exploring the Old Testament.*
   _____, *Know Your Old Testament.*
Doubleday and Co.
   Theodore Gaster: *The Dead Sea Scrolls.*
Epworth Press.
Wesley's Explanatory Notes of the New Testament.
Fleming H. Revell Co.
   S. I. Macmillan, *None of These Diseases.*
   William Smith, *Smith's Bible Dictionary.*
Harcourt, Brace and Co.
   Clive S. Lewis, *Reflections on the Psalms.*
Harper and Brothers.
   Madeleine S. and J. Lane Miller, Editors, *Harper's Bible Dictionary.*
   Clarence T. Craig, *The Universal Church in God's Design.*
   Robert H. Pfeiffer, *Introduction to the Old Testament.*
Macmillan Company.
   Andri Dupont-Sommer, *The Jewish Sect of Qumran and the Essenes.*
Moody Press.
   James Boreland, *Christ in the Old Testament.*
   Charles F. Pfeiffer and Howard F. Vos, *The Wycliff Historical Geography.*

Acknowledg-
ments
Ruth Saxe: *Studies in Hebrews.*
Charles F. Pfeiffer, Howard F. Vos and John Rea, Editors, *Wycliff Bible Encyclopedia.*
W. W. Norton and Co.
Charles Darwin, *The Autobiography of Charles Darwin.*
Prentice-Hall, Inc.
Howard Key, Franklin Young and Karlfried Froehlich, *Understanding the New Testament.*
Philosophical Library.
Vergilius Ferm, Editor. *Encyclopedia of Religion.*
William B. Eerdmans Publishing Co.
D. Guthrie, et al, *The New Bible Commentary.*
James Orr, Editor. *The International Standard Bible Encyclopedia.*
Merrill C. Tenney, *New Testament Survey.*
Erich Sauer, *The Dawn of World Redemption.*
_____, *From Eternity to Eternity.*
_____, *The Triumph of the Crucified.*
Viking Press.
Theodore Gaster, *The Dead Sea Scrolls.*
Zondervan Publishing House
A. R. Fausset, *Bible Encyclopedia and Dictionary.*
Robert H. Gundry, *A Survey of the New Testament.*
Henry H. Halley: *Halley's Bible Handbook.*
Gustav Oehler, *Theology of the Old Testament.*
Merrill C. Tenney, Editor. *Zondervan Pictorial Encyclopedia of the Bible.*

Journals

Time Magazine, Sept. 5, 1955, "Dead Sea Jewels."
Christianity Today. Exploring New Testament Backgrounds.
A Special Survey of the New Testament Books presented by *Christianity Today.* n.d., *Christian Advocate,* Aug. 22, 1968, "The Apostles' creed says it best."
6. The following authors:
Wallace A. Alcorn, David Alexander, Pat Alexander, Henry A. Appenzeler, Gleason L. Archer, James D. Bales, Edward M. Blaiklock, Harvey J. S. Blaney, Edgar J. Banks, Stephen Barabas, James Boreland, W. Russell Bowie, Wick Broomall, Charles S. Browder, F. F. Bruce, Millar Burrows, Cannon R. J. Campbell, Charles W. Carter, William O. Carver, Shirley J. Case, John Chennick, E. Betram Clagg, Adam Clark, Walter G. Clippenter, S. Maxwell Coder, Robert O. Coleman, Leo G. Cox, Clarence T. Craig, Frank M. Cross, Arthur E. Cundall, Charles Darwin, John D. Davis, J. Newton Davies, T. Wilton Davies, Percy Dearmer, D. D. Deere, Franz J. Delitzsch, Robert B. Demsey, C. Fred Dickason, Charles H. Dodd, Huber L. Drumwright, Handley Dunelm, Walter M. Dunnett, Ralph Earle, Frederick C. Eiselen, E. Earl Ellis, Norton S. Enslin, Joseph S. Exell, A. R. Fausset, Charles L. Feinberg, Adam F. Findley, Hobart E. Freeman, Karlfried Froehlich, Ward W. Gasque, Theodore Gaster, Norman L. Goddard, William C. Graham, Frederick C. Grant, J. Harold Greenlee, J. Kenneth Grider, Henry R. Gummy, Robert Gundry, Donald Guthrie, Lee Haines, Bert H. Hall, Henry H. Halley, Ralston Halmer, Paul H. Halsel, Thea B. van Halsema, E. Cuyler Hammond, Howard A. Hanke, R. K. Harrison, Thomas Hastings, Darlmus A. Hays, Andrew R. Helmbold,

D. Edward Hiebert, A. M. Hodgkin, Fenton J. A. Hort, W. S. Hottel, *Acknowledg-*
Jasper Huffman, Clyde T. Hurst, John Hutchinson, William I. Irons, *ments*
Nathan Isaacs, James Iversch, S. Lewis Johnson, Daniel B. Judah,
Earl S. Kalland, Howard C. Key, R. Allen Killen, Dennis F. Kinlaw,
Weldon D. Klopfenstein, Harold B. Kuhn, J. C. Lambert, Robert
Law, Herbert C. Leopold, Adelaide L. Lewis, Cline L. Lewis, Jack
P. Lewis, George H. Livingston, Edward Lueker, Iris McCord,
A. H. McDonald, S. I. Macmillen, Allan A. Mac Rae, J. Gresham
Machen, Alfred Martin, William P. Merrill, J. Lane Miller, Madeline
S. Miller, Wilhelm Mohler, Wilhelm Moller, James Montgomery,
William G. Moorehead, Conrad H. Muehlman, Jack J. Muller, John
M. Neale, Roy S. Nicholson, William E. Nix, John Nuelsen, Gustav
Oehler, W. O. E. Oesterley, Lewis L. Orlin, James Orr, Frederick
Owen, William Pauck, J. Barton Payne, Larman M. Peterson,
Charles F. Pfeiffer, Robert H. Pfeiffer, Clark H. Pinnock, W. T.
Purkiser, George Tybout Purvis, William H. Ramsey, John Rea,
Thomas Rees, Claude A. Reis, A. T. Robertson, Benjamin W. Robin-
son, George L. Robinson, James A. Robinson, Alvin R. Rogers, Alex-
ander Ross, M. Rowton, Tryannus Rufinnus, John Rutherford,
Charles C. Ryrie, Karl S. Sabiers, John R. Sampey, Erich Sauer,
Ruth Saxe, George H. Schodde, D. Russell Scott, Samuel J. Schultz,
R. Dykes Shaw, A. B. Simpson, Charles Slemming, Stephen J. Smal-
ley, Elmer B. Smick, Charles S. Smith, Ralph L. Smith, Wilbur
M. Smith, William Smith, N. H. Snaith, Alan S. Stibbs, Nathan J.
Stone, Andri Dupont-Summer, Merrill C. Tenney, J. E. H. Thomp-
son, R. Dwane Thompson, George A. Turner, Rollin H. Walker,
W. L. Walker, Bruce D. D. Waltke, Benjamin B. Warfield, Walter
W. Wassel, Herbert Welch, John Wesley, Henry Wheeler, William
White, Jr., Thomas Whitelaw, Charles R. Wilson, Robert McL. Wil-
son, Herbert W. Wolf, Martin J. Wyngaarden, Edward J. Young,
Franklin W. Young, Pere de Vaux, Howard Vos.

13

Foreword

Most textbooks and study guides on the Bible give limited treatment to the fundamental backgrounds from which the Bible and its institutions developed. Seldom do writers deal comprehensively with the essential aspects of salvation in the Old Testament. Some authors mention but do not elaborate on how the preexistent Christ is related to the redemptive process in the Old Covenant and what the functional mechanics were for bringing the people in the Old Testament under the blood of the Redeemer.

It is the purpose of this book to deal more thoroughly with the overall redemptive pattern and to supplement and expand many of the topics in the *Thompson Chain-Reference Bible*, based on archaeological participation and study workshops in the Bible lands during the last thirty years.

This study guide is designed to be used as an Old and New Testament survey text. Included in this study are chapters on the practical use of the Thompson Chain-Reference® Bible system; the origin and growth of the Bible, tracing its development from the earliest manuscripts to the most recent versions; the canonization of the Bible; a comparative analysis of revealed religion in both the Old and New Testaments; the transmission of the Bible; the development of worship centers from the primitive stone altars to the modern church; Hebrew times, seasons, and festivals; the titles or names of God in the Bible; types of religious officials in the Bible; God's plan of salvation from Genesis to Revelation; the covenant community in the Old Testament; a Christological study of the tabernacle in the Wilderness; the political and religious events between the testaments; the Christian era and a study of Christology in both the Old and New Covenants.

In addition, Dr. Hanke has written a survey of each of the sixty-six books of the Bible. This work is well documented. It has indices of authors, scripture references, and subjects, and is illustrated with scores of pictures taken by the author in all areas of the Bible lands.

The author gives recognition to the critical-liberal views of Bible study, but maintains a conservative Bible-centered stand in matters of Bible interpretation.

This work is presented to the Bible-reading public as a source book on the Bible as well as biblical backgrounds. The several comprehensive indices and the marginal annotations with cyclopedic numbers facilitate the use of the materials presented, and may be used with or without the Thompson Chain-Reference Bible; however, the maximum benefit will be derived when the two are used together.

THE PUBLISHERS

The Thompson Chain-Reference Bible was the culmination of the scholarly research begun by Frank C. Thompson, Ph.D., and his wife in 1890. Dr. Thompson brought to his task a deep spiritual love of the Scriptures and a passionate desire to make the Bible a living Book to even the most humble lover of God's Word. His sincerity and scholarly efforts, based on the belief that the Bible is God's infallible Word, are mirrored in every page.

With the passing of years, new Bible insights and information have become available, especially in the area of biblical archaeology. With these new developments, each of the four editions has included new data as well as additional features and helps.

The Thompson Chain-Reference Bible—Fourth Improved Edition—edited by Dr. Frank Thompson has appeared on the national best-seller lists. Thousands of people have recognized the outstanding value of this Bible down through the years. Its fifty-seven unique features are found helpful by ministers, teachers, students—all who love the Word! Marginal references connected with eight departments of helps include (1) Text Encyclopedia; (2) Special Bible Readings; (3) Outline Studies of the Bible; (4) Studies of Prominent Bible Characters; (5) Bible Harmonies and Illustrated Studies; (6) Archaeological Supplement; (7) Revised Concordance; and (8) Colored Bible Atlas with Index. It is truly a biblical library in one single volume.

16   The *Thompson Chain-Reference Bible Survey* will stimulate Bible study and further the reader's understanding of the Word of God.

Part I

Preliminary Matters

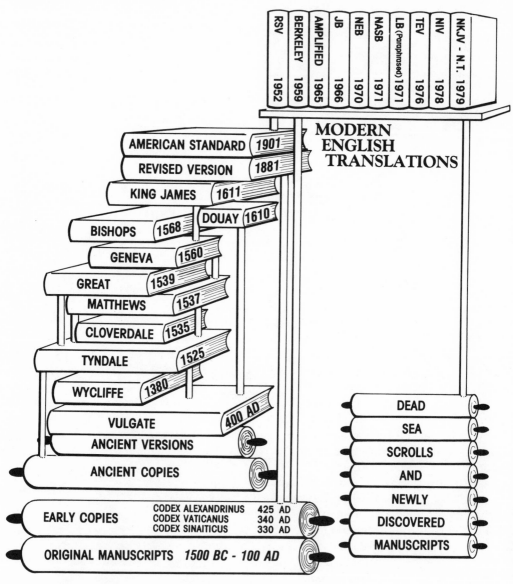

RSV	BERKELEY	AMPLIFIED	JB	NEB	NASB	LB (Paraphrased)	TEV	NIV	NKJV - N.T.
1952	1959	1965	1966	1970	1971	1971	1976	1978	1979

MODERN ENGLISH TRANSLATIONS

AMERICAN STANDARD	1901
REVISED VERSION	1881
KING JAMES	1611
BISHOPS	1568
DOUAY	1610
GENEVA	1560
GREAT	1539
MATTHEWS	1537
CLOVERDALE	1535
TYNDALE	1525
WYCLIFFE	1380
VULGATE	400 AD

ANCIENT VERSIONS

ANCIENT COPIES

EARLY COPIES
CODEX ALEXANDRINUS 425 AD
CODEX VATICANUS 340 AD
CODEX SINAITICUS 330 AD

ORIGINAL MANUSCRIPTS 1500 BC - 100 AD

DEAD
SEA
SCROLLS
AND
NEWLY
DISCOVERED
MANUSCRIPTS

Revised chart in 1979, Courtesy Back to the Bible Broadcast

1

The Origin and Growth of the Bible

I. THE FORMATIVE PERIOD OF THE BIBLE

The chart on page 180 of the TCRB Helps gives a perspective of Bible development from the most ancient manuscripts to the more recent English versions. Most of the extant Bible manuscripts are either papyrus sheets or parchment. Papyrus paper was used in Egypt for about as long a period as clay tablets were used in the Mesopotamian area. The papyrus material was more practical than clay tablets because sheets could be sewn together into continuous rolls, or made into a codex or bound book of sheets. The early manuscripts listed in the chart are either papyrus or parchment.

Origin and Growth of Bible **4220** *

Papyrus writing material was made from the papyrus reed growing along the Nile River. The bark was peeled off and the pithy interior sliced and pressed into thin strips; then the strips were laid criss-cross and pressed under heavy flat slabs of stone. (See Ch. 4, III.)

Parchment was invented in Pergamos about 190 B.C. as an emergency measure when Egypt placed an embargo on papyrus export. The Egyptian pharaoh feared that the library in Pergamos would excel the library in Alexandria. Scrolls made from parchment were used extensively until the codex or page form of book was invented in about A.D. 300. The extant ancient manuscripts are copies of copies of the autographs. All the manuscripts were handwritten and duplicated by scribes, usually under a reader; each scribe wrote down slowly what the

Pergamos **2736**

Arch. Alexandria **4325**

---

* Bold face numbers in margin throughout refer to article numbers in Helps section of the *Thompson Chain-Reference Bible.*

reader read. The number of copies that could be produced
at one time was limited only by the number of scribes in the
copying room. Brushes, pointed quills, and reeds were used
as writing instruments.

The first great advance in printing came when Johannes Gutenberg in Germany made clay molds in which to form lead
type. His first printed book was a Latin Bible completed on
15 August 1456. Two hundred copies were printed, of which
only fifty are still in existence. No change occurred in printing
until 1884 when Ottmar Mergenthaler invented and patented
the linotype—a machine with a typewriter keyboard that produced bars of lead type. This revolutionized the production
of books.

The English word *bible* is derived from the Greek word
biblion ("a little book"). The word *bible* has come to mean

Scriptures
3166

"Bible," or "The Book"—the sacred writings making up the
OT and the NT. The word *scripture* is used in the NT when
reference is made to the OT. The NT was officially canonized
in A.D. 365.

River of
Inspiration
p. VII

The Hebrew Bible is divided into a threefold classification:
the Law (Torah), the Prophets (Nebhiim), and the Writings
(Kethubim), to which the NT witnesses (Luke 24:44). The English division of the OT has five sections: the Pentateuch, the
Poetical Books, the Major Prophets, the Minor Prophets, and
the Historical Books. (For a list of both the OT and NT divisions
see River Chart on page VII, following the Preface in TCRB.)

Just when and where the OT books were written and when
they were first considered to be the Word of God is a mystery.
They were definitely written by men in the Hebrew tradition
during a span of about 1000 years. Bible book records were
in existence long before they were collected into their final

Ezra
1199, 4237

form. Much of the OT was compiled by Ezra about 536 B.C.,
and it is generally assumed that Malachi wrote the last book
in the Hebrew canon about 400 B.C. Long before the word
canon was used, the individual books of the OT were read
and circulated. These writings provided the ethical and moral
guidelines for the Hebrew people from a very early period.
They were considered to be given to the people by God

Bible Divinely
Inspired
417

through the writing prophets. "Holy men of God" received
and wrote what God revealed to them (2 Peter 1:21). Later
the books were canonized and sealed as the authoritative Word
of God (2 Tim. 3:16).

One Bible scholar remarks that "The Bible books are called
inspired as the Divinely determined products of inspired men;
the Bible writers are called inspired, as breathed into, by the

20

Holy Spirit so that the product of their activities transcends
human powers and becomes Divinely authoritative. . . . Inspi-

ration is, therefore, usually defined as supernatural influence exerted on the sacred writers by the Spirit of God, by virtue of which their writings are given Divine trustworthiness." [1]

The Isaiah scroll in the Dead Sea collection was over twenty-three feet long and ten inches wide, made of coarse sheets of parchment sewn together with linen thread. All Bible scrolls were written on separate rolls which make book study somewhat complicated. Very few individuals owned even one Bible manuscript. Usually the manuscripts were placed in centers of learning, in synagogues, and later, during the Reformation period in the sixteenth century, printed Bibles were chained to pulpits, and official readers communicated Bible knowledge to the common people, in the tradition of Ezra (Neh. 8:1–8).

Dead Sea Scrolls **4220**

Tradition holds that the Book of Job may be the oldest book in the OT, and that Moses may have had personal contact with Job while he was in Midian exile. Conservative Bible scholars assume that Moses compiled and wrote most of the materials in the Pentateuch. It is self-evident that he had access to written and/or oral traditions on the period before his time. These materials had been preserved under the supervision of the Holy Spirit until Moses could arrange them into the approximate form they are at present. The important thing is that, whatever source materials Moses may have had, the work of compilation was superintended by the Spirit of God. Only such materials as received divine approval were finally incorporated into the Scriptures. The Bible, as it is today, has passed every test of time. When the Council of Jamnia affirmed the canonicity of the OT books in A.D. 90, they were making official what had been accepted for three hundred years.

Job **1899, 4240**

Holy Spirit **1125**

Even though many old Bible manuscripts have been preserved, many papyrus documents have been lost because moisture causes papyrus to deteriorate. Other manuscripts have been lost, hidden in caves, or burned during the many times when Bible manuscripts were being sought out and destroyed. It is certain that many of the manuscripts which remain were preserved by the saints who risked their lives.

Bible Scrolls **4220**

II. THE ANCIENT MANUSCRIPTS

A. *Codex Sinaiticus*

One of the most important Bible manuscripts containing the entire NT plus most of the OT was discovered by scholar and linguist Konstantin von Tischendorf (1844) while he was visiting St. Catherine's Monastery (Greek Orthodox) at the base of Jebal Musa or Mount Sinai. In the evening, while sitting by the fireplace, he observed a basketful of printed vellum sheets written in Greek, set there to be burned. After examining some of

Codex Sinaiticus **4220**

Papyrus growing in Cairo, Egypt

Copy of Sinaiticus manuscript on display in St. Catharine's Monastery

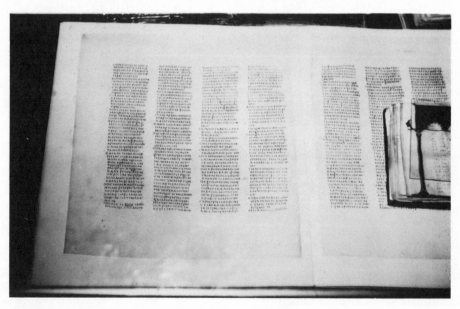

Dead Sea Scrolls in Palestinian Museum, Jerusalem

Samaritan Pentateuch in Samaritan Temple, Nabalus

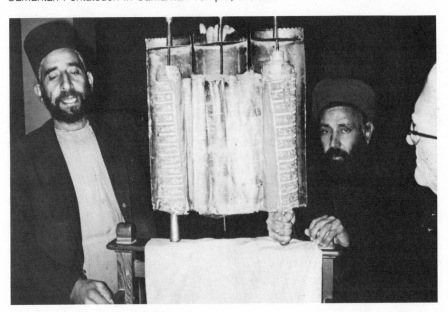

the sheets, he concluded that they were part of an ancient copy of the Septuagint (LXX—see Ch. 12, X).

Tischendorf was able to get permission from the monks to take these sheets back to Russia, where he had them published. He made another journey to Mount Sinai in 1859 and found the manuscript which came to be known as the Codex Sinaiticus. It had been written with brown ink in beautiful script on the finest vellum in the fourth or fifth century. The manuscript contained the entire NT and 199 leaves from the OT (Septuagint). It is one of the few ancient manuscripts containing all of the NT. Included in the manuscript were the Epistle of Barnabas and part of the Shepherd of Hermas on additional pages, making a total of 347 sheets. The entire manuscript was placed in the Imperial Museum in Saint Petersburg, Russia, where it remained until 1933, when it was purchased by the British Museum for $500,000.00.

B. Codex Alexandrinus

Originally the Greek Codex Alexandrinus contained the entire Bible plus the four books of the Maccabees, the Epistle of Athanasius to Marcellinus on the Psalms, and Eusebius' summary of the Psalms. Also included were fourteen canticles found in both the OT and the NT as well as the Gloria in Excelsis and the apocryphal Psalm 151. It also once contained the Psalms of Solomon. The NT section also contained most of 1 Clement and parts of 2 Clement. The codex is a very important witness to both the Septuagint and the NT. It is valuable at the point where it supplements other versions in which pages are missing, but many of its own pages are now missing. The manuscript was named for Cyril Lukaris, Patriarch of Alexandria, who gave it as a gift to King Charles I of England in 1627. It is now on display at the British Museum.[2]

C. Codex Vaticanus

Among the priceless treasures in the Vatican Museum is the fourth-century Latin Codex Vaticanus Bible, probably written in Alexandria. It was discovered on the shelves of the great library in 1481. No one knows where the manuscript came from or how long it had been a part of the Vatican collection. At the time of its discovery in the fifteenth century the manuscript was thought to contain the entire Bible but upon examination, some parts of the NT as well as parts of Genesis and the Psalms were found to be missing.

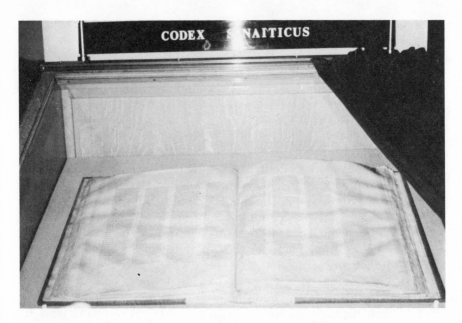

The original Codex Sinaiticus on display in the British Museum

Samaritan Pentateuch on display in Samaritan Temple, Nabalus

III. ANCIENT VERSIONS

A. *The Septuagint* (LXX)

This contained the OT in Greek and was translated in Alexandria in the third century. A detailed discussion follows on page 189.

B. *The Samaritan Pentateuch*

The Samaritan Pentateuch is the Hebrew Masoretic text written in Samaritan characters similar to those on the Moabite Stone and some of the more ancient manuscripts found in the Qumran Caves. It contains only the five books of Moses plus Joshua, which constitutes the sole scriptures for the Samaritans. The traditional date for the separation of the Samaritans from Judaism is about 440 B.C. This gives further credence to the OT having been canonized by that time. This manuscript, which was dated about the eleventh century A.D., was known only through references by such church fathers as Origen, Jerome, and other ancient writers, until Pietro della Valle discovered a copy of the Samaritan Pentateuch in Damascus in 1616. A great wave of excitement arose among the Bible scholars at first, but after careful study it was judged by Wilhelm Gesenius, the great Hebrew scholar, to be almost worthless for textual criticism. Although the Samaritans display a copy of an ancient Pentateuch, which they claim was written by Abishua, the great grandson of Aaron, this claim is questionable. There are now several editions in print and The Damascus manuscript is being reexamined by the leading scholars and compared with other manuscripts.[3]

C. *The Peshito or Syriac*

The Syriac is a translation into Aramaic, made for the Jews in Syria when Hebrew was no longer a spoken language. After the Christian Church revised it, the manuscript became known as the Peshito ("the Simple Edition"). From the fifth century onward the version has been in use by the Jacobites and the Nestorians. Many versions of this work contain books from the Apocrypha and even the Pseudepigrapha (see Ch. 12, XI and XII).

D. *The Vulgate (Latin)*

The OT portion of the Old Latin version had its origin among the Latin-speaking Jews of Carthage in about A.D. 200. Other Latin versions emerged by the late fourth century when the

Old Latin had undergone corruption "from the multiplicity of hands stirring the kettle of translations." [4]

To provide the church with a good translation of the Bible, Pope Damasus requested Sophronius Eusebius Hieronymous (A.D. 340–420), better known as Jerome from Dalmatia, to translate the entire Bible into the best Latin form. After extensive translation work on the NT, using the original Greek, Jerome began the monumental work of translating the OT directly from the Hebrew but with reference to the Greek versions. He did his work in the Grotto of the Nativity Church in Bethlehem. One of the basement rooms in this church bears a plaque in his memory. Jerome's finished work was without rival; for 1000 years it was the standard text of the Roman Catholic Church. The translation was called the *vulgate,* meaning the "common edition."

The first printed edition of the Vulgate Bible was the Gutenberg Bible, also known as the "Bible with 42 lines," because it had 42 lines on each page. Completed before August 1456 the Gutenberg Bible is believed to be the first book of importance ever printed with movable type.

About 8000 manuscripts of the various Latin versions survive. None of the OT copies are complete. A critical edition of the Vulgate has been produced by the Benedictine order and was printed by the Vatican Press.

IV. THE ENGLISH VERSIONS

During the Dark Ages (A.D. 476–1000) scarcely any Bible translation work was done. During this time civilization sank to a new low in western Europe. Academic work was limited mainly to a few cathedrals, monasteries, and palace schools. Knowledge of ancient Greek almost completely disappeared. Few people went to school, and the few writers who remained had little sense of style. In this literary darkness, popular stories and rumors were accepted as true. With the growth of papal power the Bible fell into general disuse, being supplemented by decrees and dogmas of councils and popes. However, while this literary darkness prevailed in Europe, intellectual quest existed in the Byzantine Empire (fifth and sixth centuries A.D.), where many aspects of Greek and Roman life survived. The Arabs were at their height of intellectual development, spreading civilization from Spain to the borders of India (c. 640–840). The corruption in the church was challenged in parts of France, in Spain, and in Italy by the Albigenses. By 1167 the sect had a great following in southern France, and by A.D. 1200 this movement was strong in northern Italy. The Waldensians also challenged the Roman Church by teaching that the Bible was the sole rule of authority, and thus they kindled new interest in the Bible.

A. *John Wycliffe (1320–1384)*

John Wycliffe, a teacher at Oxford, England, preached against the spiritual domination of the priesthood and the authority of the pope, advocating the people's right to read the Bible in their own language. His followers were called Lollards. Unfortunately the common people had no Bible that they could read since the Scriptures were locked within the Latin, Greek, and Hebrew tongues, which very few people knew. Wycliffe, an outstanding doctor of theology and a master at Oxford, enjoyed great favor with the pope. He was a learned man, conversant in all the biblical languages and the theology of the Roman Church. He was sent on several missions to reconcile dissenters but became a dissenter himself through his association with John Gaunt. Wycliffe eventually came to see the inconsistency of the violent struggle between the pope and clergy on one side, and the kings and nobles on the other. Both were corrupt and were dominated by self-interests.

In about 1377, Pope Gregory sent several bulls to the University of Oxford and to the Archbishop of Canterbury and the Bishop of London, in which he accused Wycliffe of teaching doctrines contrary to the church. The pope ordered Wycliffe arrested and examined, but the political parties were reluctant to take action against Wycliffe because of the great popularity he enjoyed.

The conditions in Europe gave rise to many questions: Was the pope lord over kings? Could a civil government punish a wicked bishop? Could the civil government tax the church? Did all laws have to be fair? Wycliffe concluded that "Dominion is found in grace." He applied his ideas to the popes and bishops and was brought to trial several times in church courts, but each time the English royal family saved him from condemnation.

The year 1378 was important in Wycliffe's life. He took a more aggressive stand against certain church abuses and began to question publicly the whole basis of sacradotalism and its authority. He shifted his view toward the concept which Luther later expressed in regard to the mass. Soon he made special appeals to the common people and presented Christianity as a personal faith in Christ rather than as a dogmatic system of the Roman Catholic Church. He began to send out "poor preachers" to the common people and to translate the Latin into the English of his day. Through his lay evangelists the Lollard movement gained great strength and importance.

However, after his death the Lollards suffered severe persecution.

Wycliffe was assisted in his Bible translation work by Nicholas of Hereford. The entire work was taken over and revised by John Purvey when Wycliffe died in 1384. Wycliffe's teachings were soon condemned by the Archbishop of Canterbury at Oxford. As a result many of his followers were excommunicated. Hostility against Wycliffe was so intense that in 1415 the Council of Constance ordered his body exhumed and burned and his ashes thrown into the river Swift.

It is evident that the writings of Wycliffe influenced and encouraged a number of reformers to continue his work. Many credited Wycliffe with being in the vanguard of the Reformation. It is certain that he helped the common people by translating the Bible into a language they could understand sufficently to teach their children. The chart on page 18 shows that the Wycliffe work rested entirely on the Latin Vulgate.

B. William Tyndale (1494–1536)

William Tyndale was born on the Welsh border near Gloucester about 1494. He received his education at Oxford and taught in Cambridge from 1519 to 1522. A brilliant Greek and Hebrew scholar, he was heavily burdened to make the Bible available to the common people. When he became involved with the reformers, he lost favor with the established church authorities. Later, when the local political climate became too severe, he moved to London with the idea of translating the Bible into English so that "every plow-boy might read it." After his request for help from the Bishop of London was denied, he moved to Hamburg, Germany, where he made contact with Martin Luther.

On 27 May 1524, he registered at the University of Thul and began his translation work. The printing of the Bible was started at Cologne in 1525, but it was stopped by Johann DaBeneck, a churchman who hated the Reformation. Tyndale then fled to Worms, where 6000 copies of his Bible were printed. In 1525, copies were smuggled into England in grain sacks and various other cargo, but they were sought out and burned by Bishops Worsham and Tousta.

Efforts were made to seize Tyndale, but he fled first to Marberg, and then to Antwerp in the Netherlands. Henry VIII tried to seize him for trial in England, but Tyndale escaped. However, he was captured in Antwerp in 1535 by officers of the Emperor and imprisoned at Vilivorde. Despite efforts by Thomas Cromwell to save him, he was tried for heresy, con-

The Origin and Growth of the Bible

Persecution
3480

William Tyndale
4220

Persecution
3480

29

demned, degraded from holy orders, strangled, and his body burned. His last words were, "Lord, open the King of England's eyes."

However, Tyndale's influence on England was outstanding and his life style greatly influenced the renderings in the King James Version of the Bible (1611). He was martyred before he completely finished the OT. The chart in No. 4220 of the TCRB Helps shows that his work rested upon the ancient versions and the Latin Vulgate (see page 18).

C. Miles Coverdale (1488–1568)

Miles Coverdale, born in Yorkshire and educated at Cambridge, carried on the torch of Bible translation which Wycliffe had ignited. Later Coverdale became acquainted with Tyndale on the Continent. He was not as scholarly as Tyndale, but he had initiative. His translation work depended heavily upon the Latin Vulgate and Luther's German Bible, but mostly upon Tyndale's English version. As a contributor to Bible translation, he was outstanding. He also helped to produce the Great Bible and edited the Coverdale Bible, which was published at Cologne and became the first complete English Bible in print.

In the theological turbulence in England and on the European continent, Coverdale dared to dedicate his 1535 edition to Henry VIII, the king who had tried to apprehend Tyndale. To the amazement of the scholarly world, Coverdale's Bible was given royal license by England (see page 18).

D. The Matthews Bible, John Rogers (1500–1555)

The Matthews Bible was published under a pseudonym, probably in fear of retribution. The author was actually John Rogers, a friend of Tyndale. His published work included the entire translation of Tyndale, for which Tyndale had been burned at the stake as a heretic the year before. Rogers had been educated at Cambridge and was Rector of Trinity and Lees in London. Later he served as a chaplain to the English merchants in Antwerp. Here he met William Tyndale, who influenced him to change his religious commitment. Rogers assumed the pastorate of a Protestant congregation in Wittenberg and prepared for the press the English rendering of the Bible, which included Tyndale's NT and the OT as far as 2 Chronicles.

Rogers' part in the actual translation was minimal, but his marginal notes formed the basis for an early commentary in English on the Scriptures. Three days after Queen Mary arrived in London, Rogers preached against Roman Catholicism. On 27 January 1554, he was imprisoned at Newgate on the insistence of the new bishop of London. After two examinations he was burned at the stake at Smithfield. Despite the persecution under Mary, Bible translation continued, though not without surveillance and suspicion. Through an act of Parliament, unauthorized persons were forbidden to "read the Bible aloud in a public place. Private reading was forbidden by all artificers, journeymen, servicemen, yeomen, husbandman and laborers." [5] The chart on page 180 of the TCRB Helps shows that the Matthews Bible was based on Tyndale's work (see page 18).

E. The Great Bible (1539)

The chart shows that the Great Bible was based on the Matthews, the Coverdale, and the Tyndale Bibles. At the prompting of Archbishop Cranmer, Coverdale published the Great Bible without the controversial notes contained in the earlier editions. This Bible "for the use of the church" was the only Bible that could be lawfully used in England. Because of its unusual dimensions, the Bible was chained to the church pulpit where people congregated to hear the reading of God's Word. This Bible was called "great" because of its size and its exclusive use and place in the church (see page 18).

F. The Geneva Bible (1560)

In fifty years the Reformation had swept across Europe. This was a telling blow against the Roman Catholic Church. The Council of Trent (1545–63), in session for eighteen years, abolished some moral abuses of the papacy. However, through the "Counter Reformation" the Roman Church organized for an aggressive onslaught on Protestantism, and under the brilliant leadership of the Jesuits much of the lost territory was regained. During this period many of the Protestant leaders took refuge in Geneva, where the Bible was published in 1560. Based chiefly on Tyndale and the Great Bible, the new translation was named the Geneva Bible.

Included in this version were many notes and annotations concerning those passages with strong Protestant implications. Therefore, it was highly distasteful to the established church in England but received popular support by the common people. Shakespeare used the Geneva Bible as did the Puritans of England as they went to the New World. John Bunyan drew heavily upon it in writing *Pilgrim's Progress* (see page 18).

G. *The Bishop's Bible (1568)*

When the Geneva Bible began to crowd out the Great Bible, Archbishop Parker of the Church of England set out to produce a Bible to take the place of the Great Bible. The Bishop's Bible was to be based upon the Great Bible, but actually it incorporated many elements of the Geneva Bible, which it was meant to replace. The Bishop's Bible was used extensively until 1611, when the Authorized Version (KJV) became the dominant version.

H. *The Douay Bible (1582–1610)*

After Elizabeth I became Queen of England many Roman Catholics moved to Florence and Belgium. The English Roman Catholic refugees at the University of Douay in northern France felt a need for an English Bible approved by the Roman Catholic Church. This need resulted in the Rheims-Douay Bible, of which the NT was published at Rheims in 1582 and the OT at Douay in 1610. This version was made mainly from the Latin Vulgate with some slight helps from the Hebrew and Greek originals. The English style and diction were poor compared with some of the Protestant versions, especially in comparison with the King James Version, which appeared soon after the Rheims-Douay version was completed. Eleven books of the Apocrypha were added at the Council of Trent (1545–63). See Ch. 12, XI, and page 18.

I. *The King James or Authorized Version (1611)*

King James Stuart of Scotland and, after A.D. 1603, King of England, convened the Hampton Court Conference in an effort to reconcile the religious parties in his kingdom but failed to bring the Bishops and the Puritan Party together. However, the conference did take action which brought into being a version of the Bible destined to be used for hundreds of years. A resolution was passed at the suggestion of John Reynolds, a Puritan, that a translation of the Bible be made from the original Hebrew and Greek into English with no marginal notes or comments. It was suggested that this version should become the state Bible, to be used exclusively in the public worship services of the Church of England. Not all of the conference members favored the move, but King James endorsed it, stating that none of the existing translations was accurate enough for a national Bible. The new version was to be produced by the best scholars in Oxford and Cambridge Universities, then to be reviewed by the Bishops of England and finally approved by the privy council and the king.

Fifty of the greatest biblical and linguistic scholars were assembled and instructed to divide up into six teams, two at Oxford, two at Cambridge, and two at Westminister, to work on assigned portions of the text. Afterward they were to meet together in one body for critical discussion and then again divide into committees to evaluate the recommendations submitted by the whole group. A final draft was then to be made for further critical examination by cross committees.

At that time the translators had at their disposal the best Hebrew and Greek texts available. The committee used the Tyndale, the Coverdale, and the Geneva versions as helps, and the translators' fidelity to the truth of the Scripture is remarkable. Many years later when the Revised Standard Version was completed, a spokesman of the translation committee stated: "It will be obvious to the careful reader that no doctrine of the Christian faith has been affected by the revision, for the simple reason that, out of the thousands of variant readings in the manuscripts, none has turned up thus far that requires a revision of Christian doctrine." An Introduction to the Revised Standard Bible of the New Testament by members of the Revision Committee. Luther Weigel, Chairman, 1946.

Many scholars are agreed that the KJV contains the most beautiful form of English the world has ever known, and that this translation lends itself to memorization. Perhaps something can be said for a language that has an "other-world tone." Could it be that the Word of God should have a terminology different from the language of the street? Certainly the KJV language and tone set it apart in this age of secularization and materialism.

The Authorized Version (KJV) represents the work of men in an age that did not question the integrity and authenticity of the Bible. It came at a time before the "scientific investigative technique" was applied to Bible study. One advantage of the KJV is that 95 percent of such working tools for Bible study as Bible dictionaries, encyclopedias, Bible handbooks, concordances, commentaries, and other helps are keyed to it.

As literature, the Authorized Version ranks second to none. Fortunately this version was produced at a time when the genius of language for noble prose was at its height and when a natural sense of style was not affected by self-conscious scholarship.

The KJV has been and still is precious to millions of people who have read, studied, memorized, and loved it for its simple, dignified, beautiful presentation of the Word of God. It seems unlikely that it will be supplanted by another version in the

33

near future. Interestingly enough, after all these years and after 500 Bible versions, the KJV still outsells all the other versions combined. See page 18.

J. The Revised Version (1881–1884)

By the late nineteenth century almost 275 years had passed since the publication of the KJV. The work of the biblical scholars since that time, plus the many recently discovered Bible manuscripts, generated a strong feeling within the Church of England that the Bible should be revised. This feeling was shared in America. At the request of the Church of England a group of church leaders convened to consider the matter. As a result fifty scholars from the leading Protestant denominations in the British Isles were brought together. Two committees were formed, one for the OT and the other for the NT. At the same time a committee of thirty Bible scholars was organized in America to collaborate with the English group.

It was agreed that a minimum number of changes in the KJV would be made in order to be consistent with the original texts. The basis for the revision was to be the KJV; the alterations would be made only by a two-thirds vote of the main committee. When the American and British committees met to compare notes, their disagreements outweighed their agreements. By mutual consent the British Revised Version was to be published with the use of a few suggestions from the American Committee. These suggestions were to be placed in the appendix, but without the approval of the British as to their content. The American committee agreed not to publish its work until 1901.

The British NT was published in 1881; the OT followed in 1885, and the entire Bible in one volume in 1898. About 3,000,000 copies were sold in England and in America but the KJV continued to lead in sales. See page 18.

K. The American Standard Version (1901)

The American committee honored its agreement not to publish for 14 years. In 1901 the ASV came from the press. This version benefited not only from the scholarship of England but also from the added insights of the American scholars. Many of the differences between the two versions were related to "Britishisms" or terms which were not commonly used in America.

The American committee used the term *Jehovah* instead of *Lord* as the translation for the Hebrew *YHWH*, the term *Holy Spirit* instead of *Holy Ghost*, and *love* instead of *charity*.

The ASV lacked some of the literary beauty of the KJV, but it excelled in accuracy and was based upon a superior Greek text. It has been widely used by scholars as a study Bible, but it has never enjoyed the popularity of the KJV. See page 18.

V. VERSIONS SINCE 1901

Since the current list of English versions mentioned in the TCRB, a number of new versions have been produced:

A. *Moffatt's Translation (1924–1935)*

James Moffatt was an outstanding Bible scholar and linguist, but he affirmed that he had "found freedom from the theory of verbal inspiration." This freedom is reflected in passages of both the OT and NT, where doctrinal matters are given a liberal treatment. He incorporated the JEDP Documentary Hypothesis (see Ch. 7, I and Ch. 15, I, A) by italicizing certain portions of the OT text. His liberal bias is further seen in his reference to the Virgin Birth of Christ when he refers to Joseph as "the father of Jesus." See page 18.

B. *The Smith-Goodspeed Version (1923–1931)*

Edgar Goodspeed completed the translation of the NT in 1923; H. M. Powis Smith, the OT in 1927. The entire Bible was published in 1931. This is the forerunner of the Bible in Modern English. Some sections border on paraphrase. See page 18.

C. *The Revised Standard Version (1946–1952)*

The RSV is a revision of the KJV, 1611, the ERV and the ASV (1881–1885 and 1901). The literary style is similar to that of the KJV. The copyright is owned by the National Council of Churches and it is now used by several of the major Protestant denominations. See page 18.

D. *The Confraternity Version (1948)*

This is a Roman Catholic Version in Modern English based more on the Latin Vulgate than upon the Hebrew and Greek originals. It also contains the Apocrypha (see Ch. 12, XI). See page 18.

E. *The Berkeley Version (1945–1959)*

In this version the NT was originally translated into modern English from the Greek by Gerrit Verkuyl. The OT section was the work of many scholars who carefully preserved the Messianic prophecies. The version contains numerous footnotes on difficult passages. In it the theological emphasis is evangelical, and the Scriptures are treated as the authoritative Word of God. See page 18.

F. The New American Standard Bible (1960–1971)

The NASB is a revision of the ASV supported by the best original Hebrew and Greek texts. This translation represents a ten-year project by leading scholars working in committee. The fourfold aim was (1) to be true to the original language, (2) to be grammatically correct, (3) to be understandable to the lay reader, and (4) to give the Lord Jesus Christ his proper place as accorded in the Word. The marginal cross references and the concordance make this version a useful Bible study tool. See page 18.

G. The New English Bible (1961–1970)

This is a completely new translation from the Hebrew and the Greek texts by leading British scholars from the old line denominations. Its strong point is its pleasing style and format and its rendering of the Scripture texts into contemporary English. However, it reflects a definite liberal bias. For example, in Isaiah 7:14, the rendering inclines toward a failure to recognize the miraculous. *Almah* is translated "a young woman" whereas the KJV uses the word *virgin* (Matt. 1:23).

Many of the expressions are Britishisms not familiar to the Western mind: e.g., "meal tub" in Matt. 5:15; "midge" in Matt. 23:24; "truckling to no man" in Matt. 22:16; and "who put me in the dock?" in 1 Cor. 9:3. The cross is referred to as "gallows" in 1 Peter 2:24 and as "gibbet" in Acts 10:30. Some passages border on slang: e.g., "You can take it from me that every man . . ." (Gal. 5:3) and "they all left me in the lurch" (2 Tim. 4:16). Many of the terms are more philosophical than biblical. See page 18.

H. The Amplified Bible (1958–1965)

The AB is a version in Modern English translated by a committee of qualified Hebrew and Greek scholars. The outstanding feature is the bracketed explanatory words and phrases following places where difficulty might arise. In addition, it contains footnotes to explain the more complicated passages. Thus one has the advantage of several translations in a single text. It is thoroughly orthodox and recognizes the Scriptures as the authoritative Word of God. See page 18.

I. The Good News Bible (1966–1976)

The GNB is also known as the Bible in Today's English and is published by the American Bible Society. It represents fifteen years of work by leading Hebrew and Greek biblical scholars. The version claims to be "the most faithful translation possible in vibrant contemporary English," but it has its weak points, as do all other translations. In its attempt to simplify the English language, much of the richness of biblical thought has been dissipated. Instead of "justify" the GNB has "put right"; "different tongues" is rendered "strange sounds." In referring to Christ, "blood" and "death" are frequently used interchangeably (Eph. 1:7; Acts 20:28).

Due to the GNB's wide circulation, at a very low cost, many people have become interested in the Bible and in Bible study. See page 18.

J. The Jerusalem Bible (1966)

The JB is a Roman Catholic work produced originally in French by the Dominican Fathers in Jerusalem. The English version, which is the equivalent of the French "La Bible de Jerusalem," was translated from the original Hebrew and Greek texts but supported strongly by the French version when matters of questionable interpretation arose. It is definitely a contemporary English version. The divine name Yahweh is used. The Apocrypha has been placed between Malachi and Matthew. In matters of OT criticism the version leans definitely in the direction of the JEDP Documentary Hypothesis (see Ch. 15, I, A) including the composite authorship of Isaiah and the date, 65 B.C., for Daniel. However, the Messianic prophecies are clearly noted and explained in the documentation. See page 18.

K. The New International Version (1973–1978)

This work is sponsored by the New York Bible Society, Inc. and was produced by over 100 biblical scholars mainly from the United States, Great Britain, Canada, Australia, and New Zealand. These scholars represent over a dozen main-line denominations. The translation of each book was assigned to a team of scholars. Several committees checked and rechecked each book. From the very beginning the Committee on Bible Translation was concerned that their work would be an accurate translation, clear and scholarly. The translators were committed to "the authority and infallibility of the Bible as God's

37

Word in written form." It is a balanced literary translation, true to the Word, and is being received with enthusiasm. See page 18.

L. The Living Bible (1962–1971)

This paraphrase should not be overlooked in a listing of new versions. It is the work of Kenneth N. Taylor, who saw the need of a Bible in the simplest modern English. The LB has undeniable freshness and clarity that awakens interest. Many difficult passages are qualified by use of interpretive words. For instance, in describing the faith to which James makes reference in James 2:20, the word "real" is added to "faith." The LB is referred to as a paraphrase, and in this instance it is faithful to the biblical doctrine: i.e., *paraphrase* is "to say something in different words than the author used" or a "restatement of the author's thoughts, using different words than he did." Mr. Taylor is committed to an authoritative, inerrant Bible, and in this undertaking he has made every effort to state as exactly as possible what the writers of Scripture meant. This work has been carefully checked by both Hebrew and Greek scholars and is probably one of the best paraphrase-translations on the market today. Its reception by the Bible-reading public has been phenomenal. It does communicate the divine message that "Christ died to save us from our sins." See page 18.

VI. NEW TESTAMENT VERSIONS

In conclusion, a few of the modern translations that are limited to the New Testament follow:

1. The New Testament in Modern Speech
   by R. F. Weymouth (1902).
2. The Twentieth Century New Testament
   by Mary Higgs and Ernest Malan (1904).
3. The New Testament in the Language of the People
   by C. S. Williams (1937).
4. The New Testament in Modern English
   by J. B. Phillips (1958).
5. The New Testament in the Language of Today
   by William F. Beck (1963).

The work of translation goes on. No one knows when, if ever, the perfect version will put to rest all future translation work.

2

The Canonization of the Bible

I. THE NEW TESTAMENT CANON

In biblical use, the word *canon* means a measuring rod or standard by which genuinely inspired Bible books were separated from the many spurious, religious writings, which contained biblical truth mixed with heathen philosophy and superstition. Thus the canonized books came to mean the "written rule of faith" verified by apostolic sanction.

Philosophy **2759**

The canonical New Testament books as they are today, twenty-seven in number, were generally accepted by the churches as the authentic books with apostolic authority. Jesus attested to the authenticity of the Scriptures in making frequent reference to the Old Testament books as being "the Word of God." Jesus established the authority of the NT by his reference to the OT. He referred to Moses, the prophets, the Psalms, and words and incidents of the Scriptures. Jesus further verified the message of the NT when he established his own authority. On the road to Emmaus ". . . he expounded . . . in all the scriptures the things concerning himself" (Luke 24:27).

New Testament Books **VII, VIII**

From the beginning Christian churches accepted the Old Testament as the Word of God. In fact, this is the only Bible the early Christians had.

As the Christian movement spread, the apostles and other inspired men wrote letters of instruction to the several congregations relative to doctrine, ethical and moral conduct, and the rules for ordaining church officers. Some of the letters were written to meet certain local needs as well as to clarify misunderstandings. However, these writings contained broad principles of truth which made them relevant to the problems and needs of people in every age. This fact is sometimes referred to as the "double reference" formula.

As copies of letters were received by a congregation, they were recognized as documents with a broad application, relevant to other Christian groups. Interested congregations sent their scribes to copy the letters, which were soon circulated among other Christian groups. The traditional church believed that as the Holy Spirit inspired men to write these letters, so also he superintended the preservation of these books and finally guided the minds of men in the formation of the canon. The New Testament books are listed on the River of Inspiration Chart on page VII of the TCRB, fourth edition, page 46. The historical books (the four Gospels and Acts) relate almost everything known about what Jesus said and did. Also the Book of Acts contains a record of the spreading of the gospel to other parts of the Roman world after Jesus was crucified. The Epistles deal mainly with doctrinal instruction, exhortation to Christian conduct, and rules of church polity.

Scribes
3165
Holy Spirit
1601–1614

Revelation
2500

The Book of Revelation, the last book in the New Testament canon, deals with the struggle between good and evil and the ultimate triumph of Christ at his Second Coming. It is also called the Apocalypse, meaning to "uncover" or to "reveal secret meanings."

A detailed study of each New Testament book will be found in chapter 16.

As the apostles died, and it became evident that Jesus was not coming back as soon as believers had anticipated, an urgency developed to record the gospel events. The general assumption is that all of the New Testament books were written during the first century. The Gospels and the Epistles are usually dated between A.D. 50 and 90; the Gospel of John, John's Epistles, and Revelation are dated about A.D. 90. One of the most important problems the early church officials faced was that of distinguishing between genuine apostolic writings and the apocryphal or spurious books which were written by men with heretical tendencies.

Apocrypha
p. 179

Marcion, an influential church leader in Rome with an inclination toward Gnosticism introduced a short "canon" of books to the church. He accepted only the Gospel of Luke and ten of the Epistles of Paul (excluding the pastorals). He eliminated the first two chapters of Luke because they described the miraculous stories of Jesus' birth. Marcion's compilation of New Testament materials created a serious problem in the church. Scholars are agreed that the challenge by Marcion was one of the factors which caused Christian leaders to compile a canon consistent with apostolic authority.

Another cause of concern for the early church fathers at the end of the fourth century was that such apocryphal books as 3 Corinthians, the Didache, the Epistle of Barnabas, and the Shepherd of Hermas were being circulated. The Sinaiticus Manuscript and 1 Clement were included in the fifth-century Alexandrinus Manuscript. To add to the confusion, heretical teachers were using the apocryphal books in support of their objectionable ideas. (For examples see Ch. 13, I, "The Harmony of the Gospels.") See page 194.

The Canonization of the Bible

Sinaiticus
p. 180

The church leaders felt a moral obligation to separate the spurious from the authentic books. This brought up the question of what measuring device should be used to determine the true apostolic writings from the spurious. The first consideration was whether the book had been written by an apostle or someone close to the apostolic times. There was no problem with Matthew and John. Since Mark was a close associate of Peter and Luke of Paul, it was decided that they would meet the apostolic standard. It is probable that this measure was applied to all of the twenty-seven New Testament books.

Other questions concerned whether the contents of the book were of unquestionable, high spiritual character. The apocryphal and pseudepigraphical books fell far short of this standard. (See Ch. 12, XI, XII, pages 190–192). Other considerations were whether the book had received universal approval throughout the church and whether the book had the aura of divine inspiration. This decision was difficult to determine at times. On the other hand, the contrasting inferior tone of the spurious books made proper determination less difficult. It is evident, however, that during the canonization process some of the New Testament Books were in question for short periods of time.

Apocrypha
p. 179

Inspired Word
417

In the third century, Origen classified the New Testament books into two categories: acknowledged and disputed. He placed James, 2 Peter, 2 and 3 John and Jude in the questionable category. In A.D. 326 Eusebius wrote that Hebrews and Revelation were also in dispute, the former in the West and the latter in the East. However, in the course of the canonization period the Holy Spirit permitted the process of time to be a factor in the leaders' sifting the genuine books from the false.

The writings of Justin Martyr (A.D. 150), Clement of Alexander (A.D. 165–220), and Eusebius (A.D. 326) all contained affirmation of the books as they are now in the New Testament canon. "In 367 Athanasius issued a list of twenty-seven books which tally with the twenty-seven books which are accepted by the synods of Hippo Regius (A.D. 393) and Carthage (A.D.

397–419). There was much opposition to including any of the apocryphal books." (See Ch. 12, XI). At no time were they ever included in the Protestant canon.[1] See pages 190–192.

Apocrypha
p. 179

The official canonization of the New Testament books took place at the Council of Carthage (A.D. 397) when the Council merely affirmed what the consensus of the church had been for many years.

II. THE OLD TESTAMENT CANON

How the ancient Hebrews expressed the conception of Old Testament canonicity is not known, but the idea was present long before the term was created to express it. In the New Testament the word *scripture* has specific reference to the Old Testament. The idea of the sacredness of the Scriptures is unquestionable (Matt. 21:42; John 5:39; Acts 18:24). The Rabbis considered the Old Testament books to be so sacred that, when worn out from use, they could not be destroyed or discarded as rubbish. These worn-out manuscripts were placed in a vault (called *genizah*) in some isolated part of the temple or synagogue. It is quite likely that King Josiah found a worn copy of the Law in the genizah following a wicked period of idolatry under Kings Manasseh and Amon (2 Kings 22:8).

Scripture
3166

The Old Testament books were written by men who were aware of the inspiration of the Scriptures and expressed it by "thus saith the Lord."

Inspired Word
417

These authors were divinely possessed with the idea that their writings were to be preserved and handed down to future generations as norms of faith and conduct (cf. 2 Sam. 23:2; Ps. 49:1–4; Jer. 36:27–32).

The determining factor of authenticity was based largely upon the sterling character of the writers and the belief that they were God's spokesmen. "Holy men of God spake as they were moved by the Holy Ghost" (2 Peter 1:21). The spiritual benefit which the people received from the ensuing writings corresponded with and confirmed the people's belief in the divine origin of the words. Each individual book of a prophet of the Lord was accepted as the Word of God. The pragmatic results of these books verified their authority. Their concepts and precepts actually worked in everyday life (2 Tim. 3:16). This is what made the books authoritative even before the council had accepted them. The action taken by councils attested the fact of divine origin, but the council did not initiate the selections. The council merely confirmed the authenticity of the books which the people had accepted over the years. The canon does not derive its authority from the church, whether Jewish or Christian. The office of the church is merely

Holy Men
1125

42

that of a custodian of the Scripture and a witness of its power.

The Hebrews classified the Old Testament Scriptures into three main categories: the Torah (Law), the Nebhiim or Prophets, and the Kethubim or the Writings by the Sopherim (the wise). (1) The Torah included the first five books—the Pentateuch or the Books of Moses. They were Genesis, Exodus, Leviticus, Numbers, and Deuteronomy. (2) The Nebhiim ("Prophets") embraced the four so-called former prophets: (a) Joshua, Judges, 1 and 2 Samuel (counted as one book); 1 and 2 Kings (also counted as one book) and (b) the four so-called latter prophets, Isaiah, Jeremiah, Ezekiel, and the twelve minor prophets which counted as one book. (3) The Kethubim or Writings included Psalms, Proverbs, Job, and the Five Rolls, Songs, Ruth, Lamentations, Ecclesiastes, and Esther, plus the historical books, Daniel, Ezra, and Nehemiah (counted as one book) and 1 and 2 Chronicles (counted as one book).

History does not reveal why the books are grouped as they are. The arrangement was evidently based on content and the possibility that one section of the canon was closed before the other. However, the importance of classifying the books is secondary to the fact that they are a part of the canon. Although the step-by-step process of canonization is shrouded in the unknowable, the action was evidently so gradual that there was no awareness of it. However, there are valuable hints as to how the Bible was preserved. In Exodus 40:20 the "testimony" or the tables of the Law containing the Ten Commandments were placed in the Ark of the Covenant for safekeeping. The Laws of Deuteronomy were delivered to the sons of Levi to be deposited beside the Ark. In 1 Kings 8:9 the record states that when Solomon brought the Ark up from the City of David to the temple, the tablets were still its sole contents. Another possible means of preserving the Word came through Hezekiah whose men were credited with copying a large number of Proverbs (Prov. 25:1). Later, in a period of apostasy, Josiah instituted a religious reform when the "Books of the Law," as previously mentioned, were found hidden away in the temple (2 Kings 22:8ff.). Here is an instance where some parts of the Law (how much is unknown) have been preserved. The Words of the Lord are recognized in it (2 Kings 22:13,18,19). Its authority is undisputed yet there is no mention of canon.

In the time between the Testaments, when Hebrew was a forgotten language, it was considered important to have the Hebrew Scriptures translated into Greek (Septuagint), the common language of that day. (For additional information on the Septuagint see Ch. 12, X, p. 189.)

The New Testament furnishes important evidence of a fixed canon to which authoritative appeal could be made. Most im-

The Canonization of the Bible

Bible Books
p. VII, VIII

Scriptures
3166

New
Testament
Books
p. VIII

43

portant are the Old Testament writings referred to by the authors of the New Testament. References to "the Scriptures," "the Holy Scriptures," "The Law and the Prophets," and so on are numerous: Matthew 5:17, 17:12, 22:29,40; Luke 16:16, 24:44; John 19:36, 10:34–35, 12:34, 15:25; Acts 13:15, 18:24, 28:23; Romans 1:2; 1 Corinthians 14:21; 2 Timothy 3:15; 2 Peter 1:20. These citations certainly assume that Jesus and the apostles had a great regard for the Old Testament, as separate and fixed. Luke 24:44 gives clear evidence of the threefold division of the Old Testament canon. Jesus suggests the final order and arrangement of the books of the Old Testament canon thus: "From the blood of righteous Abel, unto the blood of Zacharias" (Matt. 23:35; cf. Luke 11:51). This expression is used in the same sense in which one would say "from Genesis to Malachi." The frequent references in the New Testament to Old Testament books constitute a closed canon before the New Testament was canonized.

Spiritual
Ignorance
2037

Nicodemus
2588

New Birth
2154

Jesus expresses amazement at the people's ignornance of the Scriptures. "And have ye not read this scripture?" in his forthright question as he quoted Psalm 118:22 to show that the rejection of the Messiah by the people was already foretold in Scripture (Mark 12:10). In another instance Jesus chides Nicodemus for his lack of spiritual understanding: "Art thou a master of Israel, and knowest not these things?" (John 3:10). Jesus makes reference to the new birth, as having been taught in the Old Testament (Ezek. 36:26).

When the spiritually dead temple leaders criticized the common people, who, ignorant of the Scriptures (John 7:49), uttered the Hosannas, Jesus questioned, "Hearest thou what these say?" He followed this query with, "Have ye never read, Out of the mouth of babes and sucklings thou hast perfected praise?" (Matt 21:16).

Scriptures
3166

Resurrection
2407–2416

In his divine knowledge Jesus knew the Scriptures to be true. They were the source of his authority. After his resurrection he reproved those foolish and "slow of heart" who did not believe all that was written in the Scriptures (Luke 24:25). To Jesus, "Thus it is written" was sufficient. At the Rabbinical Council at Jamnia (A.D. 90–118) the final limit of the Old Testament canon was affirmed and authenticated.

The Jews were people of the Book. This unquestioned and confident authority won many heathen people from their impotent and impoverished superstitions to the True and Living God.

3

The River of Inspiration

I. THE BIBLE RIVER—AN INTERPRETATION

The River Chart presents a very basic presupposition that the OT and the NT river source is one and the same. The water of inspiration which flows into the tunnel on the OT side is the same that emerges on the NT side. Thus the basic revelation and inspiration in the OT must be the same as that in the NT.

River of Inspiration p. VII

An examination of each of the thirty-nine books in the OT and the twenty-seven in the NT discloses that there is complete unity within the books. The thought of biblical integrity rests on the proposition that the authors of the Bible books had divine illumination. Paul expressed this concept in these words, "All scripture is given by inspiration of God, and is profitable for doctrine, for reproof, for correction, for instruction in righteousness" (2 Tim. 3:16). Peter supports this affirmation: "For the prophecy came not in old time by the will of man: but holy men of God spake as they were moved by the Holy Ghost" (2 Peter 1:21).

List of Bible Books p. VII, VIII

Inspired Word 417, 1774–1776

Thus it is quite obvious that Bible authority and its veracity are directly connected with the character of the writers. If they were "holy men," they were trustworthy and their character was unquestioned. This being true, the entire Bible is the infallible Word of God. Regardless of any theory of inspiration of how men produced and preserved the Bible, apart from the question of how much is to be interpreted literally and how much figuratively, or what is historical or what may be poetical, we accept the Bible for what it claims to be, the Word

Holy Men 1125 Bible 414–445

45

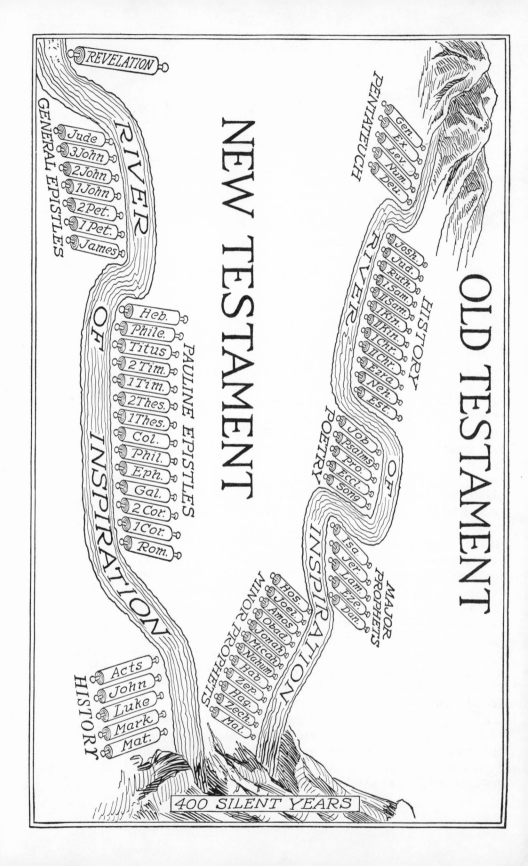

of God; it becomes the vehicle unto salvation to all who believe.[1] From Genesis to Revelation the message in the Bible changes the hearts of human beings from a bent to sin to a passion for holiness and love.

There is current today a view that the Bible is the record of man's ever upward reach to find God, that God did not really speak, but that men put their ideas about God into written form. Thus some have reduced the Bible to a system based on human speculation or rationalization with only a pretense of it being divine. This idea is vehemently rejected by most conservative Bible scholars who hold that the Bible is the record of God's continual quest for man, even from the time in the Garden when God said, "Adam, where art thou?" According to scholars, the Bible was written over a fifteen-hundred-year period by more than thirty different writers, and yet the cross reference system shows that unity of thought and purpose remain consistent in all sixty-six books. The promise of salvation can be traced like a scarlet thread through the Bible from Genesis (3:15) to Revelation (7:14).

The inspiration of the Bible is affirmed by the men who wrote it; they asserted "Thus saith the Lord" and similar expressions; the Word was written in the hearts of men; it has been a source of light and strength to people of all ages; saints have loved it. Internal evidence proves to the devout believer that indeed "holy men of God" wrote the Bible.

II. A COMPARATIVE ANALYSIS OF REVELATION IN THE OLD AND NEW TESTAMENTS

It is obvious that divine revelation, whether in the OT or in the NT, is substantially the same and manifests itself through common agencies and means; the basic principles of redemption are essentially the same regardless of the time or place, because God transcends time; he never changes. The bruising of the seed in Genesis refers to the divine sacrifice, already planned (3:15). *The sacrifice by Abel illustrated God's acceptance of the blood sacrifice (Gen. 4:4); thus the blood ritual continued until Christ validated it by his own supreme sacrifice on the cross. The written word explains the sacrifice of blood as it was portrayed in the OT and fulfilled in Christ, and the Holy Spirit witnesses to the fact in the believer's heart.*

Through revelation man lays hold of divine truth, which he cannot fully comprehend by reason alone, nor can he reduce it to everyday life without the direct aid of the Holy Spirit. The Scriptures contain a body of truth, known as the deposit of faith, which God seeks to communicate to man. The Bible

The River of Inspiration

Inspired Word
417

Word of God
410, 417, 418, 421, 422–425

Divine Inspiration
1774–1776

Methods of Revelation
2495–2504

Sacrifices
3107–3111

Holy Spirit
1601–1614

Scriptures
3166

Bible
414–445

47

*Preliminary
Matters*

Saints
3055–3060

Incarnation
720

reveals the message to those who have a will to know the truth and to act upon it.[2] This is "the faith which was once delivered unto the saints" (Jude 3).

When man received and recorded redemptive revelation during the period preceding the Incarnation, the Savior was already an active participant with the Father in Administering the plan of salvation through the Holy Spirit. God, through Christ the Lord, was the Redemptive Agent in the OT dispensation, whereas in the NT synoptic period, he, Christ, became the redemptive coordinator and witness.

As foretold in the OT, the NT is a historical verification of God's plan for man (Matt. 21–42; Mark 14:49; Luke 24:32). Eventually a fully canonized set of writings describing the events in the lifetime of Jesus the Savior was made and were acknowledged as having equal authority with the OT.[3]

James clearly states that by revelation the prophets spake in the name of Christ (5:10). Luke writes that the law and the prophets were until the coming of John the Baptist (16:16). In speaking of Jesus Christ, Philip said, "We have found him, of whom Moses in the law, and the prophets, did write" (John 1:45). Certainly the Lord in the OT is identical with Jesus Christ in the NT.[4] Peter states positively that "all the prophets witness" to Christ, "that through his name" all believers "receive remission of sins" (Acts 10:43). Paul, in his message to Agrippa, bases salvation on belief in the Messiah of whom the prophets testified (Acts 26:27). When Paul arrived in Ephesus the people were being initiated into the faith by "John's Baptism." Paul interprets John's baptism as having a relationship to belief in Jesus Christ who had not yet arrived on the scene. Paul said, "John verily baptized with the baptism of repentance, saying unto the people, that they should believe on him . . . that is, on Christ Jesus" (Acts 19:4). This raises the question: At what point in history, before Jesus came, could people be saved through faith in Jesus Christ? If they could be saved a few months before he came by exercising faith in him who was to come (foretold by the prophets), it seems logical that they could be saved by faith one year, ten years, yes one hundred years from the time "the Lamb [was] slain from the foundation of the world" (Rev. 13:8; see also 2 Tim. 3:15; Titus 1:2).

When John the Baptist said, "Repent ye: for the kingdom of heaven is at hand" (Matt. 3:2), he made a statement that was applicable to every age. The Kingdom and the King have always been at hand; the Fountain of David has always been open with the invitation that "whosoever will may come." In this connection Jesus made it clear that there was no other way into the Kingdom: "I am the way, the truth, and the life: no man cometh unto the Father but by me" (John 14:6). This

John the
Baptist
1903–1906

Agrippa
1580–1581

Prophecy
Fulfilled pp.
246ff.,
2892, 2893

Messianic
Prophecies
2890, 2891

Spiritual
Kingdom
2007–2013

"I Am"s of
Christ
4166

is a statement of fact not subject to any tense of time. The Great "I AM" is speaking.

The writer of Matthew's Gospel definitely relates the kingdom to him "that was spoken of by the prophet Esaias" (3:3), that is to him who was in existence before and during the life time of Esaias, although he did not take upon himself the form of man and become manifest or physically visible until the "fulness of the time was come" (Gal. 4:4). Christ is the principal theme in the Scriptures, and it is he whom God "promised before by his prophets" (Rom. 1:2). The Spirit of Christ, which was in the prophets, testified of the sufferings of Christ and the glory that should follow (1 Peter 1:10–11). It is obvious that the men of God in ancient times thought of Christ as the one through whom salvation was provided (cf. Ps. 51:12 and Matt 21:22; Isa. 7:14 and Matt. 1:18; Zech. 9:9 and John 12:13,14).

Christ's Suffering **713, 3489**

When Philip talked to the Ethiopian he opened the "Scriptures" at a passage spoken by the prophet Isaiah (Isa. 53:7,8), and "preached unto him Jesus" (Acts 8:35). As soon as Paul was able to do so after his conversion, he also "preached Christ in the Synagogues, that he is the Son of God" (Acts 9:20). Even the children of Israel had Christ preached to them (Acts 10:36). Throughout the Bible, Christ is the eternal focal point; he is the Redeemer and the dispenser of salvation in every age. He is always one with the Father, whether he is called LORD God in the OT or Jesus in the NT.[5]

Philip **2753**

Jesus established his divinity to preach, to overcome temptation, to expose false leaders and to teach Christian concepts, particularly those of the Sermon on the Mount and by quoting and referring to the OT Scriptures. These Scriptures offer positive proof that Christ has always been eternal and co-creator with the Father. Paul testified that the Incarnation of the Lord fulfilled his historical portion of the redemptive plan: "When the fulness of the time was come, God sent forth his Son, made of a woman, made under the law, to redeem them that were under the law, that we might receive the adoption of sons" (Gal. 4:4,5).

Temptation **3587**
Sermon on the Mount **3237**

When the Lord walked with the disciples on the Emmaus road, He said, "O fools, and slow of heart to believe all that the prophets have spoken: Ought not Christ to have suffered these things, and to enter into his glory?" (Luke 24:25,26). Luke adds these words, "And beginning at Moses and all the prophets, he expounded unto them in all the scriptures the things concerning himself" (Luke 24:27). When the Lord came to Nazareth, he read a passage from the Book of Isaiah: "The Spirit of the Lord is upon me, because he hath anointed me to preach the gospel to the poor; he hath sent me to heal

Emmaus **1119**

the brokenhearted, . . . to preach the acceptable year of the Lord" (Isa. 61:1; cf. Luke 4:18,19). He concluded with these words: "This day is this scripture fulfilled in your ears" (Luke 4:21).

While the disciples were locked in their hideaway chamber, the resurrected Jesus appeared in their midst and said unto them, "These are the words which I spake unto you, while I was yet with you, that all things must be fulfilled, which were written in the law of Moses, and in the prophets, and in the psalms concerning me" (Luke 24:44).

Christ's
Temptation
3587

During the temptation in the wilderness, Jesus made exclusive reference to the Scriptures (OT) in his conflict with Satan (Deut. 6:16; cf. Matt. 4:1–11). Furthermore all the great truths spoken by the Lord were based on OT theology; he went about "teaching . . . and preaching the gospel of the kingdom" (Matt. 4:23), as revealed in the OT (Pss. 22:28; 103:19; Dan. 4:3).

To illustrate these parallels between the OT and the NT, the Book of Matthew is an appropriate source, particularly the Sermon on the Mount. Almost every idea presented in Matthew can be traced to the OT; a similar result would be obtained using other NT books. There are many references for each idea in Matthew, but due to space limitation only a few will be presented here.

Sermon on the
Mount
4222

The Sermon on the Mount was a presentation of "old gospel wine" in new theological wineskins (cf. Matt. 5:3 with Ps. 51:17; Prov. 16:19; cf. Matt. 5:4 with Isa. 61:2,3; cf. Matt. 5:5 with Ps. 37:11; cf. Matt. 5:6 with Isa. 65:13; cf. Matt. 5:7 with Ps. 41:1; cf. Matt. 5:8 with Ps. 15:2). The terminology used in this sermon was appropriate for the worldwide or universal gospel mission to which divine revelation was directed. The Master gathered the ideas and concepts of the "Kingdom" as they had been preached in the OT by "men of faith" (Jude 3) into a homily especially suited to the need at hand. By so doing, Jesus Christ linked the NT Church to the OT. His statement, "Ye are the light of the world" (Matt 5:14), is another way of saying "The path of the just is as the shining light, that shineth more and more unto the perfect day" (Prov. 4:18). The command to turn the "right cheek" (Matt. 5:39) is clearly the spirit of the statement in Isaiah (50:6).

Kingdom
2007–2013

Closet
778

When Jesus made reference to entering the closet, he no doubt restated a principle of private devotion known to Elisha when "he went in . . . and shut the door . . . and prayed unto the LORD" (2 Kings 4:33). The entire Sermon on the Mount, including the Lord's Prayer, is a restatement of divine concepts well known in the OT (cf. Matt. 6:9 with Deut. 32:6; Isa. 6:3; cf. Matt 6:10 with Ps. 103:20; cf. Matt. 6:11 with Prov. 30:8).

Fasting as taught by our Lord (Matt. 6:16) was a common practice among OT saints (Ps. 35:13; 69:10; Isa. 58:3; Jer. 14:12; Zech. 7:5). The warning against laying up treasures on earth is obviously drawn from the Proverbs (23:4; 28:20). Seeking first the "kingdom of God" (Matt. 6:33) is a divine principle illustrated in the inauguration of Solomon as king (1 Kings 3:11ff.). "False prophets" in Matt. 7:15 were a problem in Moses' day (Deut. 13:3). The healing power manifested by Jesus (Matt. 8:14ff.) is the same that healed people in the OT. It is certain that the healing ministry of Christ was already in operation long before the Incarnation. Use of the past tense supports this thought in Isaiah 53:4,5, "He hath borne our griefs . . . he was wounded . . . he was bruised . . . , with his stripes [already provisionally existing] we are healed" and people were healed in OT times (Num. 21:9; 2 Kings 5:14).

All of the redemptive provisions (healing for the body and soul) were contained in the provision made in the crucified Savior who was projected in the fore-knowing mind of God. Rebuking the winds and the sea (Matt. 8:26) was a prerogative Christ the Lord had during the OT period (Job 38:8–11; Ps. 65:7). The concept that mercy was more desirable than sacrifices (Matt. 9:13) was an accepted truth in the OT (1 Sam. 15:22; Ps. 51:16,17; Isa. 1:11; Hosea 6:6). The principle of God providing words for an hour of need (Matt. 10:19) was well known to Moses and Jeremiah (Exod. 4:12; Jer. 1:7). The idea that a person receiving a prophet would receive a prophet's reward (Matt. 10:41) is illustrated in the relationship between the widow and Elijah (1 Kings 17:10ff.) and between the woman and Elisha (2 Kings 4:8).

John the Baptist was comparable to Elijah in the OT (Matt. 11:12–14). Christ shows from the Book of Malachi that John was another Elijah (Mal. 4:4–6); John the Baptist was to the NT church what Elijah was to the OT church. Jesus Christ came to emphasize the spirit of the law which had been lost by Pharisee-Sadducee Judaism. These leaders of the counterfeit church had substituted the "doctrines and commandments of men" for the spiritual interpretation of divine revelation (cf. Isa. 29:13 with Matt. 15:9 and Titus 1:14). The "apostate vipers" in the temple had perverted the faith of Abraham, Moses, and Elijah to such an extent that formal worship was mere shallow mockery. With few exceptions, Jesus Christ was making reference to "commandments and doctrines of men" when he said, "Ye have heard" or similar expressions. Of their legalistic application and interpretation he said, "from the beginning it was not so," but rather, "it is the spirit that quickeneth; . . . the words that I speak unto you, they are spirit, and they are life" (John 6:63). Space does not permit further illustration of the

The River of Inspiration

Fasting
3212–3214

Treasures
2814

Kingdom
2007–2013

False Prophets
2100

Healing
1538–1543

Salvation in OT
3116

Mercy vs. Sacrifice
3108

John the Baptist
1903–1906

Pharisees
3171

Sadducees
3172

Apostates
1236

False Traditions
3652

51

point. By use of the TCRB Cyclopedia of Topics and Texts and Concordance this analytical study can be continued.

Outline of the
Bible
4219

Revelation
2494–2497

III. THE STAGES OF REVELATION

On page 53 the progressive nature of revelation is illustrated in chart form where seven books are stacked, one upon another. From this it can be seen that God has always made himself available to man and man has had an option on salvation from the time God sought Adam and Eve in the Garden. The first edition of revelation was written into the very structure of the universe: "In the beginning God created the heavens and the earth." Thus in the creation God left his fingerprints on all of his work. The idea of revelation in nature is clearly seen throughout Scripture for those who have a "will" to see: "Whosoever will" may come (see John 3:16; Rev. 22:17).

Nature's
Revelation
2498 and
p. 178

One of the strongest claims to natural revelation comes in Psalm 19:1 where the Psalmist states, "The heavens declare the glory of God; and the firmament sheweth his handywork." The psalmist also proclaims in verse three that there is no language [or nation] where the voice of heavenly revelation is not heard. (See also Ps. 97:6; Acts 4:17; Rom. 1:20.) The Living Bible expresses these ideas beautifully: *"The Heavens are telling the glory of God; they are a marvelous display of his craftsmanship. Day and night they keep on telling about God. Without a sound or word, silent in the skies, their message reaches out to all the world"* (Ps. 19:1–3).

The New International Version renders these passages thus:

> The heavens declare the glory of God;
>   the skies proclaim the work of his hands.
> Day after day they pour forth speech;
>   night after night they display knowledge.
> There is no speech or language
>   where their voice is not heard (Ps. 19:1–3).

Conscience
824

God's redemptive plan was also imprinted on man's conscience (Rom. 2:15). The word "conscience" does not appear in the OT, but it is used thirty times in the NT. It must be assumed that the essential idea of "conscience" is resident in the OT, perhaps through the Hebrew word for "heart." Some scholars see in the word *reins* a sounding board for the conscience.

Reins
2984

As the basic natures of God and man have not changed, it is obvious that the NT references to conscience are equally relevant to OT man. Conscience, as a phase of human intelligence, places a burden of responsibility on man. Conscience is stimulated for good or evil, depending upon the stimuli to which it is exposed. Conscience is the medium through which

God can speak to man, but it must be divinely oriented. Although it is the voice of God in the soul, man's conscience can be influenced by experience, reason, intuition, authority, and revelation. Of course it must be acknowledged that the devil can interfere with God's communication. All of these considerations contribute their share to the reservoir of ethical insight or guiding principles. The NT makes reference to a "convicted conscience" (John 8:9), a "good conscience" (Acts 23:1), a "conscience void of offence" (Acts 24:16), a "conscience of the idol" (1 Cor. 8:7), "conscience being weak" (1 Cor. 8:7b), a "pure conscience" (2 Tim. 1:3), and an "evil conscience" (Heb. 10:22).

The River of Inspiration

The Law was written on tables of stone and given to Moses on Mt. Sinai (Exodus 24:12), representing the third edition in the process of revelation. The chart below shows the fifth edition of the Scriptures as being "Christ the Illustrated Edition." He demonstrated through his humanity that the redemptive life is possible. This edition is followed by the "Holy Spirit Edition," which engraves the word on the heart of man (Heb. 8:10), who, in turn, becomes the living epistle, "letters read by all men." The Christian is the "Shoe Leather" version as he demonstrates the Christian life in community outreach (2 Cor. 3:2,3).

Law
435–445

Holy Spirit
1601–1614

No. 4219   SEVEN EDITIONS OF DIVINE LAW

7th EDITION	THE OUTWARD CHRISTIAN LIFE LIVING EPISTLES	II COR. 3:2,3
6th EDITION	WRITTEN ON THE HEART	HE. 8:10
5th EDITION	CHRIST THE ILLUSTRATED EDITION	JN. 1:14
4th EDITION	THE ENTIRE SCRIPTURES	RO. 15:4
3rd EDITION	WRITTEN ON TABLES OF STONE	EX. 24:12
2nd EDITION	WRITTEN ON CONSCIENCE	RO. 2:15
1st EDITION	WRITTEN ON NATURE	PS. 19:1

IN this drawing the divine method of the gradual revelation and publication of the law is illustrated.

It was first written upon nature, next upon man's conscience, then the fundamental principles upon the tables of stone.

Later the entire Scriptures contained a larger and more complete edition. In due time Jesus appeared as the perfect embodiment of the truth which he illustrated in his own sinless life.

It was the divine purpose that the law, at last, should be written in the hearts of men, and the final publication of its precepts be found in their outward lives.

53

4

The Transmission of the Bible

I. THE MISSING AUTOGRAPHS (NT)

When scholars speak of verifying a biblical subject by the original Greek or Hebrew text, they do not mean to imply that they will actually read an original autograph. Unfortunately no autographs have been preserved; only copies of copies of originals remain. Almost all of the ancient copies which have survived are hand copied and are on deposit in school libraries, in museums, and in a few private collections. Photographic reproductions provide a base for scholarly studies.

In 1450 Johannes Gutenberg produced the first printed Bible in Latin. Of the 200 copies he printed, only about 48 are believed to be still in existence. The University of Texas purchased one of these copies in 1978 for $2,400,000. The total collection of NT manuscripts in existence today numbers about 5000, of which 76 are written on papyri, 250 are uncials; over 2500 are minuscules and about 2500 are lectionary editions which are divided into reading sections for each day.[1]

About 95 percent of the NT minuscles date between the eighth and thirteenth centuries. The rest are uncials dating from the second to the seventh centuries. Each year additional biblical manuscripts are discovered and added to this depository. Even though many manuscripts are lost, the number of NT manuscripts surviving is phenomenal, compared to the surviving copies of other ancient books. Some of the early nonbiblical books are known only by the references to them, and by quotations from other writers. Papias (A.D. 70–150) was a pupil of John the Beloved, but his writings exist only through quotations in Iranaeus (A.D. 130–200), Eusebius (A.D. 264–340), and others.

All but about 50 of the surviving manuscripts are incomplete, containing from only a few verses to all but a few chapters. No two manuscripts are exactly alike, but scholars can arrive at the accurate approximation of an autograph by comparing one manuscript with another. Actually the variant readings are so insignificant that no basic Christian doctrine is affected; all of the manuscripts communicate the full redemptive message.

II. TEXTUAL PROBLEMS (NT)

The early manuscripts were copied by hand on papyri or parchment sheets and sewn together to form rolls up to 30 feet long. Even though great care was exercised for accuracy, it was humanly impossible to copy such lengthy manuscripts by hand without some scribal error. Unrolling the manuscripts frequently caused much wear, and eventually they became fragile and broke up into small pieces. Because these manuscripts were carried to many areas in the world by ship, caravan, and on foot and because Christianity was an outlawed movement in some parts of the world for the first three centuries after Christ, readers had little opportunity to bring manuscripts out into the open for comparison. However, with the advent of Constantine (A.D. 313) and his Edict of Toleration, it was no longer necessary to keep NT manuscripts concealed. Soon thereafter, in making comparisons, scholars discovered variant readings. Many of these variants were unintentional or accidental, in areas of sight, of writing, and of judgment. Sometimes errors were caused by the confusion of letters or pairs of letters that looked very much alike. Sometimes an abbreviation might be mistaken for a full word, or a similar word. An error might be caused by faulty hearing when a group of scribes copied manuscripts by dictation. Sometimes intentional changes were made by the scribe to correct what he thought was a mistake in the manuscript. However, "there is virtually no evidence of a scribe's intentionally weakening the theology or purposely introducing heresy into his manuscripts." [2] Generally speaking, the scribes were professional men and took great pride in their accuracy and in the fact that they were men with a holy mission.

Even more complicated are the texts themselves. There were no chapter and verse divisions in the manuscripts, but in 1228 Stephen Langston worked out a chapter division for the entire

Christ
725, 4139

Scribes
3165

55

Bible. In 1551 Robert Stephens divided the NT into verses. About A.D. 700 the Masorites had begun to work out a verse division for the OT.

Another type of error resulted from the absence of word separation: ancient manuscripts neither separated words nor used punctuation. Thus John 1:3 would read: "ALLTHINGSWEREMADEBYHIMANDWITHOUTHIMWAS NOTANYTHINGMADETHATWASMADE." It is self-evident that errors could develop within this kind of composition.

In addition to the genuine manuscripts there were many NT apocryphal writings which were attempts to express and perpetuate heathen theogony in canonical form. The Gospel of Peter was a book supporting the Docetic heresy that Christ only seemed to have a human body. The Epistle to the Laodiceans was a mixture of the Epistle to the Philippians and heathen myths and philosophies. The only apocryphal epistles approximating Paul's letters were 3 Corinthians and the Epistle to the Laodiceans. The apocryphal Apocalypse of Peter was the only rival to the Book of Revelation by St. John. By assuming the name of those in whose spirit they professed to write, the apocalyptic approach provided heathen philosophers a vehicle in which to shroud their ancient superstitions. The inferior quality of these writings and the lack of true apostolic background were quite marked. These NT apocryphal books were never compiled in a form comparable to the OT apocryphal books. Only the heretical sects placed them on a par with the canonical books.[3]

OT Apocrypha
See p. 179

Bible readers are very much indebted to the scholars of the ages who sifted, compiled, edited, and, through a system of synthesis, have produced from the "raw materials" remarkably accurate biblical documents.

III. WRITING MATERIALS (NT)

Most of the early manuscripts were written on papyrus sheets, made from the papyrus reed growing along the Nile River in Egypt. This is the term from which the word "paper" comes. A small amount of the reed still grows in the Lake Huleh near the Sea of Galilee. To process, the papyrus reed was peeled; the pith inside was sliced and rolled into thin strips, laid criss-cross in sheets, and then pressed between two heavy flat surfaces. After a few days these sheets became writing material, which was in use in the Old Kingdom of Egypt as early as 2700 B.C. Some of this ancient papyrus has been preserved in the sands and tombs of Upper Egypt. The Edwin Smith surgical documents of 5000 years ago were written on Egyptian papyri.[4]

The early hard-sewn manuscripts were joined together in a continuous roll. With hard use these rolls became brittle and broke into pieces like a jig-saw puzzle. Some museums have large quantities of these fragments and at times it is difficult to find two pieces which fit together. The invention of the codex (page) form of book greatly facilitated the use of the ancient manuscripts. Some have perished in fires and floods, and many were deliberately destroyed during periods of religious persecution. Parchment made from skins was also used.

IV. WRITING INSTRUMENTS (NT)

Writing instruments in early times were brushes, pointed quills, and slender sticks of papyri. The papyrus pens were ideal because the pithy interior could absorb ink through capillary action. This is perhaps the forerunner of the modern fountain pen, or felt-tipped pens. The writing fluid was an ink made of charcoal, gum and water.

V. THE NEW TESTAMENT MANUSCRIPTS

When scholars study ancient manuscripts, they now use accurate photographic copies. The originals are stored in humidified vaults.

A. *Papyrus Manuscripts*

Most of the Papyrus manuscripts have been discovered since 1890 and of these the most important are the Chester Beatty papyri found in Egypt. Mr. Beatty, an English scholar, had the good fortune to discover NT papyrus sheets in Egypt in 1930–31. They came from what was originally a three-volume codex manuscript consisting of thirty-two sheets from the Gospels and the Book of Acts, eighty-six leaves from a codex of Paul's epistles, and ten leaves of an original thirty from the Book of Revelation. These manuscripts were especially valuable because they date back to the third century and provide an early form of the NT.

B. *Types of Greek Letters*

1. Uncials (fourth–tenth centuries)

The word "uncial" means "inch-high." The uncial manuscripts, dating from the fourth to the tenth century, were so called because they were written in large square Greek letters on a leather material called vellum or parchment. Probably in the autographs of the Gospels the writers used uncial letters, as they appear in the earliest and most reliable extant manuscripts of the entire NT. The Vaticanus and the Sinaiticus manuscripts were both written in this script.

2. Minuscules (ninth–fifteenth centuries)

The minuscles are the manuscripts written in small Greek letters closely joined together, which belong to a much later date than the uncials, from the ninth century to the fifteenth century. Of all the NT manuscripts, about 95 percent are minuscules. "The disparity in the numbers of the surviving manuscripts doubtless points to the fact that the minuscle handwriting, more like modern longhand, made the copying of manuscripts a much more rapid and less expensive process." [5] The variant readings in the minuscules are in the area of grammar, spelling, word omission, word duplication, omission of a line, and the addition of a line. The really significant variations amount to only about "a thousandth part of the entire text."

Some of the best-known texts for Greek NT studies are the following:

(1) Westcott and Hort (1881–82);
(2) Erberhard Nestle (1898);
(3) Greek New Testament produced by the United Bible Societies (1966).[6]

VI. THE OLD TESTAMENT MANUSCRIPTS

The problems pertaining to the OT are similar to those of the NT. There are, however, some technical differences. The OT manuscripts were entrusted to scribes trained in Rabbinical and Mosaic Law and above all else, in accuracy. They were "letter of the law" scholars, who frequently discarded a manuscript on which an error had been made. They were totally obsessed with the idea that they had the responsibility of transmitting and preserving the "Word of God" exactly, in every "jot" and "tittle," the two smallest consonantal forms in the Hebrew alphabet (Matt. 5:18). But with all these precautions it was inevitable that an unintentional error would creep in occasionally. These errors, similar to those in the NT documents, were insignificant. Some of the errors or variants resulted from a variety of causes:

1. Haplography—The writing of one word, letter, or syllable only once where it should have been written more than once.

2. Dittography—Writing twice what should have been written only once.
3. Metathesis—Reversing the proper position of words.
4. Fusion—The combining of two separate words into one.
5. Fission—The dividing of a single word into two words.
6. Homophony—The substitution of a word which has the same pronunciation, e.g., "two" for "to."
7. Misreading—Many Hebrew consonants are almost identical in shape as, Daleth and Beth; Tzaddi and Ain; He, Cheth and Tau; Caph and Pe. Vowels can also be mistaken for consonants of a similar shape. Until about A.D. 700 the Sopherim (Wise Men's) texts had no vowel pointings or pronunciation marks for the consonantal Hebrew text. At that time the Jewish scholars of Babylon and Palestine, called the Masorites, worked out a system of vowel points and divided the Hebrew Bible into verses. The most famous Masorites lived in Tiberias in Galilee (A.D. 700–1100).
8. Homeoteleuton—The omission of the next line or lines when the scribe's eye skipped from one line to another of similar ending further down the page.[7]

There are three basic "families" of OT manuscripts: the Masoretic, the Septuagint (LXX), and the Samaritan Pentateuch. The finding of the Dead Sea Scrolls in 1947 has given scholars additional Hebrew Bible Books which are much earlier than any extant manuscripts. Some of these Scrolls date back to about 200 B.C. Almost all of the Bible books have been discovered in this area, and this late discovery leaves the earlier manuscripts intact. Comparing the Dead Sea Scrolls of Isaiah with the Masoretic (i.e., medieval) text reveals a 95-percent word-for-word identity. The remaining 5 percent variants deal mainly with the slip of the pen or spelling. The noted Yale professor, Millar Burrows, says "that the Isaiah Scroll is very important for establishing the best possible text of the Old Testament. By and large it confirms the antiquity and authenticity of the Masoretic Text." [8]

The entire Bible has been checked and double checked by the test of time to such an extent that there is no longer any reasonable doubt about it. The noted scholar and archaeologist, Kathleen Kenyon, is assuring at this point:

> The Christian can take the whole Bible in his hand and say without fear or hesitation that he holds in it the True Word of God, handed without essential loss from generation to generation, throughout the centuries.[9]

The Bible as it has been given to the Church is indeed the revealed Word of God.

5

Places of Religious Worship

Places for
Worship
4316

Worship
3422–3952

I. DEVELOPMENT OF WORSHIP CENTERS

The word *worship* in the Christian religion means showing respect and honor to God. The first recorded instance in the Bible of a planned worship service was the one in which Abel offered a sacrificial animal. This act of worship was an expression of homage and faith toward God. Eventually the places of worship became more formal. Five main developments in this area are significant.

The Altar
120

A. *The Altar*

In the beginning when worship centers were first set up, the altar was merely a site or location where man sought communication with his God. Worshipers in the patriarchal period built altars wherever they pitched their tents (Gen. 8:20; 12:7; 22:9; 35:1,7). Almost any kind of marker used in communication with deity became an altar. Frequently it was nothing more than a stone or several stones laid one on top of another, or it might have been a mound of earth. Sometimes an altar was made of metal (2 Kings 16:14). The altar was in a measure a testimony or a witness to the heathen world that surrounded early Yahweh worshipers.

Noah
2597
Immediately after Noah left the ark, he built a simple stone altar on which he offered sacrifices unto the Lord, who responded favorably and promised Noah many great blessings. Abraham built altars in several places as he went from Ur of the Chaldees to Haran and on into Canaan and Egypt (Gen.

60

12:7,8; 13:18). Jacob made an altar out of the stone that he had used for a pillow while he was camping in Bethel (Gen. 28:18,19; cf. Gen. 33:20; 35:7). As time passed the need for a more formal place of worship developed.

Places of Religious Worship
Jacob
1837

Bethel
406, 4337

B. The Tabernacle in the Wilderness

The Israelites would be spending forty years as nomadic travelers in the Sinai desert and would need a portable center of worship. This took the form of a tabernacle for which God gave Moses minute construction specifications. Every construction detail was carefully delineated (Exod. 36:1ff.). For a detailed discussion of the tabernacle see Ch. 11.

The Tabernacle
3528, p. 304

C. The Temple

In the course of time the people needed a more permanent type of worship center. The tabernacle was moved from place to place as the patriarchal tribes traveled from Mount Sinai to Canaan.

Temple
3577–3579,
pp. 304, 306, 307

The next development for a place of worship was the temple, a permanent structure for use after the children of Israel had settled on their assigned land allotments in Canaan. The plan for a permanent place of constant worship was given to David, but because of his sin with Bathsheba and his involvement with war, he was not permitted to build the temple. The task of constructing it was delegated to Solomon, David's son. The temple of Solomon was one of the most beautiful and expensive buildings ever constructed. The tabernacle had been drab, covered with animal skins, whereas the temple was glorious and golden. It contained over 1,000,000 talents of silver and 100,000 talents of gold. To these Solomon added 3000 talents of gold and 700 talents of silver from his own private fortune. The princes contributed additional gold and silver. In modern times the value of the gold and silver would be equal to billions of dollars.

Fine Lebanese cedar wood was imported from Tyre. Large work crews, transported to the mountains of Lebanon, cut and shaped the cedar wood. One hundred and fifty thousand Canaanites were drafted to hew stone. The temple was erected on Mount Moriah, where Abraham, many years before, had expected to offer Isaac and where Aranuah, the Jebusite, had had his threshing floor (2 Chron. 3:1). The general plans for the temple were like those for the tabernacle, but the dimensions were doubled and the ornaments were richer. The stones were cut to size in the quarry beneath the city. All the timber was shaped and finished before it arrived at the temple site.

Cedar
651

Preliminary
Matters

Holy Place
1600

Candlestick
637

Holy of Holies
1599

High Priests
2064

Laver
2051

Temple
3577–3579

Gentile
Believers
4038

Synagogue
3521–3523

It was probably the first prefabricated building in the world: certainly it was the largest and most beautiful. The interior was overlaid with gold.

The Holy Place, within the temple, which contained the golden candlestick, was symbolic of God, the Light; the table of shew bread symbolized spiritual bread; the altar of incense suggested man communing with God through prayer. A veil separated the Holy of Holies or the Inner Sanctum from the Holy Place. Behind the veil was the Ark of the Covenant with its two cherubims ten cubits high. Once each year, on the Day of Atonement (Yom Kippur), the high priest entered here and officiated for the people. Before the priests could minister inside either sanctuary, they were required to undergo a ceremonial cleansing at the brazen laver located outside the entrance to the Holy Place. The laver, made out of brass, contained water for the ablution ritual. Scripture records show that the brazen laver was made of the "looking-glasses of the women" (Exod. 38:8). Giving up their mirrors symbolized the women's complete dedication.

A place in the temple complex was provided for the Gentiles who desired to receive religious instruction which would lead to conversion to Judaism. Such converts were called proselytes. The temple served the worship needs of the people until it was destroyed by Nebuchadnezzar in 586 B.C.

D. The Synagogue

When the Babylonians took the Jews into captivity they totally destroyed the temple which was not rebuilt until after Cyrus liberated the Jews. During the 70 years in captivity the Jews were deprived of using the temple; expediency led to the development of a functional worship center for their use during this period. The steps in the development of the synagogue are not known but it is known that the Jews brought it from Babylon. The synagogue was an all-purpose worship center, a place for prayer and Bible study as well as fellowship. No provision was made for animal sacrifice. Synagogues ranged in size from the small home unit to special structures where large numbers could gather. Only ten heads of families or households were needed to organize a synagogue. The house synagogue which could accommodate a family and a few friends may be compared to the "house churches" in the Christian era (Philem. 2). There are fifty references to the synagogue in the NT. The term occurs only once in the OT (Ps. 74:8). When the Jews were dispersed throughout the Roman Empire, they took with them their synagogue and their Scriptures. Frequently synagogues were built by one man, as was the case

of the centurion in Capernaum (Luke 7:5). Later these syna- *Places of*
gogues provided preaching places for the traveling missionar- *Religious*
ies. *Worship*

It has been estimated that the Jews had over 1000 synagogues in the Mediterranean world by A.D. 70. After the destruction of the temple under Titus (A.D. 70) the synagogue and Jewish worship spread. All animal sacrifices ended in the same year because Christ, the Savior, the Jew's Messiah, had made the final and eternal sacrifice on the cross.

The architectural lines of the synagogue carried over into the church structure. The distinguishing mark of the synagogue is the Star of David; of the church it is the cross. Church services are quite similar to those in the synagogue: the congregation sang the Psalms, had responsive readings from the Scriptures, prayed, taught lessons from the Scriptures and their leaders preached sermons. Their hymn book, the Psalms, became the hymnbook of the Christian Church. In fact, the Book of Psalms is the only hymnbook the church had for the first 1500 years of its history. Thus, the church has much in common with the synagogue. When a complete break came between the believers in Christ and those who rejected him, the Christians began to develop an institution which was more nearly suitable to the need of the combined Jewish-Gentile membership. Since animal sacrifices had ended with the destruction of the temple, worship took on a new meaning in the Christian-Messiah movement (1 Sam. 15:22; Ps. 51:16,17; Hosea 6:6).

E. The Church

Church
726–761

The next place of worship to evolve was the church; however, the term *church* is used only three times in the Gospels, once in Matthew 16:18 and twice in Matthew 18:17. The first-century Christian was distinctly Jewish; Christianity was definitely a movement within Judaism (Matt. 13:54; Mark 6:3). Jesus, as well as his apostles, (Matt. 13:54; John 6:59; Acts 13:5) taught in the temple and in the synagogues. Gradually as the rift widened between the Jews who accepted Jesus as the Messiah and those who did not, the Messianic Christians began to worship in home churches, such as Philemon had in his home (Philem. 2). Some sizeable underground chapels give evidence that the early Christians had worship services also in the catacombs. Over the ages many Jews have become "fulfilled Jews" by accepting Jesus Christ as their Messiah.

It is also quite evident that the believers in the Messiah drew their authority from the OT. The NT is filled with instances of Jesus and the Evangels reinforcing their teachings with quotations from the OT. Even though the NT books were in circula-

Messiah
695, 4186

tion from about A.D. 60 and onward, they did not attain full canonization status until A.D. 397 at the Council of Carthage. (For specific instances see pages 39–42.)

Although a synagogue quorum required ten heads of families or households the membership for a Christian church seems to have been reduced by the Lord to "where two or three are gathered in my name, there am I in the midst of them" (Matt. 18:20). The Bible contains no reference to a church building or denominational church. The ekklesia, the church mentioned in the NT, always referred to the body of believers in the Lord as Christ, the Messiah. The church was both visible and invisible and was composed of all who were really united to Christ (1 Cor. 1:2; 12:12,13, 27,28; Col. 1:24; 1 Peter 2:9,10). The first historical reference to a church building was made by Alexander Severius, who reigned as Roman emperor A.D. 222–235.[1]

In the third and fourth centuries the word *basilica* took on a Christian tone. The term means a public building ending in a semicircular apse. It was used in Roman times for a court of justice or a public assembly hall. Frequently basilicas were converted into places of worship, especially in the period following Constantine's conversion. This architectural design has been perpetuated throughout the centuries. Even today such basilica terms as narthex, nave, aisle, apse, and transept are used to describe various parts of a church building.

Thus has come the evolution of the worship center, from the most primitive pile of stones to the modern cathedral with its stained glass, church spires, and pipe organs.

The preceding paragraphs explain the absence of church ruins from first- and second-century. Extensive church buildings did not come into existence until Constantine made Christianity a state religion (A.D. 275–337). When the Roman aristocracy insisted on adhering to their pagan religions, Constantine moved his capital to Byzantium and called it Constantinople, New Rome, capital of the New Christian Empire. He made Sunday the official rest day, and forbade ordinary work. This new order of rest, one day in seven, meant much for the slaves as well as for all working people. (See next chapter.)

6

Hebrew Times, Seasons, and Festivals

I. THE SABBATH

One of the greatest blessings which has come down to man is the idea of the Sabbath, a rest day, one in seven days. Various sociological experiments have been conducted regarding this practice, but no system has proved so beneficial as the one-day-in-seven formula.

In ancient times the poor, and especially the slaves, were required to work every day. Life expectancy was low. People were expended, literally worked to death, in mines, in building projects, and on farms.

When Moses proclaimed the Fourth Commandment, the introductory words, "Remember the Sabbath Day," suggest that the Sabbath did not originate on Mount Sinai, but rather that the people should adhere to, preserve, and observe a practice forgotten or neglected. Actually the idea of one rest day a week is implied when God rested from his labor on the seventh day of creation (Gen. 2:2) and required his people to do likewise (Exodus 23:12; 16:23).

This great blessing, one rest day a week, has been transmitted to the Christian world. Even in officially atheistic countries, like Russia, and Moslem countries, such as Turkey, Sunday is the official rest day. There is something in the warp and woof of nature that demands recognition of this formula. Man's history has demonstrated his need for the recuperation of his physical, mental, and spiritual energies once every seven days. The Sabbath was to be observed by all: the servants, the beasts of burden, the members of the Hebrew household, their guests,

Sabbath
3098 ff., 4317

Rest
3010

Poor
2799–2804

Slave—Bond
Servant
2138

Death
2158–2163

Moses
2420–2421

Command-
ments
444

and the visitors within their gates—all were commanded to stop work and rest on this day (Deut. 5:14,15). Verse 15 implies that the captives in Egypt did not have the benefit of the Sabbath rest.

The priests were to set the table in the Holy Place on the Sabbath. The rite of circumcision was to be performed on the Sabbath if it was the eighth day after the child's birth (Lev. 12:3; John 7:22). A "Holy Convocation" or the assembly of the community for religious purposes was within the bounds of Sabbath activity. However, the church fathers of the second and third centuries were very much opposed to the legal aspects of the Sabbath. The rift between the Jews who rejected the Messiah and those who accepted him became so great that everything Jewish was looked upon with hostility.

Following the reforms under Nehemiah and Ezra, the Jewish leaders developed an elaborate code of regulations and restrictions. The rabbis worked out a table of thirty-nine main divisions of labor forbidden on the Sabbath Day. In their zeal for the law, the rabbis increased the commandments of the written law to include 613 precepts. "Of these, 365 are negative—things a Jew must not do—the number corresponding to the number of days in the solar year. The remaining 248 are positive—things a Jew must do—the number corresponding, according to the Rabbinic view, to the 248 bones in the human body." [1] It is evident that under this interpretation the Sabbath would become burdensome.

A. Sabbath Day's Journey

The law of "A Sabbath Day's Journey" has no direct scriptural validity. It is a device invented by the rabbis to protect the Sabbath and to keep the people in close proximity to the center of worship on the Sabbath. Only a casual reference is made to this rabbinical ordinance in Acts 1:12 which states that the distance between the Mount of Olives and Jerusalem was a "sabbath day's journey." Where this law began is uncertain, but no doubt a need developed in history to define the limits of labor on the Sabbath. Walking, as well as working, consumed human energy, so the rabbis determined that the permissible distance for travel on the Sabbath should be 2000 cubits ($\frac{2}{3}$ of a mile). In the Jerusalem Targum is the statement, "Let no man walk from the place beyond 2000 cubits on the Sabbath Day." This is an arbitrary demand and has no basis in the levitical code. However, keeping the Sabbath Day holy is clearly stated in the rabbinical ordinance, which possibly had its origin in the Mosaic period, when the Israelites were not to leave camp to gather manna on the Sabbath.[2]

Arch.
Jerusalem
4381

Sabbath Day's
Journey
3139, 3533

Cubit
3533

At the beginning of the NT period the true meaning of the Sabbath had become obscured and shrouded in oppressive ordinances. Jesus sought to clarify the real meaning of the Sabbath by showing the original purpose of the institution: "The sabbath was made for man, and not man for the sabbath" (Mark 2:27). The early Christians were loyal Jews. They worshiped daily in the temple at Jerusalem (Acts 2:46); later they attended the synagogue and heard sermons.

Hebrew Times, Seasons, and Festivals
Synagogues
3521, 3523

B. *The Christian Sunday*

The origin of the Christian Sunday is not easy to determine. The change from the seventh day to the first day was gradual. To the Christian, the Resurrection Day was the most important of days, and one can assume that this feeling contributed to the change. Nothing could be more appropriate than to commemorate the Resurrection Day once each week and to link it with the day of rest and worship.

Christ
Resurrection
2410–2416

When Christianity was predominantly Jewish, the Sabbath was accepted as the day of rest and worship. However, when Christian congregations finally became predominantly Gentile, the Sabbath was abandoned and Sunday became the official rest day.[3]

Sabbath
3098

Gentiles
2383–2384

The ruler, Constantine, further established the observance of Sunday. After he had a vision of the Cross in the sky (27 Oct. 312) he decided to fight under the banner of Christ. When he won the battle he became a Christian. In his Edict of Toleration in A.D. 313, he legalized Christianity and filled his chief offices with Christians. Constantine had fifty Bibles copied for his churches and by edict made Sunday the official day of rest and worship in his kingdom. When the Roman aristocracy insisted on their pagan religions, Constantime moved his capital to Byzantium and called it Constantinople.

II. THE SIX ANNUAL FEASTS

Jewish Feasts
1256–1261

A. *Passover*

Passover
2686

The Passover was a day inaugurated in Egypt to commemorate the deliverance of the Israelites. This was the night when the death-angel smote the first born in the land of Egypt but passed over the houses of the Israelites where the blood had been sprinkled on the door posts and the lintel. The festival began on the fifteenth day of Ahib at evening with the sacrificial meal. A lamb was slain, roasted whole, and eaten with unleavened bread, accompanied by bitter herbs, to commemorate the Israelites' exit from Egypt in haste, not waiting for their bread to rise (Exod. 12:18; 1 Cor. 5:8). The festival lasted for

Unleavened
Bread
539

Preliminary
Matters

Sabbath
d73098

Feast of
Passover
1256

seven days. The first day was kept as a Sabbath and likewise the seventh. On the second day of the festival the priest waved a sheaf of barley before the Lord to consecrate the opening harvest. The Passover has a powerful Christian implication. The Passover lamb was a foreshadowing of Christ, the Lamb of God (1 Cor. 5:7). Like the paschal lamb, he was without blemish (Exod. 12:5; 1 Peter 1:18–19)—not a bone was broken (Exod. 12:46; John 19:36). His blood was presented to the Lord (Exod. 12:13). As the Israelites ate the Passover with each other, so also Jesus ate this memorial meal with his disciples (Luke 22:1–18).

B. Pentecost or the Feast of Weeks

Feast of
Pentecost
1257, 2722

Tabernacle
3528

Sabbath
3098

The Book of Exodus contains the first reference in the OT to Pentecost (Exod. 23:16ff). It was the second of the annual feasts at which every male was required to appear before the Lord at the Tabernacle, and the first of the two agricultural festivals (Exod. 34:22,23; 2 Chron. 8:12,13). The Feast of Weeks was so called because it came seven weeks after the harvest consecration and featured offering a sheaf of the first ripe barley. The sheaf was waved on the morrow after the Sabbath, or for seven complete weeks plus the morrow which would make the fiftieth day—Pentecost. On the Sabbath, the forty-ninth day, no work was permitted; so the physical effort to wave the grain before the Lord was postponed until the morrow or the first day of the week. No one could eat new grain until he had waved the sheaf before the Lord or until after the priest had blessed it for the Lord.

Pentecost was set aside as a special Sabbath in which no ordinary work should be done. All activity was limited to the needs of the Holy Convocation.

According to tradition, the Day of Pentecost commemorated the giving of the Law on Mount Sinai, fifty days after the Passover. According to Christian tradition, Pentecost came fifty days after the Resurrection of Jesus. The correlation is indeed impressive. Some scholars suggest that the church was "born" in the Upper Room on the Day of Pentecost. However, to avoid confusion, one may consider those assembled in the Upper Room as believers and, in a sense, already the church. It would be more correct to say that the church was baptized with the Holy Spirit to empower it for world evangelism (Acts 1:4) and to give it inner resources with which to stand up under the forthcoming persecution. Peter is perhaps the outstanding example of the change within a person after he is baptized with the Holy Spirit. It would be correct to say that the church received its commission and authority to witness throughout

Church, the
Flock
746–748

Baptism with
Holy Spirit
1605

the world "when the day of Pentecost was fully come" (Acts 2:1).

C. The Feast of Trumpets (Lev. 23:24)

The Feast of Trumpets, inaugurated by Moses (Lev. 23:24ff.), ushered in the new civil year. It was celebrated at the first New Moon of Tishri, the first civil month and the seventh sabbatical month in the religious year. People were summoned to the holy convocation by the sound of trumpets. Special offerings were presented and no common work was done on this day.

D. The Feast of Tabernacles (Lev. 24:34)

The Feast of Tabernacles, occurring five days after the Day of Atonement, was known as the Feast of Ingathering (Sukkoth). It came when the moon was full in the seventh month, Tishri (September or October) and lasted seven days. On the eighth day it culminated in a "holy convocation" (Lev. 23:34–36). This autumn festival (Deut. 16:13–17) was important as the beginning of the new civil year. It came at the end of harvest after all the fruits and grain were gathered in. This crowning event of the year was a great homecoming time of family reunions and celebration when families lived in booths made from tree branches. There was thanksgiving to the Lord for a good harvest and also paying of respect to their nomadic forefathers who had lived in tents in the wilderness. This autumn feast resembled New England Thanksgiving festivities and is also reminiscent of the old-fashioned camp meetings. In the fall when crops were harvested, our forefathers gathered in the woods for religious services and family reunions. They, too, erected temporary dwelling places—brush arbors and tents.[4]

E. The Feast of Dedication or Lights (Hanukkah)

The Feast of Dedication began on the New Moon on the twenty-fifth day of Chislev, the ninth sacred month, which came in late November and/or early December, and continued for eight days. In the ceremony the people carried torches or candles which they put in homes and places of worship, hence the title, Feast of Lights. It commemorated the purification of the temple and the restoration of the altar in the temple by Judas Maccabaeus in 165 B.C. The historical source is one of the Apocryphal books, Maccabees 4:52–59. Josephus, the historian, makes mention of this feast (Ant. XII.7.7). This Feast of Lights was similar to the Feast of Tabernacles, celebrated

Feast of Trumpets
1258

Feast of Tabernacles
1259

Day of Atonement
305

Convocation
837

Thanksgiving
1457

Feast of Dedication
1260

69

by the carrying of boughs, palms, and branches and the singing of the Psalms. The use of lights during the Hanukkah celebration has always been a significant ritual in the homes, synagogues, and streets of Palestine. The feast is observed near the time when Christians are celebrating Christmas with lights on the tree.[5]

F. *The Feast of Purim (Lots)*

The Feast of Purim is held on the fourteenth and fifteenth of the twelfth month, Adar or March. Mordecai instituted it to commemorate the deliverance of the Jews of Persia from national slaughter by Haman as recorded in the Book of Esther.

The celebration is also referred to as the Feast of Lots because Haman had cast lots to ascertain on which day he would carry out the murderous decree.

This festival is celebrated with "feasting and joy, and of sending portions [of food] one to another, and gifts to the poor" (Esther 9:20–22). Its popularity with the Jews is attested to by Josephus (Ant. XI.6.13). Services in the synagogue on Purim include the reading of the Book of Esther.

Day of
Atonement
305

Atonement
304

High Priest
2064

III. THE DAY OF ATONEMENT (YOM KIPPUR)

The initial instruction by Jehovah to Moses for the Day of Atonement is given in Exodus 29:33. Further directions are given in Exodus 30:10, where it is stated that Aaron the High Priest is to make an atonement upon the horns of the altar once a year with the blood of the sin offering which is used for the purpose of an atonement for sin. This ritual is further amplified in Leviticus 23:26–32. According to Leviticus 25:9, the Year of Jubilee begins with the Day of Atonement.[6]

In the NT the Day of Atonement is referred to as "the fast" (Acts 27:9), and is the supreme act of national atonement for

sin. Fasting was commanded from the ninth until the evening of the tenth day in the seventh month, Tishri (Lev. 23:27). The ritual was divided into two parts: one for the priesthood and one for the people. On the Day of Atonement the high

priest arose and laid aside his high priestly garments, after which he underwent a ceremonial cleansing with water at the laver. Following this ritual, he dressed himself in a holy white linen garment and presented a young bullock for a sin offering for himself and his house, after which he slew the sin offering and entered the Holy of Holies with an incense burner. The cloud of incense coming from the brazier filled the room and

covered the ark. Next the high priest sprinkled the blood of the sin offering upon the mercy seat and seven times before the mercy seat, for the symbolic cleansing of the Inner Sanctum or the Holy of Holies. After making atonement, he returned to the court of the sanctuary.

The high priest then presented two goats to the Lord at the door of the tabernacle as a sin offering for the people. He cast lots over them, one marked for the Lord and the other for Azazel, the scapegoat. The goat on which the lot fell was slain and the priest repeated the sprinkling of the blood as before (Lev. 16:17).

Scapegoat
3160

In the second stage of the ceremony the high priest laid his hand on the scapegoat's head and ceremonially transferred the sins of the people to the goat through a ritualistic prayer. The goat was then led into the wilderness to perish among the wild beasts, never to return again. Thus Jesus, the crucified Christ, is identified as the sinner's "scapegoat," the innocent one taking the sins of the guilty. Some authorities suggest that the goat was led to a cliff and tossed over. His expiatory death was symbolic of ridding the people, the priests, and the sanctuary from all impurity. In later Judaism the Day of Atonement has been observed as a day of penitence and prayer.[7]

IV. THE SABBATICAL YEAR (EXOD. 21:2; 23:11; NEH. 10:31)

Sabbatical Year
3104

The sabbatical year was the first year in a cycle of seven years within the Hebrew calendar, set aside as a year for resting: for the soil, for man and beast, and for the care of the poor. It was also the year when all debts were remitted or cancelled and all slaves were set free. Apparently an Israelite could sell himself for a certain sum, to serve a fellow Israelite as a slave, but his servitude could last for no more than six years (Jer. 34:14). In the seventh year all slaves were freed. During the Sabbatical year the land was to remain uncultivated so that poor people and wild animals could live on it (Lev. 25:4–7).

Sabbatical Year
3104

In the seventh year everyone could return to his own family estate. The only properties exempt from the law were houses which were not redeemed within one year (Lev. 25:29–31) and the houses of the Levites, the priestly tribe (Lev. 25:32–34). In the Book of Deuteronomy the sabbatical year is called the "year of release" or the "year of cancellation." All debts between Israelites were cancelled with a warning against refusing to lend to a poor neighbor, in view of the nearness of the sabbatical year (Deut. 15:7–11). The law, in effect, was given for a special period of time but eventually it became obsolete by default. Later, when undue hardship developed from the letter-of-the-law interpretation, the Jews invented a system of credit which enabled the debtor to spread his obligation over a longer period of time.

71

Preliminary
Matters

Jubilee
1953

Slaves Set
Free
2137

Stewardship
3451, 3452

Sabbatical
Year
3104

V. THE YEAR OF JUBILEE (LEV. 25:10–54)

The year of Jubilee was ushered in by a trumpet blast on the tenth day of the seventh month (Tishri) on the Day of Atonement (Lev. 25:9). The Israelites were to keep the day holy and proclaim liberty throughout the land (Lev. 25:10). This year is mentioned in only three chapters, Leviticus 25 and 27 and Numbers 36. Most of the ordinances were parallel to those in the sabbatical year: e.g., the land was to rest, land was to revert to its original owners, and slaves were to be freed.

The whole idea behind the sabbatical year and the year of Jubilee was to give relief to labor, both human and animal, and to avoid enslavement, either financial or physical. These rest days were safeguards against usury and profiteering. The pattern is similar to developing countries where a few landed men own the land and the common people are reduced to serfdom or tenant farmers. In some areas the tenant farmers are always so deeply in debt to the landlords that they are never free from obligation. Under the Law of Jubilee the landed man was the steward, not the owner. Under the theocratic order, God owned the land and "the cattle on a thousand hills." The value of the land was based on the number of years remaining before the Jubilee year. It appears that the forty-ninth and fiftieth years were both free years. Perhaps the forty-ninth year under this circumstance was purely a calendar event. The Mishna takes the view that the year of Jubilee was abolished after the exile. Josephus, the historian, does not mention the year of Jubilee or its abolishment, although he makes reference to the sabbatical year.[8]

7

The Titles and/or Names
of God in the Bible

I. INTRODUCTION

A careful study of the OT reveals that Deity is referred to by several different titles and/or names, among them God, LORD, and Jehovah. This variation did not, however, become a serious problem to scholars until 1756, when Jean Astruc, a French physician, published a book entitled *Conjectures on the Original Memoirs which Moses Seems to Have Used in Composing the Book of Genesis.* He observed that in the Book of Genesis the divine names YHWH (translated Jehovah in ARV and LORD in KJV and RSV) and Elohim (translated God in most English versions) were not used interchangeably and that one was more predominant in some sections than others.

In pursuing this problem, the liberal theologians in Germany took the lead in constructing a documentary hypothesis by employing the "investigative technique" as is used for evaluating secular literature. They concluded that two separate and distinct deities were involved, not recognizing or considering the possibility that these designations or titles of deity related to the various functions of God.

According to their theory, the consonantal form of YHWH referred to the "Thunder God" of Mount Sinai; later this deity became the God of the Southern Kingdom (Judah). References to him in the Scriptures were grouped into a section specified as the "J" documents (J standing for Jehovah, the ARV rendering of YHWH). The divine name Elohim, translated "God" in almost all English versions, indicated the God of the Northern Kingdom Israel. To this theory were added the "D" docu-

Lord
2514

God
**884, 885,
2515**

Sinai
2444

73

ments which related to the legal codes or the law. The parts of the Pentateuch dealing with priestly affairs were labeled the "P" documents. These theories were combined into what is now known as the JEDP hypothesis, subscribed to generally by the liberal scholars but acknowledged as untenable by many within their own ranks. This theory leaves little, if any, place for Mosaic authorship or divine inspiration of the compilers and/or writers of the Scriptures.

One leading scholar gives an appraisal of this theory: "Scholars pursued this theory until they thought there had originally been five or six documents." Later many fragments of documents were pieced and fitted together, and then altered and added to by still later editors so that "according to some writers, some of the stories . . . in Genesis and other books were made of parts of stories from various documents and fragments. Moses was denied authorship of most of the Pentateuch. The theory was carried to such lengths of absurdity that it was far more difficult to believe, than the simple, plain declaration of the Bible itself, that Moses wrote these things. . . . They could see no other basis . . . for the use of different names for God in the OT than a literary significance which is no significance at all for the spiritual mind. There is, however, a functional significance in the use of these different names. It is much more 'rational' to believe that the great, infinite and eternal God has given us these different names to express different aspects of His being and the different relationships He sustains to His creatures." [1]

Name
2513

Nathaniel
344

Adonijah
42

Samuel
3188, 4231,
4232

Esau
1149

Martha
2258

Jesus
695, 1891

In Bible times people placed great value on the name of a child. They frequently gave it symbolic or character meaning. Hebrew is especially relevant in this connection. Modern names are intended merely as identification, but most Bible names, in addition to identifying the person, are also descriptive and often prophetic. Frequently religious significance resided in the name parents gave their child. Sometimes the name suggested the service the child should render to Deity. Perhaps the name commemorated the favor of God in the gracious gift of the child: for example, Nathaniel, "gift of God"; Adonijah, "the Lord is God"; Samuel, "heard of God." The name Jacob meant "the supplanter," Sarah, "a princess," Shallum, "recompense," Nabal "foolish or churlish," and Esau, "hairy." Martha signified "lady or mistress." Some names were given prophetically, as that of Jesus, because he was to be the Savior (Matt. 1:21). When character had developed, a new name was sometimes given as being expressive of it, as Israel, "He strove with God," and Cephas, "Rock."

The name Jesus (*Iesous*—Gr.) is the equivalent of the Hebrew Joshua *(Yehoshua)* meaning YAHWEH, "salvation." This is the personal name of the Lord in the Gospels and in Acts. In the Epistles, Jesus, with a few exceptions, takes on a compound form, Jesus Christ, or Christ the Lord. In the first case the

74

human name, Jesus, is linked with Christ, the divine name.

Divine direction concerning a name is illustrated by the name specified when the angel appeared to Mary and declared, "Thou shalt call his name Jesus, for he shall save his people from their sins" (Matt. 1:21). This was indeed he of whom Moses and the prophets spoke.

II. Various Names of God

Because some problems exist concerning the names applied to God, a short analysis of these names may provide a better understanding of his nature.

El-Shaddai means "the God who is manifested in his mighty acts" or "God Almighty." In the Septuagint the Hebrew name Shaddai is translated a number of times as the Greek word *ikanos,* which can be translated "all sufficient." Rabbinical tradition points out that the word consists of two participles, which when combined means sufficient or self-sufficient. Thus in this name, Shaddai or El-Shaddai, the idea is conveyed of the sufficiency of the Almighty One (Phil. 4:19; Deut. 2:7; 1 Kings 19:6; 2 Kings 4:6; 7:8).[2]

The name Almighty God speaks of the inexhaustible stores of his bounty, of the riches and fullness of his grace in self-sacrificing love pouring itself out for others. It reveals that every good and perfect gift comes from God, that he never wearies of bestowing his mercies and blessings upon his people (James 1:17). But it must not be forgotten that his strength is made perfect in weakness and that his sufficiency makes it possible for believers to have "a well of water springing up into everlasting life" which they can share with a thirsty and needy humanity (John 4:14).

Adonai is translated "Lord" in the English Bible, only the first letter being capitalized. It is used over 300 times in the OT, almost always in the plural and the possessive form.

The name Adonai signifies ownership or mastership and indicated the truth that God is the owner of each member of the human family [sic], and that He consequently claims . . . obedience of all. . . . The first occasion of its use, as with the name El-Shaddai, is with Abraham in Gen. 15:2. . . . After the rescue of Lot, and Abram's military achievement (Gen. 15:1) the word of the Lord came unto Abram in a vision saying, 'Fear not, Abram; I am thy shield, and thy exceeding great reward.' Abram then makes his reply, addressing God as Adonai—Lord—an acknowledgment that YHWH is also Master. Certainly Abram understood what this relationship meant; . . . Lordship meant complete possession on the one hand and complete submission on the other. . . . In addressing the Lord as Adonai he acknowledges God's complete possession and perfect right to all that he was and had.[3]

El 'Elyon designates the God of Israel as the "highest, the most high" among the gods (Gen. 14:18–20). In some passages God is referred to as the "Rock" (Deut. 32:4; 32:18; Ps. 18:31; 2 Sam. 23:3). Paul states in his letters to the Corinthians that the "Rock" was Christ (1 Cor. 10:4). This sheds some light on the question of who the "Rock" was in Christ's dialogue with Peter at Caesarea Philippi (Matt. 16:18).

There are many other names/titles for Deity in the OT. However, the main concern here is with the two principal names, YHWH and Elohim. A biblical explanation for the existence of these two names within the context of monotheism follows.

III. ELOHIM (GOD)

The divine name Elohim appears first in Genesis and over 2500 times in the OT. Its form is plural, but the meaning is uniformly singular. The plural form expresses "Majesty" or "Mightiness"—the One who brought order out of chaos. It is a generic rather than a specific personal name for Deity. Elohim is the impersonal transcendent Creator-God, not subject to the historical process and above the world of phenomena. He is the nonpersonal Almighty Mind. There is a hint of his trinitarian nature when he says: "Let us make man in our image, after our likeness." Perhaps it would be correct to say that Elohim is the Great Almighty King, who stays in the background while he manifests and relates himself to man through the second and third persons of the Trinity.

IV. YHWH/ADONAI (LORD)

The consonantal divine name YHWH, translated LORD in the KJV, Jehovah in the ASV, and Yahweh in some modern English versions is the most significant name of God in the OT and appears over 6000 times. In the post-exilic period, when a strong Messianic hope developed among the Jews, the name was not pronounced for fear of committing blasphemy; the penalty for doing so was stoning (Lev. 24:16). In theological terminology Adonai was substituted for this most holy personal name of God.

The Jewish Masoretic scholars combined the consonantal form of YHWH with the vowels from Adonai to remind the synagogue readers that they were to pronounce only the term Adonai. From the combined form of the two terms for Deity the name Jehovah developed. The imposition of the vowels of Adonai upon YHWH provided an approximate pronunciation of this word of four letters YHWH, namely Yahweh or Jehovah.

The meaning of this awesome name, YHWH, was shrouded in mystery and speculation. During the OT period the temple leaders gave credence to the idea that YHWH was the name of the Messiah and that the meaning and the pronunciation of the name would not be revealed until the advent of the Messiah. The Scribes, Pharisees, and other temple leaders never spoke the name Jesus. Since they could not utter the name of Jesus as Lord and Savior, they could not utter it at all.

"In the Gospels and throughout the NT, Jesus appears as the goal of OT revelation and the point to which all providential development tended. Paul said, [He came] in 'the fulness of time' (Gal. 4:4). It has often been shown in history how politically, intellectually, and morally everything in the Graeco-Roman world was ready for such a universal religion as Jesus brought into it." [4]

On the occasion of God's commissioning Moses to deliver the "children of Israel" from Egypt, Moses asked God how he should respond to the Hebrews when they asked the name of the God who had sent him. God told Moses to answer: "I AM hath sent me unto you" (Exod. 3:14).

Jesus, in addressing the Jews, related himself to and identified himself as "I am." Here Jesus was clearly saying that he was the One who appeared to Moses on the backside of Mount Horeb (Exod. 3:1,2; John 8:58; see also Rev. 1:18). This interpretation is strengthened by the reaction it drew from the Temple leaders. They were ready to stone Jesus for claiming that he was the "I am" or God (John 8:58,59).

At the time the Hebrew OT was translated into Greek, the combined name YHWH-Adonai was rendered Kurios. When the Greek NT was translated into English, the term was LORD. R. Alan Killen explains that "Adonai is an honorific title used both as an intensive plural of rank meaning 'Master,' 'Sovereign,' or 'Lord,' and as an appellative meaning 'My Lord.' Its alternate form occurs in Ps. 110:1 which reads: 'The Lord (Yahweh) said unto my Lord (Adonai).' Matthew 22:41–45 shows how Christ identified this title with Himself. The Greek equivalent is Kyrios [Kurios] 'Lord.' representing both Yahweh and Adonai in the OT Septuagint. In the NT it is applied to Christ equally with the Father and the Spirit." [5]

The combined YHWH and Adonai is always rendered LORD (with capital letters). A noted professor puts it thus: "The name Kurios (LORD) occurs very frequently. It seems to gather into itself the combined significance of Adonai, of which it is the equivalent, and Yahweh or Jehovah. The name is applied with equal clarity to God the Father and to Jesus Christ. Thus in the unfolding of the redemptive message of the New Testa-

The Titles and/or Names of God in the Bible

Prophecy Fulfilled
2892, 2893

Chosen People Israel
1808

"I Am"
1738

"I Am"'s of Christ
4166

Jehovah-jireh
1868

Substitute
3361

Rams
183

Jehovah-nissi
1869

Altar
120–123

Sanctification
3140–3141

Worship
3921–3924

Gideon
1414, 4294

Jehovah-
shalom
1870

Canaan
626–634

ment, the richness of Old Testament nomenclature for the Deity is presupposed." [6]

V. THE JEHOVAH-LORD TITLES

God's special relationships to Israel are expressed in the many divine names/titles recorded in the OT. Some of the most meaningful are the Jehovah or LORD titles. These include:

A. LORD-jireh which means "LORD our provider" (Gen. 22:14), associated with the times of great crisis in the life of Abraham and Isaac, commemorating the great deliverance of Isaac through the provision of a ram as a substitute sacrifice (Gen. 22:13). The ram as a substitute can typify Christ on the cross.

B. LORD-rophe means "LORD that healeth thee." Here Christ (LORD) is presented as the great Physician, not only of the body but also of the soul. This title is first used in Exodus 15:22–26, in reference to the LORD's healing of the bitter waters.

C. LORD-nissi denotes "LORD is my banner" (Exod. 17:15). Moses gave this name to the altar which he built to memorialize the defeat of the Amalekites at Rephidim (Exod. 17:16). The Amalekites, descendants of Esau, were avowed enemies of Israel. The uplifted rod in Moses' hand became the symbol of the LORD's strong arm or banner.

D. LORD-m'kaddesh expresses spiritual completeness, "I am Jehovah that sanctifies you" (Exod. 31:13). Frequently referred to in the book of Leviticus, the name indicates the importance of sanctification. A well-known Bible professor makes this comment: "Leviticus is the book of life, or the walk and worship of a people already redeemed. Therefore, sanctification is its most appropriate theme. It could not appropriately be presented until redemption was fully accomplished. It . . . sets forth that holy way in which a people already redeemed should walk worthy of their calling (Eph. 4:1) and the spiritual worship which the LORD demands of them. Thus in connection with their moral and spiritual purity, this title of God is repeated six times in the two chapters following its first appearance." [7] It is the indwelling LORD sanctifier that enables people to live a holy life (Exod. 28:36; Lev. 19:2; 20:8; 22:32; 1 Cor. 1:30; Eph. 4:24; 2 Tim. 1:9; Heb. 3:1; 12:14).

E. LORD-shalom, "The LORD is peace," was the title Gideon gave to the altar he built at Ophra, in response to the word spoken to him by the LORD, "Peace be unto thee" (Judg. 6:23). The land of Canaan had long been possessed by the Hebrews. Joshua was dead and the people had entered into their Canaan rest.

F. LORD-tsidkenu translates as "the LORD, our righteousness" and appears in Jeremiah's prophetic statement of a "righteous Branch" and a "King who is to come." "And this is his name whereby he shall be called, THE LORD OUR RIGHTEOUSNESS" (Jer. 23:6). The prophecy was given when Judah was about to fall—to be taken into captivity. The nation had sinned so greatly that judgment was inevitable, but in that day of darkness Jeremiah gave a word of encouragement to the people. Even though punishment was to come upon them, it was to be inflicted by the LORD, who loved them. Their immediate present was dark and hopeless; nevertheless, as the LORD is righteous, in the end righteousness will prevail.

The Titles and/or Names of God in the Bible
Jehovah-tsidkenu
1872

Jeremiah
1877, 4246

This designation appears hundreds of times in the Scriptures and is used in the sense of rendering justice and making right. The LORD himself is perfect righteousness or the perfectly Righteous One. He then, is a tsadik, a righteous One, wrote the psalmist (129:4). As an El-tsadik, a righteous God, there is none to compare with him, declared Isaiah (45:21). He is the Rock whose work is perfect, all of whose ways are just; tsadik is righteous and "right is he" (Deut. 32:4). His "righteousness is an everlasting righteousness," and his testimonies are righteous forever (Ps. 119:142,144). Righteousness and justice are the very foundations of his throne (Ezek. 43:1–7). Therefore in all his dealings he is righteous.

Judgment
1351–1353

Testimonies
3598

G. LORD-rohi means "The LORD is my shepherd" (Ps. 23:1), the outstanding example being found in the twenty-third Psalm. This title probably has brought more comfort to people's hearts than any other. It is in the name of the LORD-rohi that this relationship finds its highest and tenderest expression, for the LORD is the Shepherd of his people. No other name of the LORD has the tender intimate touch of this one name.

Shepherd
3264, 3265

Some scholars recognize seven titles of the LORD, in principle, in the twenty-third Psalm: (1) LORD-jireh "our provider," v.5; (2) LORD-rophe "our healer," v.5; (3) LORD-m-kaddesh "our sanctifier," v.6; (4) LORD-shalom "our peace," v.6; (5) LORD-tsidkenu "our righteousness," v.3; (6) LORD-rohi "our shepherd," v.1; (7) LORD-shamma "the LORD is there," v.4.

H. LORD-shammah conveys the meaning; "The LORD is there" (Ezek. 48:35; see also Ezek. 43:1–7). This title is perhaps the most fitting one with which to climax the OT. By his various titles the LORD revealed himself in the power and majesty and glory of his person in meeting all human needs. His name Elohim revealed him as the Creator of the universe. His name LORD revealed his special relationship to man.

Jehovah-shammah
1871

God's Power
3808

The LORD-shammah is the promise to complete the pledge to bring man to his final rest and glory, for "man's end is to glorify God and to enjoy Him forever. For, as Paul states,

Preliminary
Matters

Justification
1203, 1985,
1986

Temple
3577–3583

Egypt
1100

God Appearing
206

'Whom he called, them he also justified: and whom he justified, them he also glorified' (Rom. 8:30), a past tense, but the language of eternity."[8]

The reference by Ezekiel (48:35) appears at the very end of his message. Even though Israel's temple was destroyed and the people were separated from Jerusalem, they were assured of the LORD's presence with them.

Erich Sauer says,

> Throughout the Old Testament the LORD-Messiah is regarded as 'the coming One.' . . . Exactly the same verbal form Christos was used in the third century before Christ's birth in the Bible of the exiled Jews in Egypt, the Septuagint, the Greek translation of the OT prepared by the Jews. It is to be found in such passages as Ps. 2:2; Isa. 2:10; Dan. 9:25. . . . In the old covenant the Gospel is coming into being, (formative period) . . . the OT is the dawn of morning. The dawn belongs to the sun. Thus the OT belongs to Christ, and tells what Christ is. The NT tells who He is and in such a way that it becomes manifest that He alone knows who the Christ is; He is Jesus. So do the two Testaments correspond to the two chief names of the Redeemer; the Old to the name of His vocation; Christ, the New to His personal name, Jesus. But both are inspired by one Spirit and explain each other. Before He became man, Christ [was] is already the center of the history of salvation. His anticipatory presentation in the OT is at the same time a self-presentation, for the 'Spirit of Christ' was in the prophets (1 Pet. 1:11). The pre-Christian history of revelation is a 'history of Christ' before He came (Isa. 25:9; 33:2).[9]

Thus it can be seen that each divine name or title has a special meaning in the "God-to-man" and "man-to-God" relationships.

VI. THEOPHANY

The compound divine name YHWH-Adonai, translated LORD, is the name used when OT people came face to face with the deity. Such appearances by deity to man are called theophanies or Christophanies. Both of these words are compound Greek words meaning "God appearing" or an "appearance of God" (or Christ). *Theos* is the Greek term for God, *Christos*, the Greek term for Christ, and *Messiah* is the Hebrew equivalent. The idea of theophany comes from the Greek religions in which the priests showed the images of their gods to the people. At the festival of Delphi the statues of Apollo and other gods were prominent. Since the theophanies in the OT predate heathen religions, it is obvious that they borrowed the idea from Biblical revelation. Certainly no event in history would precede the appearance of God to Adam and Eve. The noted scholar James A. Borland has written a scholarly book on this subject: *Christ in the Old Testament.* He states: "All Old Testament theophanies that involve the manifestations of

God in human form were appearances of the Second Person of the Trinity, and as such, their purpose was not only to provide immediate revelation but also to prepare mankind for the incarnation of Christ." [10]

There are many different kinds of divine manifestations; this discussion is limited to a few of "those unsought, intermittent and temporary, visible and audible manifestations of God the Son in human form, by which God communicated something to certain conscious human beings on earth prior to the birth of Jesus Christ." [11] This study deals with the manifestation of the Second Person of the Trinity known as Christophany. According to James Borland the purposes of Christophanies suggest the following long-range implications:

Trinity
3694

1. "God the Son anticipated His future incarnation, intimated its possibility, prefigured its human form and even prophesied its coming royalty."

Incarnation
720

2. "God was using a form of revelation suited to His purposes in the early history of His redemptive plan."

3. "God connected His work in the Old and New Testaments by appearing in human form in both."

4. "God was able to reveal aspects of His person in this way that no other form of revelation allowed."

5. "God may have sought to intimate Christ's Deity and the Trinity." [12]

In the light of such statements by Jesus as "all things must be fulfilled, which were written in the law of Moses, and in the prophets, and in the psalms, concerning me" (Luke 24:44), it is needful to show without equivocation that Christ is indeed a living reality in the OT. Matthew states that Jesus Christ was the son of David and the son of Abraham (Matt. 1:1). John declared that it is not the Elohim GOD who had been made manifest but the "only begotten Son, he hath declared him" (John 1:18).

One divine said that

> The angel of the Lord came in 'human' form to Abraham, Hagar, Moses, Joshua, Gideon and Manoah. While any angel sent to execute the commands of God might be called the angel of the Lord (2 Sam. 24:16; 1 Kings 19:5,7), yet mention is made of an angel under circumstances that justify one in always thinking of the same angel, who is distinguished from the Lord, and yet identified with Him (Gen. 16:10,13; 22:11,12,15,16; Exod. 3:2,4; Josh. 5:13–15; Zech. 1:10–13), who revealed the face of God (Gen. 32:30), in whom was the Lord's name (Exod. 29:21), and whose presence was equivalent to the Lord's presence (Exod. 32:34; 33:14; Isa. 63:9). The angel of the Lord thus appears as a manifestation of the LORD Himself, one with the Lord and yet different from Him. [13]

Angel of the Lord
141

Further, Thomas Rees says, "The angel *(Malakh)* of God is a frequent mode of God's manifestation of Himself in human form, and for occasional purposes. In many passages it is as-

81

sumed that God and His angel are the same being, and the names are used synonymously" (Gen. 16:7–13; Exod. 3:2–7).[14]

The angel's identification with the Messiah and the Logos (Word/Christ) is obvious, the latter terms being more definite in their expressions of God's revelation to man. Here the Lord carries on the office of Redeemer in behalf of God's overall plan during the OT period. However, the Advent of Christ did not finalize the plan of salvation. Without the death and resurrection there would have been no salvation. Without shedding of blood, there is no remission for sins. If Christ had not resurrected from the dead, all humanity would still be dead in trespasses and sins.

At the Advent it is YHWH, the LORD, who finally appears in Jesus Christ, the God-Man. When Paul writes to Timothy, he speaks of eternal life as something "which was given us in Christ Jesus before the world began" (2 Tim. 1:9; Titus 1:2). There are over 200 titles in the Bible for Christ. These reveal the fullness of his nature and the many-sided relationships he has with his people. When God would make a special revelation of himself in the OT, he used the name YHWH-LORD, expressing his moral and spiritual attributes of love, holiness, and righteousness.

The historical display of the divine essence lies essentially in the idea of the LORD who enters into the phenomenon of space and time in order to manifest himself to mankind. All expressions which refer to revelation occur almost entirely in connection with the LORD: a few exceptions are found in the Elohistic Psalms 69 and 75 and in the Elohistic sections of 2 Samuel.

VII. THE TRINITY

A study of the Trinity in the OT affords further insight into the nature of the triune God. The Scriptures teach that God is the Creator and the Keeper of the Universe, the Father of the Lord Jesus Christ, and that He does not change (Mal. 3:6;

Heb. 1:12; 13:8; James 1:7). The idea of the Trinity is of course suggested in a passage previously quoted from Genesis, "Let us make man in our image" (Gen. 1:26). The reason for the delay in the full revelation of the Trinity may have been to

avoid conflict with the polytheistic culture of OT times. To establish firmly the concept of monotheism, one God, the idea of the Trinity was not developed until Jesus the Messiah came, and then the disclosure was gradual.

Reference to the Spirit, or the Spirit of God, or the Holy Spirit, is found in many books of the Bible. The word for Spirit in the Hebrew Bible is *ruach*, meaning "the breath of God." In the NT the Greek word for Spirit is the verb *pneuma*, meaning "breathe" and has the same basic meaning as that of the Hebrew *ruach*. The Spirit of God "moved upon the face of the waters" (Gen. 1:2) in the precreation period and at the command of Elohim (God) order was brought out of chaos (see Ps. 36:6).

The Spirit of God worked in the OT period but was divinely limited to the leaders. Even though the ministry of the Holy Spirit was restrained in the OT, his work did prepare the way for the full demonstration of the Holy Spirit on the day of Pentecost. The prophet Joel had a vision of this event (2:28,9). The Spirit of the Lord came upon Othniel (Judg. 3:9–11), upon Gideon (Judg. 6:34) and upon Jephthah (Judg. 11:29). On the other hand, the Spirit departed from Saul (1 Sam. 16:14). For comprehensive information on the ministry of the Holy Spirit see Nos. 1601–14 in TCRB Helps.

Even though God is trinitarian in nature, he is still one God (Deut. 6:4). The Father, Son, and Holy Spirit are distinct from each other and are able to send and be sent by one another (John 13:20). The unity of Father, Son, and Holy Spirit constitutes the one Godhead.

Day of Pentecost
2722

Othniel
2664

Gideon
1414, 4294
pp. 260–261

Jephthah
1876

Saul
3158

VIII. ANGELS

The word *angel* is derived from the Hebrew *Mal'akh* and the Greek *aggelos,* meaning messenger. Angels are mentioned 100 times in the OT and 193 times in the NT. The Scriptures define angels as supernaturally created beings, separated from the creation of man (Ps. 148:2–5; Col. 1:16), who enjoy God-given power (2 Kings 19:35). Holy angels comprise "an innumerable company" (Heb. 12:22). Jesus makes reference to the legions of angels under his command (Matt. 26:53); their great number is further suggested in Revelation 5:11.

The function of the angels is to serve God, to supervise men's activities, and to dispense divine grace and intelligence (Exod. 14:19; Dan. 6:22; Acts 12:7; Heb. 1:14). They are also commissioned to carry out God's decrees of judgment: death, pestilence, and military defeats (Gen. 19:15–26; Judg. 5:23; 2 Kings 19:35; Acts 12:23). These messengers are spirit beings who usually appear in quasi-anthropomorphic (human) form (Acts 1:10; Heb. 1:14; 13:2) and are usually visible only to those whom they address (Num. 22:22; 1 Chron. 21:16).

In general, angels are holy and serve Christ or God, but there are some evil angels over whom Satan presides, who defy or challenge God's authority and who inflict harm upon the children of God because of God's temporarily permissive will (Job 1:6–12; 2:1,2; Isa. 14:12,13). Apparently Satan was once called Lucifer and had heavenly status before he rebelled against God and was cast out of heaven (Isa. 14:12–19). In the

Angels
143–149

Ministering Angels
143

Angels of Judgment
146

Names and Titles of Satan
3638

83

Book of Revelation Satan is referred to as the dragon, the leader of the evil forces in battle against the divine army (Rev. 12:7–9). Satan and his followers are represented as being consigned to eternal damnation in hell (2 Peter 2:4).

As to the general designations given to angels, there are two exceptions. Reference is made to "the angel of the LORD" (Gen. 16:7; 21:17), and the "angel of his presence" (Isa. 63:9). As indicated earlier in this chapter, the "angel of the LORD" is not a created being but is the Creator himself—the very Son of God. This "angel of the LORD," considered to be Jesus Christ, was higher than the angels, but when he took on the human body he condescended to become a being "a little lower than the angels" (Ps. 8:5,6; Heb. 2:7,8). After his earthly humiliation he was exalted above the angels with "glory and honour" (Heb. 1:4,6: 2:7).

The Scripture refers to a hierachy of angelic beings:

1. *Cherubim.* These creatures are mentioned 90 times in the OT and once in the NT. Cherubim appeared in Ezekiel's vision by the river Chebar in Babylon (Ezek. 10:1–22). He describes these creatures as having wings, hands, and many eyes and being surrounded by spinning wheels (Ezek. 10:8–12). These angelic beings once guarded the tree of life in the garden (Gen. 3:24). Golden cherubim had a place in the tabernacle in the Wilderness (Exod. 25:18–20; 37:7–9) and also in Solomon's temple (1 Kings 6:23–28; 8:7; 2 Chron 3:10–13; Heb. 9:5).

In the Apocalypse John makes reference to creatures similar in appearance to those described in Ezekiel's vision (Ezek. 10:16; Rev. 4:6). According to the figurative description in the latter reference, cherubim are assumed to have the intellect of man, the strength of an ox, the courage of a lion, and the free movement of an eagle.

2. *Seraphim.* These angelic beings appear twice in a worship service around the Lord's throne (Isa. 6:2,6). They had three pairs of wings, which contributes to their unusual appearance (Isa. 6:2,3,6).

3. *Beasts.* The term *beast* usually refers to members of the animal kingdom who have no divine worship instinct, but in Revelation the term is used in connection with heavenly beings who worship around the throne of God and are to be considered to be something more than common beasts of the field. The word *beast* in Revelation 4:6–9 is used in a similar context as that of Isaiah and Ezekiel where they describe cherubim and seraphim (Isa. 6:2–6; Ezek. 10:1–23).

Both the Hebrew *chay* (Gen. 1:24) and the Greek *zoon* (Rev. 4:6) can be translated "beast" or "living creature." Contextual consideration of the heavenly function of the "beasts" in Revelation 4:6,9 indicates that "living creatures" or "living beings" would be the better translation.

The RSV renders *zoon* as "living creature" to distinguish it from a beast of the field. The term "clean and unclean" beasts in Genesis 7:2 comes from the Hebrew *behemoth*. The appearance of the creatures in Revelation 4:6 may have influenced the "beast" translation.

4. *Holy Angels*. These are referred to frequently, especially at times of important events. They were the "morning stars" and "the sons of God" who shouted for joy at God's Creation (Job 1:6a; 38:4–7); the angels were present at Jesus' birth (Luke 2:13,14); they "ministered to him" on the Mount of Temptation (Matt. 4:11), they strengthened him during his agony in Gethsemane (Luke 22:43); they were present at his resurrection and ascension (John 20:12; Acts 1:10,11), and they will form the vanguard at his Second Coming. These holy angels serve as "ministering spirits" for the redeemed (Heb. 1:14; Matt. 18:10; Ps. 34:7). They appear first in Genesis 16:7 and last at the twelve gates of pearl in the Apocalypse (Rev. 21:12).

5. *The Angels of the Seven Churches*. A careful study of those passages in the Scriptures referring to angels (messengers), shows that the term does not always imply the same idea. At times the Scripture refers to a heavenly messenger, in others the word applies to man.

The supernatural is suggested in Daniel 12:1, Acts 12:7–10, and Revelation 7:1,2. However, the word clearly applies to an ordinary messenger as referred to in 1 Samuel 11:3, also Luke 9:52 and John 2:25, to prophets in Isaiah 42:19, Haggai 1:13, Malachi 3:1a, and to priests in Ecclesiastes 5:6 and Malachi 2:7. Under the general sense of messenger, the term *angel* may be applied to Christ as the great angel or messenger of the covenant (Mal. 3:1b), to the ministers of his gospel (Matt. 11:10), the overseers (pastors) and members of his church (2 Cor. 8:23).

In Revelation the Seven Angels (messengers) of the Seven Churches received seven letters. It is thought that the seven angels were men—probably the bishops or pastors who presided over these churches (Rev. 2:1; 2:8; 2:12; 2:18; 3:1; 3:7; 3:14). The mystery of this figurative language is further intensified by identifying the seven angels with seven stars (Rev. 1:20). For additional information on the Seven Churches see Ch. 25.

Identification of the angels by name is limited to two: (1) Gabriel (Man of God) seems to be God's special delivery messenger in both the OT and NT (Dan. 8:16; 9:21; Luke 1:19,26), (2) Michael (the Archangel who is like God) is referred to as a prince (Dan. 10:13–21) and the only angel with the title "archangel" (Jude 9). Michael disputed with Satan over the body of Moses (Jude 9) and is mentioned as the commander-in-chief in the heavenly war (Rev. 12:7). Michael appears to be first in rank among the angels of heaven and is perhaps the presiding angel in the court of heaven.

Beasts
150

Christ's Temptation
3587

Christ's Ascension
678

Ministering Angels
143

Divine Messengers
694

Angels of the Churches
149

Mysteries
2486–2504

Gabriel
1377

Michael
2335

85

Religious Officials
2058–2063,
4318

Religious Officials

I. THE PRIESTS

Priesthood
2863–2864

Patriarchs
2696

Sinai
2444

Command-
ments
444

Aaron
1

Priests
2058

Altars
120–123

Urim and
Thummin
2497

Laws
concerning
Priests
2059

Before the establishment of the levitical priesthood at Mount Sinai, individuals like Cain and Abel and patriarchs such as Noah, Abraham, Isaac, Jacob, and Job performed the essential office of priest for the family and tribe. The religious head, who was divinely ordained as mediator between God and the people, had the responsibility of ritual and administration. When the Hebrew nation was organized at Mount Sinai, a religious order of an unusual nature came into being. Here the Jewish religion became institutionalized with a priesthood, a worship center, and a religious code, including the Ten Commandments and sundry ordinances.

The priests were ordained to care for the religious needs of the people. Aaron and his sons were appointed to that office and Aaron was ordained High Priest. The tribe of Levi, of whom Aaron was a descendent, was designated as the priestly tribe. It was hereditary and restricted to the one family (Exod. 28:1). All the sons of Aaron were priests unless banned by legal disabilities (Lev. 21:16ff.). The high priestly family had special duties which included (1) officiating at the altar, (2) teaching the law to the people in the tabernacle services, and (3) using the Urim and Thummin, objects placed under the breast plate, for the purpose of determining God's will in doubtful matters concerning the nation (Exod. 28:30; Num. 27:21; Deut. 33:8; Ezra 2:63; 1 Sam. 14:36–42).

86   The priests were subject to very strict laws pertaining to their personal lives (Lev. 10:6ff.); they also had to wear special

priestly garments (Exod. 28:40–42).[1] (For detailed information on the tabernacle see Ch. 5, I, B, and 11, XI.)

II. THE PROPHETS

The prophets were usually laymen divinely called to deliver a special message from God to the people. Prophets were inspired foretellers or forthtellers, who declared and interpreted divine revelation. Moses stands out as the chief prophet and father of the prophetic movement.

The OT does not explain how divine revelation was disclosed to the prophets; but when it was revealed, they became burdened to deliver the message even in the face of opposition. Usually a prophet's message was a serious warning from God against the sinful practices of the people (Hosea 9:17). As a result, many prophets suffered bodily harm and persecution for their efforts (Jer. 37:15). The prophets of the Lord were men of integrity and absolute honesty. Their message was consistent with the moral nature of the God they represented and their message was reinforced with "thus saith the Lord." The revelation given them was not human but divine in origin (2 Peter 1:20,21). The prophet Micah claimed that he was filled with the Spirit of the Lord to make known to the nation of Israel its sin (3:8). As a counter-action to the continuous duplicity of the Canaanite soothsayers and diviners, God promised to send Israel men who would declare the whole counsel of God (Deut. 18:15–22). As the priests took the needs of the people before God, the prophet took special messages from God to the people (Amos 3:7ff.; cf. Exod. 4:16; 7:1).[2]

Many of the prophets came from among the people; they were men with a sincere concern for the community who felt that they were commissioned by God to warn their contemporaries of the judgment to come and to give guidance concerning moral issues.

History has no parallel to the courageous witness the prophets of Israel gave the people, such as was demonstrated by Amos in 750 B.C. Under God, the prophets created Israel's spiritual greatness. They were "holy men of God."

The prophet addressed himself to pressing issues at hand, but his message had in it the ring of eternity. The prophets saw the outcome of Israel's national crisis and her evil pattern of living; they made it clear that Israel must either repent or be severely punished.

The prophets of Israel emphasized the holiness of God, fearlessly criticized the immorality of their day, and tried to point their people to a nobler way of life. In the courts of Israel the prophets boldly rebuked the rulers, as Nathan did David

(2 Sam. 12), and Jeremiah, the princes of Judah (Jer. 26). They did not hesitate to castigate the selfish rich (Amos 4:1; 6:4–6).

The prophets were extremely patriotic and scornful of all who would invade their lands. Their written messages declare the ultimate triumph of good and the certain downfall of evil, but they had pity for the penitent and a charitable concern for the wayward (Isa. 1:18). They kept believing that a righteous remnant would survive (Isa. 10:20–22; 37:32; Ezek. 6:8). Some of their pronouncements were bright with hope of a Messianic age.[3]

The major prophetic books in the OT are Isaiah, Jeremiah, and Ezekiel. The writings of the minor prophets include Hosea, Amos, Obadiah, Jonah, Micah, Nahum, Habakkuk, Zephaniah, Haggai, Zechariah, and Malachi. These prophetic books are called major and minor because of the length of their writings. There were also women in the prophetic office. Among them were Miriam, the sister of Moses and Aaron (Exod. 15:20,21), Deborah (Judg. 4:4), and Huldah (2 Kings 22:12–20).

Bible
414–434

For Analysis of
Books—See
Nos. **4223ff.**

In the Hebrew canon the former prophetic books comprise Joshua, Judges, 1 and 2 Samuel, and 1 and 2 Kings and contain information on the period from the occupation of Canaan (thirteenth century B.C.) to the fall of Jerusalem in 587 B.C. The Book of Daniel is usually referred to as a prophetic book. It follows Ezekiel in sequence, but in the Hebrew canon it is placed in the third division, the Writings. This book was not put with the other prophets, although Daniel was called a prophet (Matt. 24:15). Daniel was marvelously gifted with the spirit of prophecy. He had the gift of prophecy but not the prophetic vocation; rather he was an official statesman and spent his life in the business of the state. He does not use the common prophetic declaration, "thus saith the Lord," nor does he exhort his contemporaries as it was the function of prophets to do.[4]

Scribe
3165

III. THE SCRIBES

The word *scribe* has a very broad application. From ancient Babylonian and Egyptian times the scribe held a place of prominence. In the Hebrew nation the scribes were neither a religious sect nor a political party but a professional group. *Lawyer, scribe,* and *teacher* are synonymous terms.[5]

Lawyer
2054

In a day when education was not generally available to the common people, the scribe served as a public stenographer, secretary, and legal advisor for the people who needed personal, social, and legal services. In the days of walled cities the scribe usually kept a desk near the outside of the gate where he could make his services available to the people. It

The figure of a
seated scribe
found in an
ancient Egyptian
tomb

can be presumed that Boaz transacted business in the presence
of a scribe (Ruth 4:1ff.). There are also instances where the
scribe was called upon to read and write letters for the illiterate.
Scribes can still be seen near the gates of some walled cities.

The scribes were the learned men of that day, well versed
in social decorum and legal matters. As a royal official or a
secretary with cabinet status, such scribes might serve as state
record keepers (2 Chron. 26:11; 2 Kings 25:19; 2 Sam. 8:17;
1 Kings 4:3).

In the biblical context the scribe would be thoroughly trained
in all aspects of legal matters dealing with the legal codes of
Moses and biblical laws in general. The Talmud laid down strict
rules for handling biblical manuscripts. The scribes were metic-
ulous in their efforts to make an exact copy of the biblical
text being copied, carefully giving attention to each "jot" and
"tittle." Every word was checked and double checked. "It was
customary for them to count the words and even the letters
in each scroll, noting the middle word and letter, to guard
against both omissions and additions of any kind." [6]

Mosaic Law
949

89

Never has the world known more painstaking copyists than the Jewish Sopherim or scribes. Ezra was both a priest and a scribe who contributed greatly by compiling the holy oracles and who studied and taught the law to Israel (Ezra 7:6,11). After the exile, when the writing prophets had completed their work, scribal activity in the area of biblical manuscripts increased greatly. By the second century B.C. the scribes were recognized as members of an honored profession. They were the religious scholars and theologians with the responsibility to maintain the purity of the Scriptures.

During the time of Christ the scribes were active in politics and exerted a powerful influence. Because they were the teachers of the Law and because of their ability to make judicial decisions based on scriptural exegesis, they occupied important positions in the Sanhedrin. However, by that time the scribes and the Pharisees had perverted the meaning of Scripture into pure legalism disregarding the spiritual intent. The scribes together with the Pharisees and Sadducees opposed Jesus when he tried to bring the religious community back to the spirit of the Law. The problem is clearly stated by Jesus in Matthew 23:13–35.

IV. THE ELDERS

The word *elder* could relate to any area in life in which the matter of seniority was concerned. The Bible makes reference to at least three categories of elders: those in government, Jewish religious elders, and officers in the Christian Church. The biblical definition is an "official, who, so far as can be judged, had, by virtue of his right as firstborn, succeeded to the headship of a father's house, of a tribal family, or of the tribe itself (1 Kings 8:1–3; Judg 8:14–16)." [7]

Generally, the title indicated an official of the highest rank with great authority (Deut. 27:1; Ezra 10:8). The designation "elder" might be synonymous with the chief of a tribe. The word *elder* in Hebrew *(zaqen)* means "one who is bearded," suggesting a man of maturity and distinguishing him as having a certain official rank and position among the people. In the period from Moses to Ezra and on into the intertestamental era, elders were recognized as the highest authoritative body over the people. Their responsibility included both religious and political matters and the settling of intertribal disputes (Joshua 22:13–33).[8]

After Genesis 50:7 the next biblical reference to elder appears in Exodus 3:16–18 where elders were appointed by Moses to be the body of officials to receive the announcement of liberation from Egypt. Later, the covenant was ratified by the seventy elders at Mount Sinai (Exod. 19:7; 24:1,9,14). When Moses' burden of government became too great, the elders were selected and the spirit which was upon Moses was also upon them to govern the people (Num. 11:16,17). In case of legal infraction, the elders were to represent the people in making an atonement (Lev. 4:13–15). While the Jews were in Babylon, the elders were the center of authority in the Jewish community. This prominence continued after the Jews returned to Jerusalem (Ezra 5:5,9; 6:7,8,14).

In the Greek period the elders developed into the "great assembly" (Knesset) of the Jews. Later the Great Sanhedrin, of seventy elders in number, was the supreme legislative body.[9]

In the Christian church elders became officials and at times seemed to have been interchangeable with presbyters and bishops. By the early period in Acts elders existed in the church at Jerusalem (Acts 11:30).

On his missionary journeys Paul appointed elders in every church (Acts 14:23). It is quite evident that the official nature of the Christian elders was influenced by that of the Jewish elders; these men were invested with the same kind of authority. To become a Christian elder meant ordination, a formal attestation by the church officials (1 Tim. 4:14). Aptness to teach was one of the qualifications for this office. In the Book of Revelation twenty-four elders are mentioned. Some scholars see in this number a symbolic meaning of unity between the twelve tribes of Israel and the twelve apostles (Rev. 4:4,10; 7:11–13; 11:16; 19:4).[10]

Divine
Teachers
3556

V. THE APOSTLES

The word *apostle* signifies "one sent forth" as a messenger or ambassador. The definition for *disciple* is a "pupil" or "scholar." It is a broad term used to indicate those with Christian faith. The twelve Jesus chose to be his followers were called disciples. Such a designation is seen in Matt. 10:1, but in the next verse the same twelve are referred to as apostles. They are Peter, Andrew, James, John, Philip, Bartholomew, Thomas, Matthew, James, Thaddeus, Simon the Canaanite, and Judas. Sometimes this group is referred to as "the twelve." In Matthew 10:1,2 the terms *disciple* and *apostle* are interchangeable. Frequently, in broad usage, the term *apostle* or *disciple* seems to include all believers in Christ, but in Acts 1:21,22 a narrow definition would include only those who had been with Jesus from the time of his baptism. This definition of *apostle* is borne out by Acts 1:21–26 where Matthias replaces Judas. The "lot" fell upon Matthias and he was numbered with the eleven apostles (Acts 1:21–26).

Apostles
2080–2082

Disciples of
Christ
2080–2082

Matthias
2266

Judas
1959–1963

91

The number twelve appeared to be important because when "Judas by transgression fell" the disciples elected Matthias to fill the vacancy. Matthew and Mark used the word *apostle* only once each for the twelve (Matt. 10:2 and Mark 6:30). Luke refers to them as apostles almost exclusively. When speaking of the twelve, Paul employs the term *apostle* in a broader sense, for "messenger" or "agent" (2 Cor. 8:23 and Phil. 2:25). John speaks of false apostles (Rev. 2:2).[11]

VI. THE DEACONS

The word *deacon* means "to serve," "to wait upon tables," which suggests a very personal service, a service of love. In Greek tradition the term had demeaning implications, but to Jesus it meant the highest attainment in the kingdom. Jesus demonstrated this at the foot washing (John 13:14,15). However, in the NT *deacon* is only found four times (Phil. 1:1 and 1 Tim. 3:8,10,13). The word is not employed in Acts 6:1–3 when the seven men were designated to "serve tables" and to take care of the widows. It is evident that service transcends terminology; Jesus placed much importance on service.

In the church the term *deacon* is associated with a special office. To qualify for the office meant that one must be "proved worthy" (1 Tim. 3:8,9). The historical development of the office, which has a high standard, is linked with that of bishop: "[he must not be] doubletongued, not given to much wine, not greedy of filthy lucre; . . . being found blameless . . . the husbands of one wife, ruling their children and their own houses well" (1 Tim. 3:8–16).[12]

9

God's Plan of Salvation from Genesis to Revelation

"I am not ashamed of the gospel of Christ: for it is the power of God unto salvation to every one that believeth; to the Jew first, and also to the Greek" (Rom. 1:16).

I. The Essence and Nature of Salvation

A Bible scholar once said: "What is unfolded in Scripture is one great economy of salvation—*Unum Continuum Systema*—an organism of divine acts and testimonies, which, with the beginning of Genesis with creation, advances progressively to its completion in the person and work of Christ, and is to find its close in the new heaven and earth predicted in the Apocalypse; and it is only in connection with this whole that the details can be properly estimated. . . . He who has not learned to understand the Old Testament in its historical connection . . . lacks the key to its meaning." [1] Some modern theologians have a tendency to divorce OT religion from any direct connection with the NT, placing it in the same category with other pre-Christian religions, such as that ascribed to Homer and the theology of Marcion. To this school of thought, the LORD of the OT is a dim and distant figure who has nothing to do with the redemptive process in the NT.

This point of view is closely related to that of the Gnostics, who considered the God of the OT to be an inferior god, a kind of "demiurge," who had created the evil world of matter, in contrast to the spiritual realm that Jesus had come to reveal. To this impersonal, transcendent god, love, mercy, and justice were completely foreign. [2]

Salvation
3116–3123

Testimonies
3598

Creation
884–886

Works of Christ
3913

Book of Revelation, The Apocalypse
4288

However, the facts of revelation do not substantiate these conclusions. "The relationship of the NT to the Old is of such nature that they both stand or fall together. The NT assumes the existence of the OT law and prophecy as its positive presupposition . . . We cannot have the redeeming God of the New Covenant without the creator and 'covenant God' preached in the Old; we cannot divorce the Redeemer from the OT predictions which He came to fulfill. The genesis of all the ideas of the NT relating to salvation lies in the OT." [3]

There is not a flower of truth blooming in the NT whose seed was not sown in the soil of the Old; and there was not a seed of truth planted in the OT which does not come to full fruitage in the NT. The very breath of the OT is the same breath that prayed, dying, on Calvary.

The heavenly council met in extraordinary session in behalf of man's redemption long before the racial catastrophe [the Fall] took place. God the Father, with the Son and the Holy Spirit, constituting the Trinity, had the bridge of salvation built before man actually came to it. While the details of the plan of redemption were not known from the beginning, there was no uncertainty as to the [basic] facts . . . The Christ, promised [to man] in Eden, was the [eternal] Saviour of the world, making it possible that the first woman who yielded to the temptation of disobedience, might through faith in the promised Redeemer become a subject of His redemptive grace.[4]

A noted Bible scholar captured the significance of this truth in these words: "Before the first man sinned, God provided a way by which he might escape the death penalty and be made perfect again. That was through the atoning work of Christ Who . . . was 'slain from the foundation of the world' " (Rev. 13:8b).[5]

In Matthew 25:34 reference is made to the inheritance of "the kingdom prepared for you from the foundation of the world." With regard to the eternal relationship of Christ to salvation the Bible affirms that "God had appointed His Son to be the Mediator of salvation. The Son is the Lamb, without blemish before the foundation of the world was laid (1 Peter 1:19,20). Christ is the Mediator of world redemption, for it was the good pleasure of the '. . . Father that in him [Christ] should all fulness dwell . . . to reconcile all things unto himself' (Col. 1:19,20). His death on the Cross was an offering of Himself to God" (Heb. 9:14).[6]

The Bible, from Genesis to Revelation, reveals one God, the Creator of the heavens and earth. He is presented in the NT as a God of love and mercy, and it was he whom Jesus came to reveal.

As God is holy and eternally the same, his hatred for sin and his love for holiness have always been consistent. With him is "no variableness, neither shadow of turning" (James 1:17). The psalmist had this in mind when he said, "Thou art the same, and thy years shall have no end" (Ps. 102:27). Malachi, as a spokesman for the Lord, emphasizes this conclusion, "For I am the LORD, I change not" (Mal. 3:6). Parallel to this plain teaching of Scripture is the fact that God does not have two redemptive plans, one for the people in the OT and one for those in the NT. It is not likely that God exposed the human race at any time to hopeless fate. Because of God's foreknowledge and love, a recovery plan would be imperative. When Adam and Eve sinned, they had a standby plan of salvation provided for them (Rom. 4:13; 9:6–8).

After their transgression, Adam and Eve, suddenly realizing that they were sinful and naked, made aprons from fig leaves for a covering. Afterward "did the Lord God make coats of skins, and clothed them" (Gen. 3:21). The account indicates that the price of this covering was the life of an animal. This seems to foreshadow the innocent dying for the sinner. Thus

> the covering of their nakedness was a gracious token from . . . God, that the sin which had alienated them [Adam and Eve] from Him, . . . was henceforth to be in His sight as if it were not. It was done . . . to denote the covering of guilt from the eye of Heaven, an act which God alone could have done. But He did it, . . . by a medium of death, by a sacrifice of the life of those creatures which men were not yet permitted to kill for purposes of food, and . . . with grace which laid open the prospect of recovered life and of blessing for the fallen. It is probable that Adam and Eve appropriated God's redemptive provision before they died.[7]

Adam's faith was expressed by the name he gave Eve.

> From the first, Adam believed in the original good news of the coming seed of the woman (Gen. 3:15). This is suggested by the name Eve (Hebrew *Chavva*, "life") which he gave to his wife (*Isha*, fem. of *Ish*, "man") directly after the original promise, and immediately before the expulsion from Paradise (Gen. 3:20ff.). "Sunken in death he nevertheless gave his wife so proud a name" (Calvin), and thereby expressed his faith in the conquest of death by life. So it was an "act of faith that Adam named his wife Eve" and from that time the new name of his wife was for man the "reminder of the promise of God's grace." [8]

Adam called her "woman" in Genesis 2:23 (taken out of man) and "Eve" in Genesis 3:20, "because she was the mother of all living."

Luther says of the original good news: "On this, Adam trusted and thereby was saved from his fall. That Eve also in faith took her stand on the ground of the word of promise is shown by her statement in Genesis 4:1." [9] The redemptive acceptance is most strongly reflected in Abel whose righteousness cannot be doubted (Matt. 23:35). On the other hand, Cain is presented

God's Plan of Salvation from Genesis to Revelation

Eternal
2481

Salvation for All
3119

Adam
34

Eve
1159

Guilt
1763

Sacrifice
3107–3111

Abel
4

Cain
618
95

as one who rejected God's requirement as evidenced by his act of murdering his brother (Gen. 4:5–15). Abel accepted God's plan "by faith" (Heb. 11:4); Cain rejected it by doubt. Abel's faith was evidenced by righteousness; Cain's sinful rebellion, by his crime. In brief, "By their fruits ye shall know them" (Matt. 7:20).

Murder
2449, 2450

Knowledge
2020–2035

Offering
Acceptable
2625

Blood Sacrifice
516

"Cain must have been in a position to have the same knowledge of sin and mercy as did Abel, but the offering which he brought was rejected. In what way did the two offerings differ? One offering, that of Abel, was of such a nature that it required the shedding of blood. The other was bloodless." [10] The blood sacrifice (Rev. 13:8b) was sufficient ground for the faith of Abel. "It is quite evident that we have an intimation, at least, in the sacred records, that the sacrifice in its earliest history, was instituted by God Himself, either by example or immediate command. . . . The shedding of the blood of the sacrifice, and the yielding up of its life, must repeat continuously, to stupid, fallen humanity of every generation, the message of man's guilt, of divine justice and God's mercy. The promise made in Eden should be fulfilled." [11] The loss of life is the penalty of sin, and its typical vicarious surrender was necessary to remission (Heb. 9:22). "The blood of animals was used in all offerings for sin . . . (Lev. 17:11). The 'blood of Jesus,' the 'blood of Christ,' the 'blood of Jesus Christ,' or the 'blood of the Lamb,' are figurative expressions for His atoning death (1 Cor. 10:16)." [12] Scripture points out that Noah took clean animals into the ark (Gen. 7:2ff.), evidently for sacrificial purposes, and after the flood,

> Noah built the Lord an altar and offered burnt offering. . . . To Him the hearts of the pious lift . . . To heaven. . . . must their offering and prayers ascend, if they are to reach His throne.
>
> So as to give this "upward" direction to the sacrifice, . . . there were erected . . . high places and altars from which [the prayers] should 'ascend' heavenwards in the fire. The presence of God is indeed everywhere and is not restricted by the boundaries of an above or beneath (Ps. 139). . . . The clean animals offered, as well as the sacrifices from the beginning of the world, themselves point to the sacrifice on Golgotha, the Lamb, without blemish and without spot (1 Peter 1:19,20) who is in truth the fountain of all preservation and salvation of the world.[13]

It is evident that this blood symbolism is reflected in the OT rite of circumcision. This act was a covenant sign between Abraham and the Lord. "In order that Abraham might become 'the friend of God' he was commanded that he should be circumcised as a token of the covenant between him and God (Gen. 17:10,11). The blood exuding from the operation was a testimony of faith in God's blood atonement." [14]

96

The use of blood in the OT is "everywhere vested with cleansing, expiatory, and reverently symbolic qualities. . . . From the OT to the NT we see an exaltation of the conception of blood and ceremonies. In Abraham's covenant [circumcision] his own blood had to be shed. . . . There must always be a shedding of blood. 'Apart from shedding of blood there is no remission' (Heb. 9:22). The exaltation and dignifying of this idea finds it highest development then in the vicarious shedding of blood by Christ Himself (1 John 1:7)." [15]

Noah was a faithful follower of the Lord, and of him it was said that he "found grace in the eyes of the Lord." He was a "just man and perfect in his generations, and Noah walked with God" (Gen. 6:8,9,22; 8:20; 9:1,9). In the interest of exegetical integrity the question of Noah's drunkenness must not be evaded. There are several approaches to the question; of these, two categories will be considered, e.g. (1) that he was guilty of sin and was restored, and (2) that he did it innocently.

1. It must be recognized that devout people have succumbed to temptation and have committed sin (even getting drunk), but because of the mercy and grace of God, "If we confess our sins, he is faithful and just to forgive us our sins, and to cleanse us from all unrighteousness" (1 John 1:9). Those who acknowledge this aspect of God's grace would be inclined to give Noah the benefit of the doubt. David sinned and was forgiven (2 Sam. 11:3,4; cf. Ps. 32:1–5).

2. It is generally agreed that revelation of grace—its details—has been progressively revealed, e.g., man's understanding of grace is broadened through personal experience and the example of others (1 Cor. 10:6).

   Wine is not mentioned before the Noah incident (Gen. 9:20,21), nor is there a prohibition for the use of it prior to the time when "Noah began to be a husbandman"—a man of the ground, a farmer. This may have been the first time the wine [grape vine] was cultivated; and it is probable that the strength or intoxicating property of wine was never known before. The process of fermentation might have overtaken Noah without him being aware of the fact or its effects. A right-minded person would hesitate to deprive Noah of innocence for doing something (end in itself) like this without knowing the consequences.

   In the interest of charity and candor it would seem that Noah should be given the benefit of the doubt, especially since Noah's name is still listed on the roster of faith when the Book of Hebrews was written (Heb. 11:7). Adam Clarke gives some thought-provoking observations at this point. [16]

In his devotion to God, Noah observed the requirements given by God to the Adamic generation. Adam Clarke states that,

The old world began with sacrifice, so also did the new . . . (Gen. 8:20). The proper mode of worshipping the divine Being is the invention or institution of God Himself; and sacrifice, in the act and design, is the essence of religion. Without sacrifice, actually offered or implied, there never was, there never can be any true religion. Even in the heavens, a lamb is represented before the throne of God as newly slain (Rev. 5:6). The design of sacrifice is two-faced, the slaying and the burning of the victim point out: first, that the life of the sinner is forfeited to divine justice; secondly, that his soul deserves the fire of perdition.[17]

The Jews have a tradition that Noah built his altar on the same spot where Adam built his worship center and where Abel later offered his sacrifice. It is thought that this place was Mount Moriah in Jerusalem, presently called the Dome of the Rock, where Abraham offered Isaac.[18]

Abraham was also a child of faith. Accordingly Abraham "believed God. . . . By this heroic faith, was he justified. . . . Abraham believed; he had faith in the Lord and the Lord reckoned it to him as [righteousness]. . . . This is one of the mountain peaks of Scripture. It is higher than Sinai. It joins together the two Testaments. Already it reflects the light of Christ. . . . Abraham, is now at peace, and [has] lived on in faith." [19] The most significant event in Abraham's life was the revelation he received on a starry night when God concluded the covenant of faith with the patriarch (Gen. 15:5, 18). That was the time

when Abraham received the divine declaration of justification, and it is there that in the annals of salvation the very first plain and express mention is made of the justification by faith of a sinner (Gen. 15:6).

It is evident, however, that all responses to God required an act of faith, and it has been by faith in God's provision that people of all the ages have been justified. The reality of "justification" transcends its theological statement.

The question should be raised: When was faith reckoned

to Abraham for righteousness? Was it before or after his circumcision (Rom. 4:10)? The answer is: Not less than thirteen years before he was circumcised, because the covenant of circumcision was first introduced when Abraham was ninety-nine years old (Gen. 17:1–14); but the covenant of faith and justification

took place even before the birth of Ishmael, and therefore before Abraham's eighty-sixth year (Gen. 17:1,11). Consequently Abraham had been justified already thirteen years before he was circumcised.

It is significant that Paul builds his case for justification by faith upon the OT. In Romans he draws liberally upon the Hebrew Scriptures to prove that justification is through faith (Rom. 3:21ff.; 4:1ff.). Abraham's justification prior to circumcision is prophetically significant because through it Abraham was to become the father of all such as were without circumcision but, through faith alone, should become justified. By this fact it became evident that circumcision was not necessary for salvation but only a "seal of righteousness" by faith. To obtain salvation the Gentiles were not required to pass through the anteroom of the Jews—that is, through the law—but must first pass through the anteroom of that faith which Abraham already had before he was circumcised. Thus the Scriptures teach salvation is without human merit, that redemption is of grace, a free gift entirely by faith, and that the gospel of the church age was foreshadowed in the covenant with Abraham; the "new covenant" is the continuation and glorious perfection of the covenant with Abraham (Rom. 4; Gen. 3:9,14).

Abraham's faith in God's resurrection power was also manifested in his willingness to sacrifice his son, Isaac, upon whom so much depended, for he reckoned "that God was able to raise him up, even from the dead" (Heb. 11:19). The words of Abraham to his servants attested his confidence: ". . . and I and the lad will go yonder and worship, and come again to you" (Gen. 22:5). Thus Abraham's faith became the type of faith manifest in the NT resurrection.

"The sacrifice which represented, in the fullest measure, Christ in His work of expiation and atonement was the particularly great offering of the Levitical system . . . Whether from the herd of cattle, the flock of sheep or goats, or the clean fowl, . . . without blemish. . . . This represents Christ, the choice one of heaven, the unblemished one, whose life was sacrificed, and consumed, as it were, upon the altar of divine justice, in behalf of sinful men." [20] From the beginning, offering the sacrifice was a testimony to saving faith in God's promise.

In addition to Abraham's faith, Isaac, Jacob, Joseph, and Moses (Heb. 11:20) also believed the promises. Of these men of faith it is said: "These all died in faith, not having received the promises, but having seen them afar off, and were persuaded of them, and embraced them, and confessed that they were strangers and pilgrims on the earth" (Heb. 11:13). Faith has always been the basic fundamental in a sinner's redemption. By faith and repentance a sinner can be reconciled to God. Faith was the key to salvation not only for OT penitents but for Paul and Silas as well. The writer of Hebrews states: "Without faith it is impossible to please him: for he that cometh to God must believe that he is, and that he is a rewarder of them that diligently seek him" (Heb. 11:6). The faith here expressed is faith in the atoning merits of the blood of "the Lamb" (1 Peter 1:18,19; Rev. 13:8b). If "Jesus Christ [is] the same yesterday, and to day and for ever" (Heb. 13:8), his relationship to the redemption of man is the same always.

In speaking to the "people of Israel" about Jesus Christ, Peter says, "This is the stone which was set at nought of you builders,

Gentle
Believers
4038

Salvation by
Grace
1447

Resurrection
Promises
2407

Isaac
1802

Isaac
1802

Jacob
1837

Joseph
1937

Moses
2420, 2421

Paul
2697

Silas
3288

99

Preliminary
Matters

Name of the
Lord
2513–2517

Salvation by
Faith
1206

Salvation
Possible to All
3119

which is become the head of the corner. Neither is there salvation in any other: for there is none other name under heaven given among men, whereby we must be saved" (Acts 4:11,12). Here the statement projects this truth into every age. It is evident that salvation has never been available through any other name. Only by faith in God's Christ can anyone be saved, and people who will be gathering around the "Great White Throne" in heaven will be there because they exercised saving faith in him. Abel, Abraham, Isaac, Jacob, and Joseph will be there; Moses, Gideon, Barak, Samson, David, and Samuel will all be there, as well as a multitude of other OT saints. Matthew, Mark, Luke, John, Peter, and James will be there along with Paul, Silas, and Timothy. Moody, Sankey, Wesley, Calvin, and Knox will be there with hosts of others. All will be there because of the saving faith they exercised in God's Christ. All who have exercised this faith in Christ will be there. Faith as a prerequisite to salvation is well presented in the eleventh chapter of Hebrews.

God the
Creator
884–886

Songs of
Victory
2477

God is the Creator of all and he has a standing offer of pardon to all men who turn from their evil ways and do that which is right (Ezek. 33:11–14ff.). The song of redemption and of personal salvation is the eternal theme in the hymnbook (Psalms) of the OT church and in the books of the prophets. This shows that OT saints enjoyed a conscious realization of sins forgiven; "Let the God of my salvation be exalted" (Ps. 18:46); "For thou art the God of my salvation" (Ps. 25:5); "The LORD is my light and my salvation" (Ps. 27:1); "The salvation of the righteous is of the LORD" (Ps. 37:39). Obviously the psalmist makes salvation personal when he says: "The law of the LORD is perfect, converting the soul" (Ps. 19:7) and "Re-

store unto me the joy of thy salvation. . . . Then will I teach transgressors thy ways; and sinners shall be converted unto thee" (Ps. 51:12,13). Certainly the psalmist cannot be an evangel until he himself is forgiven and restored. The prophet Isaiah adds a note to the certainty of redemption: "God is my salvation" (Isa. 12:2), and the prophet Micah joins in the refrain: "I will wait for the God of my salvation" (Mic. 7:7). (See Synagogue and Church, Ch. 5, I, D–E, pages 62, 63.)

II. THE WORK OF THE HOLY SPIRIT IN THE OLD AND NEW
TESTAMENTS

It can be further assumed that God the Creator, Yahweh the Lord, and Ruach the Spirit of God are the "Three in One" in the OT. The Spirit of God in the OT is the Holy Spirit in the New; he reveals divine truth in both testaments. Peter definitely attributes the inspiration of the OT to the Holy Spirit (2 Peter 1:21).

God's Plan of Salvation from Genesis to Revelation

Inspiration
417, 1774

A study of the work and nature of the Holy Spirit's work shows that his coming upon persons in the OT was limited to specially selected leaders such as prophets, priests, priestesses, and kings (Judg. 6:34; 1 Sam. 10:10), and "it is in the prophetic period that He becomes the organ of the communication of God's thoughts to men." [21]

It is only through the Spirit that divine revelation penetrates the heart and mind of man. The Spirit is represented as proceeding from the Lord and imparted by him, to a person, to be bestowed upon others (Num. 11:17,25). A person can also lose the Spirit as Saul did (1 Sam. 16:14). In Isaiah the Israelites "rebelled, and vexed his holy Spirit" (Isa. 63:10). It is evident that as the Holy Spirit progressively revealed himself, the latter forms of his revelation are more distinct, appearing in a more personal way after the founding of the Theocracy.

Holy Spirit's Work
1611–1614

Dr. Oehler says that the Holy Spirit unfolds himself in proportion as the outward Theophany disappears (see Ch. 7, VI, page 80) and that it is the same with the course of revelation in the NT, especially since "Christophanies continued for some time after the ascension of our Lord [and] then disappeared and made room for the revelation of the Lord in the inwardness of the Spirit." [22] In the OT the Spirit's work in the divine kingdom is rather that of endowing the organs of the Theocracy (government under God) with the gifts required for their calling, and these gifts of office in the OT are similar to the gifts of grace in the NT (1 Cor. 14:12ff.).

The Spirit of God bestowed upon Moses and the seventy elders the gift of divine wisdom in guiding the people (Num. 11:17ff.); which was given also to Joshua (Deut. 34:9), the judges (6:34), and the kings (1 Kings 3:12). Obviously this work is parallel to the work of the Spirit as promised by Jesus Christ. "When he, the Spirit of truth, is come, he will guide you into all truth . . . and he will shew you things to come" (John 16:13). It would appear from this evidence that the full revelation of the Trinity and the Holy Spirit in particular in the New Testament is foreshadowed by the restrained work of the Spirit through the OT prophets, priests, and kings.

Elders
2078

Trinity
3694

The NT Church of the future, on the contrary, is founded upon the outpouring of the spirit upon all [saved] flesh (John 12:28ff.). . . . The direct personal communication with God which is effected by the Spirit, and which afforded the prophets an insight into the divine counsels, is to become the possession of all members of the Church (Num. 11:29). The impartation of the Holy Spirit, besides communicating a vital knowledge of God, purifies the heart and creates a readiness to fulfill the Divine Will (Ezek. 36:25–27), . . .

Holy Spirit
1601–1614

thus the end of the OT educational work is attained; the holy people of God are also a . . . holy church.[23]

III. THE NATURE OF THE ATONEMENT

Atonement
304

In the Gospels, Christ Jesus himself foretold his anticipated "death on the cross" to be one phase of the Atonement that was provisional from the beginning. Theologians of the early NT Church—such as Iranaeus, Origen, Athanasius, and Augustine—interpreted the death of Christ as a ransom, paid to the devil, and assumed that Christ was the divine Logos Incarnate. Anselm in his book, *Cur Deus Homo?*, argued that the death of Christ, the God-man, was a reparation or satisfaction paid to God for the sins of mankind. Luther and other reformers attested that the suffering of Christ was the divine punishment for the sins of the world.[24] All of these views present segments of the doctrine of the Atonement predicated upon the assumption that man had sinned and that he could regain favor with God only by becoming justified, i.e., restored to a condition as though he had never sinned.

Justification by
Faith
1203, 1985

Messianic
Hope
4186

Justification in turn was possible only by faith, a concept stated in the OT and reaffirmed in the New (Hab. 2:4; Rom. 1:17). In the OT, salvation was acquired by faith in Christ, the Messiah, who was foreordained "before the foundation of the world" (1 Peter 1:20), but was manifest "when the fulness of the time was come" (Gal. 4:4). The OT church had a prophetic look at the cross; the NT church has a backward historical look at the cross to which God committed his Son. Prophets, priests, and holy men of the OT as well as ministers and evangelists in the NT strove to interpret the Atonement God made for man. There is no question that the Lord and all of his NT interpreters present the Atonement as it has existed essentially from the beginning.

Salvation
Promised
3122

Contingent upon repentance, confession, and faith, "He appointed all men in love unto sonship and holiness (Eph. 1:4,5). But therewith 'before all time' He also promised them life (Titus 1:2), and therefore, from the standpoint of God as above time, His grace is thus given to us 'before the world began' " (2 Tim. 1:9).[25]

It is an accepted fact that "Christianity" had its beginning with the Incarnation of Jesus Christ. But provisionally the principle of "Christianity" was a reality when God established a plan for man's redemption. The believers during and before the earthly ministry of Jesus were in fact "Christians" at heart because they exercised saving faith either in the promised or provided Savior. They were Christians in spirit before they were so called at Antioch (Acts 11:26). By assuming the name

"Christian" they did not subscribe to a new religion, they merely accepted a new name. The foundation for salvation has always been rooted in the Atonement made for man: "Jesus Christ was in the divine purpose appointed from the beginning of the world to redeem man by His blood." [26]

Every student of the Bible is aware that in Christ "all the prophets witness, that through his name whosoever believeth in him shall receive remission of sins" (Acts 10:43). "Christ is the theme of the OT; He said so Himself (Luke 24:25-27,46); so His greatest apostle testified (Acts 26:22,23). It is only from the King of Scripture, that the testimony of His preceding heralds can be understood: it is only from the NT that the question as to the OT solves itself." [27] Any intelligent interpretation concerning the Atonement must take into consideration the fact that there is only one Atonement—both in the OT and NT, and that the blood of animals in the OT was symbolic of the blood which was shed by the "Lamb of God," which was provisionally, and prophetically, provided before the OT period.[28] "In the NT the initiative is of God, who not only devises and reveals the way of reconciliation but by means of angels, prophets, priests, and ultimately His begotten Son, applies the means of atonement and persuades men to accept the proffered reconciliation. . . . It follows that atonement is fundamental in the nature of God in His relations to men, and that redemption is in the heart of God's dealing in history." [29]

The OT contains a counterpart to the various elements recorded in the NT. Sacrificing the animal was a testimony to the fact that the worshiper had truly repented of his sins and that by faith he was trusting in God's promise. The ritual of the Day of Atonement, the Good Friday of the OT, expresses the very essence of God's plan. Mohler says:

Divine Promises
2878-2888

Day of Atonement
305

Holy Place
1600

> As the tabernacle, the sacrificial system, the entire law, thus too, the Day of Atonement in particular, contained only the shadow of future good things, but not these things themselves (Heb. 10:1), and is "the figure of the true" (Heb. 9:24). Christ himself entered the Holy Place, which was not made with hands, namely, into heaven itself, and has now appeared before God, by once for all giving Himself as a sacrifice for the removal of sin (Heb. 9:23ff.). By this act the purpose of the OT and its highest development, the Day of Atonement, understood in its typical significance, has been fulfilled. . . . Accordingly, our hope, too, like an anchor (Heb. 6:19), penetrates to the inner part of the veil, i.e., to Heaven.[30]

The Day of Atonement did not make its appearance until the era of tabernacle worship, but its functional principle was found in the worship system current in earlier days. A progressive element of refinement is to be recognized in the history of redemption. Early worship had as its center the altar without benefit of a building; later came the tabernacle, which was followed by the temple; during the exile the synagogue came into existence. All of these places of worship were different in design but were, by purpose and function, similar. In each of these places of worship there was the idea of God meeting man, where sinful man met the condition of salvation.

Abraham appropriated the benefits of the Atonement through faith and became a believer in Christ the coming Messiah. The benefits of this faith are reflected in the collective names of the promise (Rom. 4:13) and the blessing (Gal. 3:14), mercy (Luke 1:54), as well as holiness (Luke 1:73–75) and the covenant (Acts 3:25). The way in which Abraham responded to this particular goodness of God makes him the type of the Christian believer. It is declared that he "saw" Messiah's "day" (John 8:56). His faith in the divine promise of the Atonement was for him unsupported by any evidence of the senses: this type of faith led to his justification (Rom. 4:3), and therefore in this sense again he is the "father" of the Christians, as believers (Rom. 4:11,12). For that promise to Abraham was, after all, "preached before the gospel," in that it embraced "all nations" (Gal. 3:8).

By faith Abraham appropriated personal salvation, and he is one with all believers in God's Christ. [31] Even though the formal "Day of Atonement" had not been instituted, Abraham was indeed a kind of spiritual child made possible through the blood Atonement, laid, in principle, in the Adamic generation (Gen. 4:4; cf. Heb. 11:4). Abraham looked ahead 2000 years and believed what God had promised; today believers look back 2000 years and believe what God provided.

The Atonement is symbolized in the Passover, which was instituted to commemorate the sparing of the Israelites in Egypt (Exod. 12:3,12,46; 23:15). That night the Angel of the Lord smote all the firstborn in the land of Egypt but passed over the houses of the Israelites where the blood of the Paschal Lamb had been sprinkled. Sauer says:

> The Israelites pleading the blood, mindful of the afflictions from which they awaited deliverance, and putting away wickedness, were the people of the Lord in holy, glad communion before him. . . . Celebrations of the Passover are recorded at Sinai (Num. 9:1–14), on entering Canaan (Josh. 5:10); under Hezekiah (2 Chron. 30:1–27); with reference to Solomon in v. 26, under Josiah (2 Chron. 35:1–19); and in the days of Ezra (Ezra 6:19–22); (Matt. 26:17). The Passover was to be observed as an ordinance forever (Exod. 12:14–24) and the true church has continued this rite to the present time.

> Naturally the details were impressed on the minds of the people and lent themselves to symbolic and homiletic purposes (1 Cor. 5:7), where the Paschal Lamb is made to typify Jesus Christ (Heb. 11:28). The best known instance of such symbolic use is the institu-

tion of the Eucharist [Lord's Supper] on the basis of the paschal meal.[32]

It should be pointed out that the words used in the narratives of the NT institution of the Lord's Supper are similar to those in connection with the Passover, e.g., "body," "blood," "covenant," "given," "poured out," "for you," "for many," "unto remission of sins," "memorial" (Exod. 24:6–8). The "immediate background of the Lord's Supper is the Passover, and that without prejudice as to whether the Lord Christ was at the paschal meal with His disciples before he instituted the Lord's Supper, as seems most probable (Luke 22:7–18), or whether he died upon the day of its observance. . . . The Passover was at once a covenant-recalling and a covenant-renewing sacrifice, and the Lord's Supper, as corresponding to it, was instituted at the time of its yearly observance, and of the Immolation of the true paschal lamb, of whose death it interpreted the value and the significance" (Exod. 2:23–28).[33] The use of bread and wine in the Eucharist is suggestive of the accustomed use in the OT (Exod. 29:38–42). Feeding upon the paschal lamb was an expression of faith in God's Paschal Lamb, Jesus Christ.

Information coming from the *Manual of Discipline*, discovered in the Dead Sea Caves, shows that the OT church (of which the Essenes were evidently a part) definitely observed a sacrament similar to the Christian Last Supper. The Lord's Supper or Eucharist confession of this church closely resembles that of the present Christian church. If the records of the OT church strike a frankly Christian note, it is because they proclaim that Christianity is near.

IV. THE NATURE OF THE NEW BIRTH

An important question revolves around the problem of personal salvation in the OT. Is one to say that the just man not only walked in the faith of a future fulfillment of the promise and a future redemption, but also rejoiced in the present possession of salvation, and had the assurance that his sins were forgiven?

From the evidence gathered in the OT comes the conclusion that people enjoyed salvation before Christ's incarnation. It is assumed that the disciples and others were saved men before the crucifixion. Both the OT and NT teach and illustrate that all individuals experience divine forgiveness who have repented of their sins and who have turned to God in saving faith (Ezek. 43:27; Acts 10:34–36). David, as an individual, testified to personal forgiveness and salvation when he said,

"Blessed is he whose transgression is forgiven, whose sin is covered" (Ps. 32:1). On another occasion the psalmist said: "There is forgiveness with thee" (Ps. 130:4; cf. Is. 55:7).

Many other instances are given in the OT of individuals repenting and being restored to God's favor (2 Kings 22:19). "The sin of Israel is recognized as the sin of the individual, which can be removed only by individual repentance and cleansing. This is best seen from the stirring appeals of the prophets of the exile. . . . This cannot be understood otherwise than as a turning of the individual to the Lord." [34]

There was no merit in the animal sacrifice brought by the individual worshiper, for "it is not possible that the blood of bulls and of goats should take away sins" (Heb. 10:4). It was only as the sacrifice symbolized and testified to faith in the blood of God's "Lamb" that sins were remitted. The "interposition of divine grace" is represented under the figure of a ceremonial washing and sprinkling from all iniquity and sin (Isa. 1:18). Proselytes embracing Judaism had to repent and submit to the same ritual before they could be fully received into the covenant of Israel.

In the teachings of our Lord, the concept of the "new birth" or regeneration is resident in the OT; the teaching is clear at this point and is graphically asserted by Jesus Christ in his conversation with Nicodemus (John 3:1–21), "a man of the Pharisees . . . a ruler of the Jews." He was well versed in the Talmud and the Midrash as well as other great rabbinical teachings. Above all, he was a student of the Scriptures; and yet, despite this fact, Nicodemus was apparently ignorant of the OT teachings on "the new birth." He is a type of church member who has not been regenerated, that is, "born again." Jesus takes this occasion to chide Nicodemus for his ignorance. "Art thou a master of Israel, and knowest not these things?" (John 5:10). Adam Clarke paraphrases this verse thus: "Hast thou taken upon thee to guide the blind into the way of truth; and yet knowest not that truth thyself? Dost thou command proselytes to be baptized with water as an emblem of a new birth; and art thou unacquainted with the cause, necessity, nature, and effects of that new birth?" [35] Here Jesus Christ is speaking about a divine necessity existing before the crucifixion was actually carried out. Nicodemus could not become a member in the "kingdom" until he had experienced salvation, namely, the "new birth." The Incarnation did not in any way change the conditions by which believers entered the "congregation of the righteous" (Ps. 1:5; see also Ezek. 11:19).

Professor Sauer says,

The whole pre-Christian revelation of salvation divides into two chief sections: the covenant of promise and the covenant of law—

the sinner is to be redeemed, and to this end renewal and new-birth are needful. But this new-birth has man's conversion as a presupposition, and conversion is twofold: a turning from and a turning to, a "No" to ourselves and a "Yes" to God, or as the NT puts it, repentance and faith. Only here is revealed . . . the true meaning of the OT histories: throughout centuries God spoke the word "faith" into the history of salvation, this is the meaning of the covenant with Abraham. Through two thousand years it was an education in faith. Throughout centuries God spoke the word "repent" into the history of salvation; this is the meaning of the law of Moses. Through one thousand, five hundred years it was an education in repentance. "Repent" and "believe" the gospel (Mark 1:15) says Christ. . . . This is the NT purpose of the OT. [36]

God's Plan of Salvation from Genesis to Revelation

Justification by Faith **1203, 1985**

For the OT Church the rite of circumcision was the symbol of faith by which believers were distinguished from the heathen; the rite effected admission to the fellowship of the covenant people, securing for the individual his share in the promises and saving benefits provided by God from the beginning (Rev. 13:8b).

Circumcision **765–767**

Born Again **2154**

It is evident that ethical demands are made on the adult who is spiritually circumcised, namely "born again"; he is obliged to obey God, whose covenant sign he bears in his body, and to walk blamelessly before him (Gen. 17:1). Thus circumcision is the symbol of heart purification after the new birth (Col. 2:11). The spiritual significance is brought out in the use of the phrase "uncircumcision of heart" to note a want of receptivity to the things of God (Lev. 26:41, Jer. 9:25; Ezek. 44:7); "while, on the other hand, the purification of the heart, by which it becomes receptive to the things of God and capable of executing God's will, is called circumcision of the heart" (Col. 2:11–13: cf. Deut. 10:16).[37]

New Creature **2582**

From this evidence it is apparent that the physical operation (circumcision) is symbolic of the spiritual change wrought in the heart by the Holy Spirit, "circumcision of heart," or the "new birth" (see Rom. 2:25ff.).

It can be noted that Abraham was "spiritually circumcised," or "born again," before he submitted to the physical operation of circumcision (Rom. 4:11).

Gradually baptism with water superseded circumcision. Reference to sparkling of water and cleansing from filthiness is found in the OT (Num. 8:7; Ezek. 36:25). It is certain that John the Baptist found in such passages the ground for his practice of baptizing the Jewish believers who sought "to flee from the wrath to come" (John 1:25–28; Matt. 3:7). The time period of the Gospels took place in the OT era. The NT Period did not come into being until after the death of Jesus Christ. The baptism of John was a connecting link between the OT and the NT churches because John ministers in the synoptic OT period—before Jesus died.

Moral Filthiness **957**

John's Baptism **760**

It has always been necessary for sinful man to accept the promised salvation proffered by the Lord. The cleansing so often referred to is in reality the circumcision of the heart (Deut. 30:6) rather than of the flesh. As God takes the initiative in making the covenant, it is apparent that human sin and depravity can be effectively eliminated only by the act of God himself renewing and transforming the heart of man (Hos. 14:4).[38]

People were lost in "trespasses and sins" from the day the first sin was committed. They all, without exception, needed to be saved—to be "born again." Jesus Christ came to "seek and to save that which was lost" (Luke 19:10), but he had always been "seeking to save the lost" (Gal. 4:4). Christ came in the person of Jesus to reveal God the Father more clearly, and to die on the cross. The principle, "new birth," is reflected in the story of the prodigal son; he is declared to have been "dead" and to be "alive again" (Luke 15:24).[39]

The teaching on the "new birth" in the NT reiterates a truth that is, was, and always will be, effective; it is timeless. Moreover, every sermon and doctrine in the NT is initiated by the Spirit of God. Inspiration for the two Testaments came from a common source (2 Tim. 3:16; 1 Peter 1:10,11). Paul distinctly reaffirms the basic OT concept

that a new life is in store for those who have been spiritually dead; that at conversion a spiritual resurrection takes place. This regeneration causes a complete revolution in man. He has thereby passed from under the law of sin and death and has come under 'the law of the Spirit of life in Christ Jesus' (Rom. 8:2). The change is so radical that it is possible now to speak of a 'new creation,' of a 'new man,' that 'after God is created in righteousness and true holiness' (Eph. 4:24) and of 'the new man which is renewed in knowledge after the image of Him that created him' (Col. 3:10) and the image to which the sinner in the NT is renewed is the image of the OT God.[40]

To Paul, regeneration was a personal knowledge of God's Christ whereby the sinner acquired the imprint of the divine nature. Peter affirms, through OT phraseology, that by the "new birth," believers become "a chosen generation, a royal priesthood, an holy nation, a peculiar people" (1 Peter 2:9). Behind the race, the priesthood, the holy nation, stand the redeemed ones—the born-again believers who constitute the church in every age. According to popular interpretation, the "new birth" is associated with the post-crucifixion period, but it must be pointed out that people were redeemed, that is, people were "born again" before Jesus Christ was crucified. Jesus' encounter with Nicodemus took place during the OT period. A never-changing God cannot have a double standard, one for the OT and another for the NT. Some examples are given of people who were converted before the crucifixion.

1. In his high-priestly prayer Jesus Christ recognized the redeemed nature of his followers when he said, "I have given unto them the words which thou gavest me; and they have received them, and have known surely that I came out from thee, and they have believed that thou didst send me. I pray for them: I pray not for the world, but for them which thou hast given me; for they are thine" (John 17:8, 9). The Redeemer follows this testimony by saying: "Those that thou gavest me I have kept, and none of them is lost, but the son of perdition" (John 17:12), and here the apostasy of Judas is verified. Eleven of the original twelve were still faithful; one had, by transgression, fallen from the faith (Acts 1:25).

God's Plan of
Salvation
from Genesis
to Revelation

Christ's Prayer
2834, 2835

Apostosy
1235

2. There can be no doubt but that Zaccheus was converted, i.e., born again, the day Christ visited him. The Scriptures clearly provide the evidence: "Jesus said unto him, This day is salvation come to this house" (Luke 19:9). Following the Master's visit, Zaccheus brought forth works meet for repentance. The fruits of his life gave witness that he had experienced a "new birth;" he had come to a place in his life where old things had passed away and all things had become new (Luke 19:1ff.).

Zaccheus
3977

Salvation
3116–3123

3. To those already considered can be added the "many [that] believed in his name" (John 2:23), "the Samaritans of that city [who] believed" (John 4:39), "the man [that] believed the word of Jesus had spoken" (John 4:50), "many of the people [that] believed on him" (John 7:31), and the "many [that] believed on him there" (John 10:42), as well as Peter, the profane fisherman, whose shadow later healed others (Matt. 26:74; Acts 5:15).

Arch. Samaria
4409

Salvation
for All
3119

The Master is explicit and insistent upon sinners being genuinely converted. "Verily I say unto you, Except ye be converted, and become as little children, ye shall not enter into the kingdom of heaven" (Matt. 18:3). Conversion has always been a prerequisite for membership in the living church. The statement, "He that hath the Son hath life; and he that hath not the Son of God hath not life" (1 John 5:12), applies to all time. "Ye must be born again" (John 3:7) is the irrevocable formula whereby sinful man is translated from death to eternal life. This divine truth, the "new birth," has been forever in effect for both the Jew and Gentile alike (Rom. 15:8–12).

Conversion
834–836

V. THE MECHANICS OF SALVATION IN THE OT PERIOD

One of the Articles of Religion in many Protestant churches reads, in part: "The Old Testament is not contrary to the New; for both in the Old and New Testaments everlasting life is offered to mankind by Christ."

The problem of how Christ could save the people in the

OT before the crucifixion is one which few writers have really faced. Some of the writings on this subject leave the impression that God has used a vacillating "trial and error" method—environment, influence, and example—but failed to save man until he finally conceived the idea of sending his Son. Some writers convey the idea that the sacrificing of animals, and/or obeying the Law, were sufficient to bring salvation. Still others have developed a complicated system of morality and ethics closely related to Greek philosophy and Liberation theology. These

False Prophets
2100

indefinite theories should not be. God is absolute in all areas of his being, and it little behooves man to place God in a labyrinth of uncertainty.

It is evident that the Scriptures present a simple plan of salvation from Genesis to Revelation; it is not necessary for man to superimpose his personal theories before he can have a rudimentary knowledge of salvation. There is a unity in the

Good
Doctrines
1029
God's
Immutability
2480
God's
Impartiality
1979, 1980

OT and NT in the basic Christian doctrines; and the NT doctrines amplify those in the OT.

God is eternally the same, and he has saved men throughout the ages by an act of faith in his promise (Ezek. 18:31,32). God is "no respecter of persons," and he looks upon the human race as a whole, without regard to national or racial distinctions. The only chosen people God has are those who have responded to his invitation and have accepted their election to salvation. "God so loved the world that he gave . . ." (John 3:16).

Chosen
Vessels
2073

Redemption
2978–2979
Enoch
1135
Noah
2597
Abraham
15
Melchizedek
2284

Although the early Genesis record includes little formal teaching about redemption, the Book presents enough to show that a theology based on blood was common knowledge. The same pattern of redemption is discernible in the lives of such early Old Testament characters as Enoch, Noah, Abraham, and Melchizedek.

Before going further in this study, certain basic assumptions should be considered, namely that:

1. Man's constitution and moral nature have not changed from those of fallen Adam (Rom. 5:12).
2. Man's need for salvation from sin has never changed (Rom. 3:23).
3. God's provision for man's salvation has been eternally the same.
4. By virtue of God's absolute nature, the plan of salvation could not be one thing for one generation and something else for another.
5. Jesus Christ, the Covenant Agent, is the same yesterday, today, and forever (Heb. 13:8).
6. The act of faith has always been the means whereby man has been able to appropriate salvation (Heb. 11:6).

The educational process which God adopted for man is basically the same as that used in modern education. In his curriculum, God has slowly unfolded over a period of time the details of this provision. Even though the basic plan of salvation was revealed in the beginning, the Scripture spells out the details, "precept upon precept; . . . line upon line; here a little, and there a little" (Isa. 28:10). "First the blade, then the ear, after that the full corn in the ear" (Mark 4:28; cf. Matt. 13:35).

God's Plan of Salvation from Genesis to Revelation

Learning Process
2028

At the appropriate time "God sent forth his Son, made of a woman, made under the law, to redeem them that were under the law" (Gal. 4:4,5). Here is a specific reference to God's clock, pointing to high noon—to an hour when the time was full. This noon hour was revealed in the Advent of God's Son. It is evident there was a period in history when the time was not full; the fullness of time was preceded by a period of preparation.

The "dawn of redemption" compares favorably to the dawn of a new day. There is a moment when the sun becomes visible but before that time, the light and life-giving properties of the sun have started to become effective. Sufficient light appears whereby man can find his way about. The benefits of the sun are effective long before it reaches its zenith or apex.

By analogy then, the dawn of God's revelation in his Son was prior to man's fall into sin. In other words, God's cure was provided for man before the need arose. However, there is a difference between the fundamental provision and man's full understanding of this provision.

In God's plan the fullness of this revelation was to be manifest in the incarnation, which was not practicable until an educational process could prepare the mind of man for the fuller revelation.

Incarnation
720

The idea that salvation was provided for man from the beginning is suggested in Isaiah 53. Whatever the provision was, it had already been made in the mind of God as seen in the use of past tense: "he *hath* borne our griefs, and *carried* our sorrows: . . . he *was* wounded for our transgressions, he *was* bruised for our iniquities: the chastisement of our peace *was* upon him; and with his stripes we are healed" (Isa. 53:4,5). This same tense is also expressed in John 3:16 at a time when Christ was still actively engaged in his human ministry. The statement is clear: "God so *loved* the world, that he *gave* his only begotten Son, that whosoever believeth in him should not perish, but have everlasting life" (John 3:16).

See Isaiah's Portrait of Christ
4301

These references, in addition to Revelation 13:8, certainly indicate that the provision of salvation in Christ was made long before the actual crucifixion on Golgotha. This still leaves unanswered the question: How could God save a man before

Arch. Golgotha (Calvary)
4347

the crucifixion? This question can best be answered with an analogy from life.

Through the use of a note at a bank, a penniless man can enjoy all the financial benefits he would have if he already had the money. The maker of the note agrees to redeem it, to make full settlement at some future date, and on the basis of this promise the banker opens his vault and makes the funds available. By this analogy, God's redemptive promissory note was given to the human race. God, who "cannot lie," promised or pledged to redeem the note at some future date by the payment of his Son on the cross. The date of this note was "the fulness of time." God's note was sufficient legal tender

Kingdom of
God
2009

for people to enter the kingdom of God. The only requirement was that the people should repent of their sins and have faith

Faith
1203, 1985

in the Maker of the note. By faith, the saints of the OT were able to draw checks of salvation on the bank of heaven with full realization that the note would one day be fully redeemed. Ultimately this "faith" was justified when God redeemed his promissory note at the cross.

The blood of animals did not atone for man's sin. The offering of these animals had been only a testimony, a symbolical expres-

Atonement
304

sion of the faith the believer had in the blood of the atoning Savior who would die for humanity. How well these early believers understood the theology of Atonement is not known. However, the people of the OT found satisfaction in the same "redemptive fountain" at which the present generation finds satisfaction for their souls today. This was verified when Moses and Elijah joined hands with Jesus, Peter, James and John (Matt. 17:1–3). The Savior of the OT period is the same as that of the New (Isa. 43:11,12).

VI. SALVATION SYMBOLIZED IN THE EXODUS

On pages 240–241 the Journey Maps show the Journeys of Israel through the wilderness under the leadership of Moses,

Moses
2420, 2421

a type of Christ. Since the early formative years of the Christian church, Bible scholars have been able to see the plan of salvation prefigured in Exodus. This is clearly evidenced in 1 Corinthians 10:1–4.

The OT abounds in rich dispensational and doctrinal symbolism. In addition to the tabernacle a most interesting redemptive pattern is found in the Exodus experience of the Hebrews. Grace Saxe points out that the Epistle to the Hebrews "explains the significance of the whole Jewish ritual" and that a study of the Exodus through the barren wilderness presents God

as protecting the Israelites from danger, supplying their needs, teaching them, training them, and eventually bringing them into the rich land of Canaan, their permanent home. So Christ is, at this time, gathering together a people for his name, taking them through a hostile world, protecting, teaching, training, and preparing them for their eternal home.[41]

The apostle Paul tells the Corinthians that "all our fathers were under the cloud, and all passed through the sea; and were all baptized unto Moses in the cloud and in the sea; and did all eat the same spiritual meat; and did all drink the same spiritual drink: for they drank of that spiritual Rock that followed them: and that Rock was Christ" (1 Cor. 10:1–4). Paul concludes that "all these things happened unto them for ensamples: and they are written for our admonition" (1 Cor. 10:11). The word *ensample* is translated from the Greek word *tupos* meaning literally "a figure, image, or pattern prefiguring a future person or thing."

In the brief space allotted to this study only a few of the places, persons, and events will be examined to show their symbolical meaning.

1. *Egypt.* This land of bondage symbolizes sin. The Hebrews who were slaves in Egypt found their plight was almost hopeless. They could not deliver themselves but were dependent upon help from the outside such as God gave to them through his servant Moses.

Egypt
1100

Physical Bondage
2138

2. *Pharaoh—a type of Satan.* This Egyptian king ruled Egypt with an iron hand. Exodus 1:8–22 presents an account of Pharaoh's oppression of the Hebrews. He, a "prince of the world," held his slaves in bondage. "Israel sighed by reason of the bondage, and they cried, and their cry came up unto God . . ." (Exod. 2:23). Is this not a picture of distressed and burdened people who, when they cry out to God in sincerity, get a sympathetic response from God?

Pharaoh
2747, 2748

3. *The Children of Israel.* The Hebrew children typify the people, who, being dissatisfied with the unjust treatment and the tyranny of the king, long for deliverance. When people are ready to turn from sin to righteousness, there is a leader who is ready to take them from Egypt to Canaan. Even one sinner is important enough to be led to the promised land. The Lord not only delivers but he gives continual guidance.

Israel
1808

4. *Moses.* Moses, compared to Christ, the Great Deliverer (Deut. 18:15), leads the people out of the land of sin. Moses was given to the people at the proper time, even as Christ came forth when the "fulness of time was come." He, who was called the son of Pharaoh's daughter, chose "rather to suffer afflictions with the people of God, than to enjoy the pleasures of sin for a season" (Heb. 11:24,25). As the son of Pharaoh's daughter, he was in line for the throne. Although he had all the social and economic advantages of Egypt at his command,

Moses
2420, 2421

See TCRB
pp. 254, 255

he chose privation with his people. Jesus, too, "was rich," yet for our "sakes he became poor, that [we] through his poverty might be rich" (2 Cor. 8:9; Phil. 2:5–8).

Moses, like Jesus, was rejected by his people. When Moses received his call to service, he said, "Behold, they will not believe me, nor hearken unto my voice: for they will say, The LORD hath not appeared unto thee" (Exod. 4:1). Jesus also "came unto his own, and his own received him not" (John 1:11).

God gave credentials to Moses so that the people might know that he was sent from God. Moses performed miracles as did Christ although of a different nature. However, the miracles of Christ, like those of Moses, were intended to give credence to his divine commission.

From the narrative about the Hebrews' desire to sacrifice unto God comes the insight that man cannot build his altar of worship in "the land of sin." They could not sacrifice because the Egyptians wanted to keep the people in Egypt. Pharaoh wanted the people to offer their sacrifices within his borders. Moses was divinely compelled to go "three days' journey" from the land (Exod. 8:25–28). "Moses said . . . there shall not an hoof be left behind" (Exod. 10:26).

It is also necessary for true believers to separate themselves from Egypt. "Friendship with the world is enmity with God" (James 4:4, RSV). It is impossible to serve the God of heaven and the god of the world at the same time. Man must serve either one or the other (Matt. 6:24).

5. *Pharaoh's Imitators.* Pharaoh called his magicians together and they duplicated some of the miracles of Moses. Satan also has a counterfeit religion which is so close to the genuine that many are deceived. Satan is willing for people to be religious. As long as he can keep the people satisfied with a bloodless religion, he is happy. Imitating real religion is much more effective than promoting outright infidelity. Religion with some semblance of reality is always dangerous because there is enough truth in it to make it attractive. God wants forthright Christians, not people who compromise. Moses stated the case plainly and to the point, "There shall not an hoof be left behind" (Exod. 10:26). God demands complete separation from the world, sin, and the devil.

6. *The Passover.* The redemptive work of Christ is evident in the Passover (Exod. 12:1ff.). The lamb was to be without spot or blemish, and its blood was to be sprinkled upon the door post and the lintel so that the death angel could see it. The applied blood was necessary to life: without the blood, death was certain. Paul states that "Christ our passover is sacrificed for us" (1 Cor. 5:7). The importance of Christ's blood is

symbolized by the blood of the passover lamb. The Lord informed the people that "the blood shall be to you for a token upon the houses where ye are: and when I see the blood, I will pass over you" (Exod. 12:13). Many people of Egypt were good, moral, law-abiding citizens, but this was not enough. Only the blood availed.

With the assurance of safety, the Hebrews were able to feast upon their lamb with peace of mind. They enjoyed communion and fellowship such as only the redeemed can have. The feast is not for unbelievers, but for those who have been redeemed by the blood of the lamb.

7. *The Pillar of Cloud* (Exod. 13:21,22). The pillar of cloud speaks of the presence of God through his Holy Spirit. During the day the pillar took the shape of a mushrooming cloud so that the Israelites might be guided as well as be protected from the hot desert sun. At night the pillar turned into a column of fire so that the people might have evidence of God's presence. It is of importance that the pillar was a light for the Hebrews but utter darkness for the Egyptians. So it is with Christians versus sinners. The believer receives light and revelation from God, but to the sinner this mystical presence is foolishness (1 Cor. 2:11–14).

Pillar of Cloud
2501

When the Hebrews began to move out of Egypt, Pharaoh and his army gave pursuit. So it is when a seeker starts to leave the bonds of Egypt. Satan always makes it difficult for the repentant soul to escape. He always attempts to keep the captive from crossing the "Red Sea."

8. *The Red Sea* (Exod. 14:9ff.). In preparation for their escape from Egypt the children of Israel had been delivered by the blood. At the Red Sea they were delivered from Egypt by the power of God. The Red Sea (symbolizing a separation from the forces of sin) opened a path for the Hebrews, but when they had crossed, the waves closed upon Pharaoh and his men. The Red Sea means death. The Red Sea experience might symbolize a type of water baptism marking the end of service to Satan and the beginning of service to God (1 Cor. 10:1–4).

Red Sea
2975

9. *The Redemption Song* (Exod. 15:1–21). When the Hebrews saw that Pharaoh and his army had been drowned in the sea, they sang a song of victory. A similar response occurs when a repentant sinner crosses the Red Sea and obtains salvation. Does he not find within him a compelling urge to sing the songs of Zion as an expression of praise and thanksgiving to God for saving him from his enemy, Satan? When he looks at Calvary and sees that his own sins are gone, he, too, enters into an understanding of the hymns that have been sung by the saints of other days. The Song of Moses is a type of Christian hymn.

Songs of Victory
2477

10. *The Wilderness* (Exod. 17:1ff.). After the people had been
redeemed the trials and hardships began to press in upon them.
During these physical hardships, many began to think about
the flesh pots and the garlic of Egypt. The human outlook
for survival was dark. Wilderness testings came to them from
every hand. This experience symbolizes the experiences many
believers go through who do not hasten on to complete consecration. Neglecting prayer, Bible study, and personal service
are some of the wilderness dangers that believers must avoid.
Every Christian should become established by making his complete dedication to God, going on without delay to possess
his Canaan land. This is the believer's reasonable service (Rom.
12:1,2).

11. *Canaan.* This was the ultimate goal of the Israelites, that
God had promised to the Hebrew children; it was a land flowing
with milk and honey, where the grapes of Eschol grew so large
they touched the ground. This land was their reward for com-
pleting the conquest, not just going part way.

God also offers the "milk and honey" experience to all believers who consecrate themselves completely to him. They can
live in the land where pomegranates and grapes abound. Paul
gives the formula: "I beseech you therefore, brethren, by the
mercies of God, that ye present your bodies a living sacrifice,
holy, acceptable unto God, which is your reasonable service"
(Rom. 12:1).

It is the will of God that all believers should be filled with
the Holy Spirit and this can come about only by obeying the
divine injunction: "wait for the promise of the Father."

When the members in the infant church in Jerusalem met
the condition, "they were all filled with the Holy Ghost." This
Canaan experience is a believer's privilege, his birthright, and

his responsibility, but it is more than this, it is the believer's
obligation. God has provided it, and he expects every believer
to appropriate it.

A complete surrender to God with the resultant infilling of
the Holy Spirit will save Christians, both old and young, from
wasting many precious years in the wilderness. It was God's
desire for the Hebrews to go immediately to possess the land,
but because of their unbelief, they doomed themselves to aim-
less wanderings in the snake-infested desert. What folly! Why
should any believer spend tortuous years in the wilderness
when the murmuring brooks of Canaan and the grapes of Es-

chol beckon him on.

God intends for every believer to be radiant, happy, and
victorious. Pentecost changed the early believers from a state

of uncertainty to one of victory and joy. What God did for
the early Christians he can do for any Christian.

10

The Covenant Community in the Old Testament

I. THE ESSENTIAL CHRISTOLOGY OF THE OLD TESTAMENT

The OT contains a religious system which has blessed mankind throughout generations (see Ch. 14). It is the basic source for the concept of a monotheistic holy God and the dignity and worth of a human being. Jesus and the early Christians quoted the OT extensively to support their message. The moral, ethical, and religious standards of the Christian faith were drawn from the OT legal code which God gave to Moses and the Israelites on Mount Sinai about fourteen hundred years before the advent of Christ.

One God **2649**

Mosaic Law **949**

Both the OT and the NT include the teaching that the basic requirement is one's love for God and love for man. When a lawyer asked Jesus, "which is the great commandment in the law?" (Matt. 22:36), Jesus quoted God's words to Moses, "thou shalt love the LORD thy God with all thine heart, . . ." (Deut. 6:5) and "thou shalt love thy neighbor as thyself" (Lev. 19:18; cf. Matt. 22:37–39). This is perhaps the simplest statement of what Christianity is all about, and it puts OT religion on a lofty plane.

Preeminence of Love **2209, 4182**

Jesus concluded his statement thus: "On these two commandments [love God; love man] hang all the law and the prophets" (Matt. 22:40). In the Good News Bible (American Bible Society) this passage reads: "The whole Law of Moses and the teachings of the prophets depend on these two commandments." In fact, Paul tells the Christians of Jewish origin in Galatia that, "all the law is fulfilled in one word, even in this; Thou shalt love thy neighbour as thyself" (Gal. 5:14). John adds this test of

Commandments **444**

117

discipleship, "By this we know that we love the children of God, when we love God, and keep his commandments" (1 John 5:2; see also 1 John 4:11–17). With this love in his heart, man will not disobey either the first four commandments dealing with man-to-God obligations, or the other six referring to man-to-man relationships (Deut. 5:6–21).

In OT times God placed upon Moses the responsibility of implementing and recording the plan whereby man could approach God and meet his requirements (Exod. 19:3; Deut 4:14).

The Decalogue (Exod. 20; John 7:19) and carefully constructed rules governing sacrifices, offerings, and the treatment of community members and strangers were designed to make of the Israelites a holy nation, if they would be obedient (Exod. 19:5,6). The OT contained symbolism which expressed faith in God's promise of redemption and which was finally fulfilled in Christ. The law was only a shadow of the good things to come, but even a shadow presupposes an object and that object was Christ.

Man in his sinful state (Rev. 7:14–21) is unable to achieve the high standard instituted by God through Moses, and later reemphasized by Jesus: to love God with his whole heart and his neighbor as himself. The enablement to fulfill the divine commandment of love must come from God, because he is love (1 John 4:8). To this end he made provision by the promise

of a Savior.

Even before Christ came, some persons were enabled to experience saving faith such as was referred to by Habakkuk, "The just shall live by his faith" (Hab. 2:4) and which was reaffirmed by Paul (Rom. 1:17; Gal. 3:11) and the writer of Hebrews 10:38.

There is even evidence of experiencing "Sermon on the Mount" love as seen in the story of Jacob and Esau. In order

to escape Esau's vengeance (Gen. 27:41) for stealing his birthright, Jacob fled to Padan-aram in Haran (Gen. 28:6). Years later Jacob decided to return home but he fully expected his brother to vent his hostility upon him. Jacob's scouts told Jacob that his brother Esau was coming to meet him with 400 men (Gen. 32:6). Jacob, under conviction for his sin, probably imagined each man was fully armed and ready to do battle. Jacob was "greatly afraid" and organized his tribe into battle formation (Gen. 32:7,8). He put his fighting men in the front ranks and placed his wives and children in the rear (Gen. 33:1–3). Jacob rationalized that he could buy his brother off with gifts (Gen. 32:13–20).

When Jacob came face to face with Esau, a miracle of love happened. Instead of Esau showing hostility and hate toward Jacob, he showed compassion and love. "Esau ran to meet him, and embraced him, and fell on his neck, and kissed him: and they wept" (Gen. 33:4). Instead of seeing the face of a vengeful brother, Jacob viewed his brother's face as though he "had seen the face of God" (Gen. 33:10b).

Years later this love attitude is again expressed by Joseph when he confronts his brothers in Egypt (Gen. 45:1–5). Certainly this attitude of love expressed by Esau and Joseph gives rationale to the love commandment given by God through Moses (Deut. 6:5; Lev. 19:18; cf. Matt. 22:37–40).

When the Savior came, one of his first declarations was that he had not come to destroy the Law which God had provided in the past, but that he would fulfill or establish "the Law." NT teachings clarify his meaning as to his ability to accomplish this expectation in three principal areas: his relationship to the Law and his authority regarding it; his function as a perfect sacrifice; and his fulfillment of the Messianic prophecy.

Christ, the Lord, as envisioned by the Prophet Isaiah, had the power to make the ritualistic Law effective: "He will save us" (Isa. 33:22). The Scriptures provide further proof that Christ was indeed the source of the Law (Isa. 51:4). The visible evidence of the Covenant (Tables of the Law) made by God was to be placed within the Ark (Deut. 10:2). Hence, Christ, author of the Law, and Son of God, could fulfill the Law of the Old Covenant and usher in the "New Covenant" (Jer. 31:31–33; cf. Heb. 9:1–28).

When the incarnate Christ (God, the Son in human flesh) came, he presented a new understanding of the Law. His purpose was to establish the Law (Rom. 3:31), which included the Decalog that God had given Moses, but he did eliminate the levitical ritual and the animal sacrifices, which were to serve only in the pre-Advent period: these he fulfilled in his own death on the cross.

The inner heart relationship now became more important and religion more personal. The Law, once written on stone tablets, was written within men's hearts (Jer. 31:33; 2 Cor. 3:3). Christ did not repudiate the Law, for its use in past generations had been directed by God (Lev. 18:3,4). In fact it was by reference to the Old Covenant that Christ could explicate and establish the meaning of the New. The old Law, observed by use of ritual, was a means, not an end. The Law was to guide God's people, until the time when all the Law would be fulfilled; when the Prophet, who is Christ, "the end of the law for righteousness" would appear (Rom. 10:4).

Paul said, "I had not known sin but by the law" (Rom. 7:7). So the Law was put in charge to lead us to Christ that we might be justified by faith. Now that faith has come, we are no longer under the supervision of the Law (Gal. 3:24,25).

Law
437, 949, 4055

Commandments
949

Incarnation
720

Law in the Heart
438

New Covenant
881

Purpose of Law
4055

119

Christ also fulfilled the Law because he was the perfect priest, the sacrifice, and the promised Redeemer. Thus Christ transcended the ritualist law of the OT in providing a better way to man's salvation. He was the sinless priest—the High Priest, who did not need "to offer up sacrifice . . . for his own sins" (Heb. 7:27) as the levitical priests were required to do daily (Heb. 7:16; 10:10,12). There was no permanence in the sacrifices offered by the regular priests (Heb. 7:23); these offerings had to be repeated. Nor could "the blood of bulls and of goats . . . take away sins" (Heb. 10:3,4). OT prophets had acknowledged this fact (1 Sam. 15:22; Jer. 6:20; Ps. 40:16; 51:16). In

the NT John declared that Jesus is "the Lamb of God, which taketh away the sin of the world" (John 1:29).

The blood of Christ as the perfect offering was "as of a lamb without blemish and without spot" (1 Peter 1:19). "Through the offering of the body of Jesus," believers are "sanctified . . . once for all" (Heb. 10:10,14). Finally, the coming of Jesus

Christ the
Messiah
695

Messianic
Prophecies pp.
246–249

Christ fulfilled all the Messianic prophecies which the faithful Jews had waited for (Deut. 18:15,18; Zech. 9:9; Dan. 9:25; John 1:45).

Another area of vital importance in the Christocentric message of the Scriptures is God's attitude toward sin and its punishment. God, by his very holy nature, cannot tolerate sin. Adam and Eve's disobedience in the Garden introduced sin

into the world and separated man from God. Some scholars see sin as having its origin in heaven.*

The entire plan of salvation was designed to bring sinful, rebellious humanity back to obedience and fellowship with the Creator. God's law was for man's good. The Command-

ments must become a "way of life" if man is to survive. As to civil and social codes as well as moral ones, Jesus insisted that citizens must obey the law (Matt. 22:21; see also Rom. 13:1; Titus 3:1; 1 Peter 2:13,14). He certainly affirmed the validity of the Commandments when he said, "Thou shalt do no

murder, Thou shalt not commit adultery . . ." (Matt. 19:18). Paul also recognized the binding claim on man to observe the Commandments: "Thou shalt not commit adultery, Thou shalt not kill, Thou shalt not steal, Thou shalt not bear false witness, Thou shalt not covet; and if there be any other commandment it is briefly comprehended in this saying, namely, thou shalt

---

* "Some theologians see an intimation in the Book of Isaiah that Lucifer was Satan who once resided in heaven and was expelled because of selfish ambition or rebellion (Isa. 14:12–19; cf. Luke 10:18). On the other hand, some see the name Lucifer to mean the planet Venus, the morning star or evening star in its east-west relationship to the sun." (John D. Davis, "Lucifer," in *Davis Dictionary of the Bible*.)

love thy neighbour as thyself" (Rom. 13:9; see also 1 Peter 4:15; 1 John 3:15).

As to punishment for murder, the OT is very specific: "Whoso sheddeth man's blood, by man shall his blood be shed" (Gen. 9:6; see also Exod. 21:14,15). OT history is replete with instances which show that sin leads to destruction.

The prophet Amos vigorously denounced the sins of Israel (Northern Kingdom). Ignoring his warning resulted in complete destruction of the nation and enslavement to the Assyrians. The punishment was harsh, but it was commensurate with Israel's sins. Ezekiel gives a description, in dramatic and figurative language, of the frightful consequences when a nation forsakes God and turns to unrestrained sin (Ezek. 20). The standard of punishment prescribed in the OT may seem severe, but who is to pass judgment on these laws? History clearly reveals what happens when a nation defies God and breaks the laws embodied in the Ten Commandments.

The essential substance of law in all civilized countries is reflective of the Mosaic code. No one has improved upon these laws because they are the perfect legal code given by God to Moses and in some form to earlier societies. There is danger in every age of civilization abandoning or modifying the laws of God. Scripture teaches that law is ordained by God (Rom. 13:1), that it is the duty of man to obey the law, and the duty of duly appointed officials to administer punishment for breaking the law (1 Peter 2:13,14).

As both the OT and NT are the infallible Word of God, it is obvious that Christianity has not repudiated, indeed cannot, repudiate the moral and ethical laws of the OT (2 Tim. 3:16,17).

Since the Advent of Christ, the grace of God has been more strongly emphasized, but grace does not abolish the moral law. Some Christians have raised questions of OT-NT unity concerning the incident of the "woman taken in adultery" (John 8:3). After the men had made their accusation and Jesus had written in the sand, no one remained to press charges against her. Jesus said, "Neither do I condemn thee: go, and sin no more" (John 8:11). God's mercy and grace can always be extended to the penitent sinner, even when he must be punished. Salvation sometimes comes to men before they are sent to, or while they are in, prison. Even those who have been given the death penalty can receive forgiveness from God and salvation before they die. This is the beauty of grace; regardless of how sinful a person has been, by repentance and faith he can receive instant pardon from God. At this point the OT is clear: those who repent are promised escape from God's judgment (2 Chron. 7:14; Isa. 55:7; Ezek. 18:21). The entire Book of Judges

Murder
2450, 2451

Punishment
3047, 3048

Mosaic Law
949

Purpose of Law
4055

Grace
1445–1449

Divine Foregiveness
1314, 2300, 3345

121

gives examples of Israel being forgiven after the people repented.

When Jesus spoke about men forgiving one another, he was referring to man-to-man interrelationships. God forgives anyone who repents; man is to do likewise, even to the extent of forgiving "seventy times seven" (Matt. 18:21,22; see also Mark 11:25; Luke 17:41; Eph. 4:32; Col. 3:13; Jonah 3:5–10).

Important in the case of the woman taken in adultery is the question of motive on the part of the men who brought the woman to Jesus. The legal issue (their bringing only the woman) suggests that their paramount concern may not have been what the woman had done; their motive was evidently to trick Jesus into an answer that would conflict with the law of Moses. If they accomplished this, they could accuse Jesus

Blasphemy
473, 474

of blasphemy which was punishable by death (Lev. 24:16). In any case they certainly had no legal authority to take the woman to Jesus for a crime which was punishable by death, because Jesus was not a civil judge nor did he claim to be. He always insisted that citizens should give to Caesar (civil law) that which was Caesar's (Matt. 22:21; see also John 18:36). If the men truly had had concern for the law, they would have taken both the man and the woman to a duly appointed magistrate.

The conclusion of the events surrounding this woman illustrates divine mercy and forgiveness, but the outcome did not

Punishment
3047, 3048

waive the punishment which Theocratic law (government by God) demanded for this particular offense. Under the circumstances the charges were so clearly one sided that legal action was impracticable. Law is intended to be inherently fair and just; the woman could not be punished alone (Lev. 20:10). Under modern law, the case would have been dismissed on legal technical grounds arising from the absence of the other offender. However, irrespective of legal technicalities, when one violates moral law, there are consequences within the human conscience. Certainly the woman experienced psychological and sociological sufferings. The same can be assumed for the man who probably was living in constant fear that he too might be taken into custody at any time.

Some people have a problem in reconciling the OT law of

Retaliation
2279, 2280

"eye for eye, tooth for tooth" (Exod. 21:24), with the teaching of Jesus on turning the other cheek (Matt. 5:39), and forgiving the offending brother "seventy times seven" (Matt. 18:22). The "eye for eye" law, rightly interpreted, means that the punishment must be commensurate with the crime. Divine law states that he who murders a man, forfeits his right to live (Gen.

9:6).

In many instances a clear distinction should be made between the redemptive teachings in the OT and the "traditions of the elders" by which temple matters were decided. This structure of "traditionalism" had in it so many additions that the pharisaical legal code had little resemblance to the basic teachings of the OT. In any case the Judaism of Jesus' day was a flagrant departure from the religion of the OT. Peter, Paul, and Jesus all denounced the nonbiblical interpretation the temple leaders superimposed upon the plain teachings in the OT (Matt. 15:3–6; Mark 7:7,8; Col. 2:8; Titus 1:14; 1 Peter 1:18).

Jesus came to reinstate the spirit of the law which, in his day, had been twisted into "letter of the law legalisms." Jesus pointed out that acts of murder, adultery, or other infractions are the result of mental assent before the thoughts are put into action (Ps. 37:8; Prov. 14:17; 16:32; 19:11).

He explained that in the sight of God, the sin has already been committed when man conceives the act in his mind (Matt. 5:21, 27ff.). These references show the unity of the entire legal structure between the OT and NT, and that the plan of salvation, basically and substantially, is the same in both Testaments. God foreknew that man would sin and therefore he planned salvation before man was created (2 Tim. 1:9; Titus 1:2). However, after the essence of God's redemptive plan was initially revealed, there was a progressive unfolding of revelation with succeeding generations gradually receiving additional light on the various phases. "When the fulness of the time was come," the final details of God's plan were manifested in Jesus Christ.

The authority by which Jesus taught came from the OT, his message was the "Good News" that the Messiah "written in the law of Moses, and in the prophets, and in the psalms" had come (Luke 24:44). (For a more thorough study on OT Christianity see Ch. 14, I, page 205.)

II. THE QAHAL IN THE OLD TESTAMENT

There have always been religious congregations from the earliest times. There is a sense in which Adam and Eve were a congregation when they had a conversation with God among the trees of the Garden (Gen. 3:8–21). In this regard there is unity between the teachings in the OT and the NT, as indicated in the first part of this chapter, which rests upon the assumption that there has always been a body of believers in all ages who were essentially Christian in belief, to the extent of the revelation they had.[1] The Scriptures clearly show that an assembly of people or a church worshiping the Living God is of early origin; it may have been in operation by the time of Abel (Gen. 4:4).

The Covenant Community in the Old Testament

Traditions
3652

False Teachers
2101

Legalism
2990

Anger
3956

Redemption
2978, 2979

Revelation
2495–2498

Congregation
820, 821

123

124

In the OT, the assembly of believers was called the *qahal* of God. In the Greek OT this term was translated *ekklesia,* and in the English it is rendered *church.* So it would seem that any objection to recognizing the OT church would be more semantic than real. (For general reference to both the OT and the NT church see Nos. 726–752 in the TCRB Helps.)

A noted church historian observes that, "If we are to understand the nature of the church, we must begin with the OT. According to Acts 7:38 there was already a church in the wilderness when God redeemed His people out of Egypt. Terms such as 'new Israel' and 'Israel of God' would be pointless except against the background of a nation which had been so conceived as the people of God. If Christians were the 'true circumcision' (Phil. 3:3; cf. Ezek. 44:7) and the 'real sons of Abraham' (Rom. 4:16), this OT background is presupposed. A people of a New Covenant presupposed an Old Covenant." [2] The Chosen of God enjoyed this blessed relationship because individuals had conformed their lives to God's will and design. They were the "children of the most High" (Ps. 82:6), "the congregation of the righteous" (Ps. 1:5), the constituency of the OT church. Thus the "basic conception" of an organized congregation or church goes back to the OT. The "true remnant" about which the prophets had spoken had found fulfillment in the Christian community. The words of the Savior following Peter's affirmation, "Thou art the Christ, the Son of the living God" (Matt. 16:16), "Upon this rock I [Christ] will build my church" (Matt. 16:18) suggests the continuity of the church from the OT to the NT.

The church in the OT can be compared to the foundation and basement of a new church building. Occasionally churches first appear as roofed-over basements, where all the functions of the church and worship are carried on. Later the superstructure rises, but the basic function in the roofed-over basement, as compared with the completed building, is essentially the same. Christ built his message and teachings upon the foundation of the patriarchs and prophets. In Matthew 16:18 Christ presents himself as the (future) Builder of the church and as he became the "corner Stone" so he was and also is the Foundation. No foundation, other than Christ, can support the redemptive structure (1 Cor. 3:11). He, who was the foundation of the plan of redemption from the beginning, has been ingrained in the work of salvation, and this redemptive work is the same, regardless of time. Christ is the Lord of eternity, the "Alpha and the Omega." In speaking of the church, the Lord used the thought patterns of his day to fit the current need. By adopting the term "church," Christ did not imply the abandonment of the purpose of the synagogue and the temple. He was merely reshaping terminology to fit the day when the Gentiles would enter the fellowship of believers, the church.

The Covenant Community in the Old Testament

Church
726–749

When the word *church* comes to the mind of the average person, it evokes a variety of responses. Some people think in terms of a church building in which people worship God, while others think of denominational groups, but these ideas would have been strange to the early church. "Amid the ruins of war-torn cities many modern Christians are discovering anew that the Church is not made of stone or brick. The living stones of the true Temple of God are those who worship Him in spirit and in truth." [3] The church is, by definition, the "people of God" and the idea of more than one denomination was not present in early Christianity. In Jesus Christ all believers in God are one and belong to the same mystical body called the church. In the true church all human discrimination is abolished (Gal. 3:28; Col. 3:11). The unity of the Christian faith is indicated in "One Lord, one faith, one baptism, one God and Father of all" (Eph. 4:5,6) which unifies all believers and makes them a part of the glorious church.

"One can hardly say . . . that Jesus founded the Christian Church. For centuries there had been a people who looked upon themselves as set apart for God. When Christians applied the term ekklesia to themselves they redefined the qahal of God, in terms of the new acts and revelation of God in Jesus Christ for their redemption. It was not to be identified with Israel after the flesh, but with individuals from every tribe, nation, people and tongue" (Rev. 7:9).[4]

Flesh
1290

A noted German scholar puts it this way: "Before the foundation of the world, God conceived the counsel of salvation for the church, . . . from eternity, that amazing structure that . . . was determined by the Redeemer. Therefore, 'from before the ages,' the Christ mystery was . . . hidden in God for the Gentiles who would be fellow-heirs and fellow-members of the body of Jesus Christ our Lord" (Eph. 3:6).[5]

III. THE EKKLESIA IN THE NEW TESTAMENT

According to the conception of historic Christianity, the Ekklesia or the church is made up of people who have committed their lives by faith to God through Jesus Christ and who witness to the work of the Savior among the communities of mankind. "It is the whole spiritual commonwealth of God's children, the company of all faithful people. It is represented by the organized or visible church in any or all ages." [6] The Greek word *ekklesia*, though not a religious term, has its own pre-Christian history. In the Septuagint (Greek OT) it is used to describe the "body of believers" in the OT times. The Septu-

Witness
**689, 703,
1606, 3855A**

agint translators' use of the word *ekklesia* to render the Hebrew *qahal,* denotes the "Congregation" or the "Community of Israel" (Job 30:28; Ps. 149:1). The term "OT *church*" is the functional equivalent of all other terms used in the NT to designate believers.

The term *ekklesia* is never used to mean a building or house of assembly but to designate a body whose unity does not depend on its meeting together in one place. It is not merely an assemblage of individuals but of members in their several places united to the one head, Christ, and forming one organic living whole (1 Cor. 12). It is referred to as the Bride of Christ (Eph. 5:25–32), the household of God (Eph. 2:19), and the temple of the Holy Ghost, made up of living stones (Eph. 2:22; 1 Cor. 3:16; 1 Peter 2:5).[7]

IV. THE KINGDOM OF GOD

Christ made reference to the church three times in two verses (Matt. 16:18; 18:17). In fact "the gospels clearly indicate that the central message of Jesus did not semantically deal with the church but was concerned with the 'kingdom of God' and the repentance which was necessary if men should enter in by the gracious mercy of God (Mark 1:14,15). Jesus announced the nearness of the kingdom of God, a message which gave tremendous urgency to His ethical demands. A crisis was at hand; men must stand ready to pay the price to enter God's Kingdom (Luke 14:25–33). The term 'kingdom' was common in the old covenant and was understood to mean 'children of Zion' (Ps. 149:2), 'congregation of the saints' (Ps. 89:5), or 'those who had faith in the Lord.' "[8]

Kingdom of
Heaven
2008–2013

Christ's
Glorification
682

John the Baptist and Jesus were not the first who spoke of the kingdom of heaven. Indeed "they adopted the language of the OT and of Judaism around them, filling the same expression with new meaning as in Luke 15:21: 'Father, I have sinned against heaven, [i.e., God], and in thy sight'; Matthew 21:25: 'the baptism of John, whence was it? from heaven, [i.e., God], or of men'; Matthew 26:64: 'ye [shall] see the Son of man sitting on the right hand of power [i.e., of God].' Therefore, with the Lord the prevailing description of the kingdom of God is the kingdom of heaven."[9]

The expression "kingdom of heaven" is found only in Matthew (32 times) and was originally intended for Jews; the other Gospels, written for Gentile readers, used the expression "kingdom of God" (for example, Luke 32 times; Matt. 13:31,33, cf. Luke 13:18–21; Matt. 19:14, cf. Luke 18:16,17). Thus the "kingdom of heaven" and the "kingdom of God" are identical.[10]

V. The Jew vs. the Gentile

It is evident, however, that the Savior's ideas of the kingdom certainly cannot be explained in the framework of the Jewish-pharisaic conception, which assumed that "the choice of Israel" was based upon a superiority of this people. Rather, the "choosing of Israel" conforms to the lowly outward appearance of the divine revelation. Nowhere in the OT is there any approbation of racial exaltation of the unregenerate Jew. On the contrary, it is precisely the OT that is full of direct glowing words of judgment denouncing the holy wrath of God against apostate Israel.[11]

Some Bible scholars interpret the OT to be uniquely and exclusively for the Jews but this position is not tenable. There is evidence to show that "the OT is not the book of Jewish national religion but it is the Book of God and of His revelation. Jewish-Talmudic-Pharisaic moralizing and the OT are not one and the same; the OT purports to be the testimony of the Holy Spirit to the sons of all men, and to the grace of God which pardons the repentant believing sinner. This grace is available to all men alike, Jew or Gentile (see Rom. 2:10ff.)."[12] Perhaps the greatest evangelical appeal recorded in the OT was given to the Gentiles with the preaching of Jonah (Jonah 3:1ff.). Christ gave recognition of this effort and drew some parallels from the event to illustrate the need of his day. Here is an obvious instance in which Jesus presents his own objectives in the same light as that of an OT preacher. In both cases the urgent business at hand for Jew and Gentile alike was to repent and be saved (Matt. 12:39; Luke 11:29).

God has no favorites (Acts 10:34–36). His grace extends as freely to Gentiles as to Jews (Acts 15:9; Rom. 2:11,13; 3:22,29; 10:12,13; 1 Cor. 12:13; Gal. 3:28; Eph. 2:13,18; 3:6). Now this truth is evident, but to Peter it was revolutionary. God does not favor a Jew; he has never shown special consideration to an apostate or nonbelieving Jew. Grace always has come by faith and faith alone, to the Jew and to the Gentile alike. In speaking of this matter, Paul raises a question and then answers it in the light of his established premise: "Is he the God of the Jews only? is he not also of the Gentiles? Yes, of the Gentiles also: seeing it is one God, which shall justify the circumcision by faith, and uncircumcision through faith" (Rom. 3:29,30). Judaism had a dual nature; it was the suspension agent for both the "holy seed" (Ezra 9:2; Isa. 6:13) or the church, and the "congregation of evildoers" (Ps. 26:5), referred to later in this chapter as the counterfeit church. The latter group had the erroneous idea that God would not and did not extend his grace and favor to the Gentiles "and that the descendants of

God's Judgment
1966–1969

Universal Father
1247

God's Impartiality
1979

Grace
1445–1449
Faith
1201–1213

False Profession
2989

127

Preliminary Matters

Arch Joppa
4382

Universal
Opportunity
4180

Jacob were the only ones who enjoyed his peculiar favor and benedictions," even though people were redeemed before the founding of the Jewish race.

Apparently for Peter this narrow Pharisaic viewpoint prevailed until he had the heavenly vision at Joppa (Acts 10:9ff.). He was then convinced that "God was no respecter of persons" (Acts 10:34), and that "we must all appear before the judgment seat of Christ; that every one may receive the things done in his body, . . ." (2 Cor. 5:10); so no one nation, or people or individual could expect to find more preferential favor with God. He is absolutely just and could not ignore the pious prayers, fastings, and benevolent almsgiving of Cornelius. The biblical record shows that "the noblest spirits (of Israel) did not restrict salvation to Jews but insisted that God wanted Israel to be a light to the nations of the world" (Isa. 45:22; 49:6; Zech. 8:20ff.).[13]

So it has always been, "Whosoever will" may come. This is the truism of the ages. It must be remembered that the redemptive plan was given in its essential form to Adam and Eve and that all nations are included in its spiritual benefits. The Hebrews did not live in a vacuum, but they circulated throughout the heathen nations and scattered abroad the message of salvation. The Diaspora was one of the means by which the message of the Bible spread to many parts of the world (see Ch. 12, IX, page 187).

In his letter to the Romans, Paul presents the basic requirement for salvation: "For therein is the righteousness of God revealed from faith to faith: as it is written, The just shall live by faith" (1:17; see also Hab. 2:4). On the basis of this truth, Abraham, the founder and father of the Jewish people, was justified by faith, even before the Mosaic law was given; trusting in God, Abraham and all his believing descendants have been justified. "And thus the faith of the old covenant led to the faith of the new covenant, which shows that salvation has been by faith . . . from the beginning. All that were just or righteous in the earth became so by faith, and by this principle alone they were enabled to persevere; as it is written: 'the just shall live by faith.'"[14] This has been the redemptive hope for all men in all ages—Jew or Gentile.

Wrath of God
3132
Godlessness
3082–3085
Methods of
Revelation
2495–2498

128

Paul states that "the wrath of God is revealed from heaven against all ungodliness and unrighteousness of men" (Rom. 1:18) whether they be Gentile or Jew. Paul was no longer spiritually blind; his eyes had been opened, and he could see that salvation has always been available to Gentile and Jew alike. This realization is evidenced in these words: "Because that which may be known of God is manifest in them [the Gentiles]; for God hath shewed it unto them. For the invisible things of him from the creation of the world are clearly seen, being understood by the things that are made, even his eternal power and Godhead; so that they are without excuse" (Rom. 1:19,20). Although the Gentiles had no written revelation, yet what could be known of God was everywhere manifest among them (see Ps. 19). The Gentiles were constantly exposed to the Jewish religion; the Court of the Gentiles in the temple provided a teaching media. It is assumed that the publican prayed in the Court of the Gentiles (Luke 18:9–14). (See also TCRB, p. 306.)

When Peter attained the state of grace where he could say, "of a truth I perceive that God is no respecter of persons" (Acts 10:34), he saw God as he really was and always had been and realized that Christ is "Lord of all." Both Jew and Gentile have always been eligible for membership in the kingdom, by faith. "There is no other way of obtaining life and salvation. . . . The law condemns all men as being under sin. None therefore is justified by the works of the law." [15] Therefore justification is by faith and faith alone, and so it has always been since time began.

Universal Call
1791

VI. THE COUNTERFEIT COVENANT COMMUNITY

In the Scriptures a false, counterfeit religious system is clearly discerned. John infers this: "I know the blasphemy of them which say they are Jews, and are not, but are the synagogue of Satan" (Rev. 2:9). The conflict between the forces of good and evil in the world is evident on every hand. All means and methods are used by Satan and his angels to frustrate and destroy God's program (see Job 1:7ff.; Luke 4:6; Acts 26:18; 2 Cor. 4:3,4; Eph. 6:12; 2 Thess. 2:9). Satan's most effective efforts have been made through imitation, half truths, and counterfeit. Satan has counterfeits for all the good things of God; there is in the world today a counterfeit church made up of people (inside the visible church and out) who are, consciously or unconsciously, motivated by Satan. The "church in the wilderness" (Acts 7:38) had to contend with this "counterfeit group" known as the "mixed multitude." [16]

False Religion
2988-2991

Directing this counterfeit church are the false prophets and ministers who perpetuate a counterfeit system, with its seductively beautiful allurements, its ritualistic appeal, its easy religion without repentance or abandonment of sin, and "many there be which go in thereat" (Matt. 7:13).

Mixed
Multitude
2388

It is a well-known fact that counterfeits and adulterations are difficult to detect, and many are deceived thereby. The counterfeit church propounds a kind of humanistic, rationalistic salvation which discards "all dependence upon anything outside of man himself for the attainments of the good life . . . .

129

Whatever satisfaction he is to enjoy he must achieve by his ability to control the physical world about him or through his manipulation of social forces which can thus be made to serve him. He is entirely this worldly in his outlook. Science is the key to his hope of a better world." [17]

The counterfeit church consists of people who serve and worship their own self-interests. They are found in the visible church, the demominational groups, with all the appearances of pious saints. They use the forms and terminology of the church, but at the same time are "denying the power thereof" (2 Tim. 3:5). They claim the name "Christian" but are not in union with Christ (Eph. 5:23–27; Heb. 12:22,23). At times representatives from this group have been able to take control of the visible church and to direct its functions and affairs; while at other times they are associated with other institutions, de-

finitely satanic. They live a kind of "Dr. Jekyll and Mr. Hyde" life. The "mystical body of Satan" and the "mystical body of Christ move along in history, within the framework of the visible Church, sometimes within each other and sometimes parallel to each other. These two lines run through all ages; the ripening of the great 'world' for the tempest of judgment and the preparing of the 'little flock' for deliverance out of misery and distress." [18]

The two will be closely related until the end of time, even as the wheat and tares are closely related until harvest. "The attempt to sever the tares from the wheat prematurely has led to many schisms, which have invariably failed to accomplish anything and only generated fresh separations. We must wait till Christ's manifestation for 'the manifestation of the sons of God' " (Rom. 8:19; Col. 3:4).[19] Jesus' parable of the wheat and

tares is applicable here (Matt. 13:30). At the judgment "the angels shall come forth, and sever the wicked from among the just" (Matt. 13:49).

Goats
169
Sheep
184

Last Judgment
1351

A very familiar scene in Palestine has always been the mixed flock. The black goats and white sheep pasture together, but there comes a time when the shepherd separates his sheep from his goats. Christ draws an analogy: On the day of judgment a separation will be effected, and to the "sheep on his right hand" he will say "Come, ye blessed of my Father, inherit the kingdom prepared for you from the foundation of the world" (Matt. 25:31ff.). But the goats on his left hand are addressed thus: "Depart from me, ye cursed, into everlasting fire, prepared for the devil and his angels" (Matt. 25:41ff.). Christ further illustrates the physical association of the good and evil until the judgment day: "I tell you, in that night there shall be two men in one bed; the one shall be taken, and the other shall be left. Two women shall be grinding together;

the one shall be taken, and the other left. Two men shall be in the field; the one shall be taken, and the other left. . . . Whereesoever the body is, thither will the eagles be gathered together" (Luke 17:34–37). Obviously, at this point the spiritual wheat and tares, the good and evil, are forever separated.

This division will take place at the judgment. Obviously, political Judaism was the OT agent in which both the true church and the counterfeit church were found. God's plan to redeem man used the shedding of animal blood, which was typical of the "Lamb slain from the foundation of the world" (Rev. 13:8b). By offering blood sacrifices as God had commanded, the believers gave evidence of their faith in God's redemptive provision. These early believers expressed faith in the Lord and were thus saved. Favor with God has always depended upon the sinner's acceptance of God's son, Christ the Lord. When the Savior said, "No man cometh unto the Father, but by me" (John 14:6), he clearly revealed that he had always been the way by which sinners obtained favor with the Father.

Abel represents the church; he brought an acceptable blood sacrifice. Cain, who offered no animal sacrifice, represents the counterfeit church; he brought merely an expression of his own rationalization, falsely assuming that the products of his field could substitute for the blood sacrifice which God required. Thereby he became the prototype of all who dare to approach the sanctuary of God without the shedding of blood (Heb. 9:22).

Cain must have known the true way since he was reared in the same home with Abel. He was religious but he had a religion of the flesh and he was irreverent and selfish (Gen. 4:9). He was deluded into depending upon his own way; this was the thinking of the first murderer. But on the other hand, the "way of Abel" was to humbly acknowledge that sin necessitates death, and that the guilty rely on the sacrifice appointed by God.

When the Messiah appeared, the degenerate "followers of Cain" put our Lord on a cross (Acts 3:15) and persecuted his followers (Acts 4:1–3). By rejecting Christ they proved that they did not know the Father (Acts 3:14,15,17). They claimed to be the true people of God, but really they were the children of the devil (John 8:44). These God-denying church leaders were also referred to as members in the "synagogue of the Libertines" (Acts 6:9).

In Jesus' day religious affairs were no longer controlled by true Jehovah worshipers; the priests, scribes, Pharisees, and other officials possessed the key to the temple precincts, but they were impostors and counterfeits.

It is evident that God has never been dependent upon any

Judgment Seat
1965

Salvation through Christ Only
3117

Abel
4

Cain
618

Jesus the Messiah
695

Corrupt Priests
2102
False Prophets
2100

131

visible ecclesiastical organization for preserving the faith. At times the church has been temporarily forced underground, but through "ordained" and/or "lay" representatives, God has had his witnesses in every age and dispensation. Interesting information comes, at this point, from the Dead Sea Scrolls. *The Manual of Discipline* was revered by the Sect of the Covenant at Qumran, an intensely separatistic sect; they rigidly avoided the "Sons of Darkness," contact with whom meant defilement and impurity. In *The Manual of Discipline* the expression "to be separated from all unrighteous men" (or "men of error") appears repeatedly (1 QS V:1,a,10; VIII:13, etc.).[20]

It is quite probable that these faithful believers, referred to at times as the "children of the prophets" (Acts 3:25), withdrew from the formal temple precincts to escape the evil

threats of the corrupt leaders whom they opposed and to establish themselves in wilderness caves and dens so that the "faith which was once delivered unto the saints" (Jude 3) could be preserved and that a way might be prepared for the coming of the Christ-Messiah. Millar Burrows adds this sidelight: "the moral ideals of the covenant members at Qumran are much like those of similar monastic groups in other religions, but quite unlike those of orthodox Judaism at many points. They are the ideals of a group that has withdrawn from the world

into a separate life or rigid discipline and purity, going into the desert to prepare the way of the Lord by the study of the Law." [21]

Asceticism and mysticism, represented by purely Jewish sects, were active in the century before the Incarnation.[22]

Little is known about the earthly life of our Lord from age twelve until he assumed his public ministry; his activity and whereabouts are shrouded in mystery and darkness. Nothing specific is said about the Lord's contact with the Essenes, but it is evident that his ministry and teaching were closely related to this pious "holiness group." It is evident he divorced himself completely from the Pharisee-Sadducee system of legalistic Judaism. At the Jordan river John introduced Jesus as the "Lamb of God, which taketh away the sin of the world" (John 1:29).

In certain historical periods "the faith which was once delivered unto the saints" (Jude 3) was severely resisted, but God has never been without a witness. At times "the faith" has made tactical retreats and has made its abode with small groups and sects, but it has always revived and flowered into revival movements in some localities. In the political world, the democratic ideal has at times been lost as far as the visible outline

132

was concerned, but it continued to "glow" in the hearts and minds of the common people, later to manifest itself again, perhaps under a new name. So it has been with the "faith" throughout history.

The entire ecclesiastical hierarchy of Pharisee-Sadducee Judaism of the Savior's day stood condemned before God. Professing themselves to be the servants of God, they were instead administrators of murder. Instead of accepting the Lord, in the person of Jesus, they rejected him, the "chief cornerstone" (Acts 4:10–12). Instead of serving the church, these "false prophets" served the "synagogue of Satan" (Rev. 2:9). A further inquiry might be made relative to the identity of these apostles of evil. Did Christ call them by name? Jesus identified these "false prophets" and called them the "children of the devil" (John 8:44–47; see also Matt. 23). The Gospels indicate that these servants of Satan were none other than the scribes, the Pharisees, the Sadducees, the chief priests, the elders, and the rulers who were in charge of the religious program in the temple.

Cornerstone
692

False Prophets
2100

Apostasy
1235, 1236

Their interest in religion was limited mainly to use as a cloak behind which to hide their evil designs. Sin, to them, became a lucrative business. The poor were oppressed and driven into slavery; dishonest trading and bribery were common; public and private virtue were almost forgotten; the courts of justice were notorious; immoralities were practiced without shame or compunction. The appetites of the greedy temple authorities were such that they made the house of God "a den of thieves" (Matt. 21:13, see also Matt. 23). However, a few of these leaders did accept Christ (John 3:1; Acts 26:5; 15:5).

Through faith the "congregation of the saints" (Ps. 89:5), the church, stood up under persecution and abuse by these "children of the devil" (1 John 3:10), i.e., the counterfeit church. The faithful believers were subjected to disgrace and indignity as indicated in Hebrews (11:37–40). Some examples of what Jesus said about the religious leaders are given below:

1. In addressing the scribes and Pharisees in Jerusalem, Christ called to mind the fact that Isaiah had pronounced condemnation upon the religious leaders of his day. The Lord then applied this condemnation to their descendants: "This people draweth nigh unto me with their mouth, and honoureth me with their lips; but their heart is far from me. But in vain they do worship me, teaching for doctrines the commandments of men" (Matt. 15:8,9). Isaiah had referred to this group as an "abominable branch" (Isa. 14:19); "rebellious children" (Isa. 30:1; see also 30:9). Teaching traditions of men instead of divine truth has always been characteristic of false prophets.

2. Jesus advised the people to ignore the temple authorities because they did not discern spiritual issues. Said Jesus: "Let

them alone: they be blind leaders of the blind. And if the blind lead the blind, both shall fall into the ditch" (Matt. 15:14). Certainly no blind man wants another blind man to lead him across the street, nor does one sinner care to have another sinner attempt to lead him into the way of salvation.

3. On another occasion the Pharisees and the Sadducees came to tempt Jesus with their trick questions, whereupon Jesus called them "hypocrites" (Matt. 16:1–3).

Hypocrites
2995

4. The people are warned against the leaders: "Take heed and beware of the leaven of the Pharisees and of the Sadducees" (Matt. 16:6). By leaven, Christ meant the "traditions of the elders" as opposed to the doctrines of God. As leaven has a tendency to permeate the dough, so these false teachings endangered the entire religious body.

5. Evidence of corruption and perversion within the ranks

Corrupt Priests
2102

of the priests and elders was seen in the manner in which they challenged the authority of Christ (Matt. 21:23). The fact that they did not recognize the Savior as the Son of God showed their ignorance of the Father (John 8:19).

Apostates
1236

6. The demon-possessed nature of these leaders is further shown in the efforts of the chief priests and Pharisees to lay hands on the Savior in order to harm him, even to kill him.

False
Teachers
2101

7. To further evaluate the status of the temple authorities the following facts should be considered: Jesus called the scribes and Pharisees "stumbling blocks" to the kingdom of heaven; they refused to go in, and they prevented others from so doing (Matt. 23:13). They devoured widows' houses (literally robbed the widow of her home and living) and then hid behind long sanctimonious prayers in public places (Matt. 23:14). This same group took great pains to convert the heathen to their way of life which made each of them "twofold more the child of hell" (Matt. 23:15). These false teachers were referred to as

Self-exaltation
3194

fools who pervert God's Word by their false teachings regarding the temple and the altar (Matt. 23:16–18).

Murderers
2450

The Pharisees, intoxicated with their own self-righteousness, boasted: "If we had been in the days of our fathers, we would not have been partakers with them in the blood of the prophets" (Matt. 23:30). But Jesus countered their claim: "Wherefore ye be witnesses unto yourselves, that ye are the children of them which killed the prophets" (Matt. 23:31). By their deeds and attitudes they witnessed to their true nature. Jesus then called them "serpents" and "vipers," the key symbol of sin, and asked the question: "How can ye escape the damnation of hell?" (Matt. 23:33). He next described prophetically the persecution and murder to which they would give themselves

134

in their conflict with God's righteous forces (Matt. 23:34ff.). Our Lord gave the scribes and Pharisees a preview of their future wickedness: "Behold, I send unto you prophets, and wise men, and scribes: and some of them ye shall kill and crucify; and some of them shall ye scourge in your synagogues, and persecute them from city to city: that upon you may come all the righteous blood shed upon the earth, from the blood of righteous Abel unto the blood of Zacharias son of Barachias, whom ye slew between the temple and the altar" (Matt. 23:34–35).

The Covenant Community in the Old Testament

But this is only part of the evidence of their wrong doing: "Now the chief priests, and elders, and all the council, sought false witness against Jesus, to put him to death" (Matt. 26:59). This same crowd violated their own law by holding our Savior's trial at night. The chief priests and elders used methods of bribery and political intrigue and "persuaded the multitude" that they should ask for the release of Barabbas rather than Jesus (Matt. 27:20).

Apostates **1236**

False Witnessess **3856, 3857**

Finally the chief priests, scribes, and elders mocked him as he died on the cross (Matt. 27:42). How unlike was their attitude to the spirit of the Beatitudes, as given by the Master: "Blessed are the merciful" (Matt. 5:7). The temple authorities, by their rejection of Christ evidenced the fact that they did not know the Father and that the love of God was not in their hearts (John 8:19ff.). The leaders made much of their faith in Moses, but Jesus told them that they stood condemned by Moses (John 5:45,46). If they had been true spiritual descendents of Moses, they would have accepted Christ as the Messiah. He said to them: "For had ye believed Moses, you would have believed me: for he wrote of me" (John 5:46).

Mocking Christ **3493**

Rejected Christ **2965**

So perverted and blind to spiritual truth were the temple rulers that they rebuked some of their own number for believing in Christ. Said they, "Are ye also deceived?" (John 7:47). When the officers came back empty handed from their mission to take Christ, the authorities asked: "Have any of the rulers or of the Pharisees believed on him?" (John 7:48). This is a familiar oriental custom, making a strong affirmative statement in the form of a question. The obvious inference is that few if any of the temple rulers or the Pharisees had openly professed belief in Christ. By their denial of him as the Christ-Messiah they gave testimony that their hearts were not right. Jesus told these "Satanic apostles" that they would die in their sins (John 8:24). The leaders of the temple said much about Abraham being their father, but Jesus challenged them: "If ye were Abraham's children, ye would do the works of Abraham. But now ye seek to kill me, a man that hath told you the truth, which I have heard of God; this did not Abraham" (John 8:39,40). It is true, they were physical descendants of Abraham but they were not his spiritual descendants (see Rom. 2:28,29).

Evil Children **3063**

Instead of being children of God they were children of the devil (John 8:44; 1 John 3:10).

The leaders continued to boast that they had "one Father, even God" (John 8:41), but the Master said to them: "If God were your Father, ye would love me: for I proceeded forth and came from God; neither came I of myself, but he sent me. Why do ye not understand my speech? even because ye cannot hear my word" (John 8:42,43; Matt. 11:27).

In a final address Jesus made the indictment in these words:

"Ye are of your father the devil, and the lusts of your father ye will do. He was a murderer from the beginning, and abode not in the truth, because there is no truth in him" (John 8:44). Jesus then asked the question of them: "Which of you convinceth me of sin? And if I say the truth, why do ye not believe me?" (John 8:46). Jesus then gave the answer: "He that is of God heareth God's words: ye therefore hear them not, because ye are not of God" (John 8:47).

Moorehead states that "When Pharisaism, with its rigid legalism, with its intolerable burdens, became dominant, all liberty of worship and spontaneous service largely disappeared. The religious life of Israel stiffened into a dreadful monotony." [23]

This certainly is a serious indictment of those who were clad in ecclesiastical garb; it has been noted that Jesus did not identify the natural descendants of Abraham (see Rom. 2:28,29) as the "Israel of God" (Gal. 6:16). The Jews became members

in the "household of faith" (Gal. 6:10) only when they accepted Christ as their Lord; only then did they become "quickened" by the Spirit (Eph. 2:5; see John 5:21) and have a spiritual relationship with Abraham (Gal. 3:7). In reference to the "enemy of all righteousness" (Acts 13:10) Paul attested the union of Elymas, the sorcerer, and the devil.

They (Pharisees) expressed ignorance and unbelief of the work and mission of Christ. Without accepting Jesus they could not have known the Father (Matt. 11:27; see also Acts 3:14, 15,17). It is evident that the scribes, Pharisees, Sadducees, and other false ecclesiastical leaders are types and examples of whom each generation has its counterpart (see Deut. 13:1–3; Jer. 14:14; Matt. 7:15; 24:4,5,11,24; Mark 13:5; Luke 21:8; 2 Peter 2:1–3). Abel is referred to as a righteous prophet who was slain by Cain (Luke 11:50,51), a type of all succeeding "enemies of the cross" (Phil. 3:18).

VII. THE TRANSITION FROM THE OLD COVENANT TO THE NEW
TESTAMENT CHURCH

"He taketh away the first, that he may establish the second" (Heb. 10:9). The story of the church is as old as creation, but ever new in its adjustment to each age. A historical perspective of this redemptive institution reveals a progressive development from its pristine origin in Genesis to its full culmination in Revelation. At first, its ritual and form were adapted to the simplicity of nomadic life, but gradually, as society developed in its various complexities, the church made adjustment to developing sociological needs. One of the earliest shrines, or places of worship, was a heap of stones, or a pillar (Gen. 28:18) which was followed by a more carefully made stone altar (Gen. 8:20). Thus the OT church continued its corporate relationship with God, under a changed order of worship, and after the crucifixion of Christ no further animal sacrifices were necessary. The symbolic meaning of the sacrificial system was fulfilled when Jesus Christ died on the cross (see 1 Sam. 15:22). (For detailed information on the development of worship centers from the altar to the temple see Ch. 5, page 60ff.)

During this period God led his people a step nearer to the spiritual reality behind the sacrifices. By then the people were able to comprehend better a personal holy life as an expression of faith. The whole sacrificial ritual was intended only to point out the infinite mercy of God to fallen man, in his redemption by the blood of the new covenant. God wanted to show his people—his church—that they should look for the mercy and salvation prefigured by the sacrifices. This concept was expressed by many of the OT divines. God touched upon this thought through Hosea: "I desired mercy, and not sacrifice; and the knowledge of God more than burnt offerings" (Hosea 6:6). The ultimate end of the levitical ritual was for man to communicate love. The Lord pointed this out when a scribe questioned him about the commandments. Said he: "Thou shalt love the Lord thy God with all thy heart, and with all thy soul, and with all thy mind, and with all thy strength: . . . Thou shalt love thy neighbour as thyself." "This," the Master said, "is more than all whole burnt offerings and sacrifices." (Mark 12:30–33). "God prefers an act of mercy . . . to any act of worship to which the person might be called at the time (Matt. 9:13)." [24]

During the first century B.C. the faithful Jewish believers at Qumran, "the Israel of God," recognized the uselessness of the sacrifices. (See Ch. 12, VII, B, page 68.) In *The Manual of Discipline*, IX 13–15, appear these words: "When these things shall come to pass in Israel, at these destined times, the institution founded by the Holy Spirit for eternal Truth shall make atonement for the guilty, rebellious and sinful infidelities, and to obtain divine Grace without the fat of sacrifices. But the offering of the lips shall be as a fragrance of righteousness and the perfection of my way shall be as the free-will gifts of an acceptable offering." [25]

The praise of God, evidenced in a life of true holiness by

The Covenant Community in the Old Testament

Fuller Revelation
2499, 4155

Places of Worship
3538, 3577, 3580

Insufficient Sacrifices
3108

Love
2201

Arch. Dead Sea Scrolls
4356

Praise to God
1451

137

faith in the Lord, the supreme sacrifice which a pure soul offers God, involves a complete, personal dedication. The OT worshiper brought an animal without spot or blemish: just so today, only a person with sins forgiven is a fit subject for consecration at God's altar (see Rom. 12:1).

From the time of the Exile, the synagogue as a place of worship became more and more prominent, and by the time the temple was destroyed under Titus in A.D. 70 the "ideal sacrifice" was so well ingrained in the thought pattern of the church that the temple and its traditional sacrifices were no longer important; they had served their purpose. The church

described in the Synoptic Gospels found the synagogue adequate, and within the framework of this institution the NT church developed. It seems evident from the NT that Jesus gave his disciples no formal prescription for the organization of the church. In the first days after Pentecost (Commemoration of the Law at Sinai) believers had no thought of separating themselves from the religious life of Israel and the OT church, and did not realize the need of any distinct organization of their own. The temple worship was still adhered to (Acts 2:45; 3:1), though it was supplemented by apostolic teaching, by prayer and fellowship, and by the breaking of bread (Acts 2:42–46). Organization was a thing of gradual growth, suggested by the needs as they arose. Religious services were held mainly in the Jewish synagogues, and the oldest Christian meetings and meeting places were thus modeled on the pattern of the sister institution. In the synagogue can be recognized the transitional step from the temple to the modern church. Sacrifices were not offered in it; rather it was used for exposition of the Law, and in time, prayers and preaching were added to the services. (For further information see Ch. 5, I, D.)

For many years the NT church continued to use the physical agencies and edifices of the OT church. The synagogue was the place where the believers in Christ, the Messiah, assembled; the OT was their Bible. Later, opposition by decadent Judaism became so intolerable that the NT church abandoned the visible institution of Judaism and eventually built its own houses of worship. The apostles had maintained a close bond between the Jewish synagogue and the Christian church until resistance to the truth by the rejecting Jews led Christians to leave the

term synagogue to them exclusively.[26] Many years after the apostolic period "Christian Churches were built resembling

synagogues, with the holy table placed where the chest containing the law had been; the desk and pulpit were the chief furniture in both. Common to both church and synagogue were

the discipline (Matt. 18:17), excommunication (1 Cor. 5:3–5), and the collection of alms (1 Cor. 16:2)."[27] The similarity of the Christian church building to the synagogue gives credence to the affinity and common historical background of the two.

The Dead Sea Scrolls provide much information on this transition period. Père de Vaux was one of the pioneer scholars in a study of these Scrolls. He says:

> The Essenes must have lived at Khirbet Qumran, except for a few years, from about 100 B.C. or a little before, to A.D. 66–70. . . . The most startling disclosure of the Essene documents so far published is that the sect possessed, years before Christ, a terminology and practice that have always been considered uniquely Christian. The Essenes practiced baptism and shared a liturgical repast of bread and wine presided over by a priest. They believed in redemption and the immortality of the soul.[28]

Earthly life was to the Essenes a war between the powers of light and darkness. Many of the rites and concepts of worship among the Essenes are similar to those in the NT, particularly in the Gospel of John and the Pauline Epistles. John the Baptist's use of baptism has led scholars to believe that he was either an Essene, or strongly influenced by the sect.

The unity and affinity of the OT and the NT church is further affirmed by Frank M. Cross, Jr., of the American School of Oriental Research: He points out that there are undeniable correlations between the writings of the Essenes and the NT church and that this is reflected in all aspects of christian institutional life.[29] (See also Dead Sea Scrolls, Ch. 12, VII, B.)

It is difficult to explain why God chose to close the period of written revelation with Malachi and omit almost four hundred years of unrecorded divine activity, but it is evident that this period was rich in religious values. The period around 200 B.C. produced valuable writings known as pseudepigrapha, mainly of Jewish origin and apocalyptic in nature (see Ch. 12, XII). Many of them are quoted by the Christian Fathers; some of them are cited by the New Testament writers (Jude 14). The whole of these works has been preserved for us through Christian means, e.g., the Ethiopic Church. The OT Apocrypha was preserved through the Septuagint (Greek OT) and the Latin Vulgate. These were never canonized and were called "deutero-canonical." They contain information on events during the silent period. (See Ch. 12, XI, page 62.)

This period was prominent in the political and religious pursuits of the Judaistic sects, the Pharisees, Sadducees, and Essenes. The Essenes, however, are never mentioned by name in the OT or NT. The Pharisees assumed a strict letter-of-the-law, legalistic position; the Sadducees accepted only the Pentateuch as being authoritative and had no share in the Messianic hopes of which the Prophets spoke at length. They believed in neither angels nor spirits and had no hope of immortality

(Acts 23:8). On the other hand, "nothing could be farther removed from the Essene spirit and doctrines as recorded in the apocalypses. The Messianic hope bulk largely: angels are prominent; their hierarchies are described and their names given. The doctrine of immortality is implied, and the places of reward and punishment are described." [30]

It is a matter of historical record that the believers in Christ were separated from traditional Judaism as represented by the Pharisees and Sadducees. True Israel (the church) was closely linked with those who looked for the Messiah and who accepted him when he came. The NT church is indeed an extension or continuation of the OT church to whom the faith was once delivered (Jude 3). This precious faith has been preserved by mystical groups such as the Essenes and the Therapeutae (Jewish monks and other like groups to which Philo makes reference in his treatise "De Vita Contemplativa"). One noted scholar observes that "the Essenes and the Therapeutae were given over to a study of the laws and sacred oracles of God enunciated by the holy prophets, and hymns, and psalms and all kinds of other things by reason of which knowledge and piety are increased and brought to perfection." [31] It is evident these intertestamental groups help one to make closer contact with that spiritual Judaism out of which Christ the Messiah came. From this, one can see that the temple hierarchy rejected Jesus but at the same time other Jews accepted Jesus and became the vanguard for the Christian church.

At times in history the Christian faith was not evident, but there were always minority groups ("the Israel of God," Gal. 6:16) in which the faith was nurtured and preserved. Thus God is not dependent upon "ecclesiastical cloth" for the preservation of the faith (Acts 13:27ff.). In periods of spiritual darkness God has preserved the faith within the hearts of humble people. Is it possible that Simeon and Anna, living at the beginning of Jesus' earthly life, were acquainted with the Essenes and at the end of his life, Joseph of Arimathea also? It seems reasonable to suppose that these groups were Essene in spirit, but perhaps bearing another name. Thompson points out that the "term 'Methodist' was derived from a purely temporary characteristic of the society that gathered around Wesley. As the name Essene is not found in the NT it is possibly a nickname, as the term 'Quakers' was, applied to the Society of Friends." [32]

Another significant fact is that Essenism disappeared with the advent of Christianity. Could it not be that Christianity became a continuation of this "Mosaic ideal" nurtured by the Essenes? Is it not possible that the terminologies and the practices of the Essenes, such as baptism carried over into the institution known as the Christian church? It is evident from the

Faithful
Servants
603

Rejected
Jesus
2965

Spiritual
Darkness
2179

140

data presented that the Essene literature at Qumran provided a very logical transitional link between OT Judaism and NT Christianity. A renowned Bible scholar says, "If we are to understand the Palestine in which our Lord's ministry was carried on, we must comprehend the place occupied by the Essenes." He continues with this very surprising statement: "The Essenes are brought forward as the very flower and perfection of Mosaism. . . . They use a threefold criterion—love of God, love of virtue and love of man. . . . No one can fail to be struck with the resemblance all this has, in the first place, to the teaching of the Sermon on the Mount and to the practice of the early church." [33]

The Covenant Community in the Old Testament

Church Divinely Instituted 731

Both the Essenes and the Christians were inspired and influenced by the Messiah: The Essenes looked forward to the promises of the OT prophets; for the Christians those promises had become a reality. The essence of redemption in the OT is the same as that in the NT. The Essenes and the Christians both developed their ritual from the sources which inspired Abel, Enoch, Joseph, Daniel, and the other spiritual giants in the OT. Cross says:

Messiah 695

Messianic Hope 4186

> The New Testament and Essene writers . . . draw on common sources of language, common theological themes and concepts and share common religious institutions. . . . For God chooses to give meaning to human history, not to suspend it. This means he uses its continuities, its language, its events, its institutions in speaking to men and in building His church. . . . No Christian need stand in dread of these tests.[34]

Distinction must be made between the apostate religious leaders (Matt. 23; John 8:36–59) and those pious ones, the Essenes and other "like groups" (Matt. 5:9; 24:22; Isa. 35:10) who refused to compromise on the moral, ethical, and social standards clearly taught in the OT. These OT principles were frequently quoted by Jesus (Matt. 22:36–40; cf. Deut. 6:5; Lev. 19:18) and the NT writers.

Apostates 1236

Faithful Servants 603

From the Scriptures it is evident that the revelation of Christ was gradually unfolded over the centuries so it was natural and normal that the basic ritual would undergo slow changes in order to fit itself to the changing culture, economy, and functional needs of the people. (See Ch. 12, VIII on "The Sacraments and Their Changing Modes," page 180.)

Fuller Revelation 2499, 4155

These changes in the ritual facilitated the passing of "Spiritual Judaism" into the Christian era and into the Gentile world.

Most important is the fact that the final establishment of Christianity was contingent upon the birth, life, death, and especially the resurrection of Jesus Christ. Paul says, "If Christ be not raised, your faith is vain; ye are yet in your sins" (1 Cor. 15:17).

The promises by God of a Savior could not fail, because "God cannot lie" (Titus 1:2; Heb. 6:18); it was a promissory note with God's signature, redeemable immediately by an act of faith, and by this faith they were justified (Gen. 15:6; Hab. 2:4; 2 Chron. 20:20).

History shows that God redeemed the note on the due date, "When the fulness of the time was come" (Gal. 4:4), exactly as Moses and the prophets had foretold. The NT is a record of this fulfillment.

11

A Christological Study of the Tabernacle
(Hebrews 9:1–28)

A Christological study of the tabernacle has been popular for Christians throughout the ages. In the Bible, many of the more than 212 references to the tabernacle specifically foreshadow Christ. At least 25 references to the tabernacle appear in the NT. In Hebrews 9:11 the writer states that Christ became "an high priest of good things to come, by a greater and more perfect tabernacle, not made with hands."

Tabernacle
3528

In God's wisdom he revealed the full plan of redemption progressively through the life and experiences of the Hebrews. Thumbnail sketches of the Anointed One begin in the third chapter of Genesis and continue to Malachi. (For a more detailed study of fulfilled Messianic prophecies see page 209.) The tabernacle in the wilderness is one of the great object lessons in the OT on Christ the Savior (see work of Christ in the OT, Ch. 9, God's Plan of Salvation from Genesis to Revelation, page 93).

I. THE TABERNACLE (Exod. 25:9ff.)

Tabernacle
3528

The architectual wonders of man grace various nations of the earth. Greece boasts of its Acropolis and Parthenon; Italy, its leaning Tower of Pisa; and France its Eiffel Tower. In the United States are the Empire State Building and the Washington Monument. Only the Jews can boast of a structure planned, designed, and revealed by God. "The instructions were given to Moses on Mt. Sinai to build 'according to all that I shew thee, after the pattern of the tabernacle, and the pattern of all the instruments thereof, even so shall ye make it' (Exod.

Mt. Sinai
2444
143

25:9). The construction details for the tabernacle are specific. Over fifty times it is said, 'As the Lord commanded Moses, so did he.' " [1] A study of the tabernacle shows that God chooses to accomplish the greatest number of ends by the fewest and simplest means possible. Every detail has special spiritual significance.

The kind of wood, the colors, the skins, the rings, the stones and embroidery, the lamps and the candlestick, even the priests' robes—all were to convey divine truth, not only for Moses and his people but for those of future generations. It is significant that God gave only two chapters in the Bible to the creation of the world and the fall of man, while he set apart no less than fifty chapters for the subject of the tabernacle. Many of the details in the tabernacle prefigure the Lord Jesus Christ, who became flesh and tabernacled among men.

The outside of the tabernacle was commonplace and unattractive. It was made of drab badgers' skins "but when we come inside, we find ourselves surrounded by shining gold: looking up to the curtained roof, we see the wings of the cherubim woven in blue and purple and scarlet and fine twined linen . . . . So it is with Christ Himself. The natural man, beholding Him, sees no beauty that he should desire Him [Isa. 53:2b], but to those who know the Lord Jesus Christ, His beauty satisfies their souls." [2] Building materials for the tabernacle such as acacia wood, hair, and skins were obtainable in its immediate vicinity. Gold, silver, brass, and linen were brought from Egypt (Exod. 25:3–7). The tabernacle in the wilderness was a movable sanctuary which served as a dwelling place for God among his people (Exod. 25:8). The Ark of the Covenant was the focal point. It was the appointed meeting place between the Lord and the priests, who represented the people (Exod. 25:22).

The tabernacle contained two rooms designated as the Holy Place and the Holy of Holies. The table of shewbread (Exod. 25:23–30), the golden candlestick (Exod. 25:31–40), and the altar of incense were placed in the Holy Place. The Holy of Holies accommodated the Ark of the Covenant. The veil was made out of white, blue, purple, and scarlet colored materials, and separated the two rooms. Over the Ark rested the Shekinah glory (Exod. 26:31–35). Inside the Ark was placed Aaron's rod that budded, the tables of the Law, and a pot of manna—all objects of veneration for the Hebrews. The brazen laver stood in front of the Holy Place (Exod. 30:17–21) and the brazen altar just inside the "eastern gate." The tabernacle was within, in a curtain-enclosed court, rectangular in form, 100 cubits long and 50 cubits wide with a wall 5 cubits high (Exod. 27:11–19).[3]

The arrangement of the fixtures is suggestive of the cross.

The brazen altar, the brazen laver, the altar of incense, and the Ark of the Covenant form the upright of the cross. The golden candlestick on the left and the table of shewbread on the right form the cross piece. Here is seen one of the many prophetic implications of Christian symbolism in the OT.

The Levites were responsible for the maintenance of the tabernacle and the court, and pitched their tents around its walls. Moses and Aaron camped near the entrance while the tribe of Judah had its standard flying just beyond the eastern gate. The other tribes were located in their appointed places around the outer edge of the linen fence.

A Christological Study of the Tabernacle (Heb. 9:1–28)

Levites
2114

II. THE TRIBE OF JUDAH (NUM. 2–3)

Judah
1955, 1956

The prophetic implications found in the position of the camp of Judah is very significant. Its location to the east is not accidental but intentional (Num. 2:30). From early times in Hebrew history the people looked for a great Leader. Ancient biblical records gave sketches about the Holy One that was to come. Moses was inspired to prophesy that the Messiah would come out of the Tribe of Judah (Gen. 49:10). The location of the camp of Judah suggests the idea that as the sun rising in the east ushers in the dawn of a new day, so the tribe of Judah located eastward would usher in the "Son of Righteousness" with healing for the nations.

Judah
1956

Moses
2420, 2421
Judah
1955, 1956

Beyond the tribe of Judah was located the continually burning fire which consumed the bodies of the sin offerings and the refuse of the camp. Here the fire becomes representative of the eternal fires that will ultimately torment the souls of men who have not settled the problem of sin at the brazen altar (cf. Deut. 32:22; Ps. 55:15; 86:13).

III. THE LINEN FENCE AND THE GATE (EXOD. 27:9–19; 38:9–20)

Linen
2185

The linen fence served as the line of demarcation between the world of sin on the outside and the redemptive court on the inside. Entrance could be made into it only by way of the gate (Exod. 27:9–21). Efforts to gain admittance over the fence would result in death, for touching the fence was fatal. "It was made of fine twined linen, white and might speak typically of the righteous requirements of the law, as linen symbolizes righteousness. There is no chance of getting into God's presence by law keeping" [4] (v. 9). The eastern gate was the one and only way into the court of God's favor. Jesus said on one occasion, "He that entereth not by the door into the sheepfold, but climbeth up some other way, the same is a thief and a robber" (John 10:1). Climbing over the fence could be representative of man's attempt to gain salvation through humanistic efforts. Some have considered plans to avoid Christ and his cross, but none of these have met God's standard. The fence around the tabernacle with its one gate is suggestive of Christ as the only door to salvation. Jesus said, "I am the door: by me if any man enter in, he shall be saved" (John 10:9). In

another place he said, "no man cometh to the Father, but by me" (John 14:6).

Linen
2185
Purple
2929, 2930
Scarlet
3161
Blue
518

Over the one and only entrance to the court there was a curtain "of blue, and purple, and scarlet, and fine twined linen" (Exod. 27:16), which symbolized the character of Christ. Each of the four colors suggest figurative significance. The blue speaks of Christ's heavenly character, the purple tells of his kingly or royal nature, and the scarlet symbolizes his atonement, while the white speaks of Christ as the Spotless One who dwelt among men. The curtain before the gate marked the place where men could step from the world of sin into the world of true righteousness. No one guarded this gate. It was always ready to admit those who would repent and be saved. "Whosoever will may come" was and will always be the divine invitation.

IV. THE BRAZEN ALTAR (EXOD. 27:1–8; 38:1–9)

Just inside the gate was located the brazen altar where a penitent dealt with the problem of sin before he could go into the redemptive court (Exod. 27:1–8). "The only way the sinning Israelite could be right with God, and safe from the penalty due His sins, was through the sacrifice offered on the brazen altar [symbol of the cross of Christ], and the mediation of the high priest who took the blood of the sacrifice into the Holy of Holies on the great day of atonement." [5]

To punish the Israelites in the wilderness for their rebellious conduct, God sent "fiery serpents" into their midst; many were bitten and died (Num. 21:6). For their relief, Moses lifted up

a brazen serpent on a pole with a cross piece (to keep the serpent from sliding down) (Num. 21:9); when, in obedience and faith, the people looked upon the serpent, they were healed, and by looking unto Jesus (Heb. 12:2) a sinner may receive spiritual healing. Christ gave the analogy that "as Moses lifted up the serpent in the wilderness, even so must the Son of man be lifted up: That whosoever believeth in him should not perish, but have eternal life" (John 3:14–15). Here it is seen that the serpent on the pole symbolized Christ on the

cross. As the serpent symbolized sin (and sin's origin) so Christ, having taken our sins upon himself, symbolized the sins of the world. Christ promised, "If I be lifted up from the earth, [I] will draw all men unto me" (John 12:32).

The brazen altar stood directly in the entrance, and no one could gain admittance to the court without presenting a sin offering without spot or blemish (Exod. 12:5; Num. 19:2; Deut. 15:21). Does this not suggest the requirement for salvation—that of repenting for sin and confessing Christ before one can come unto a saving experience?

The Hebrews presented a choice animal as a sin offering whereas post-Advent penitents plead the atoning merits of the Lamb, slain for all mankind. The pattern of animal sacrifice dates back to Abel (Gen. 4:4) and then to the days of the flood when Noah stepped out of the ark and offered sacrifices to God (Gen. 8:18–20). This practice was continued by the Jewish church until the Lamb of God was offered on the cross.

Slemming puts it well when he says, "Even so we must ourselves visit the 'altar' and see our 'sacrifice' dying for us ere we can step into any blessing of a Christian walk or know anything of the fellowship of a living Christ . . . . As a Holy God He has irrevocable claims which must be fully realized before He can show forth mercy: sin must be punished, either in person or substitute. The lamb, goat, and bullock were Israel's substitute, and God accepted them at the altar. These great claims of God have since been met to the full in Christ at Calvary when He became the Offering, the Altar, and the Priest." [6]

V. THE BRAZEN LAVER (EXOD. 30:17–21; 38:8; 40:7)

Between the brazen altar and the tabernacle stood the brazen laver (Exod. 30:18–21). The laver was located beyond the altar; this altar spoke of atonement and expiation for sins. For the priests the laver was a basin for symbolically cleansing themselves in preparation for service and worship.

The brazen laver was made from the looking glasses of the women (Exod. 38:8). This is significant. Their giving these symbolized the complete consecration God requires. Life is a treasure, the prized possession that God asks of his servants.

As the priest approached the laver, he could see his reflection in its shiny surface. Seeing himself reminded him of his sinful nature and his need for cleansing. "And the Lord spake unto Moses, saying, Thou shalt also make a laver of brass, and his foot also of brass, to wash withal: . . . and thou shalt put water therein. For Aaron and his sons shall wash their hands and their feet thereat. When they go into the tabernacle of the congregation, they shall wash with water, that they die not; or when they come near to the altar to minister, to burn offering

A Christological Study of the Tabernacle (Heb. 9:1–28)

Brazen Altar
122

Abel
4
Noah
2597

Die to Self
3504

Laver
2051

Consecration
3508

Spiritual Cleansing
962

Burnt Offering
2626
147

made by fire unto the Lord" (Exod. 30:17–20). This washing symbolized the priest's ceremonial cleansing and fitness for administration before God on behalf of Israel.

The brazen altar was for the people. The brazen laver was for the priest who presented himself before the Lord within the Holiest Place. The priest rendered for the people a service they could not perform for themselves. Since the veil has been rent in twain, every believer in this dispensation may become a priest to offer spiritual sacrifices. Peter declared that, "Ye also . . . are . . . an holy priesthood, to offer up spiritual sacrifices, acceptable to God by Jesus Christ" (1 Peter 2:5).

James stated that those who would draw near to God must cleanse their hands (James 4:8), typified by washing at the brazen laver. Preparation for worship and service demands a clean heart. No state of grace permits active and willful sin. Holiness unto the Lord is the minimum that is acceptable unto God (1 John 3:6).

McCord points out that "If we would serve Him, then we must be vessels purged, sanctified and thus made meet 'for the master's use, and prepared unto every good work' (2 Tim. 2:21). Or if we would worship Him in song, prayer, praise, Bible study, or in any way whatever, we must go into His presence by way of the laver. A holy life is the Christian standard; but 'if any man sin, we have an advocate with the Father, Jesus Christ the righteous: and he is the propitiation for our sins: and not for ours only, but also for the sins of the whole world' (1 John 2:1,2)." [7]

Substitution 3361

Holiness 1598

Holy Place 1600

VI. THE HOLY PLACE (EXOD. 26:35–37)

The Holy Place was the outer room of the tabernacle separated from the inner room by the veil which symbolized the flesh of Jesus Christ (Heb. 10:19,20). In the sanctuary immediately in front of the veil that separated it from the Holy of Holies, stood the altar of incense. In this apartment also were the table of shewbread on the right hand, and the golden candlestick on the left. Each of these objects has divine significance and prefigured the work and office of the Lord Jesus Christ.

"Let us proceed now with bowed heads and reverent hearts into those sacred precincts, reserved for priests unto God, pausing . . . first to examine ourselves. Are we really entitled to such a close relationship with God? Have we come by the way of the cross of Calvary, typified in the brazen altar? Have we been washed at the laver? If so, there is but one thing still needed, and that is to step, by faith, within the door. We cannot behold God's glory until we come into His presence." [8]

Holy of Holies 1599

Self-examination 3197

Arch. Calvary 4347

148

A. The Golden Candlestick

A Christological Study of the Tabernacle (Heb. 9:1–28)

The candlestick of gold has a base and a perpendicular shaft with six branches, three coming out of one side and three out of the other (Exod. 25:31–39). The candlestick and its associated vessels were to be made exactly as directed on the mount (Exod. 25:40).

Candlestick
637

Light is a very important provision in the creation, and light was created first in the natural world. Physical light dispels darkness, and spiritual light dispels spiritual darkness. Light is essential to existence. "It is that which clothes everything with beauty and color. It is that which gives glory to the rainbow and the ruby. It is that which makes the diamond anything but a bit of charcoal. It is that which makes the human face so full of loveliness; and it is that which gives us everything that is beautiful in our human relationships and in all the wonder of the natural world." [9]

Light
2165–2180

Rainbow
2943

Many of the figures used in the Bible in relation to God are figures of light. The pillar of fire and the burning bush are reminders of the words of Jesus Christ when he said, "I am the light of the world" (John 6:12).

Pillar of Fire
2501

The golden candlestick was the first object that the priest saw as he entered the tabernacle. God wants the pure light of his divine illumination to shine forth in his church, so that his light may shine through believers.

Candlestick
637

The light on top of the candlestick is a reminder that Christ is the light of the world. The flame was fed with oil which symbolizes the Holy Spirit who makes manifest the light of Christ. In a sense the base symbolizes Christ and the branches suggest the Christian's relationship to Christ. In the Sermon on the Mount Jesus said, "Ye are the light of the world." As the flame was fed by the oil, so the Christian's light must be fed by Christ through the Holy Spirit.

Christ the Light
2168

Light
2166–2170

The lights on the candlestick also symbolize the light of the believers' testimony. The purpose of the church is to radiate the light that comes from above.

Testimonies
3598

The only light in the tabernacle was the candlestick which illuminated the room and the objects in it. The candlestick symbolizes the light of Christ which Christian believers radiate into the world.

There is one more important fact; the candlestick had to be filled with oil each day. The officiating priest had to trim the wick and keep it clean. This may be a symbol of the Christian's need to attend to his spiritual condition each day by prayer, the study of God's Word, and service so as to keep his light burning brightly at all times.

Oil
2638

Prayer
2816
149

B. The Table of Shewbread (Exod. 25:23–30; Lev. 24:5–9; Heb. 9:2)

The table of shewbread got its name from the bread placed upon it. "Shewbread" in Hebrew is "bread of faces," faces signifying presence. The bread stood in the divine presence always before the face of the Lord. Here it is suggested that all the supplies for the children of Israel, both material and spiritual, come from the Lord. Believers, too, have the assurance that Jesus will supply all their needs (Phil. 4:19).[10]

The table stood on the right side upon entering the outer room, just opposite the candlestick. The bread is suggestive of Christ, the spiritual food. The table on which the loaves were placed each Sabbath was made of acacia wood, which grew in the desert where there was little else. This is perhaps emblematic of the lonely adverse conditions under which the Son of God was born and reared. The gold with which the table was overlaid speaks of his divinity.

Twelve fresh loaves were placed on the table each Sabbath by the officiating priests. The loaves were arranged in two rows, each loaf sprinkled with a small amount of frankincense as a memorial unto the Lord. The week-old loaves were eaten by the priests (Exod. 25:30; Lev. 24:5–9; 1 Sam. 21:6; Matt. 12:4). The bread is a type of the word of God, that is Christ the Written Word, who is also seen as Christ the Living Word (John 6:35,41).

The fine beaten flour out of which the loaves were made can symbolize the mill of suffering through which Christ passed. "As bread must be crushed in the mill stones and kneaded in the baker's hand, and baked in the fierce heat of the oven, so . . . the heavenly bread has been prepared under the crushing pressure and in the consuming flame of suffering. As the bread passed through the hot oven, even so Christ passed through the fire of Calvary and came out the Bread of Life to satisfy those who trust Him." [11]

The shewbread was eaten by the priests representatively for the twelve tribes of Israel. As there was a loaf for each tribe, so there is a satisfying loaf for every believer, who becomes a priest in the faith and is privileged to eat of that bread which is Christ. In Christ adequate provision has been made for the whole church. Truly, it is a miracle that as bread satisfies the physical so Christ, the bread from heaven, satisfies every repentant soul.

The loaves of bread served a twofold purpose. First, they were offered to God as an oblation, and second, they were eaten by the priests. "When we offer ourselves in complete dedication, God responds by giving us a satisfying portion of

His heavenly manna, and makes us a blessing to others. Peace that passes human understanding comes over us as we make our consecration complete. Every day requires new strength, and grace, and one must have 'daily bread.' The whole of the true believer's life is a Sabbath in the sense that he has entered into rest, rest from sin and self in Christ, and in the enjoyment of his peace he can sing: 'I shall not want. He maketh me to lie down in green pastures. He leadeth me by the waters of rest.' " [12]

A Christological Study of the Tabernacle (Heb. 9:1–28)

C. The Altar of Incense (Exod. 30:1-10, 34-38; 37:25-29)

The receptacle holding the incense is the last of the three main objects in the Holy Place. It was also made of acacia wood overlaid with gold and stood in the center of the Holy Place just outside the veil which concealed the Holy of Holies. Each morning while the priests dressed the lamps, smoke from the altar of incense ascended toward heaven. Once each year, on the Day of Atonement, the High Priest took the censer into the Holy of Holies where incense was burned in connection with his ministration at the mercy seat.

Incense
1747

Censer
652

The smoke was typical of the intercession of the appointed high priest as well as of the prayers of the saints. This principle applies to the psalmist's request that his prayer might be set forth before the Lord as incense (Ps. 141:2), and also to the worshipers praying outside the temple while Zacharias offered incense within its walls (Luke 1:10). In the Apocalypse an angel was seen burning incense on the golden altar in connection with the prayers of the saints (Rev. 8:3–5).

Intercession
1785

Zacharias
3979, 3980

Great things happened at the hour of prayer when incense was being offered. "And it came to pass at the time of the . . . evening sacrifice, that Elijah the prophet came near, and said, Lord God of Abraham, Isaac, and of Israel, let it be known this day that thou art God in Israel. . . . Then the fire of the Lord fell" (1 Kings 18:36–38).

Incense
1747

Fire
1282–1285

The smoke from the burning incense filled the sanctuary, making it fragrant with perfume, and it helped the priest to realize that he was standing on holy ground (Exod. 30:34–38). The formula for this incense was used exclusively for its intended purpose. Using it for other purposes involved serious consequences.[13]

Perfume
2624

The ascending smoke is suggestive of various spiritual truths. The central message for us is its symbolization of prayer and communion with God. "There is something in the sense of smell which is perhaps finer than any other of the senses. The perfume which this sense appropriates is almost like the breath of nature, expressing the finer sensibilities of the soul of the

151

natural world. And the fragrance became an expression of the sweet breath of prayer and it is the chosen emblem of the heart's homage to our heavenly Father.[14] The perpetually burning fire in the censer is a reminder of our Lord's continual intercession at the right hand of God the Father Almighty (Heb. 7:25).

Holy of Holies
1599

VII. THE HOLY OF HOLIES (EXOD. 26:31–33; Heb. 10:20)

The central part of the tabernacle complex was the tabernacle itself, composed of two rooms. The outer room, the Holy Place, was twice as large as the inner room or the Holy of Holies (see Part VI in this chapter). The Holy of Holies is sometimes referred to as the "inner sanctum." This room was beyond the veil (cloth curtain separating the two sanctuaries) where God met the high priest on the Day of Atonement.

Veil
3745, 3746

A. *The Ark of the Covenant*

Ark of the
Covenant
216

Incense
1747

The Ark of the Covenant was the only piece of furniture in this sanctuary, except on the Day of Atonement when the altar of incense was taken inside for the day. The Ark served also as the mercy seat. The acacia wood out of which the ark was made is again suggestive of Christ's humanity, and the gold with which it was overlaid symbolized his deity. "The Ark being placed in the Holy of Holies is a type of Christ in glory in the presence of God the Father." [15] The Shekinah glory, typifying God's presence, hung over the Ark of the Covenant (Exod. 40:35).

Holy of Holies
1599

Shekinah
2502

Mercy Seat
2303

Moses was instructed to begin the construction of the tabernacle by making the Ark of the Covenant. The lid covering it was called the mercy seat. The two cherubim of gold on the cover were symbols of the presence and the approachableness of the Lord (Exod. 25:10ff.). God began the redemptive plan from the focal point, while man appropriates it from the peripheral. God initiates the redemptive plan at the mercy seat while man appropriates the redemptive provision at the

Brazen Altar
122

Laver
2051

Incense
1747

Shewbread
3269

Candlestick
637

brazen altar. At the altar the sin problem is settled for time and eternity.

The steps in the tabernacle blueprint were sevenfold. "First, the seeker made a decision at the gate; second, he made provision for his acceptance at the brazen altar; third, he was ceremonially cleansed at the brazen laver; fourth, he made intercession at the altar of incense; fifth, he had communion and fellowship at the table of shewbread; sixth, he testified at the golden candlestick, and seventh, his faith turned into sight within the veil." [16]

The ark contained three objects:

1. The Two Tables of the Law (Exod. 19; 20:1–17; Matt. 22:36–40)

These tables were a testimony to the law of God as given to Moses and recorded in the Pentateuch (Exod. 20:1–17). The law of God contained three areas, namely the moral law, the civil law, and the ceremonial law. "The law, which man could not keep, was deposited within the ark of the covenant and beneath the mercy seat." [17]

2. The Golden Pot of Manna (Exod. 16:11–31; Num. 11:1–9)

The manna supplied the physical needs of the people on their pilgrimage even as Christ supplies the Christian's spiritual needs as he goes on his journey to the "promised land." The manna came down from heaven as Christ himself came down from above. As Christ came in a supernatural manner, so the manna fell in a miraculous way. As the manna came in the night time, so the Lord came in the world's night of sin, when man was steeped in formalism and the "traditions of men" rather than in true repentance and faith (Matt. 15:1–9).

3. Aaron's Rod that Budded (Num. 16–17)

Aaron's rod "budded . . . and bloomed . . . and yielded almonds" (Num. 17:8). The budding of this rod confirmed a God-chosen priesthood.

The room in which the ark was located was a perfect cube. Above the ark hovered the Shekinah glory. Once each year, on the Day of Atonement, the high priest carrried the names of the people on his breast and shoulders and made peace with God for their sins. The Holy of Holies was the secret place of the Most High where all repentant sinners were represented through the high priest. A view of the inside was obstructed by the veil. Now the veil has been rent in twain and all believers are priests in the faith and may go personally to the mercy seat. When the sinner meets the condition of repentance for sin at the foot of the cross, the veil for him becomes "rent in twain" and it is then that he can rejoice over the invitation: "Having therefore, brethren, boldness to enter into the holiest by the blood of Jesus, by a new and living way, which he hath consecrated for us, through the veil, that is to say, his flesh; and having an high priest over the house of God; let us draw near with a true heart in full assurance of faith, having our hearts sprinkled from an evil conscience, and our bodies washed with pure water" (Heb. 10:19–22).

On the Day of Atonement the high priest sacrificed a bullock for himself and his fellow priests. The censer with live coals

A Christological Study of the Tabernacle (Heb. 9:1–28)

Tables of Stone **3543**
Testimonies **3598**

Manna **2248**

Traditions **3652**

Rod **3092, 3093**

Ark **216**

Holy of Holies **1599**

Veil **3745, 3746**

Flesh **1290**

Day of Atonement **305**

153

was placed inside the Holy of Holies so that the smoke might cover the mercy seat. The priest then sprinkled blood from the bullock upon the mercy seat and the floor.

After the high priest made an atonement for himself and his house (Lev. 16:6), he presented two goats "before the LORD at the door of the tabernacle of the congregation. And Aaron . . . cast lots upon the two goats; one lot for the LORD, and the other lot for the scapegoat. . . . And Aaron shall lay both his hands upon the head of the live goat, and confess over him all the iniquities of the children of Israel, and all their transgressions and all their sins, putting them upon the head of the goat, and shall send him away by the hand of a fit man into the wilderness: and the goat shall bear upon him all their iniquities unto a land not inhabited: and he shall let go the goat in the wilderness" (Lev. 16:7,8,21,22).

The blood of the goat killed for a sin offering was taken within the veil and sprinkled upon and before the mercy seat "because of the uncleanness of the children of Israel, and because of their transgressions in all their sins" (Lev. 16:16).

The time the high priest spent behind the veil was always an occasion of anxiety and suspense. As long as the high priest moved about behind the veil, the golden bells gave forth a tinkling sound and the people knew that all was well. Silence in the inner sanctum indicated that the priest had completed his ministration before the Lord, and he was standing before the mercy seat waiting for the Lord to indicate his pleasure by a movement of the Shekinah or pillar of cloud.

Tradition has it that a scarlet cord was tied around the high priest's leg so that he could be dragged out if he suffered death inside. It meant certain death for the high priest if he went into the presence of the Lord without being ceremonially clean and fit to officiate for the people. Only holy, set-aside people could come into the presence of the Lord God (Exod. 19:22; cf. 2 Sam. 6:7,8).

There was a season of rejoicing among the worshipers when the short period of silence was broken by the tinkling bells. The sounding of the bells meant that all was well and that sin had been expiated for that year.

VIII. THE VEIL (EXOD. 25:31–37; HEB. 9–10)

The inner veil separating the two sanctuaries was a thing of beauty and is a reminder of Christ. It hung upon four pillars and on it were embroidered golden cherubim (Exod. 27:31) which indicated that this was the dwelling place of deity. The white in the curtain symbolized Christ's purity; the blue his flawless character, the purple his royal nature, and the scarlet his sacrifice for sin. The Epistle to the Hebrews states that the veil was a type of the flesh of Christ (10:20). The human frame that Christ took upon himself was a veil which hid the inner glory of the divine life. Once during his life on the earth that glory burst through the veil, on the mount of transfiguration.[18]

A Christological Study of the Tabernacle (Heb. 9:1–28)

Veil
3745, 3746

IX. THE HIGH PRIEST'S ROBE (EXOD. 28)

A study of the tabernacle would not be complete without directing some attention to the symbolic truth in the high priest's robe. Every part and appointment were designed to convey spiritual truth. Moses was commanded to "make holy garments for Aaron" (Exod. 28:2). These served as object lessons in God's plan of redemption:

Garments
1050

A. The Ephod and the Robe (Exod. 28:6ff.)

The ephod was an upper garment worn by the high priest during his official ministrations. It contained the same brilliant colors as those found in the veil. Heretofore the white, blue, purple, and scarlet were manifest only in the hangings of the tabernacle and court, but now the colors are brought into a more personal relationship. The high priest wore these brilliant colors upon his own body, which is suggestive of the personal relationship all believers have to Christ. The ephod was suspended by two shoulder straps, one over each shoulder. On each shoulder strap was an onyx stone encased in a setting of gold and engraved, each with the names of six tribes of Israel (Exod. 28:9; 39:6,7).

Ephod
1143

The robe was distinct from the ephod itself and was fringed at the bottom with bells of gold alternating with pomegranates of blue, purple, and scarlet (Exod. 28:31–35; 39:22–26). "The small golden bells were attached to the lower part of the official blue robe of the high priest in order to send forth a sound that might be heard when he went into the holy place before the Lord" [19] (Exod. 28:35).

Priest's Robe
1050

B. The Girdle (Exod. 28:8)

The girdle is functional as well as emblematic of service. Truly, service characterizes the life of Christ. "He went about doing good." The lame were healed, the palsied were made whole, the blind were given their sight, and the demon-possessed were restored to sanity. Even now his good work continues "seeing he ever liveth to make intercession for [us]" (Heb.

Girdle
1420, 1421

7:25). Christ is a "minister of the sanctuary, and of the true tabernacle, which the Lord pitched, and not man" (Heb. 8:2).

C. The Onyx Stones (Exod. 28:9,14)

Onyx
2856

The onyx stones were mounted on the shoulder pieces and on each stone were engraved the names of six tribes of Israel "according to their birth" (Exod. 28:10). The stones were to be in plain view of everyone and gave continual testimony to the watchful care of the priest over his people. They were kept constantly before the Lord. The high priest was divinely instructed to "put the two stones upon the shoulders of the ephod for stones of memorial unto the children of Israel" (Exod. 28:12).

Memorial
3004

This concern of the high priest for his people is suggestive of Christ the high priest's continual care. "He ever liveth to make intercession" for his own (Heb. 7:25). The name of each child of God is engraved in the Lamb's book of life and it is comforting to know that "he cares for us."

Intercession
1785

Breastplate
540, 541

D. The Breastplate (Exod. 28:15–29)

The breastplate, made out "of gold, of blue, and of purple, and of scarlet, and of fine twined linen" (Exod. 28:15) was square. Twelve precious and semiprecious stones were mounted on it. Moses was commanded to "set in it settings of stones, even four rows of stones" (Exod. 28:17).

Each tribe had its own stone on which its name was engraved. No two were alike. There was a sardius (ruby), a topaz, a carbuncle, an emerald, a sapphire, a diamond, a ligure, an agate, an amethyst, a beryl, an onyx, and a jasper (Exod. 28:17ff.).

The breastplate was suspended on the high priest's chest by two chains of gold. By divine instruction Aaron was to "bear the names of the children of Israel in the breastplate . . . for a memorial before the Lord continually" (Exod. 28:29). The breastplate had a function somewhat related to the onyx stones on the shoulders of the high priest, but assigned a single stone to each tribe. For Israel this symbolized the watchful care of the Lord, not only over Israel as a nation but over individual tribes. For the believers this is suggestive of the personal interest God directs to each individual.

Urim and
Thummin
2497

156

E. The Urim and the Thummin (Exod. 28:30)

The Hebrew meaning of these words is "lights" and "perfections." These objects were placed underneath the breastplate next to the high priest's heart. With Urim and Thummin the high priest learned the will of God in doubtful cases. Through these devices the perfect will of God was ascertained for the nation. This is suggestive of Christ, the High Priest who reveals the Father's will. "What satisfaction it is to know that the One who . . . pleads man's cause with the Father has unlimited power, fathomless love, and unsearchable wisdom. What a settled peace should be ours in the consciousness of this!" [20]

A Christological Study of the Tabernacle (Heb. 9:1–28)

F. The Mitre and the Plate of Gold (Exod. 28:36–38)

Mitre
2387

The Lord instructed Moses to "make a plate of pure gold, and grave upon it, like the engravings of a signet, HOLINESS TO THE LORD" (Exod. 28:36). This plate was to be suspended upon Aaron's forehead. The head of the high priest was "crowned with the symbol of holiness and righteousness, an important factor for those who hold the responsibility of leadership and particularly those who lead in religious affairs. This was decidedly true of the Lord Jesus Christ the great High Priest. His was holiness in the . . . fullest sense of the word." [21] As believers in Christ what could be a more fitting heart attitude than holiness to the Lord?

High Priest
2064

G. The Linen Coat and Breeches (Exod. 28:39–43)

Linen
2185

The high priest and his sons wore the linen coat and breeches. "The linen typifies righteousness, and . . . God, clothes each believer with the righteousness [Rev. 19:8] that is in Christ. . . . Is there anything about us to indicate to others that we are sons of God? Do we have in our lives a well-balanced fruitage and testimony represented by the alternate arrangement of the pomegranates and bells? . . . Are we consecrated to His service, holy unto the Lord? These are some of the questions all believers might ask themselves." [22]

The Political-Religious Events
Between the Testaments

I. The Pre-Persian Period (1000–430 B.C.)

Israel
1807–1829

Judah
1956

Apostasy
1235
Assyrians
300
Asa
265
Uzziah
3744
Hezekiah
1585
Josiah
1923

Zedekiah
3988, 3989

Babylon
329–331

Arch. Babylon
4334

Synagogues
3521–3523

158

The Golden Age of Israel was ushered in by David and Solomon about 930 B.C. Eventually the United Kingdom was divided into two parts—the North (Israel) and the South (Judah). Jeroboam, an Ephraimite, ruled the Northern Kingdom, and Rehoboam, the son of Solomon, reigned over the South. All of the kings of the North gave their allegiance to the heathen Baal gods. Worshiping idols finally led to the destruction of the Northern Kingdom. In 721 B.C. the Assyrians conquered Israel and took many of its leading citizens into captivity. Judah had its idolatrous kings, too, but a few God-fearing kings such as Asa, Jehosaphat, Uzziah, Hezekiah, and Josiah were able to bring the nation back from the brink of disaster. However, these times of revival were finally overshadowed by four evil kings, who brought about the downfall of Judah. During the reign of Zedekiah the conquering hordes of Babylon broke down the city walls and levelled both the temple and the city to the ground in 586 B.C.

Most of the inhabitants were taken into captivity in Babylon. To all outward appearances, the nation's political and religious existence had been dealt a mortal blow. But the result was that the captive years for Judah became actually a period of spiritual growth; the synagogue developed during this time, giving the Jews worship centers within easy reach of all members in the community. (See page 62.) Many of these small centers were in the homes, and thus the people lost their dependence upon the temple and its hierarchy. The synagogue was basically a layman's institution, another example of laymen preserving the faith in troubled times.

Under Ezra the holy records were codified and organized into what later became the OT. Another benefit accruing from the captivity was that the Jews lost interest in Baal worship. There was no longer a question as to who the God of Abraham, Isaac, and Jacob was. For them Yahweh was the living God, the creator of the universe. Another benefit came from the miraculous power which God manifested in their midst. During the seventy years of captivity, God revealed his supernatural power in the lives of Daniel and the three Hebrew children. God demonstrated that he could preserve faith in the lion's jaws as well as in the heat of the fiery furnace (Dan. 3:27). Finally God showed his mighty power by sending a friendly nation to conquer Babylon and set the captives free.

Ezra
1199
Baal
3936

Daniel
914

II. THE PERSIAN PERIOD (430–332 B.C.)

Following the Jews' return to Palestine, many of them scattered all over the Tigris-Euphrates river area including Persia, taking with them their faith, their synagogue service, and their holy oracles. They gave witness to the true and living God in the far outreaches of the heathen world.

Persia
2744

Through the conquest of Babylon by Cyprus, God provided a sympathetic deliverer for the Jews in exile. During Belshazzar's feast in the great banquet hall in Babylon, detached fingers of a man's hand wrote a frightening message on the wall. It read: "MENE, MENE, TEKEL, UPHARSIN," which meant: "God hath numbered thy kingdom and finished it. Thou art weighed in the balances, and art found wanting. Thy kingdom is divided, and given to the Medes and Persians" (Dan. 5:5,25–28). During the night the great king of Babylon was slain. Persian engineers had diverted the bed of the Euphrates River around the city. The next morning, under the direction of Cyrus, the Persians marched their army over the drained riverbed and captured the city. Both Darius and Cyrus, Persian kings, are mentioned as rulers of Babylon.[1] (For more information on the Cyrus-Darius problem see page 308.)

Babylon
329–331, 4334

God's Judgment
1966–1974

Cyrus
907
Darius
915–917

When Babylon was conquered, Cyrus immediately decreed that the Jews were free and that they could return to Judea. It seems clear that the hand of God was at work to provide a new political power that would be friendly to the Jews. By the Edict of Cyrus (Ezra 1:2–4) the prophecy of Jeremiah was fulfilled to the letter (Jer. 25:12,13). However, many of the Jews were well established in business and in the political life of Babylon and Persia and had no interest in going back to Jerusalem. On the other hand, priests and the religious party

Jeremiah
1877

159

wished to reestablish temple worship. The older people and the poor had nothing to lose but a great deal to gain by returning to Jerusalem; so they joined the religious group for the trek back to the land of their forefathers.[2]

In addition to providing financial help for the venture, Cyrus returned to the Jews the sacred gold and silver vessels which

Nebuchadnezzar had taken from the temple. An offering was received from "the chief of the fathers of Judah and Benjamin" (Ezra 1:5,6; see also 6:1–5). Not only did the people and the priests take an offering among themselves, but also Darius and his counselors offered expense money for tribute, bullocks, lambs, and rams for their sacrifices, as well as silver and gold for the reconstruction of Jerusalem (Ezra 6:8,9; 7:15,16).

The question has been raised: Why did Cyrus befriend the Jews? Some have suggested that Daniel showed Cyrus some of the prophecies which had been fulfilled by Babylon's conquest (Jer. 25:11,12; 29:10). The prophecy by Isaiah concerning the "dry river" must have attracted the king's attention (Isa.

44:26–28). It seems that Cyrus was a willing and ready agent whom God could use to carry out his divine purpose. Cyrus freely acknowledged the hand of the Lord in these words: "The LORD God of heaven hath given me all the kingdoms of the earth; and he hath charged me to build him an house at Jerusalem, which is in Judah" (Ezra 1:2).

Under the friendly dominion of Persia and with little or no political or military responsibility, Jerusalem once again became the center of Jewish national life. However, when the Persians extended their military power into Greek territory, they suffered a crushing defeat at Salamis in 479 B.C. The decisive battle was at Issus when Alexander defeated Xerxes; this ended Persian influence in Europe. When Greece finally gained control of Palestine from the Persians, the Jews continued to enjoy favor and freedom.

III. THE GREEK PERIOD (331–167 B.C.)

The origin of the Greek state is uncertain. A scholarly guess is that it began in about the twelfth century B.C., about the

time the Hebrews arrived in Canaan under Joshua, or perhaps in the period of the Judges. The Trojan war occurred in 1193–

1184 B.C. The Homeric age was parallel to the time of David and Solomon's reign (1043–933 B.C.). Reliable history makes reference to the first Olympiad in 776 B.C. The Hellenistic states were formed in the period between 776 and 500 B.C. Then came the Persian wars, culminating with the battles of

Thermopylae and Salamis in 480 B.C. In 336 B.C. Alexander the Great, at the age of 20, assumed command of the Greek army and swiftly conquered Egypt, Syria, Babylon, Persia, and the lands beyond. After reaching the Indus Valley (326 B.C.) he is said to have wept for more worlds to conquer. Throughout the conquered area Alexander established Hellenism—the dissemination of Greek ideas, learning, dress, customs, festivals, and athletic contests. The Greek language became the *lingua franca,* the common language of the realm.

The Political-Religious Events Between the Testaments

The Egyptian city of Alexandria was founded in honor of the great conqueror and became an example of Hellenistic culture and learning. At the invitation of Alexander, multiplied thousands of Jews moved to Alexandria, where they were introduced to Greek culture and the Greek language. Many of the Jews developed a Hellenistic form of Judaism. In the middle of the third century B.C. the Greek-speaking Jews produced the Septuagint—the Greek Old Testament (see X of this chapter).

Alexandria
114, 4325

Dispersed Jews
1023

When Alexander died in Babylon at the age of 33, his empire was divided among his several generals. Most prominent were the two whose dynasties would have lasting importance for the Near East area. Seleucus gained control of Syria and Ptolemy took control of Egypt. Palestine went first to Syria and then to Egypt, where it remained until 198 B.C. Under the kings of Egypt, called the "Ptolemies," the Jews enjoyed peace and tranquillity. They built many synagogues in Alexandria, and through their economic and political participation the city became a great center of Judaism.

Syria
3524

Egypt
1100

Antiochus III (the Great) (223–187 B.C.) reconquered Palestine in 198 B.C., and it reverted to the kings of Syria, called the "Seleucids." When Antiochus IV (175–164 B.C.) ascended the throne, he assumed the name of Antiochus Epiphanes (the manifest [god]). Bitterly opposed to the Jews, he made a determined effort to strengthen Hellenism. At the same time he took steps to exterminate the Jews and their religion. The final break came in 167 B.C. shortly after Antiochus was forced to withdraw from Egypt on Roman orders. Treating Jerusalem as an enemy city, he loosed his army upon it; the result was widespread death, looting, and destruction.[3] This utter lack of feeling and respect for the Jews made the ensuing rebellion of 166 B.C. inevitable (1 Macc.).

IV. THE MACCABEAN (INDEPENDENCE) PERIOD (167–63 B.C.)

In 198 B.C. Palestine passed back to Syrian control under the Seleucids (see the Greek Period, III in this chapter). Later, in 175–164 B.C. a violent outrage developed against the Jews under Antiochus Epiphanes III. Being hard pressed for funds to carry on his feud with the Ptolemies, Antiochus increased the tax levy against the Jews and offered the position of high priest to the highest bidder. He removed the rightful high priest, Onias, from office and installed a man named Jason, who agreed to assist Antiochus in his effort to Hellenize the Jewish nation. Jason built a gymnasium in Jerusalem and forced some of the Jewish males to submit to surgery to disguise their circumcision and then to participate in the sports in the nude (I Macc. 1:14–15). Many of the Jews were horrified. To chal-

lenge this blasphemous practice, an opposition party, called Hasidim (Pious ones) was organized. The Hasidim fought bravely against efforts to impose Greek customs upon them because to them these practices were very immoral. In desperation, Antiochus finally decided to destroy the religion of the Jews by forbidding the practice of Judaism in all of its forms and by erecting in the Jewish temple an altar to Zeus and

offering upon it the flesh of a sow. Heathen altars were set up all over the country. The Jews were commanded to worship at them and to eat food forbidden by the Torah, but the Hasidim refused to obey.

Finally the Jews revolted under the leadership of a priest named Matthias and his five sons. Foremost among the sons was Judas. Matthias summoned all the faithful Jews to join him in a war of resistance against Antiochus. Immediate support came from the Hasidim. Matthias died shortly thereafter and his leadership was quickly assumed by Judas, whose nickname was Maccabeus—"the Hammer."

In December 164 B.C., three years after the temple was desecrated, Judas defeated the forces Antiochus had dispatched from Syria to Jerusalem and declared a state of independence. Judas immediately fortified and garrisoned the city. He gave his attention to cleaning up the temple and rededicating it to God. This event, which comes near Christmas, has been celebrated ever since as the feast of Hanukkah. The Independence period lasted about a hundred years (167–63 B.C.).

V. THE ROMAN PERIOD (63 B.C. TO A.D. 638)

The eighth century B.C. saw the founding of Rome, and the fifth century, the organization of a republican form of government. Two centuries of war with the North African rival city of Carthage ended in victory for Rome (146 B.C.). The great Roman general and statesman, Pompey, conquered Jerusalem in 63 B.C., making it a part of the greater Roman Empire. Rome's representative in Syria, Hyrcanus II, a son of Alexandra and her husband Alexander Janneus, was appointed high priest.

Antipater, an Idumean (descendant of Esau), was appointed ruler of Judea; he faithfully carried out the policies of Rome.

In 40 B.C., Herod became ruler of both Judea and Samaria, with the title of king. However, disturbances in Jerusalem made it impossible for him to ascend the throne until 37 B.C., after which he ruled until 4 B.C., the time of Jesus' birth. During Herod's rule, Peraea in Trans-Jordan, Galilee, and the territory north and east of the sea of Galilee were added to his kingdom. Because of his political skill, Herod proved to be one of the most successful of Rome's puppet rulers. He came to be known as Herod the Great. Under him a degree of law and order was restored in troubled Palestine. He set the country as a buffer state between Rome's territories and the hostile Arab tribes, who constantly threatened Rome's lines of communication.

Herod gave support to the imperial cult and built many temples honoring Augustus Caesar. He also built gymnasiums, theatres, and stadiums to encourage the Hellenistic way of life.[4] However, to maintain a semblance of peace in his territory, Herod was forced to show some favor to the Jews. To gain their cooperation, he lowered their taxes and rebuilt the temple with great splendor. But behind the facade of friendship he filled the land with secret officials and took ruthless vengeance on any Jew who created visible dissension. He even had his favorite wife, his brother-in-law, and his two sons murdered because he was suspicious of their loyalty. When it was reported that a new king was born in his realm, he sent his soldiers out to slaughter all the male children in Bethlehem up to two years old.

In his will Herod designated his sons as his successors. The Jews, in their anxiety not to have a continuation of the Herodian dynasty to rule them, sent a petition to Rome requesting a nullification of this will. With encouragement from the Hasidim, the Jews began to riot in protest. In addition to the Hasidim there were the extremely fanatical zealots who helped to keep the spirit of the rebellion at the boiling point. To counteract this, the Roman governor in Syria was sent to put down the uprising, and shortly thereafter Augustus Caesar approved Herod's will, dividing the kingdom among his three sons.

Judea was turned over to Archelaus (4 B.C.–A.D. 6); Herod Antipas was to rule over Galilee and Peraea; and Iturea was given to Philip. During the troublesome period between A.D. 6 and 66, Rome sent at least 14 procurators to Judea. The increased tension and Jewish rejection of Hellenism made the rulers' task progressively more difficult. Many of the procurators were low-grade politicians who sought only their selfish interests. To these men, graft and immorality of every kind were an accepted way of life. They had difficulty in comprehending the Jews' religious faith and devotion to God. Pontius

Preliminary
Matters

Images
3934–3947

Samaritans
3135, 3136

Pilate (A.D. 26–36), before whom Jesus appeared, is a good example of how the procurators failed to understand the Jewish mind and heart.

Pilate's acts of poor judgment, such as bringing the military insignia, with its image of Caesar, into the holy city of Jerusalem and commanding his soldiers to attack a group of defenseless Samaritans, forced Rome to remove Pilate from office.

In A.D. 66 the situation became so critical that a revolt broke out in Jerusalem. The misrule of Florus, the last of the procurators, brought things to a climax. When the revolt raged beyond local control, Nero dispatched his star general, Vespasian, to crush the revolt with military force. Vespasian had been in command only a short time when he was proclaimed Emperor of Rome to succeed Nero. The general returned to Rome to assume the seat of government and placed military command in the hands of his son, Titus, who marched on Jerusalem and completely destroyed all resistance in Jerusalem by A.D. 70. The temple and city were completely leveled. A pall of smoke hung heavily over the ruins of what was once the proud city of Jerusalem. This brought an end to temple worship and its sacrificial system. The synagogue became the sole place of worship. Rome continued to have political influence and power in Palestine until the Mohammedan Arabs gained control of Jerusalem (A.D. 638).

VI. THE POLITICAL-RELIGIOUS PARTIES

A. *The Religious-Philosophical Background*

Generally speaking, the Jewish community was bound together by the Torah and the temple. However, as the Jews were dispersed throughout the Mediterranean world, they became more and more divorced from close association with temple worship. Out in the empire they were exposed more strongly to Hellenistic influences than in their homeland, and consequently some major differences developed which were foreign to strict Judaism with its emphasis on the teaching of the Torah and the "tradition of the elders."

Before the time of Philo, the Jewish philosopher (20 B.C.–A.D. 54), the Hellenized Jews had begun to blend the concepts of Greek philosophy with the teaching of their own sacred books. They developed the idea that the Pentateuch itself was the source of inspiration from which the Greeks developed their own philosophy. Through this syncretistic process they endeavored, by allegorical interpretations of their own books, to find indications of the profoundest doctrines of philosophy in the simplest stories of the Pentateuch.

Philo grew up in this philosophical atmosphere. He based

his own philosophy and much of his religious interpretation on certain systems of Greek philosophy, especially on that of Plato, which best harmonized with the Hebrew Scripture. Philo held that the attributes of God mentioned in the Scriptures were to be understood only figuratively. Like Plato, Philo believed that even though God was the Creator, he was extremely transcendent and too far removed to be personally involved in his own creation.[5] During the Christian era, some scholars directly borrowed from Philo, but it is doubtful whether he had ever heard of Jesus.

Alexandria, Egypt, continued to be a great center of learning and attracted many Greek as well as Hebrew philosophers. To most of the Jews in Alexandria the Hebrew language was dead. Greek had become the popular language, and consequently many Jews investigated the Hellenistic philosophies written in Greek. Clement, a bishop of Rome (A.D. 95), came to Alexandria in middle life to study philosophy. Basilides, a Greek agnostic, taught in Alexandria (A.D. 117–138). Origen (A.D. 185–254), a Christian scholar with wide travel experience and learning, was born in Alexandria and spent his life there in the study and the reproduction of the Scriptures.

Alexandria
114, 4325

Out of this changing philosophical background three reactionary parties developed, represented by the Pharisees, the Sadducees, and the Essenes. All of these were said to have had their origin during the so-called 400 silent years.

B. The Pharisees

Pharisees
3171

The Pharisees were laymen (not priests) dedicated to preserving the Mosaic Law. Their origin is not known but there is evidence that they were in existence in the time of Ezra when heathenism threatened Judaism. Their presence is more clearly pronounced during the Maccabean Revolt when heathen philosophies were creeping into Jewish religious life.

> The Pharisees . . . . [were] esteemed most skillful in the exact application of their laws . . . . but were not apt to be severe in punishments favoring "stripes and bonds" but not death.[6]

The Pharisees were the strict legalists. They stood for the rigid observance of the letter of the law, including the traditions. There were some sincere men among the Pharisees, but in the main, they were known for their self-righteous attitudes. Their aim was sometimes commendable, but by stressing the letter of the law and neglecting the spirit, they became victims of extremism. Because the Pharisees were concerned about preserving the law, they neglected that which the law intended to protect, the rights of the individual. The nature of their

Legalism
2990

Pharisees
3171
165

legalistic confusion is reflected in the Gospels, especially in the twenty-third chapter of Matthew where the Pharisees and scribes came in direct conflict with Jesus, who taught and emphasized the spirit of the law.

A more moderate spirit among the Pharisees prevailed in Gamaliel, a doctor of the law, who advised moderation when the apostles were brought before the council for teaching in the name of Jesus (Acts 5:34–39). Some Pharisees accepted Jesus as the Messiah. Among them was Saul of Tarsus (Acts 23:6ff.).

C. The Sadducees

In their origin the Sadducees seem to have been contemporaries of the Pharisees. They are mentioned by the historian Josephus.[7] Unlike the Pharisees, the Sadducees reacted against Jewish Legalism, but they favored the philosophical speculation inherent in Hellenism. They took no part in the Maccabean revolt. Although they were religious officials, at heart they were very irreligious. They were wealthy, worldly, and prominent

in the Sanhedrin. They placed high value on the law of Moses but relegated the prophetic writings to a place of lesser importance. They rejected the belief in angels, demons, evil spirits, and Jesus' resurrection. They were the extreme liberal philosophers of their day. Both the Pharisees and the Sadducees ac-

knowledged the Supremacy of the Torah, but the Sadducees held only to the written law and did not accept the traditions of the elders. Both the Sadducees and the Pharisees opposed Jesus (see Matt. 23).

D. The Essenes

Even though not mentioned in the Bible, the Essenes were active in the Jewish community during the last two centuries B.C. Their presence in the Dead Sea area is attested to by Philo, the Jewish Philosopher; Flavius Josephus, a historian of the first century A.D.; and by the Damascus Document.

The ancient historians state that the Essenes also had their origin in the period of religious protest about the same time

the Pharisees and Sadducees became active. In the days of Jesus the temple was under the control of the priests, the Pharisees, the Sadducees, and probably the Essenes. The Sanhedrin was the highest Jewish authority in matters of religious law. The Pharisees were so legalistically minded that eventually the law became an end in itself. Most of the activities in the temple were "letter of the law" legalisms. The moral and ethi-

cal teachings of the Scriptures had been abandoned long ago. One hardly finds a favorable reference to the Pharisees and

Sadducees in the NT. When Jesus arrived at the temple, he referred to it as a "den of thieves" instead of a house of worship.

The Political-Religious Events Between the Testaments

The Essenes were caught in the legalistic cross fire of the religious parties. It is not known exactly when the Essenes separated themselves from the temple and its activities and withdrew into communal settlements where they could have freedom of worship. Some scholars view the Essenes as the true "holiness people" in whom God kept the Messianic hope alive. They believe there is evidence to show that both Jesus and John the Baptist may have had contact with these people.

Messianic Hope 4186

Certainly the Savior and John the Baptist had more in common with the Essenes than with the temple hierarchy.

John the Baptist 1903

Why the Essenes are not mentioned in Scripture is only conjecture. In the first place, they were a minority group, perhaps less than 4000. Their protest against the temple hierarchy, both political and religious, culminated in a radical withdrawal from normal social and religious associations in Jerusalem. Such religious extremists were not popular and probably not thought to be worthy of public attention. Their separation and withdrawal soon resulted in complete oblivion. A parallel to this would be the absence of any reference in Egyptian records to the Hebrew residency or to the Exodus.

The prebaptism ministry of both Jesus and John the Baptist took place in Essene territory. Regardless of what the final judgment about the Essene community might be, it is obvious that, although there were differences, there are sufficient similarities between the teachings of these people and the later teachings in the Gospels, especially those of John, to form a bridge of communication between the Old and the New Covenants.

John the Baptist 760

VII. The Bridge between the Testaments

A. The Political Arena

The space of time between 400 B.C. and the birth of Christ is often referred to as the silent period because recorded OT prophecy came to an end. Divine revelation which resulted in the written word had ceased. Malachi had completed the last book in the OT canon about 400 B.C. However, this so-called silent era was one of the most active times in history.

Historical Bridge p. 179

During this interval God was setting the world stage for the presentation of his Son, the King Messiah. The prophets had told in great detail the various aspects of his coming. Some traced his lineage to Abraham, while others named the tribe of Judah as the one from which he would come. Some made reference to his miraculous conception; one prophet stated that he would be born of a virgin; another sage named Bethle-

Messianic Prophecies pp. 246–249

hem as the place where he would be born. There was a general air of expectancy in some strata of society. Simeon and Anna awaited his coming with anticipation. Heathen religions had been largely discredited. Philosophy no longer held the imagination of the people. God had already sent Jewish forerunners to every part of the Mediterranean world. These Jews, who had been scattered to the "four corners of the earth," had taken with them the synagogue, the Bible written in Greek, the universal language of that day, and also the messianic expectation. Rome, by its conquests, had made the Mediterranean an "inland sea." *Pax Romana,* the peace of Rome, eliminated international wars. Rome put the "world" under one flag. Roman roads extended to all parts of the empire, and safety, to some degree, was assured for the traveler by the Roman legions stationed along the way.

The next section presents a study in depth on the Dead Sea Scrolls. The evidence is strong to support the conclusion that the dwellers at Qumran were indeed Essenes.

B. *The Dead Sea Scrolls*

The discovery of the Dead Sea Scrolls is one of the most significant archaeological finds of the twentieth century. These scrolls constitute some of the earliest OT manuscripts known to man, dating back to within several hundred years of the autographs. In addition, there are extrabiblical books which give heretofore unknown information about the pre-Christian Jews and the "pre-Advent church." The particular scrolls to which this study makes reference are definitely of the B.C. period and have in them vivid glimpses of the period not covered in the Bible. The last few centuries before the coming of Christ are shrouded in a peculiarly silent darkness as far as written revelation is concerned. These scrolls and the OT, as well as the noncanonical apocrypha and the pseudepigrapha, give some information on the events during that period.

Many volumes have been written on the Dead Sea Scrolls, with varying shades of interpretation. An objective look at the scrolls reveals startling similarities between the pre-Messianic dwellers at the scroll community (Qumran) and the early Christian church. In the following pages, the subject materials present the affinity of the scrolls with the gospel records. On this similarity most scholars are agreed, but there are a great many differences in the interpretation of these materials.

It is quite evident that the people living in the Qumran community before the Advent practiced rituals which were similar to those of the post-Messianic church. It would be strange if this were not true, because after all, these people (probably Essenes) were representative of the devout believers in spiritual pre-Advent Judaism, as expounded by the prophets. These people were the "spiritual Israel of God."

Supervision and direction of formal temple worship had been taken over by the apostate ecclesiastical leaders within Judaism to such an extent that true worshipers found it difficult to carry on their form of worship within the religious system of the temple. A scholar of note relates that "in the Qumran texts and Damascus Document we now have considerable quantity of literature cherished and produced by a dissident group of Jews during the time when the Temple was standing, just after the composition of the latest books of the Old Testament. . . ." [8]

The pre-Advent apostasy within the established ecclesiastical temple hierarchy was so great after Christ began his public ministry that it was considered a serious religious offense to acknowledge Jesus of Nazareth as the Messiah. Offenders were removed from synagogue membership without question (John 9:22; Acts 7:51,52). Many of the faithful believers who anticipated the imminent coming of the Messiah withdrew to the Judean wilderness where they worshiped more in accordance with Judaism in the days of the prophets. The Dead Sea Scrolls and the religious movement which they represent help Bible students to comprehend and to reconstruct the spiritual situation of pre- and post-Advent Christianity. By enriching one's knowledge of Judaism in the period in which Christianity arose, the Dead Sea Scrolls supply material for a better understanding of the NT and of early Christianity.

Excommunication
752

Spiritual
Corruption
**843, 1814,
2545–2549**

Advent
1346–1348

It is significant that it was in the wilderness area, in the proximity of the Qumran community, rather than in the temple, that John the Baptist and Jesus inaugurated their public ministries. One of the scholars who took an initial lead in scroll translation and interpretation points out that instead of looking for the Jewish substrata of Christian doctrines in Pharisaic and Talmudic quarters, as had hitherto been done, henceforth the same search must be conducted from the direction of Essenism as revealed by the new documents. The gospel does not emerge out of Pharisaic Judaism. On the contrary, in the gospel accounts, Jesus was the target of the Pharisees' hostility. They spared him neither the strongest criticism nor the bitterest invective (see John 8:44).

Little is known about the background of John the Baptist and about the prebaptismal years of Jesus, but the Scripture states that in due time John presented Jesus of Nazareth as the Messiah, "the Lamb of God, which taketh away the sin of the world" (John 1:29).

Many scholars of the Dead Sea Scrolls are in agreement that

it should not be surprising to find similarity in language and thought between the early church and the Qumran community. Jesus was baptized by John the Baptist in the Jordan River during the time when the community of covenanters was flourishing not many miles away. It is further agreed that there are many points at which John's ideas resemble those expressed in the Dead Sea Scrolls. Like the covenanters he was devoted to preparing the way of the Lord in the wilderness. He insisted that without previous spiritual cleansing, bathing in water could not signify the removal of guilt. There is also a striking similarity in that the "conception of a Messianic baptism by the Holy Spirit is present also in the scrolls. The statement in the *Manual of Discipline* that at the end of this age God will cleanse men by sprinkling upon them the spirit of truth recalls John's proclamation that the Messiah will baptize His people with the Holy Ghost" [9] (Matt. 3:11; John 2:28,29; Acts 2:16–21).

Since the similarities which exist between the Gospels and the Qumran texts are striking, one can conclude that there may have been association of the two. This conclusion is justified because the dwellers at Qumran were representatives of the pre-Christian (Messianic) religion as revealed in the OT. An objective examination of the scrolls may dictate the conclusion by Burrows that "Christians should have no reluctance to recognize anticipations of Christianity in the Dead Sea Scrolls. The Gospel was given as the fulfillment of what was already revealed. God who spoke in many and various ways to the fathers by the prophets, spoke more clearly and fully in His Son." [10]

From the scribal tables and benches, as well as from the scrolls and the thousands of scroll fragments found, comes the evidence that the Qumran community was a literary center. Many of these scrolls and fragments are biblical in nature. One of the most important scrolls in this group is the Scroll of Isaiah which portrays most graphically the vicarious sufferings of the Messiah to whom these holy people were dedicated. The prophet Isaiah states, "Surely he hath borne our griefs, and carried our sorrows. . . . He was wounded for our transgressions, he was bruised for our iniquities . . . with his stripes we are healed. . . . He was oppressed, and he was afflicted" (Isa. 53:4–7).

Many of the messianic passages are in the past tense. This particular tense is also used in John 3:16, which clearly states that salvation had been provided before Christ actually died on the cross. There is a sense in which Jesus Christ had already been crucified and had already been resurrected—that is, in the mind of God—long before the Incarnation. The redemptive promise by God was as good as its ultimate fulfillment. And by faith, pre-Advent humanity could be saved.

In addition, the nonbiblical scrolls found in the Qumran area abound in matters relevant to the doctrine of redemption. According to the testimony given in the scrolls, the people residing in the covenant community believed that they constituted the "Israel of God," the spiritual seed of Abraham (Rom. 9:6; 11:5) or the remnant which preserved "the faith which was once delivered unto the saints" (Jude 3). They believed that God always had his faithful witnesses and that they were, in fact, the successors to previous "remnant" groups professing the true messianic faith.

They thought of themselves as the spiritual descendants of Moses. They were looking for a new covenant but also for the reaffirmation of the Old, which had been given in Eden and was periodically reaffirmed, not alone at Mount Sinai, but to all believers in all ages.

They considered themselves the "elect" or "chosen people," not because of their lineal descent from the patriarchs, but rather because they had responded to and had met the condition of God's redemptive plan. They had gained membership in the "household of God" by virtue of their professed faith in God's promised Messiah.

These people were not attempting to change the legal code they already had. It was their aim to assert the law and "to deliver it from the realm of darkness in which it had become engulfed . . . . and perverted by 'false expositors.' " [11]

These spiritual children of Abraham endeavored to exemplify and promulgate the spiritual intent of the Scriptures. In their writings they made reference to a teacher, not just a teacher, but a godly, righteous teacher who would come. This teacher was probably typified by the true prophets, but all of these types pointed forward to the One who would fulfill all righteousness, even the Messiah (Deut. 33:9,10; see also Acts 3:17–23). The true and righteous teachers, in contrast to the false prophets, taught the people that as Moses was raised up a prophet and teacher, to lead the church through the wilderness, so God would soon raise the Great Prophet and Teacher, the Messiah, to lead the church through the wilderness of the world. The Messiah would proclaim that which the people in the pre-Advent period had appropriated by faith and expressed. The Book of Deuteronomy asserts this view: "The LORD thy God will raise up unto thee a Prophet from the midst of thee, of thy brethren, like unto me; unto him ye shall hearken . . ." (18:15ff.; see also Acts 3:17–23). Special significance is seen in the fact that some of the fragments found in the caves indicated passionate messianic expectation.

The Political-Religious Events Between the Testaments

Salvation Promised **3122**

Chosen People **1808**

The Elect **2724**

False prophets **2100**

171

The doctrine of the new birth was understood at least in principle by these faithful believers and was considered definitely a part of divine revelation. The Qumran dwellers taught that man could see and receive the deep spiritual things of God only through an inner enlightenment. The term "remnant" had a very peculiar significance to these people because in their thinking they were actually the small remnant that would welcome the Messiah. In their *Book of Hymns,* reference to the "shining faces" identifies the people with the special enlightenment.

The Essenes believed that this enlightenment accrued membership for them, not only in a consecrated earthly brotherhood, but also in an eternal fellowship with God. This is certainly consistent with the teachings of the OT (Job 19:25–27; Dan. 12:2,3; Pss. 16:10,11; 17:15; 23:6).

The supreme authority in all theological matters was assumed by the priests ("right teachers"). The administrative functions were handled by a group of officials whose counterpart today would be stewards, deacons, elders, or presbyters. A noted scholar of the scrolls points out that "these Presbyters were known as 'the men of special holiness' and they had to undergo a year's probation before appointment" (Acts 6:1ff.).[12]

This Covenant community might be compared to the Waldensian brotherhood of the twelfth and thirteenth centuries. From a religious viewpoint the comparison is indeed suggestive of the common reaction both groups had against the doctrinal degeneration of the established hierarchy.[13] The Qumran sect held an annual conference for the discharge of community affairs which was provided for in the *Manual of Discipline,* similar to the regulative discipline which church denominations have today.

It is clear that these Covenant people present the forms of pre-Advent religion or Christianity. Here is the introduction to an order of religion and worship which took on new forms and terms after the Advent of the looked-for Messiah. Here is the religious and cultural background in which John the Baptist carried on his work and to which Jesus may have been related to a certain extent. In the Dead Sea Scrolls are the authentic forms and idioms reflected in the Gospel of John and other NT writings. It is possible that the ritualistic ideas expressed in the scrolls helped to formulate a blueprint of the religious organization which later developed in the post-Advent church. This is evidenced by the Dead Sea scriptures in which NT parallels are numerous.

The affinities between the thought and language of the Dead Sea Scrolls and that of the NT may best be gauged by a representative list of examples. By permission from the publisher a few excerpts given below show how the Dead Sea Scrolls provide a long-needed document portraying the forerunner of Christianity. In these scrolls one of the many bridges is provided over which religious entry can be made from the OT Church to the New. Gaster's work cites the following parallels:

1. The members of the community styled themselves "the elect" or "the elect of God." Compare Titus 1:1.
2. The truth of God, as revealed in His law, is constantly called the light. Compare John 1:7–9 and 8:12.
3. The "enlightened" members of the community describe themselves as "Sons of Light." Compare John 12:36.
4. In the *Book of Hymns*, the faithful frequently declare that they stand in the eternal congregation of God, and hold direct converse with Him, and share the "lot of the holy beings." Compare Eph. 2:19.
5. A basic tenet is the doctrine of the "remnant," the belief that their community constitutes the true "relic" of Israel, faithful to the Covenant. See Rom. 11:3–5.
6. The spiritual leader of the community is called "teacher" or "right teacher." In John 3:2 Jesus is hailed as the teacher sent by God. . . . So too in John 16:13.
7. In the *Manual of Discipline* is the statement that "if the community abide by the prescribed rules it will be a veritable 'Temple of God, a true holy of holies.'" Compare 1 Cor. 3:16–17.
8. In the *Manual of Discipline* there is a long passage describing the Two Ways, viz., of good and evil, light and darkness, which God sets before every man. See Matt. 7:13ff.
9. The *Manual of Discipline* quotes the famous words of Isaiah in Isa. 40:3. . . . In John 1:23, the Baptist quotes exactly the same passage in exactly the same context.[14]

A leading scholar summarizes the linkage between the OT and the NT thus:

These scrolls provide a link between the Old and New Testament periods . . . unlike the pattern of life prevailing in the Judaism of the Temple. This community observed poverty, chastity, and obedience as rigid disciplines and practiced daily baptisms. Admission to membership was highly selective. They flourished when the Christian movement was taking root. . . . It is possible that the import of this group and others like them was much stronger on Judaism (and thus on Christianity) than we had imagined before finding the scrolls.[15]

C. The Book of Psalms

Psalms
4241

The Book of Psalms provides us with another bridge over which saints pass from the OT church period into the New. This book was the hymn book of the church during the Old Covenant period and served almost exclusively as the basic hymnbook of the NT church for over fifteen hundred years. The Psalms provide a union of spirit in the church through

Praises to God
1451–1454
173

the ages. Believers find here a vehicle of expression for the soul as it endeavors to praise God for salvation. Every redemptive emotion finds an avenue of expression in the Psalm book and the Christian finds that he has a common emotional experience with his brethren of the OT. Believers can meditate upon this book and feel the same heartfelt inspiration that they receive from reading the Gospels.

Truly, the Psalms have been an exceedingly important instrument for the expression and spread of doctrine and devotion, both in the OT and the NT church periods. Expressions of praise and thanksgiving to God for the joy of salvation are found on every page. First it blesses a man, and then it offers glory to God; finally it culminates in a grand "hallelujah chorus."

In addition to praise and thanksgiving there is also present in the Psalms a prophetic spirit which recognizes the reality of Christ. Jesus certainly affirms the fact that the Psalms have Christological content when he says: "all these things must be fulfilled, which were written in the law of Moses, and in the prophets, and in the Psalms, concerning me" (Luke 24:44). In many of the Psalms one discovers elements of religious life and experience that are thoroughly Christian (Pss. 146–150). While Jesus hung on the cross his mind turned to Psalms 22:1; 31:5; 69:21. In this book a composite picture of the suffering Savior is clearly revealed. In it we read that he was patterned after the order of Melchizedek (Ps. 110:4); that he would be betrayed by a friend (Ps. 41:9); that another person would be elected to Judas' office (Ps. 109:7,8); that false witnesses would accuse him (Ps. 27:12); that he would be hated without a cause (Ps. 69:4); that his hands and feet would be pierced (Ps. 22:6–8); that he would be given gall and vinegar (Ps. 69:21); that his prophetic words would be repeated in mockery (Ps. 22:8); that he would pray for his enemies (Ps. 109:4); that soldiers would cast lots for his garments (Ps. 22:18); that not a bone would be broken in his body when he was crucified (Ps. 34:20); that he would be resurrected from the dead (Ps. 16:10); that he would ascend to heaven after his resurrection (Ps. 68:18). Many of these statements can be applied to Jesus without misconstruing their meaning.

C. S. Lewis says, "In a certain sense Our Lord's interpretation of the Psalms was common ground between Himself and His opponents. The question . . . how David can call Christ 'my Lord' (Mark 12:25–37), would lose its point unless it were addressed to those who took it for granted that the 'my Lord' referred to in Psalm 110 was the Messiah, the regal and anointed deliverer. . . . The 'scriptures' all had a 'spiritual' or second sense. Even a gentile 'God-fearer' like the Ethiopian eunuch (Acts 8:27–38) knew that the sacred books of Israel could not be understood without a guide, trained in the Judaic tradition, who could open the hidden meanings. Probably all instructed Jews in the first century saw references to the Messiah in most of those passages where Our Lord saw them; what was controversial was His identification of the Messianic King . . . with Himself." [16]

Wonderful, indeed, is the bond which unifies worshipers in the OT period with that of the New. This bond is exemplified by "Christ and the Eleven singing the second half of the Hallel (Pss. 113–118) after the transition from the Passover to the Lord's Supper; of the disciples at Jerusalem 'praising God' (Acts 2:47); of Paul and Silas imprisoned at Philippi, where 'at midnight they prayed and sang praises (Psalms) unto God' (Acts 16:25); of James urging his readers, when cheerful, to 'sing praises' (James 5:13); and of Paul similarly emphasizing the place of 'psalms and hymns and spiritual songs' . . . the NT inferentially suggests that the Church will do wisely, nevertheless to retain a large place in its liturgy for the Psalter, as a precious inspired gift of God, for the use of the NT Church." [17]

In Paul's address to the church at Corinth he observed, "when ye come together, every one of you hath a psalm . . ." (1 Cor. 14:26); and in his letter to the Ephesian and Colossian believers, a similar reference is made (Eph. 5:19; Col. 3:16).

Before the period of the Reformation, church services were usually opened with the reading or singing of a psalm. The Hebrew practice of singing psalms continued in the post-Advent church (see Pss. 62:4; 111:1; 132:16; Jer. 33:11; Ezra 3:11, and so on).

After the Reformation the Psalter was re-emphasized "so that Christ's people might once again drink freely of this fountain of salvation . . . the Psalter gave joy, courage, and strength in days of trial and danger." [18] In addition to their use in singing, many churches made a wide use of the Psalter in responsive reading. It is thought that the Psalter has contributed more to biblical unity than any other portion of the Bible, and its importance as devotional literature is seen in the fact that most editions of the New Testament include the Book of the Psalms at the end. One divine says that along with the NT, the aged Christian desires a copy of the Psalms. He passes easily from the Gospel to the Psalter and back again without the sense of shifting from one spiritual level to another. Religious experience was enjoyed and was portrayed by the ancient psalmist so well that no Christian book in the apostolic period was composed to displace the Psalms.[19]

The Political-Religious Events Between the Testaments

Gentile Believers
4038

Praises to God
1451

Singing
2472–2477

The Psalms
4241

175

D. The Hymnody of the Church

As the Psalms bring the Old and NT church together, so the Christian hymns evolving after the Reformation attest their OT ancestry. The frequent references to OT places, persons, and things in Christian hymns suggest a common theology, doctrine, and background. "I will sing my great Jehovah's praise" and "When I see the blood I will pass over you" or "Just inside the Eastern Gate" are just a few of the terms and phrases compatible to the OT church. Our hymnody contains many selections whose terminal points are found in the Book of Isaiah: "Holy, Holy, Holy" comes from Isaiah 6:3; "O Zion Haste" was inspired by Isaiah 12:6; "Heralds of Christ" came into being out of Isaiah 40:3–5; Toplady's "Rock of Ages" owes its origin to Isaiah 32:2; "Savior, Like a Shepherd Lead Us"

was born out of Isaiah 44:28, and "All Hail the Power of Jesus' Name" came from Isaiah 28:16. Many other great Christian classics in the realm of music find their inspiration in the Book of Isaiah. Foster's solo, "Fear not, I am with Thee" has Isaiah 43:5 for its foundation; Simper's anthem, "Sing, O Heaven," comes from Isaiah 44:23; and Harker's solo, "How Beautiful upon the Mountains," finds expression in Isaiah 52:7. The solo by Roberts, "Seek ye the Lord," is keyed to Isaiah 55:6, and Handel's *Messiah*, the greatest of all musical compositions, draws over one-third of its texts from the Book of Isaiah.

Isaiah is influential in our Christian hymnody because he was dedicated to the Christ of the Bible. Most of our Protestant hymnals contain many references to the OT subjects including the saints. For example, one of the poets related Jesus to a common heaven with the prophets of the OT: "Jesus my all, to heaven has gone . . . the way the holy prophets went." In another hymn we read: "Hail to the brightness of Zion's glad morning, long by the prophets of Israel foretold." Another poet refers to the common loyalty of the OT prophets and the apostles to Christ, the Word: "For our Prophets and Apostles, Loyal to the living Word; For all heroes of the Spirit, Give we thanks to Thee, O Lord." In another hymn we read about the affinity between the two Testaments:

> Join, O Man, the deathless voices,
> Child of God, lift up thy head!
> Patriarchs from the distant ages,
> Saints all longing for their heaven,
> Prophets, psalmists, seers and sages,
> All await the glory given.

The NT poets not only emphasize the theological unity between the Testaments but also make reference to "The God of Abraham . . . who was, and is, and is to be . . . the same one Eternal God." Another poet shows that "poet, prophet and saint received his word from this one Eternal God." In another hymn OT and NT saints have a common cause: "Finding, following, keeping, struggling, Is He sure to bless? Saints, apostles, prophets, martyrs, Answer, Yes." In some hymns OT saints and their relationship to the Savior are projected into NT thought patterns: "Hail to the Lord's annointed, Great David's greater Son!" [20] (See VII. C. of this chapter for a discussion of the Psalms.)

E. The Liturgy of the Church

In the liturgy of the church one again finds compatibility with the religion of the OT. In our responsive readings frequent reference is made to the Psalms and other OT texts. On Palm Sunday we read responsively selections from Psalms 40 and 45, and on Good Friday we read from Psalm 22. Ascension Day calls for readings from Psalm 21. Selections from the Psalms and/or other OT books appear in almost every responsive selection, and this is as it should be since the entire OT abounds in references to Christ. It is Christ, and only Christ, who makes the OT alive and pulsating with redemptive life; take Christ out of the OT and we have remaining only a lifeless religious shell.

Many other bridges could be cited which provide free and easy passage between the Testaments. The Lord's Supper is a bridge over which participants in the Passover can readily pass. Baptism is a bridge over which the circumcised in heart of the OT can readily travel; and transfiguration of our Lord provided a bridge over which Moses and Elijah could pass to earth from the heavenly shore.

Lord's Supper
761

Baptism
Enjoined
756

F. The Ekklesia (Church) (Also see Ch. 10, III.)

A single word can be a most powerful link between periods of time. The Greek word *ekklesia* is such a term, forming an undeniable bridge between the church in the OT period and the church in the NT period.

This word *ekklesia* comes to us from the classical Greek, meaning an assembly such as a political group or gathering. The ecclesiastical writers appropriated this term to designate a religious community comprising members on earth or saints in heaven or both. Strictly speaking, it is used when reference is made to the "called out ones" or the "believers in the Lord's Christ-Messiah." This term is never used to designate a church building, nor is there reference in the NT to such a structure.

In the third century before Christ the Greek language be-

Church the
body of Christ
726

177

came dominant in the Mediterranean world, and in the middle of this century the Hebrew Bible was translated into Greek because Hebrew was an almost forgotten language among the dispersed Jews. When Paul and the early missionaries began their journeys to announce the glad tidings that Jesus of Nazareth was indeed the Messiah, they went to the synagogues in which the Greek OT was used. It can be demonstrated that most of the OT quotations in the NT use the terminology of the Septuagint (Greek OT) rather than the Massoretic text (Hebrew OT). It can be said that even the Greek language provided a religious inter-Testament bridge. The ekklesia in the NT takes its name and primary idea from the qahal of the OT. The qahal of the OT is a continuing idea in the NT and becomes the ekklesia (church).

Although the term "church" is understood by many to mean an institution brought into existence on the day when the Holy Spirit baptized a certain group in the Upper Room, let us ask ourselves: Were these Holy Ghost–baptized people saints or sinners? Does the Holy Spirit baptize sinners? Obviously not. Those in the Upper Room already bore the mark of the cross and had the blood applied before they assembled there.

Let us consider the facts. The English word *church* appears many times in the Authorized (King James) Version of the NT. To be specific, it appears three times in the Gospels and about seventy-eight times in the entire NT. However, the fact that *church* in the English language is used in reference to both a building and the body of Christ, has caused no end of confusion—perhaps more than has been caused by any other key term of the NT.

It can then be asked which Greek word has been translated "church." The answer is *ekklesia,* which means the "called out ones." The term defies translation, and should be transliterated in all versions and tongues. The ekklesia is the institution in which saints of all ages find their repose. This term is equally at home in the Greek OT and the Greek NT.

Fenton Hort, once Professor of Divinity at Cambridge and cocompiler with Brooke Foss Westcott, of the Greek text, makes this observation: "The English term 'church,' now the most familiar representative of 'Ekklesia' to most of us, carries with it associations derived from the institutions and doctrines of later times, and thus cannot, at present, without mental effort, be made to convey the full and exact force which originally belonged to Ekklesia." [21]

Scholars are generally agreed that the Greek word *ekklesia* could also be translated "congregation," and was thus rendered in most English versions throughout Henry VIII's reign. The Geneva revisers translated *ekklesia* to read "church," and it was the accepted rendering in the authorized version of 1911. The general conclusion among scholars is that the only neutral word to denote the church is the transliteration of *ekklesia*, pointing back to the beginning of Christianity. It is impossible to fully understand the actual ekklesia of postapostolic times without first gaining some clear impressions of the ekklesia of the apostles from which it came. In the lifetime of our Lord such language was peculiarly likely to be misunderstood by the outer world of Jews, and therefore it is not surprising if it formed no part of his ordinary public teaching.

As a final consideration, let it be noted that the passage in Matthew 18:17 uses the term *ekklesia* in a sense of something already in existence. Here the Lord is speaking not of the future but of the present, instructing his disciples how to deal with an offending brother. In a functional sense the ekklesia was already in existence during the lifetime of our Lord, as it was in the wilderness with the Hebrews on their way to Canaan (Acts 7:38).

In the major passages of Matthew 16:16–18, Jesus addresses Peter in Caesarea Philippi, and evokes from him the confession, "Thou are the Christ, the Son of the living God." In turn the Lord says to Peter: "I say also unto thee, That thou art Peter [*Petros*] and upon this rock [*petra*, Peter's confession] I will build my church [*ekklesia*] and the gates of hell shall not prevail against it." Here there is no question of a partial or narrowly located ekklesia. The congregation of God in the OT is what the disciples must have come to understand to be the meaning of the church which was, for the present, mysterious. If one may venture for a moment to substitute the name "Israel" and read the words as "on this rock I will build my Israel," one may have at least an approximation of the probable sense. The ekklesia of ancient Israel was the "ekklesia of God," and since Jesus was confessed to be God's Messiah, our Lord could, without risk of grave misunderstanding, claim the ekklesia as his own. The ekklesia (the called out ones) of the apostles has antecedents in facts and words recorded by the Evangels and historically in the institutions and teachings of the OT.

Exhaustive Concordance of the Bible by James Strong defines the word *ekklesia* thus: "a calling out . . . . a popular meeting, especially a religious congregation (Jewish Synagogue, or Christian community of members on earth or saints in heaven, or both): assembly, church." The precise meaning of the term in the OT is a common one. The Greek OT (Septuagint) renders the OT term *qahal* as "ekklesia." Two important words are used in the Hebrew OT for the gathering of the people of Israel or their representative heads: *edhah*, translated "congregation"; and *qahal*, rendered "assembly" in the Revised Ver-

The Political-Religious Events Between the Testaments

God a Rock
3178

Apostles
2080–2082

179

sion. "Synagogue" is the usual, almost the universal, Septuagint rendering of *edhah;* "synagogue" is also the usual translation of *qahal* in the earlier books of the Pentateuch (see Ch. 10, II). It is well to remember that the use of these terms in a biblical sense has to do with a group of people who are followers of God.

Fenton Hort says, "In the NT period the term 'Ekklesia' already has a history of its own, and was associated with the whole history of Israel. . . . Its antecedents, as . . . used by our Lord and His Apostles, are of two kinds, derived from the past and present respectively. The most important meaning came from its ancient, or religious use. This is the sense in which it was used in the Jewish Scriptures. This was combined with the senses in which it was still current in the everyday life of the Jews . . . ." [22]

The actual word *ekklesia,* as many know, is confined in the Gospels to two passages in Matthew (which was written to the Jews) where Peter's name is used in connection with building the Messiah's ekklesia. Thus the way was paved for the use of this term by the apostles in that it was founded on an impressive saying of Christ the Lord. What he declared that he would build was in one sense old, and in another new. It had a true continuity with the ekklesia of the Old Covenant; the building of it would be a rebuilding, as suggested in Acts 15:16, where James quotes Amos 9:11, "In that day will I raise up the tabernacle of David that is fallen, and close up the breaches thereof; and I will raise up his ruins, and I will build it as in the days of old." Hence, this single word, *ekklesia,* forms another bridge between the OT and the NT. The chart on page 181 (p. 179 of TCRB) shows some of the inter-testamental relationships.

VIII. The Sacraments and Their Changing Modes

Baptism and the Lord's Supper (referred to by some as "sacraments" or "ordinances") are related to something sacred, consecrated, and, in a sense, shrouded in mystery. This word *sacrament* does not appear in the Bible, but it has a biblical connotation and is used to denote a religious ceremony or an act observed and instituted first by divine revelation and later by Christ the Lord. By participating in the sacrament or ordinance the recipient acknowledged his salvation faith and testified to the world around him that he had received divine grace. By the very nature of the sacraments, they are usually conferred upon the recipient by an ordained minister—a man who has gone through the disciplines of grace and has the seal of approval by his own people and also by the church officials

THE HISTORICAL BRIDGE

SPANNING THE INTERVAL BETWEEN THE OLD AND NEW TESTAMENTS, 400 B.C.--4 or 5 B.C.

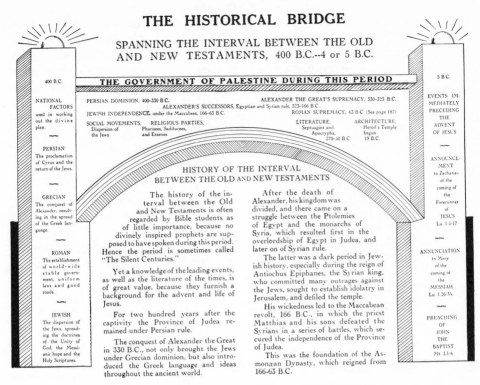

400 B.C.

THE GOVERNMENT OF PALESTINE DURING THIS PERIOD

5 B.C.

NATIONAL FACTORS used in working out the divine plan.

PERSIAN DOMINION, 400-330 B.C.
ALEXANDER'S SUCCESSORS, Egyptian and Syrian rule, 323-166 B.C.
JEWISH INDEPENDENCE. under the Maccabees, 166-63 B.C.

ALEXANDER THE GREAT'S SUPREMACY, 330-323 B.C.
ROMAN SUPREMACY, 63 B.C. (See page 187)

EVENTS IMMEDIATELY PRECEDING THE ADVENT OF JESUS

SOCIAL MOVEMENTS,
Dispersion of the Jews

RELIGIOUS PARTIES,
Pharisees, Sadducees, and Essenes

LITERATURE,
Septuagint and Apocrypha,
270-50 B.C.

ARCHITECTURE,
Herod's Temple begun
19 B.C.

PERSIAN
The proclamation of Cyrus and the return of the Jews.

GRECIAN
The conquest of Alexander, resulting in the spread of the Greek language.

ROMAN
The establishment of world-wide stable government, uniform laws and good roads.

JEWISH
The dispersion of the Jews, spreading the doctrines of the Unity of God, the Messianic hope and the Holy Scriptures.

HISTORY OF THE INTERVAL
BETWEEN THE OLD AND NEW TESTAMENTS

The history of the interval between the Old and New Testaments is often regarded by Bible students as of little importance, because no divinely inspired prophets are supposed to have spoken during this period. Hence the period is sometimes called "The Silent Centuries."

Yet a knowledge of the leading events, as well as the literature of the times, is of great value, because they furnish a background for the advent and life of Jesus.

For two hundred years after the captivity the Province of Judea remained under Persian rule.

The conquest of Alexander the Great in 330 B.C., not only brought the Jews under Grecian dominion, but also introduced the Greek language and ideas throughout the ancient world.

After the death of Alexander, his kingdom was divided, and there came on a struggle between the Ptolemies of Egypt and the monarchs of Syria, which resulted first in the overlordship of Egypt in Judea, and later on of Syrian rule.

The latter was a dark period in Jewish history, especially during the reign of Antiochus Epiphanes, the Syrian king, who committed many outrages against the Jews, sought to establish idolatry in Jerusalem, and defiled the temple.

His wickedness led to the Maccabean revolt, 166 B.C., in which the priest Matthias and his sons defeated the Syrians in a series of battles, which secured the independence of the Province of Judea.

This was the foundation of the Asmonæan Dynasty, which reigned from 166-63 B.C.

ANNOUNCEMENT to Zacharias of the coming of the Forerunner of JESUS
Lu. 1.5-17

ANNUNCIATION to Mary of the coming of the MESSIAH
Lu. 1.26-35.

PREACHING OF JOHN THE BAPTIST
Mt. 3.1-6

THE BOOKS OF THE APOCRYPHA

I ESDRAS	THE WISDOM OF SOLOMON	THE HISTORY OF SUSANNA
II ESDRAS	ECCLESIASTICUS	BEL AND THE DRAGON
TOBIT	BARUCH	THE PRAYER OF MANASSES
JUDITH	THE EPISTLE OF JEREMIAH	I AND II MACCABEES
ADDITIONS TO ESTHER	THE SONG OF THE THREE HOLY CHILDREN	III AND IV MACCABEES

The word APOCRYPHA means hidden, or secret.

ORIGIN. The term Apocrypha is generally applied to a collection of books, from eleven to sixteen in number, which appeared in the interim between the Old and New Testaments.

They have come down to us in more or less close connection with the canonical books of the Bible.

They have had a strange history. Ecclesiastical opinion in different periods has differed widely as to the value of the literature.

The Jews of the Dispersion in Egypt placed a high estimate upon these books, and included them in the Greek translation of the Old Testament, called the Septuagint, but they were rejected from the Hebrew canon by the Jews of Palestine.

THE ROMAN CATHOLIC CHURCH in the Council of Trent, 1546 A.D., declared eleven of the books to be canonical, and they appear in the modern Catholic edition of the Scriptures.

THE VIEW OF THE PROTESTANT CHURCH

It is commonly agreed that some of these books contain material of literary merit, and historical value.

But their canonicity has been rejected, and they have been gradually omitted from the modern editions of the Protestant Bibles, for the following reasons:

1. They are never quoted by Jesus, and it is doubtful if they were ever alluded to by the apostles.

2. Most of the early Fathers regarded them as uninspired.

3. They did not appear in the Ancient Hebrew canon.

4. The inferior quality of most of the writings as compared with the canonical books, stamps them as unworthy of a place in the sacred Scriptures.

CHARACTER OF THE BOOKS

Authorities differ as to the classification of these books.

The Epistle of Jeremiah is often incorporated in the Book of Baruch, and III and IV Maccabees are often omitted.

HISTORIC;—I and II Maccabees and I Esdras.

TRADITIONAL;—Additions to Esther, Susanna, Song of the Three Holy Children, Bel and the Dragon, Judith and Tobit.

PROPHETIC;—Baruch and the Prayer of Manasses.

APOCALYPTIC;—II Esdras and IV Esdras in the Latin Vulgate.

INSTRUCTIVE;—Ecclesiasticus, and the Wisdom of Solomon (in style like the Proverbs).

at large who have the responsibility to supervise and maintain the integrity of the church and its functions.

The general Protestant view is that the sacraments are merely visible symbols of grace, that there is no inherent virtue in them or in the administrator, and that the sacraments are relevant only to those who have made a profession of faith in Christ as their Lord and Savior. By receiving the sacraments, the believer gives testimony to the "whole world around him" that Jesus Christ is his source of salvation. Also by participating in the sacraments, the believer commemorates what Christ did for him on the cross. In addition, it is a time of thanksgiving for the believer; he expresses thanks to God for the redemptive blood that was shed on Calvary's cross. Because of the very nature of baptism and the Lord's Supper, differences of interpretation have developed. There is, however, general agreement that they are outer expressions of an inner work of grace made possible by the atoning blood of Jesus Christ.

It should be acknowledged that some Protestant groups have their own interpretations regarding the relationship between OT, circumcision and NT baptism. It is our purpose to point out the bridge relationship or transition from the OT to the NT concerning these two sacraments.

Most Protestants recognize only (1) baptism and (2) the Lord's Supper. Justification for this view is based on the fact that these two rites are the only ones the Lord directly initiated and in which he participated.

Most Baptists and many Independent groups consider these rites to be ordinances rather than sacraments. The initiatory rite is called believers' baptism because it is received only when a person attains the age of accountability and makes a profession of faith in Jesus Christ. The mode of baptism is immersion. Those of other persuasions accept both immersion and sprinkling. The biblical justification for water baptism is found in such passages as Matthew 28:9; Acts 2:37,38; Mark 2:4,5; for the Lord's Supper in Matthew 26:26–30; Mark 14:22–25; Luke 22:19,20; 1 Corinthians 10:16,17; 11:23–27.

Baptism
756–760

Lord's Supper
761

Because of the twofold nature of the sacraments, there must be a twofold division: first, there is the need for an immediate relationship between the individual and God; this is called the personal. Above all other considerations, man owes personal fealty to God. Second, man is not only an individual with a personal obligation, he is also an integral part of the social community; this is called the social relationship.

Circumcision
765–767

In the OT the initiatory rite was circumcision. But this does not mean that the mode of administering the sacraments must always be the same. Indeed, a little reflection will show that the mode could not be the same before Christ's human life and death. Certain external religious actions or rituals used in teachings and inculcating religious truths and doctrines obviously had to be changed at the coming of Christ. These changes do not rest upon any arbitrary command or ordinance but upon the practical nature and development of the plan of redemption from before the Advent until after Christ the Messiah was crucified and ascended into heaven.

Basically the need for the sacraments or ordinances existed from the time salvation was first presented to man. Many believe that the plan and the promise (Gen. 3:15) were presented to Adam and Eve. Abel, their son, certainly gives evidence that he had been taught the way of salvation and the acceptable sacrifice. The stages of the religious ritual are revealed in the Bible. Since salvation could not be fragmented, one may assume that salvation was complete from the time God presented the plan to man, and essentially it has not changed.

Two sacraments were practiced in the OT—circumcision and the Passover; the one was initiatory, the other commemorative. Before these sacraments were introduced, there may have been other rites which God had established to fulfill this purpose. Before the Advent, all the rituals and ceremonies referred to the time when circumcision and the Passover were inaugurated. However, they also looked toward the Messiah's coming.

Salvation in the OT as well as in the NT required faith: a forward look of faith in the promised Messiah and a backward look of faith in the provided Savior satisfied the redemptive requirement. Some of the ritual, customs, and modes, exceedingly useful and appropriate before Christ's Advent, were inappropriate and useless afterward. The Bible record reveals changing forms and modes of the ritual. The OT forms of circumcision, the Passover, the Day of Pentecost, the Sabbath, all take on new significance after the advent of Christ.

Substantially Christ was and is the center of all salvation relevance in both the OT and the NT. In the OT he is referred to as the coming King and Savior; in the NT he is presented within the context of history. He had come; this was the Good News. In the OT, Christ stands in the prophetic tradition, illustrated by the animal sacrifices, symbolizing faith in him who was spoken of by Moses and the prophets. In the NT Christ is the fulfillment of all that the prophets foretold (Rom. 1:1–5). When Jesus said, "I am the way, the truth, and the life: no man cometh unto the Father, but by me" (John 14:6), he made a statement which is timeless. It was a statement of eternal truth. There never was a time when this statement was not true. He always stands in the same relationship to sinners and saved men (Heb. 13:8), but in the one case the literal consummation of his great atoning acts was in the proph-

The Political-Religious Events Between the Testaments

Sacraments
756–761

Salvation Promised
3122

Circumcision
765–767

Passover
1256

Advent
1344–1348

Messianic Hope
4186

Circumcision
765

Passover
1256

Fulfilled Prophecy
2892, 2893

etic future, and in the other, in the historical past. In the NT, the OT sacraments continue, but the mode changes from circumcision to baptism and from the Passover to the Lord's Supper. Each one will be considered separately:

A. *Circumcision—Baptism*

Circumcision
765

Baptism
756

Sinners
4025

Saved
1358

The word *circumcision* comes from the Hebrew word *mula* and from the Greek word *peritome*. Both have the basic meaning of "cutting around." The natures of the "natural man" and the "redeemed man" are such that in society it is necessary for the redeemed man to have a mark of identification and a symbolic witness. Circumcision was the mark chosen by God to identify believers in the days of Abraham (Gen. 17:1–10). It was understood to be a mark of separation from the practices of the sinful world in which the believers lived. History affirms that circumcision was an early Semitic institution and the idea was borrowed by some other religions. It is assumed that the worship of Elohim-YHWH (God the Lord) was the first religious system and that the other religious systems are corrupted "spinoffs" from this pure religion.

The ritual always commemorated the historical event but it also looked forward to the reality which it symbolized. Circumcision was definitely a vital part of God's plan as it was unfolded in the time of Abraham from Genesis to Malachi. The validity of the event was dependent upon the prophetic event to which it looked forward. The coming of the Messiah, a future event of grace, was always an integral part of OT religion. The person who submitted to circumcision thereby sealed a promise to God and the qahal, or the OT church, to carry out and observe all the things implied in OT church "membership." The believing Jew was under this obligation, and the rite was the seal which bound him to be true to the faith.

Now if the sacrament of circumcision was necessary, why did it not continue after Christ? The sacrament of initiation did continue uninterruptedly, but in a different form. Nothing changed but the form in which the sacrament was administered, and this was done for most obvious and necessary reasons. The particular form in which the sacrament was administered before the coming of Christ had peculiar significance and appropriateness to the blood-letting in the animal sacrifices. The significance of all this was the forward look, to the cross, which foreshadowed "the Lamb of God" who died once for all. Since the animal sacrifices looked forward to the redemptive event, they no longer had relevance. It was now necessary to change, to introduce a sacramental mode which would be historical. The "Lamb of God" on the cross took the place of the "slain animal," and water baptism as an historical attestation was adopted as the mode of the initiatory rite.

Of course sacramental modes do not change suddenly. There is a gradual, preparatory phase so the people can become adjusted to the change. As an example, the use of the metric system is being introduced gradually, and both the mile and the kilometer are on sign posts and speedometers. Since circumcision was the sacramental mode before the Advent, it had no real relevance after the Advent because what it had pointed to was fulfilled in Christ. Paul repeatedly explains this in his Epistles to the Galatians and to the Romans. "Behold, I Paul say unto you, that if ye be circumcised, Christ shall profit you nothing. For I testify again to every man that is circumcised, that he is a debtor to do the whole law" (Gal. 5:2,3). Circumcision of the flesh now becomes "spiritual circumcision" of the heart of which baptism is the symbol (Rom. 2:28,29, Deut. 10:16; Jer. 4:4; 9:25,26).

Spiritual
Circumcision
766

Even in the OT, physical circumcision was intended to be the outward sign of inward grace, the circumcised heart (Ezek. 44:7), and in the NT, it is the new birth. It is well to bear in mind that the introduction of water baptism as an initiatory rite developed gradually in a time when both circumcision and water baptism were used concurrently. Ritualistic washing with water was well known in the OT (Exod. 24:4; 30:20; 40:12; Lev. 15; 16:26–28). John the Baptist used water in his initiatory rite, and it is significant that both John and Jesus ministered during the OT period. The NT period did not start until after the death of Christ on the cross, as previously indicated.

Water for
Spiritual
Cleansing
961–966

B. The Passover—Lord's Supper

For information on the OT background of the Passover, read Ch. 6, II, A, page 67. The concern in this section will be the relationship between the Passover and the Lord's Supper. Again one observes how an OT rite gradually changed to fit the religious need of the New Covenant. Sometimes it is difficult to focus on the point at which the actual change took place, but in retrospect the change becomes evident.

The Gospel record contains several accounts of Jesus going to Jerusalem to celebrate the OT Passover. The earliest instance occurred when Joseph and Mary took the boy Jesus to Jerusalem (Luke 2:41ff.). John the Beloved gives an account of the three separate Passover feasts attended by our Lord during his formal earthly ministry (John 2:13,23; 6:4; 11:55; 12:1; 18:29,39). The Synoptic writers make it clear that Jesus was crucified on the first day of the Passover (Matt. 26:17; Mark 14:17; Luke 22:14).

Feast of
Passover
1256

John gives a vivid description of Jesus' last Passover with his disciples (John 19:41ff.).

John associates Jesus with the "Passover Lamb" in his reference: "Behold the Lamb of God, which taketh away the sin of the world" (John 1:29). In Paul's letter to the Corinthians he stated that "Christ our passover is sacrificed for us" (1 Cor. 5:7). In John's account of Jesus' last Passover with his disciples, Jesus states that he is the "bread of life"; this fits well into the Paschal context (John 6:31–35; cf. Matt. 26:26–29). The early church recalled the analogy between the Jewish Passover and the death of Christ (Matt. 26:17ff.; Mark. 14:12ff.; Luke 22:7ff.). Like a Paschal lamb, he was without blemish (Exod. 12:5; cf. 1 Peter 1:18,19); not a bone was broken (Exod. 12:46; cf. John 19:36). In 1 Corinthians 5:7,8 reference is made to the unleavened bread of sincerity and truth within the context of "Christ our passover who is sacrificed for us." Jeremiah's reference to the New Covenant of the future led the NT Church to interpret the death of Jesus as a prophetic fulfillment (Jer. 31:31).

It becomes progressively clear that the annual celebration of the OT Passover was adopted as the vehicle in which the NT celebrated the death of Christ but under a new name, the Lord's Supper. It is still a sacrament but has been changed to the NT context. Note that in both instances the central point is the "shed blood." In the OT the blood was sprinkled on the visible door post, in the NT the blood is mystically applied to "the door post of the heart." In each celebration the idea of freedom from enslavement is present—the Israelites from Egyptian bondage, the church from the bondage of sin.

The OT Passover has no significance for the Christian who wishes to commemorate the Savior's sacrifice. It commemorates the deliverance from the bondage of Egypt. Of necessity there had to be some changes in it, or the rite would become meaningless. These obvious changes were that, first, the Passover had looked forward to the shedding of Christ's blood, and now that has been accomplished. Something must be substituted for the Paschal lamb, which prefigured Christ. Second, the Passover had looked forward to the great deliverance by Christ, so long anticipated by every act of worship. The acts of worship must now be continued by the NT church and in remembrance of him (Luke 22:19; 1 Cor. 11:24,25).

The OT Passover is now behind; it is history. Christian believers cannot commemorate the Paschal lamb because the "Lamb of God" has died on the cross, has arisen from the grave, and is now at the right hand of God the Father (Mark 16:19; Heb. 1:3). Like that of baptism the name of the sacrament became changed at the time of Christ. He, "the Lamb of God, which taketh away the sin of the world" (John 1:29) has taken the place of the Paschal lamb of Egypt.

The liturgical section of most denominational hymnals includes a responsive reading on, "Christ Our Passover." The response quoted below is from the United Methodist Hymnal (1966):

CHRIST OUR PASSOVER

Christ, our paschal lamb, has been sacrificed. Let us, therefore, celebrate the festival,
   not with the old leaven, the leaven of malice and evil, but with the unleavened bread of sincerity and truth.
For we know that Christ being raised from the dead will never die again; death no longer has dominion over him.
   The death he died he died to sin, once for all, but the life he lives he lives to God.
So you also must consider yourselves dead to sin and alive to God in Christ Jesus.
   Christ has been raised from the dead, the first fruits of those who have fallen asleep.
For as by a man came death, by a man has come also the resurrection of the dead.
   For as in Adam all die, so also in Christ shall all be made alive.
   1 Corinthians 5:7b–8; Romans 6:9–11; 1 Corinthians 15:20–22

IX. THE DIASPORA (ITS CONTRIBUTION TO RELIGION)

The Hebrew word *golah* has come into English use as *dispersion,* and means "forced exile." By the time of Christ more Jews lived outside of Palestine than lived in Judea. The dispersion of the Jews came when Assyria took the Israelites into captivity (721 B.C.). In 586 B.C. the natives of Judea were taken into Babylon and with the fall of Jerusalem in A.D. 70 Titus took many Jews to Rome as slaves. Some Jews went voluntarily into other lands for economic opportunities. Egypt had one of the largest Jewish communities in the Near East. Over 1,000,000 Jews lived in Egypt in the days of Christ. Syria also had large concentrations of Jews, and there is evidence of Jews living in Asia Minor, Achaia, and Corinth. It is said that Antiochus III moved 2,000 Jewish families to Asia Minor. The Book of Acts gives evidence of the presence of Jews and their synagogues when Paul and the early missionaries began to evangelize these parts. Jews in Rome were persecuted by Tiberias Caesar. In Corinth, Paul met Aquilla and Priscilla, who had been driven out of Rome by Claudius (Acts 19:1,2). The islands of the Mediterranean also had Jewish settlements. Cyprus was the home of Barnabas, and Titus ministered to Jews on Crete.

The scattered Jews maintained strong ties with Jerusalem and the temple until A.D. 70. At Pentecost, Jewish representa-

Assyrians
299, 300

Babylon
4334

Egypt
1100

Syria
3524

Asia
272

Synagogues
3521–3523

Tiberias
Caesar
612

Cyprus
907

187

tives "out of every nation under heaven" were present in Jerusalem on this memorable day (Acts 2:5–11). The close relationship of the dispersed Jews with the temple in Jerusalem is further evidenced by their monetary support. Gifts of money were sent regularly with the pilgrims going to Jerusalem. The temple was made rich and beautiful by the treasures contributed from abroad. There was very little local treasure. Ancient chronicles tell about Methridates, King of Pontus in Asia Minor, confiscating 800 talents of silver collected by the Jews for transmission to Jerusalem. On another occasion Pomponius Flaccus confiscated 100 pounds of gold bound for the Temple.[23]

The cause of God was greatly enhanced through the Diaspora. If it had not been for the dispersion of the Jews there might not have been a Septuagint (Greek OT, see Ch. 1, III, A, also X, next page). Since the Greek language had become universal, the availability of the Jewish Scriptures in Greek greatly facilitated Bible religion. The Diaspora also produced the Targums, the Aramaic translations of portions of the OT, which communicated the scriptural message of the Lord to the Babylonian area.

The Apocrypha and other extrabiblical writings were developed by the dispersed Jews (see XI in this chapter). These works are not considered to be canonical, but they do preserve much knowledge about the times and events in the "silent period."

The synagogue is another institution which developed while the Jews were in Babylonian captivity. Following the destruction of the temple and the separation of the Jews from Jerusalem by hundreds of miles, they could no longer practice the

levitical sacrifices; a substitute place of worship became a necessity. Out of this need the synagogue developed. It was indeed a very practical solution to the problem. As slaves, the Jews were limited in their movement; they could not go to a central worship center. They were scattered throughout Babylon and needed local worship centers. A synagogue could accommodate a small group and could be located in a home, or in a large building.

By the time the Jews came back from Babylon to Jerusalem,

the synagogue had become an established part of their religious life (See Ch. 5, I, D, page 64). Synagogues were built in every community, large or small, so that worship could be carried on without going to the temple in Jerusalem. The synagogue also provided an easy transition for the Jews when the temple was destroyed under Titus in A.D. 70.

An additional advantage was that the synagogues abroad provided easily accessible preaching places for the early missionaries. Since the Christ-Messiah movement was Jewish, it was logical and reasonable for the missionaries to make their local contacts in the synagogues. Frequently Paul and the early evangels "reasoned in the synagogue every sabbath, and persuaded the Jews . . ." (Acts 18:4) and "straightway he preached Christ in the synagogues, that he is the Son of God" (Acts 9:20).

There is no way to measure the witness the Jews gave for the Lord in the many areas in which they were scattered; they had the institutional organization for transmitting the religion of the Bible. After Christ came, the synagogues became natural preaching places in which the "Good News" could be proclaimed.

The conviction of sin was quickened and personal experience in religion was increased; the Scriptures were taken to all parts of the Empire and biblical concepts and precepts of ethics and morality were promulgated, but there was persecution and opposition to the gospel. A universal outlook of a common human heritage became known through the mixing and mingling of Jew and Gentiles. The Messianic expectation of the Jews had prepared the world at large for the message of Christ.

The Political-
Religious
Events
Between the
Testaments

Sabbath
3098

Witness
704

Conviction of
Sin
1764

X. THE SEPTUAGINT (LXX)

The Septuagint (LXX) came into being when the Hebrew language had been almost forgotten, especially among the dispersed Jews in the Roman Empire. Hebrew language began to decline during the Babylonian captivity (606–536 B.C.), and was practically dead in the Roman Empire outside Jerusalem and its environs. The Aramaic Targums developed as oral paraphrases to Scripture reading in the postexilic synagogue. Aramaic words are especially noticeable in the exilic books of Daniel and Ezekiel.

The Greek language became the vernacular in most of the eastern Mediterranean world after the conquest of Alexander the Great (334–323 B.C.), with the exception of priestly circles. By 250 B.C. the Jews were left without a Bible they could read. A Jewish Bible for Greek-speaking Jews in the educational and cultural library in the city of Alexandria, Egypt, was not available. The need for a Jewish Bible in the commonly spoken Greek language of the day became so great that a special appeal was made to the King of Egypt to authorize a translation of the Hebrew Bible into Greek.

Bible
414–434

Alexandria
114, 4325

Knowledge of just how the Septuagint (LXX) came into being is not clear. According to a little-known scholar in Alexandria, Aristeas, the Jews brought pressure upon the king, pointing out that his great library was incomplete without a Jewish Bible in the common language. Following this request, Ptolemy Philadelphus III is said to have ordered seventy-two Jewish scholars shut up in a monastery to undertake the translation separately, each without comparing notes with his neighbor. When the work was finished, each man's translation was in total agreement, word for word. Thus, the translation was called the New Greek Septuagint (LXX), after Aristeas' romantic story of the seventy-two scholars. The truth probably is that some Hebrew-Greek scholars in Alexandria began translating the Torah in about 250 B.C., and eventually completed the entire OT.

In the Greek-speaking world of that day, the Septuagint became a powerful force in spreading Bible knowledge in a heathen world. Later it became a ready vehicle for the spread of the Messiah-Christian religion.

XI. THE APOCRYPHA

The chart on page 181 gives a short digest of the Apocrypha. To this information should be added the following:

The word *apocrypha* means hidden or secret and is the name given to fourteen books of a religious nature which contain information on events between 400 B.C. and the Advent of Christ. Even though they contain information on matters of religion, these books are considered to be noncanonical, especially by most Protestants. At the Council of Trent in 1546 the Roman Catholic Church adopted all but three of the Apocryphal books as canonical. I and II Esdras and the Prayer of Manesseh were omitted. They are called Deutro-canonical and not apocryphal in the Douai Version—the official Roman Catholic Bible.

The apocryphal books were written in Greek between the first and the third centuries A.D. and were never a part of the Hebrew canon, which concluded with Malachi about 400 B.C. However, the Apocrypha was included in Wycliffe's translation. Likewise, Luther recognized these works as having literary value but placed them between the OT and the NT with this notation: "These books are not held equal to the sacred scriptures and yet are useful and good for reading." As far as content is concerned these writings do not contain anything new in the area of redemptive Revelation. All the necessary redemptive information is contained in the sixty–six Books of the Protestant Canon.

The apocryphal books bear the following titles:

1 Esdras. The purpose of the books was to present Cyrus and Darius to the Jews as being benevolent persons. It contains the debate of the three soldiers who concluded that the truth is the greatest thing, and parts from Ezra, 2 Chronicles, and Nehemiah with legends about Zerubbabel.

2 Esdras. In this book Ezra is said to have had visions of a new world government and the coming of a new age.

Tobit. A romantic novel about a young Israeli captive in Nineveh who was led by an angel to wed a "virgin widow."

Judith. This book is a supposedly historical account of a rich, beautiful Jewish widow who, in the days of the Babylonian invasion, went to the tent of a Babylonian general and cut off his head to save the city.

The Rest of Esther. These are fragments of accounts gathered by Jerome to show the hand of God in the OT Book of Esther.

Wisdom of Solomon. A mixture of Hebrew thought and Greek philosophy was written by an Alexandrian Jew who claimed to be Solomon.

Ecclesiasticus. A book of proverbs and wise sayings by Jesus, the son of Sirach, gave rules of conduct for civil, religious, and domestic life.

Baruch. A book of paraphrases from Jeremiah, Daniel, and other prophets. It appears to have been written in Babylon by Baruch, the scribe of Jeremiah.

Song of the Three Holy Children. This song is an addition to the Book of Daniel, giving the prayers of the three Hebrew children while they were in the fiery furnace. It also contains their triumphal praise for deliverance.

History of Susanna. As another addition to Daniel, this narrative tells about the wife of a wealthy Jew in Babylon who was cleared of a charge of adultery by the wisdom of Daniel.

Bel and the Dragon. Intended as an addition to the Book of Daniel, this writing includes Daniel's proof that the idols of Bel and the Dragon are not gods.

Prayer of Manasses. The volume contains the supposed prayer of Manasses when he was a captive in Babylon, referred to in 2 Chr. 33:12,13.

1 Maccabees. The Maccabees is recognized as a historic book of great value, containing an account of the heroic struggle by the Jews for independence (175–135 B.C.).

2 Maccabees. This book is also an account of the Maccabean struggle (175–166 B.C.), supplementing 1 Maccabees. It is said to be an abridgment of a work written by Jason of Cyrene, of whom nothing is known.

In general these were written by unknown authors and were added to the Septuagint which was composed about the same time. Several reasons exist for rejecting the Apocrypha as part of the bible canon:

1. The books were not in the Hebrew OT and were written after the Hebrew canon was closed.
2. Josephus rejected them as a whole.

191

3. They were never recognized by the Jews as Hebrew scripture.
4. They were never quoted by Jesus or by anyone else in the New Testament (see Pseudepigrapha, XII in this chapter).
5. They were never recognized by the early church as having canonical authority nor as having been divinely inspired.
6. When the Bible was translated into Latin (Catholic Bible) in the second century, its OT was translated from the Greek OT (Septuagint) and not the Hebrew. When the Protestants rejected the Apocrypha, the Catholic Church affirmed it as Scripture at the Council of Trent in A.D. 1546, in an effort to stop the Protestant movement. The apocryphal books are still in the Douay [Douai] version.
7. A final reason for rejecting these books as canonical is that the quality of the writings is inferior to the canonical Scripture. The dignity and integrity of the writers of the canonical books is lacking. Identification of authorship is almost impossible in the Apocryphal Books.

XII. THE PSEUDEPIGRAPHA

These books were written by Jewish authors between 200 B.C. and A.D. 100. The word *pseudo* means "false" or "hidden." Even though the works deal with religious subjects, they are far below the quality of the canonized Bible books. Some of the books include the following:
A. Palestinian Books Written in Hebrew in 200–100 B.C. The Testaments of the Twelve Patriarchs contain legends, moral codes, and apocalyptic expectations which the twelve patriarchs are said to have passed down to their descendants.
(a) The Psalms of Solomon, written about 40 B.C.
(b) The legendary lives of the Prophets, dating A.D. 1–100.
B. Palestinian Books Written in Aramaic, about 200–1 B.C.
(a) The Book of Jubilees, a legendary account of Genesis and Exodus through Ch. 12.
(b) The Testament of Job (legends).
(c) The Book of Enoch (apocalyptic). This is quoted in Jude 14–15.
It is acknowledged that even these books contain some truth. Where passages are singled out under the leading of the Holy Spirit they are true, as in the aforementioned quotation from Jude.
C. Books and Legends Written A.D. 1–100
(a) Legends with Christian additions

(b) The Martyrdom of Isaiah

(c) The Additions to Jeremiah

(d) The Life of Adam and Eve

(e) The Assumption of Moses

(f) The Apocalypse of Abraham

D. Alexandrian Books Written in Greek 200 B.C.–A.D. 100

(a) Written about 200–75 B.C. Letter of Aristeas giving a legendary account of the translation of the Pentateuch into Greek in about 250 B.C. (See special section on the Septuagint, page 189.)

(b) 3 Maccabees written in 75–1 B.C. Gives an account of the miraculous deliverance of the Egyptian Jews from a death sentence.

(c) 4 Maccabees is a philosophical and historical demonstration of the stoic statement, "Devout reason is master of the passions." Written in A.D. 1–100.[24]

These writings are anonymous. Appended names of canonical authors were used to give dignity to the heretical writings.

13

The Christian Era

Harmony of
the Gospels
pp. 269ff.

I. THE HARMONY OF THE GOSPELS OR THE SYNOPTIC PROBLEM

Messianic
Prophecies
pp. 246ff.

God had spoken to the prophets during the centuries about the coming of the Messiah. Every minute prophecy concerning the "great prophet like unto Moses" was fulfilled when Jesus was born in Bethlehem while Herod the Great was king.

Gospels
1440–1442

To describe the historical fulfillment of these prophecies it was necessary to create a new type of literature. The four Gospels became the means of communicating the birth, life, teachings, death, and resurrection of the Lord. *Gospel* means "good news"; the good news was that "He of whom Moses and the prophets spoke" had arrived. Thus the gospel records are especially important; they are the "divine package" in which all of the dependable information about Jesus and his life has been preserved. The first-century Jewish historian, Josephus, the Roman writer, Pliny the Younger, as well as Tacitus, the Roman historian, Suetonius, the Roman biographer, and Lucian, the Greek satirist and critic of the Christian religion, make reference to Jesus. However, these statements are so brief that they are valueless in an attempt to reconstruct the life of Jesus. They do confirm, nevertheless, that he lived, became a public figure, and died under Pontius Pilate, and that within a dozen years of his death, worship of him spread as far as Rome. [1]

There were some apocryphal and pseudepigraphical NT books which are inferior in quality and sometimes ridiculous in content (see pages 190–193). Among the apocryphal NT

194

books dealing with Christian events are the Acts of Peter, the Acts of Paul, the Acts of Andrew, and separate books of the gospel including the Gospels of the Edomites, the Egyptians, the Twelve Apostles, Barnabas, Nicodemus, and Joseph the Carpenter. One of the books teaches that "conjugal life is sinful and that women should reject the society of their husbands" (Apocryphal Acts). The implication is that only celibate people can go to heaven.

Many other subjects are devoid of delicacy of feeling and are always out of touch with reality. The writer of Apocryphal Acts regards the earthly life of Jesus as only an appearance and unreal. In another book Peter heals his daughter for a short time and then requests her to resume her illness, where-upon her old disease returns (Acts of Peter).

Falsehood
3702

Those gospels concerning the infancy and childhood of Jesus deal with the miraculous power Jesus supposedly possessed in childhood. On one occasion Jesus and his playmates were playing on a rooftop. After one of the boys died as a result of a fall, the boy's mother accused Jesus of pushing her son off the roof. Jesus is said to have replied, "No, I did not push him off," after which he restored the boy to life. When Jesus asked the lad, "Did I push you off the roof?" the boy replied, "No, I slipped and fell." Then, according to the account, the boy lay down and died again. On another occasion, Jesus and his friends were making mudpies. After drying them, the boys sailed the flat patties through the air; however, when Jesus threw his discs, they turned into birds and flew away. [2] The intellectual level of these books at best is very low.

False
Witnesses
3856, 3857

The recording of the gospel events and teachings was delayed for several reasons. The disciples of Jesus saw no need of a written record as long as Jesus was with them. Initially their understanding had been that the "Kingdom of God" on earth was soon to be realized.

Also because they considered Christ's ministry to be exclusively Palestinian, they saw no need for a written account of his life. Since the Christian movement was strictly a Jewish phenomenon at that time, there was aversion to writing religious books other than the OT, which was regarded as being sufficient.

Other reasons for the hesitancy to write included the fact that the OT was the source from which Jesus, the apostles, and the early missionaries quoted, to affirm their message. Jesus frequently cited the OT passages for his authority (see Ch. 14, I). In addition, eyewitnesses attested what Jesus said and did. Finally, as the leaders in the Christian movement were, in the main, poor, and writing materials were very expensive, it was not feasible for the disciples to engage in literary activity.

195

*Preliminary
Matters*

Chart:
Harmony of
the Gospels
pp. 269ff.

They placed much emphasis upon the "inner life of the spirit" rather than upon the "written letter of the word."

On pages 269 and following in the TCRB Helps, "The Harmony of the Gospels" opposite the "Tree of Jesus' Life" includes a comparative analysis of the specific content of the four Gospels. At first glance the "Synoptic Problem" becomes apparent: Why are the Gospels so similar and yet so unlike?

First, each Gospel writer had his own personality, as well as social and economic background. Second, each Gospel was written to a different group of people. (For a discussion of each book see pages 349ff.) It will be sufficient at this point to say that the Gospel according to Matthew was written by a Jew to the Jewish community, as a piece of evangelistic literature. The Gospel written by Mark was to the Romans, the people of action. Their ability as engineers and builders is attested by their great engineering projects still standing. The Gospel recorded by Luke was directed to the intelligentsia of that day, the Greeks. The literary quality of this book gives ample testimony that its author was a man of "letters." John wrote the Gospel which bears his name about thirty years after the synoptic Gospels (Matthew, Mark, and Luke) A.D. 90. The author, John, assumes that the basic fundamentals of the gospel were well established and that there was a need for a more spiritualized interpretation, especially for the Hellenized Jews. Matthew, Mark, and Luke are more nearly alike. They are called the synoptic Gospels because, viewed together, they are parallel to each other, and their content is similar.

Luke
2216

John
392, 1902

Matthew
2265
Mark
2253

The four columns on pages 269–272 of the TCRB Helps list all of the Gospel events in the left-hand column. In glancing across the page, it is seen that the subject listed in the left-hand column under III, "The Christ of Obscurity," are not all discussed by the four Evangels. The subjects under Nos. 39, 40, and 41 are mentioned only by Luke. "The Visit of the Wise Men" under No. 42 is recorded only in Matthew, as is also the case with "The Flight to Egypt" under No. 43; however "The Return to Nazareth" under No. 44 is mentioned by both Matthew and Luke. The subjects from Nos. 47–56 are listed only in John, whereas "The Early Galilean Ministry" under No. 56 is a subject of discussion by all four Evangels.

A glance at page 270 shows that the reference numbers extend from 61 to 140, and of these 79 subjects John mentions only 8. Of the eight, only five of the references are by John alone. In glancing at page 271 the same principle applies. It is clear that the Gospel reports in John are 90 percent different from the other Evangels.

Beginning with No. 215 on page 272, "The Agony in the Garden," the entries take on a new degree of similarity. From

Nos. 215 to 257 one sees that the four Evangels have a similarity of emphasis on the suffering, death, and resurrection of Christ. It is in this area that the four Evangels are most in harmony and agreement. Carefully studying these pages will bring its reward of inspiration and enlightenment.

The Christian Era

Christ's Death
3367

Christ's Resurrection
2407–2415

It is evident that each writer sets forth the event as he witnessed it, without reference to the other two. With the exception of Luke 1:1–4, nothing is said about the authors' sources.

Scholars are still unable to give definite answers concerning the synoptic problem. Serious discussions have continued and larger issues have been raised, but no adequate solutions have been found. Three scholarly theories have evolved out of these debates:

A. The Oral Tradition

This theory assumes that each gospel writer obtained his materials independently, not from written records, but from oral narratives of the sayings and activities of Jesus, which, through repetition, had assumed a relatively fixed form.

B. The Mutual Use Theory

Many variations of this theory exist. The basic assumption is that a single source, one of the Gospels, was used by the other writers. In this approach each of the Gospels has been put first, each second, and each third, and each in turn has been regarded as the source of the others.

C. The Source Theory

Those who hold to the source theory assume that there was a common depository of some kind (oral or written) from which all three synoptic writers drew their information; however, there is no consensus on this theory among scholars. The source in this theory is believed to be very similar to, if not identical with, the Gospel of Mark. Some studies conclude that 90 percent of the content in Mark was incorporated in the other two Gospels and that in the order of events Matthew and Luke have mainly followed Mark. Consideration is also given to the idea that there was a second source in addition to Mark, now generally called "Q" after the German word *quelle*, meaning a "spring" or "source." Some scholars raise the question as to why "Q" has not survived? To this there is no answer available.

Gospel of Mark
4263

Gospel of Matthew
4262

Gospel of Luke
4264

It has been suggested that the "Q" document comprised the "in-class notes" which Matthew recorded and that later Matthew as well as Mark and Luke used these notes in compiling their gospel records. In these early days the writers freely borrowed from each other without benefit of footnotes because, in the first place, gospel information was in the "public domain," and, second, in this early day there was no concept of plagiarizing or copyright. It is evident that the materials of which the Gospels were composed existed before they were put in final form. At least thirty years elapsed from the time Jesus ascended to heaven until the Gospels, in their present form, were written. Of the three synoptic writers, only Matthew was an apostle and the sole eyewitness. Mark and Luke obviously had access to Gospel materials of some kind. Mark was in close contact with Peter, and Luke was a frequent companion of Paul, who is considered to be an apostle because of his personal encounter with the resurrected Lord on the Damascus Road. [3]

Peter
746

Irrespective of human instrumentality it must be acknowledged that the compilation of the gospel record was superintended and directed by the Holy Spirit. The promise is that "He shall teach you all things, and bring all things to your remembrance" (John 14:26). It is logical to assume that materials of an oral or written nature would be valid gospel material as long as the Holy Spirit sanctioned the selection.

Luke
2216

Divinely
Inspired
417, 1774

Luke established authority in this area: Note Luke 1:1–4. Luke, a physician, was a man of literary ability. Under the leadership of the Holy Spirit, Luke made extensive research in his preparation for writing the Books of Luke and Acts. For a detailed study of the nativity event see Ch. 19, IV on the Gospel of Luke, page 362.

From these observations comes the conclusion that God used four men of unquestioned integrity and piety to make a record of the events surrounding the "birth, life, death and resurrection" of Jesus Christ. The fact that these Gospel documents have stood the test of time for almost two thousand years, gives credibility to the belief that in them mankind has trustworthy redemptive information from the eternal, living God.

II. CREEDS OF THE CHRISTIAN FAITH

In a religious context the word *creed* means a concise, biblically based expression of the Christian faith. Creeds were formulated as the church grew and administrative affairs became more complicated. Because heathen philosophies, Gnosticism and Hellenism had crept into the church, it was necessary to make a plain affirmation of the fundamentals of the faith. Learned men of the church convened councils to study the Scriptures and to formulate credal statements. New Testament writers had provided the materials in their clear-cut affirmation

Vain
Philosophies
2759

One God
2649

of the oneness of God, the unqualified deity of Christ, and the personality of the Holy Spirit.

A. *The Apostles' Creed*

The Apostles' Creed is the most widely known statement of faith in the church universal. This creed states clearly all of the basic fundamentals of the Christian faith. Each element in it can be verified by the Scriptures.

The creed arises out of the "mists of antiquity." It originated early in the history of the church when its faith was challenged by many heathen philosophies. It was in use in some form as early as A.D. 150. According to tradition each one of the twelve apostles wrote one phrase of the creed, but this is not generally accepted by modern scholars.

One early tradition on the origin of the Apostles' Creed was perpetuated by Tyrannius Rufinus (A.D. 345–410), who wrote a commentary on the Apostles' Creed, translated *Church History* by Eusebius, and finally established a monastery on the Mount of Olives in Jerusalem. [4] According to Rufinus:

> Tradition says . . . on the eve therefore of departure from one another, they first mutually agreed upon a standard of their future preaching, lest haply, when separated, they might . . . vary in the statements which they should make to those whom they should invite to believe in Christ. Being all therefore met together, and being filled with the Holy Ghost, they composed . . . this brief formulatory of their future preaching, each contributing his several sentences to one common summary; and they ordained that the rules thus framed should be given to those who believe. [5]

Reference is also made to this tradition by Johannes Cassianus (A.D. 360?–435?), an early monk and theologian with extensive travel experience in the Jerusalem-Bethlehem area, as well as by Saint Jerome (Eusebius Hieronymus), translator of the Latin Vulgate. [6]

It is quite likely that the Apostles' Creed, as it is today, underwent many revisions. The Athenian philosopher, Aristides (A.D. 126), wrote a Christian defense to Emperor Hadrian. It contains what is believed to be an approximation of the original Apostles' Creed:

> Now, the Christians trace their origin from the Lord Jesus Christ. And he is acknowledged by the Holy Spirit to be the Son of the Most High God, who came down from heaven for the salvation of men. And being born of a pure virgin, unbegotten and immaculate, he assumed flesh and revealed himself among men that he might recall them to himself from their wandering after many gods. And having accomplished his wonderful dispensation, by a voluntary choice, he tasted death on the cross, fulfilling an august dispensation. After three days he came to life again and ascended into heaven.

199

. . . He had twelve disciples who, after his ascension to heaven, went forth into the provinces of the whole world and declared his greatness. [7]

It is generally agreed that some form of the Apostles' Creed was given to early converts at their baptism. This creed is a common denominator of theology upon which most Christian groups can agree.

The text of the Apostles' Creed with appropriate Scripture verification follows:

THE APOSTLES' CREED

I believe in God the Father Almighty, [1] maker of heaven and earth; [2]

And in Jesus Christ his only Son our Lord: [3] who was conceived by the Holy Spirit, [4] born of the Virgin Mary, [5] suffered under Pontius Pilate, [6] was crucified, [7] dead, [8] and buried, [9] the third day he rose from the dead; [10] he ascended into heaven, [11] and sitteth at the right hand of God the Father Almighty; [12] from thence he shall come to judge the quick and the dead. [13]

I believe in the Holy Spirit, [14] the holy catholic Church, [15] the communion of saints, [16] the forgiveness of sins, [17] the resurrection of the body, [18] and the life everlasting. [19] Amen.

1. Isaiah 64:8; Matt. 6:9	11. Luke 24:51; Acts 1:9
2. Gen. 1:1	12. Luke 20:42; Acts 2:55
3. Matt. 17:5; Acts. 2:36	13. Acts 10:42; 2 Tim. 4:1
4. Luke 1:30–35; Matt. 1:20	14. Matt. 1:18; Luke 1:35
5. Matt. 1:18–25	15. Eph. 5:27
6. Matt. 27:12,24	16. 2 Cor. 13:14
7. Matt. 27:35; 1 Cor. 2:2	17. 2 Chron. 7:14; 1 John 1:9
8. Luke 23:46; John 19:33	18. 2 Cor. 4:14; 1 Thess. 4:16
9. Matt. 27:59,60	19. John 3:16
10. Luke 16:9; John 20:9	

For additional references see subject index and concordance in TCRB.

B. The Nicene Creed

As the church developed and questions arose it was necessary to make concise declarations of the basic doctrinal beliefs. "To put these truths together was the great theological achievement of the clear thinking and vigorous debate which led to the Council of Nicaea (A.D. 325) and on to the Council of Chalcedon" (A.D. 451). [8] The Council of Nicaea was called by Emperor Constantine to settle the theological controversy between Arius and Athanasius. Arius of Alexandria argued that Christ was a high creature but that he was not eternal and he was not of the nature of God. Athanasius "saw clearly that the issue at stake was the distinctiveness of Christianity and the reality of the Incarnation. He recognized that to worship a Christ who is not quite God is an open door to a return to polytheism." [9]

The controversy was settled in Athanasius' favor. The Council adopted a creed which stated in part that God was the Father Almighty and that Jesus Christ the Lord was the only begotten of the Father, who was made flesh, suffered, rose from the dead, and ascended into heaven.

Notwithstanding the victory of Athanasius, the Arian heresy did not die completely. It still appears in some strains of liberal theology. However, the Nicene creed became the "established standard for the normative Christian understanding of Christ throughout the ages."

THE NICENE CREED

I believe in one God: the Father Almighty, maker of heaven and earth, and of all things visible and invisible;

And in one Lord Jesus Christ, the only begotten Son of God: begotten of the Father before all worlds, God of God, Light of Light, very God of very God, begotten, not made, being of one substance with the Father, through whom all things were made; who for us men and for our salvation came down from heaven, and was incarnate by the Holy Ghost of the Virgin Mary, and was made man, and was crucified also for us under Pontius Pilate; he suffered and was buried,* and the third day he rose again according to the Scriptures, and ascended into heaven, and sitteth on the right hand of the Father; and he shall come again with glory, to judge both the quick and the dead; whose kingdom shall have no end.

And I believe in the Holy Ghost, the Lord, the giver of life, who proceedeth from the Father and the Son, who with the Father and the Son together is worshipped and glorified, who spake by the prophets. And I believe in one holy catholic and apostolic Church. I acknowledge one baptism for the remission of sins. And I look for the resurrection of the dead, and the life of the world to come. Amen.

C. Other Statements of Faith

The Creed of Athanasius became the third defensive statement of the Christian church. This creed was formulated to explain in detail, the Nicene Creed, and dealt mainly with the doctrine of the Trinity and the Incarnation. Even though Athanasius spent many years defending the Nicene Creed, it is generally agreed that he did not write the creed bearing his name. Scholars are of the opinion that the creed, as we have it today, was not formulated in its present form until the time of St. Augustine.

---

* Traditional use of this creed includes these words: "He descended into hell."

The next theological controversy was over original sin. St. Augustine (A.D. 354–430) challenged the position of Pelagius, who said that "man was created in a neutral condition, neither sinful or holy and with capacity for good or evil. His will was free and undetermined—each succeeding man is born in the same condition as Adam before the fall and is free from guilt or pollution at birth." [10] In opposition to this view, Augustine contended what is known as the biblical doctrine of original sin. This controversy resulted in "Augustine establishing, deep in Christian thought, the conviction that salvation is by faith alone, a grace given to creatures who have inherited a racial predisposition to sin, and who therefore could never in themselves please God." [11]

Statements of faith in the fourth and fifth centuries were called creeds, while similar statements in the sixteenth and seventeenth centuries were called confessions, based mainly on the idea of reconciliation. These confessions were limited in scope and theological range. We list a few:

1. The Confessions of Gennadius, a statement of faith for the Muslims.
2. The Answers of Jeremiah were replies from the patriarchs of Constantinople in answer to Lutheran theologians.
3. The Orthodox Confessions of Peter Magila set forth the teachings of the Eastern Orthodox Church.

The sixteenth-century reformation period produced the Augsburg Confession, setting forth beliefs of the Lutheran movement. The Reform movement under Zwingli and Calvin, as distinguished from the Lutheran group, produced the Tetrapolitan Confession by Martin Bucer in 1530 and John Calvin's Consonsus Tigurinus in 1549, both designed to present the Calvinist view.

In 1646 the Westminster Confession was produced to set forth doctrinal articles for the Presbyterians in England and Scotland. During the reign of Henry VIII in England The Articles of 1536 and The King's Book of 1543 were published. Then came the Forty-two Articles showing clearly the Protestant influence on the English Church. The Thirty-Nine Articles reflected the theological posture of the English Church under Queen Elizabeth.[12]

The twentieth century produced several creeds, of which the Korean Creed and A Modern Creed are best known.

D. The Korean Creed

202 Henry Gehard Appenzeller and Horace Grant Underwood together were the vanguard of organized missions in Korea.[13]

They were both men of letters with unquestioned dedication
to the cause of Christ and missions. Under their scholarly leadership the Bible was translated into the native tongue and
Tract Societies, Theological Seminaries, and Christian Colleges
were founded.

At the time the Korean Methodist Church was organized
(1930), it was felt that a supplementary credal statement should
be formulated. Bishop Herbert Welch was appointed to make
a rough draft of such a statement expressing the basic essentials
of the Christian faith in nontechnical language. In consultation
with Bishop James C. Baker and the leaders of the Korean
church a final draft was made, presented and approved by
the first General Conference of the Korean Methodist Church.
This creed has been used extensively in the National Church
of Korea.[14]

THE KOREAN CREED

We believe in the one God, maker and ruler of all things, Father
of all men, the source of all goodness and beauty, all truth and
love.

We believe in Jesus Christ, God manifest in the flesh, our teacher,
example, and Redeemer, the Savior of the world.

We believe in the Holy Spirit, God present with us for guidance,
for comfort, and for strength.

We believe in the forgiveness of sins, in the life of love and prayer,
and in grace equal to every need.

We believe in the Word of God contained in the Old and New
Testaments as the sufficient rule both of faith and of practice.

We believe in the Church as the fellowship for worship and for
service of all who are united to the living Lord.

We believe in the kingdom of God as the divine rule in human
society, and in the brotherhood of man under the fatherhood of
God.

We believe in the final triumph of righteousness, and in the life
everlasting. Amen.

E. A Modern Creed

Edwin Lewis, the great theologian at Drew Theological Seminary, formulated A Modern Affirmation during the time when
the liberal-conservative theological controversy was at its peak,
in the mid 1930s. About this time his own theological position
was changed to the conservative side.[15] His Affirmation is
quoted below:

A MODERN AFFIRMATION

We believe in God the Father, infinite in wisdom, power, and
love, whose mercy is over all his works, and whose will is ever
directed to his children's good.

We believe in Jesus Christ, Son of God and Son of man, the gift of the Father's unfailing grace, the ground of our hope, and the promise of our deliverance from sin and death.

We believe in the Holy Spirit as the divine presence in our lives, whereby we are kept in perpetual remembrance of the truth of Christ, and find strength and help in time of need.

We believe that this faith should manifest itself in the service of love as set forth in the example of our blessed Lord, to the end that the kingdom of God may come upon the earth. Amen.

It is to be acknowledged that this and other newer creeds are limited in scope and content and should not be used exclusively. Bishop Nolan B. Harmon of the United Methodist Church says,

> No one can object to these modern affirmations being used occasionally as explanations of certain truths of creed, provided—and this is an important proviso—that the one who uses them, and the people who are led to repeat them, know exactly how far they go and do not go. . . . What I object to is to give the impression by the sonorous introduction and the constant use of these affirmations as a church-wide worship that they embody anything like the comprehensive faith of the Christian Church. . . . These 20th century-affirmations which sound so lofty and leave out so much. If they supplement, yes; if they supplant, no. Let the Apostles' Creed be used and let its verities be explained and preached—the whole Gospel to the whole world.[16]

A Study in Christology

I. CHRISTIAN THEOLOGY IN THE OLD TESTAMENT

In reading the OT one soon finds evidence that it is a collection of holy writings, describing a unique religion (2 Peter 1:2). In these inspired words one discerns a God of mercy (Jonah 4:2) and love (Jer. 31:3), as well as one of judgment (Isa. 30:18). The religious system described in the OT had a priesthood (2 Chron. 11:13) directed by a high priest (Exod. 21:10). The deity is monotheistic (Deut. 4:3; 6:40) but presented in three persons: *Elohim,* "God" (Gen. 1:1); *YHWH,* "Lord" (Gen. 3:23); and *Ruach,* "Spirit" (Gen. 6:3; cf. Luke 4:18), corresponding to the NT Father, Son, and Holy Ghost or Spirit (Matt. 28:19) (see Ch. 7, II–IV, VII, pages 75–83).

Bible
414–434

The spiritual well-being of the Hebrew people is supervised by a group of evangelists, called prophets (2 Kings 5:8). The people of God were called the qahal—the Congregation—the "called out ones" (Ps. 82:1; 87:5), corresponding to the ekklesia of the NT "church" (Matt. 18:17; Acts 2:47). The worship centers manifested progressive development from the simple altar (Gen. 8:20) to the tabernacle (Exod. 26:1) followed by the temple or House of the Lord (2 Sam. 7:13; 1 Kings 5:5), and finally the synagogue (Matt. 12:9). In these centers of worship the Holy Writings were presented to meet the moral, ethical, and religious needs of the people "for doctrine, for reproof, for correction, for instruction in righteousness" (2 Tim. 3:16b).

The hand of God is seen at work in many places under many different circumstances (John 2:9; 4:46; Mark 1:26). Repentance is the heart attitude by which the pentient gains favor with

Repentance
2706–2710
205

God in both the OT and the NT (Exod. 13:17; Jer. 18:8; cf. Matt. 3:2; Acts 3:19).

This raises the question: what religion is this? The traditional answer would be that it is Judaism, the religion of the Jews. But this is too simplistic. It is more than that. In a real sense OT religion was Christianity in embryonic form. It was a system by which people in the OT escaped the penalty for sin and gained fellowship with their Creator. In this system one sees all the aspects of the "church" as it was before the coming of Christ the Messiah.

The essential nature of worship is the same in both the OT and the NT; the cohesive force in both is love. This is clearly enunciated in a Mosaic address: "Thou shalt love the LORD thy God with all thine heart, and with all thy soul, and with all thy might" (Deut. 6:5), and "thou shalt love thy neighbour as thyself" (Lev. 19:18).

When a lawyer asked Jesus what the most important commandment was, he restated the OT formula quoted above and discussed in par. 2, 3, page 117. These two commandments are the key to a happy relationship with God and man. This love fulfills all the demands of law. Jesus said, "on these two commandments hang [depend] all the law and the prophets" (Matt. 22:40). The message is simple: the commandment of love satisfies and fulfills all the other commandments of God.

The OT contains basically the religious system called Christianity; but like any other system of truth comprising beliefs and practices, there was a need for a fuller explanation of the religious concepts and precepts in the OT. The NT illuminates the prophetic revelation of salvation in the OT.

The NT writers regarded the OT as comprising a complete system of revealed religion. Indeed the apostles did not pretend to teach any doctrine, tenet, or truth which they were not ready to prove by the then existing Scriptures, the OT. If they preached the gospel, they drew it from the OT. They not only preached no other gospel than that contained in the OT, but they repudiated everything contrary to the OT teachings, declaring every addition to it to be false. "Though we, or an angel from heaven, preach any other gospel . . . let him be accursed" (Gal. 1:8). A few passages substantiate this claim: "Did ye never read in the scriptures, The stone which the builders rejected, the same is become the head of the corner?" (Matt. 21:42). Here the appeal is made to Psalm 118:22 and Isaiah 28:16. Jesus himself declared, "I was daily with you in the temple teaching, and ye took me not: but the scriptures must be fulfilled" (Mark 14:49; Ps. 22:6–8). "And beginning at Moses and all the prophets, he expounded unto them in all the scriptures the things concerning himself" (Luke 24:27); "Then opened he their understanding, that they might understand the scriptures . . . Thus it is written [in the Scriptures], and thus it behoved Christ to suffer . . ." (Luke 24:45,46).

When the Apostle Paul evangelized the Jews he "went in unto them, and three sabbath days reasoned with them out of the scriptures" (Acts 17:2). The Jews in Berea are commended because they "were more noble than those of Thessalonica, in that they received the word with all readiness of mind, and searched the scriptures daily, whether those things were so" (Acts 17:11). When Paul preached, "he mightily convinced the Jews, and that publickly, shewing by the scriptures that Jesus was Christ" (Acts 18:28).

OT teachings show that the death of Christ was according to the Scriptures (1 Cor. 15:3; see also Acts 10:43; 26:22,23). The Word states that a man who is not saved in accordance with the OT cannot be saved at all (see Luke 16:29–31; Isa. 8:20). The holy Scriptures are fully sufficient to make one "wise unto salvation through faith which is in Christ Jesus" (2 Tim. 3:15).

Holiness for Christians is commanded by the OT teachings (1 Peter 1:16). The Gospels contain the fulfillment of the promises recorded in the OT (Rom. 1:2); these Scriptures reveal the laws, statutes, and judgments of God (Exod. 24:3,4; Deut. 4:5–14); they testify of Christ (John 5:39; Acts 10:43; 1 Cor. 15:3); they are sufficient for all religious needs and profitable for both doctrine and practice; they were written for instruction (Rom. 15:4); they are not to be added to, nor is aught to be taken from them (Deut. 4:2); they work effectually in all who believe (1 Thess. 2:13); Christ enables the believer to understand them (Luke 24:45); the Holy Spirit likewise enlightens them (John 16:13; 1 Cor. 2:10–14); everything must be tried by them (Acts 17:11); they are designed for the regeneration of mankind (James 1:18; 1 Peter 1:23), for converting the soul and making wise the simple (Ps. 19:7), and for sanctifying the soul (John 17:17; Eph. 5:26) as well as producing Christian hope (Ps. 119:49; Rom. 15:4) and obedience (Deut. 17:19,20). The Scriptures are good for cleansing the heart (John 15:3; Eph. 5:26) and for promoting growth in grace (1 Peter 4:11); they are a source for verifying truth (1 Peter 1:16).

This examination of many passages indicates that there is no essential doctrine nor teaching known in the NT which is not drawn directly from the OT. Paul expressly declared that he preached nothing else, and he instructed Timothy to follow the same rule (2 Tim. 3:15–17; 4:2). However, Paul was accused of preaching false doctrines (Acts 24:5,6; 25:7). Paul's imprisonment was the result of his commitment to the ancient faith of the OT church, and not to any "new" views, tenets, or practices. "For the hope of Israel," the apostle exclaims, "I am bound with this chain" (Acts 28:20). "And now I stand and

A *Study in Christology*

Prophecy Fulfilled
2892, 2893

Christ's Teachings
3558

Sabbath
3098

Scriptures
3166

Preached Christ
2089

Believers
1212

Regeneration
2154

Sanctification
3140, 3141

Grow in Grace
995, 996

Hope
4186

207

am judged for the hope of the promise made of God unto our fathers: unto which promise our twelve tribes, instantly serving God day and night, hope to come. For which hope's sake, king Agrippa, I am accused of the Jews" (Acts 26:5–7). The Epistle to the Hebrews is an argument refuting the charges against its author and his associates, that they had imbibed new religious tenets. From the beginning to the end, the writer contends for the unity of Apostolic Christianity with the Judaism of their fathers and the ancient church, but presents Christianity as better than Judaism.

At the time of Christ, and for many years previous, the church possessed its Bible, the OT, which was held in the highest veneration. No people ever lived who held their sacred books in greater respect than did the Jews before, and at the coming of, Christ. But there was no printing, and the books were all handwritten. They were few and only in the hands of the learned. Many of the people could not read; indeed, reading and writing were skills attained by only a select group. A knowledge of what the Scriptures contained was communicated to the people through the church by readings on the Sabbath and by means of the sculpture and paintings in the church.

The chief complaint against the apostles was that they preached things new, things not taught in Scriptures and therefore false. To have done this would have been a great offense against revealed religion, and if the apostles or anyone else had taught and preached things not found in the Scriptures, the accusations against them would have been just. But the apostles constantly denied the charges and contended that they were made only by those who did not understand the Scriptures, that they set forth exactly what the OT taught and nothing more. An examination of what the twelve and Paul did teach and a comparison of their teachings with the OT reveal that they did not violate the integrity of the Scripture. They explained and elaborated, but they dared not, nor did they, add to them one new idea.

Frequently the "Christian religion" and the "Jewish religion," in these express terms, are "contrasted" with each other, but there is no real contrast—they are the same in Spirit. Of course one must distinguish between the OT teachings and the "traditions of the elders" (Mark 15:3; 7:8; Col. 2:8; Titus 1:14; 1 Peter 1:18).

II. THE TREE OF JESUS' LIFE

This chart presents a complete perspective of Jesus' life from the beginning of creation in Genesis to his second coming as recorded in Revelation. The various periods of his existence and life are depicted in the tree system from the roots to the topmost branch.

A *Study in Christology*

III. THE PREEXISTENT CHRIST

Pre-existent Christ
709, p. 269

Christ has been a living reality with the Father and the Holy Spirit from all eternity. The Savior proclaimed that he was one with the Father who "is in me, and I in him" (John 10:30, 38; 17:11). In his high priestly prayer he petitions the Father: "Glorify thou me with thine own self with the glory which I had with thee before the world was" (John 17:5).

Christ Glorified
682

IV. THE PROPHETIC CHRIST

Prophetic Christ
pp. 246, 269, 282

The most conclusive proof that the Bible is a divinely inspired Book is found in the fulfilled prophecies from the OT which are windows through which God admitted light on future events. One of the most fruitful areas of Bible study deals with the Messianic prophecies, given over a 1500-year period by about 30 different authors in many different locations. These prophecies form a complete representation of Christ. It is unreasonable to assume that the prophets could give such a minute, accurate view of the Messiah without divine inspiration.

The prophecies of the coming Messiah begin early in the Genesis record (Gen. 3:15). The prophets state that the Messiah Christ would be revealed or made manifest, not created at some future date. Jesus Christ, who is the same "yesterday, today, and forever," is coexistent and eternal with God the Father. Through the progression of revelation God gave a composite picture of the Messiah, the Christ, who would take away the sin of the world. Apart from Christ's virgin birth there could be no fulfillment of these prophecies because the supernatural conception of Jesus shows God's power to fulfill his prophecies.

Messianic Prophesies
2890

Virgin Birth
4217

Prophecies
2890

In one of the first Messianic prophecies in the OT, God, speaking to Satan, prophesied, "And I will put enmity between thee and the woman, and between thy seed and her seed; it shall bruise thy head, and thou shalt bruise his heel" (Gen. 3:15). It is evident that this prophecy refers to Christ because he did truly bruise Satan's [the serpent's] head. Paul, in his letter to the Galatians, states that "when the fulness of the time was come, God sent forth his Son, made of a woman, made under the law, to redeem them that were under the law" (Gal. 4:4).

Initially, when Christ hung on the cross, and finally at the resurrection, he bruised Satan's head, even as satanic forces, incarnate in man, bruised Christ's heel when the cruel spikes were driven through his quivering flesh. Finally, he will cast Satan into the lake of fire and the defeat of Satan will be complete. The writer of Hebrews tells the Jewish converts that, "as the children are partakers of flesh and blood, he [Christ] also himself likewise took part of the same; that through death he might destroy him that had the power of death, that is, the devil" (Heb. 2:14). Jesus was "declared to be the Son of God with power, according to the spirit of holiness, by the resurrection from the dead" (Rom. 1:4).

In the Genesis reference, one recognizes the promise of him who was to be born of a woman and whose seed was to be at odds with the seed of Satan. The enmity that prevails between the righteous on the one hand and the evil forces on the other is continually manifesting itself. A war has been going on between the forces of righteousness and those of evil since this judgment of God was pronounced (2 Cor. 10:4; 1 Tim. 1:18; 6:2; 2 Tim. 2:4).

The Scripture (Gen. 3:15) is addressed not to Adam and Eve, but to Eve alone; the consequence of this purpose of God was that Jesus Christ was born of a virgin. This is what is implied in the promise. Jesus Christ died to redeem sinful man by the sacrifice of himself, and eventually to destroy him who had the power of death, that is, the devil. Although Satan will be defeated, Christ indicated that Satan is now the prince of this world and that he goes about seeking whom he may devour, or as an "angel of light" deceiving the very elect. Even though he is a potentially defeated foe, he is still active (1 Cor. 2:6; 1 Peter 5:8). In destroying Satan's power and lordship over mankind, God enabled man to turn the power of Satan unto God (Acts 26:18), and Satan bruised his heel. God so ordered it, because salvation could only be brought about by the death of Christ. By woman sin was introduced into the world, and by woman a Savior from sin was given (Gal. 1:14; 4:4).

The prophetic statement in Genesis 18:18 assured Abraham that he would be the progenitor of a nation which would be a spiritual blessing to the nations of the earth. In retrospect the Bible student can see that this blessing has come to the world through Christ, who was a descendant of Abraham. It is said of Abraham that he saw the promises "afar off," and that he was "persuaded of them," and "embraced them" (Heb. 11:8–13). Paul tells the Galatians that Abraham was justified by faith, that the gospel was preached to Abraham (Gal. 3:8), and that the believers in Christ are the spiritual children of Abraham.

The Messiah was to be of the promised seed of Isaac and Jacob (Gen. 17:19; Num. 24:17). He would be a descendant of the tribe of Judah (Gen. 49:10), one of the twelve tribes. When Jesus was born in Bethlehem of Judaea, the other tribal nations had vanished. It is most singular that the prophet was able to designate Judah, the only tribe with a political identity at the time of Jesus' birth. Certainly only divine inspiration could have foreseen this outcome (Gen. 49:10).

A Study in
Christology

Arch.
Bethlehem
4339

Inspiration of
Bible
417

The Messiah was to be "heir to the throne of David," and so he would be born in David's hometown, Bethlehem (Micah 5:2); Daniel indicates the time of the Advent (9:25). By giving the world a virgin-born Messiah, God eliminated the possibility that a counterfeit or false Messiah could come. Only the virgin-born would be able to lay claim to this position. The fact that this person was to be called Immanuel, meaning "God with us," is a clear indication that a "sign" would accompany the manifestation of the Redeemer, clearly set forth in prophecy. This divine name could not have been given to an ordinary human being; it could have been given only to the God-man Jesus Christ, who truly was born as the prophets had foretold.

Immanuel
1741
Redeemer
2977

World history does not reveal another human being of whom it could be said he is "God with us." This reference "can refer only to Christ because Christ is God. Thus Christ is the Only One who can be rightfully called Immanuel, 'God with us.' This is indeed an appropriate name for His coming to earth. He is God . . . manifest in the flesh (1 Tim. 2:16). He (Christ) 'was made flesh and dwelt among us' (John 1:14). Christ is the Immanuel, a name which carries with it the true meaning of the Incarnation, namely God with us in human flesh." [1]

Son of God
707

Isaiah is specific; the prophecy clearly stated that the Messiah to come was to be a son, born of a virgin. No one in history, other than Christ, can be found who has this identification. It is to be acknowledged that the Isaiah 7:14 passage is couched in a historical reference pertaining to the prophet's own time. Critics of the "Messiah interpretation" at this point ask: "How can the coming of Christ seven centuries later be made to establish the time for the forsaking of the land of Israel and Syria? What relevance does this text have to King Ahaz?"

Messianic
Prophecies
pp. 246ff.

Some prophetic and especially messianic texts in the Old Testament are found in a setting quite foreign to their nature; they appear as kind of prophetic parentheses (Pss. 34:20; 41:9; 69:21; 110:4). Frequently these prophetic texts have the same relationship to the context as does a precious stone in the native ore in which it is imbedded. This idea is further illustrated in such messianic prophecies as Psalms 22:16,18; 34:20; 41:9; 69:21 and Zechariah 9:9; 11:12,13.

From a literary point of view the Scriptures cannot be made to conform to the "scientific investigative techniques" which are so commonly applied to secular literature. The Scriptures

Scriptures
3166

211

are uniquely "God breathed" and are designed to convey redemptive revelation inherent in the Christ Messiah. "Holy men
of God spake as they were moved by the Holy Ghost" (2 Peter
1:21); the ways of God are foolishness to the natural or sinful
man (see 1 Cor. 2:10–14). Certainly Matthew understood the
passage in Isaiah 7:14 to mean the virgin-born Christ (Matt.
1:23).

J. Gresham Machen says,

> It is certainly clear that something more than the Israelitish people
> is meant by the figure of the "Servant of Jehovah" in the latter
> part of Isaiah: and it is certainly clear that something more is meant
> by "Immanuel" in our passage than the child of the prophet or of
> Ahaz or of any ordinary young woman of that time. A really sympa-
> thetic and intelligent reader can hardly . . . doubt but that in the
> "Immanuel" of the seventh and eighth chapters of Isaiah, in the
> "child" of the ninth chapter, whose name shall be called "Wonder-
> ful, Counsellor, mighty God, everlasting Father, Prince of Peace,"
> and in the "branch" of the eleventh chapter, one mighty divine
> personage is meant. The common minimizing interpretations may
> seem plausible in detail; but they disappear before the majestic
> sweep of the passages when they are taken as a whole.[2]

During the first century most of those who embraced the
Christian faith were Jews—Jews in the strict spiritual sense—
who anticipated the Messiah and accepted him when he came.
To what extent they understood all the intricate details of Jesus'
birth is a matter of conjecture, but the fact remains that they
recognized him as the Messiah.

Adam Clarke observes that:

> According to the original promise there was to be a seed, a human
> being, who should destroy sin; but this seed or human being, must
> come from the woman alone; and no woman alone could produce
> such a human being without being a virgin. Hence, a virgin shall
> bear a son, is the very spirit and meaning of the original text, inde-
> pendent of the illustration given by the prophet; and the fact re-
> corded by the evangelist, is proof of the whole. But such a reading
> of prophecy will not be induced, in those who have abandoned
> it, by any considerations that we can now bring forth; indeed, it
> will come only when there is a mighty revulsion from the shallow-
> ness of present religious life, and when men are again ready to
> listen to the voice of the living God.

> It may perhaps at first sight seem strange that if Isaiah 7:14 is
> really a prophecy of the virgin birth of the Messiah, the later Jews
> should have so completely failed to interpret it in that way. But a
> parallel in the Old Testament which seems to the Christian heart
> to be a prophecy of the redeeming work of Christ . . . is that match-
> less fifty-third chapter of Isaiah. We read it today, often in prefer-
> ence to New Testament passages, as setting forth the atonement
> which our Lord made for the sins of others upon the cross. Never,
> says the simple Christian, was there a prophecy more gloriously
> plain.[3]

It is evident that the Isaiah 7:14 passage relates to Jesus Christ because reference is made to the divine name *Immanuel* ("God with us"). (The name which appears as *Immanuel* in the OT shows up as *Emmanuel* in the NT because of alphabetical peculiarities between Hebrew and Greek.) Emmanuel is indeed "God with us" to comfort, enlighten, protect and to give inner resources to sustain faith in the hour of persecution and death. Believers throughout the ages have testified to saving faith in Jesus Christ, and many have died in defense of their faith.

Other prophetic Scriptures referred to the infants whom Herod would murder in his effort to destroy the Christ child (Jer. 31:15); to the flight by the holy child to Egypt to escape Herod (Hosea 11:1); and to Christ's ministry in Galilee (Isa. 9:1,2). In Deuteronomy 18:15 the writer spoke of the Messiah as a great Prophet; the psalmist associated him with Melchizedek (110:4; Heb. 6:20). Isaiah foretells his rejection by the Jews (53:3), but the Spirit of the Lord was to be upon him (Isa. 11:2). Another prophet saw Christ riding on an ass into Jerusalem on Palm Sunday (Zech. 9:9).

The psalmist mentioned Judas, who was to betray the Savior (41:9), and Zechariah wrote of Judas selling Christ to the priests for thirty pieces of silver (11:12), the betrayal money to be used to buy a potter's field where the poor could be buried (Matt. 27:7). This land was the dump where broken pottery was discarded (Zech. 11:13). The psalmist referred to the incident in the Upper Room, where the vacant office of Judas would be filled (109:7,8).

False witnesses who accused the Messiah were foretold in the Psalms (27:12). Another prophet described his silence when he was accused, telling how he was smitten and spat upon (Isa. 50:6). The psalmist prophesied that the Messiah would be hated without a cause (69:4), and Isaiah saw him as he was smitten and afflicted in the torture of the Crucifixion (53:4,5). According to Psalm 22:6–8, he was to be mocked and insulted and given gall and vinegar to drink on the cross (Ps. 69:21). His prophetic words were repeated in mockery (Ps. 22:8), but he prayed for his enemies (Ps. 109:4). Still another prophet saw the pierced side of the Savior on the cross (Zech. 12:10). The psalmist prophesied that soldiers would pierce his hands and feet and would cast lots for his garments (22:18) but noted that not a bone in his body would be broken (34:20), as was usually done with the crucified. He was to be buried with the rich (Isa. 53:9) and rise from the dead (Isa. 33:10). He was to ascend into heaven (Ps. 68:18). When all these prophecies are viewed together, they result in a perfect portrait of Christ in his redemptive work. Truly this is the son of God.

V. THE CHRIST OF OBSCURITY

Jesus was mentioned only three times before John presented him at the Jordan River:

(1) at his birth (Luke 2:1–7);
(2) at his presentation in the temple (Luke 2:22–24);
(3) at his visit to the temple when he was twelve (Luke 2:41–50).

The years between age twelve and his baptism are shrouded in silence. Scripture does not reveal how long Joseph lived or what Christ did until he began his formal ministry. Some writers have suggested that he worked in Joseph's carpenter shop.

VI. THE MINISTERING CHRIST

Jesus' public ministry began immediately after his temptation experience (Matt. 4:1–11). His inaugural introduction was given by John the Baptist: "Behold the Lamb of God, which taketh away the sin of the world" (John 1:29). (References under No. IV, p. 269 of the TCRB Helps may be helpful.)

VII. THE SUFFERING SAVIOR

The sufferings of Christ began during passion week. On Palm Sunday Jesus made his triumphal entry into Jerusalem. At that time the crowds proclaimed "Hosanna to the son of David: Blessed is he that cometh in the name of the Lord; Hosanna in the highest" (Matt. 21:9). During this week Jesus drew the battle line when he drove the sellers of animals and the moneychangers from the temple (Matt. 21:12,13).

It is again suggested that the reader trace all references under No. V on page 271 of the TCRB Helps. The instances of Christ's suffering are listed in this section. Jesus is betrayed and arrested in the garden, No. 216; he is taken before the High Priest as a malefactor, No. 218; he suffers indignities and false accusations before Pilate, No. 221; Jesus is mocked and abused, No. 227; he is led away to be crucified, No. 229; and he is crucified on Golgotha, No. 232.

VIII. THE RISEN SAVIOR

On page 272 of the TCRB Helps all of the Scripture references dealing with the resurrection of Jesus Christ are listed. The very heart of the Christian faith is based on the bodily resurrection of the Lord. Salvation came only because of

Christ's resurrection. Paul declared that "If Christ be not raised . . . ye are yet in your sins" (1 Cor. 15:17). Also in Romans 4:25 Paul affirmed that Chirst was "raised again for our justification." This is indeed the "good news." The Gospels find their climax in the description of Jesus' resurrection (Matt. 28; Mark 16; Luke 24; John 20,21), and the early church focused its faith in the resurrection (Acts 2:24–32; 3:14–16,26; 4:10; 5:30; 7:55ff.; 10:39–43). In Paul's letters, resurrection is also the central point (1 Cor. 6:14; Gal. 1:1; Col. 2:17).

A Study in Christology

Postresurrection
2415

IX. THE GLORIFIED SAVIOR

Glorified Savior
p. 272

After his resurrection there was sufficient likeness to his earthly body that the disciples were able to recognize him as their Lord. He showed the disciples his hands, feet, and side, which bore evidence of the crucifixion (Luke 24:39; John 20:27,28). Thomas was convinced of Christ's identity by this evidence. There are, however, mysterious elements in the appearance narratives, because he could appear and disappear at will, as was the case on the road to Emmaus; he "vanished out of their sight" (Luke 24:31); a sudden appearance of Jesus in the midst of the disciples is indicated in Luke 24:36,37.

Christ's Postresurrection Appearances
2415

John verified the supernatural when he wrote that Jesus appeared in the midst of the disciples while "the doors were shut" and they were hiding from the Jews (John 20:19). Another mysterious element was that persons did not always recognize him at first sight. "Some doubted" and others had difficulty identifying Jesus as the Christ (Matt. 28:17). Mary Magdalene thought Jesus was the gardener (John 20:14ff.). Apparently Jesus had the power to withhold his identity at will. When Jesus appeared after His resurrection, his was a "spiritual body" mentioned by Paul (1 Cor. 15:44; Phil. 3:21). This word "spiritual" does not mean "immaterial" but some kind of "material" under spiritual control. In speaking of spiritual entities, one cannot explain this phenomenon in scientific terms. For one with faith in the integrity of the Scriptures such an event is spiritually discerned.

Great Mysteries
2486

Spiritual Body
4003

The following devices available in the TCRB Helps will be useful study aids in exploring the events and significance of Jesus' life. The Scripture references in No. VII on page 272 and the chart map on page 273 deal with the life and ministry of Jesus.

In No. 4303 on page 243 a study in the Gospel of John is presented using a gallery of well-known paintings to illustrate the various offices of Christ. Deeper insights can accrue from a study of the numbers from the TCRB Helps that are listed below for each chapter of the Gospel of John.

Preliminary
Matters

John 1—The Son of God, Nos. 701–718
John 2—The Son of Man, Nos. 710–723
John 3—The Divine Teacher, No. 3555
John 4—The Soul-Winner, No. 3908
John 5—The Great Physician, No. 1539
John 6—The Bread of Life, No. 1308
John 7—The Water of Life, No. 3788
John 8—The Defender of the Weak, No. 4145
John 9—The Light of the World, No. 2168
John 10—The Good Shepherd, Nos. 3264–3267
John 11—The Prince of Life, No. 4136
John 12—The King, No. 3421
John 13—The Servant, No. 3901
John 14—The Consoler, No. 784
John 15—The True Vine, No. 1338
John 16—The Giver of the Holy Spirit, No. 4165
John 17—The Great Intercessor, No. 1783
John 18—The Model Sufferer, Nos. 3489–3495
John 19—The Uplifted Saviour, Nos. 3360–3368
John 20—The Conqueror of Death, No. 4136
John 21—The Restorer of the Penitent, No. 3025

For additional commentary, analysis, and outline see TCRB Helps No. 4308 and the following pages.

Part II

The Old Testament

NEW TESTAMENT

#	Topic	Reference
1	REALIZATION	Jn. 1.45
2	REDEEMER	Gal. 3.13
3	OUR FATHER	Mat. 6.9
4	LAST THINGS	II Pet. 3.10
5	RISING SUN	Jn. 8.12
6	SATAN'S DEFEAT	Rev. 20.10
7	SIN'S REMEDY	Jn. 3.16
8	LIFE ETERNAL	Jn. 5.24
9	CHRIST, THE LAMB	Jn. 1.29
10	LIBERTY	Rom. 8.2
11	GOSPEL	Rom. 1.16
12	SUBSTANCE	Heb. 10.34
13	INWARD EXPERIENCE	Luk. 24.32
14	THE SPIRIT	Gal. 5.5
15	FULFILLMENT	Acts 3.18,19
16	OUR SAVIOUR	Luk. 2.11
17	PARADISE REGAINED	Rev. 22.14

400 SILENT YEARS

CHRIST

OLD TESTAMENT

1	LONGING	Job 23.3
2	CREATOR	Gen. 1.1
3	MAJESTIC GOD	Ex. 19.18
4	FIRST THINGS	Gen. 1.1
5	SPIRITUAL DARKNESS	Ps. 82.5
6	SATAN'S VICTORY	Gen. 3.6
7	SIN'S CURSE	Gen. 3.17-19
8	DEATH REGNANT	Gen. 3.19
9	BLOODY SACRIFICES	Ex. 12.3-7
10	BONDAGE	Pr. 5.22
11	LAW	Ex. 20.1-17
12	TYPES AND SHADOWS	Heb. 8.5
13	OUTWARD CEREMONIES	Heb. 9.10
14	THE LETTER	Rom. 7.6
15	PROPHECY	Isa. 11.1, 2
16	EXPECTED MESSIAH	Mal. 3.1
17	PARADISE LOST	Gen. 3.23

CONTRAST BETWEEN THE OLD TESTAMENT AND THE NEW TESTAMENT

NOTE: Follow the topics by numbers across the page.

No. 1 Longing (in the Old Testament) corresponds to No. 1 Realization (in the New Testament).

The Pentateuch (Genesis–Deuteronomy)

I. INTRODUCTION

The word *Pentateuch*, a title for the first five books in the OT, is a Greek term and literally means "the five-volumed book." The Hebrew word for these books is *Torah*, meaning "The Law," or "teachings."

River of Inspiration p. VII

The Pentateuch is of great importance because it contains the foundations and background for divine revelation. It is evident that there is a decided chronological and historical continuity from one book to another. Many of the writers of the OT books quote from the Pentateuch as did the writers of the NT. The Pentateuch is the keystone which gives unity to and holds the entire Bible together.

The Pentateuch delineates the mighty work of God. Divine intervention is noticeable on its pages. As one travels the route of the Exodus, it becomes clear that, apart from divine supervision, there could not have been an Exodus. The absence of food and water supplies and the extreme climate create conditions so hostile that such a large number, estimated by some to have been 3,000,000 people, could not possibly have survived without the manna and the quail.

Miracles of Moses and Aaron 2361

The miraculous elements in the Pentateuch are the basis of attack by scholars whose philosophical suppositions rule out the possibility of God's supernatural intervention in history.[1]

Manna 2248 Quail 464

These scholars have attacked the Pentateuch at a vital point, Mosaic authorship. In the early days of liberal criticism the assertion was made that Moses could not have written the Pentateuch because the art of writing had not yet evolved. Of course this feeble claim has been put to rest by many archaeo-

219

logical discoveries of writing dating many centuries before Moses.

The Mosaic character of the Pentateuch is evidenced by the growing body of literature coming from the ancient ruins of long forgotten cities. These documents show that "Genesis is deeply rooted in Mesopotamian culture of the third millennium and the early half of the second millennium B.C. Without a doubt, there came to Moses . . . materials containing knowledge of God's dealing with ancient man, . . . particularly the Patriarchs. Research has revealed that not only the cuneiform script of Mesopotamia and the hieroglyphics of the Nile Valley were ancient and widespread in Moses' time but [that] alphabet writing had long since been developed into an effective medium of communication. There is nothing which need prevent Moses or some other scribe from recording whatever God commanded him to write." [2]

Patriarchs
2696

A. The Documentary Hypothesis

Lord
2514

God/Creator
884, 885

Modern rejection of Mosaic authorship began with a French physician, Jean Astruc, who did not deny the origin of the book but raised some questions about the non-interchangeable divine names of YHWH (LORD) and Elohim (God), which were most frequently used in the Book of Genesis. He suggested that Genesis was a compendium of two ancient documents which he identified as the YHWH (Jehovah) sources and the Elohim sources. In a few decades the German scholar Johann Eichhorn developed a documentary hypothesis about Genesis and Exodus which ruled out the possibility that Moses had any part in writing these books. He designated the YHWH (Jehovah) sources as "J" and the Elohim sources as "E." Such other German scholars as J. S. Vater, H. Hupfeld, A. Dallman, K. H. Graf and J. Wellhausen systematically organized this theory to include legal documents designated as "D" and priestly ordinances as "P" documents. This theory included all five books of the Pentateuch and became known as the Graf-Wellhausen JEDP documentary hypothesis. Based on anthropological theories the "J" documents were dated about 850 B.C.; the "E" documents, about 750 B.C.; the "D" documents, about 650 B.C.; and the "P" documents, about 550 B.C. (For additional information on this theory and a biblical analysis of this problem see page 73 in this book: "Titles or Names of God in the Bible.")

B. Mosaic Authorship

220   Moses is credited with the authorship of the Pentateuch by both biblical and extra-biblical witnesses. The caption at the

beginning of the first book reads: "The First Book of Moses called Genesis." Some critics object to Mosaic authorship because of the account of Moses' death in the last chapter of Deuteronomy. Certainly the literary content and continuity in Deuteronomy 34 is such that it could easily fit at the head of Joshua's Chronicle. Some scholars suggest that Joshua wrote the postscript for Deuteronomy. It is possible that Joshua was present when Moses died.

The internal evidence for Mosaic authorship is overwhelming, and should forever refute the idea that Deuteronomy is a secular book.

The last four books of the Pentateuch revolve around the contact Moses had with the Lord. In dozens of passages the "LORD spake unto Moses" and "the LORD said unto Moses" (Exod. 30:22,34), and in reverse "Moses said unto the LORD" (Exod. 33:12; Num. 11:11). The instances in which God commanded Moses to write are numerous (Exod. 17:14; 34:27; Deut. 31:9). Later David referred to "the law of Moses" (1 Kings 2:3), and in the synoptic period Luke used the same expression (Luke 2:22). Jesus made frequent reference to the writings of Moses (John 5:46,47; 7:19). Since Moses did not live until the twelfth or the eleventh century B.C., he obviously obtained documentary data and/or oral traditions for the Genesis account from sources outside his own experience. There is internal evidence to support the supposition that Ezra was involved in biblical compilation and editing; however, it is probable that Genesis was already in the Mosaic form in which it appears today and that Ezra did work on other biblical books closer to his own time.

"The issue of Mosaic authorship of the Pentateuch is important to any one who [considers] the NT as a truthful record of Jesus Christ's words and work. Faith in Christ and in the books of the OT canon stand or fall together. Christ and His apostles not only [consider] the Pentateuch as [having] Mosaic [authorship] but put their seal on it as Holy Scripture, as they did for the entire Jewish canon of their day (Rom. 1:2; 2 Tim. 3:16)." [3]

One noted scholar concludes this discussion with these words: "There is no valid reason to dispute the Mosaic authorship. The scriptures uphold it, and the style of the Pentateuch is in harmony with other records originating at an earlier date than the beginning of the Hebrew monarchy. . . . Besides it is altogether possible that Moses used earlier documents and annals, such as 'The Ten Generations' . . . and compiled them into one account. Suffice it to say, whether compiled or originally composed, Moses was guided by the Spirit, as the Bible indicated, to write a redemptive or a religious history of 'first things.' " [4]

The Pentateuch (Genesis–Deuteronomy)

Genesis
4223

Moses, Lawgiver
2053

Scriptures
3166

Holy Spirit Guides
1611

221

C. The Organic Evolutionary Hypothesis vs. Divine Creation

By definition, "organic evolution" assumes that man ascended from the animal world. Some biblical scholars have developed the theory of "theistic evolution" to explain the Genesis account of creation. They see no conflict between divine creation and the evolutionary hypothesis. On the other hand, many traditional biblical scholars do not accept this theory because it is contrary to the plain teachings of an authoritative and infallible Bible and does not accommodate itself to the biblical claim that "holy men of God spake as they were moved by the Holy Ghost" and that "all scripture is given by inspiration of God" (2 Peter 1:21; 2 Tim. 3:16). Certainly the Holy Spirit knew what the facts were, and he could have revealed the evolutionary process, if there had been one.

Since the theory of evolution is contrary to the integrity of biblical revelation, the following reasons show why biblical creation and organic evolution are incompatible. The Bible clearly teaches that Christ co-existed with God the Father from the beginning, but according to the "evolution" theory, Christ is considered to be, if he is considered at all, the culmination of a process. Hence, this theory holds that his preexistence was limited to successive stages, from the lower to the higher, until he achieved some semblance of deity.

This radical theory of "organic evolution" seems to have a destructive effect upon the faith of men. In the early nineteenth century Charles Darwin was preparing for the Christian ministry. Darwin says, "Whilst on board the Beagle I was quite orthodox, and I remember being heartily laughed at by several of the officers (though themselves orthodox) for quoting the Bible as an unanswerable authority on some points of morality." [5] However, when evolution became his belief (1836–1839) the first casualty of his Christian commitment was belief in the Bible as the infallible Word of God. Soon thereafter he abandoned the Christian faith in which he had been reared. He wrote:

> I had gradually come, by this time, to see that the Old Testament from its manifestly false history of the world . . . and from its attributes to God [of] the feelings of a revengeful tyrant, was not more to be trusted than the sacred books of the Hindoos, or the beliefs of any barbarian. . . . I gradually came to disbelieve in Christianity as a divine revelation. . . . Thus disbelief crept over me at a very slow rate, but was at last complete. The rate was so slow that I felt no distress, and have never since doubted even for a single second that my conclusion was correct. [6]

Evidently Darwin lost his faith because of an apparent conflict between plain Bible teachings and a dogmatic scientific approach to biblical interpretation based upon the scientific investigative technique. R. Laird Harris concluded that "it is the feeling of many biblical scholars that this conflict is due to misconception of the Bible's teaching and its relation to scientific theory. . . . Much of the scientific-religious conflict can be avoided if extremes of scientific dogmatism on the naturalistic nature and animal origin of man are avoided." [7]

The Pentateuch (Genesis– Deuteronomy)

Genesis states that God created things "after their kind." It seems reasonable to assume that "kind" as used in Genesis has to do with types which can interbreed. There has been change but there is a lack of evidence to support the evolutionist's claims that all living forms found today come from one common ancestor. God created life after "their kind," as the Bible states plainly. Above all, man was created separately and in the "image of God" in a specific creative act and not through a process of evolution from a single-celled animal.

Creation **884–886**

Image of God **4044**

James D. Bales gives an interesting statement at this point:

It will be observed that the Bible does not say how God formed man's body from the dust of the earth, nor how long it took. However, it does not seem that [this] silence of the Scriptures . . . gives us any grounds, when we consider some other passages, for assuming that it was by an evolutionary process via the animal route.

First, although animal flesh was already in existence—and it, too, was formed of the ground (Genesis 2:19)—yet the passage of Genesis 2:7 does not say that man was formed from animal flesh but of the dust of the ground. Both animal life and dust existed when God created man. God made man from dust and not from living creatures. [8]

Second, Genesis 1:24,25 shows that God created animals and enabled them to bring forth "after their kind." "And God said, Let the earth bring forth the living creature after his kind, cattle, and creeping thing, and beast of the earth after his kind: and it was so. And God made the beast of the earth after his kind, and cattle after their kind, and every thing that creepeth upon the earth after his kind: and God saw that it was good" (Gen. 1:24,25). The law of reproduction in this passage reveals that the animals, who were created before man was created, were to reproduce after "their kind." However, if man came by evolution via the animal route, some animals would have had to produce not their own kind, but mankind.

Beasts **150**

It is quite clear that the doctrine of organic evolution is antagonistic to that of creation and as Huxley says, "Evolution, if consistently accepted, makes it impossible to believe the Bible."

Organic evolution is unchristian and diametrically opposed to the Christian system of thought. Seven considerations substantiate this conclusion:

(1) The theory of organic evolution excludes a transcendent God, thus leading to pantheism instead of theism.

(2) The theory of organic evolution nullifies the idea of creation as clearly stated in the biblical record.

(3) The theory of organic evolution degrades man in that it denies the direct divine origin of man. Instead of recognizing man as having been created in God's image, the evolutionist believes that man evolved from a lower form.

(4) The theory of organic evolution invalidates Bible authority. Darwin, in his *Life and Letters,* states, "For myself, I do not believe that there ever has been any revelation." Thus the Bible is reduced to a book conceived and produced by man without action on the part of God.

Methods of
Revelation
2495–2504

(5) The theory of organic evolution denies the truth of Christ as to his incarnation and virgin birth and puts him in the same category with other men but somewhat higher up on the evolutionary scale. If Christ was a culminating figure in the ever upreaching scheme of evolution, why did not the human race continue from there to become 100-percent Christ-like characters. Apart from the virgin-born Son of God, the human race is basically the same now as it was before the birth of Christ. Evolution cannot accommodate the bodily resurrection of Christ nor his second coming. It would seem that the plainly stated biblical record is much more compatible with the facts than the theory of evolution.

Resurrection
2410–2416

(6) The theory of organic evolution invalidates the Christian interpretation of sin and defines evil as "the working out of the fundamental forces of life itself." Thus the logic of organic evolution destroys not only the doctrine of original sin but also the holiness of God, for it makes God the author of sin.

Sin, Universal
3340

Holiness of
God
1597

(7) The theory of organic evolution is incompatible with ethics. If the principle of living is merely the "survival of the fittest," as among the beasts, the Christian teachings of love, service, and growth through self-sacrifice would have no effect in preventing selfish struggles against others.

Jesus Christ
677–723

There is no place for Jesus Christ in the evolutionary program because Jesus Christ, in the view of the evolutionist, is an exception in nature. This is supported by the fact that the so-called "upreach" of evolution ended with Jesus Christ. Humanity still has not evolved to the state of perfection demonstrated by the Savior. Man, who is still basically sinful, needs the divine intervention as expressed in the new birth. Evolution would deny the reality of miracles, including the new birth and the virgin birth.

224

A theistic evolutionist could be saved, but the theory that man evolved from a lower form of life is incompatible with the biblical record of man's origin. That Adam and Eve were created initially by God as two human beings is obvious in the Genesis account. However, in a day when study of the Bible is neglected and ignorance of the Bible is apparent, it is possible for the deceptive and subtle theories of liberalism to take up residence in one's mind.

To refresh one's memory it is well to cite the instances in the Bible where Adam is definitely presented as a historical person and not "a symbolical term for all mankind."

D. The Historicity of Adam

The fact that Adam and Eve were actual, historical human beings is clearly affirmed in both the Old and New Testaments including the clear-cut affirmation by Jesus Christ. In the following paragraphs some Scripture references substantiate this claim and show the absurdity of the "symbolic" theory:

Adam
34, 1240

A. *Genesis 1:27.* Here it is stated that "God created man in his own image"; "male and female created he them." Jesus affirms this action: "Have ye not read, that he which made them at the beginning made them male and female" (Matt. 19:4).

Creation
884–886

B. *Genesis 2:19.* "God formed every beast of the field, and every fowl of the air; and brought them unto Adam" to name.

C. *Genesis 2:21,22.* "The LORD God caused a deep sleep to fall upon Adam, and he slept: and he took one of his ribs, and closed up the flesh instead thereof; And the rib, which the LORD God had taken from man, made he a woman, and brought her unto the man."

D. *Genesis 3:1ff.* Here it is stated that Adam and Eve committed the sin of disobedience.

Disobedience
2620, 2621

E. *Genesis 4:1.* "Adam knew Eve his wife; and she conceived, and bare Cain." Later Abel and other children were born.

F. *Genesis 5:1–3.* "This is the book of the generations of Adam. In the day that God created man, in the likeness of God made he him; male and female created he them, and blessed them, and called their name Adam, in the day when they were created. And Adam lived an hundred and thirty years, and begat a son. . . ."

G. *Genesis 5:5.* Here the scripture states that Adam lived 930 years.

H. *Deuteronomy 32:8.* In this reference Moses clearly affirms the historicity of Adam. The nations of the earth are referred to as the "sons of Adam."

I. *Joshua 3:16.* In this passage a city is named after Adam.

J. *First Chronicles 1:1.* Here the name Adam is listed as the first in a chronology of the human race.

K. *Job 31:33.* Job clearly acknowledges Adam as a person and compares his own transgression to that of Adam.

L. *Luke 3:38.* Luke acknowledges Adam as a person and lists him as the first human being in his chronology of the human race.

M. *Romans 5:12.* Paul tells us that "by one man sin entered into the world, and death by sin; and so death passed upon all men, for that all have sinned."

**Sin
3340**

N. *Romans 5:14,18.* Paul clearly acknowledges Adam to be a historical person: "Nevertheless death reigned from Adam to Moses, even over them that had not sinned after the similitude of Adam's transgression, who is the figure of him that was to come. . . . Therefore as by the offence of one judgment came upon all men to condemnation; even so by the righteousness of one the free gift came upon all men unto justification of life."

**Death
2158**

O. *First Corinthians 15:22.* "For as in Adam all die, even so in Christ shall all be made alive."

P. *First Corinthians 15:45.* "And so it is written, The first man Adam was made a living soul; the last Adam was made a quickening spirit."

Q. *First Timothy 2:13.* "For Adam was first formed, then Eve."

R. *Jude 14.* Jude affirms that Adam was a person: "And Enoch also, the seventh from Adam, prophesied of these [things]. . . ."

**Animals
150**

S. *First Corinthians 15:39.* Paul clearly tells the Corinthians that the flesh of animals is different from that of man: "All flesh is not the same flesh: but there is one kind of flesh of men, another flesh of beasts, another of fishes, and another of birds." If this is true, how can there be a biological relationship between the beasts and man whom God made in his image?

It is obvious that the theory of organic evolution (man from animal) and the plain teachings of Genesis are incompatible. Furthermore, the evolutionary hypothesis would make Mosaic authorship irrelevant and there would be no basis for Scriptural authority.[9]

**Bible Outline
4222**

II. GENESIS

A. *The Name*

**Book of
Genesis
4223**

The word *genesis* does not appear in the Hebrew Bible, but is derived from the Hebrew *bereshith* as used in Genesis 1:1, "In the beginning God created the heaven and the earth."

The Greek word *genesis* means variously: "birth," "origin," "genealogy" or "generation." The translators of the Greek version of the Scripture, Septuagint (see page 189), used the word *genesis* as the name for the first book in the Bible. The term is most appropriately used in this connection because the Book of Genesis answers "the question of how the world originated, how sin came into the world, how man fell from grace, how God gave hope of redemption to fallen man, how sin spread, how a great judgment was visited upon the sinful world in the Flood, how a remnant of the human race was providentially saved, how the human race again spread abroad still proudly asserting itself." [10]

Thus the name "Genesis" is given to a book which contains a record of the origin or beginning of all things.

The Pentateuch (Genesis–Deuteronomy)

Creator
884, 885

B. Authorship and Date

Moses
2420, 2421

There is no direct internal evidence that Moses wrote the Book of Genesis, but tradition has preserved the idea of Mosaic authorship. The name of Moses has been closely bound to the authorship of the Books of the Pentateuch, which are referred to as "The Five Books of Moses." The caption at the head of the first book in the OT is "The First Book of Moses, called Genesis." This pattern follows through to Deuteronomy which is called the "Fifth Book of Moses."

There are sufficient statements in the other books of the Pentateuch to give Mosaic authorship to at least portions of Genesis as well as the other books in the Pentateuch (see Exod. 17:14; 24:4–7; 34:27; Num. 33:2).

There are at least thirty-five instances in the Book of Leviticus when such expressions as "the LORD spoke to Moses (and Aaron)" are used. If the exact words that the LORD spoke are employed, the measure of probability is high that they were converted to writing as soon as spoken (see Deut. 1:1; 17:18; 27:1–8; 31:9,24).[11]

In the NT, Christ adds to the validity of Mosaic authorship in his reference to the threefold divisions of the Hebrew Bible, with these words: "all things must be fulfilled, which were written in the law of Moses, and in the prophets, and in the psalms, concerning me" (Luke 24:44; see also Luke 16:29,31; cf. John 5:46,7; Matt. 5:17). In this statement about "Moses" Jesus is making reference to the Pentateuch or the Five Books of Moses.

Prophecy fulfilled
2892, 2893

One writer affirms that "the apostles also used terminology which supports this contention (Acts 26:22; 28:23). Christ referred to many items in the Genesis record as inspired Scriptures (Matt. 19:4–6; 24:38; Luke 17:32; John 7:22). It is clear that the apostles held to the Mosaic authorship of Genesis. The Jewish historian Josephus expressly stated the same view

Apostles
2080–2082

227

in about A.D. 90 (Against Apion 1.8). No ancient authority of value brings this view into question." [12]

Mosaic authorship is important to the conservative, evangelical Christian because the entire system of doctrinal and scriptural integrity rests on this question. To discount Moses as the author of the Pentateuch places a low estimation on the divine inspiration and the authority of the Scriptures.

It cannot be denied that Genesis covers a period of time before Moses was born, but it is reasonable to assume that in the dialogue between Moses and God, a revelation of the creation account could have been given. However, it is also reasonable to believe that under the leading of the Holy Spirit, Moses had access to the divine oracles, in oral tradition or in written form, or both. Written documents now in the hands of scholars go back ot the third and second millennium B.C. Hence, to assume that Moses had available to him written documents is reasonable.

C. Background, Purpose, and Content

The exact stages in which the Book of Beginnings developed are unknown. To outline this book is a difficult task because it is possible that the Book of Genesis had its beginning with the family records referred to as the "Ten Generations." The original part of Genesis was probably the preface and the Creation Hymn (Gen. 1:1–2:3).

The Ten Generations referred to in Genesis follow:

1. The Generation of the Heaven and Earth (2:4–4:26)
2. The Book of the Generations of Adam (5:1–6:8)
3. The Book of the Generations of Noah (6:9–9:28)
4. The Book of the Generations of the Sons of Noah (10:1–11:9)
5. The Book of the Generations of Shem (11:10–26)
6. The Book of the Generations of Tereh (11:27–25:11)
7. The Book of the Generations of Ishmael (25:12–18)
8. The Book of the Generations of Isaac (25:19–35:29)
9. The Book of the Generations of Esau (36:1–43)
10. The Book of the Generations of Jacob (37:2–50:26)

Moses probably used these family records as a basis for compiling the Book of Genesis in its present form.

The Book of Genesis is a vast storehouse of knowledge, embracing many subjects. Only a select few can be considered in the space allotted. This Book is, in a measure, the keystone of all redemptive doctrines. The very need of salvation rests upon the origin of sin as described in Genesis. Without the

Excavations at Ur, home of Abraham

Mosque of the Patriarchs where Abraham purchased cave in which to bury Sarah (Gen. 29:9–19). Later he was buried here (Gen. 25:9). Eventually Isaac, Rebekah and Leah were also buried here (Gen. 49:31–33)

Ur Junction where tourists coming from Baghdad by train to visit Ur of the Chaldees disembark

Bedouin tent in Negev desert, typical of type used in Abraham's day

Genesis record there could not have been the other sixty-five books in the Bible. All of these books base their theology on what happened in Genesis. This book is the sourcebook in which the message of the "cross" is prefigured through the lives and experiences of such men as Abel, Enoch, Noah, Melchizedek and Moses. The wilderness journey, the tabernacle, and finally the entrance of the "Jacob tribes" into the "Promised Land" are object lessons of God's grace. The Book of Genesis tells man where he came from and where he is going.

It is evident that the worship of YHWH (LORD) was known in Babylon and beyond Ur of the Chaldees when Abraham was called out to become the progenitor of the Christ-Messiah who would come more than a thousand years later. It is assumed that Abraham and Hammurabi were contemporaries. The evidence of divine revelation is reflected in the similarity between some of the Codes of Hammurabi with the Mosaic Laws. Moses was given a formal set of the Ten Commandments on Mount Sinai. One of them stated: "Remember the sabbath day, to keep it holy." Thus, it would seem that the Sabbath had been neglected or forgotten and that they were to revive a custom not practiced in Egypt.

When Abram arrived in Salem (Jerusalem), Melchizedek was "the priest of the most high God." Melchizedek was high enough in the priestly hierarchy to make demands on Abram (Gen. 14:18–24). "Apparently from the approving manner in which this mysterious king-priest is mentioned here, the way in which Abram himself used his name for God (v. 22), and the place given him in biblical typology (cf. Ps. 110:4 with Heb. 5:6–7), he had somehow risen above the pagan worship of his environment and was serving the True God by this significant name . . . God Most High. . . . He proceeded to bless Abram in that name of God which he commonly used, and Abram gave him a tenth of all." [13]

The Book of Genesis is the frequent target of a certain type of "scientist." This book is not a scientific text book, but at the same time it does contain scientific truth. "Genesis is clear that God made the worlds and is the Lord of nature as well as of spirits; therefore where the Bible touches on science, it must be held to be correct. When fairly and accurately interpreted, the Bible in Genesis 1 and elsewhere declares that God created the worlds out of nothing. Matter is not eternal; with this view the current theories of science have no quarrel." [14]

There are at least two theories on the creation days: (1) the creation days are twenty-four-hour days, and (2) the creation days referred to in Genesis are long periods of time. It is true that God's redemptive plan does not "rise or fall" on whether

The Pentateuch (Genesis–Deuteronomy)

Redemption through Crist
2978, 2979

Messianic Hope
4186

Decalogue
949

Abram
13
Jerusalem
1881–1885

False Gods
3924

Scoffers
3037

Creator
884–886

231

Blowing the Shofar. This announced the beginning of the Sabbath every Friday evening

A Bedouin camel market in Beersheba

A ziggurat—an artificial mound built on the plains of Babylon
where shrines to the gods were erected

The mound of Dothan partially excavated. Dothan was a small
town near Shechem on the caravan route (Gen. 37:14, 17, 25;
2 Kings 6:13). Joseph was cast into the pit here and sold to
the Midianites by his brothers (Gen. 37:17–28)

the creation days were twenty-four-hour days or longer periods of time. "The word 'day' has variable meanings. In Gen. 1:5 it is used as a term for Light. In 1:8,13 it seems to mean a day of 24 hours. In 1:14,16 it seems to mean a twelve-hour day. In 2:4 it implies the whole creation period. In such passages as 2 Tim. 1:12 it seems to refer to the era beyond the Lord's Second Coming, and in Ps. 90:4 and 2 Peter 3:8 'one day is with the Lord as a thousand years, and a thousand years as one day.' " [15]

Concerning the Flood, science and the Bible both agree that the earth was once covered with water. This agreement is apparently verified by the fact that fossils and sea shells are found at high elevations. Science says that water covered the earth millions of years ago and that cataclysmic upheavals created the mountains. The Bible states that the earth was covered with water in Noah's day; so there is no conflict here.

Flood
973

Tithes
2123

It is a matter of record that the paying of tithes had its origin in the early part of Genesis. It is another phase of the animal sacrifices which the worshiper of the Lord was to make as an expression of his devotion to and faith in his Creator.

The word *tithe* comes from the Hebrew word *ma'aser* (Gr. *dekato*) and means giving a tenth part of the produce. Later when the medium of exchange became money, a tenth part of the money was to be given to the cause of the Lord. The Jews had the custom of tithing long before it became a means of support for the Levitical tribe under the Law of Moses. The first direct reference to tithing appears in Genesis 14:17–20, where Abram paid tithes to Melchizedek, "king of Salem [Jerusalem] . . . and . . . the priest of the most high God." Giving the tithe carries with it the idea of commitment and dedication, as in the case where Jacob made a covenant with God and promised to pay his tithe to the LORD (Gen. 28:22). The tithe also implied "not the least and the last" but the "first and the best" for the LORD. Also, in it is the idea of paying rent to the LORD, the owner of all things. Someone has suggested that the "Divine Landlord" is most generous in that he permits the tither to keep 90 percent.

Free Will
Offerings
2628

The idea of "free will" is at the heart of the tithe and is an expression of thankfulness as well as an acknowledgment of God's claim on one's possessions. However, by the time Jesus came, the institution of tithing had degenerated into an expression of self-righteousness (Luke 18:11,12). Jesus rebuked the scribes and Pharisees who tithed their "mint and anise and cummin, and have omitted the weightier matters of the law, judgment, mercy, and faith" (Matt. 23:23).

234

Actually the tithe is a part of one's self because in giving the tithe a person gives a vital part of himself. In working to

On the seven-foot-high stele, known as the Code of Hammurabi, Shamash the sun-god is shown in the act of giving the code of laws to King Hammurabi. Courtesy, Oriental Institute, Chicago

earn substance, one burns up vital energy. Tithing is also a way by which a person develops interests outside and beyond himself, thus avoiding selfishness. No one can maintain a spiritual outlook on life when "self" is the end. One should love one's self but not to the exclusion of loving his neighbor. Jesus said, "Love thy neighbor as thyself." A normal relationship with God includes a normal relationship with man. Jesus ex-

pressed it this way, "Thou shalt love the Lord thy God with all thy heart, and with all thy soul, and with all thy mind. . . . Thou shalt love thy neighbour as thyself" (Matt. 22:37–39). This standard of man-God relationship has been in force from the very beginning. Actually the quotation above was an OT standard which Jesus quoted from Deuteronomy 6:5

and Leviticus 19:18. The Ten Commandments support this idea because the first four commandments have a man-to-God

relationship and the other six are man to man. It becomes clear that the practice of tithing in "the spirit of free will" helps the worshiper to develop a devotion to God and an interest in others.

In conclusion, the Book of Genesis ends with a glorious reference to the time when Shiloh, the great Messiah-King, coming out of the tribe of Judah, will gather his people together into a glorious fellowship (Gen. 49:10).

III. Exodus

A. The Name

In the Hebrew Torah the Book of Exodus, the second book in the Pentateuch, is called *We'elleh Shemoth,* meaning "these are the names." This expression, however, does not really describe the book. The English is a transliteration of the Greek word *exodus* and means "going out" or "departure." The title *Exodus* is used in the Greek OT (Septuagint).

B. Authorship and Date

The Book of Exodus, as part of the Pentateuch, is attributed to Moses. He is the central human figure in the book. Internal evidence indicates that

the author must have been originally a resident of Egypt (not of Palestine), a contemporary eye witness of the Exodus and wilderness wanderings, and [must have] possessed a high degree of education, learning and literary skill. No one else conforms to these qualifica-

tions as closely as Moses, the son of Amram. . . . The author was well-acquainted with Egyptian names, titles, words and customs. He correctly referred to the crop sequence for lower Egypt (Exod. 9:31,32). He spoke only of the shittim tree or acacia, the one known

A view of the Great Sphinx, over 4,000 years old

The ruins of Tanis, one of the treasure cities built by Joseph.
This is a statue of Rameses II, probable Pharaoh of the Exodus

Bricks made of straw as they were in Pharaoh's time

Plain on which the children of Israel camped at Mt. Sinai (called the Valley of Jethro)

desert hardwood tree in the Sinai peninsula, as the source of lumber for the tabernacle (Exod. 25:5, etc.); . . . the badger skins used as the outer cover for the tabernacle (Exod. 25:5; 26:14). . . . He knew about the reeds in the marshes of the Nile delta (Exod. 2:3) and that the desert sand begins abruptly at the edge of the cultivated fields (Exod. 2:12). He seems to have been an eye witness of the events . . . ; he listed for no apparent reason the exact number of springs (12) and of palm trees (70) at Elim (Exod. 15:27).[16]

The Pentateuch (Genesis–Deuteronomy)

Nile
2591

Finally, the proof of Mosaic authorship is strengthened by Jesus' reference to rising from the dead. He states "as touching the dead, that they rise: have ye not read in the book of Moses, how in the bush God spake unto him, saying, I am the God of Abraham, and the God of Isaac, and the God of Jacob?" (Mark 12:26; see also Luke 20:37). The Book of Exodus may have been written while Moses and the Israelites camped around Kadesh-Barnea.

C. Background, Purpose, and Content

The starting point for the Exodus is Rameses, as indicated in Exodus 12:37 and Numbers 33:5, and is associated with the eastern edge of the fertile delta area called Goshen (Gen. 47:6).

Rameses
2946

Goshen
1439

The Book of Exodus is thoroughly redemptive in its content. It is the period when the passover was instituted, foreshadowing Christ, "the Lamb of God." For a Christological analysis of the tabernacle see page 143. The outline theme of the book deals with liberation from enslavement, idolatry, and death. It continues to develop revelation concerning man's redemption, which is introduced in brief capsule form in Genesis.

Slavery (Bond-servants)
2138

In the Book of Exodus, YHWH, the LORD, the second person in the Trinity (see Ch. 7, I, II, III), declares himself to be "Israel's Covenant God." He delivers the Israelites and brings them out of the land of Egypt; he takes them to himself to be his people and to be their God; and he will bring them into the land promised to Abraham, Isaac, and Jacob (Exod. 6:6–8).[17]

As a background for Israel's monotheism there stands the Polytheism of Egypt. There appears to be a time in ancient Egypt when a monotheistic type of religion was practiced, but by the time of the historic period, a religion had developed in which each native tribe adopted its own god represented by an animal.

Polytheism
3928–3947

One God
2649

Among the animals in the Egyptian pantheon were the bull, cow, vulture, falcon, hawk, crocodile, goat, ape, frog, beetle, and serpent.

False Gods
3934–3941

The Book of Exodus begins about 430 years after Jacob and his sons migrated to Egypt (Exod. 12:40,41). During this time the population of Egypt had increased appreciably. At the time

239

JOURNEYS OF THE CHILDREN OF ISRAEL FROM EGYPT

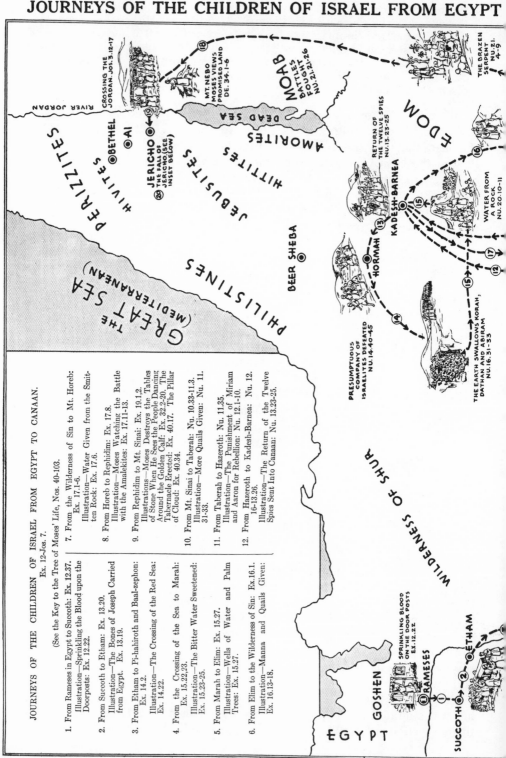

JOURNEYS OF THE CHILDREN OF ISRAEL FROM EGYPT TO CANAAN. Ex. 12-Jos. 7.

(See the Key to the Tree of Moses' Life, Nos. 40-103.)

1. From Rameses in Egypt to Succoth: Ex. 12.37.
   Illustration—Sprinkling the Blood upon the Doorposts: Ex. 12.22.

2. From Succoth to Etham: Ex. 13.20.
   Illustration—The Bones of Joseph Carried from Egypt: Ex. 13.19.

3. From Etham to Pi-hahiroth and Baal-zephon: Ex. 14.2.
   Illustration—The Crossing of the Red Sea: Ex. 14.22.

4. From the Crossing of the Sea to Marah: Ex. 15.22,23.
   Illustration—The Bitter Water Sweetened: Ex. 15.23-25.

5. From Marah to Elim: Ex. 15.27.
   Illustration—Wells of Water and Palm Trees: Ex. 15.27.

6. From Elim to the Wilderness of Sin: Ex.16.1.
   Illustration—Manna and Quails Given: Ex. 16.13-18.

7. From the Wilderness of Sin to Mt. Horeb: Ex. 17.1-6.
   Illustration—Water Given from the Smitten Rock: Ex. 17.6.

8. From Horeb to Rephidim: Ex. 17.8.
   Illustration—Moses Watching the Battle with the Amalekites: Ex. 17.11-13.

9. From Rephidim to Mt. Sinai: Ex. 19.1,2.
   Illustrations—Moses Destroys the Tables of Stone When He Sees the People Dancing Around the Golden Calf: Ex. 32.2-20. The Tabernacle Erected: Ex. 40.17. The Pillar of Cloud: Ex. 40.34.

10. From Mt. Sinai to Taberah: Nu. 10.33-11.3.
    Illustration—More Quails Given: Nu. 11. 31-33.

11. From Taberah to Hazeroth: Nu. 11.35.
    Illustration—The Punishment of Miriam and Aaron for Rebellion: Nu. 12.1-10.

12. From Hazeroth to Kadesh-Barnea: Nu. 12. 16-13.26.
    Illustration—The Return of the Twelve Spies Sent Into Canaan: Nu. 13.23-25.

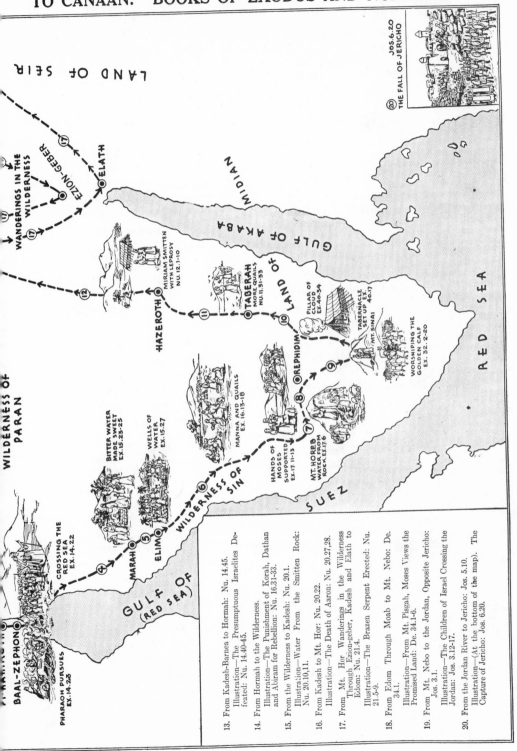

JOS. 6.20
⑳ THE FALL OF JERICHO

LAND OF SEIR

WANDERINGS IN THE WILDERNESS

⑰ EZION-GEBER

⑰ ELATH

LAND OF MIDIAN

GULF OF AKABA

MIRIAM SMITTEN WITH LEPROSY NU. 12.1-10

HAZEROTH

⑪

TABERAH MORE QUAILS NU. 11.31-33

RED SEA

PILLAR OF CLOUD EX. 40.34

⑩ REPHIDIM

TABERNACLE SET UP EX. 40.17

MT. SINAI

WORSHIPING THE GOLDEN CALF EX. 32. 2-20

WILDERNESS OF PARAN

BITTER WATER MADE SWEET EX. 15.23-25

WELLS OF WATER EX. 15.27

MANNA AND QUAILS EX. 16.13-18

HANDS OF MOSES SUPPORTED EX.17.11-13

MT. HOREB WATER FROM ROCK. EX.17.6

⑨

⑧

⑦

⑥ WILDERNESS OF SIN

SUEZ

BAAL-ZEPHON

CROSSING THE RED SEA EX. 14.22

④

⑤ MARAH

ELIM

GULF OF (RED SEA)

PHARAOH PURSUES EX. 14.23

13. From Kadesh-Barnea to Hormah: Nu. 14.45.
    Illustration—The Presumptuous Israelites Defeated: Nu. 14.40-45.

14. From Hormah to the Wilderness.
    Illustration—The Punishment of Korah, Dathan and Abiram for Rebellion: Nu. 16.31-33.

15. From the Wilderness to Kadesh: Nu. 20.1.
    Illustration—Water From the Smitten Rock: Nu. 20.10,11.

16. From Kadesh to Mt. Hor: Nu. 20.22.
    Illustration—The Death of Aaron: Nu. 20.27,28.

17. From Mt. Hor Wanderings in the Wilderness Through Ezion-geber, Kadesh and Elath to Edom: Nu. 21.4.
    Illustration—The Brazen Serpent Erected: Nu. 21.5-9.

18. From Edom Through Moab to Mt. Nebo: De. 34.1.
    Illustration—From Mt. Pisgah, Moses Views the Promised Land: De. 34.1-6.

19. From Mt. Nebo to the Jordan, Opposite Jericho: Jos. 3.1.
    Illustration—The Children of Israel Crossing the Jordan: Jos. 3.12-17.

20. From the Jordan River to Jericho: Jos. 5.10.
    Illustration—(At the bottom of the map). The Capture of Jericho: Jos. 6.20.

of the Exodus the Israelites numbered more then 600,000 men over 20 years of age, besides women and children (Num. 1:45,46). According to the best scholarly estimate, that would place the total population at about 3,000,000. Some scholars object to this high figure but for 70 persons to reach this number in 430 years it would only be necessary to double the population about every 25 years.

D. The Highlights of the Book of Exodus

The outline in the TCRB Helps No. 4224 gives four main subtopics for the content of the Book of Exodus:

Physical
Bondage
**1820, 2141–
2143, 3478**

1. *The Period of Bondage.* The oppression of Israel began under the new Pharaoh. The great increase in the Israelite population made this Pharaoh feel insecure. To slow their increase the Israelites were subjected to oppression and abuse. The Book ends with the marriage of Moses while he was in exile.

Deliverance
968–972

2. *The Period of Deliverance.* This topic includes the call of Moses at the burning bush, the twelve plagues, the deliverance under Moses from Pharaoh, and the institution of the Passover.

Discipline
497

3. *The Period of Discipline.* In this division is an account of Israel's travel experiences from Egypt to Mount Sinai.

Commandments
444

4. *The Period of Legislation and Organization.* During this period the Lord gave the Ten Commandments, the ordinances, and the plans for the tabernacle to Moses. YHWH, the LORD, gave the Israelites three religious institutions at Mt. Sinai:

   a. The tabernacle for a formal worship center (see Chs. 5, I, B and 11, I).

   b. The levitical priesthood, that was to supervise all religious activities.

Ordinances
2662

   c. The Ten Commandments and the ordinances which ultimately were incorporated into the Jewish Bible.

A Modern Pilgrimage to Mt. Sinai

See Map of
Wilderness
Journey
pp. 256, 257

It is possible for a religious pilgrim to retrace the steps of Moses and the Hebrew children from Egypt to Canaan provided there are no international border restrictions. For a map showing the traditional route of the Exodus, see pp. 240–241. Twelve to fifteen hours of hard driving are involved in a journey from Cairo to Mount Sinai. The traveler crosses the same bleak, desolate desert wilderness the children of Israel traversed over 3000 years ago. The sand, the desert insects, the rocks, the dreary ridges, and the rugged mountain peaks are still there. Much of the journey is through a dry river bed with marks of erosion on either bank.

IV. LEVITICUS

A. *The Name*

The Book of Leviticus deals largely with the levitical priesthood and the national festivals and ordinances which developed
during the first month of the second year after the Israelites
left Egypt. The word *leviticus* comes into the English version
from the Greek OT (LXX) where the term is rendered *leviti-
kon.* The Hebrew title, *Wayyiqra,* is actually the first word
in the Book of Leviticus (Hebrew) meaning "and he called."
The term is descriptive of the content in the Book.

B. *Authorship and Date*

The Book of Leviticus is placed third in the Pentateuch,
the Five Books of Moses. The question of authorship is related
to the continuing narrative from Genesis to Deuteronomy. In
the Book of Leviticus, as well as in Exodus, Numbers, and Deuteronomy, Moses is the central character. The name Moses is
mentioned in each of the 27 chapters of this book, except chapters 2 and 3, over 80 times in all.

The caption at the head of the Book of Leviticus, "The third
Book of Moses called Leviticus," was placed there by scribes
at a very early date to preserve author identification.

The liberal view ignores these considerations and classifies
Leviticus as "the priestly code." This code is known as "P"
within the "JEPD" documentary formula which assumes that
the book was compiled by priests in Jerusalem between 500
and 450 B.C. Robert H. Pfeiffer presents this view: "The priestly
code is a fifth century Midrash or historical commentary on
the embrionic Pentateuch (JED), including a series of narratives often illustrating legal precedents and a codification of
ritual laws based on earlier codes." [18] Dating the book about
600 years after the events it described was based on a wish
to view the history of the OT religion and literature in terms
of the liberal philosophies of the age. For example, Julius Wellhausen laid down the principle that the sense of sin in Israelite
sacrifice was a decidedly late development.[19] Robert O. Coleman addresses himself to this consideration: "The fact that
there would have had to be regulations before there could
have been orderly worship by the priests and people demands
a central controlling force and a fixed time. We can best understand this as the role of Moses at the establishment of tabernacle
worship . . . ; there is no need to believe that this fixing of
rites in worship of Jehovah was a gradual one of evolution or
that the record of Leviticus is a late invention of Ezra's day." [20]
Thus the JED formula has very little place for Moses or the
historical setting the Book of Leviticus describes. (For a discus-

The Old Testament

Inspiration
1774 Also see
417, 4173

Hebrew Festivals
1276

Worship of God
3921

Holiness
1596–1598

Insufficient Sacrifice
3108

Holiness
1596–1598

Polytheism
3928–3947

sion of the JEDP Documentary Hypothesis see page 220.)

The conservative position is that the writers of the Bible books were inspired by the Holy Spirit, and the events they set forth are factual and relevant to the period in which the described events took place. Even though Leviticus does not state that Moses wrote the book, the many instances of the use of the words, "The Lord spoke to Moses" (Lev. 4:1; 5:14, 6:1,8,19,24; 7:22,28) and the relationship Moses had in the establishment of the grand national festivals of the Jews such as the Passover, Pentecost, and the Feast of Tabernacles lead conservative Christians to accept the traditional view that Moses wrote the Book of Leviticus sometime before arriving on the plains of Moab. The historical review Moses gave there verifies the existence of Leviticus in some form. A well-organized plan of worship was already in use, based on the levitical ordinances and national feast days.

Thus one can see that the general subject matter of Leviticus is so intertwined with the content of other books in the Pentateuch that to deny Moses' authorship of one book would affect the entire Pentateuchal structure. Leviticus is definitely Mosaic in its subject matter, style, scope and terminology.

C. Background, Purpose, and Content

The general theme of Leviticus is holiness, both as to the nature of God and as a way of life for his subjects. God's divine injunction to the people was "Sanctify yourselves therefore, and be ye holy: for I am the LORD your God" (Lev. 20:7). In the OT the people were commanded to bring their sacrifices to the Tabernacle but in the NT Paul told the Hebrew Christians that "it is not possible that the blood of bulls and goats should take away sins" (Heb. 10:14). What then, was the worth of the blood sacrifices? It is believed that the value was symbolic. The true spiritual worshiper of the Lord brought his blood sacrifice as an expression of his love and devotion to God. It is obvious that the bringing of a sacrifice was not adequate (see 1 Sam. 15:20–22; Ps. 51:15,16), but that it merely symbolized the worshiper's obedience and devotion to God. Holiness of heart is carried through into the NT and expressed forcibly in Peter's sermon: "But as he which hath called you is holy, so be ye holy in all manner of conversation; because it is written, Be ye holy; for I am holy" (1 Peter 1:15,16); the latter part is a quotation from Leviticus 11:44.

The entire Book of Leviticus is designed to deter Israel from the polytheistic culture of Egypt and to establish a unified monotheistic concept of divine worship. The TCRB divides the Book of Leviticus into four main sections to show how

244

God endeavored to hold Israel's attention to the claims of the living God. The first division outlines "The Way of Access to God." The chief principle the LORD wanted Israel to learn was that they should approach God only at the altar designated. To this end the tabernacle with its altar was built.

The Pentateuch (Genesis–Deuteronomy)

One God
2648

The offertorial ceremonies were developed to help romanticize the worship of the Lord and to help Israel keep its undivided attention upon God. This provided a dramatic expression through which the worshipers could manifest their faith in God.

To help the Israelites express their inner motivation, God gave them a priesthood and a high priest to lead them. The worshiper might bring one of the five ceremonial offerings.

Priesthood
2863, 2864

1. The Burnt Offering

Burnt Offerings
2626

This offering was the first ritualistic ceremony (Lev. 1:2–9). It was designed to help Israel express undivided devotion to God by a complete dedication of themselves. As the animal "without spot or blemish" was offered to God on the altar by fire, the worshiper's own dedication would result in "self" being purified and directed by God. No one can give a more complete offering than himself. Paul illustrates this principle well in Roman 12:1,2.

Self-Abasement
3193

2. Meat or Meal Offering

Meal or Meat Offering
2630

The second ceremony (Lev. 2:1–16; 6:8–14) was designed to develop appreciation and thankfulness. Spiritual grace is a measure of a free gift from God; it is unmerited. Thus the recipient of a gift was to show his appreciation. God did not demand expensive sacrifices from poor people, but he expected each one would give freely according to his means. Even a pigeon or a small wafer was acceptable to the Lord as long as it was from a "broken spirit . . . and a contrite heart" (Ps. 51:17). So, when a worshiper made an offering, no matter how small, that person was giving a part of himself because some energy had to be expended to earn the cost of a small offering. Jesus summarized this principle in his reference to the "widow's mite" (Mark 12:42).

Pigeons
463

Mite
2386

3. Peace Offering

Peace Offering
2631

The third ceremony was the peace offering (Lev. 3:1–17; cf. 7:11–18). This ceremony was designed as a fellowship experience with God. One part of the offering was consumed by fire on the altar; the other part was reserved for a meal with

245

close friends and loved ones. The human association symbolized their joyful fellowship with the Lord.

4. Sin Offering

The fourth ceremony, the sin offering, was a means of expressing to the Lord guilt for sin (Lev. 4). All sins, whether intentional or unintentional, had to be atoned for by the prescribed blood sacrifice and confession.

5. Trespass Offering

The fifth and last ritual in this series was the trespass offering designed for the intentional offender, who was an offense against God and man, both of whom had to be satisfied. It required not only a sacrifice for sin but also restitution with compensation to the person offended. The idea of atonement was involved in both the sin and the trespass offering. In this section are some requirements for the priest: their cleansing, their holy garments, and their official duties. (See Lev. 8–10.)

The next section in the fourfold outline is "Special Enactments Governing Israel" (see the TCRB Helps No. 4225, II). This part deals with such practical matters as food, cleanliness, sanitation, purity of life as being conditions for divine favor, and the purity of the priests and the offerings (see Lev. 11–22).

Feasts:
Passover
1256
Pentecost
1257
Tabernacles
259

Section III in TCRB Helps No. 4225 deals with the "Five Annual Solemnities, or Feasts" (Lev. 14–24). This division concerns the Feasts of Passover, Pentecost, Trumpets, Tabernacles, and the Day of Atonement. (For a detailed discussion of these feasts see Ch. 6, II, III.)

Section IV deals with "General Enactments and Instructions" (Lev. 25–27), and discusses the Sabbatical year, the Year of Jubilee, and some miscellaneous laws and ordinances. (For a development of these subjects see Ch. 6, IV, V.) As noted in TCRB, the Book of Hebrews is the NT companion to Leviticus (see No. 4280 in TCRB Helps).

V. NUMBERS

A. The Name

The title of this book in the Hebrew canon is *Bemidgar*, a term found in the first verse which means "in the wilderness." In the Greek OT the term is rendered *Arithmoi,* from which the English word arithmetic is derived. In the Latin Vulgate the word is translated "number." Although the Book of Num-

Pillars at Baalbek, north of Damascus. This was once a center
of Baal worship. Six of the original columns still stand. They
are 66 ft. high and 22 ft. in circumference. They were brought
from the quarries at Aswan, Egypt, 1200 miles away

A 1200 ton stone at Baalbek

bers suggests a census, the actual numbering of the tribes occurs only in chapters 1, 2, 3, and 26.

B. Authorship and Date

The Book of Numbers is the fourth book of the Pentateuch, and Mosaic authorship is tied in with the assumption that Moses is the author of the Pentateuch. The name "Moses" appears 245 times in the Book of Numbers, and many of these references have the words, "the Lord spake unto" or "Moses spake." Certainly Moses was eminently qualified to write this book because he was present and a participant in the drama which unfolded in the Sinai desert.

One writer points out that certain passages in Numbers have the "appearance of having been written by Moses, . . . those which bear evidence of having been intended for a people not settled in cities but dwelling in tents and camps, e.g., Numbers 1–4, describing the arrangements for the census and the formation of the camp; the high priestly benediction is given in Numbers 6:24–26; orders for marching and halting the host are given in Numbers 10:35,36; the direction for the sounding of the silver trumpets in Numbers 10:1–9; the legislation which obviously presupposes the wilderness as the place for its observances (Num. 19:3,7,9,14). . . . It is not too much to say that the preponderance of evidence lies on the side of the substantial Mosaicity of the Book of Numbers." [21]

C. Background, Purpose, and Content

The Twelve Tribes of Israel have behind them the Passover (Exod. 12:22), the crossing of the Red Sea (Exod. 14:22), the experience of the bitter waters at Marah (Exod. 15:23–25), the sweet water wells at Elim (Exod. 15:27), the giving of the Law (Exod. 20:1–21), the tabernacle (Exod. 25:1–9), and the priesthood (Exod. 28:1–5) at Mount Sinai; their next main encampment was at Kadesh-Barnea (Num. 13:26; 32:8).

A brief analysis of the book shows that the tribes received organization and legislative instruction and that they prepared to break camp at Sinai and resume their journey toward the Promised Land. Every tribe was identified by the name of one of the twelve sons of Jacob. The two sons of Joseph, Ephraim and Manasseh, were designated as half-tribes (Num. 1–2). After the tribes were numbered and organized, they were assigned with respect to the service which they were to render in maintaining and moving the tabernacle (Num. 3). Each male from 20 to 50 years was to serve in some official capacity. Strict rules for camp sanitation were given (Num. 5). Rules for commemorating the Passover were defined (Num. 9).

Moses
2420, 2421

Tents
3596

Trumpets
2466–2467

Passover
2686

Marah
2249

Elam
1104, 4362

Tabernacle
3528

Priesthood
2863, 2864

Sinai
2444

Kadesh
1989

Ephraim
1144–1147

Manasseh
2244, 2245

It becomes evident that all the members in the tribe were not true Jehovah worshipers. There was in their midst a "mixed multitude or the Counterfeit Church" (see Ch. 10, VI). Judgment was pronounced upon those who murmured and doubted God's promises (Num. 11). The marriage of Moses to a Cushite wife resulted in sedition by Aaron and his sister, Miriam (Num. 12). Twelve men, one for each tribe, were sent into Canaan to spy out the land (Num. 13). The pessimism produced by the majority spy report caused rebellion in the camp. God decreed that all Israelites of twenty years and older were to perish in the wilderness (Num. 14). God established worship guidelines (Num. 15). The earth swallowed Korah, Dathan, and Abiram for their part in the insurrection against Moses (Num. 16). The authentic priesthood was to be determined by the budding rod (Num. 17). The priests were to be supported by tithes and offerings (Num. 18); the red heifer ordinance outlined the ritual of purification for sin (Num. 19). Miriam died and Moses was informed he would not be permitted to enter the Promised Land (Num. 20).

Many of the people, bitten by serpents, were healed by looking up to the brazen serpent, a type of Christ (Num. 21; cf. John 3:14). The Israelites faced Balak and the prophet Balaam (Num. 22) and had a running encounter with Balaam, the false prophet, until they arrived at the plains of Moab (Num. 22–25). The second census was taken; Joshua, Caleb, and Moses were the only adults who had survived from the first count (Num. 26). The inheritance laws were revised, and Joshua was appointed as Moses' successor (Num. 27). The laws relating to burnt offerings, the Sabbath, and the Passover were restated (Num. 28). Additional instructions were given regarding the feast days (Num. 29,30), and Israel's victory over the Midianites followed (Num. 31).

Reuben, Gad, and Manesseh settled for a tract of land on the east side of Jordan (Num. 32). Israelite history was reviewed (Num. 33), and a formula for dividing the land was worked out (Num. 34). Forty-eight cities were assigned to the Levites, including four cities of refuge (Num. 35); inheritance laws were given (Num. 36,37). The period in Exodus covered between 38 and 39 years.

VI. DEUTERONOMY

A. The Name

The name, Deuteronomy, is derived from the Septuagint (Greek OT) and means the second law.

The title Deuteronomy in the English is an Anglicized form of the Greek compound word *Deuteronomion*, which means "second

Mixed Multitude
2388
Miriam
2375

Korah
2043
Dathan and Abiram
918

Balak and Balaam
333, 334

Passover
2686

Book of Deuteronomy
4227

law" (*deutros* = second; *nomos* = law). This Greek term is an interpretative paraphrase of the Hebrew *Aleh (Hadebarim),* which means, "These be the words" (Deut. 1:1). In some of the Hebrew Commentaries the rabbis call this book *Misneh Torah,* which means "the repetition of the law." Others call it *Sepher Tukhhuth,* which means "the book of reproofs." This book is rightly referred to as the "second law" because it contains the Levitical laws and ordinances in a more concise and systematic form than previously given.[22]

B. Authorship and Date

The Book of Deuteronomy is the fifth book in the Pentateuch and is linked to Mosaic authorship. This view was held by both Jewish and Christian scholars until liberal scholars developed the Documentary Hypothesis, known as the JEDP theory (for a discussion of this theory see page 220 in this chapter). Jesus and the NT writers alluded to the Book of Deuteronomy over 100 times, usually indicating that the reference came from Moses (Mark 12:19; Matt. 19:8; Rom. 10:19). The name of Moses is frequently mentioned, and he is the central figure in Deuteronomy.

C. Background, Purpose, and Content

The Book of Deuteronomy covers a period of five weeks, from the first day in the eleventh month of the fortieth year after the Israelites left Egypt, ending one lunar month later.

It consists mainly of the three great addresses of Moses to the new generation that had grown up since the law was given at Mount Sinai. The rebellious generation, twenty years old and upward (Num. 14:29), had died; of the adults only Joshua, Caleb, and Moses were still living.

In his first great address (Deut. 1–4) Moses reviewed the events of the wilderness and reminded the people of God's

faithful protective care from Sinai to the plains of Moab.

In his second address (Deut. 5–20) Moses gave a commentary

on the Ten Commandments, which had been given at Mount Sinai (Exod. 20). In this discussion he emphasized that the love of God is the practical formula for obeying the Commandments (Deut. 6:5; 10:12; cf. Matt. 23:36–40; Lev. 19:18). Moses also

pointed out that the idea behind the initiatory rite of circumcision is spiritual circumcision of the heart (Deut. 10:16; see also 30:6; Jer. 4:4; Rom. 2:29; Col. 2:11). (For additional information on circumcision see page 184.) In this address Moses explained the importance of such feast days as the Passover, Pentecost,

and Tabernacles, reminding the people that the covenant God had made with Abraham, Isaac, and Jacob was equally binding

Wadi Musa, entrance to canyon at Petra. Known as Moab's Rock
Fortress. Moses was denied passage through Moab

An ancient mosaic map of Jericho. It shows fish in the Jordan
River turning around after contacting the Dead Sea. This map
is located on the floor in the church at Madaba, Jordan

for the new generation. Many of this generation were old enough to remember that obedience resulted in rewards and that the penalty for disobedience was punishment (Deut. 6:1–9; 7:12–27).

To insure justice, six levitical cities of refuge were set aside where the law violator could be protected until legal machinery could be set up for a just trial (Num. 35:9ff.).

The parents were cautioned to provide religious training for their children. The priests were urged to read the Law to the people once every seven years. In this address Moses warned the people against the temptation of spiritual adultery or idolatry.

In his third address (Deut. 27–30) Moses directed his attention to the future, thereby expressing his faith in God's providential plan for the people after they crossed the Jordan river. The leaders were instructed to call a judicial council after arrival in Canaan for the purpose of ratifying and renewing commitment to the covenant given the patriarchs.

Moses blessed each of the twelve tribal leaders (Deut. 33). Moses was permitted to view the promised land from "Pisgah's lofty height," the highest point in the Mount Nebo range, but was not permitted to enter because of his indiscretion in the desert (Num. 20:7–13).

Deuteronomy 34 contains an account of the death of Moses: some critics object to Mosaic authorship of Deuteronomy because of this death account (see section I of this chapter). Certainly the literary content and continuity in Deuteronomy 34 is such that it could easily fit at the head of Joshua's chronicle. Some scholars suggest that Joshua wrote the postscript for Deuteronomy. It is possible that Joshua was present when Moses died.

16

The Historical Books (Joshua–Esther)

I. JOSHUA

A. The Name

The Book of Joshua is named for one of the faithful spies who, with Caleb, brought back a true report from Canaan. Joshua is the first book of the second group of Hebrew writings known as "The Former Prophets." Other writings in this series include Judges, 1 and 2 Samuel, and 1 and 2 Kings. The name Joshua underwent a progressive change in spelling. When Joshua was listed with the other eleven spies, he was called "Oshea the son of Nun" (Num. 13:8). Before the spies departed on their mission, Moses called Oshea "Jehoshua" (Num. 13:16). When the spies returned, Jehoshua became "Joshua" (Num. 14:6). He was so called from that time on.

In the NT the name Joshua is Grecized and appears as Jesus (Acts 7:45; Heb. 4:8). Why this change of spelling came to be is uncertain, but it is known that Hebrew custom was to change the name of a person at a time of crisis or in changed relationships: for example, Abram was changed to Abraham; Jacob to Israel; and Saul to Paul. It is possible that Joshua's name was changed to reflect the continuing revelation of the messianic hope. As a leader, Joshua is a type of Christ. The name Oshea, meaning, "helper," was changed to Joshua meaning "Jehovah the helper." (For a discussion of the various divine names see page 75ff. under "The Titles and/or Names of God in the Bible.") Joshua's character is reflected in his consecration (Num. 14:6–8); he is notable for his spiritual mindedness (Josh.

Book of
Joshua
4228

Spies
3429

Joshua
1922, 4293,
pp. 258, 259

Messianic
Hope
4186

Joshua's
Character
Study
4293

253

3:5; 8:30), his godly reverence (Josh. 5:14), his courage (Josh.
10:25), and his obedience (Josh. 11:15).

Joshua was an Ephramite (Num. 13:8) who settled in Tim-
nath-serah (Josh. 9:50) and was buried in the hill country of
Ephraim.[1] Because of his loyalty to Moses and his spiritual integrity the Lord appointed Joshua to succeed Moses (Deut.
31:22,23) and to lead the children of Israel into Canaan. Joshua
was eminently qualified for this office, having served as personal
minister to Moses (Exod. 24:13; 32:17). He was in attendance

when the Lord communicated with Moses (Exod. 33:11); he
learned about the power of the Holy Spirit from Moses (Num.
11:27–29). His experience as a spy familiarized him with the
Canaanites' territory in Palestine.[2]

B. Authorship and Date

According to tradition, the Book of Joshua was written by
the man whose valiant achievements it relates. Both Jewish
and Christian scholars have held to this view. Joshua certainly
is the central human figure throughout the entire Book. His
name appears at least once in every chapter except the sixteenth. With the advent of the Documentary Hypothesis this
book suffered literary alteration along with the books of the
Pentateuch. (For a discussion of this liberal theory see page
219ff.)

The most likely answer to authorship is found in the "Deuter-
onomist Theory" which supposes that Joshua preserved a record of events, written and/or oral, which was later compiled
and edited to form the book as it appears in the Bible. There
may have been an editor after the time of Joshua because the
book contains a record of Joshua's death and burial (Josh. 24:29–
31).[3]

C. Background, Purpose, and Content

The Book of Joshua continues the historical narrative begun
in the Pentateuch, and it is sometimes called the last book in
the Hexateuch.* As to subject matter, Joshua is more closely
related to the Pentateuch than to the books of the Former
Prophets of which it is a part.

---

* Hexateuch consists of the five books of the Pentateuch plus Joshua, which
form a six-book literary unit having historical continuity. Some believe that
the Hexateuch preceded the Pentateuch as a literary unit and that the Book
of Joshua was removed about 400 B.C. on religious and theological grounds,
namely to emphasize the importance of the Torah—the Pentateuch—as
the Five Books of Moses (Ferm, *Encyclopedia of Religion*, Philosophical Library).

Excavation at Jericho showing various strata of civilization

Seven-pronged candlestick originally placed in the Tabernacle

Excavation at Hazor, city destroyed by Joshua

Hazor—cultic objects and statue from "C" temple

"House on the wall" in Ankara, typical of house where Rahab
lived in Jericho

The Book of Joshua records the crossing of Jordan, the people's encounter with the fortress city of Jericho, and the establishment of the twelve tribes in their homeland (a privilege Jacob's descendents did not have for four hundred years). All of the tribes received their land allotment except the priestly tribe of Levi, who controlled only the six cities of refuge.

The Historical Books (Joshua–Esther)
Jericho
1878, 4380

Joshua was faithful in carrying out the instructions of Moses. The covenant made by God with the fathers was reaffirmed (Josh. 24:14–33). Joshua proved himself to be a strong leader (Josh. 1:2–9). The words in Joshua's farewell address challenged the tribes as well as they have countless followers of the Lord: "Now therefore fear the LORD, and serve him in sincerity and in truth . . . . as for me and my house, we will serve the LORD" (Josh. 24:14,15).

Important information about the early topographic details of Palestine have been preserved in this book. Archaeological evidence in many parts of Palestine confirms the accuracy of the book of Joshua. (See Archaeological section in TCRB Helps, No. 4324—Ai; No. 4370—Gerizim; No. 4378—Hazor; No. 4380—Jericho; No. 4388—Lachish; No. 4411—Shechem; No. 4412—Shiloh.)

II. JUDGES

A. The Name

Book of Judges
4229

The title of the Book of Judges was derived from the special rulers, the Judges, appointed by God to assume governmental control after the death of Joshua. Judges is the eighth book in the OT and the second in a group called "The Former Prophets."

Judges of Israel
1821, 1822
Joshua
1922

The name Judges comes from the Hebrew *shaphatim* (pl.) and refers to men who ruled and directed the affairs of state in Israel from the death of Joshua until the crowning of Saul as king (Judg. 2:16). The term *shaphatim* (pl.) is unlike the term *shaphat* (sing.), meaning "one who judges controversies in court."

Saul, King of Israel
3158

B. Authorship and Date

Phinehas
2760
Ezra
1199
Hezekiah
1585
Samuel
3138
257

The authorship of the Book of Judges is unknown. Some scholars suggest that each judge maintained a diary or executive log and that eventually some redactor (editor) compiled the book into the form as it appears in the Bible. "Some ascribe it to Phinehas, to Samuel, to Hezekiah, and some to Ezra. But it is evident that it is the work . . . of a person who lived posterior to the time of the judges . . . and most probably of

Excavation at Megiddo shows a circular altar dating back to the Canaanite period

Temple steps at Baalbek (Lebanon). The steps leading to the temple were cut out of solid blocks of stone weighing 600–1000 tons each

Samuel." [4] Others have suggested that the final compilation of the book may have come after the Josiah reform.[5]

Charles R. Wilson writes that "the dates for the period of the Judges may be set between 1250 and 1050 B.C. This includes the history of Israel from the death of Joshua to the rise of the monarchy under Saul. Joshua's death may be dated in 1417 B.C., as seen from comparing the following references: Exod. 17:8ff.; 16:35; Josh. 24:19; 1 Kings 6:1. This would make the period of the Judges roughly 367 years." [6]

C. Background, Purpose, and Content

No leader had been provided to succeed Joshua; so when he died the nation of Israel was without a central government or an executive head. The nation soon degenerated and began to serve the gods of the heathen nations. Law and order became a personal matter and soon ceased to exist. "Every man did that which was right in his own eyes" (Judg. 17:6). Repeatedly God intervened and provided a judge to deliver the people from their life of bondage.

The office of judge was not hereditary nor were the judges elected by the people. They were special rulers chosen by God and were always selected by him in a supernatural way. Adam Clarke says:

> They [the judges] had no power to make or change the laws; they were only to execute them under the direction of the Most High God; therefore God was king in Israel: the government was a theocracy; and the judges were his deputies. The office, however, was not continual, as there appear intervals in which there was no judge in Israel. And, as they [the judges] were extraordinary persons they were only raised up on extraordinary occasions to be instruments in the hands of God [in] delivering their nation from the oppression and tyranny of the neighboring powers.[7]

The pattern of Israel's apostasy was consistent. When the "children of Israel did evil in the sight of the LORD and forgat the LORD their God, and served Baalim and the groves . . . . The anger of the LORD was hot against Israel." The Lord turned them over to a heathen rule for a season (Judg. 3:7,8,12; 4:1; 6:1).

The pattern of deliverance was also consistent. When the people repented and cried unto the Lord, the Lord raised up a deliverer for the children of Israel, to conquer the enemy and to deliver the people from bondage (Judg. 3:9,15; 4:3; 6:7). At times of victory some of the leaders composed and sang a ballad of triumph (Judg. 5:1ff.; see also Exod. 15:1ff.).

The general teaching of Judges is consistent with the law as revealed to Moses by God. The Book of Judges constantly

Baal
3936

Anarchy
2551

Book of the Law
525

Deliverance
968–971

Apostasy
1235

Repentance
2706–2710

Songs of Victory
2477

259

The Old Testament

Discipline
497

Samuel
3138

Book of Ruth
4230

manifests the discipline which the Lord had imposed upon his people. In the national development of Israel, the cycle of sin, sorrow, repentance, and salvation occurred repeatedly.

The instability in the national and religious affairs of Israel continued until the days of Samuel. This last judge, and the first prophet, led the way for Israel's spiritual and national renewal.

III. RUTH

A. The Name

The name Ruth is not a translation but a transliteration of a Moabite name into Hebrew characters. This is one of the few instances where the meaning of a name in Hebrew is unknown. No Hebrew stem can be positively identified. The fact that Ruth was not a Jew may account for a lack of etymological identification. The book was obviously so named because Ruth is the central character. In the Hebrew canon Ruth is one of the Five Scrolls *(Megilloth)* and is listed in the category of the Writings (Heb., *kethubim;* Gr., *hagiographa*).

B. Authorship and Date

According to Jewish tradition, Samuel wrote the Book of Ruth, but certain internal information raises the question of whether Samuel was the sole author. It is, however, quite possible that Samuel helped to preserve information on the events in Ruth. The reference to (King) David (1000–960 B.C.) in Ruth 4:17–22 makes it unlikely that Ruth in its present form was written in Samuel's lifetime. The opening words in the book suggest a backward look: "It came to pass in the days when the judges ruled" seems to indicate that the period of the judges was a comparatively distant event (Ruth 1:1). Miller and Miller say, "It is believed to have been written in the post-exilic period (c. 400 B.C.); the chief reasons for assigning it to this period are (1) the language it employs; (2) the obsolete customs it depicts which must be explained to its readers (Ruth 4:7); and (3) its implied protest against Nehemiah's and Ezra's censure of the mixed marriages so popular after the exile (Ruth 1:4; Neh. 13:1–3,23–27; Ezra 10)." [8]

Book of
Judges
1821

Nehemiah
2577
Ezra
1199

Book of
Judges
4287

C. Background, Purpose, and Content

The Book of Ruth is one of the shortest books in the OT, but few books surpass it for historical background. It is a natural sequel to the Book of Judges. Adam Clarke suggests that it might have originally been an appendix to the Book of Judges.[9]

The description of King David's ancestry makes the Book of Ruth a connecting link with later historical books. The friendly relationship expressed in the Book of Ruth by the Moabites toward this Jewish family is again manifested when David placed his mother and father in the care of the king of Moab (1 Sam. 22:3,4; cf. Matt. 1:5).

The Historical Books (Joshua–Esther)

David
919, 4296

One of the motives for this book probably was to combat racial prejudice. This story shows that "God is no respecter of persons" (Acts 10:34) and that all nationalities are welcome into the kingdom when they repent and have faith in Jehovah. Ruth is an example of one who separated herself from her people, the Moabites, and became loyal to the nation and religion of Israel. In this book the Moabitess, Ruth, became a link in the messianic line.

Racial Prejudice
4083

Ruth
3097a

Concerning the Book of Ruth, Arthur E. Caudell wrote, "It enshrines so much of what is basic in human relationships and in true Israelite religion. It is a story of a loyal, disinterested relationship which secured its just reward. . . . The upright, considerate, and industrious Boaz was a model Israelite. It demonstrated an overruling Providence and the all-embracing love of God, illustrating the fact made explicit in Acts 10:34–35. It is a story of ordinary people [who] . . . appeal to the heart.

True Religion
2985–2987

It speaks a word of hope to the hopeless, the desolate, and the bereaved." [10] Perhaps the spirit of the book is expressed in Boaz's statement to Ruth: "It hath fully been shewed me, all that thou hast done unto thy mother in law since the death of thine husband: and how thou hast left thy father and thy mother, and the land of thy nativity, and art come unto a people which thou knewest not heretofore" (Ruth 2:11,12). The Book of Ruth also communicates the providential care by the Lord Jehovah for two widows, Ruth and Naomi, in desperate circumstances, and the ancient customs of courtship and marriage.

Boaz
520

Book of Ruth
4330

The ethical values of the book must not be overlooked. Here a good example is presented of "steadfast filial piety." The loyal commitment of Ruth to Naomi and her God brought to Ruth prosperity, happiness, a good husband, and the honor she received as an ancestress of the House of David.

Piety
2986

IV. 1 AND 2 SAMUEL

A. *The Name*

Books of First and Second Samuel
4231, 4232

The name Samuel comes from the Hebrew *Shemuel*. The two books of Samuel originally formed a single book called by that name; 1 and 2 Kings were also one book. It is evident

261

The Old
Testament

Saul, King of
Israel
3158

Kingdom

2008–2012

that both Samuel and Kings books are a continuation of the Book of Judges because they contain an account of the last judge and the election of Saul, as well as the chronicles of the kings of Israel and Judah.

Herbert W. Wolf explains that when the OT was translated into Greek (Septuagint, early third century B.C.) the books of Samuel were divided into two books, called the "Books of Kingdoms." "In similar fashion Kings became 'Kingdoms III and IV'. . . . Jerome affixed the title 'Books of the Kings'. . . . His modification of 'Kingdoms' to 'Kings' was intended to reproduce the Hebrew title for the present 1 and 2 Kings . . . . Eventually the Latin Vulgate reverted to the name 'Samuel' for the first two books." [11]

The Rabbinic Bamberg Bible, published in 1516, divided the Samuel Book into Parts 1 and 2. When the Bible was translated into English, Jerome's modified arrangement of 1 and 2 Samuel and 1 and 2 Kings was adopted.

B. Authorship and Date

It is impossible to ascribe the authorship of the Samuel books to any one person. The name Samuel was probably given to these books because of the prominent place that the prophet has in the first twenty-five chapters; his death is recorded in chapter 25.

Elmer B. Smick remarks that

> There are indications in Scriptures that the prophets Samuel, Nathan, and Gad were the authors. 1 Samuel 10:25 says that Samuel wrote a book and laid it up before the Lord, while 1 Chronicles 29:29 states that the acts of David were 'written in the book of Samuel, the seer, and in the book of Nathan, the prophet, and in the book of Gad, the seer' (cf. 2 Chron. 9:29 are the acts of Solomon). It is not likely that Samuel could have been responsible for more than the early part of 1 Samuel since his death is recorded in Ch. 25. 2 Samuel 5:5 speaks of the complete reign of David in the past tense, so someone who outlived David wrote the section.[12]

Reference is also made to the Book of Jesher (2 Sam. 1:18) (now in print but its origin is questioned). The books of Nathan and Gad are no longer in existence; therefore, verifying their content is impossible. However, since the books are referred to in Scripture, one may assume that they contained reliable information. It is possible that the final edition of the Samuel books, under the leading of the Holy Spirit, drew some information from these sources as well as from the royal records such as those David preserved (1 Chron. 27:24). It is evident that much of the material in 1 Samuel is contemporary with the prophet Samuel. These noncanonical sources are very important and have much historical value.

C. Background, Purpose, and Content

Since the Books of Samuel deal at length with Samuel's life, a biographical sketch follows. Scripture records that Samuel, whose name means the "name of God," was the last of the judges (1 Sam. 7:15; Acts 13:20) and the earliest Hebrew prophet after Moses (2 Chron. 35:18; Jer. 15:1). Samuel's father was Elkanah, a Levite, who with his family lived in the hill country of Ephraim (Josh. 21:5; 1 Chron. 6:66). Hannah, Samuel's mother, was barren, but after special prayer she gave birth to Samuel, whom she dedicated to the Lord. While he was yet a child, Samuel ministered in the tabernacle at Shiloh, living in a chamber in or near the tabernacle. The Lord revealed himself to Samuel in his early boyhood (1 Sam. 3:4ff.). By the time the youth had reached manhood, he was revered and respected by Israel from Dan to Beersheba (1 Sam. 3:20,21).

Samuel was unlike some of the prophets who succumbed to the temptation of rendering pleasing prophecies during times of stress (Jer. 14:13,14; 27:1,10,14; see also Amos 7:10–17). He and the other prophets (Jeremiah, Ezekiel, Daniel, Amos) shunned this temptation; they obediently proclaimed the whole counsel of God. The Books of Samuel had a twofold purpose: first, to narrate the historical events preceding the prophet's time and, second, to teach the moral and spiritual lessons portrayed in God's revelation. Charles R. Wilson comments,

> The authenticity and completeness of the history of Israel recorded in the books of Samuel give great emphasis to the significance of history in the Bible. It was through the outworking of the historical process that God revealed His acts. The compiler of Samuel was aware of that and perceived that what had happened in the course of Israel's history was vital to his contemporaries for their instruction and admonition concerning God's activity in their time.[13]

The Books of Samuel record the reformation work begun by the prophet following the confusion and apostasy recorded in the Book of Judges. This revival began when, during Samuel's tenure as judge, Israel was delivered from the Philistines at Mizpah (1 Sam. 7:3–14).

Even though it was not God's choice, the people insisted on having a king. With Samuel's guidance, Saul was selected as Israel's first king (1 Sam. 11:15). Even though Saul began his reign under favorable circumstances, he soon showed con-

Samuel
3138

Elkanah
1118

Hannah
1495

Shiloh
3271, 4412

Beersheba
388, 4335

False Prophets
2100

Godly Prophets
2074

Morality
572, 573

Reformers
2076
Revivals
312–315
King Demanded by Israel
2966
263

tempt for his obligations. Saul was commanded to totally destroy the war booty taken from the Amalekites, but he disobeyed God and chose to save the best oxen and sheep (1 Sam. 15:9). After his loss of fellowship with God, Saul was troubled by an evil spirit (1 Sam. 16:14–16). When Saul's condition continued to deteriorate, his servants urged him to "seek out a man, who is a cunning player on an harp" (1 Sam. 16:16).

Evil Spirits
3156

King Saul
3158

Jealous
1851
Fortune
Tellers
2230, 2231

Samuel chose David, the son of Jesse, to be Saul's comforter. David's superior qualities aroused Saul's jealousy. As a result, Saul determined to murder David (1 Sam. 19:1). After the danger to his life became great, David left the court and became a wanderer (1 Sam. 18–20); he even aided the Philistines in their warfare against Israel (1 Sam. 29–30).[14]

Eventually Saul sought the counsel of the witch at Endor (1 Sam. 28:7ff.), who brought Samuel back from the dead, but instead of friendly reunion Samuel rebuked Saul (1 Sam. 28:15). Finally Saul's loss of fellowship and communion with God led to his suicide (1 Sam. 31:4). David was anointed king by the men of Judah.

V. 1 AND 2 KINGS

A. The Name

The word for king comes from the Hebrew *melakhim*. The other meanings or titles of the Book of Kings have been many. The earliest title, consisting of the first three words in 1 Kings, "Now king David" (1 Kings 1:1), is similar in origin to the title for the book of Genesis, which came from the first word, *bereshith*, which translates "in the beginning" (Gen. 1:1).

In early times the Samuel and Kings books were 1 and 2 Kings (the Samuel Books) and 3 and 4 Kings (the Kings Books). These divisions were justified on the basis that all of these writings were one continuous religious-political unit. The Books of Kings cover a period of about 400 years.

In the original Hebrew there were only consonant forms (without vowels). After A.D. 600 the vowel points were added and with this addition the scrolls doubled in size. Dividing the scrolls into two parts may have been functional, i.e., to facilitate their use.

B. Authorship and Date

The author of the Kings books is unknown. Some scholars suggest that Ezra was the compiler or editor. As a priest, Ezra was a zealous servant of the Lord, a reformer opposing the corruption which had filtered in. He was also approved and accepted by the Jews.[15] Others suggest that a prophet in Babylon wrote the book during or after the Exile, in about 550 B.C. The "synchronism between the northern and southern kingdoms throughout the Kings books favors the idea that these records were kept by the prophets." [16] The material for the compilation of these books may have come from public and private records similar to the Samuel books.

Some scholars suggest that Isaiah and Jeremiah may have participated in the compiling and editing of these books because of the similarity of several chapters in both prophetic writings to some in 1 and 2 Kings. Compare 2 Kings 18:19,20 with Isaiah 36, 37, 38, and 39; and 2 Kings 24:18 and 25:1 with Jeremiah 52:1. An alternate view is that the prophets perhaps used some material from the Kings books.[17] The uniformity of the style and the connection of the events suggest a single author or editor. That this person had access to ancient documents is suggested by his own words, "the rest of the acts . . . are they not written in the book of the chronicles of the kings of Judah?" (1 Kings 11:41; 14:19,29; 15:7,23,31; 16:5,14,20,27).

C. Purpose and Content

The First Book of Kings begins with the close of David's reign. His son Solomon took the kingdom into its golden age during which time the temple was built. At Solomon's death the territory was divided into the Southern Kingdom (Judah) and the Northern Kingdom (Israel). The writer of these books usually gave the length of each king's reign and the name of the queen of the king of Judah. As to the spiritual history, the writer stated each king's relationship to God. The whole viewpoint is Deuteronomic, with emphasis on loyalty and obedience to Jehovah.

David
919

Solomon
3414

Kings of Judah
1824
Kings of Israel
1823

The Books of the Kings show that the rulers of Israel did not hesitate to violate the Davidic covenant (2 Sam. 7:8–16) nor the covenant God made with Israel at Shechem (Deut. 29:1–22).

Shechem
3258, 3259, 4411

The Kings books started with a stable kingdom and ended with a total collapse and deportation of the people, the net result of rebellion and idolatry.

Idolatry
3928–3933

The chart on page 194 in TCRB Helps shows the moral heights and depths in the lives of the kings of Judah. As the people followed the example of their rulers, it pictures the causes of the downfall of the kingdom which led to the primary cause of the Babylonian captivity.

The Old Testament

Books of First
and Second
Chronicles
4235, 4236

David
919

Solomon
3414

VI. 1 AND 2 CHRONICLES

A. The Name

The Chronicles, once a single continuous scroll, and written in chronological order, are so named because of their historical account of the reign of the kings of Judah and Israel. There is no structural reason for dividing the books into two parts; the beginning narrative in book two is a continuation of the kingly line which ends in book one with the death of David and begins in book two with the reign of Solomon, David's son and successor. In the Hebrew canon the Chronicles books are listed under the category of the Writings (Heb., *kethubim;* Gr., *hagiographa*).

These books have had several names. One of the great commentators writes:

> In Hebrew they are denominated . . . *dibrey haiyamim;* literally, "The Words of the Days," i.e., the Journals, particularly of the kings of Israel and Judah. . . . The Septuagint (Greek OT) has . . . "of the things that were left omitted" which seems to suggest that these books were a supplement either to Samuel and the books of Kings, or to the whole Bible. . . . In our English Bible these words termed "Chronicles from the Greek . . . A History of Times, Kingdoms, States, Religion, etc. with an Account of the most memorable Persons and Transactions of those Times and Nations." [18]

In the Greek OT the word *paralipomena* is used for Chronicles and means "of the things that were left or omitted."

B. Authorship and Date

The authorship of the Chronicles books is unknown. Some think that they are the work of different authors. There is internal support for this view in a number of references. The Jews took great care to record their civil, military, and religious transactions, and to ascertain that the men who did the recording were indeed "holy men of God" who wrote "as they were moved by the Holy Ghost" (2 Peter 1:21). The reign of David was recorded by Samuel, Nathan, and Gad (1 Chron. 29:29); the acts of Solomon were written by Nathan, Ahijah, and Iddo (2 Chron. 9:29). Some of the acts of Jehoshaphat were written by "Jehu the son of Hanani" (2 Chron. 20:34); Isaiah recorded the royal records of Uzziah (2 Chron. 26:22), and those of Hezekiah (2 Chron. 32:32). Other references to authors are found in 2 Chronicles 28:9 and 33:19. Frequently the prophets were closely associated with the kings and had scribal responsibility. However, one commentator concludes that "the uniformity of the style, the connection of the facts, together with the recapitulation and reflections which are often made, prove that they are the work of one . . . person." [19] Both Jews and Christians have long had the opinion that Ezra was the man who finally organized, edited, and compiled the Chronicles as they appear in the Bible. Some suggest he was assisted by Haggai, Zechariah, and Malachi.

Second Chronicles concludes with the reference to Cyrus, the Persian king who conquered the Babylonians and set the Jewish captives free (2 Chron. 36:23). Ezra, Haggai, Zechariah, and Malachi were prominent and active at the time when Cyrus published his emancipation decree included in the Book of Ezra, which follows 2 Chronicles. Some of the terms in these postexilic writings which do not appear in prior writings may have been acquired in exile: e.g., "golden cups" in 1 Chronicles 28:17 and in Ezra 1:10, 8:27 and "a drachma" or drams in 1 Chronicles 29:7; Ezra 2:69; Nehemiah 7:70; "rafts" or floats, 2 Chronicles 2:16 and 1 Kings 5:9. Calmet considers these words as strong evidence that these books were the work of Ezra, which he penned after the captivity.[20]

Ezra returned to Jerusalem in about 457 B.C., and Nehemiah assumed the position of governor in about 444 B.C. The temple had been rebuilt in 520–515 B.C. Then followed a period of extreme Jewish laxity in matters of Mosaic law and indifference to religious obligations. No positive date for the Chronicles books has been determined. All specific dates are at best only suppositions. Ezra may have written the Chronicles at a time of a low spiritual level, possibly the time he went from Babylon to Jerusalem and after the walls were rebuilt, between 450 and 397 B.C. As to the date of the writing, debate continues among the scholars.

C. Background, Purpose, and Content

It was during this time that Ezra felt a pressing need for a religious revival. To stimulate and challenge the people, Ezra may have been prompted to write a historical homily to remind his readers of their rich heritage and the providential oversight which the Lord Jehovah had provided for them throughout the generations. This may explain why the Chronicles books are historical sketches and not complete history. They may have been written specifically to promote revival.

The Chronicles books are neither solely a record of events occurring at that time, nor are they a supplement to previous books. The writer relates in them many things which had already occurred, but he also omits some important events in the history of Israel. However, he includes little that is not recorded in other books. Genealogy predominates until the tenth chapter in 1 Chronicles, which begins abruptly with the

Looking down into Hezekiah's tunnel

Central avenue in Tadmor, 150 miles northeast of Damascus, outpost under King Solomon. Street is almost a mile long and has 750 columns each 55 feet high (2 Chron. 8:4). Under Rome the name was changed to Palmyra

unsuccessful battle of Saul and his ensuing death. The writer gives many details in the life of David, but he omits reference to David's adultery with Bathsheba and the consequences. Nothing is recorded about the incest of Amnon and his sister Tamar nor of the rebellion of Absalom.

The purpose of the books was to give the people a partial genealogy from Adam to about 500 B.C. (1 Chron. 1–9) and to establish family descent (cf. Ezra 2:59); to review the Kingdom of David (1 Chron. 10–29), and to enumerate the principles of the ideal theocratic state.[21] Second Chronicles 1–9 portrays the glory of Solomon with emphasis on worship in the temple. Second Chronicles 10–36 gives a history of the Southern Kingdom with its "religious reforms and the military victories of Judah's more pious kings." [22]

Religious Reforms 316–318

See chart on page 194 of TCRB Helps, showing the moral heights and depths in the lives of the kings of Judah. As the people followed the example of their rulers, it pictures the causes of the downfall of the kingdom, which led to the primary cause of the Babylonian captivity.

VII. EZRA

A. The Name

The Book of Ezra derives its title from the man who is thought to have been the compiler and author. In Hebrew the name is "Ezra" and appears fourteen times in the book. In the Hebrew canon the historical Book of Ezra is listed in the category of the Writings (Heb., *kethubim;* Gr., *hagiographa*).

Book of Ezra 4237

B. Authorship and Date

There is evidence to support the conclusion that the Books of Ezra and Nehemiah were originally one book. Furthermore, the style, continuity, connective links, and approach suggest that these two books, forming a large, single scroll, also included the Chronicles books. It is significant that the last two verses of 2 Chronicles are almost identical to the first two verses in Ezra.[23] Charles R. Wilson points out that "Ezra and Nehemiah have affinities with I and II Chronicles. The most satisfactory explanation is that these writings are the work of one compiler . . . . Two sections in Ezra are in Aramaic (4:7–6:18; 7: 12–26) . . . . If these sections represent the Aramaic language of Babylon that was prevalent during that part of the period of the restoration included in the Old Testament narrative, these writings may be dated between 430 and 397 B.C." [24] The

Ezra 1199 Nehemiah 2517

Aramaic content would indicate that the author was familiar with the language of Babylonia, the country in which the Jews were enslaved. "Ezra was a very holy man; so also was he a very learned man, and especially skilled in the knowledge of the Holy Scriptures; and therefore he is said to have been a very ready scribe in the law of God, for which he was so eminent that Artaxerxes takes [sic] particular notice of it [sic] in his commission." [25] Certainly Ezra was well qualified to write the books of Ezra and Nehemiah as well as the Chronicles books. One may assume the date of the books to be somewhere between 430 and 397 B.C. However, among the scholars the debate on the issue has not been resolved.

C. Background, Purpose, and Content

Backsliding
993

In 2 Chronicles and 2 Kings we are given an account of the disaster which befell both the northern kingdom (Israel) and the southern kingdom (Judah) because of their backslidings and rebellions. Israel was carried into captivity by the Assyrians, never to regain its political identity. Judah, a less idolatrous country, was taken into Babylonian captivity for seventy years.

Cyrus
907

When Cyrus, the Persian king, conquered Babylonia, the Jews were emancipated and were permitted to return to Jerusalem. The Books of Ezra and Nehemiah tell how Judah was restored— how the workers rebuilt the Jerusalem altar, temple, and walls. A scholar of note observes that

> In the beginning of the year 458, before the Christian era, Ezra obtained of King Artaxerxes and his seven counsellors a very ample commission for his return to Jerusalem, with all of his nation, the Jews, that were willing to accompany him . . . . giving him full authority there to restore and settle the state, and reform the Church of the Jews, and to regulate and govern both according to their laws.[26]

Persia
2744

It is interesting to note that the Persian king was so intent on the resettlement of the Jews in Judea that he gave freely from the treasury of the state to help rebuild "the house of their God" (Ezra 7:15,16; see also 2 Chron. 36:23).

Jewish
Dispersion
1023

There is no way to measure the extent of the influence the dispersion of the Jews had in the spreading of the Jewish faith. It is evident that sometime during the seventy years of the Babylonian captivity the Jews settled all over Babylonia as well as in Persia. God's providential hand was at work to provide a deliverer for the Jews in Cyrus. It seems apparent that Cyrus had been greatly influenced by the Jewish religion, so much so that he provided economic and military support for their cause. "Some suggest that Daniel showed Cyrus the prophecies that were thus fulfilled by his conquest (Jer. 25:11–12; 29:10)

Babylon
329–331, 4334

Cyrus
907

and also the prophecies of Isaiah, who 200 years before, had called Cyrus by name, stating that under him the Jews would return and rebuild Jerusalem (Isa. 44:26–28; 45:1,13). No wonder Cyrus had high regard for the Jew's God." [27]

The Historical Books (Joshua–Esther)

VIII. NEHEMIAH

A. The Name

Nehemyah is the Hebrew word for Nehemiah, which appears seven times in the book. The Book of Nehemiah is so named because Nehemiah, the author, is its principal figure. Unlike Ezra the priest, Nehemiah was a layman—a zealous builder who became the civil governor with authority from the Persian king to rebuild the walls of Jerusalem.[28] In the Hebrew canon the historical Book of Nehemiah is listed under the category of the Writings (Heb., *kethubim;* Gr., *hagiographa*).

Book of Nehemiah **4238**

Nehemiah **2577**

Ezra **1199**

Persia **2744**

B. Authorship and Date

For authorship and date see commentary on Ezra.
Author: Ezra.
Date: 430–397 B.C.

C. Background, Purpose, and Content

In about 444 B.C. Hanani visited his brother in the palace at Shushan. Hanani brought sad tidings about the reconstruction program in Jerusalem. Through enemy intrigue the rebuilding program had stopped (Neh. 4:7–13). Nehemiah was the king's cupbearer who tasted the food and wine as a precaution against the king's being poisoned.

Hanani **1482**

"Nehemiah was a man of prayer, patriotism, action, courage and perseverance. His first impulse always was to pray (Neh. 1:4; 2:4; 4:9; 6:9–14). He spent 4 months in prayer before he made his request to the king (Neh. 1:1; 2:1)." [29] With a heavy heart Nehemiah communicated his concern for Jerusalem to the king (2:1–3). Sympathetic to the request of Nehemiah, the king sent Nehemiah to Jerusalem with letters of identification and recommendation bearing the king's seal. To insure the execution of the king's intent, "captains of the army and horsemen" were sent to accompany Nehemiah (2:4–9). Upon arrival in Jerusalem, Nehemiah made a secret inspection of the walls and found breaches in them, and many of the gates destroyed. In spite of the hostility from his enemies, the Moabites, Ammorites, Ashdodites, Arabians, and Samaritans, Nehemiah began the rebuilding of the walls. Notwithstanding the opposition,

Prayer **2816**

271

they were finished in 52 days. Jerusalem was again a city enclosed with walls 142 years after its destruction in 581 B.C.[30]

The next phase in the reconstruction period was spiritual:
Ezra and his helpers called a special convocation and read
God's law to the people. This effort resulted in a great wave
of repentance and in turn a great revival and a new commitment to keep God's law (Neh. 9–10). The wall was dedicated
and temple service was reorganized (Neh. 9–12).

After numbering the priests and Levites, Nehemiah condemned the practice of marriage between Jews and heathen
wives. He reminded the people of the sin of Solomon and the
evil effects these heathen women had upon Solomon and the
nation (Neh. 13:26–31).

Nehemiah supervised the rebuilding of the wall, but his most
important contribution was spiritual in nature. He made the
people realize the intimate relationship they had with God
and that his message was a practical implementation of the
exhortation of the pre-Exilic prophets such as Jeremiah, Ezekiel, Habakkuk, and Zephaniah. In addition, the people began
to realize the faithful stewardship of Nehemiah. As a layman,
he had come to Jerusalem to deal with an almost impossible
task, as well as with vigorous opposition.

"With the help of the Lord, he revived a desolate Jewish
Community and sought to make it well-pleasing to God through
reforms. He toiled diligently and sacrificed personal popularity
in order to gain the divine approval 'Well done.' His deep
desire was expressed in his prayer: 'Remember me, O my God,
for good' (Neh. 13:31)." [31]

IX. ESTHER

A. The Name

The name "Esther," from the Hebrew 'ester, comes from
the Jewess Esther, who became queen of Persia. In the Hebrew
canon, the Book of Esther is one of the five scrolls (Megilloth)
and is listed in the category of the Writings (Heb., kethubim;
Gr., hagiographa).

B. Authorship and Date

The authorship of the Book of Esther is unknown. The terminology in Esther 9:29–32; 10:3 seems to eliminate Mordecai
as a contender for authorship. Mordecai is the subject being
discussed by the writer, whoever he may be. The writer is
obviously a Jew who is familiar with the palace and with Persian
customs. He quotes the legal documents written by Mordecai.

Revivals
312–315

Repentance
2706–2710

Second
Temple
3578

Opposers of
Religion
1567, 1568

Book of Esther
4239

Esther
1152

Mordecai
2401
Persia
2744

272

The Hebrew style of writing closely resembles that in the Books of Ezra and Nehemiah, and the Chronicles books. This similarity of style suggests that Ezra may have been the author.[32]

It is estimated that Esther became queen of Persia in 478 B.C. and that she saved the Jews from destruction in 473 B.C. "Esther appears about 40 years after the temple was rebuilt and about 30 years before the wall of Jerusalem was rebuilt." [33]

From this historical background one may conclude that a likely date for the Book of Esther is in the mid fifth century B.C.[34]

C. Background, Purpose, and Content

The purpose of the Book of Esther is to relate the origin of the Feast of Purim. (For a detailed discussion of the Feast of Purim see page 70.)

The liberal view is that this book is a historical novel and that "the story has not been confirmed by any Persian records nor is it referred to by any New Testament writers." [35]

Although the name of God is not mentioned in this book, the author communicates the spiritual element of God's overruling providence. Mordecai's stand against the evil Haman is typical of the three Hebrew children's resistance to the edict of the king and the evil Chaldeans (Dan. 3:8–12). The courageous action of Mordecai to expose Haman's plan for revenge because of Mordecai's refusal to bow down to Haman is a reminder of God's intervention for his people.

"The outstanding religious motive is divine providence. The Jews learned under God's affliction what they would not learn under His forbearance . . . . No Jew could have penned this without the intention of presenting the providence of God in the sparing of His people." [36] If Haman's plot had succeeded there would have been no Jewish race from which Christ the Messiah came.

Another evidence of Jewish observances is the appointing of a fast by Esther (Esth. 4:16; 9:31; Ps. 69:10; Isa. 58:3; Jer. 14:12; Joel 1:14; 2:12). The Feast of Purim is so ingrained into the history and customs of the Jews that the historicity of Esther cannot be doubted.

Feast of Purim
1261

Haman
1478

Divine Providence
2905–2913, also **2493**

17

Poetry and Wisdom Literature
(Job–The Song of Solomon)

I. JOB

A. The Name

The name Job comes from the Hebrew *'iyobh* meaning "object of enmity" or "he who turns." The Book of Job derives its

name from its central character Job, whose name appears 55 times in the book. Because of its antiquity the etymology of the name defies literary analysis. Some scholars note that an early form of Job in ancient literature is *Ayyab* meaning "where is father" or "no father." The translation suggests that Job may have been an orphan or perhaps an illegitimate child.[1] In the Hebrew canon the poetical Book of Job is listed in the category of the Writings (Heb., *kethubim;* Gr., *hagiographa*).

B. Authorship and Date

The Book of Job has been the center of literary debate from earliest times. Scholars have presented various theories: some say Job is a fictional character; others say the Book of Job is about a real person, while some deny that Job existed. However, the evidence is strong that the work is historical and factual.

It is impossible to determine an author or a date for the book of Job because of its antiquity, but the identity of such a character as Job is established in the Old Testament and in

nonbiblical sources. The book is first noted in Hebrew literature in the Old Testament. The name of Job is mentioned in extra-

biblical literature such as the tell-el-Amarna tablets from Egypt, in the clay tablets found at Mari on the Middle Euphrates,

and in the Ugaritic texts from Ras Shamra on the Mediterranean coast of Syria. These places are widely separated, but
they were all stopping places for the Hebrew people. Job's
name appears in Ezekiel with the names of two other righteous
men—Noah and Daniel (Ezek. 14:14,20). A Job is also mentioned in the genealogical table of the tribe entering Egypt
with Jacob, where Job is catalogued with the sons of Issachar
(Gen. 46:13). His historicity is confirmed by James who has
memorialized Job's patience (James 5:11).

Jewish tradition says that Job was a descendent of Abraham,
Isaac, and Jacob. The fact that the Book of Job has a place in
the OT canon further confirms that Job has a place in history.
Because of the divine inspiration accorded canonized books,
the integrity and authenticity of Job is further confirmed.

The writer of Job was obviously well acquainted with the
desert east of the Jordan river as well as with the cultural
background of Egypt. A well-known scholar says of Job: "There
are several indications that he [Job] lived in the patriarchal
age: the longevity of Job (he apparently lived two centuries),
the flourishing of true religion, supported by special divine
revelation outside the community of Abraham's covenant, and
certain early, social and ethnic features such as the still nomadic
status of the Chaldeans and the patriarchal form of worship
and sacrifice." [2]

Jordan
1915, 1916

Patriarchs
2696

With respect to authorship a noted writer states that "the
case for a Hebrew author rests largely on references to civil
and moral prescriptions (Job 22:6; 24:9; cf. Exod. 22:26; 25:2;
cf. Deut. 19:14), familiarity with a few OT writings and mention
of the name of the God of Israel. Yahweh is in the prologue
and epilogue and in the superscriptions of God's speeches and
Job's answers." [3]

OT Morality
572, 573

Authorship of the book of Job has always been debated:
learned men have suggested the names of Elihu, Job's friend,
Solomon, Isaiah, Ezra, and others, but the evidence available
points to Moses as the possible author. According to Hebrew
tradition, the Book of Job was compiled/edited/written by Moses in Midian exile. It is thought that Moses had direct contact
with Job, or with those who knew Job intimately and who possessed authoritative information, oral or written, on the material in the Book of Job.[4]

Midian
2338–2340
Moses
2420, 2421

Adam Clarke gives the consensus of the great scholars in
his day with reference to authorship. The conclusions still remain valid.

That Moses was the author of Job has been the opinion of most
learned men . . . the writer of this poem must, in his style, have
been equally master of the simple and the sublime: that he must
have been minutely and elaborately acquainted with astronomy,

natural history and the general science of his age; that he must
have been a Hebrew by birth and . . . that he must have flourished
and composed the work before the exodus . . . every one of these
features is consummated in Moses and in Moses alone. . . . Instructed in the learning of Egypt, it appears . . . that he composed
it during some part of his forty years residence with the hospitable
Jethro, in that district of Idumea which was named Midian. . . .
In addition to these external proofs of identity . . . a little attention
will disclose to us an internal proof of peculiar force, in the close
and striking similarity of diction and idiom which exists between
the Book of Job and those pieces of poetry which Moses is usually
admitted to have composed . . . the order of creation, as detailed
in the first chapter of Genesis is precisely similar to that described
in Job XXXVIII:1–20, the general arrangement that occupied the
first day; —the formation of the clouds, which employed the second;
—the separation of the sea, which took up a part of the third;
—and the establishment of the luminaries in the skies which characterized the fourth . . . the combined simplicity and sublimity of
Gen. 1:3 "and God said, Be light! and light was," has been felt
and praised by the critics of every age . . . and has by all of them
been regarded as a characteristic feature of the Mosaic style.[5]

C. Background, Purpose, and Content

Uz
3742

The Bible states that Job lived in the Land of Uz (border
between Palestine and Arabia) and that he was a very wealthy
and influential sheik or desert rancher. Scripture relates that
he was "perfect and upright, and one that feared God, and
eschewed evil" (Job 1:1). Disaster struck in quick succession.
"His vast herds of camels were stolen, and their attending servants killed, by a band of Chaldean robbers. At the same time,
his herds of oxen were stolen and their attending servants killed
by a band of Sabean robbers. . . . About the same time his
7000 sheep and their attending servants were killed by a thun-
derstorm, and . . . his family of ten children were all killed
by a cyclone. . . . A little later Job himself was smitten with
Diseases
1506–1521,
also **4011**
the most hideous and painful disease known to the ancient
world." [6] This evidence supports the assumption that Job was
a historical figure and that the message in the book has a legitimate claim to a place in historical literature.

Wisdom
3846

The book of Job is the first in a group of four books known
in the OT canon as wisdom literature and is in dialogue form
with a narrative prologue and an epilogue in prose. Its poetical
form employs parallelisms, rhythmic expressions, and synonymous or antithetical couplets. The other wisdom books are
Psalms, Proverbs, Ecclesiastes, and Song of Solomon; they are
all classified as poetical books.

Outstanding literary men have paid high tribute to the book
276 of Job as being the greatest of all literary compositions. Victor
Hugo said, "The Book of Job is the greatest masterpiece of

the human mind." Thomas Carlyle referred to Job as "one of the greatest things ever written." Philip Schaff said, "It rises like a pyramid in the history of literature." [7]

Poetry and Wisdom Literature

The Book of Job presents both philosophical and theological problems. It deals with the age-old question: "Why do the righteous suffer?" "Is God unjust because the righteous Job is punished so severely—nigh unto death?" A misinterpretation of the Mosaic law assumed that a good man would always be rewarded without experiencing punishment but the wicked man would always be punished with no material rewards. The true biblical view, however, is that "it rains on the just and the unjust." The righteous man can suffer from the elements as much as the wicked man. A hailstorm can wipe out the crop of a good man as well as that of a bad man. The facts are that disease will strike in all families regardless of their moral state.

Mosaic Law
949

Further insight results from the account of the conversation between God and Satan.* The Book of Job illustrates Satan's attack on man (Job 1:6–9,12; 2:1–7). He is no mythical figure but personal and real with power to inflict harm upon human beings. Peter gives a dramatic description of Satan in these words: "your adversary the devil, as a roaring lion, walketh about, seeking whom he may devour" (1 Peter 5:8). Satan's purpose and design is to do evil continually. He is the enemy of the soul of man, opposing goodness of every kind. He is the chief opponent of God and man and is determined to undo the work of God and persuade men to sin (Luke 22:3). One writer says,

Satan
3149–3154

Satan's Ambition
4095

> When permission is granted him [Satan] to carry out his evil plots, it is only that he may become an instrument in furthering the divine plan. In Job's case, the vain efforts of Satan to induce the patriarch to sin resulted in disciplining his character and maturing his faith in God. In the fully revealed doctrine of Satan, which is seen in the NT, he is the god of this world who has access to the hearts of men, deceives them, and receives their willing or unwilling obedience (Luke 22:3; Acts 5:3; 26:18; 2 Cor. 4:4; 2 Thess. 2:9; Rev. 12:9).[8]

An overview of the Book indicates that the story revolves around Job and three dogmatists, Eliphaz, Bildad, and Zophar, who assume that Job's difficulty was attributable to secret sins. It is the contention of Eliphaz that no innocent man will be chastised through affliction and that God destroys only the wicked. The speeches of Bildad and Zophar support this thesis (Job 8:3–7; 18:5–21; 22:3–11). Job insisted that he was not a wicked man (Job 10:7), that God is no respecter of persons and that he sends affliction on the righteous as well as upon

Eliphaz
1115
Zophar
4000

Respect of Persons
1984

---

* The name "Satan" is used in both the OT and NT while "Devil" is used only in the NT. However, the two terms can be used interchangeably.

the wicked (Job 9:22); in moments of despair and intense pain
Job regretted his birth (Job 10:18–22). Zophar countered with
the assertion that Job's punishment should be more severe (Job
11:6) whereupon Job became sarcastic and challenged the assumptions of his comforters (Job 12:13).

As the dialogue proceeded each became more caustic than
the other (Job 13:3,4). Job rebuked his friends for being unmer-
ciful and insisted on his innocence (Job 16:17). Bildad reproved
Job for his presumption and impatience (Job 18). In his agony
Job expressed his faith in the resurrection (Job 19). Zophar
and Eliphaz continued their attack on Job (Job 20,22). Job

agreed that in the end the wicked suffer (Job 21) but insisted
upon his own innocence (23,24). Bildad made his last speech
(Job 25). Job concluded his rebuttal and grew more confident
of his innocence (Job 26–31).

In Job 32 the whole dramatic scene changed. The three comforters ceased to reprove Job; Elihu, a fourth member of the
team, entered the controversy and rebuked the original three
comforters for their inability to subdue Job. Elihu took the
position that suffering is intended by God to be corrective
rather than punitive.

God, in a whirlwind, spoke against ignorance, impatience,
helplessness, and the infinitesimal smallness of man as compared to God and asked question after question, which "awed"
Job into silence and drove him to his knees (Job 38–41). In
the last chapter, the Lord reprimanded the three comforters
for the wrong they had done to Job. God commanded them

to give a special burnt offering of seven bullocks and seven
rams and informed them that Job would pray for them (Job
42:8).

It becomes clear that Job's fortunes changed when he
"prayed for his friends" (Job 42:10). Perhaps this indicates that
Job should have prayed for his friends in the beginning instead
of arguing with them. The concluding verses give an account
of the great prosperity Job enjoyed after his deliverance. The
Scripture states that "the LORD gave Job twice as much as
he had before" (Job 42:10b).

II. PSALMS

A. *The Name*

The Hebrew title is *Sepher Tehillim,* meaning "book of
praises." In the Greek OT (LXX) it is rendered "Psalmoi" and
in the English Bible it is translated "Psalms"; the title means
"Songs set to Music." In the Hebrew canon the poetical Book

of Psalms is listed in the category of the Writings (Heb., *kethubim;* Gr., *hagiographa*).

B. Authorship and Date

Tradition says that David was the principal author of the Psalms; seventy-three are ascribed to him. Asaph, a Levite skilled in playing the cymbal and a leader in David's choir, was the author of thirteen (50, 72–83); eleven are ascribed to Korah, probably a family of musicians (42, 44–49, 84, 85, 87, 88). Solomon is credited with two (22, 127), Moses with one (90), Ethan with one (89), and forty-nine are anonymous.

The Targum has assigned two psalms of the anonymous group to Adam (92, 139), one to Melchizedek (110), and one to Abraham (89). Some psalms may be ascribed to the author of the previous psalm. New Testament writers assumed that at least some of the psalms were written by David (Luke 20:42; Acts 1:16). The Hebrew prepositions, "of," "to," and "for" make identification difficult. A psalm may have been dedicated "to David" or it may have been a psalm "for David"; on the other hand, it may have been a psalm "of David."

No doubt David was the author of some of the anonymous psalms or those which have uncertain authorship. It seems quite probable that David was the author of over one-half of these psalms, making him the major contributor.

C. Background, Purpose, and Content

The Book of Psalms is the first in the category of writings called the poetical books. The language in some of the psalms is figurative. Hebrew poetry and hyperbole are used to express ideas (Ps. 58:10). The primary interpretation of the psalms is usually found within the historical context, or in the immediate setting, but because of their nature, the psalms are applicable to any age. As one reads the psalms, he becomes aware that they are speaking to him. They are devotional in nature and are designed to satisfy the need of the human heart.

Since early times, men have engaged in music by which the soul expresses its emotion and may reach to God in prayer. The mood in the psalms ranges from the deepest sorrow and grief to the highest expression of joy (1 Peter 1:8).

Music
2454–2477
Sorrow
1944
Joy
1926–1938

D. The Structure of the Psalms

The Book of Psalms has five sub-divisions: Book One, chs. 1–41; Book Two, chs. 42–72; Book Three, chs. 73–89; Book Four, chs. 90–106, and Book Five, chs. 107–150. Each book closes with a doxology (Pss. 41:13; 72:18–19; 89:52; 106:48; 150:6). The Lord (Jehovah) is the predominant divine name used in the Book of Psalms (see page 73 in this book). From

The Old
Testament

ancient times the fivefold division has been indicated in both the Hebrew and Greek (LXX) and is thought to be comparable to the fivefold division of the Pentateuch.

The headings of the psalms give the key to their musical rendition with the title being determined by the superscription: For example "To the chief Musician upon Gittith" (Pss. 8, 81, 84). "To the chief Musician on Neginoth" indicated that the psalm was to be sung with stringed instruments (Pss. 4, 6, 54, 55, 67, 76). "To the chief Musician upon Nehiloth" signified that wind instruments were to be used (Ps. 5), and "A song upon Alamoth" designated a musical composition to be sung by some young women (Ps. 46). The refrain of the choral response is included in the second part of each verse in Psalm 136. Such other words as "Maschil" (Ps. 32) and "Michtam" (Pss. 16; 56–60) furnish further musical direction. Some psalms were to be sung antiphonally (responsively) (Pss. 15, 24). The familiar words "Hallelujah" and "Amen" were congregational responses.

There are eight main categories of psalms:

1. The Psalms of Praise

Songs
2476, 2477

The Bible is replete with songs of praise and thanksgiving to Jehovah. Both Judaism and Christianity engage in singing. Finally, in heaven the redeemed will continue to sing God's praises (Rev. 5:9–14).

Hebrew
Festivals
1276

Music and ritual played a prominent part in the festive occasions of Israel. Upon the completion of Solomon's temple and the placing of the Ark of the Covenant in the Holy of Holies, the chronicler described the event: "the priests that were present were sanctified [set aside and cleansed for holy service].

Levites
2114

. . . The Levites which [sic] were the singers . . . being arrayed in white linen, having cymbals and psalteries and harps, stood at the east end of the altar, and with them an hundred and twenty priests sounding with trumpets. It came even to pass, as the trumpeters and singers were as one, to make one sound to be heard in praising and thanking the LORD" (2 Chron. 5:11–13).

Trumpets
2466, 2467

The 150 psalms contain expressions of joy and praise. Moses and Miriam composed and sang a psalm of thanksgiving on the banks of the Red Sea after being delivered from the host of Pharaoh (Exod. 15), a song which may be typical of those sung on their journey to the Promised Land (Num. 21:17) (see Ch. 9, VI, 9). The victory of Deborah and Barak over Sisera resulted in a song of praise (Judg. 5:1ff.); Hezekiah's singers put the words of David to music (2 Chron. 29:28–30). When the inaugural convocation was held for King Solomon, the

Victory Songs
2477

Scripture states that "four thousand praised the LORD with the instruments which [David] made . . . to praise therewith" (1 Chron. 23:5).

The Hebrew word *hallelujah* is a compound word meaning "praise Jehovah" or "praise the Lord" (*hallel* means "praise" and *JAH* means "Jehovah"). The Greek form is *alleluia*. Because of alphabetical differences between Hebrew and Greek, these words are usually transliterated in the various languages and would be understood in almost any country by its religious community. The expression "hallelujah" in any country would be understood to mean "praise the Lord." Its use is indeed universal. The psalms beginning with "hallelujah" or with "praise the Lord" include Psalms 106, 111–113, 117, 135, 146–150; those ending in praise are Psalms 104–106, 113, 115–117, 135, 146–150. Jesus and the disciples sang at the Last Supper (Matt. 26:30); Paul and Silas sang in prison (Acts 16:25). The *hallel* psalms were sung at family devotions during the Feasts of the Tabernacles, Pentecost, and Dedication.

The use of psalms as a hymnody was carried over into the NT church (Matt. 26:30; Mark 14:26). Jesus was familiar with the Psalms and used them frequently. Even on the cross he used phrases of the Psalms in his dying agony (Pss. 22:1, 31:5; cf. Matt. 27:46; Luke 23:46); thus he affirmed the Christological content of the Psalms (Luke 24:44).[9]

Psalm 119 is sometimes called an acrostic or alphabetic psalm because there are in it twenty-two divisions, each with eight verses; each section begins with one of the twenty-two Hebrew consonants; i.e., verses 1–8 use the Hebrew character *aleph*. Each of the eight verses in this section begins with an *aleph*. Verses 9–16 employ the second consonant in the Hebrew alphabet—*beth*— and each of the eight verses in this section begins with a *beth*. This formula continues throughout the psalm to verses 169–176 (the twenty-second section) which have *tau* as their superscription, and each of the eight verses begins with a *tau*. Almost all of the 176 verses in the psalm make reference to the Word of God in some form: "testimonies," "thy word," "precepts," "statutes," "law," "judgments," and "commandments" are a few of the terms used.

2. The Psalms of Degrees (120–134)

The Psalms of Degrees are said to be postexilic and were used as a source of inspiration in the days of Nehemiah by the laborers while they were rebuilding the walls of Jerusalem. The laborers kept a sword in one hand and a trowel in the other (Neh. 4:17, 18). The title may well signify "Songs of going up, upon the walls," because the songs were short and

Poetry and Wisdom Literature

Praise to God
1451

Nehemiah
2577

281

A shepherd watching his sheep on the shore of the Sea of Galilee, reminiscent of David's words in Psalm 23

Camel on threshing floor treading out wheat as it was done in Old Testament times

could easily be sung from memory by the workmen and the guards.[10]

3. The Nature Psalms (19, 29, 50, 65, 104)

There is a natural transition from the praise of the Creator to the praise of creation. The psalmist was able to see God reflected in the creation all around him—the things the Creator made for man to enjoy.

Creator
844

In Psalm 19 the sweet singer of Israel sees God's redemptive revelation portrayed in the heavens. "The heavens declare the glory of God; and the firmament sheweth his handywork." He sees in the sky a revelatory language which can be understood by persons around the world. He pointed out that there is no language in the world in which this revelation of the sky would not be understood. He calls the heavens the "tabernacle for the sun." All is governed by "the law of the LORD" and leads to "converting the soul." The fear of the Lord is to be the natural consequence of this revelation. He concludes with a benediction which many Christians have known from their youth: "Let the words of my mouth, and the meditation of my heart, be acceptable in thy sight, O LORD, my strength, and my redeemer."

Creation
884–886

Nature's Revelation
2498

Redeemer
2977

In Psalm 29 the psalmist describes in poetical ecstasy the glory and beauty of the environment around him. He is awed and inspired by the waters and thunder, the cedars of Lebanon, the flames of fire, the wilderness, and the flood. In all of this natural phenomenon the psalmist sees God in the beauty of his holiness.

Nature's Beauty
4074

The majesty and glory of God the Creator is the theme in Psalms 5, 65, and 104. Because the glories of the Lord cannot easily be described or expressed in ordinary speech, the psalmist uses much figurative language.

4. The Historic or National Psalms (14, 44, 46, 53, 66, 68, 74, 76, 79, 80, 83, 85, 87, 108, 122, 124–126, 129)

The God of Israel is preeminent in both the national and religious affairs of Israel. It is through the nation of Israel that Christ the Messiah appeared on earth. In these psalms the writer reviews God's providence in the lives of Abraham, Isaac, and Jacob. Jerusalem, the holy city of Zion, is mentioned many times.

Messiah
695, 2890, 4186

Some of the psalms deal with the events in the lives of the kings of Israel (Pss. 18, 21, 22, 89, 101, 110, 144). However, some psalms, reflecting critical national situations, have a tone of woe and despair (Pss. 44, 74, 79, 80, 137).[11]

Exodus
4224

Disobedience
2620–2621

Psalm 80:8 deals with the Exodus from Egypt; Psalms 78 and 105 speak of the ten plagues; the crossing of the Red Sea is mentioned in Psalm 66, 74, 78; God leading Israel through the wilderness is the subject in Psalm 78; the Promised Land comes into focus in Psalm 105. The psalmist acknowledges that when Israel disobeyed God, they suffered the consequences, as at Shiloh (Pss. 78:10,37,60). Every aspect of life is touched in these psalms, including the times of peace and prosperity as well as times of war, stress, famine, and disaster.[12]

5. The Social Psalms (8, 78, 104, 139, 146)

Social Duties
2527, 3778,
3393–3410

Although the purpose of the Book of Psalms is not to be a sociological study, the book does contain many insights into the origin and activities of the human race. Man is a special creation of God (100:3). Adam was to rule over God's creation (8:5,6). In Psalm 8 the poet looks up to the heavens and sees the glory of God and observes the fingers of God at work. The observer looks down to the fields and sees the result of the works of God in the animal world. The sheep and the oxen and the beasts of the field are all God's creation and subjects for praise by the psalmist.

Man, as an individual, received new life from God (Ps. 139:13); the eternal destiny of man has been recorded in the Bible (Ps. 139:16). Man has a physical body and yet he is a spiritual being made in the image of God (Pss. 8:5; 103:14) and has an immortal soul (Ps. 31:5). The security of the redeemed soul is described in Psalm 4:8.[13]

6. The Imprecatory Psalms (52, 58, 59, 69, 109, 137)

Sinfulness
3340

Vengeance
3131

The Imprecatory Psalms are the most difficult to interpret because in them man invokes the wrath of God upon his enemies. Perhaps these statements acknowledge the evil which rises up in man's heart at times. These prayers do not reflect the pronouncement of God's attitude but are prayers by men for vengeance upon evildoers. Some feel this is in direct contradiction to the teachings of Jesus that one should love his enemies. One writer explains these psalms thus:

> In the Old Testament God's purpose was to maintain a nation and to pave the way for the Coming of Christ. He was working with human nature as it was, and did not necessarily endorse everything that even His most devoted servants did or said. Some of these Psalms are Battle Hymns, expressing intense patriotism . . . life and death struggles with powerful enemies to help the nation to survive. With the Coming of Christ, God's Revelation of the meaning of human life, and its standards of conduct were completed; and God shifted the direct emphasis of His work from the mainte-

284

nance of a nation to the transformation of individuals into the kind of persons He wants us to be.[14]

Christians frequently pray for the defeat of the enemy in wartime, as if the enemy were a spiritual one, the personification of Satan and his forces of darkness. In a measure, the imprecations against the enemy are actually directed against the principle of evil and not so much against the person. When righteous people are persecuted or oppressed, there is justification for the righteous to make an appeal to God for deliverance and victory.

God has an abhorrence of sin, the cause of all trouble in the world. Liberals have criticized the OT for the national destruction commanded by God on nations, as found in the OT, but an evil society can finally forfeit its right to survive, as man can forfeit his right to live in a decent, law-abiding society when he commits murder (Gen. 9:6). It is acknowledged that there is a difference between righteous indignation and defensive action for one's own personal interests. The Imprecatory Psalms seem to have been expressed in terms of concern for causes of righteousness and not for personal vindication. J. Barton Payne points out that: "three things must be observed positively: that the Psalms and other Biblical imprecations are not hasty, emotional expressions, but carefully written literature; they are prayers and songs . . . written in good conscience; and that they are not, in the last resort, human products, but are rather inspired works of the Holy Spirit." [15]

7. The Penitential Psalms (6, 32, 51, 102, 130, 143)

Even though the psalmist David succumbed to the temptation of the flesh, he was sensitive to sin and its serious consequences. A noted scholar offers this definition of sin and its implications:

"Transgression" denotes an overt act of stubborn revolt and wilful defiance of a known law. "Iniquity" is an unnatural, distorted state due to the presence of a life-sapping, deadening, evil force which eventually will destroy all ethical qualities, leaving one in a state of helplessness. "Sin" indicates missing the mark, falling short of the goal . . . these companion words are used in the appeal for pardon. "Blot out" means to erase or expunge, as words from a manuscript or data from a careful record, the misdeeds of the past. "Purge" and "wash" are strong terms used to describe the completeness of the purification needed. "Cleanse me" is a familiar phrase carried over from the ritual of the priests in the purification of lepers, and here given a wider application. The power of God alone could bring such deliverance.[16]

285

Penitence
2706–2718,
2884–3025
Original Sin
3339

Divine
Forgiveness
2300, 3345

The Penitential Psalms give expressions of regret or remorse for committed sin. The instances in the Psalms of human wrong-doing, repentance, and forgiveness are many. Man's iniquity is presented as original and Adamic which is transmitted from generation to generation (Pss. 51:3; 58:3).[17]

The outstanding example of sin committed and forgiven by God is that of David's adultery with Bathsheba, the wife of Uriah, the Hittite, a soldier in Israel's army (2 Sam. 12ff.). After David committed sin, the prophet Nathan called upon the king and related that a wealthy citizen in his realm had taken from a poor man his only pet lamb and had served it to his guest (2 Sam. 12:1–4). Upon hearing the story, David was greatly angered and pronounced the penalty of death upon the guilty offender (2 Sam. 12:5). By the words, "Thou art the man," David was made to realize that he was the sinner, that he had taken the wife of another man (2 Sam. 12:6–11) and committed adultery (2 Sam. 3:5,13–16). Nathan told David that

for this sin the Lord would exact punishment upon him and the the sword would never depart from his house (2 Sam. 12:9–11).

Psalm 51 records David's confession of his sin and his plea for the mercy of God. In vv. 1–4 David admits his transgression, acknowledges his sinful nature and asks God to cleanse him thoroughly. In v. 10 he pleads for a "clean heart" and "a right spirit." Psalm 32 is an expression of the "blessedness" David

experienced after his sins were forgiven and he was restored to God's favor. David is quite outspoken in his testimony. In verse 1 he says, "Blessed is he whose transgression is forgiven, whose sin is covered." In verse 2 he indicates his justified state

in these words, "Blessed is the man unto whom the LORD imputeth not iniquity, and in whose spirit there is no guile." This declaration reflects the joy explicitly stated in the NT (1 Peter 1:8).

8. The Messianic or Royal Psalms

A noted scholar sums up the Messianic content of the Psalms in these words:

> No one can read the Psalms without being aware that the individual verses have a deeper, further significance beyond the simple meaning of the words. The Messiah is not mentioned by name, but his figure is foreshadowed, as later generations of Jews came to realize. And the New Testament writers are quick to apply these verses to Jesus as the prophesied Messiah.

Other psalms depict human suffering in terms which seem far-fetched in relation to ordinary experience, but which proved an extraordinarily accurate description of the actual sufferings of Christ. Under God's inspiration, the psalmists chose words and pictures which were to take on a significance they can hardly [sic] have dreamed of. Psalm 22, the psalm Jesus quoted as he hung on the cross (verse 1, Matthew 27:46), is the most amazing example. Compare verse 16 with John 20:25; verse 18 with Mark 15:24. (See also Psalm 69:21 and Matthew 27:34,48.)[18]

Poetry and Wisdom Literature

For additional information on the Christology in the Psalms see Ch. 12, VII, C.

Portraits and Prophecies of Christ
4301–4305
pp. 246–249

III. PROVERBS

A. *The Name*

Book of Proverbs
4242

The Book of Proverbs derives its name from the first two words in the first chapter: "The Proverbs." The word *proverbs* is derived from the Hebrew word *mashal,* meaning "a comparison of one thing to another."

In the Hebrew canon the poetical Book of Proverbs is listed in the category of the Writings (Heb. *kethubim;* Gr., *hagiographa*).

B. *Authorship and Date*

David
919
Solomon
3434

Internal evidence links "Solomon the Son of David, king of Israel" with the authorship of Proverbs (1:1). Tradition credits Solomon with writing most of the Book of Proverbs; however, it is apparent that some other authors participated in the compilation of this book. Among those mentioned in the book are "the men of Hezekiah," who copied out and compiled some proverbs which apparently were written by Solomon (Prov. 25:1). The name Agur appears as a caption at the head of chapter 30. Lemuel is credited with chapter 31.

God's Wisdom
3839–3846

A careful study of the Proverbs indicates that these wise sayings were collected over the years and that Solomon was one of the wise men who collected, compiled, added to, and edited these sayings of wisdom. That there is repetition would indicate that several men shared in the compilation, all possibly drawing materials from the same general source. Presumably these sayings were preserved in oral and written form by many different people and ultimately recorded by a Spirit-filled editor, as they now appear.

Internal evidence shows that these maxims or proverbs were collected over the ages and were finally compiled by Solomon in about 950 B.C. The proverbs copied by Hezekiah's men and those written by Agur and Lemuel were probably added in about 700 B.C.

C. Background, Purpose, and Content

The Book of Proverbs contains aphoristic literature, duplicated in other parts of Scripture but only on a fragmentary
basis (Psalms, Ecclesiastes, Job). The entire Book is made up
of short epigrams (wise sayings) which are concise and easy
to memorize. It is possible that in Israel maxims constituted
a large part of the early childhood training which parents probably instilled in their children and may have formed the basis
for the earliest educational curriculum. Likewise the proverbs
were recited by men and women in all strata of life—from
the learned and rich to the poor and ignorant. They were
repeated while men worked in the fields, in shops and on the
roads, as well as in the schools.

The proverbs are definitely influenced by Deuteronomic social and religious ideals. They were a personification of law
and order: OT wisdom grew out of experience and action in
life, but the "fear of the Lord" was the first step in gaining
wisdom. One writer speaks of the Book of Proverbs as "a Manual of Sanctified Common Sense." He says,

> The main object that the writers of our book had in view was
> to teach men how to live happy and contented lives as long as
> they were on earth: for this reason they deal very largely with
> the relationship between man and man, between parents and chil-
> dren, husband and wife, friend and foe, rich and poor, high and
> low; they teach what is right behaviour in every phase and occupa-
> tion of life; how to accept adverse fortune, and the fitting attitude
> of him who enjoys wealth; to practice self-control in all things, to
> cultivate consideration for others, and so on, in a word, how to
> live to the best advantage, to do right, because it brings its own
> reward, to avoid wrong doing because it entails disadvantages. . . .
> It is pointed out that wisdom and godliness are really the same
> thing and that the origin and essence of the highest form of wisdom
> is the fear of the Lord.[19]

The Wise Man vs. the Prophet and Priest

The wise men shared in the religious educational process
with the priests and prophets.

The priests interpreted God and his law of sacrifice to the
people. The many different feasts (Tabernacles, Passover, Pentecost) were vehicles devised to teach the people the intricacies
of God's plan of redemption. Through the ritual the deeper
meanings of worship were communicated to the people. The

blood in the animal sacrifices symbolized the great redemptive
sacrifice of Christ the Messiah and was the heart of the worship

service.

The prophets (the *Nebhiim*) were the divinely inspired foretellers of the consequence of a certain course of action. They intuitively felt the will of God for the people. The prophets were laymen, priests, statesmen, farmers, and shepherds—they came from many walks in life, but they all spoke with conviction that they were speaking for God. These spokesmen brought special messages from God to individuals, to groups, and to nations. They "spake as they were moved by the Holy Ghost" (2 Peter 1:21), dealing with immediate issues as well as the future. These men assumed that tomorrow was inherent in today. They were fearless and spoke their divine message irrespective of consequences.

Poetry and
Wisdom
Literature

Holy
Witnesses
1606

The wise men endeavored to enlarge on the teachings of the priests and the prophets. They condensed the essence of truth into short and pithy sayings, so they could be grasped and understood by the common people. One writer puts it thus:

> The wise men attempted to present a composite picture of the ideal man. It is not a sentimental, apologetic saint they portray, but a man of red blood and practical ability. He is a devoted husband, a true friend, a wise counselor and a charitable neighbor. He is industrious, honorable and righteous. His insight into life is simple, yet profound. Above all he is sane, normal, and motivated by a sound faith in God and a desire to evidence his loyalty to God by living in accord with the divine precepts. He is happy and content.[20]

Devout
Mothers
1670

The ideal mother and wife is presented as a virtuous woman, industrious, ever desiring to provide for the well-being of her family. She is respected and admired and is a leader in the community for the causes which will strengthen and bless society. Wisdom was dispensed wherever people met, because schools or institutions as known today had not yet developed. Through memorization, truth was communicated, not only by "wise men" but also by the father and mother to the children and by the children to each other. A large body of axiomatic truth floated in the minds of the people. These wise sayings influenced and became a part of the cultural pattern.

Men of wisdom collected these wise sayings and compiled them into written form as they appear in the wisdom books of the Bible. Hebrew wisdom had in it a striking difference to speculative Greek philosophy of the Western world. The wise men dealt with divine revelation; the philosophers, with human reason. The Jews had their "wise men"; the Greeks had their "philosophers." The "wise men" dealt with everyday practical truths; the philosophers dealt with abstract theories. The "wise men" were concerned with ethics and morality, based on divine revelation, whereas some of the "philosophers" based the test of validity upon whether certain courses of action

Vain
Philosophy
2759

289

were reasonable and pleasurable. W. T. Purkiser sums up the difference between the "wise men" and the "philosophers" thus: "While reason was the method of Greek Philosophy and argumentation its form, intuition or insight was the method of Hebrew wisdom and the epigramic proverb its form. The Jewish wiseman had no argument to sustain, no chain of reason to follow. He presents his truth with the simple assurance of one who has seen." [21]

Book of
Ecclesiastes
4243

IV. ECCLESIASTES

A. The Name

A precise name for the Book of Ecclesiastes does not appear in the Bible text. The name is derived from the second word in the first chapter of both the Hebrew and Greek Old Testament. In the Hebrew Bible the word is *qoheleth*, meaning a presiding officer or one who speaks to an assembly, a school or a religious body such as a synagogue.

Assembly
275

Synagogues
3121–3123

The word in the Greek OT is *ekklesiastes*, meaning a member of or a presiding officer of an *ekklesia* (a religious body) or a preacher. A scholar of note phrases the meaning thus: "The English title Ecclesiastes is taken from the Greek translation of the Hebrew word *Qoheleth* and means 'one who gathers an ekklesia,' *ekklesia* being the Greek word for 'church' or 'assembly.' From this, Luther interpreted it as meaning 'the preacher,' a title which found its way into our English version." [22] Luther translates the word *qoheleth* as *prediger*, (German), which in English means "preacher."

Church
726

In the Hebrew canon the Book of Ecclesiastes is one of the Five Scrolls *(Megilloth)* and is listed in the category of the Writings (Heb., *kethubim;* Gr., *hagiographa*).

B. Authorship and Date

Positive identification of the author of the Book of Ecclesiastes is not given in the Bible text; however Jewish tradition has always assumed that Solomon was the author.

The introduction refers to "the Preacher" (Heb., *qoheleth*), the son of David, king of Jerusalem (Prov. 1:1). Verse 12 states that "I the Preacher was king over Israel in Jerusalem."

Solomon
3414

Solomon, with all of his royal glory and wealth, was eminently qualified to describe the experimentation and the conclusion portrayed in this book. He probably wrote the manuscript in his declining years when he could look in retrospect upon his life with its varied experiences of wealth, power, royal prestige, and every conceivable sensuous pleasure. Solomon died in 931 B.C., after a reign of forty years.

C. Background, Purpose, and Content

The general purpose of Ecclesiastes may be to communicate the unhappy consequences of a life given to seeking wealth, power, political prestige, and unrestrained self-indulgence. The key to this pessimistic conclusion is found in these words: "Vanity of vanities, saith the Preacher, vanity of vanities; all is vanity" (Eccl. 1:2). Solomon's conclusion seems to deal with periods when God had little or no place in his life.

Vanity
1120

Solomon presents some of the great beauties of life, but the predominant tone of this book is desperation, futility, and melancholy. He had grown up under a father (David) who faced difficulties, hardships, and struggle but was forever proclaiming "Rejoice" and "Praise the Lord." David had brought Israel to the brink of the "golden age" with its wealth, power, and glory. Solomon was "born with a silver spoon in his mouth," as it were, and he never confronted the realities of life. Though he gave his heart "to seek and search out by wisdom concerning all things that are done under heaven" (Eccl. 1:13), all he found was gloom: "I have seen all the works that are done under the sun; and, behold, all is vanity, and vexation of spirit" (Eccl. 1:14). He adopts a defeatist attitude toward life; though he claims to have had great "wisdom and knowledge," he knows only the "vexation of spirit" (Eccl. 1:17); to him wisdom and knowledge "increaseth sorrow" (Eccl. 1:18).

Uncertainty of Life
2147

Wealth
2805–2811

Solomon set out to buy happiness with his great wealth. He wrote, "Whatsoever mine eyes desired I kept not from them, I withheld not my heart from any joy" (Eccl. 2:10). He gave himself to "enjoy pleasure," to "laughter" and "mirth" and the "wine cup." He planted great "vineyards," "gardens," "orchards," and "trees," and made "pools of water," with which to irrigate them. In his lifetime Solomon acquired many "servants," "maidens," wives, and concubines (1 Kings 11:3) as well as great cattle ranches. He accumulated much gold (1 Kings 10:14–17). He was entertained by great musicians with many instruments, but in spite of what he had, he was not satisfied.

Sorrow
1944, 3490

Earthly Happiness
1940

Earthly Riches
2806

Musical Instruments
2454–2469

He expresses his stark pessimism in these words, "Then I looked on all the works that my hands had wrought: . . . and behold all was vanity and vexation of spirit, and there was no profit under the sun" (Eccl. 2:1–11). The term "under the sun" is interpreted to mean that he sought and enjoyed all these things by his own efforts and not as blessings from God.

The attitude of Solomon is typical of a man in any age who has the "golden platter" placed in his lap. He soon discovered that without struggle and hardship the fruit of fame and fortune is futile and empty. His riches were his sufficiency; he seemed to think he had no need for God. He was in a position to

Disappointment
1190

taste the fruits of luxury and pleasure in every area of life, but found them bitter and meaningless. The unceasing refrain in the entire Book is the word "vanity," which occurs 37 times.

The King of Israel saw earthly life at its best; he could gratify every sensuous desire. He made it his business to taste every earthly pleasure, but he found it all to be vanity and vexation of spirit. Even though the name of God is mentioned twenty times in the book, the main thrust is that he sought satisfaction and meaning in life through his own efforts (Eccl. 1:2–2:23). To Solomon, God seemed to be abstract, impersonal and transcendent, so far away that Solomon was not conscious of God's availability.

Solomon found life disappointing (Eccl. 4:1–16). The worldly attainments proved to be futile and inadequate (Eccl. 6:1–7). Yet, shrouded in philosophical speculation, there are some suggestions of hope. He gives words of wisdom for living in a world where all is vanity (Eccl. 7:1–12:8). He does not totally ignore the Deuteronomic Law—"obey the earthly king and fear the heavenly king" (Eccl. 8:1–17). He makes honorable mention of death (Eccl. 9:1–12). The writer admits that wisdom is better than folly (Eccl. 9:13–10:20); that hard work and benevolence in a troubled world may bring satisfaction (Eccl. 11:1–8). He exhorts youth to "Remember now thy Creator" (Eccl. 12:1,2). Apparently the writer, now in his old age, comes to the conclusion that his own humanistic approach is vain, that others should not follow his example, and that the way to start life is with God.

Solomon himself appears to be so much confused in his "humanistic prison that he cannot break out." He seems to maintain his pessimistic view of life—"Vanity of vanities, saith the preacher; all is vanity" (Eccl. 12:8). Finally in the last two verses a burst of light comes forth. He concludes that to "Fear God, and keep his commandments" is the best way to live (Eccl. 12:13).

A legitimate question may be asked: why was such a book included in the canonized Scripture? No absolute answer is available, but succeeding generations can and should profit from Solomon's experience. "God gave Solomon wisdom and unparalleled opportunity to observe and to explore every avenue of earthly life. And, after much research and experiment, Solomon concluded that, on the whole, humanity found an unutterable yearning for something beyond himself [sic]. Thus the book, in a way, is humanity's cry for a Saviour. With the coming of Christ, the cry was answered. The vanity of life disappeared. No longer vanity, but joy, peace, gladness prevailed. . . . In Christ humanity found the Desire of the ages: Life, Abundant, Joyous, Glorious Life." [23]

Vain
Philosophy
2759

Precious
Wisdom
3842

Fear God
3034–3036

Christ Our
Savior
3360–3368

Fruit of Spirit
Gal. 5:22–26,
1337

292

V. THE SONG OF SOLOMON

A. The Name

The Song of Solomon is frequently called "The Song of Songs" or "Canticles." The book derives its name from the first verse in the book: "The song of songs, which is Solomon's" (Song of Sol. 1:1). In the Hebrew Bible this title appears as *Sir hassirim;* in the Septuagint as *Asma;* and in the Latin Vulgate as *Canticum* or *Canticorum.* In the Hebrew Canon the Song of Solomon is one of the Five Scrolls and is listed in the category of the Writings (Heb., *kethubim;* Gr., *hagiographa*).

B. Authorship and Date

Traditionally, the Song of Solomon has been attributed to Solomon because of the reference to Solomon in the first verse and other parts of the book (Song of Sol. 1:1; 3:7,9,11; 8:11,12). This opinion is consistent with the view that the Bible is the authoritative Word of God. A likely date for this book is about 950 B.C., the middle of Solomon's reign, which ended in 931 at his death.

The first verse is vague, according to the Hebrew idiom. It could mean that Solomon was the author or that the song was about Solomon. This uncertainty is acknowledged, but the probability is that Solomon was the writer.

C. Background, Purpose, and Content

The Song of Solomon has been a difficult book for the religious community to deal with because of its general eroticism. The language is passionate and sensuous; the description of man and woman relationships are in intimate terms. It is made more difficult because there is not a religious sentence in it nor is the name of God ever used.

However, it is a book in the canon, and this is the basis for accepting it as a part of the inspired Word of God. Therefore readers must seek a wholesome, positive interpretation of this Song. The Jewish church has always cherished the Song and used it as a part of the ritual on the eighth day of the Passover, in memory of the Exodus when God, the Bridegroom, espoused Israel as his bride. In the third century A.D., Origin introduced this book to the Christian church as representing the blissful relationship between Christ, the Bridegroom, and his bride, the church. It is obvious that the study of the Song of Solomon demands a pure, sanctified attitude, especially in an age of sexual permissiveness and perversion.

Poetry and Wisdom Literature

The Song of Solomon
4244

Solomon
3414

Sensuality
667

Feast of Passover
1256
See also **2686**

Christ as Bridegroom
736

293

There are at least five major approaches to, or interpretations of, the Song of Solomon.

1. The Cultic View

Some persons assume that this book presents a liturgy of Baalism, the Canaanite fertility cult, prevalent in Palestine when the tribes arrived. This cult had as its purpose the stimulation of nature. The priest and priestess performed a sexual ritual in the temple. This observance was supposed to have a magical influence upon the fertility of the land and the productivity of the herds.

2. The Lyrical View

According to this interpretation, the book contains a series of love songs, in which the sensuous beauty of the bride is discussed and dramatized.

3. The Literal View

There are several versions of the literal view. The most popular one is the "conjugal love version," which portrays the beauty and sacredness of sexual love within holy matrimony, a husband-wife relationship sanctified by God. The sacredness of marriage is further enhanced by the participation of Jesus in the marriage at Cana of Galilee (John 2:1ff.).

One writer justifies this love poem in these words:

> Even if Canticles is merely a collection of songs describing the bliss of true lovers in wedlock, it is not thereby rendered unworthy of a place in the Bible. . . . If Canticles should be rejected because of its sensuous imagery in describing the joys of passionate lovers, portions of Proverbs would also have to be excised (Prov. 5:15–20). Perhaps most persons need to enlarge their conception of the Bible as a repository for all the things that minister to the welfare of men. The entire range of man's legitimate joys finds sympathetic and appreciative description in the Bible. Two lovers in Paradise need not fear to rise and meet their Creator should He visit them in the cool of the day.[24]

4. The Dramatic View

This view is sometimes referred to as the "Shepherd Hypothesis," a view popular a few decades ago. It was assumed that the "Song of Solomon" is one of the few survivors of ancient Hebrew art. This theory is strengthened by the "stage directions" found in the Codex Sinaiticus. In this biblical manuscript various verses are assigned to "different speakers such as 'the

bride to maidens,' 'the maidens to the bride' and 'the bridegroom to the bride.' Clearly some sort of drama is here
presupposed." [25]

*Poetry and
Wisdom
Literature*

Bride
737
Bridegroom
546

A further analysis suggests a

drama in fine arts, thirteen scenes. There are three main characters
and three choruses—court ladies—citizens of Jerusalem. The play
opens with the Shulamite girl yearning for her absent lover. Solomon
tries to woo her but is unsuccessful. She replies that "there is a
true love that cannot be excited artificially." The simple country
maiden has no adequate conception of palace life and conduct.
She answers Solomon in language borrowed from the shepherd
life familiar to her. She draws imagery from the pastoral and horti-
cultural mountain life.

In the second act the Shulamite describes a date she had with
her shepherd lover in the mountains. She tells about a dream she
had since coming to the palace and how she searched the streets
of Jerusalem for her lover until she found him.

In the third act Solomon enters dressed in all his splendor in
an effort to overwhelm the maid, but in her inner subconsciousness
she hears only the passionate pleas of her absent lover; this is followed by another dream about her lover.

In the fourth act the social set in Jerusalem express their surprise
at her rejection of the king. Solomon then renews his efforts to
win the maiden, telling her how he first saw her in a nut orchard,
but she maintains her loyalty to her shepherd lover and in the
last act she is permitted to return home to be reunited with her
lover. Some ancient sages point out that through this experience,
Solomon is converted to higher ideals because of the loyalty the
maid demonstrated for her lover under the most severe entice-
ments; she demonstrated to Solomon that pure love is more powerful than sensual love.[26]

5. The Allegorical View

Perhaps the most popular and abiding interpretation of the
Song of Solomon is the allegorical view, which presupposes
that the Song portrays the love relationship between Jehovah
and Israel. Jehovah is the Bridegroom and Israel, is the bride.
It is probably this view that made the canonization of this
love poem possible. The allegorical view is supported in the
oldest Jewish sources such as the Targum, Talmud, and Midrash. It is a matter of record that marriage is the symbol in
the OT illustrating the relationship between Jehovah and Israel.
The Jews expressed this belief in their use of this poem during
the Passover Feast. When Israel turned its face from God and
worshiped the gods of Canaan, they were called adulterers;
this was spiritual adultery. The terms "whoredom" and "whoredoms" are frequently used in citing Israel's spiritual infidelity
(Jer. 3:9; 13:27; Ezek. 16:17; 16:33; Hosea 1:2; 4:10).

Christ as
Bridegroom
736

Passover
Feast
1256

295

Isaiah makes clear the idea embraced by the allegorical position: "As the bridegroom rejoiceth over the bride, so shall thy
God rejoice over thee" (Isa. 62:5). Other prophets affirm this
position (Hosea 2:18–22; Jer. 3:1–10; Ezek. 16 and 23). The
application of Jehovah, the bridegroom, and Israel, the bride,
was transferred to Christ and his church. Jesus made frequent
reference to the bridegroom and bride imagery and did not
hesitate to identify himself as the bridegroom, who would one
day complete the age and take unto himself his bride, the
church.

Christian scholars readily adopted and developed the Jewish
allegorical interpretation, for the figure of wedlock is used in
the NT by both Paul and John to represent the ultimate and
vital union of Christ and his church (2 Cor. 11:2; Eph. 5:22,23;
Rev. 21:2–9). One writer has contributed this explanation:

> The pure spontaneous, mutual love of a great king and a humble
> maid was seen to exemplify the mutual affection between Jehovah
> and His people. And the story was told, not merely because it was
> beautiful, but chiefly because it was typical of this great religious
> truth. The Song of Songs is thus analogous to Messianic Psalms,
> which are based on the personal experiences or official position of
> David and Solomon, and exhibit truths regarding the great king.
> The comparison of the mutual love between the church and its
> divine head to that of the bride and bridegroom frequently occurs
> in the NT (Eph. 5:25–33; Rev. 9:7–9; 21:9, etc.).[27]

The Prophets (Isaiah–Malachi)

I. ISAIAH

Book of Isaiah
4245

A. The Name

The name Isaiah is derived from the Hebrew *yeshayahu*, meaning "Jehovah saves," or "Jehovah is salvation." The Greek form
"Esaias" is used in the English NT. In the Latin Vulgate the
rendering is the same as the Greek—"Esaias." The title of the
book originated from the reference in the first verse, "Isaiah
the son of Amoz," as explained in the next section of this chapter under "Author and Date." The name Isaiah also appears
a number of times in various sections of the book as well as
in other parts of the OT.

Isaiah
1803

Isaiah is the first of the Major Prophets in the English Bible
and the first of the "Latter Prophets" in the Hebrew canon.
For a general discussion of "The Prophets" see Ch. 8, II.

Prophets
2065–2070

B. Authorship and Date

The authorship of Isaiah (758–698 B.C.) was not questioned
by scholars in Judaism and traditional Christianity until the
development of biblical criticism in the eighteenth century.
One supposition of this approach was that the prophets always
spoke only in immediate historical situations, that there was
no miraculous intervention by God, and that the prophets could
not foretell the future. On the basis of this assumption, the
book of Isaiah, the book of Daniel, and other sections of the
OT which contain reference to miracles and prophetic state-

ments of future events have been reassigned to dates later than the historical events these writings describe.

As most of the content in chapters 1–39 was considered to be unified and within the period of Isaiah's ministry, most critics have been willing to grant authorship of these chapters to the prophet. However, chapters 40–66 contain some references to events not in his lifetime; consequently these chapters were assigned to writers living in a later period, after the predicted events had become history. An imaginary second Isaiah (Deutero-Isaiah), supposedly living after the Babylonian captivity (536 B.C.), was credited with writing the chapters in question. Because of differences in historical background, a third Isaiah (Trito-Isaiah) was created. Since then, other Isaiahs have been suggested to deal with the so-called textual problems. At the present time the book of Isaiah is "in large part distributed among various writers from Cyrus to Simon (538–164 B.C.)." [1] The process of this arbitrary division of the book of Isaiah by such extreme critics as J. Wellhausen, B. Stade, A. Kuenen, F. Ruckert and others is well presented by Robert H. Pfeiffer.[2]

The messianic prophecies were either ignored or disposed of by the use of a "gloss"—an imaginary explanation.* This approach brought into question the whole idea of Scriptural integrity. According to this approach, certain passages relating to "universal peace" (Isa. 11:1–9); "universal judgment upon the whole earth" (Isa. 14:26), and the Apocalyptic chapters (Isa. 24–27) transcended Isaiah's range of thought; so these passages were lifted out of their chronological context and reassigned to a later date, when, it was supposed, these concepts had developed.

Another argument used in favor of multiple authorship, but not developed in this study guide, is style; i.e., internal and linguistic evidence in matters of diction and tone. Some critics have favored the assigning of two or more Isaiahs in the authorship of the book because of the variations in content and style that they have noticed in certain passages. A study of various authors' works sometimes shows a difference in style within the individual author's writing. His style may vary with content and emotion. Might not such variation within Isaiah's long ministry support the view of single authorship of the Book of Isaiah?

Both Jewish and Christian tradition accepted Isaiah as the author of the entire Book bearing his name. Isaiah is the recognized author in both the Talmud and in the writings of the Early Church Fathers. Not only is the author of the book identi-

---

298 * Gloss: "to make appear right and acceptable: WHITEWASH. . . . to dispose of (as a difficult problem) by false or perverse interpretation. . . ." Webster's New Collegiate Dictionary, 1973, p. 490.

fied in the first verse, his name is mentioned sixteen times in the body of the book with such notations as, "then said the LORD unto Isaiah" (Isa. 7:3); "Isaiah said unto them" (Isa. 37:6); and "then came the word of the LORD to Isaiah" (Isa. 38:4). Jesus referred to Isaiah at least four times as the author (Matt. 13:14,15; 15:7; Mark 7:6,7; and Luke 4:17; cf. Isa 6:9,10; 29:13; 61:1,2). Philip identified Christ, with the passage of Isaiah that the Ethiopian eunuch was reading (Acts 8:28,29; cf. Isa 53:6–8). Paul affirmed that Isaiah is the author of the book of Isaiah (Acts 28:25–27; Rom. 9:27,29; 10:16; 15:12).

Philip
2754

Paul
2697

The evidence for a single author and the traditional view that the prophet Isaiah wrote the Book of Isaiah is overwhelming. Isaiah's prophecies follow a general chronological order from chapter one to sixty-six. In Isaiah 6:1 the writer refers to the death of King Uzziah (740 B.C.); in Isaiah 20:1 to the Tartan's arrival in Ashdod (711 B.C.); in Isaiah 36:1 he makes reference to the fourteenth year of Hezekiah's reign when Sennecherib came to attack Jerusalem (701 B.C.). Chapters 40–61 were written soon after 701 B.C.[3]

Uzziah
3744

Hezekiah
1585

In addition to the Book of Isaiah, Isaiah wrote two other books: *The Life of Uzziah* (2 Chron. 26:22) and *The Book of the Kings of Judah and Israel* (2 Chron. 32:32). the best information available is that Isaiah's prophetic life extended from 758 to 698 B.C.[4]

C. Background, Purpose, and Content

Isaiah was the "stately gentleman," equally at home in the palace (Isa. 7:3) or in the temple (Isa. 8:2). He served the court of Jerusalem for about sixty years under the reign of four kings: Uzziah, Jotham, Ahaz, and Hezekiah. When Sennacherib, the conqueror of Assyria, demanded Jerusalem's surrender, King Hezekiah "prayed before the Lord." God sent an answer to King Hezekiah through the words of the prophet Isaiah. During the night God answered by sending the death angel to destroy the 185,000 Assyrian troops (2 Kings 19:15,20,35). Sennacherib hastily retreated to his capitol, Nineveh, where his two sons assassinated him (2 Kings 19:35,36).

Jotham
1924, 1925
Ahaz
103

As a prophet, Isaiah ranks above the other seers. He was the prince of all the prophets; his writings excel in their scope and in prophetic insight; he is a man of God. Isaiah's major theme was, "salvation by faith" (Isa. 43:10). He is the St. Paul of the OT, and the book by his name is often referred to as the fifth Gospel because of its Messianic content. When all of Isaiah's prophetic statements are assembled into a composite collection, a perfect portrayal of Christ emerges, showing Jesus in his various sufferings and death. The fifty-third chapter alone

299

Portraits of
Christ
4301

Galilean
Ministry
pp. 273–277

Nazareth
2571, 4398

Prophetic
Christ
4308

Spiritual
Highway
1563

Zion
3996

Isaiah Scroll
4356

contains sufficient Christological information to keep a Bible student occupied for a lifetime.

Handel drew much of his imagery for his great oratorio, the *messiah,* from Isaiah. So fully does he (Isaiah) describe the person and office of the coming Messiah that from the time of Jerome he has been known as the evangelist of the old Testament.[5] Through his "prophetic telescope" Isaiah views the Messiah as the heir to the throne of David (Isa. 9:7); his virgin birth is clearly predicted (Isa. 7:14; cf. Matt. 1:18; also see page 209).

The mention of the Messiah's ministry in Galilee (Isa. 9:1) is an unusual prediction, because the Messiah was expected to set up his kingdom in Jerusalem, in the very heart of Judaism. Isaiah's prediction proved to be true; Jesus did grow up in the lowly village of Nazareth (John 1:46), in the very heart of Galilee—far removed from the temple hierarchy. It was here that he selected his disciples and conducted much of his earthly ministry. He was expected to redeem Israel, yet Isaiah accurately predicted that he would be rejected by the Jews (Isa. 53:3; cf. John 1:11); that he would be anointed by the Holy Spirit (Isa. 11:2); and that he would be cruelly abused. All this the prophet Isaiah clearly foretold (Isa. 53:4–7). The prediction of his crucifixion between two sinners (Isa. 53:12) and other prophecies give a perfect preview of Christ's suffering and death.[6] For a review of the messianic prophecies see page 209.

Some of the ideas presented throughout the book are peculiar to Isaiah. He refers to Jehovah as "the Holy One of Israel" twenty-five times. This phrase appears only six times in other parts of the OT. The "highway" is an expression peculiar to Isaiah (Isa. 35:8; 40:3; 49:11; 62:10) and is found throughout the book; also note such terms as "remnant" and the position occupied by "Zion." "Pangs of a woman in travail," the "wrath of Jehovah hath spoken it," and "streams of water" are expressions used at intervals from chapter 1 to chapter 66 and appear nowhere else in the OT. These phrases are indicative of the probable single authorship of the book of Isaiah.

The discovery of the Isaiah scroll at Qumran greatly strengthened the conservative view. A scholar of note concludes that "Essentially, it is the same as the book of Isaiah in our Bible, a voice from 2000 years ago, preserved in the wondrous providence of God, confirming the integrity of the Bible."[7] The existence of the Isaiah scroll is no doubt the greatest biblical discovery of this century. Albright places the date of the scroll in the second century B.C. Another well-known scholar expresses the same opinion in these words: "This makes it [the

Isaiah scroll] the oldest known complete Hebrew manuscript of any Biblical book, and it agrees in almost every respect with our traditional Hebrew texts, as used in the translation of the King James Version of our Bible." [8]

Another scholar evaluates this view:

> To deny to Isaiah of the 8th century [B.C.] all catholicity of grace, all universalism of salvation or judgment, every highly developed Messianic ideal, every rich note of promise and comfort, all sublime faith in the sacrosanct character of Zion, as some do, is unwarrantably to create a new Isaiah of greatly reduced proportions, a mere preacher of righteousness, a statesman of not very optimistic view, and the exponent of cold ethical religion without the warmth and glow of the messages which are actually ascribed to the prophet of the 8th century.[9]

II. JEREMIAH

A. *The Name*

Book of
Jeremiah
4246

The name *Jeremiah,* derived from the Hebrew, *Yirmeyahu,* and abbreviated *Yirmeyah,* means "Jehovah founds or establishes." In the Greek OT (LXX) the word appears as *Iermais* and in the later Vulgate as *Jeremias.*

The name of the Book of Jeremiah is taken from the first verse: "The words of Jeremiah the son of Hilkiah" (1:1). There are other places in the book where the name Jeremiah appears. (See next section for further development on the name and authorship.) Jeremiah is the second of the major prophets in the English Bible and the second of the latter prophets in the Hebrew canon.

Jeremiah
1877

B. *Authorship and Date*

According to both Jewish and Christian tradition, Jeremiah is the author of the book bearing his name. The basis for this assumption is strengthened by the prominence of Jeremiah's name in 34 of the 52 chapters, for a total of 132 times. Other parts of the OT mention Jeremiah's name 15 times. It is quoted once in the NT as "Jeremias" (Matt. 16:14).

Jeremiah was a native of Anathoth, a small community about six miles northeast of Jerusalem. This village was located in the area belonging to the tribe of Benjamin and was appointed by Jehovah for use by the priests, the descendants of Aaron (Josh. 21:13–18).

Anathoth
138, 4327
Benjamin
401

Jeremiah received his call to the prophetic office, possibly at the age of 20 (Jer. 1:6) in the thirteenth year of King Josiah's reign (Jer. 1:2), about 626 B.C. He was active in Jerusalem until its fall in 586 B.C.[10]

Josiah
1923
301

C. Background, Purpose, and Content

A student of Jeremiah soon discovers that the structure and content of the book are not arranged chronologically. Apparently Jeremiah circulated individual scrolls, each one illustrating some aspect of his total message. Later the scrolls were compiled into a single book. The names of the five kings under whom Jeremiah served are listed below:

Jeremiah 1:2	*Josiah*, 639–608 B.C.
22:11	*Shallum (Jehoahaz)*, 608 B.C.
	(as *Shallum* in 1 Chron. 3:15)
	(as *Jehoahaz* in 2 Kings 23:30)
1:3	*Jehoiakim*, 608–597 B.C.
22:24	*Jehoiachin*, 597 B.C.
1:3; 32:1–5	*Zedekiah*, 597–536 B.C.

It is evident from the list above that there is a difference between the order of the chapters and the dates.

One writer describes this chronological irregularity:

> It will be seen that the book is not arranged in chronological order. Some late messages come early in the book, and some early messages come late in the book. The messages were delivered orally and perhaps repeatedly, for years, possibly, before Jeremiah began to write them. The writing of such a book was a long and laborious task. Writing parchment, made of sheep skin was scarce and expensive. It was made into a long roll, and wound around a stick. This may account, in part, for the lack of order in Jeremiah's book. After writing an incident or discourse, some other entrances delivered previously would be suggested, and he would write them down, in some cases, without dating them, thus filling up the parchment as he unrolled it.[11]

God called Jeremiah to the prophetic office especially to warn the people of Judea to repent and turn to God. Because of their idolatry, the Northern Kingdom had fallen to the Assyrians. Next, Judah was about to be attacked by Nebuchadnezzar, the Babylonian conqueror. Most of Judah had been conquered, only the capital of Jerusalem remained, and it was surrounded by hostile forces. One commentator describes the moral and spiritual state of Judah in these words:

Assyria
299
Nebuchad-
nezzar
2573
Idolatrous
Altars
3948
Ammonites
129
Baal gods
3936
Habakkuk
1472
Zephaniah
3990

> Altars to Baal were erected, and asherim were built. Moloch, the Ammonite deity, was acknowledged by the sacrificing of children in the Hinnom valley near Jerusalem. Worship of stars and planets was instituted. Official approval was given to astrology, divination, and occultism. The Temple itself was desecrated with graven images of Asherah, the wife of Baal. God was openly deified at altars in the court of the Temple where the host of heaven was worshiped (cf. Jer. 19:13). Innocent blood was shed. . . .[12]

A brief analysis of the book shows that Jeremiah and his fellow prophets, Habakkuk and Zephaniah, made desperate attempts to warn Judah to repent and "flee from the wrath to come" but the religious and political leaders persisted in moral and spiritual degradation. Jeremiah likened Judah to an unfaithful wife who has forsaken her husband and has become a prostitute. Not only was sexual promiscuity and adultery common among the people (Jer. 5:7,8), but also the nation was given to spiritual adultery, so called because of their unfaithfulness to Jehovah and their worshiping of pagan gods. The people scoffed at the prophet's warning (Jer. 5:12); the leaders did not hesitate to oppress and rob the people (Jer. 5:26–28); the government was corrupt (Jer. 5:30,31); the leaders listened to the false prophets (Jer. 5:31), but they ignored the men of God.

The Prophets (Isaiah–Malachi)

Jeremiah
1877

Adultery
1662

Robbery
3089

False Prophets
2100

Habakkuk
1472

Zephaniah
3990

Jeremiah, a man of sorrows, found a people totally abandoned to everything vile; they were a "wicked and adulterous" generation.[13] Even Pashur the priest cast his lot with the evil forces. When Jeremiah's severe warnings persisted, he was put in prison and in stocks (Jer. 20:2). Finally when Jeremiah advised the Jewish leaders to surrender and take their punishment, he was accused of treason (Jer. 37,38). The advice of the false prophets was contrary to that which Jeremiah gave the people. Jeremiah predicted that Jerusalem would be destroyed and that Judah would be taken into captivity for 70 years (Jer. 25). Jeremiah, again placed on trial and accused of treason by the priests and the false prophets, barely excaped execution (Jer. 25–26).

After preaching for twenty-three years, Jeremiah wrote his prophecies in a book so that his warnings could be read to all the people, but King Zedekiah burned the book and again imprisoned the prophet (Jer. 38:6). Soon thereafter Nebuchadnezzar destroyed Jerusalem (Jer. 39) and appointed Gedaliah governor to rule over the remaining citizens; however, in three months Gedaliah was assassinated by the rebellious element who then fled to Egypt, forcibly taking Jeremiah with them (Jer. 40–43). In Egypt, Jeremiah continued his warning (Jer. 44) and foretold the destruction of Egypt. When Nebuchadnezzar had completed the destruction of Judea, he attacked and conquered Egypt, according to the prophet's prediction (Jer. 43:8–13). After the conquest of Egypt, Jeremiah predicted the fall of Babylon (Jer. 50:37–43).

Jeremiah 50 and 51 were copied in a separate book and sent to Babylon. The book was to be read to government officials. Then in solemn ceremony the chapters were sunk in the Euphrates river with these words: "Thus shall Babylon sink, and shall not rise from the evil that I will bring upon her . . . thus far are the words of Jeremiah." [14] To this day the empty ruins remain.

Arch. Babylon
4334

303

III. LAMENTATIONS

A. *The Name*

The original title of Lamentations was taken from the first word in the book. In the Hebrew canon it is called *Ekkah* (1:1), meaning "How" or "Alas!" A modern expression might be "how come" this disaster. In the Greek OT (LXX) the word is rendered *threno*. In Latin it is *thren*, meaning "lamentations." This book has a collective name which tradition has applied to the five elegies in the Hebrew canon lamenting the fate of destroyed Jerusalem. In the Hebrew canon the Book of Lamentations is one of the five scrolls *(Megilloth)* and is listed in the category of the Writings (Heb., *Kethubim;* Gr., *Hagiographa*).

B. *Authorship and Date*

Many scholars believe that Jeremiah wrote the Book of Lamentations. The style and phraseology of the entire book appear similar to the writings in the Book of Jeremiah.

Jeremiah certainly was qualified to write the dramatic description of horror and destruction. Only an eyewitness could do this.

C. *Background, Purpose, and Content*

Jeremiah lived in Jerusalem for about forty-five years under most trying conditions. He had suffered persecution in an effort to save Jerusalem from destruction and the people from captivity. Tradition says that Jeremiah took a position on the western slope of the Mount of Olives and mourned as he watched the city of Jerusalem being burned to the ground.

The composition of this poem is very technical. Chapters 1, 2, 4, and 5 each have twenty-two verses. They are called acrostic or alphabetic because each of the twenty-two Hebrew consonants is used as the initial letter for one of the twenty-two verses. For instance, in chapters 1, 2, 4, and 5 the first verse begins with the *aleph*, verse two with the *beth*, the third three with a *gimel*, verse four with *daleth*, and so on to the end of each chapter.[15]

Chapter 3 has sixty-six verses or three sets of twenty-two verses. In this chapter the first three verses begin with an *aleph*, the second three with a *beth*, the third three with a *gimel*, and so on to the end of the chapter. The order of *ain* and *pe* in chapters 2 and 4 is reversed. This arrangement is comparable to Psalm 119 which is an alphabetic poem with twenty-two eight-verse sections. One scholar describes the sadness of this poem in these words:

> One would think . . . that every letter was written with a tear; every word the sound of a breaking heart: that the author was compacted of sorrow; disciplined to grief from his infancy; one who never breathed but in sighs, nor spoke but in a groan. . . .
> All the expressions and images of sorrow are here exhibited in various combinations. . . . Misery has no expression that the author of Lamentations has not employed. . . . Take him through his life to his death, and learn from him what true patriotism means. The man who watched, prayed and lived for the welfare of his country; who chose to share her adversities, her sorrows, her wants, her afflictions, and disgrace, when he might have been a companion of princes, and have sat at the table of kings; who only ceased to live for his country when he ceased to breathe;—that was a patriot, in comparison with whom almost all others are obscured, diminished and brought low, or totally annihilated.[16]

IV. EZEKIEL

A. The Name

The name Ezekiel is derived from the Hebrew *Yehezkel* meaning "God strengthens." In the Greek OT (LXX) it appears as *Iezehiel* and in the Latin Vulgate as *Ezechiel*.

The name of the Book is taken from Ezekiel 1:3 "The word of the LORD came expressly unto Ezekiel."

The Book of Ezekiel is the third of the major prophets and the third of the Later Prophets in the Hebrew canon.

B. Authorship and Date

Ezekiel 1:3 records that the prophet was the son of a certain Buzi and that he was also a priest as well as a prophet. This identification would presuppose that Ezekiel was a man of letters, well-versed in the rabbinical law of his day. Some writers see special levitical elements in Ezekiel 40–46, and high-priestly characteristics in his portrayal of the Messiah (Ezek. 25:25f.; 45:22).[17]

C. Background, Purpose, and Content

Ezekiel was taken into Babylonian captivity with King Jehoiachin during Nebuchadnezzar's second attack upon Jerusalem in 597 B.C., eleven years before the city was totally destroyed. His place of residence in Babylon was in the vicinity of the Chebar river, "the great ship canal branching off from the Euphrates north of Babylon and running through Nippur to the Tigris." [18]

When Ezekiel arrived in Babylon, Daniel had already at-

Jehoiachin
1859
Babylon
329–331, 4334
Jerusalem
1881
Euphrates
1157
Ezekiel
1197
305

tained great fame. Daniel was the prophetic statesman in the palace, and Ezekiel was minister to the captives in the slave areas. Ezekiel was of aristocratic rank, a member of the priestly tribe, accustomed to association with the upper echelon of society. In Babylon he was suddenly thrust into the society of the poor, indeed a new experience for him. Before he assumed parish responsibility among the common people, he lived in their midst to work and eat as they did for a time. This experience put him in a better position to understand the problems of the people so that he could say, "I sat where they sat" (Ezek. 3:15). In spite of all his pleading, the people were still rebellious and refused to turn to the Lord (Ezek 2:1–5). Ezekiel's revelation from God came in the form of a scroll (Ezek. 2:9–10) which the prophet was commanded to eat (Ezek. 3:3).

The people who had gone into exile with Daniel (606 B.C.) were hopeful that Ezekiel's arrival (579 B.C.) would signal a return to Jerusalem, but their hopes were dashed when Ezekiel told them that the city of Jerusalem would soon be destroyed by fire and that more captives would be arriving. Ezekiel made it clear that the people would be homeless for many years and would stay in exile until they repented and accepted God (Ezek. 4–7).

Ezekiel had many visions of the final destruction of Jerusalem (Ezek 8,9), but he prophesied that there would be an eventual restoration after the exiles were humbled, and ceased their idolatry (Ezek. 10–12).

The Prophecy in chapter 12 describes accurately the fate which would befall king Zedekiah five years later. Zedekiah was forced to see his sons put to death. Then his captors put out his eyes and led him as a slave to Babylon to join the other captives. Zedekiah, no doubt, was the victim of the advice given him by the false prophets (Ezek. 13,14).

Ezekiel had a vision of a burning vine tree which symbolized the burning of Jerusalem (Ezek. 15). Through the symbol of a bride, the prophet gave a vivid description of Judah's idolatry (Ezek. 16). The parable of the two eagles symbolized the destruction of Jerusalem under Zedekiah (Ezek. 17), the result of the national and personal sins of Judah. In the parable of the lion cubs, the prophet lamented for the princes of Israel (Ezek. 19). The elders' continual rebellion against God (Ezek. 20) eventually resulted in their destruction (Ezek. 21–23). A cauldron symbolized the siege of Jerusalem and the dispersion of the people (Ezek. 24). Nations other than Israel were also subject to divine punishment. The prophet directed his prophetic attention against Ammon, Moab, Edom, and Philistia (Ezek. 25), later against Tyre and Sidon (Ezek. 25–28).

Ezekiel's prophecy of judgment upon Tyre is unusual. The

Ruins of the Hippodrome at Tyre from Ezekiel's time

Wall decoration of a guard in the palace at Babylon now in the Berlin Museum. Daniel was taken as a youth into Babylon

prophet predicted that Nebuchadnezzar, king of Babylon, would set his engines of war against the walls of Tyre, that with axes he would break down the walls, and that the conqueror would put stones, timber, and the dust of Tyre into the sea (Ezek. 26:7–12). When Nebuchadnezzar's army approached Tyre, the leading citizens and the government moved to an island a mile or so off the coast. It took the Babylonian conquerors thirteen years to destroy the city on the shore (585–573 B.C.). Years later, when Alexander the Great conquered the city in 332 B.C., the island city had become a formidable fortress.

Alexander was a land soldier without ships, so to attack the city on the island he built a causeway to the island with the stone and timbers from the old city. The need for fill-in material became so great that he literally scraped the dirt from the surface down to the bare rock to complete the project.[19] Bible scholars see in this episode the minute fulfillment of Ezekiel's prophecy that the "stones," the "timber" and "dirt" would be put into the water (Ezek. 26:12).

Ezekiel next pronounced judgment and desolation upon Egypt (Ezek. 29–30) and Assyria (Ezek. 31). Shortly thereafter Ezekiel lamented when his prophecy against Egypt was fulfilled (see Ezek. 29–30; 32). For centuries the site of the former city was a bare rock, just as Alexander the Great had left it. It was a place where the fishermen spread their nets to dry. Thus the prophecy of Ezekiel was fulfilled in detail (Ezek. 26:4,5,14).[20] When news of the fall of Jerusalem reached Babylon, Ezekiel received a new call to prophesy (Ezek. 33). He pronounced judgment upon the shepherds of Israel who fed themselves but did not "feed the sheep" (Ezek. 34). Edom was the next nation to fall because of the help the people gave Nebuchadnezzar when their Jewish cousins were being slaughtered by the Babylonians. (See Obadiah for further pronouncements of doom upon Edom.)

In the "vision of dry bones" Ezekiel saw the resurrection of Israel, the return of the Jews to Judah (Ezek. 37) and the destruction of the enemies of Israel (Ezek. 38, 39). Ezekiel's concluding prophecies deal with the rebuilt temple and the restoration of offerings and sacrifices (Ezek. 40–48).

Book of Daniel
4249
Daniel
Character
Study
4300

V. DANIEL

A. The Name

The name "Daniel" is derived from the Hebrew *Daniyel* and means "God is my judge." In the Greek OT (LXX) this name is rendered *Daniel* corresponding to the form used in English. The book is so called because Daniel is the principal character. His name is mentioned 75 times in the book, appearing in all but chapters 3 and 11. The Book of Daniel is the fifth book of the Major Prophets, but it is listed in the category of the Writings (Heb. *Kethubim*, Gr., *hagiographa*).

B. Authorship and Date

The Bible refers to three Daniels: (1) a son of David and Abigail (1 Chron. 3:1), (2) a priest in the days of Nehemiah (Ezra 8:2; Neh. 10:6), and the celebrated Jewish prophet in the Babylonian Court.

Babylon
329–331, 4334

The Daniel in the book by this name was taken, as a youth, into Babylon with the other captives in the first deportation during the reign of Jehoiakim (606 B.C.). In Babylon he and his companions were selected to be trained and to serve as liaison officers between the captives and the Babylonian government. Men in all ages since have been inspired by Daniel's loyalty to God (Dan. 1:5). Daniel stands out as a man of intelligence, integrity, and dedication to Jehovah.

Jehoiakim
2862

The Book of Daniel, like the Book of Isaiah, has been vulnerable to attack by certain critics. However, both Christian and synagogue scholars have been committed to the assumption that the book was written by Daniel. Around him the account centers. The words in Daniel 12:4 indicate that Daniel wrote a book and was instructed to seal or conclude it (see Dan. 7:2).

The Book of Daniel deals with the prophet's relationship to government officials and people in the Babylonian-Persian area. The Book also contains prophetic statements concerning the development of future nations and predictions relating to the coming of the Messiah and the founding of his kingdom.

Prophesying
1894

The authorship of Daniel remained unquestioned until, in the third century Malchus Porphyry (or Porphyrius) attacked the historical integrity of Christianity and the Book of Daniel (A.D. 233–304). He vented his antagonism against the Christian religion in his fifteen books entitled: *Against the Christians.*[21] In the twelfth book the critical thrust was against the apocalyptic sections in the Book of Daniel, and the foretelling of future events.

False Prophets
2100

Porphyry, a scholar, was educated in the heathen philosophy of Athens and Rome. "With Platinus, he believed in good and evil demons and respected Greek mythology with its philosophical tenets. He relied upon enchantment as a means of acquiring power over demons and the souls of the dead, believing that all matter was polluted."[22]

309

The translation of the Latin Vulgate version of Jerome assists

Wall decoration from the palace of Babylon (above) and lion wall decoration from the same place. Both are now in the Berlin Museum

the student to a better understanding of Porphyry's opposition to revealed truth. Jerome interprets Porphyry's view thus:

> he went through the various kings in order, stated the actual number of years involved and announced beforehand the clearest signs of events to come, and because Porphyry saw that all these things had been fulfilled and could not deny that they had taken place, he overcame this evidence of historical accuracy by taking refuge in this evasion, contending that whatever is foretold concerning the antichrist at the end of the world was actually fulfilled in the reign of Antiochus Epiphanes (175–164) because of certain similarities to things which took place at his time. But this very attack testifies to Daniel's accuracy. For so striking was the reliability of what the prophet foretold, that he could not appear to unbelievers as a predictor of the future, but rather a narrator of things already past. . . . Porphyry makes his objection to us concerning the Book of Daniel, that it is clearly a forgery, not to be considered as belonging to the Hebrew Scriptures but an invention composed in Greek. . . .[23]

Prophecy fulfilled **2892, 2893**

Of course, Porphyry was mistaken in assuming that the Book of Daniel had its origin in Greek and not in Hebrew; he initiated the destructive criticism of the Bible which followed. The references in the Bible which foretell the future and give an account of the miracles which occurred, have been the focal point of attack by some critics. They assumed that the prophets could not foretell the future; those who disbelieved placed the prophetic section at a date subsequent to the actual event.

When modern theological rationalism developed in the seventeenth and eighteenth centuries, the critics adopted Porphyry's approach to Daniel. Instead of leaving the Book of Daniel in its historical context (606–535 B.C.), they placed it in the period of Antiochus Epiphanes or during the Maccabean Revolt (175–164 B.C.), even though Antiochus is not mentioned in the book. They assumed that the people needed encouragement in those troublesome times. Consequently a clever scribe was invented who used the figure of Daniel to write a kind of fictional historical novel to stimulate loyalty to God and to maintain enthusiasm for the national cause against the Seleucid ruler, Antiochus Epiphanes. Thus historicity of the events described in the Book of Daniel became totally irrelevant. These critical scholars have classified a respectable book in the OT canon with a group of spurious books akin to the Pseudepigrapha. So it has been with all scholars such as Emil K. Kraeling in *Encyclopedia of Religious Knowledge,* page 216; Robert R. Pfeiffer in *Introduction to the Old Testament,* page 420; and others.

Archaeological Supplement pp. 309ff.

In recent years archaeological and other kinds of new discoveries have strengthened the traditional, conservative view. Clyde J. Hurst concludes that,

Despite prevalent critical opinion against the 6th century dating of the book [Daniel] a gradual trend is discernible toward earlier dating. The discovery of Belshazzar's (q.v.) name on Babylonian clay tablets, and the probable identification by Whitcomb of Darius the Mede (q.v.) with Gubaru (Gr: *Gobryas*) have gone far to validate the 6th cent. historical accuracy of the book. Alleged linguistic and exegetical problems have been more than adequately answered by conservative scholars. . . . Qumran fragments of the Book of Daniel (150 B.C.) are also weighing heavily in pushing back the date of the authorship of the book toward the conservative date.[24]

The many references in the Book of Daniel to the immediate Babylonian and Persian background indicate that the writer was present to make these cultural observations. The internal evidence is supplemented by the external.

It is evident that Jesus considered Daniel to be a historical person and the author of his Book and that what Daniel had

said about the "abomination of desolation" was important (Matt. 24:15; Mark 13:14; cf. Dan. 9:27).[25] William Smith writes: "The book represents, in many respects, a startling and exceptional character, yet it is far more difficult to explain its composition in the Maccabean period than to connect the peculiarities which it exhibits with the exigencies of the Return."[26]

C. Background, Purpose, and Content

The Babylon to which Daniel and his friends were carried was one of the mighty cities of antiquity located in the general area where civilization had its beginning, in the Garden of Eden. The tower of Babel was built at Borsippa, 10 miles southwest from the center of Babylon. Archaeologists have discovered the remains of a great tower which some scholars identify as the foundation of the original tower.[27]

Historians agree that the city of Babylon was square—15 miles to each side—and that the walls were 300 ft. high and 80 ft. thick with 250 watch towers.[28]

A brief analysis of the Book of Daniel shows that Daniel was the young prophet who won court favor in Babylon because

Persia
2744
Greeks
1464
Shadrach
3247
Meshach
2305
Abednego
3

of his intellectual, physical, and moral excellence. Even though he was challenged several times for his faith, he apparently retained his official relationship as well as his spiritual and moral integrity for about seventy years.

Through his dream-image Daniel prophetically identified the four on-coming world powers: Babylonia, Persia, Greece, and Rome. Between the time of Daniel and the coming of Christ each prediction was minutely fulfilled (Dan. 2). After Daniel and his three friends had been in Babylon twenty years, Shadrach, Meshach, and Abednego defended their spiritual integrity. For this allegiance they were thrown into the fiery furnace;

through divine intervention the three emerged from the furnace unsinged (Dan. 3). Daniel showed his courage when he told the king that his dream meant that the king would temporarily lose his sanity, join the animals in the field, and eat grass (Dan. 4). Following this experience the king made a profession of faith in Daniel's God (Dan. 4:37).

The Prophets (Isaiah–Malachi)
Daniel 914

After Daniel had been in Babylon seven years, Belshazzar put on a "royal feast." During that time a mysterious hand began to write on the wall. That same night Cyrus, the Persian king, took the city, marching his troops into the city over the dry river bed. Historians state that Cyrus's engineers diverted the course of the Euphrates river around the city. No additional historical record has been found so far which mentions Darius the Mede or any other ruler between Nabonidus, Belshazzar, and Cyrus, nor have the various identifications of Darius satisfied all scholars. This does not mean that Darius did not exist (Dan. 5). Some scholars suggest that Darius was a sub-king under Cyrus.

Cyrus 907

Darius 915–917

Because of Daniel's popularity in the court, his political enemies determined to attack him through his religion (Dan. 6:5). Daniel was ordered not to face Jerusalem while praying, but he persisted. For his disobedience he was cast into the lion's den, but God protected Daniel just as he had preserved the life of his friends who were cast into the fiery furnace (Dan. 6). Chapter 7 records Daniel's vision of four beasts coming out of the sea—a lion, a bear, a leopard, and a nameless beast with iron teeth and ten horns. The four beasts are usually interpreted to represent the four world empires, Babylon, Persia, Greece, and Rome. The ten horns are thought to represent the ten kingdoms into which the Roman Empire was divided.

Visions 2495

Babylon 329–331, 4331
Persia 2744
Greeks 1464
Rome 3095

In this vision Daniel seems to have been carried into the "end time" or the final judgment (Dan 7:9,10,13,14). The eighth chapter is a continuation of chapter 7. In the ninth chapter Daniel has a vision of "The Seventy Weeks." J. W. Purkiser presents a commonly held interpretation among evangelicals:

Angels 143–149

> The angel . . . reveals to Daniel that the seventy years in reality stand for seventy weeks (of years), or a period of seventy times seven years. Of these seventy weeks, sixty-nine ("seven weeks, and threescore and two weeks") represent the time "from the going forth of the commandment to restore and build Jerusalem" to the coming of the Messiah (9:25). The remaining week seems to refer to the reign of the Antichrist and to be delayed until the time of the end (9:27). The command referred to is commonly thought to be the commission given to Ezra by Artaxerxes, king of Persia, in 458 or 457 B.C. (Ezra 7:11–28). If the latter date is used, we note that the time from Ezra's commission until the beginning of Christ's ministry in A.D. 26 was exactly 483 years (sixty-nine times seven years)—a remarkable fulfillment of prophecy)! [29]

Messianic Prophecies 2890

A reconstruction of Babylon after Unger with the Ishtar Gate in the foreground. Reproduced by permission of the Oriental Institute of Chicago

Daniel's last vision took place two years after the Jews returned to their homeland (434 B.C.). God showed Daniel some of the hidden conflicts which were going on in the unseen world. Michael and his angels were at war with Satan and his angels (Dan. 10). Chapter 11 presents a continuation of the four great empires from the time of Daniel to Christ. These revelations seem to be progressive, culminating in the "end of time." There is to be a time of trouble such as had never occurred before. In Chapter 12 Daniel brought a glorious message on the resurrection: "and many of them that sleep in the dust of the earth shall awake, some to everlasting life, and some to shame and everlasting contempt" (12:2).

Finally, Daniel was commanded to seal the book, presumably the one he had written and which is to be opened at "the time of the end" (Dan. 12:4).

VI. HOSEA

A. The Name

The Hebrew name for Hosea is *Hoshea*, probably meaning "Help, God," or "God is help." It comes from a Hebrew verb from which *salvation* is derived. In the Greek OT the name is rendered *Osee*. The title for the Book of Hosea comes from the book itself where the name appears once in the first verse and twice in the second verse.

The Book of Hosea is listed in the English Bible as the first of the Minor Prophets, probably because Hosea's book is the longest of those of the minor prophets. In the Hebrew canon it is listed as that of the fourth Latter Prophet.

B. Authorship and Date

Authorship has been ascribed to Hosea in both Jewish and Christian tradition. Verse 2 states: "The beginning of the word of the LORD by Hosea." Verse 1 identifies Hosea as the son of Beeri, and states that the Word of the Lord came to him in the days of Uzziah (787–735), Jotham (749–734), Ahaz (741–726), and Hezekiah (726–697), kings of Judah, and in the days of Jeroboam (790–749). It is evident that Hosea had a long life span; his ministry lasted for about fifty-seven years (782–725). Hosea was one of the eighth-century prophets and "was a younger contemporary of Amos, an older contemporary of Jonah and Micah." [30]

C. Background, Purpose, and Content

The Book of Hosea has presented problems concerning moral principles to both Jewish and Christian scholars. The text of

The ruins at Babylon with the Ishtar Gate

The ruins of the main street in Jerash, one of the cities of the Decapolis (ten cities) near the border between Jordan and Syria. Some feel Joel's ministry may have taken place in this area

Hosea clearly states: "The LORD said to Hosea, Go, take unto thee a wife of whoredoms and children of whoredoms" (Hosea 1:2). Verse 3 records that Hosea "went and took Gomer the daughter of Diblaim; which conceived, and bare him a son" (Hosea 1:3). The remaining part of chapter 1 and chapter 2 deal with the children conceived in this union, and the meaning of the names given them, as well as the judgment God proposed for Israel. It is apparent that Gomer continued to practice her prostitution while she was married to Hosea, for the writer stated the offspring are the children of whoredoms and "their mother hath played the harlot: she that conceived them hath done shamefully: for she said, I will go after my lovers" (Hosea 2:5). Gomer left her husband's home to associate herself with a lover who could better satisfy her fondness for luxury.

Despite Gomer's infidelity, Hosea continues to love his wife. The Lord commanded Hosea to bring his wife back. When the lover refused to release Gomer without monetary compensation, Hosea redeemed her for fifteen pieces of silver and some barley (Hosea 3:1,2). The rest of Hosea deals with the various aspects of judgment which are to befall Israel. Students of the Bible have an interest in the interpretation of this story. For what purpose was it considered to be the infallible, inspired Word of God? Of the many theories, there are two leading ones:

1. *Allegorical.* According to this view, the story is purely allegorical (having hidden meaning), designed to communicate a truth, but has no actual authority. However, if the events did not occur, it would be difficult to know what is truth and what is fiction. The Book of Hosea does not support the assumption that the account is merely an allegory. The story is told clearly and simply: What God said and did and what Hosea said and did.

2. *Literal.* The literal interpretation presupposes that Hosea loved Gomer and thought that he could reform her. Casual thinking would lead one to wonder how God could command Hosea to violate the very commandments he had instituted at Sinai.

To better comprehend God's direction to Hosea, one needs to recognize something of the extent of the apostasy and immorality which prevailed in Israel. Jehovah, the true and living God, had been forsaken; in his place the people worshiped the Baals—the nature gods and goddesses. The pagan temple ritual involved sexual immorality in which the people participated, the outstanding example being the Baal priests and the temple harlots or prostitutes. The belief was that to influence the productive forces of nature, the priest and priestess must engage in sexual orgies. Male prostitution and homosexuality

Fidelity
1230–1232

Apostasy
1235

Heathen
630, 1546
Baal gods
3936

were included in the ritual. Thus, the people were completely under the control of the Baal gods.

About forty years before Hosea, Jezebel, a dedicated champion of the Baal religion, married Ahab, the king of Israel. As the queen, she brought hundreds of Baal priests and prophets into the royal court and started a systematic persecution and murder of God's prophets. She threatened the great Hebrew prophet Elijah, who escaped death at her hands only because of God's providence. One scholar describes Jezebel's reign:

> She was a devoted worshipper of Baal, and intolerant of other faiths. To please her, Ahab reared a temple, and an altar to Baal in Samaria, and set up an Asherah (1 Kings 16:32,33). . . . She slew all the prophets of Jehovah on whom she could lay hands (1 Kings 18:4–13). When she planned the death of Elijah (1 Kings 19:1,2), and afterward effected the judicial murder of Naboth, she similarly ignored the king's authority, though he condoned the deed (1 Kings 21:16–22).[31]

The moral and religious degradation which existed in Israel resulted in disregard for social and ethical values. Corruption had affected every segment of society. In fact, this total disregard for righteousness finally resulted in a disaster for the nation such as could be compared only to the Canaanite nations who perished under Joshua. Israel embraced the very system which had brought total judgment upon the heathen nations (see Josh. 1–2).

The Baal religion was one of the most depraved religions in the world. Even young girls were expected to give themselves to the temple hierarchy for sexual purposes before marriage. Their service was usually for a month or more.

One reason God commanded Hosea to marry a prostitute may be that most, if not all, marriageable young women had served their time in the temple as religious prostitutes. Halley writes: "The idolatrous worship of the land was so universally accomplished with immoral practices (Hos. 4:1–14) that it was hard for a woman to be chaste, and 'whoredome,' in its literal sense, was probably true of most of the women of the time. For Hosea, possibly, it was that kind of woman, or none at all." [32]

Although the story of Hosea and Gomer is repulsive to the pure mind, history shows that God can use the evil experiences of men for his glory. Some parables drawn from this story show that as Hosea continued to love Gomer, despite her infidelity, so Jehovah continued to love his bride, the children of Israel, even though they had turned their faces from him and committed spiritual adultery. One writer summarizes the matter thus:

Whatever the difficulties of determining the correct interpretation may be, the basic message of the prophet is clear, Israel is the wife of Yahweh (Hos. 2:19,20; cf. 2:2). She has entered into this holy relationship by way of a covenant (Hos. 6:7; 8:1). However, like Gomer, the nation is guilty of spiritual infidelity, having been corrupted by Baal worship (Hos. 2:8,13,17; 4:13; 11:2).

More fundamental than their idolatry is the people's lack of personal knowledge of their God (Hos. 4:1,6; 5:4; 6:6; 13:4). They have rejected a close, warm contact with His loving heart (Hos. 4:6); in return they must press on to know Yahweh (Hos. 6:1–3). Coordinate to their infidelity and the spurning of His love is the absence of covenant loyalty and devotion . . . on their part (Hos. 4:2; 6:4,6). . . . A revival of its observance is essential (Hos. 10:12; 12:6).

Even though Israel has fallen to this despicable level, Yahweh still loves her with yearning compassion (Hos. 11:8,9; 14:4). If she will but repent (Hos. 10:12; 12:6; 14:1), He will have mercy and restore her. . . . Just like Luke writes of the prodigal son, so Hosea tells of the prodigal wife.[33]

VII. JOEL

A. The Name

In Hebrew, the name Joel is *Yoel* and means "Jehovah is God." In the Greek OT (LXX) this name is rendered *Ioel*. Nothing is known about this prophet other than that he was the son of Pethuel (Joel 1:1). This particular Joel is not mentioned in the OT other than in the book bearing his name. In the English Bible the Book of Joel is listed under the Minor Prophets in second place; in the Hebrew Canon it is the fifth under Latter Prophets.

B. Authorship and Date

Both Jewish and Christian traditions attribute authorship of the Book of Joel to the prophet whose name it bears. The first verse states: "The word of the LORD that came to Joel."

Joel gives a description of destruction by famine and insect hordes (Joel 1:4), but this reference does not contain a statement as to the date of its writing or its author. Natural disasters happened frequently in Judea, e.g., the famine mentioned in the Book of Ruth and the one in Genesis which occurred in the days of the patriarch Jacob (Gen. 41:54ff.). The book contains passages similar to those in Jeremiah (46:10), Isaiah (2:12), Ezekiel (7:19), and Amos (5:16,20), especially with reference to an apocalyptic event. Joel is considered to be an eighth-century prophet. McRae suggests that Joel began his ministry in 837 B.C. and ended it in 800 B.C.[34]

The name Joel is quite common in the OT but in each instance the reference is to a Joel other than the prophet, e.g.,

a Levite in the family of Kohath, the father of Heman, the
singer (1 Chron. 6:33); the older son of Samuel (1 Sam. 8:2);
a Gershomite Levite who helped carry the Ark (1 Chron.
15:7,11,12); a chief of the tribe of Issachar (1 Chron. 7:3); a
brother of Nathan and a soldier under David (1 Chron.
11:26,38); a son of Pedaiah and ruler in the tribal domain of
Manasseh (1 Chron. 27:20); a chief Gadite in Basham (1 Chron.
5:12–17); a Reubenite (1 Chron. 5:4,8,9); a Kohathite Levite
during Hezekiah's reign (2 Chron. 29:12); one of the Simeonite
princes (1 Chron. 4:35–44); a son of Nebo (Ezra 10:43); and a
Benjamite in Jerusalem under Nehemiah (Neh. 11:9).[35]

C. Background, Purpose, and Content

There is almost no narrative in the book, except a short passage in 2:18. The first part of the book is an account of the
invasion and destruction caused by the palmerworm, the lo-
custs, the cankerworm, and the caterpillar. Each successive
invader ate what the other had left. These insects grew rapidly
from larva to winged adult (Joel 1:4) and at every stage their
appetite increased so that when they had finished no green
thing remained.

Pestilence
1971, 1972

In warning the nation Joel used the insect swarms as a symbol
of enemy hordes of the north that would sweep across the
land leaving it scorched and desolate. He affirmed that no one
need fear God's judgment if he would repent and turn his
face to God (Joel 2:11–13). Joel pled with the whole nation
to repent and assured them that God was merciful (Joel 2:13–
17). Upon their repentance, God promised to rid the land of
the insects and to restore it to a bountiful supply.[36]

God's
Judgments
1966–1974

The second part of the book is apocalyptic; Joel describes
prophetically a distant day when the Lord, their God, "will
pour out [his] spirit upon all flesh," without regard to social
distinction (Joel 2:28–31). In this day "Whosoever shall call
on the name of the LORD shall be delivered [saved]" (Joel
2:32). On the Day of Pentecost Peter quoted this passage as
a prophetic statement which was being fulfilled in the Upper
Room (Acts 2:16–21).

Retribution
3049, 3050

Joel prophesied that a day of retribution would come for
those who had inflicted evil upon God's "chosen people" (Joel
3:2–8) and that the final destiny of people and nations would
be determined on the Judgment Day. After an earthquake
and fire God would abolish all evil and make his home in the
City of Zion (Joel 3:16–18).

320

In his prophetic vision Joel saw a day when God's people
would dwell forever in a heavenly Jerusalem (Joel 3:20).[37]

VIII. AMOS

A. The Name

In Hebrew the name Amos is *amos* and means "burden or burden bearer." In the Greek OT (LXX) the name appears as *Amos*. The prophet Amos is mentioned seven times in the Book bearing his name but never mentioned in the rest of the OT. Another unknown Amos is mentioned in the NT (Luke 3:25). The Book of Amos appears in the English Bible as the third Minor Prophet; in the Hebrew Canon it is the sixth Latter Prophet.

B. Authorship and Date

Both Jewish and Christian tradition attribute authorship of the Book of Amos to the Amos referred to in the book. The first four words of the book read, "The words of Amos." Other references to him appear in Amos 7:8,10,11,12,14.

Amos 1:1 states that Amos prophesied "in the days of Uzziah [787–725 B.C.] king of Judah, and in the days of Jeroboam [II] the son of Joash [806–790 B.C.] king of Israel. . . ." The reference to the earthquake cannot be linked positively with some known historical event. One writer interested in antiquity concluded that the earthquake "was coincident with the imposition of Uzziah's leprosy (2 Chron. 26:16–21), according to which, Amos's prophecy was about 751 B.C." [38] The best estimate is that Amos discharged his prophetic office between 750 and 760 B.C.

C. Background, Purpose, and Content

Amos was not a professional prophet, and his prophetic experience seems to have been limited to one time. He said that he was not a prophet nor the son of a prophet but only a "herdman, and a gatherer of sycomore fruit" (Amos 7:14). The sycamore tree in Palestine grows to a great height, 40 to 50 feet, and is not related to the sycamore tree of the Western world. This tree bore a pithy quality of fig, edible for both man and beast.

Amos was a layman in the small community of Tekoa in Judah, about ten miles south of Jerusalem. God called him with a message for Israel, the Northern Kingdom, approximately 200 years after the founding of the Kingdom. Israel was in the midst of great national prosperity but in a state of extreme apostasy. Calf worship had become the religion of Israel, now further corrupted with Baal-worship which brought with it many of the abominable practices of Canaanite idolatry. Elijah and Elisha had pleaded with the nation to repent but to no avail.

When Amos arrived at Bethel, the center of religious apostasy in the Northern Kingdom, he employed a psychological approach. Instead of stating his prophecy against Israel at once, he pronounced judgment on Israel's neighbors in Damascus (Amos 1:3), Gaza (1:6), Tyrus (1:9), Edom (1:11), Ammon (1:13), Moab (2:1), and Judah (2:4). The denunciation Amos directed toward Judah must have created a favorable receptivity in the minds of the leaders. However, when Amos began his condemnation of the social and religious sins of Israel (Amos 2:6), the leaders soon directed their hostility against Amos.

The evils in their religious practices were paralleled by their social sins. Drunkenness and adultery were common practices (Amos 2:7,8); the righteous were scorned, chastened, mocked, and sold as slaves for a few pieces of silver; the poor were sold for the price of a pair of shoes (Amos 2:6,7). Apparently the rich religious-political leaders lived in luxury while the poor struggled to survive (Amos 3:15).

Amos denounced the sins of Israel. In reproving the Israelites he addressed them as the cows or "kine of Bashan" (Amos 4:1). They were like fatted animals awaiting the slaughter, for one of their sins had been the oppression of the poor.

Amos pleaded with the leaders of Israel to repent and turn to God (Amos 5:4–9). Apparently they were willing to offer sacrifices to God but without repentance. Amos looked with contempt on their offerings as sheer mockery. The Lord said,

"I hate, I despise your feast days. . . . Though ye offer me burnt offerings and your meat offerings, I will not accept them; neither will I regard the peace offerings of your fat beasts" (Amos 5:21,22). Even their songs were an abomination to God (Amos 5:23).

Finally the nation reached the point where God would pronounce his judgment. Punishment in the form of Assyrian captivity was to be their lot (Amos 6:7–14). Soon they were led away "with hooks."[39] The religious and political leaders were equally involved in the degenerate practices of the nation. When Amos declared that the impending judgment could not be avoided, "Amaziah the priest of Bethel sent to Jeroboam king of Israel, saying, Amos hath conspired against thee in the midst of the house of Israel: the land is not able to bear all his words. For thus Amos saith, Jeroboam shall die by the sword, and Israel shall surely be led away captive out of their own land" (Amos 7:10,11).

Amaziah commanded Amos to leave the country and return to "the land of Judah, and there eat bread, and prophesy there:

but prophesy not again any more at Bethel: for it is the king's chapel, and it is the king's court" (Amos 7:12,13). The homily of Amos on the grasshoppers foreshadowed the destruction of Israel. Amos interceded for the people and God extended the grace period (Amos 7:1–3). The message on fire also symbolized destruction (Amos 7:4–6). Once again Amos interceded for the people, and God relented. In the message on the plumb line the city was measured for destruction (Amos 7:7–9). By that time the grace period had ended and the fate of Israel was sealed. The message of summer fruit (Amos 8:1) symbolized that the kingdom was ripe for destruction. Additional details of the destruction follow in the succeeding passage (Amos 9:1–8). Amos described what it would be like when there is a famine of hearing the Word of God (Amos 9:8–12).[40]

The Prophets (Isaiah–Malachi)

Prophets Sent by God
2074

Fire, Instrument of Judgment
1283

IX. OBADIAH

A. The Name

Book of Obadiah
4253

In Hebrew the name Obadiah is *Obadyah* and means "Serving the Lord," or "A Servant of the Lord." It is a compound name from *Obed*, "servant," and *Yah*, an abbreviated form of YHWH, pronounced *Adonay* by the Jews. In the Greek OT the word is *Obidou*.

The name Obadiah is used nineteen times in different OT passages, but only one reference, in the book by this name, pertains to the prophet. The other Obadiahs are: a steward or prime minister under Ahab (1 Kings 18:3–16), a descendant of David (1 Chron. 3:21), a leader in the tribe of Issachar (1 Chron. 7:3), a descendant of Saul (1 Chron. 8:38), a Levite (1 Chron. 9:16), a Gadite (1 Chron. 12:9), a Zebulunite (1 Chron. 27:19), a teacher of the law (2 Chron. 17:7), a supervisor under Josiah (2 Chron. 34:12), a leader from Babylon under Ezra (Ezra 8:9), a scribe under Nehemiah (Neh. 10:5), and a gate keeper in Jerusalem (Neh. 12:25).[41]

Ahab
102

David
919

Ezra
1199

The Book of Obadiah appears in the English Bible as that of the fourth Minor Prophet; in the Hebrew canon it is the seventh in the list of the Latter Prophets.

B. Authorship and Date

The only link of identification for the writer of this book is found in the first verse: "The vision of Obadiah. Thus saith the Lord GOD concerning Edom." There is no consensus as to which Obadiah wrote this book, but because the narrative deals with the Edomites when Jerusalem was being burned by the Babylonians, the most likely Obadiah is the one living

Visions
503–509

323

The Book of Obadiah is addressed to the Edomites who lived in the rock city fortress of Petra. This photo shows tourists on horseback in front of the fortress

The entrance to Petra

during the reign of Zedekiah (597–586 B.C.). See 2 Chronicles 36:11–21; Psalm 137:7.

The Prophets
(Isaiah–
Malachi)

Zedekiah
3988, 3989
Jeremiah
1877
Obadiah
4253

One commentator calls attention to the parallel passages in Jeremiah and Obadiah. He says, "The first nine verses of this shortest of all Old Testament books closely parallels parts of Jeremiah 49, though the sequence of the material is different (cf. Obad. 1–4 with Jer. 49:14–16; Obad. 5,6 with Jer. 49:4,10; Obad. 8,9 with Jer. 49:7,22). The question is: which prophet is dependent upon the other? The most likely answer is that both writers used an earlier well-known prophecy. Doubtless the present arrangement in this book is the work of Obadiah." [42]

Both Jewish and Christian traditions credit Obadiah, the prophet, with authorship, between 586 and 583 B.C.

C. Background, Purpose, and Content

Obadiah's prophecy is directed against Edom, a country south of the Dead Sea. The Edomites were the descendants of Esau and were cousins of the Jews whose progenitor was Esau's brother, Jacob. Their capital was Petra, a fortress city situated in a bowl-shaped depression surrounded by high sandstone mountains. The only approach to Petra was, and still is, through the Seq, a crack in the mountain range caused by an earthquake, through which the Wadi Musa flows, entering on the east side and exiting toward the west, emptying into the Aravah, a valley connecting the Gulf of Akaba and the southern end of the Dead Sea.

Edom (Esau)
1149, see Map
7 at the south

Jacob **1837**

Petra was an almost impregnable cliff city which was easy to defend and difficult to attack. Through the years the Edomites prospered by raiding caravans enroute from Mesapotamia to Egypt, and then retreating into their fortress city.

The descendants of Esau (Edomites) and the descendants of Jacob (Jews) were always bitter enemies and jealous of each other (Gen. 25:23; 27:41). The Edomites refused passage to Moses and the twelve tribes while they were enroute to Canaan (Num. 20:14–21). The Edomites were always ready to aid an enemy attacking the Jews. When the Israelite tribes were fighting the Canaanites, the Edomites aided and abetted the enemy. Again they assisted the Babylonian army when Jerusalem was under siege (Obad. 11–14). Obadiah pronounced judgment upon the Edomites for this treachery; they would have to suffer the same fate as the ones defeated (Obad. 15).

Man's
Jealousy
1851

Treachery
3660

Within four years after the fall of Jerusalem, the same Babylonians, whom the Edomites aided, attacked this mountain stronghold, conquered it and carried most of the inhabitants to Babylonia as slaves.

325

A note of hope for the restoration of the Jewish nation is prophesied in the closing verses (Obad. 17,18), but the "house of Esau" was to be reduced to ruin (Obad. 15). This has been literally fulfilled. Jerusalem continues to be a thriving city while the capital city of the Edomites, Petra, is only a mass of vacant ruins.

X. JONAH

A. The Name

The Hebrew name of Jonah is *Yonah*, meaning "dove"; in the Greek OT (LXX) it is *Ionas*. In the English OT it is rendered *Jonah* and in the NT *Jonas*. The name appears eighteen times in the Book of Jonah, beginning in verse one: "Now the word of the Lord came unto Jonah the son of Amittai. . . ." The same Jonah is referred to in 2 Kings 14:25 where it is said that his home community was Gath-hepher, now known as Galilee. In the NT Jonah's name is used ten times under the name of "Jonas" (Matt. 12:39,40,41; 16:4; Luke 11:29,30,32; John 21:15).

The Book of Jonah appears in the English Bible as that of the fifth Minor Prophet; in the Hebrew canon it is the eighth in the list of the Latter Prophets.

B. Authorship and Date

Determining the authorship of a work is sometimes related to its historical verification. The conservative view takes into consideration the historical-internal evidence and has concluded that the book is historical. The liberal view tends to interpret Jonah as fictional. This view is probably best represented by Robert H. Pfeiffer: "the story of Jonah is neither an account of actual happenings, nor an allegory of the destiny of Israel, or the Messiah (cf. Matt. 12:40); it is fiction—a short story with a moral—like the Book of Ruth, . . . or legendary character like Daniel." [43]

Some liberal views would take issue with Pfeiffer and insist that the book is an allegory which assumes that Jonah was identified with Israel and that the mission of Israel was to declare God's truth to the world. According to this view the fish is Babylon who swallowed the Israelites and took them into exile. The fish expelling Jonah on the beach represented the Jews returning from exile. Jonah's negative attitude to Nineveh's repentance represents the Jews after returning from exile. [44]

However, the Book of Kings makes reference to Jonah as a

historical person and identifies him as a son of Amittai (1 Kings 14:25). Halley points out:

> Jesus unmistakably regarded it as a historical fact (Matt. 12:38–41). It takes considerable straining to make anything else out of the language. He called it a "sign" of the resurrection. He put the repentance of the Ninevites, his resurrection and the Judgment Day in the same category. He surely was talking of Reality when he spoke of his resurrection and the Judgment day. Thus Jesus accepted the Jonah story. For us that settles it. We believe that it actually occurred, just as recorded; and that Jonah himself, under the direction of God's Spirit, wrote the book . . . and that the book, under the direction of God's Spirit, was placed among the Sacred Writings in the Temple as a part of God's unfolding revelation of Himself.[45]

"By accepting the historicity of the book, which is clearly asserted in both the OT and NT, it seems that Jonah must have written the book during the reign of Jeroboam II (782–753). Traditionally he has been considered an 8th century prophet." [46]

Jeroboam
1879, 1880

C. Background, Purpose, and Content

Nineveh was the capital of Assyria, a world empire for about 300 years (900–607 B.C.). The Assyrian capital was a center of vice, corruption and heathen immorality. These vices are not specifically described in the book but the city was widely known as a center of fertility cult worship and of cruelty to its war victims.[47] The book makes reference to the wickedness of Nineveh (Jonah 1:2), and the fact that God sent Jonah to Nineveh on an evangelistic mission suggests spiritual need.

Baal gods
3936

Jonah was obsessed with the idea that the Jews were God's chosen people without any consideration to moral or spiritual obligation, and that they were not to associate with the heathen gentile world. Peter, too, had this problem until his experience on the housetop at Joppa where his ministry to Cornelius had its inception (Acts 10).

Chosen
Instruments
2013

Jonah tried to escape his prophetic duty by taking a ship to Tarshish (probably in southern Spain). However, at sea, God intervened and had Jonah thrown overboard. After a large fish swallowed Jonah, and disgorged him on the beach, he went in haste to Nineveh. For those who have problems with the fish, it can be pointed out that there are several instances where a large fish swallowed a man; thus the claim that a whale (large fish) could not have swallowed Jonah is not well taken. The account states that God prepared a great fish for the task (Jonah 2:17). The Hebrew word here used is *da'g* meaning fish, not whale. Two other words in the Hebrew OT are translated whale: *tanniym* in Job 7:12 and *tan* in Ezekiel 32:2, but in all three instances the intended meaning is a large fish, or

Nineveh
2593, 4400

327

sea monster. In the NT the translators rendered the Greek word *ketos* to read "whale" but it can mean either a great fish or a whale. The word whale is frequently used as a descriptive adjective.

The Book of Jonah is part of the inspired, infallible Word of God and has a place in the Hebrew canon, certifying its validity. This should be enough reason for authenticity to those with a high regard for scriptural integrity.

When Jonah arrived in Nineveh he found it to be a very large city. The main part, including the palace and temple area was enclosed with a high wall. The residential section extended for miles up and down the Tigris river and for many miles eastward. One archaeologist gives this description of the ruins:

> The city walls, clearly visible in outline, are eight miles long and enclose two important mounds. One is called Nebi Yonus, and according to local legend, is the tomb of the prophet Jonah [mound covers 40 acres]. It is covered by a modern village with cemetery and mosque; consequently only very superficial excavation has been possible. The northern and larger mound, Kuyunjik, is one of the largest in Mesopotamia; it is estimated that over 14 million tons of earth would have to be moved to excavate it completely. The main buildings thus far discovered are three royal palaces and two temples.[48]

The size of the city is suggested in the text: "And Jonah began to enter into the city a day's journey" (Jonah 3:4).

The modern visitor to Nineveh finds a limited number of archaeological test pits whose findings testify to the splendor and glory of this ancient city. Unfortunately, most of the important archaeological finds have been removed to museums in London, Paris, and Berlin. Currently the Department of Antiquities in Iraq is restoring some of the walls and city gates. The massive ruins as seen today indicate the tremendous size of ancient Nineveh.

Sackcloth
1950
Ashes-Dust
1058

Gentile
Believers
4038
Godly Fear
1034–1036

When Jonah arrived in Nineveh, the people took his prophecy of impending judgment quite seriously. "The people of Nineveh believed God, and proclaimed a fast, and put on sackcloth, from the greatest even to the least of them" (Jonah 3:5). Even the king joined the repentant people (Jonah 3:6). The putting on of sackcloth and sitting in the ash pit symbolized a spirit of repentance and humility. God saw that "they turned from their evil way" (Jonah 3:10) and withheld his judgment. This is the first example of Jewish evangelism reaching out to the Gentiles. It is evident that "God is no respecter of persons: but in every nation he that feareth him, and worketh righteousness, is accepted with him" (Acts 10:34,35). When Jonah saw the Ninevites repent and turn their faces to the living God, the prophet was displeased. He still carried in his heart a prejudice against Gentiles. He cared little whether or not more than 620,000 persons might be destroyed. Jonah expressed his desire to die rather than see salvation come to this great city (Jonah 4:1–3). Livingston describes Jonah's experience with the gourd vine and the hot east wind in these words:

> In order to teach the prophet a lesson, God prepares a fast growing plant to shade him from the sun, but the next night He allows a worm to destroy it. Then he set a hot east wind blowing. As a result Jonah is faint in spirit and wishes for death. The story closes with a declaration that whereas Jonah is concerned for gourds, God is concerned for the salvation of sinful men.[49]

This Book teaches that God is concerned for the salvation of souls, irrespective of nation, race, or creed. He is "not willing that any should perish" (2 Peter 3:9). The evasion of responsibility, as with Jonah, is still man's weakness; God is powerful and can change the designs and will of man.

God's judgment is always tempered with mercy; the most unlikely mission fields are the most fruitful, and finally God is anxious to extend his mercy and grace to all who repent and seek his face.[50]

XI. MICAH

A. The Name

The Hebrew name for *Micah* is *Mikkan* meaning "Who is like Jehovah?" The translation indicates Micah's character and concept of righteousness and holiness. The Greek rendering of Micah (LXX) is *Michaias*. There are thirty instances in the OT where the name Micah appears, besides the single reference in the first chapter of the book (1:1). Some of the leading persons by this name are: an Ephramite who stole 1000 pieces of silver (Judg. 17), a descendant of Reuben (1 Chron. 5:5), a son of Meribbaal (1 Chron. 8:34), a Levite during the reign of David (1 Chron. 23:20), a son of Zichri (1 Chron. 9:15), and the father of one of Josiah's messengers (2 Chron. 34:20).

The Book of Micah is the sixth of the Minor Prophets in the English Bible and the ninth of the Latter Prophets in the Hebrew canon.

B. Authorship and Date

Micah's name in the Book establishes the author's identity: "The word of the LORD that came to Micah" (1:1). Jewish and Christian tradition has credited Micah with writing this book

The ancient walls of Nineveh stretch as far as eyes can see. Greater Nineveh is said to have been 30 miles long and 10 miles wide

A section of the walls of Nineveh being reconstructed with original as well as new materials. The new walls have a modified height

although certain critics question its authenticity, especially on the basis of its prophetic content—foretelling future events. Micah lived in the days of Jotham, 749–734 B.C.; Ahaz, 741–726 B.C., and Hezekiah, 726–697 B.C., all kings of Judah. Of the three, only Ahaz was a wicked king. Micah was a native of Moresheath, about 25 miles southwest of Jerusalem along a military highway over which the Assyrians marched in 734 and 711 and again in 701 B.C.

It is difficult to ascertain the origin of certain passages in some of the prophetical books. The passage in Micah 3:12 (740–700 B.C.) is almost identical with that in Jeremiah 26:18 (627–586 B.C.). Similar phraseology exists between Micah 4:1–3 and Isaiah 2:2–4 (758–698 B.C.). The three prophets may have used a "floating oracle" or a common source for their information, probably composed by an earlier prophet of hope.[51] Micah, one of the eighth-century prophets, probably wrote the major portion of the book sometime before the fall of the Northern Kingdom (721 B.C.) since he predicts its downfall. As there were sacred oracles in circulation by that time, it is possible that through the leading of the Holy Spirit, some interborrowing of information took place. The writers then did not have the documentation ethic prevalent today.

C. Background, Purpose, and Content

Micah was a contemporary of Amos and Hosea, who prophesied in the Northern Kingdom, and of Isaiah, the prophet-statesman in Jerusalem. Micah, the country preacher, directed his prophecies to both Judah and Israel as did Isaiah, the prophet of the palace.

The idolatrous curse of the north was beginning to become a problem in Judah. Micah denounced rulers, priests, and false prophets. He condemned the exploitation of the poor and dishonesty in business as well as the apostasy which was developing in the Southern Kingdom.[52]

In the Book of Micah, which contains only seven chapters, the prophet first denounced the transgressions and sins of Israel. He predicted that Samaria would become a "heap of the field" (Mic. 1:6). In 722 B.C. the Assyrians literally made a "heap" of a pile of rubbish out of Samaria (the palace area is nothing more than that at the present time). In chapters 2 and 3 Micah challenged certain social and moral abuses in the land (Mic. 2:1–3; 3:1–3). Claude Ries describes these abuses thus:

The sins he [Micah] excoriated were those which bore upon the plain people whom he knew as farmers, agriculturists and small

The Prophets
(Isaiah–
Malachi)

Prophets
(Seers)
2069

Assyria
299, 300

Oracles of God
2500

Amos
132
Hosea
1704

Idolatry
Forbidden
3928

Samaria
**3133, 3134,
4409**

331

The Old Testament

land owners. These were made the victims of the rapacity of the wealthy . . . ; the social sins of cruelty and inhumanity bulk large in his writings.

The rulers, the wealthy, the conniving priests and prophets in the capital cities, feeling secure within strong fortifications, made the most of their power to oppress the poor. The peasants had no protection from either the Assyrians or from the "grafters" of their own nation.[53]

The religious and political rulers lived within the walled cities whereas the peasants had their homes and fields on the outside of the walls.

Prophetic Visions 2496

In chapter 4 Micah had a vision of a "warless, prosperous, God-fearing world with Zion at its head." Isaiah had a glimpse of this glorious society (2:2–4).[54] Henry H. Halley makes this observation:

> Suddenly in the midst of this rhapsody of the future, the prophet reverts to his own troublesome times and the doom of Jerusalem, which he had just mentioned (3:12), announcing that the people would be carried away captive to Babylon (4:10). It is an amazing prophecy. At the time, Assyria was sweeping everything before it. This was 100 years before the rise of the Babylonian empire. Yet, Jerusalem survived the Assyrian onslaught (2 Kings 19:35–37) and lived on until Assyria was overthrown by Babylon, at whose hands Jerusalem fell, 606 B.C.; and its people were carried away to Babylon.[55]

Messianic Prophecies 2890

In the fifth chapter Micah prophesied the coming of the Messiah (Mic. 5:2). The specific nature of Micah's prophecy was apparent—the Messiah was to come in Bethlehem. The prophet specified the political sub-division, Ephratah, originally "the tribal domain of Ephraim," in order not to confuse it with the Bethlehem located within the territory of Zebulun (Josh. 19:15), about 7 miles northwest of Nazareth in Galilee.

Ingratitude to God 1458 Idolatry 3928–3951

In chapter 6 Micah reviewed the sins of ingratitude to God, religious pretense, dishonesty, idolatry, each of which was to receive its due punishment. Micah watches the breakdown of his country. The corruption which began at government level had permeated the whole nation, and now human relationships were crumbling. Friendship and families had deteriorated; the human aspect was bleak and discouraging. But with God there is always hope. In God's mercy, love, and compassion, forgiveness and restoration were still possible, if the people would repent and turn their face to God.

Book of Nahum 4256

XII. NAHUM

A. The Name

332

The name *Nahum* in the Hebrew canon means "consolation" or "consoler," and expresses the purpose of the book, to comfort the oppressed and afflicted people of Judah. The name *Nahum* does not occur in any other OT book and it is used only once in the book by that name (1:1): "The burden of Nineveh. The book of the vision of Nahum the Elkoshite." In the genealogical table by Luke the name *Naum* appears, but it has no relationship to Nahum the prophet.[56] The book of Nahum is the seventh in the list of books by the Minor Prophets and the tenth of the Latter Prophets in the Hebrew canon.

The Prophets
(Isaiah–
Malachi)

Oppression
2005, 2006

B. Authorship and Date

Both Jewish and Christian tradition ascribe the authorship of this book to the prophet Nahum. Nothing is known about the author's ancestry or background, but he was one of the men whom God chose to write a book which became a part of the Hebrew Bible. The date for the writing of Nahum could be within the bounds of about fifty years. The tone of the message suggests that it was written shortly before Nineveh fell in 612 B.C. A most probable date is between 614 and 612 B.C., "after the Medes and Babylonians began to close in on Nineveh." [57]

Nineveh
2593, 4400

B. Background, Purpose, and Content

Nineveh was the great and mighty capital of Assyria. It was founded by Nimrod, shortly after the flood (Gen. 10:11,12) and was a rival of Babylon from the beginning. Nineveh was located in the northern part of the country on the Tigris river and Babylon in the southern part on the Euphrates river. For a description of Nineveh see the commentary on the Book of Jonah.

Nimrod
2592, 4346

Some scholars associate Nahum with the town of Capernaum, which means the "home" or "village of Nahum." It had now been about 150 years since Jonah witnessed a great spiritual revival and a turning of the Ninevites to the worship of Jehovah. By the time Nahum assumes his prophetic office the Ninevites had reverted to their heathen worship. Nahum declared that God was jealous and would take vengeance upon his enemies. The days of the nation that had destroyed the Northern Kingdom and threatened Jerusalem were numbered. The fall of Nineveh would bring rejoicing throughout the Tigris-Euphrates area. The 300 years of terror and destruction were about to come to an end for the once proud and mighty Assyria of which Nineveh was the home and capital of the militant kings.

Capernaum
641, 4349

Jonah
1909

Divine
Jealousy
1850

Assyria
299

The prophet gives a vivid description of the battle which was to take place on the streets of Nineveh (Nah. 2:3,4); when the gates opened, the palace was to "be dissolved" by the flood-

333

ing Tigris river (Nah. 2:6). (The effects of this flood damage are still visible in old Nineveh.) The destruction of the "bloody city" was at hand (Nah. 3:1–3). No power on earth would now be able to save Nineveh; it had gone to the "point of no return." The defenses of the city would be destroyed (Nah. 3:12–18) and there would be great rejoicing by the people in the neighboring countries. The prophet gives a vivid description of the battle scenes in the streets; the flaming chariots shall rage and "justle one against another" and they "shall run like the lightnings" (Nah. 2:4).

Henry H. Halley describes the total destruction of the once great city:

> Its destruction was so complete that even its site was forgotten. When Xenophon and his 10,000 soldiers passed by 200 years later he thought the mounds were the ruins of some Parthian city. When Alexander the Great fought the famous battle of Arbela, 331 B.C., near the site of Nineveh, he did not know there had ever been a city there.
>
> So completely had all traces of the glory of the Assyrian Empire disappeared that many scholars had come to think that the references to it in the Bible and other ancient histories were mythical; that in reality such a city and such an empire never existed. In 1820 an Englishman, Claude James Rich, spent 4 months sketching the mounds across the Tigris from Mosul, which he suspected were the ruins of Nineveh. In 1845 Layard definitely identified the site; and he and his successors uncovered the ruins of the magnificent palaces of the Assyrian kings, whose names have now become household words, and hundreds of thousands of inscriptions in which we read the history of Assyria as the Assyrians themselves wrote it, and which to a remarkable degree supplement and confirm the Bible.[58]

XIII. HABAKKUK

A. *The Name*

The Hebrew name for Habakkuk is *habhakkuk* and means "embrace" or "ardent embrace," "to cling." He clung to God. The Greek OT (LXX) renders this name *Hambakoum*. The only instances where Habakkuk appears in the entire Bible are the two times it is included in the Book by this name (1:1; 3:1).

The Book of Habakkuk is the eighth in the Minor Prophets; it is the eleventh in the Latter Prophets in the Hebrew canon.

B. *Authorship and Date*

Little reliable information is available as to the identity of the prophet Habakkuk other than that he had a burden for his nation and that he prayed to God for it. Most scholars are

Ruins at Palmyra, which figured in Habbakkuk's ministry

A modern plowman follows the tradition of his fathers in the Holy Land

willing to credit Habakkuk with writing the entire Book. However, some of the more critical writers are hesitant to ascribe chapter 3 to this prophet even though it mentions the prophet's name (Hab. 3:1). They argue that this chapter must have been written by a later compiler because the views are more typical of another age, that this chapter was designed to be used in the temple worship, and that the theology expressed in it reflects a period after the Exile. To support their contention they point out that the third chapter was not found in the Habakkuk manuscript at Qumran on the Dead Sea (see Ch. 12, VII, B).

The Book may have been written at some time during the early part of the seventh century B.C., during the time of Josiah (639–608) and Jehoiakim (608–597).[59]

C. Background, Purpose, and Content

The dialogue between Habakkuk and God seems to have taken place in the midst of the Babylonians' military campaigns around Jerusalem. Most of the country had been devastated and occupied by the invaders and the city had been greatly damaged. Many of the citizens, including Daniel and the three Hebrew children, had been carried into Babylon in 606 B.C.

The prophet was bewildered by the savage attack of the enemy and engaged God in a debate, similar to a conversation. Habakkuk was unable to understand how God could permit a nation more wicked than his own to savagely attack the covenant people. From God's answer the prophet concluded that in the end a nation that sins but repents will be restored by God, whereas the heathen nation, temporarily prosperous and victorious, will be ultimately destroyed. The great heathen political and religious capitals of the ancient world are still a "heap of ruins," e.g., Babylon, Nineveh, Ur, and Ephesus, while Jerusalem is a thriving city. History seems to bear out the idea that God sometimes used wicked nations to chasten his people.

From his insight into God's judgment and justice, the prophet saw that the essence of a satisfying relationship with God was faith. He formulated the statement: "The just shall live by his faith" (Hab. 2:4), and this assertion has become the base upon which the doctrine of justification by faith is developed in the NT. Paul quotes the verse twice (Rom. 1:17 and Gal. 3:11).[60] It is also repeated by the writer to the Hebrews (10:38).

Habakkuk may have been a chorister in the Levitical choir. Musical references occur in the first and last verses of the third chapter. The first verse includes a reference to *shigionoth*, which is a musical term meaning a "dithrambic ode," a lively, enthusiastic musical sequence. The last verse mentions singers and stringed instruments. The Hebrew designation for the use of stringed instruments is *neginoth* and is found frequently in the superscription of the Psalms (Pss. 4,6,55,67,76). (For additional information on the Superscriptions see page 280.)

The Prophets (Isaiah– Malachi)

XIV. ZEPHANIAH

Book of Zephaniah
4258

A. *The Name*

The Hebrew name for Zephaniah is *Sephanyah*, meaning "bides" or "Jehovah has bidden." The Greek OT (LXX) renders the name *Zacharias* as *Sophonias*. In the Scriptures the name appears a total of ten times but only once in the Book of Zephaniah. At least four other men bear this name: a Babylonian captive executed by Nebuchadnezzar (2 Kings 25:18; Jer. 52:24), a Levite, descendant of Kohath (1 Chron. 6:36), a priest in the reign of Zedekiah (Jer. 21:1; 37:3), and the father of Josiah, who returned from Babylon (Zech. 6:10,14). The single reference to Zephaniah in his book appears in the first verse. The Book of Zephaniah is the ninth in the list of Minor Prophets and the twelfth of the Latter Prophets in the Hebrew Canon.

Zephaniah
3990

B. *Authorship and Date*

Jewish and Christian tradition credit Zephaniah with the authorship of the book bearing his name. In the first verse the writer states, "The word of the LORD which came unto Zephaniah. . . ."

Some of the liberal critics give credit to Zephaniah for having written the first chapter but do not accept his authorship of chapters 2 and 3 because of the prophetic elements in these sections. This position is not acceptable to conservatives because it holds that there is no validity in prophecy, i.e., foretelling of future events.

Since Zephaniah affirmed that he had entered the prophetic office during the reign of Josiah, king of Judah (1:1) (639–608 B.C.), he was probably a leader in the reform during Josiah's reign. MacRae suggests that the prophet ministered 640–610 B.C.[61] He may have written his prophecy about two years before the first attack on Jerusalem by the Babylonians, or about 608 B.C.

Josiah
1923
Reformers
2076, 2077
See also
316–318

C. *Background, Purpose, and Content*

Little is known about Zephaniah other than that he was a fourth-generation descendant of King Hezekiah—thus a prince of royal lineage.[62] Zephaniah received his call to the prophetic office while he was quite young and was one of the first prophets

Prophets Sent by God
2074

in seventy years, after Isaiah and Micah. It is apparent that Nineveh had not yet fallen to Babylon (Zeph. 2:13).

The Book of Zephaniah divides itself "into two parts, of unequal length. Chapters 1:2–3:8 contain denunciation and threats; Chapter 3:9–20, contains a promise of salvation and glorification." [63] One scholar describes the seriousness of the national situation at the time Zephaniah (also Jeremiah) accepted his call to the prophetic office: "Zephaniah's sensitive, moral and religious spirit was overwhelmed by the impending doom that awaited the disobedient: in such a spiritual atmosphere disaster was sure. The Day of Wrath (Zeph. 1:14–18)—

borrowed from Amos (5:18–20) and Isaiah—here for the first time became apocalyptic . . . the Day of the Lord became not only the Day of Wrath, but the Last Day. . . . Zephaniah envisaged an attitude of life in which there remained nothing but judgment of an Outraged God." [64]

The basis of Zephaniah's prophecy is the impending universal judgment which God is about to unleash. The extent of the

coming destruction can be compared to that of the flood under Noah (Zeph. 1:2–4; Gen. 6:5–7). The surrounding nations would not escape the wrath of God. Judgment would come upon Philistia (Zeph. 2:4–7), Moab and Ammon (2:8–11), Ethiopia (2:12) and Assyria (2:13–15), but punishment of these nations would be no consolation for Jerusalem. Religious and political leaders had become so corrupt that the nation could not escape retribution (2:1–4).

The prophet does offer hope for a remnant who will ultimately enjoy exaltation "as a redeemed daughter of Zion." [65] Some critical scholars question the integrity of 2:1–3,4–15, which refers to the "meek of the earth" and "seek meekness."

The claim is that the concept of "meekness," as mentioned here, did not develop until the post exilic period. "There can be no question that the words occur more frequently in post exilic psalms and proverbs than in pre-exilic writings, but it cannot be proved, or even shown to be probable, that the words might not have been used in Zephaniah's day (cf. Exod. 10:3; Num. 12:3; Isa. 2:9ff.; Mic. 6:8)." [66]

In chapter 3 the prophet again denounced the "filthy and polluted" city (Zeph. 3:1–5). Nevertheless, the prophet again opened the door of hope for a surviving remnant (3:12,13).

In Zephaniah 3:9 the prophet speaks of a "pure language," "a prediction of a complete and perfect revelation of God to man (obviously meaning the Gospel of Christ) as a result of which converts from among the nations would be brought to

God, joyful with glad songs of redemption, all the earth resounding with the praise of God's people." [67] Might it also be possible that the fulfillment of this prophecy came to pass when Greek became the universal language?

XV. HAGGAI

A. The Name

In Hebrew the word for Haggai is *haggay,* meaning "festival" and may suggest he was born on a festival day or it may refer to the anticipation of the return from captivity. (For a discussion of the meaning of Hebrew names see Ch. 7, I.) In the Greek OT (LXX) this name is rendered *Haggaios.* The prophet is mentioned ten times in the entire Bible, two times in the Book of Ezra (5:1; 6:14), and eight times in the book bearing his name (1:1,3,12,13; 2:1,13,14,20). No other man by this name appears in the Bible.

The Book of Haggai is the tenth in the list of Minor Prophets and the thirteenth of the Latter Prophets in the Hebrew Canon.

B. Authorship and Date

The Book of Haggai is short and concise. The unity and continuity are such that tradition has always given the prophet credit for writing it. His name, being frequently mentioned in the book and referred to by one of his associates, Ezra (5:1; 6:14), makes authorship quite certain. R. K. Harrison comments that "There is no element in the prophecy as it now stands that points to diversity of authorship. Indeed, the weight of internal and external evidence supports the contention that the prophet Haggai was himself the author of the work attributed to him, and that he furnished a narrative of contemporary events involving himself in an objective manner." [68]

Haggai was a contemporary of Zechariah, and this fact, with the internal evidence, makes it possible to date the book as having been written in 520 B.C.

C. Background, Purpose, and Content

The prophet Haggai, as well as Zechariah and Malachi, was a post exilic prophet, so called because he prophesied after the Babylonian exile. Soon after the emancipation proclamation was given by Cyrus, the Jews began to return to Jerusalem. Haggai and Zerubbabel were two of the leaders returning with the first contingent. The reference in 2:3 is usually interpreted to mean that Haggai had seen Solomon's Temple and that he had been among the persons, including Daniel, who were de-

Malachi
4261
Cyrus
907
Daniel
914

339

ported in 606 B.C. If this is correct, Haggai was an old man—about 85 years of age—when he prophesied.

The idea of returning to their homeland, at that time devastated and occupied by their enemy, was not a popular prospect for the Jews who had become established in Babylon. Many were profitably engaged and had no desire to return. However, a group of about 42,000 (Ezra 2:64) people, including priests and religious leaders, who had nothing to lose and those with an adventurous spirit responded (Ezra 1:5). Zerubbabel (Sheshbazzar) was commissioned to be governor over the new Jerusalem community (Ezra 1:8; 5:14). Later when the returnees saw the rubble and the ruins of the old city, the initial wave of spiritual zeal and enthusiasm abated. When Haggai and his workers began to rebuild the altar and the temple, the Samaritans and the neighbors who had established "squatters rights" during the Jews' absence opposed the work and, in fact, stopped it temporarily by legal action (Ezra 4:1–6; 5:1–5; 6:1–13).

The Book of Haggai contains four main prophecies which were delivered over a four-month period:

1. After the exiles had been engaged in their building project for a short time, their attention was diverted to building their own "ceiled" houses, while the temple remained roofless. Haggai told the people that a lack of dew from heaven and their short crops had been due to God's displeasure at their indifference and religious apathy (Hag. 1:6,10). After Haggai exhorted them to resume work on the temple, they complied (Hag. 1:12–15).

2. In less than a month the work slackened. The people were discouraged because of the humble appearance of the new building as compared with the old. Haggai assured them that when completed, the glory of the new temple would be greater than that of the old. Work once more resumed (Hag. 2:1–9).

3. The third prophecy is a sequel to the first. Haggai drew an analogy: as the unclean pollutes the clean, so the work of the laborers done grudgingly and without zeal had polluted their undertaking, and God had withheld his blessings of plenty (Hag. 2:10–19).

4. The fourth prophecy is a sequel to the second. The prophet uttered words of encouragement, telling the people that God was about to shake the nations of the earth (cause revolutions and turmoil among them) with a prophetic intimation regarding the final overthrow of the heathen nations in the Day of Judgment (Hag. 2:20–22).

One scholar succinctly wrote: "The prophecy of Haggai (2:20–23) looks to the future. Furthermore, there is significance in the use of the singular 'throne.' (Hag. 2:22) . . . one may see here, along with many able expositors, a reference to the ultimate overthrow of this world system, dominated by Satan, when the rightful King, the Lord Jesus Christ, returns to take the reign of government." [69]

Haggai concluded his final message with a note of hope. Although Zerubbabel, the governor, did not fulfill the expectation of the vision (Hag. 2:21-23), nevertheless the prophet was faithful in proclaiming Messianic hope for future generations.

Evil Worldly
System
3918

XVI. ZECHARIAH

Book of
Zechariah
4260

A. The Name

The Hebrew name for Zechariah is *Zekharayah,* which means "Jehovah has remembered." It is mentioned at least twenty-nine times in the OT. The Greek OT (LXX) renders this name *Zacharias.*

Ezra makes two references to the prophet Zechariah (5:1; 6:14), and the name is included four times in his Book (Zech. 1:1,7; 7:1,8). Each instance is a definite identification, e.g., "the word of the LORD unto Zechariah" (1:1) or similar words. The Book of Zechariah is the eleventh in the list of Minor Prophets and the fourteenth of the Latter Prophets in the OT canon.[70]

Zechariah
3978

B. Authorship and Date

Jewish and Christian traditions have always considered the prophet Zechariah to be the author of the Book of Zechariah, written about 521 B.C. Some liberal critics who hold the view that prophets could not foretell the future have questioned the last six chapters because they contain messianic prophecies (these references will be discussed further in this chapter) and other references which foretell the future (Zech. 14:1-3).

Fortelling the
Future
430, 1774

C. Background, Purpose, and Content

Zechariah was first a priest by birth and then a prophet by special call, as were Jeremiah and Ezekiel. Zechariah (Jehovah has remembered) was the son of Berechiah (Jehovah blesses) and the grandson of Iddo (timely, or the appointed time) (Zech. 1:1,7; Neh. 12:4,16). The meaning of these names along with the words "jealous" and "jealously" and such terms as "in that day" and "the day of the Lord" suggest the key to the meaning of the book.

Priest
2063
Prophet
2065–2074

However, the Book of Zechariah is still difficult to understand. George L. Robinson observes: "Few books of the OT are as difficult of interpretation as the Book of Zechariah; no other book is as Messianic. . . . The scope of Zechariah's vision, and the profundity of his thought are almost without parallel

341

The Old Testament

Zerubbabel
3991

Haggai
1475

. . . his book is the most Messianic, the most truly apocalyptic and eschatological, of all the writings of the OT." [71]

The prophet Zechariah was a "contemporary of Zerubbabel, the governor, Jeshua, the high priest, and Haggai the prophet (Zech. 3:1; 4:6; 6:11; Ezra 5:1,2), and united with Haggai in exhorting the leaders of the Jewish colony to resume work on the house of God." [72] The prophet Haggai had been preaching two months and the temple work had started when Zechariah began his prophetic work. Zechariah's formal ministry lasted about three years.

Disobedience
2620, 2621

Exhort
1182

Zechariah sensed an apathy in the people's devotion and a tendency to revert to the ways of their disobedient forefathers. The prophet's concern resulted in a message which had a two-fold purpose: to exhort the people to repentance and to encourage them with visions of a glorious future (Zech. 1:1-6).[73]

The Book of Zechariah has two major divisions: 1, Apocalyptic, chapters 1-8; 2, Prophetic, chapters 9-14.

Visions
2495

During one night God granted the prophet eight visions, which inspired the people to finish rebuilding the temple:

The first vision of the myrtle trees and the horses meant that the whole world was at rest under the hand of the Persian Empire (Zech. 1:7-17). Certainly the Jews were greatly favored in the freedom granted them and the financial assistance given them by the Persian king.

The second vision of the horns and the carpenters represented the nations who had destroyed Judah and Israel and through the image of the four carpenters the prophet foretold the overthrow of Israel's enemies (Zech. 1:18-21).

Measuring Rod
2267

The third vision of the measuring line (Zech. 2), was a forecast that Jerusalem would prosper and grow until it would overflow its walls, and the nations of the world would come to seek counsel in Jerusalem.

Atonement
304

Messiah
695, 2890, 4186

The vision of Joshua, the high priest, gave a pre-vision of the atonement of Christ (Zech. 3). The filthy clothing of the high priest represented the sins of the people, and the removing of these garments symbolized that the people's sins were forgiven (Zech. 3:4-7). A foreshadowing of Christ the Messiah is seen in the BRANCH to which the prophet makes reference (Zech. 3:8-10).[74]

The fifth vision in the fourth chapter has a "double reference," the first one for the immediate time while Zechariah was building the house and the second for a later, more glorious House, to be built by a descendant of Zerubbabel. He is called "The Branch," the candlestick representing God's House, and the light-bearer to the world. The two olive trees seem to represent Joshua and Zerubbabel.

Branch
691

342

The sixth and seventh visions picturing a "flying roll" or

scroll and an ephah represent a curse against stealing and swearing (Zech. 5:1-4; 5:5-11). In the end the Lord will separate sin and the sinner from the kingdom (Zech. 5:1-11).[75]

The eighth and final vision of the four chariots (Zech. 6:1-8) is similar to the first, showing a completion of God's work (Zech. 6:4-15).

In chapters seven and eight the prophet recalls that the people fasted in the fourth, fifth, seventh, and tenth months and mourned for the temple. The people asked whether they should continue their fasts as before and Zechariah reminded them that previously their fasts had the ingredient of penitence for their former sins, but now the fast had become a mere outward rite without spiritual significance. Then the prophet changed the scenes and gave a picture of the age when fasts would become joyful (Zech. 7:5-7; 8:19-23).

The people were discouraged because their number was small and they were despised, existing only by permission of the Persian king. The prophet tried to convince the people that the day would come when the enemy nations would be broken and God's people would again prosper and rejoice (Zech. 8:3-5). All the nations would one day come to the Jews to learn about their God (Zech. 8:22,23; see also 1:17; 2:4,11; 14:8,16).

The judgment God's prophet pronounced on the neighboring nations was fulfilled. Chapters 9-14 contain references discussing the Greek wars which came 200 years after Zechariah. Chapter 9 seems to point to Judah's struggle with Greece which took place when Alexander the Great invaded Palestine in 332 B.C.,[76] and suggests the final triumph of God's kingdom.

Part two of Zechariah's work contains messianic prophecies; it is quite evident that the prophet was speaking of the coming Messiah and the establishment of Christianity. The following references reflect the nature of Zechariah's messianic insight; he predicted that Christ would enter Jerusalem triumphantly on a colt (Zech. 9:9); that he would be sold for thirty pieces of silver (Zech. 11:12); that the enemy would pierce the Savior while he was on the cross (Zech. 12:10); that his blood would open up a "fountain" in the House of David "for sin and for uncleanness" (Zech. 13:1); that his wounds would be inflicted in the house of his friends (Zech. 13:6); cf. "He came unto his own, and his own received him not" (John 1:11). In a glorious foreview Zechariah parts the curtain and shows the Savior in his triumphant arrival on the Mount of Olives (Zech 14:4).

The prophet has something to say about the Jews returning to their homeland: He will gather them "out of the land of Egypt" and "out of Assyria . . . into the land of Gilead and Lebanon" (Zech. 10:10). A severe warning is directed against

Fasting
3212-3214

Discouragement, Encouragement
1018-1020

God's Judgment
1966-1974

Messianic Prophecies
2890

343

"the nations that come against Jerusalem" (Zech 12:9). In that final day the prophet envisions that Jehovah "will pour upon the house of David, and upon the inhabitants of Jerusalem, the spirit of grace and supplications: and they shall look upon me whom they have pierced, and they shall mourn for him, as one mourneth for his only son, and shall be in bitterness for him" (Zech. 12:10).

J. Kenneth Griner says,

Some have spoken of the Gospel of Isaiah. We could also speak of the Gospel of Zechariah. It begins with a call to repentance (Zech. 1:4) even as Christ's own ministry does (Matt. 4:17); and it is inlaid all through with references to the Messiah. . . . Zechariah has more to say about Christ than all of the other Minor Prophets. . . . Nowhere else in the Old Testament is there such a concentrated and rich revelation of Messianic prophecies.[77]

Thus the prophet Zechariah projects one of the most dramatic foreviews of both the first and the second coming of Christ. Few OT writers, with the exception of Isaiah and the Psalmist, give such a comprehensive picture of the things that deal with the Messiah, the coming King and Redeemer.

XVII. MALACHI

A. *The Name*

The Hebrew name for Malachi, which appears only once in the entire Bible (Mal. 1:1) is *mal'akhi* and means "messenger," in a ministrative sense, as a "minister of religion." Some scholars suggest this form may be an abbreviation of *Malachiah*,

a Hebrew personal name meaning "the messenger of Jehovah." [78] In the English Bible the word *messenger* appears twice in the Book of Malachi (2:7; 3:1) and is rendered from the Hebrew *Mel'ak* meaning "to dispatch," as a deputy, a spe-

cial messenger or courier, and sometimes "the Angel of the Lord."

The Book of Malachi is listed in the English Bible as the twelfth work of the Minor Prophets; in the Hebrew canon it is the fifteenth of the Latter Prophets.

B. *Authorship and Date*

Tradition has ascribed authorship of this book to the prophet Malachi, mainly because of the reference to his name in verse one: "The burden of the word of the LORD to Israel by Malachi." Some scholars question the prophet's authorship because the word "Malachi" is not generally a proper noun. The meaning of the word "messenger" may imply the prophet's actual name or a pseudonym for Ezra.[79]

No other book in the OT is written anonymously, and evidence is lacking to support this deviation for Malachi. The conservative view is that the book has unity and continuity of subject matter sufficient for one to ascribe authorship to the prophet Malachi. As the prophet was a contemporary of Ezra and Nehemiah, one can assume that the book was written about 450 B.C. In his presentation Haggai frequently uses the Socratic question-and-answer, or dialogue, style.

C. Background, Purpose, and Content

There is scant information about the prophet Malachi. The single reference to this prophecy (1:1) gives no information concerning his ancestors nor the date when he prophesied. It is generally assumed that he ministered about 100 years after Haggai and Zechariah, and that he continued the reform movement which they started.

The Jews who returned to Jerusalem under the leadership of Haggai and Zechariah had rebuilt the temple; Nehemiah completed the walls thirteen years later. By this time the Babylonian experience had cured the Jews of a desire to worship the Baals. However the people had become at "ease in Zion." The people had fallen into an attitude of indifference, largely because leadership had become corrupt and self-centered. The priests were using blemished animals for sacrifice (1:8), and their neglect of duties connected with the temple caused people's interest in worship to diminish. Religion became a form without spiritual meaning.

Zechariah
3987

Baal
3936

Acceptable Sacrifices
3108

According to the Law, the Jews were to marry only within their own group, but instead, these Jews were intermarrying with the people who worshiped "strange gods" (Mal. 2:11). Older men were discarding the wives of their youth for young foreigners (Mal. 2:15).[80] God was receiving more favorable worship from the Gentiles than from the Jews (Mal. 1:11). The priests had been ordained to lead the people in truth and righteousness, but instead they were causing others to stumble in the path of righteousness (Mal. 2:8). The prophet does not spare the religious leaders from the severest condemnation and rebuke (Mal. 2:1–4).

Many scholars agree that Malachi was speaking of "the Forerunner"—John the Baptist—in his reference to the messenger (Mal. 3:1). This is in keeping with the Hebrew word used for messenger—*Mal'ak*. Some apply this name to the coming Messiah himself. The Messiah was to come with terrible judgment, but also to refine and purify his people, including the priests (Mal. 3:2–6). The messianic reference (3:1–7) is a kind of parenthesis between the prophet's condemnation of Judah's immor-

Robbery
3089
Tithes
2123

Elijah
1112

Messiah
**695, 2890,
4186**

ality (2:11–17) and the people's robbing God by withholding their tithes and offerings (3:8–10).* The people refused the challenge to bring the tithes (3:13–15). The prophet shifted back into an apocalyptic declaration in chapter four. Four times the prophet looked forward to "the Day of the Lord" (1:11; 3:1–6, 16–18; 4:1–6). The reference to "the Day" (3:2,17; 4:1,3,5) seems to mean the Christian era. In the closing prediction, Elijah is to usher in a new day. Four hundred years later the "second Elijah," John the Baptist, appeared (Matt. 3:1–12; 11:14).

"Thus closes the Old Testament. Four hundred years elapsed. Then came the Messiah, whom the Hebrew nation had been born to bring forth. As through the centuries, the Jews had rejected the prophets of God, so when the Messiah arrived, they rejected him. Since which time Jews have been homeless wanderers over the earth, the tragedy and miracle of the ages." [81]

---

* The tithe was a kind of income tax which the people were expected to pay for the upkeep of the temple and the support of the priests. However the people had refused to pay their religious obligations (Mal. 3:8,9); therefore, the prophet urged his audience to put God's promise of bounty and plenty to the test by paying their tithes (3:10).

Part III

The New Testament

19

The Gospels and Acts

I. INTRODUCTION TO THE SYNOPTIC GOSPELS (MATTHEW, MARK, AND LUKE)

Some information has been presented earlier (Ch. 13, III) on the problem surrounding the synoptic Gospels. Additional exposition of this problem is included in each of the following chapters. This introduction presents an overview of the problem. As indicated in Ch. 13 the writing of the gospel books had been delayed for approximately thirty years because there was in circulation a considerable amount of oral narration as well as some written fragments concerning gospel events. The church believed that this information would serve until the Lord returned. But with the passing of years, and the death of eyewitnesses, the need arose for preserving the gospel story in written form for use by the believers in the newly formed churches throughout the Empire. Under the inspiration of the Holy Spirit, Matthew, Mark, and Luke formulated written records which have been passed down to the present.

A critical examination of these records shows that the first three Gospels have many similarities as well as differences. Clark H. Pinnock notes some of these peculiarities: "Some 606 vv. out of Mark's total 661 appear, although somewhat abridged, in Matthew, and 380 reappear in Luke. Only 31 vv. in Mark have no parallel in either Matthew or Luke. In addition, there are some 250 vv. common to Matthew and Luke that have no parallel in Mark. Obviously, this synoptic relationship can be viewed in different ways. Many solutions

Second
Coming of
Christ
1344–1350

Matthew
2265
Mark
2253
Luke
2216

349

have been proposed, but none has won unanimous agreement." [1]

The Book of Mark contains the central core of gospel information and it would seem that Matthew and Luke were largely dependent upon Mark for their material. An alternate explanation is that there was a common depository from which all three synoptic writers may have drawn their facts. On the other hand, both Mark and Luke may have been dependent, to a great extent, for narrative on Matthew, an eyewitness. Others suggest that Mark and Luke obtained part of their information from Peter, also an eyewitness. It is of course probable that there was a sizeable amount of borrowing in the overall endeavor. However, Matthew had no need for borrowing from anyone because he was a steady companion of our Lord.

Regardless of what their literary sources were, all of the writers were directed and inspired by the Holy Spirit. The Master said, "But the Comforter, which is the Holy Ghost, whom the Father will send in my name, he shall teach you all things, and bring all things to your remembrance, whatsoever I have said unto you" (John 14:26).

In conclusion, one reason for the variation in content may be attributable to the Evangels' varied motives. These writers addressed their gospel messages to three different cultural groups. Matthew is regarded as having written to the Jews with their OT background; Mark, to the active Roman builders and engineers; and Luke, to the intellectual Greeks.

A study of the Gospel of John reveals that 90 percent of the content is different from the first three gospels. This is understandable because John wrote about thirty years later than the other writers and at a time when the churches were established. John built upon the synoptic foundation and used a philosophic approach to reveal profound truths in his presentation of the Savior.

Some critics insist that the gospel-records are merely narrative stories handed down from generation to generation, and that they do not contain trustworthy information about Jesus. However, this criticism is inaccurate because the integrity of the gospel records is verified by internal evidence, style, self-evident authorship, church fathers, and historical content which have withstood the test of time for almost 2000 years.

James Iverach asserts that "The place of the Gospels in church tradition is secure. Eusebius [264–340] places the 4 Gospels among the books that were never controverted in the church. . . . It is acknowledged that by the end of the 2nd century these 4 Gospels . . . [were] ascribed to the authors whose names they bear, [and] were in universal circulation and undisputed use throughout the church." [2]

II. MATTHEW

A. The Name

The Greek name for Matthew is *Matthios,* meaning "Gift of God" or "of Jehovah." This name appears five times in the NT and in each instance the citation relates to the apostle Matthew (Matt. 9:9; 10:3; Mark 3:18; Luke 6:15; Acts 1:13). In the second reference, the qualifying words indicate the apostle's former occupation; he was Matthew the publican (10:3). Some NT references name this same man "Levi" (see Mark 2:14; Luke 5:27). However, no satisfactory explanation for this variation is available. (For a discussion on name changes see page 74.)

Robert McL. Wilson indicates that both names are Hebrew, and he raises the question: "Could it be that he [Matthew] was the son of a man named Levi, 'Matthew ben Levi,' and that he was a Levite? Perhaps, as in Peter's case, Jesus gave him the name Matthew as a Christian-Jewish name, because it means 'a gift of Yahweh.' . . . Only God could change a tax collector named Levi into a Christian apostle named Matthew."[3]

B. Authorship and Date

The authorship of the Book of Matthew is of much importance to colloquial Christians because the message and the prophetic parts are intimately associated with an eyewitness of the gospel events. To take the book out of its synoptic context and assign it to a writer other than an eyewitness seems to violate the integrity of the Scriptures. Those of liberal persuasion usually take the position that the writer of Matthew was dependent upon Mark for his sources. If Matthew was an eyewitness of what Jesus said and did, it does not seem reasonable to assume that he needed to consult a man who was not an apostle nor a witness of Jesus' ministry. Those who have this view also assume that the book was written after A.D.70—the date of the destruction of Jerusalem—because of the prophetic statements Jesus made in this regard (Luke 19:43,44; 21:24).

The parable of the kingdom of heaven (Matt. 22:7) provides another base for assuming late authorship, but such an interpretation of this text ignores the fact that foretelling future events is an integral part of Scripture. Christians of the conservative view would not deny this power to Jesus.[4]

It is true that the Gospel does not name Matthew as the author; little is known about him. However, the ancient church attributed authorship of this book to Matthew. The caption, "The Gospel according to Saint Matthew," is not a part of the

The Gospels and Acts

Gospel of Matthew
4262
Matthew
2265

New Names
2585

Kingdom of Heaven
2013

351

The Valley of Hinnom where tradition says Judas hung himself

A beautified area around the east wall of Jerusalem

original manuscripts, but it has appeared as the title of Matthew (as have the captions in the other NT books) since the beginning of the second century A.D. and is confirmed by such other writers as Justin Martyr (A.D. 100–165) and Irenaeus (A.D. 125–202). Eusebius, writing in the fourth century, quoted Papias, the Bishop of Lyons, from Irenaeus in the second century and from Origen in the third century (*New Bible Commentary*— Eerdmans). These ancient writers say that Matthew wrote his Gospel originally in Hebrew and Aramaic. Presumably the writer had "field notes" and later, in about A.D. 60, he incorporated the abbreviated Hebrew version into a more complete Greek edition. Many Greek copies of Matthew have survived, but no Hebrew or Aramaic versions are in existence today.[5] The testimony of these ancients, who lived so close to the synoptic period, would seem to be trustworthy, especially since one of them, Papias, was a disciple of John the Beloved. No other person of that group would have been more qualified to write this book than Matthew himself.

Dating the Book of Matthew is closely related to the question of authorship. Wilson points out that "the traditional view of the time and place of writing has been that Matthew was the first evangelist to write a gospel and that he wrote in Palestine, possibly in Jerusalem itself, shortly after the events of Matthew 27:8 and 28:15 in about A.D. 60. . . . A different place now seems more plausible. . . . Antioch in Syria about A.D. 60 is both the probable and plausible time and place of writing of the first gospel." [6] This place was the headquarters and pivotal point for the early Christian church and would provide a favorable environment for writing such a book.

Syrian Antioch
197, 4328

C. Background, Purpose, and Content

Matthew, Mark, and Luke are known as the synoptic gospels because they contain much parallel material (see Ch. 13, I).

As previously mentioned, Matthew was a publican who collected Roman taxes. The office was usually sold at auction to the highest bidder. Because of the finances involved, usually only men of great wealth were able to obtain such a position.

Publican
2926

Tax Collectors
2926

The very nature of such transactions made the office of tax collector conducive to extortion and abuse, and the man an object of scorn. Frequently the tax collector farmed out portions, or all, of his territory, and this necessitated extra revenue to pay these "middle men." If Zacchaeus is an example of tax abuse, the financial hardship of the common people must have been severe (Luke 19:8).

Zacchaeus
3977

It was no accident that the Book of Matthew was placed first in the NT canon. As the Holy Spirit inspired the writers

353

Golgotha (place of the skull) near where Jesus may have been crucified

A carpenter in Nazareth, reminiscent of Joseph's shop there when Jesus was growing to manhood

and revealed to them what they should write, so the Holy Spirit could have guided the compilers in their selection and placement of the holy books. The Book of Matthew was rightly placed at the beginning of the NT canon because it correlates the OT prophecies with their fulfillment in the NT. It contains more fulfilled prophecies pertaining to the Messiah than any of the other three Gospel records. At least 60 references and 40 quotations, such as "that it might be fulfilled" and "thus it was written by the Prophet," appear—more frequent than in either of the other synoptic books.

Fulfilled Prophecies **246–249**

The Jewish community seems to have been foremost in the mind of the writer Matthew. His message is the good news that the Jewish Messiah came in the person of Jesus Christ. The first verse clearly states that Jesus Christ is a kinsman of the Jews, "the son of David, the son of Abraham," and was intended to attract the attention of the Jews. Because Abraham was the founder of the Hebrew nation and the Jews called him their Father (Matt. 3:9; John 8:33,39), they would be attracted to Jesus by this kinship. The rest of the apostles, who were Jews, and the many other people who were attracted to the Savior, came to realize that Jesus of Nazareth was he "of whom Moses in the law, and the prophets, did write" (John 1:45). Another indication that the Book of Matthew had the Jews in mind is the genealogy (mentioned also in Luke 3:23–38). Matthew's genealogy goes back only to Abraham, which was of special interest to the Jews, since they claimed Abraham as the founder of their nation.

Messiah **695, 2890, 4186**
David **919**
Abram-Abraham **15**
Apostles **2080–2082**

In the early days of the human family God chose one family line—that of Abraham—through which his Son was to enter the human family. The Hebrew nation was founded and nurtured by God to prepare them for this great mission and provided the human agency for the coming Messiah. The genealogy in Matthew is somewhat abbreviated but adequate to present the line of descent.

Genealogy of Christ **1400**

The genealogy in Luke differs from that of Matthew who, in presenting the descending line, uses the word "begat." Luke presents the ascending line using the term, "was the son of." From David, there are separate lines touching in Shealthiel and Zerubbabel. "The commonly accepted view is that Matthew gives Joseph's line, showing Jesus to be the legal heir to the promises given Abraham and David: and that Luke gives Mary's line, showing Jesus' blood descent, 'Son of David, according to the flesh,' Rom. 1:3. Mary's genealogy, in accord with Jewish usage, was in her husband's name. Joseph was the 'son of Heli,' (Luke 3:23), that is, 'son-in-law' of Heli. Heli was Mary's father. Jacob was Joseph's father. . . . Carefully guarded through long centuries of special vicissitudes, they contain a

Mary **2259**

family line through which a promise was transmitted . . . , a fact unexampled in history." [7]

Another clue to Matthew's Jewish appeal is seen in his reference to geography. One writer notes that it "is seen, incidentally, that he presupposes the reader will know the geography of Palestine and its customs, manners and ceremonies. . . . [For] instance, in the matter of washing the hands before eating bread, Matthew takes for granted that the readers are acquainted with that custom (Matt. 15:1–2); but Mark feels that he should explain to his readers that this was the tradition among the Jews (Mark 7:3). . . . He wanted the Jews to see that Jesus was the long promised Messiah." [8]

Further evidence that this Gospel was written for the Jews is suggested in the presentation of the conflict between the true concept of the Messiah and the false. The Jewish religious leaders were jealous and so absorbed with using their office for their own selfish interests that they showed hostility toward Jesus when he warned and rebuked them, which brought to the surface their false righteousness. He distinguished between the true OT teachings and the "tradition of the elders," indicating the deplorable state of the Jewish church in such statements as "O generation of vipers" (Matt. 12:34) and "ye hypocrites" (Matt. 15:7), as well as "blind leaders of the blind" (Matt. 15:14; see also Matt. 23).

The increasing resentment by the temple hierarchy is expressed in such accusations against Jesus as "this man blasphemeth" (Matt. 9:3), and "Why eateth your Master with publicans and sinners?" (Matt. 9:11), as well as "Behold a man gluttonous, and a winebibber" (Matt. 11:19), and "He is guilty of death" (Matt. 26:66).

However, there is a tone of universality in Matthew's account. He presents the first gentile pilgrims—the Magi—to the Savior (2:1–2), and mentions the faith of the Roman centurion (8:5–10). He foretells of the future inflow into Jerusalem to hear the Christ-Jehovah gospel; he cites the statement by Jesus: "many shall come from the east and the west, and shall sit down with Abraham, and Isaac, and Jacob, in the kingdom of heaven" (8:11).[9]

Religious leaders expressed strong reaction when Jesus prophetically stated that "the kingdom of God shall be taken from you, and given to a nation bringing forth the fruits thereof" (Matt. 21:43) and when he presented the Great Commission, commanding them to make disciples in all nations (Matt. 28:19–20).

There are many other Jewish distinctives in Matthew's Gospel including the term "kingdom of heaven" rather than the "kingdom of God" to avoid uttering the name of God for fear

Washing
Hands
1494

Jewish
Jealousy
4051

Traditions
3652

False
Teachers
2101

Blasphemy
473, 474
Publicans
2926

Universal
Gospel
1442

Jerusalem
1881–1885

Kingdom of
Heaven
2013

Kingdom of
Heaven
2011

of blasphemy (Matt. 13:31; cf. Luke 13:18–19) and the parable of the "wheat and the tares" (the field of the world, Matt. 13:38).

III. MARK

A. *The Name*

The Gospel of Mark was written by John Mark. His first name,
John, was his Jewish given name, translated from the Greek *Ioannes*. Mark (Gr: *Markos*) was his Roman (Latin) surname, meaning "a large hammer." He was called John among the Jews but Mark in the gentile world (Acts 12:12,25; 15:17).

John Mark's name appears five times in the New Testament (Acts 12:12,25; 15:37,39; 2 Tim. 4:11). The first three references include the names John and Mark. Twice he is called John (Acts 13:5,13). In three other places he is referred to as "Marcus" (Col. 4:10; Philem. 24; and 1 Peter 5:13).[10]

B. *Authorship and Date*

From the beginning, early church tradition credits John Mark with having written the Gospel of Mark. The caption at the head of the book, "The Gospel according to Mark," was not a part of the original manuscript but was placed there by the fathers to preserve the identification of the author. This fact is attested by such early Christian writers as Papias (A.D. 70–155), a pupil of John the beloved and Bishop of Hieropolis; John Martyr (A.D. 100–167), a philosopher and defender of Christians; and Eusebius (A.D. 264–340), the father of church history. In general, there is agreement among modern scholars that John Mark was the author of the book bearing his name,[11] and by many conservative scholars that the book was written before the destruction of Jerusalem in A.D. 70, probably about A.D. 60.

Peter
2746
Mary, Mother of Mark
2263
Paul's First Journey
p. 287

C. *Background, Purpose, and Content*

John Mark's name is mentioned first in Acts 12:12, when Peter was released from prison, and went to the house of Mary, "the mother of John, whose surname was Mark; where many were gathered together praying." John Mark appears next in Perga where, for reasons unknown, he left the company of Barnabas and Paul and returned to Jerusalem (Acts 13:13).

When Barnabas and Paul were making preparation for their second missionary journey, Barnabas was "determined to take with them John, whose surname was Mark" (Acts 15:37), but

The New
Testament

Paul
2697
Silas
3288

Paul objected. After disagreement between the two men, Barnabas took John Mark on tour independent of Paul of which nothing more is said. "Paul chose Silas" to accompany him on the second journey. Apparently John Mark later developed into a strong missionary witness. When Paul was in prison at Rome, he asked Timothy to bring Mark "for he is profitable to me for the ministry" (2 Tim. 4:11).

Most scholars are agreed that John Mark was a close associate of Peter and "that he . . . inquired of the Elders and the followers of the Elders [concerning Jesus' ministry]. . . . Having become the interpreter, he wrote down accurately all that he remembered, not, however in order, the words and deeds of Christ. . . . Mark made no mistake in thus writing down some of the things as he remembered them. For one object was in his thoughts—to omit nothing that he had heard, and to make no false statements." [12] But some ancients believe that Peter, "through modesty, would not put his name to the work, but dictated the whole account, and Mark wrote it down. . . ." [13] The Book of Mark indicates, however, that the writer follows closely and substantially, the well authenticated Gospel tradition, even though he was probably not an eye witness." [14]

The short, concise statements of fact show that Mark had remarkable organizational ability and literary skill to portray action. He gives dynamic movement to the events recorded in his Gospel with such words as "straightway" (19 times) and "immediately" (17 times). The considerable amount of data which Mark includes in his book is illustrated in the first chapter. Mark made the declaration that Jesus is the "Son of God" (v. 1); that John is the messenger of God (v. 2) as well as "the voice of one crying in the wilderness" (v. 3), the baptizer (vv. 4–8), a rugged character (v. 6), and the forerunner of Jesus (v. 7). This introduction is followed by an account of the baptism of Jesus (v. 9), at which time the heavens were opened (v. 10) and God affirmed that Jesus is the Son (v. 11). In the next verse is a reference to Jesus being driven by the spirit [sent him out—NIV] into the wilderness for 40 days (v. 12). He is "tempted of Satan" (v. 13). Following this experience, John was put in prison (v. 14). Jesus began to assemble his disciples by calling Simon and Andrew (vv. 16–18) and then added James and John (vv. 19,20). In Capernaum Jesus entered the synagogue (vv. 21,22) where he healed a man with an unclean spirit (vv. 23–27). Forthwith, Jesus went into a house and healed Simon's mother-in-law (vv. 29–31). When his fame went abroad, many others were healed (vv. 32–34). The following morning Jesus went out "into a solitary place" to pray (v. 35).

In the same chapter Mark verified that Jesus is the one anticipated by the prophets (vv. 2,3), that it would be he who bap-

Herod's North End Palace at the Masada excavation

Air view of the Herodian palace excavation east of Bethlehem

The ramp at Masada over which the Romans attacked. Dead Sea is in the background

Top view of a tomb opening with rolling stone door, similar to the one in which Christ was buried

tized men with the Holy Spirit (v. 8) and that he was a receiver of visions (vv. 9–11). He is the One to whom angels ministered (v. 13), and who preached the Gospel of the Kingdom (v. 15). Jesus also called men to become evangelists (vv. 16–20); he was a teacher with authority (v. 22) and the One who cast out demons (v. 25). He was a man of prayer, one who had compassion for the sick (vv. 30–34), and one with missionary interest (v. 39). This "action-filled" writing reflects the *dunamis* (power) or the dynamite of God. (The Greek lexicon defines *dunamis* to have inherent power, power residing in a thing by virtue of its nature, or which a person or thing exerts and puts forth, power . . . beyond our power.)

Cast out Demons **3157**

The Book of Mark contains approximately 90 percent of all the material (in condensed form) contained in the Books of Matthew and Luke. This phenomenal amount of information in Mark has created a problem for some scholars who have concluded that Mark wrote the first Gospel and that Matthew and Luke borrowed liberally from Mark for their writings. Another speculation is that there may have been a central source of information which all the gospel writers utilized, known as the "Q" document ("Q" is the symbol for the German word, *quelle*, meaning source or spring). However, no such book or manuscript is in existence.[15]

The assumption that the gospel writers copied from each other is not necessarily true. In the days of Jesus the educative process involved a great deal of memorization. Thus the gospel events were communicated orally among the people. The sayings and activities of Jesus were the subject of conversation in the marketplace and at the synagogues. Possibly some of the people may have carried fragments of written materials— one person perhaps made notes as he heard the various stories about Jesus. Of course, the Holy Spirit superintended and regulated the written gospel records. Most of the Book of Mark seems to have been written for gentile readers, probably those in Rome. The writer explains a number of Jewish customs and frequently employs Latin terms without translating them; but he does interpret a number of Aramaic terms (cf. Mark 3:17; 5:41; 7:11,34; 15:34),[16] and discusses details of life in Palestine which could have been unfamiliar to the Gentiles (Mark 7:3ff.; 12:42; 14:12,15–22,42).

Holy Spirit Guides **1611**

Internal evidence shows the author to be a Christian Jew who was intimately acquainted with the Jewish life and who had a knowledge of the Scriptures. His knowledge of the general geography of Palestine, and especially Jerusalem, gives further support to this supposition.

Gentile Believers **4038**

Unlike the Book of Matthew, with its frequent OT citations, the Book of Mark makes its appeal to Gentiles by its disapproval of Jewish dietary laws (Mark 7:2–7) and strict sabbath observation (Mark 2:28).

It is clear that there was a great need for a Gospel account with such terms as "straightway" and "immediately." The Romans were builders—the engineers of the world. Their method of construction was so thorough that many viaducts, bridges, and buildings of Roman origin are still in use.

The Romans were not interested in philosophizing. They were people of action; they built for permanency—they were more interested in what Jesus did, and less in what he said. Therefore Mark emphasized the actions of Jesus.

Mark called his writings the "gospel," using the term six times in his book (1:1,14,15; 13:10; 14:9; 16:15). He selected the word from the Greek OT (LXX), used especially in the Book of Isaiah—the Hebrew word *basar* meaning "good tidings," which is translated in the English as "gospel."

Mark did not propose to write a biography in the usually accepted sense, but a treatise with a religious-historical background. It is evident that originally, when Mark uses the word *gospel* he means the faith, not the book.

The book of Mark has a practical appeal to the modern church. J. Newton Davies puts it in these words:

> Just as the first readers in Rome, of this vivid portrayal of the Son of man, were encouraged to face cruel tortures and punishments of unheard-of severity, and above all to maintain their missionary zeal in the face of colossal obstacles and continuous disappointments, so the Christian Church today, in reading afresh the story of the life of Jesus as written by Mark, will be greatly strengthened and encouraged in its task of presenting the claims of Christ to an age bewildered by many conflicting emotions, torn by faction, burdened by many sorrows, weighed down by the spirit of materialism, and yet in its heart of hearts yearning for one who will be its guide and shepherd through the perplexing mazes of its day. The road to the future, it has been well said, is the road back to the NT. We cannot more effectively begin to walk that road than by reading and rereading this striking presentation of the Lord of life by John Mark.[17]

The entire structure of the Book is suggestive of a universal gospel.

IV. LUKE

A. *The Name*

The name Luke comes from the Greek *Loukas* and appears three times in the New Testament (Col. 4:14; 2 Tim. 4:11; Philem. 24), twice as Luke (2 Tim. 4:11; Col. 4:14) and once as Lucas (Philem. 24). He is not considered to be the Lucius who is cited twice in the NT (Acts 13:1; Rom. 16:21). Luke is not mentioned in the Gospel by his name nor is he mentioned in the Book of Acts, even as John does not mention himself in his Gospel.

B. Authorship and Date

Authorship of Luke cannot be separated from that of the Book of Acts because these books are two parts of one whole. Luke was not making a boastful statement when he said that he had a "perfect understanding of all things" (Luke 1:3) in the gospel accounts, nor in his second record when he stated that he had written "of all that Jesus began both to do and teach, until the day in which he was taken up . . ." (Acts 1:1,2).[18] Rather, the indication is that Luke conducted thorough research before he began to write his book. Only such excellence could challenge the Greek mind. In the Book of Acts, Luke gives a continuing account of what Jesus did through his commissioned evangels after his resurrection.

Although Luke's name does not appear in his books, the internal evidence provided by the use of the personal pronouns in certain parts of the Book of Acts, along with Paul's reference to Luke's name (see C of this discussion) serve to support the supposition that Luke is the author.

After Paul received his Macedonian vision, the writer of these books apparently joined Paul and Silas; this is indicated by the pronouns "we" and "us," which begin in the text at this point. They continue to appear until the party arrived at Philippi (Acts 16:10–12), where Luke apparently stayed to practice medicine and to oversee the church, while Paul and Silas continued on their journey to Thessalonica. The first person plural pronouns are suspended at this point but begin again when Paul returned to Philippi and started his journey back to Jerusalem. The recurrence of the pronouns indicates that the writer had rejoined the missionary party (Acts 20:5–21:17). Later when Paul was delivered into the hands of Julius, the centurion, to be taken to Rome, the pronoun "we" again is used, indicating that the writer had again joined Paul (Acts 27:1–28:16). These references in Luke and Acts show that Luke was the writer of the book.

From the Epistles written during Paul's first imprisonment in Rome it is evident that nine people were with Paul: Tychicus, Epaphroditus, Onesimus, Aristarchus, Marcus, Jesus who is called Justus, Epaphras, Luke, and Demas (Eph. 6:21; Phil. 2:25; Col. 4:7–14; Philem. 10,23,24).

"Since the writer of Acts went with Paul to Rome, Epaphras and Epaphroditus are ruled out because they arrived later (Phil. 4:18; Col. 4:12). Aristarchus (Acts 19:29), Mark (12:25), Timothy

Macedonia
2222
Medicine
1529
See Paul's Journeys
pp. 288–293
Luke
2216
Tychicus
3715
Epaphroditus
1146
Onesimus
2650
Aristarchus
213
Marcus (Mark)
2253
Epaphras
1139
Luke
2216
Demas
974
Timothy
3628

These nomads crossing the Sinai desert remind one of the three wise men coming to worship the baby Jesus

An inside view of the Church of the Nativity built over the traditional site of Jesus' birth

(16:1), and Tychicus (20:4) are eliminated because they are all mentioned in the third person in Acts." [19]

It is doubtful if the runaway slave, Onesimus, coming to Paul later, could have written the book. Demas is an unlikely author since he deserted Paul (2 Tim. 4:10). Only Luke and Justus remain, and since tradition does not mention Justus in this connection, it is obvious that Luke must be the author of both the Gospel of Luke and the Book of Acts.

These books are addressed to Theophilus. The cultural and educational quality of the writings and the writer's interest in sickness and in healing are additional reasons why these books were written by a man of letters as well as one with a medical knowledge (Luke 4:27; 8:29,43,49). It is thought that the Book of Luke was written about A.D. 60.

C. Background, Purpose, and Content

Of Luke's background, little is known other than that he was a physician (Col. 4:14), and that he was a companion of Paul during a part of his missionary journeys. Scholars differ as to his religious background. Some think he was a Jew converted directly to Christianity, while others suggest he was a Gentile (Greek) and that he became a proselyte to Judaism, sometime later accepting Jesus of Nazareth as the Messiah in the same way that the apostles and other Jews had done.[20]

Proselytes
2895, 2896

Apparently many people had written on what Jesus said and did, but Luke felt that there was still a need for another presentation of the gospel. The first four verses in Luke are filled with basic background information.

Luke
2216

In the first verse Luke's scholarly background is clearly evident. He could not have made this statement without having read what the "many . . . had set forth." The subject matter of these writers is identified with the Christian faith—"those things which are most surely believed among us." There is no hesitation on the part of Luke to make this declaration; what he is saying is factual and not theoretical. It must be remembered that Christian profession entailed great risks. Men were severely persecuted and even put to death for making such declarations. Luke went further to describe the character of these writings. They were documents prepared "from the beginning . . . [by] eye witnesses, and ministers of the Word." They had in them the evidence of apostolic authority.

Testimonies
3598

Apparently some gospel records had already been written, but there still was a need to satisfy Greek civilization representing culture, philosophy, reason, beauty, and education. The

Caesarea Philippi at one source of the Jordan river near the foot of Mt. Hermon

Excavation of the Herodian Fortress Palace, an artificial mountain built by Herod the Great to enclose and protect his person, a place of refuge. It became his tomb. Inside were terraced gardens, baths and a marble throne room

writer's appeal would have to be made by a brilliant scholar in excellent Greek form. Luke had the qualifications and attempted to satisfy this need.

He wrote a sympathetic, concise, and orderly account of the gospel which some call the most beautiful story every written.[21] He presented Jesus in all of his beauty and perfection as the universal Savior, who is not for the Jews alone, but for all mankind. Luke directed his message to Theophilus. The salutation, "most excellent," suggests that he was writing to a high Roman official, perhaps in the Greek community, who had embraced Christianity. The name Theophilus is a compound word meaning "Lover of God." It is apparent that Theophilus already had some Christian instruction and that Luke was writing a more concise, orderly treatise, especially with the Gentiles in mind (Luke 1:1–4).

Gospel
1440–1442

A Greek audience is further indicated by the detailed account Luke gave of the birth of both John the Baptist and Jesus. The writer deals at length with the priest Zecharias and his wife Elizabeth, the parents of John the Baptist. Luke goes into even greater detail in connection with the events surrounding the Nativity story. Luke, the physician, trained in biology, went into detail to present the virgin birth as factual. Luke showed an interest in women, e.g., Anna, the prophetess; Mary the Mother; and Mary Magdalene.

The genealogy presented by Luke is evidence of his intellectual excellence. Matthew traces the messianic line only to Abraham (Matt. 1:2) (see Ch. 19, I, C). To the Greeks this limited view of world history would not be satisfactory. They would desire a more complete account. Luke satisfied this demand by tracing the genealogy back to Adam and God (Luke 3:38).

Christ's Genealogy
1400

It is true that Matthew presented some universal aspects of the gospel, but Luke went into greater depth. He refers to Jesus as being the light of the Gentiles (Luke 2:32) and he quoted Isaiah (cf. Isa. 52:10): "All flesh shall see the salvation of God" (Luke 3:6). Luke wrote of Elias being sent to befriend a widow (a Gentile) in Sarepta of Sidon during the drought, though his mission did not include the widows of Israel (Luke 4:25,26), and of the healing of Naaman, the Syrian, without the cleansing of the lepers in Israel (Luke 4:27).

Universal Gospel
1442

Elias (Elijah)
1112

Naaman
2505

Luke centered attention upon social outcasts, the poor and repentant sinners. One outstanding illustration is the immoral woman, who, in repentance, poured expensive ointment on Jesus' feet (Luke 7:37,38). Luke mentioned that Jesus rebuked James and John for wanting to call down fire from heaven to consume a Samaritan village (Luke 9:51–56). The story of the Good Samaritan is cited only by Luke (Luke 10:25–37) as is the story of the Prodigal Son (Luke 15:11–32). Only Luke pre-

Samaritans
3135, 3136

367

served the narrative of ten lepers (Luke 17:11–19). When the self-righteous Pharisee prayed by the side of the contrite publican, Luke reports that Jesus justified the latter rather than the former (Luke 18:9–14). The account of the repentant Zacchaeus would not be known if it had not been written by Luke (Luke 19:1–10), nor would the story of the penitent thief on the cross (Luke 23:39–43).

Many other examples in Luke's account show that Christ was interested in the whole human race, not just the Jews. This universal acceptance made the Gentiles and all others, including the poor and the outcast, eligible for kingdom membership.

V. JOHN

A. The Name

The Gospel of John derives its name from the apostle John (Gr., *Johanan*) which means "Jehovah has been gracious." The author does not mention his own name but refers to himself as the one "whom Jesus loved." Study affirms that John "was recognized as the one closest to Jesus. Five times he is spoken of as the disciple 'whom Jesus loved' (John 13:23; 19:26; 20:2; 21:7,20). He must have been a man of rare qualities of character to thus attract the companionship of Jesus." [22]

John, Peter, and James, who formed the inner circle of disciples, were frequently grouped together in a triumvirate (Matt. 17:1; 26:37; Mark 5:37; 13:3; 14:33; Luke 9:28). Of the three, John most nearly fits the "beloved" description. Jesus called him the " 'Son of Thunder' (Mark 3:17), which seems to imply that he had a . . . violent temper, but he brought this under control. The incident of forbidding the stranger to use the name of Christ in casting out demons (Mark 9:38) and the desire to call down fire on the Samaritans (Luke 9:54) are . . . [phases of] his nature." [23] Even though sometimes John was intolerant and vindictive, he was the disciple who would later say, "He that loveth his brother . . ." (1 John 2:10). In spite of John's nature, he had an unquestioned devotion and love for his Master. Jesus must have recognized these qualities in John for "when Jesus was on the cross He committed Mary to the care of the 'beloved disciple.' His own brethren were not believers at this time." [24] John's desire was not for his own self-interest but to extol the Christ and his work.

For some reason, John seems to be the disciple most devoted to the Lord: it was he who sat next to the Savior (John 13:23). Perhaps his change to a loving nature explains why he is referred to as "John the Beloved." Certainly love is an important subject in the Gospel of John and in his First Epistle.

The New Testament

Pharisee
3171
Publicans
2926
Zacchaeus
3977

Gospel of John
4265

John the Beloved
392, 1902

Peter
2746
James
1842

Samaritans
3135, 3136

Brotherly Love
2200–2202

Mary
2250

John, Beloved Disciple
392, 1902

368

Fishermen on the Sea of Galilee

The Garden of Gethsemane is to the left of the church in the
upper center

B. Authorship and Date

From early Christian times John the apostle was credited with having written the Gospel of John. Early second-century writers, including Irenaeus (A.D. 125–202), Bishop of Lyons and author of *Against the Heresies;* Tertullian (A.D. 160–220), a Roman theologian and author; the theologian Saint Hippolytus (A.D. 160–223); and Origen (A.D. 185–254), a Greek philosopher and writer, ascribe authorship of the Gospel to John.

Internal evidence supports John as being the author. John, who was a Jew, frequently quoted from the OT. His writings show that he was well acquainted with Jewish feasts (John 7:2ff.), customs (John 8:3ff.), and the messianic prophecies (John 1:41). John, upon hearing Jesus' request, readily accepted and became a follower (Matt. 4:21; Mark 1:20).

Until the development of Form Criticism in the eighteenth and nineteenth centuries, authorship of the books of the Bible was seldom questioned (see commentary on Acts, page 374). Since that time unresolved problems have developed in the biblical field. A number of the books of the Bible have come under attack, especially the Pentateuch and the Gospels. In the case of the Fourth Gospel, some critics have relied upon an obscure statement by Papias, as quoted from Eusebius, and concluded that the author is a little-known presbyter in Ephesus by the name of John and not John the Apostle—since *presbyter* means "elder" and John the Beloved referred to himself as the "elder" (2 John 1:1; 3 John 1:1).[25]

This double reference to John is hardly a basis upon which to assume that the author of John's Gospel was an obscure presbyter in Ephesus (Acts 19:4). Henry H. Halley says, "The same class of critics who deny the Virgin Birth of Jesus, His Deity, and His Bodily Resurrection . . . have inferred that the author was not John the Apostle but another John of Ephesus. This [conclusion] would undermine the value of the book as a testimony to the Deity of Jesus." [26] George H. Turner says that "when both internal and external evidence is weighed, there seems no compelling reason to deny to John, the son of Zebedee, the honor of being its author." [27]

It is not known where John received his inspiration to write the Gospel of John; the only reference made to a revelation from God is the Apocalypse (Rev. 1:9). The traditional place for his inspiration is on the Isle of Patmos where John had been banished in the reign of Domitian in about A.D. 95. Scholars are not in agreement as to whether John received his revelation at Patmos for all of his books (John, Revelation, 1,2,3 John); neither are they certain that he wrote any of them on the Isle. Some scholars think that he wrote all of his books at Ephe-

False
Teachers
2101

Ephesus
1142, 4365

Jesus Divine
701, 702

Biblical
Inspiration
417

370

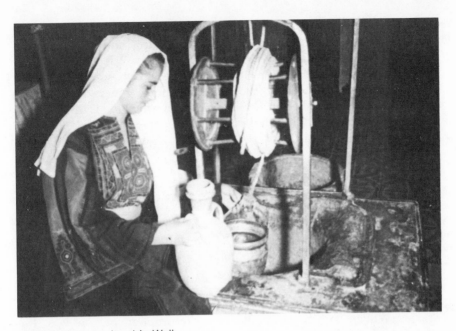

Native woman at Jacob's Well

Entrance to Lazarus' Tomb at Bethany

sus, which has a strong traditional link with the Virgin Mary, who is supposed to have lived here with John in later years. The traditional house of the Virgin Mary is located on a hill at Panaja Kapoulu, a suburb of ancient Ephesus, and it is believed that she is buried there. In John's generation a strong church flourished in Ephesus. The congregation is listed as one of the Seven Churches of Asia Minor (Rev. 2:1ff.).

It is generally assumed that the book was written about A.D. 90.

C. Background, Purpose, and Content

Biographical information about the apostle John is limited. He is mentioned three times by Matthew, ten times by Mark, and seven times by Luke. John's family was apparently wealthy because they had servants (Mark 1:19,20). From Matthew 4:21 one learns that Zebedee was his father and that Salome was his mother (Matt. 20:21), but the identity of Salome is uncertain. William Smith comments upon the problem: Salome was "the wife of Zebedee, as appears from comparing Matt. XXVII, 56 with Mark XV, 40. It is further the opinion of many modern critics that she was the sister of Mary, the mother of Jesus, to whom reference is made in John XIX, 25. The words admit, however, of another explanation, according to which they refer

to the 'Mary, the wife of Cleophas' immediately afterward mentioned. We can hardly regard the point settled, though the weight of modern criticism is decidedly in favor of the former view." [28]

The Gospel of John is selective in its choice of subject matter. Ninety percent of its content is different from the synoptic Gospels. John acknowledges that Jesus said and did many other things not included in his book (John 21:25). John included many striking miracles (signs) which could inspire a belief that Jesus Christ was indeed God's Son. John clearly states that "these are written, that ye might believe that Jesus is the Christ, the Son of God; and that believing ye might have life through his name" (John 20:31).

Differing from the writers of the synoptic Gospels, John recorded miracles, better designated as signs, of Jesus which were manifestations of this power and character. Jesus had

(1) Power over nature—changing water into wine (John 2:1–11).

(2) Power over disease—healing the nobleman's son (John 4:46–56).

(3) Power over the body—healing the lame and blind man (John 5:1–9; 9:1–41).

(4) Power over death—the raising of Lazarus and speaking of his own resurrection (John 2:19; 10:18; 11:1–46).

Only the feeding of the 5000 is common to all the gospel records.

John provides further evidence that the reader might believe that Jesus is the Christ: he spiritualizes water (John 4:10; 7:38), light (8:12; 12:35), and bread (6:35,48) and gives special significance to such terms as world (3:16; 8:23), life (10:15; 14:6), know (3:11; 13:17), love (14:15,23; 15:12), truth (8:32; 16:13), and resurrection (5:29; 11:25).

At the time John wrote the Gospel (about A.D. 90) he was the only living apostle. The period of the synoptic Gospels was now past; 30 years had elapsed since the first three Gospel records had been written. The church, then about 50 years old, had been established in much of the Roman world.

Various heathen philosophies were pressing in upon the Christians. Among the views was that of the Gnostics, which was becoming a serious threat to the Church. Those who held the view of the Gnostics repudiated the OT and made Jesus merely a creature created by God, and his death only apparent. Concerning this philosophy Conrad Henry Moehlman writes that "The Gnostic god was a philosophical abstraction with mystical trimmings and redemption a divine Comedy. In Gnosticism the same god could not be both creator and judge and redeemer. If Gnosticism had triumphed, Christianity would have become just another Graeco-Roman mystery religion." [29] Another writer termed Christian Gnosticism the "acute Hellenization of Christianity." [30]

Vain Philosophies **2759**

Greek philosophy, coupled with other aspects of Hellenism, had made deep inroads among the Jews of the Diaspora and had become the dominant way of life among the Jews. Greek had become the language of the Jews, and with the Greek language had come Greek influence. John challenged the encroaching Gnosticism and Hellenization of the Jews. The purpose of 1 John, and one purpose of the Gospel of John, was to combat error in the Christian church (especially in 1 John), the heresy of Gnosticism.

To break through the philosophical facade of the Hellenized community, John interpreted Christianity by identifying Christ with the well known and understood term *logos,* a word that was "as old as the Greek language. It was first introduced by Heraclitus of Ephesus, in the 5th century B.C. into a circle of philosophical ideas as principle of cosmic interpretation." [31]

Heresy **1577**
Christ the "Word" **700**

According to Heraclitus,

Philosophic wisdom . . . apprehends that the total process of cosmic being is subjected to the regulative control of an agency to which . . . the logos technique accounted for the orderliness of nature. He further postulated that change, if not chaos, must conform to fixed patterns; and that . . . therefore, order, law, measure and predictability, were formulations of cosmic transformations going on according to logos, thus the permanence of all things preserved, because all things observe their own measure.[32]

The Greek concept of the logos did not contain the idea of a transcendent God but only an imminent law or reason or a creativity responsible for the things as seen. There was resident in the Greek understanding a recognition that the world was a unity and "that basic to all human institutions is a spiritual, all-pervasive principle with which man must deal, i.e., the *logos.*"[33] There is a sense in which the Greek concept of the logos is in accord with the fourth Gospel but there is a difference.

At this point John removed the term logos from the realm of principle and gave it Life and Personality and made of it a Person. In the English Bible (John 1:1ff.) this term, meaning the "Living Word" or Christ, is used 22 times in the Gospel of John.

Logos "The
Word"
700

In identifying the logos as Christ, John did for the Hellenized Jews what Paul did for the Athenians when he identified their "unknown god" as Jesus Christ (Acts 17:22–31). John says in substance that the "logos and God are two appellations of one single divine reality."[34]

Thus John breathes life and Christological meaning into a term that had heretofore been a philosophical abstraction.

VI. ACTS

A. The Name

Acts of the
Apostles
4266
Codex
Alexandrinus
4220

The Book of Acts has had a variety of names: " 'The Acts or Transactions of the Apostles' is the title in the Greek BEZAE. . . . 'The Acts of the Holy Apostles' is the title in the Codex Alexandrinus [see Ch. 1, II, B] and several others. . . . By some it has been . . . [called] a 'Fifth Gospel' . . . and the 'Gospel of the Holy Apostles,' [as well] as 'The Book, the Demonstration of the Holy Spirit.' "[35]

Other ancient manuscripts give the title as "Acts," "The Acts," "Acts of the Apostles," and "Acts of the Holy Apostles."[36]

Authorized
Version
p. 181

The title, "The Acts of the Apostles," is used in the Authorized Version (1611) and the Revised Version (1881) as well as the Revised Standard Version (1946).

The patristic fathers probably assigned the caption, "The Acts of the Apostles," to the Book of Acts to preserve an account of the work of the risen Savior and its continuance through the apostles by the power of the Holy Spirit. However, the

Another view of the Garden of Gethsemane

The Damascus Gate in Jerusalem

account makes reference to the activities of only a few apostles by name. In a sense, the book is a "Fifth Gospel" because it is a continuation of the narrative begun in the Gospel of Luke. (See part C, "Background, Purpose, and Content," in this chapter.)

B. Authorship and Date

Evidence for authorship of Luke and Acts has been presented in the chapter on the Gospel of Luke. Literary style, the chronological order of the writing, and the internal and external evidence make it impossible to separate authorship of the two books from that of a single writer. This leads to the conclusion that Luke is the author of both books. Presumably the Book of Acts was completed by Luke at some time near the end of Paul's two-year imprisonment in Rome. It is apparent that Luke's principal sources of information were his immediate personal contact with Paul and the notes he had accumulated while traveling with Paul. The date of composition for the Book of Acts is uncertain but A.D. 80 seems to have the greater probability. The book could not have been written earlier than Paul's final imprisonment because the narrative is continuous to that time, nor could it have been written later because the writings deal specifically with Paul's imprisonment in Rome.[37]

A study of the Book of Acts should include comment upon the viewpoint of those critics who differ from the traditional view of establishing authorship of a book upon internal and external evidence. Some critics subject a book to question if it contains miracles, the supernatural power of Jesus, and the ability of prophets to foretell the future. The Book of Acts has been no exception to this procedure. "With [their reasoning] . . . instead of inferring the truth of the narrative from the overwhelming evidence that it is the narrative of eyewitnesses, and a contemporary, they conclude it is not the authoritative narrative because it contains . . . statements to the miracles which they are . . . [unwilling] to admit as true." [38]

Among the references not acceptable to those who use this form of interpretation are "the account[s] of the Ascension of our Lord and the Day of Pentecost . . . as well as the miracles of Peter, and John . . . and the other supernatural events throughout the book." [39]

Form Criticism is a device that the critics have created by which natural historical events can be shifted from their setting to a later date more compatible with the pre-supposed "scientific investigative technique." [40] This kind of exegesis is coupled with "rationalistic" assertions of "alleged contradictions," "in-

Tree of Paul's
Life
4309

False
Teachers
2101

Ascension
678
Day of
Pentecost
2722

376

adequate accounts," and "omissions of facts," but these assertions are never clearly defined.[41]

Another device used by these critics for nullifying the traditional view is the creation of sources which a supposed "redactor" is said to have used, including (1) a biography of Peter,
(2) a rhetorical work of the death of Stephen, (3) a biography
of Barnabas and the memoirs of Silas.[42] None of these so-called
sources have biblical, historical, or literary certainty. In conclusion it is asserted that the Book of Acts "is not historically
reliable." [43] Most of this destructive criticism was developed
by German critics of the eighteenth and nineteenth century
of which the Tubingen school is representative.

C. Background, Purpose, and Content

A parallel study of the Book of Acts can be made by consulting the TCRB Helps, pp. 280, 281.

As to the title, "The Acts of the Apostles," the book deals
only in a limited way with the activity of all the apostles. Of
the apostles, the book mentions "the eleven" (1:26), who "witnessed Christ's ascension to heaven (Acts 1) and the election
of Matthias to replace Judas (Acts 1), which was followed by
the outpouring of the Holy Spirit (Acts 2). Peter is the prominent figure in the first 12 chapters of Acts,[44] and Paul in the
later chapters. References to the events occurring after Pentecost include Peter's imprisonment (Acts 4), the tragic death
of Ananias and Sapphira (Acts 5), the healing of Aeneas, the
raising of Dorcas from the dead (Acts 9), and the conversion Dorcas
1033
Cornelius
841
Samaria
3134
Peter
2746
of Cornelius in Caesarea (Acts 10), the election of Philip to
supervise the social affairs (Acts 6), his planting of the church
in Samaria (Acts 8), and the baptizing of the Ethiopian eunuch
(Acts 8). John is mentioned as being with Peter at the healing
of the man at the temple gate and being in prison with Peter
(Acts 3). In chapters 13–28 most of the references deal with
those before, during, and after Paul's conversion on the Damascus road.

The Book of Acts is the key, not only to the continuing activity of the apostles but also to the Pauline Epistles. Information
as to Paul's Galatian ministry is contained in Acts 16 and 18,
his Philippian ministry in Acts 16, his Thessalonian witness
in Acts 16 and 17, his labors at Corinth in Acts 18 and 20,
his work in Ephesus in Acts 18 and 19, and his ministry among
the Romans in Acts 28. "No one could read Acts without realizing that Paul was a genuine apostle of Christ, independently
commissioned by Him and proving by the 'signs of the apostles'
which accompanied his ministry, the truth of his claim that
he came in no way behind 'the very chiefest apostles' (2 Cor.
12:11)." [45]

Roman baths in Ankara, Turkey

Theatre at Ephesus seating 25,000 people

The "Street called Straight" in Damascus today

Ruins of Perga in Pamphylia

Post
Resurrection
p. 281
Day of
Pentecost
2722
Judas
1959–1963

D. The Book of Acts as a Supplement to the Gospels

If the gospel records were the only source of information available on the post-Resurrection Christian movement, knowledge of the developing Jewish-Gentile church would be very limited. The prophetic statements in the OT regarding the outpouring of the Holy Spirit (Joel 2:28,29; cf. Acts 2:16,17) and the replacement of Judas (Ps. 109:7,8; cf. Acts 1:15–17) would not be understood.

In writing the Book of Acts, Luke continued that which he had so ably begun in his gospel narrative. The entire content in the Gospel makes the Book of Acts imperative.

Joseph Exell says of Luke: "It is obvious that the first preaching of the Gospel [by Luke] in Jerusalem was necessary, both to connect his second work with the first, and also because . . . the Mission of the Gentiles sprang from the Mother Church in Jerusalem. The existence and establishment of the Jewish Church was the root from which the Gentile Church grew and the Gentile Church had a common interest with the Jewish Church in these great events." [46]

1. Journeys of Paul in His Early Life (Acts 7:58–11:26)

Saul of Tarsus left his home when still a young man to study under Gamaliel in Jerusalem. His first act of persecuting the Christians was in connection with the stoning of Stephen (Acts 7:58).

On his way to Damascus to apprehend Christians, Saul's conversion took place and later he became Paul the evangelist to the Gentiles. After his conversion, Paul went into the Arabian desert (Gal. 1:17), presumably to pray and to study the Scriptures. On his return, he stayed three years in Damascus preaching and teaching that Jesus of Nazareth was indeed the Jewish Messiah, and then went to Jerusalem where he abode for fifteen days with Peter (Gal. 1:18). After this he journeyed to his home, Tarsus, where he remained until Barnabas came to escort him to Antioch, the new headquarters of the gentile church (Acts 11:25,26).

Journey Map
p. 287
Paul's
Missionary
Journeys
2382
John Mark
2253

2. Paul's First Missionary Journey (Acts 13:1–14:28)

The church at Antioch ordained Paul and Barnabas for the first missionary journey into the gentile world. Apparently young Mark accompanied them. Their first port was Salamis on the Island of Cyprus. A monastery and tomb bearing the name of Barnabas is presently located a few miles west of Salamis. Paul and Barnabas traveled overland to Paphos, on the west coast, where the proconsul Sergius Paulus became a

The Acropolis in Athens with the Temple of Zeus in foreground

The Parthenon in Athens. Photograph courtesy Agora Excavations, American School of Classical Studies at Athens

convert and Saul's name was changed to Paul (Acts 13:4–12). (See page 74 on Name Changes.)

After the missionary party landed at Perga on the southern coast of Asia Minor, Mark returned to Jerusalem (Acts 13:13). In Pisidian Antioch Paul preached in the synagogue and was violently opposed by the Jews. The missionary group continued on the Iconium. Strong persecution drove them on to Lystra where Paul was stoned and left for dead (Acts 14:19).

They traveled as far as Derbe and then, retracing their steps, came to the coastal town of Attalia. By ship they returned to the Christian headquarters in Antioch.

3. Paul's Second Missionary Journey (Acts 15:40–18:22)

Paul's second missionary journey was marked by a disagreement with his friend Barnabas. As mentioned in the Gospel of Mark, Paul did not want Mark to accompany them; consequently Barnabas and Mark went on an independent missionary journey. Paul chose Silas for his partner, stopping first in Tarsus. From there they traveled to Derbe, Lystra, Iconium, and Pisidian Antioch, all towns which he had visited with Barnabas on his first journey. At Lystra, Timothy, a young man of faith with a Christian background joined Paul and Silas (Acts 16:1–3). In Galatia, the Holy Spirit urged Paul to proceed to Troas where he received the Macedonian call.

Sailing to Neapolis, the port city of Philippi, and thence over the coastal mountains Paul and Silas reached Philippi where, on the Sabbath day, they made contact with some women praying by the river. Opposition to their ministry soon developed, which resulted in the imprisonment of the missionaries and the conversion of the jailer (Acts 16). Their next ministry was at Thessalonica where again the Jews persecuted Paul and Silas (Acts 17). In Berea the people were more kindly disposed, searching the Scriptures to ascertain if Paul's message was true (Acts 17). However, when the trouble-making Jews from Thessalonica came to Berea more opposition arose. Paul proceeded to Athens, leaving Silas and Timothy behind to establish and nurture the church.

In Athens, Paul introduced the "unknown god" to the learned men (Acts 17). At Corinth, Silas and Timothy rejoined Paul and there they ministered for eighteen months. Then they began their long journey back to Antioch, stopping briefly in Ephesus, Caesarea, and Jerusalem.

4. Paul's Third Missionary Journey (Acts 18:22–21:17)

Paul stayed only a short time in Antioch at the end of his second journey before departing on his third journey, never again to see Antioch. After a visit with the churches in Galatia,

Ruins of a Roman swimming pool in Ankara

Ruins of the temple of Augustus in Ankara (Galatia)

he continued to Ephesus. During his second visit in Ephesus the people began to destroy their idols. Demetrius and his fellow silversmiths incited the people to riot because they feared that their sale of idols would be destroyed by the people's conversion to Christianity. From Ephesus, Paul continued

Macedonia
2222

his missionary journey northward into Macedonia and Greece where several of Paul's missionary associates joined him in Macedonia.

Miletus
2346

At Miletus, Paul delivered his notable farewell address to the Ephesian elders who had come to hear him. Despite the elders' warning of danger in Jerusalem at the hand of the Jews, Paul continued on his way to face the wrath of the Jews, stopping briefly at Coos, Rhodes, and Patara as well as Tyre, Ptolemais, and Caesarea. In Jerusalem, Paul related his missionary experiences. While he was at worship in the temple the Jews seized him, but he was rescued by the Roman soldiers. After he appeared before the Sanhedrin, a certain number of Jews made a pact to kill Paul. After a series of charges and defenses before Felix, Festus, and Agrippa in Caesarea, Paul appealed to the court of Caesar in Rome.

Missionaries of the Early Church
pp. 294–295

The missionary witnesses operating in and out of Antioch were quite impressive. At least sixty missionaries are referred to by name in the Pauline epistles. The greatest number are listed in Acts and the Timothy letters.

Journey Map
pp. 292–293

5. Paul's Voyage to Rome (Acts 27–28)

Rome
3095, 4408

With other prisoners, Paul was delivered to a centurion for the sea voyage to Rome. After some stormy weather and a shipwreck at Malta, Paul was taken overland from Puteoli to Rome. In Rome he continued his ministry without further accusations by the Jews. Tradition holds that Paul ministered about two years in Rome, during which time Luke wrote the Book

Martyrs
3488

of Acts with Paul's aid, and that eventually Paul died a martyr's death.

The ruins of the Roman Forum

20

The Larger Epistles of Paul
(Romans–2 Corinthians)

I. ROMANS

A. The Name

The Book of Romans takes its name from those to whom the book is addressed. The letter was directed "to all that be in Rome" (Rom. 1:7), and to the Roman church composed of believing Jews, and the heathen who had been converted directly to the Christian faith, some of whom may have been in Jerusalem on the Day of Pentecost (Acts 2:10). From the many people to whom Paul addressed greetings it would seem that the church was a sizeable one at the time Paul wrote the book (Rom. 16:3,23). For a listing of these names see Part C of this section.

B. Authorship and Date

The Book of Romans is one of the few NT books for which Pauline authorship is seldom questioned. Such ancient church fathers as Clement of Rome, Ignatius, Polycarp, and Justin all quote from the Book of Romans and assign authorship to Paul the apostle. Even Marcion includes Romans in his list of Pauline Epistles.[1]

The place of writing (Corinth) and the date for this epistle are fixed within narrow limits. This conclusion is organically linked with certain names in the salutation. Phoebe, whom Paul commended to the Romans, was one of the deaconesses at Cenchrea, the port town of Corinth (Rom. 16:1,2). Cenchrea is the location where ships were placed on rollers and pulled

Epistle to the Romans
4267

Romans
772

Proselytes
2895, 2896

Corinth
840, 4353

Phoebe
2751

385

The dome of St. Peter's Cathedral in Rome

The pyramid of Caius Cestius. Built in 12 B.C. as a tomb, it rises 121 feet high and measures 100 feet wide at its base

by manpower across the narrow isthmus, to avoid the tempestuous waters surrounding Achaia or the Peloponnesian Peninsula.

Gaius, mentioned as an official in the church, provided lodging for Paul in Corinth (Rom. 16:23; 1 Cor. 1:14). Erastus is referred to as the chamberlain (treasurer) of the city (Rom. 16:23). Thus it seems that Paul wrote his epistle from Corinth on his third missionary journey during the winter or spring of A.D. 58 following his long residence in Ephesus (Acts 20:3). The postscript at the end of Romans affirms the place of writing as Corinth and states that the letter was to be sent by Phoebe, a faithful servant of the church at Cenchrea (Rom. 16:1).[2]

C. Background, Purpose, and Content

In the introductory verse of the Book of Romans, Paul expresses his desire to go to Rome for the purpose of imparting "some spiritual gifts" and establishing the believers in faith (Rom. 1:10–12). His statement, "I must also see Rome" (Acts 19:21) apparently implies Divine leading (Acts 23:21). He had labored in such well-known commercial and religious centers as Ephesus, Corinth, Thessalonica, and Athens. Although Paul had planned to visit the capital city of Rome, he had been prevented from going. On numerous occasions Paul had expected to go to Rome, but circumstances had prevented him from going (Rom. 1:13).

Rome
3095, 4408

Ephesus
1142, 4365
Corinth
840, 4353
Thessalonica
3610, 4420

No specific information is available as to when the Christian church in Rome developed; however, on the Day of Pentecost, after the Holy Spirit came to those believers assembled in the Upper Room at Jerusalem, there were among the crowd, "strangers of Rome, Jews and proselytes" (Acts 2:10). Evidently some of the Jews who had gone to Jerusalem to celebrate the Jewish Feast Day of Pentecost accepted Jesus of Nazareth as their Messiah. It is possible that the Christ-Messiah believers developed from the witness of these believers as well as from these who traveled throughout the Empire and came at times to Rome. The greetings in Romans 16 indicate that there was a strong Christian group in Rome when Paul wrote his epistle. Apparently those believers were so outstanding that their faith was "spoken of throughout the whole world" (Rom. 1:8).

Proselytes
2895, 2896

Day of Pentecost
2722

Faithful Servants
603, 1228, 1229

Rome was opposed to any group which endangered the political tranquillity of the empire. Claudius had commanded that all Jews should leave Rome (Acts 18:1,2). Among the exiles were Priscilla and Aquila, friends of Paul. When he arrived in Corinth, his first contact was with them. Other references to this couple show that they were effective Christians (Acts 18:18,26). The number of Christian believers in Rome is indicated in the greetings Paul sent; those names include Mary,

Aquila and Priscilla
208

387

Andronicus, Junia, Amplias, Urbane, Apelles, the household of Aristobulus, Herodion, the household of Narcissus, Tryphena, Tryphosa, Persis, Rufus, Asyncritus, Phlegon, Hermas, Patrobas, Hermes, Philologus, Julia, Nereus and his sister, and Olympas, "and all the saints which are with them" (Rom. 16:6–15).[3]

Paul suggested that all of these should salute each other with "an holy kiss," and he informed them that the other "churches of Christ salute you" (Rom. 16:16). Paul sent salutations on behalf of the saints with him, including Timotheus, Lucius, Jason and Sosipater, Gaius, Erastus, and Quartus (Rom. 16:21–23), and identified his scribe Tertius as the writer of the epistle (Rom. 16:22). This list of many coworkers is not complete by any means, but it does indicate that there were numerous believers in Rome. Paul indicates the believers were so widespread that some had even penetrated Caesar's household (Phil. 4:22). This roster of believers points out that Paul had remarkable knowledge of and acquaintance with his fellow laborers. It is not surprising that Paul found brethren in the faith waiting for him when he landed at Puteoli (Acts 28:14,15).

It was Paul's contention, verified by Scripture, that Christianity is the culmination of Judaism and that the Jewish faith came to fulfillment in Jesus Christ. Paul developed the thesis that the true Jews were the ones with spiritual circumcision of the heart (Rom. 2:28,29).

The Books of Romans, Galatians, and Hebrews emphasize "justification by faith" (Rom. 1:17; Gal. 3:11; Heb. 10:38; cf. Hab. 2:4). It is clearly stated that the plan of salvation was the same for both Jew and Gentile as God was no respecter of persons (Rom. 2:10,11). God has no double standard—one plan of salvation for the Jew and another for the Gentile (Rom. 3). Paul said that no one is without excuse and that all must come to God by Jesus Christ. No one is saved by the works of the law, but all are saved by faith in Jesus Christ (Rom. 3:22,23; cf. Rom. 3:24–31; Eph. 2:8,9).[4]

Paul described the degenerate state of humanity in Romans 1:18–32. In these passages one can see the resulting abnormality when the sexual relationship is extramarital—outside of marriage. The Living Bible describes in modern words the abominable state of this life style:

Claiming themselves to be wise without God, they became utter fools instead. . . . So God let them go ahead into every sort of sex sin, and do whatever they wanted to—yes, vile and sinful things with each other's bodies. . . . That is why God let go of them and let them do all these evil things, so that even their women turned against God's natural plan for them and indulged in sex sin with each other. And the men, instead of having a normal sex relationship

Salutations
3409, 3410

Spiritual
Circumcision
766

Justification by
Faith
1203, 1985

Depravity
2545

with women, burned with lust for each other, men doing shameful things with other men . . . (Rom. 1:22,24,26,27).

Many of the NT writers declared that every person—Jew or Gentile—can be delivered from the penalty, power, and pollution of sin through faith in Jesus Christ (Rom. 3:21–31). "The gospel of Christ . . . is the power of God unto salvation to every one that believeth" (Rom. 1:16; see also Rom. 2:25–29).

God's Impartiality
1979

Paul explained more clearly the doctrine that no one has an excuse for his sinful conduct because God has given sufficient revelation to direct man's steps into the path of righteousness (Rom. 1:20; 2:1). Paul contended that salvation is not an inheritance but a state attained by faith and that the true spiritual Jew is one who has had circumcision of the heart (the new birth) which gives man a justified relationship with God. Spiritual circumcision also symbolizes the purification of the mind, heart, and will; it gives the believer a status as though he had never committed sin.

Excuses Not Acceptable
3347

New Birth
2154

Spiritual Circumcision
766

In chapter 4 Paul recognized that Abraham and David were justified by faith and not by works of the law (Rom. 4:1–9; cf. Eph. 2:8.9). In this context Abraham is the spiritual father of all who believe and accept God's Messiah (Rom. 4:11–16). To be justified, every individual must appropriate salvation by faith in Christ's atonement. Paul says, "Therefore being justified by faith, we have peace with God through our Lord Jesus Christ" (Rom. 5:1). The high standard of grace and the key to victory over sin is expressed in Romans 6:1–12. In chapters 6–8 Paul describes the victory through the Spirit and shows that "there is . . . no condemnation to them which are in Christ Jesus, who walk not after the flesh, but after the Spirit" (Rom. 8:1). It is the dominating Spirit of Christ which frees the sinner from the law of sin and death (Rom. 8:2).

Justification by Faith
1203, 1985

No Condemnation
3124

Messiah
695

In chapters 9–11 Paul deals with the Jews' rejection of the Messiah, a Jew, and the prophetic revelation of the future Israel in the grace of God. Paul points out that there are two Israels: "For they are not all Israel, which are of Israel" (Rom. 9:6b). He also makes it clear that not all physical descendants of Abraham are his "spiritual seed" (Rom. 9:7,8). Through faith, both the believing Jew and Gentile are made one in Jesus Christ. For additional information see Ch. 10, V.

Paul gives a theological exposition of the supremacy of God (Rom. 9:15–23) and makes it clear that both Jews and Gentiles are eligible for and included in God's plan of sovereign grace (Rom. 9:24–26; cf. Rom. 9:30–33; 10:4–13). It is evident that God has a long range design for Israel as a nation because "a remnant shall be saved" (Rom. 9:27b). It is clear that the door

Return of Jews
1827

389

of grace is open to the rejecting Jew, for "God hath not cast away his people which he foreknew" (Rom. 11:2a; cf. Rom. 11:2b–32).

Prophecy of the future state of Israel is difficult. This is an area in which many prophetic interpretations have developed; only time will reveal the details. There are two aspects of Jewish history which are most unusual: the preservation of the nation and its language. These developments give reason to expect the continued fulfillment of prophecy concerning the Jews.

(1) Politically, the nation came to an end with the destruction of Jerusalem under Titus in A.D. 70. The resurrection of Israel, as a nation, in 1947 is unique. There is no instance in history where a nation has revived as a political entity after its dissolution. The passing of 2000 years definitely put Israel into the same category with other dead nations.

(2) Hebrew, as a national language among dispersed Jews, was considered to be dead by about 250 B.C., except in the immediate area of Jerusalem among those of the temple hierarchy. The scattered Jews had adopted the universal Greek language and/or the local dialects of the area in which they lived; they were out of touch with their "mother tongue." Today Hebrew is the unified language among the Jews who have assembled in Israel from over 70 language areas.

What God has in mind for the Jews and Israel remains to be seen, but it is certain that a Jew, if he is to be saved, must accept Jesus Christ the Messiah as his personal Savior.

Chapters 12–16 deal with personal duties and commitment (Rom. 12:1,2) and individual responsibility to established government (Rom. 13:1–7). As believers, each person has a duty to be charitable (Rom. 14:1–8).

Handley Dunelm presents the doctrinal nature of the Book of Romans in the following outline. It is included here to give a perspective of the general content of this book:

1. The Doctrine of Man.
2. The Doctrine of God.
3. The Doctrine of the Son of God.
4. The Doctrine of the Spirit of God.
5. The Doctrine of Duty.
6. The Doctrine of Israel.[5]

When Paul came to Rome, evidently no charges were filed against him by the Jerusalem authorities (Acts 28:21). Although Paul was "kept" by a soldier in a dwelling, apparently he was free to preach the gospel without religious or political interference (Acts 28:30,31).

II. 1 CORINTHIANS

A. The Name

The first Epistle to the Corinthians derives its name from the Corinthian church to whom the epistle is addressed.

B. Authorship and Date

The Epistle to the Corinthians is recognized to be of Pauline authorship. Both the internal and external evidence is such that no critic of note has challenged Paul as the author. Throughout the centuries tradition has insisted that these epistles contain the very *pectus Paulinum,* the mind and heart of the great apostle to the Gentiles, and preserve for the church an impregnable defense of historical Christianity. What has been said of their genuineness applies almost equally to both 1 and 2 Corinthians.[6] In A.D. 95 Clement of Rome made reference to Paul as the writer of this epistle. Ignatius and Polycarp both provide additional external evidence of Pauline authorship. The best information available indicates that Paul wrote his first letter to the Corinthians from Ephesus about three years after his first visit to Corinth.[7] Most scholars are agreed that the letter was written about A.D. 55.[8]

C. Background, Purpose, and Content

For a historical background of the Corinthian church it is necessary to consult Acts 18. The city of Corinth was favorably situated on the isthmus between Achaia, the Peloponnesian Peninsula, and the mainland of Greece, Macedonia.

Three excellent harbors provided protective facilities for both east- and west-bound water traffic as well as loading ports for the land caravans. Because of its strategic location it became the gathering place for both the best and the worst in Roman and Greek society. It was a center for arts, crafts, artificers, and tradesmen of every kind, but it also was a place frequented by prostitutes, gamblers, adventurers, vagrants, and religious cultists. Its immorality and sensuous pleasures gave the city the title of "sin city." To "act as a Corinthian" was a synonym for the gross immorality of that day. The lowest state of moral corruption was to be "corinthianized." [9]

In this morally and spiritually depraved city Paul preached the gospel. He intended only a brief stopover, but the Lord commanded him to tarry; Paul had an eighteen-month ministry there (Acts 18:9–11).

Paul founded the Corinthian church during his first visit on his second missionary journey. His first public ministerial con-

First Epistle to the Corinthians
4268

Corinth
840, 4353

Gentiles
2383, 2384, 4038

Paul's Preaching
2087

Excavation and ruins at Corinth

Acro-Corinth. 1885 feet high, about two miles south of Corinth.
On top was the temple of Aphrodite, goddess of love

tact was in the synagogue, where he reasoned with the Jews that Jesus was the Christ-Messiah (Acts 18:4,5). It appears that the church was at first a synagogue congregation. Crispus, the chief ruler of the synagogue, was Paul's first convert (Acts 18:8). However, it was at Corinth that Jewish hostility and rejection made Paul "shake his raiment" and turn to the Gentiles (Acts 18:6). When the Jews brought Paul before Gallio, the deputy of Achaia, the Jews were driven out of the Judgment Hall (Acts 18:12–16). Apparently Sosthenes, one of the chief rulers of the synagogue, was publicly flogged by a Greek mob (Acts 18:17).

At the end of his ministry in Corinth, Paul took his leave to go to Jerusalem to celebrate Pentecost (Acts 18:19–21). After a short stay Paul returned to Antioch to begin his third missionary journey (see TCRB Helps pp. 290–291). After some meetings in Galatia and Phrygia he continued on to Ephesus (Acts 19:1). During his stay in Ephesus, travelers from Corinth informed Paul of the difficulties the church was having. Ephesus, an eight-day journey by sea from Corinth, became a kind of relay station for news from Corinth. All the news concerning the Corinthian church was unfavorable.

Chloe, who had come from Corinth, reported serious contentions among church members (1 Cor. 1:11). To obtain additional information, Paul sent Timothy to Corinth (4:17). After faithful work in Corinth, Apollos joined Paul in Ephesus (3:5,6; 16:12). Apollos was followed by Stephanus, Fortunatus, and Achaicus (16:17), who supplied Paul with additional information on the conditions in Corinth. According to the reports: "The church had broken into factions, and was distracted by party cries. Some of its members were living openly immoral lives, and discipline was practically in abeyance. Others had quarrels over which they dragged one another into heathen courts. Great differences of opinion had also arisen with regard to marriage, and the social relations generally; with regard to banquets and the eating of food offered to idols; with regard to the behaviour of women in the assemblies, to the Lord's Supper and the lovefeasts, to the use and the value of spiritual gifts and to the hope of the resurrection." [10]

These gloomy reports distressed Paul greatly. His first impulse was to visit them "with a rod" (1 Cor. 4:21), but he decided to write the church a letter instead (1 Corinthians), which was delivered by Titus. Even though the Corinthians deserved the severest rebuke, Paul wrote a masterful letter in which he exercised considerable restraint. He made his appeal to the finer instincts of the church members. With commendation and praise, he fanned the small spark of goodness still remaining. In his appeal "to them that are sanctifed in Christ Jesus, called to be saints, with all that in every place call upon the

The Larger Epistles of Paul

Synagogues
3521, 3522
Persecution
3480–3484

Opposers
1567, 1568

Feast of Pentecost
1257, 2722
Antioch **197**
Galatia **1382**
Phrygia **2762**
Ephesus
1142, 4365
Corinth
840, 4353

Timothy
3628

Apollos
200, 201

Strife, Contention
3731–3735
Intemperance
3571–3576

Lord's Supper
761

Chastise
497
Titus
3641

393

Second
Coming of
Christ
1344–1350

Spiritual Gifts
486

Greeks
1464

Unacceptable
Offerings
2635, 3108

Brotherly Love
2201

name of Jesus Christ our Lord . . ." (1 Cor. 1:2), he prayed that the grace and peace of God would rest upon them (1:3), and he expressed thanks for the grace of God which had been given to them by Jesus Christ (1:4), "even as the testimony of Christ" had been confirmed by them (1:6). Paul commended them for the gifts which they had so generously given (1:7) and assured them that as they waited for the coming of the Lord, they would be confirmed by the Lord to the end and so they would "be blameless in the day of our Lord Jesus Christ" (1:7–9).

R. Dykes Shaw evaluates this letter thus: "It moves with firm tread among the commonest themes, but also rises easily into the loftiest spheres of thought and vision, breaking again and again into passages of glowing rhythmical elegance. It rebukes error, exposes and condemns sin, solves doubts, upholds and encourages faith, . . . in a spirit of utmost tenderness and love, full of grace and truth." [11]

In chapter 12 Paul presented his extraordinary insight on spiritual gifts. In chapter 13 he developed a treatise on love. This is truly the greatest statement on love ever penned. It is the "high water mark" of all sacred literature.

Shaw says that the First Corinthian letter has three outstanding features:

1. The first is Paul's earnest warning against a factious spirit. The Corinthians were obsessed with a party spirit of Greek democracy and were influenced in their religious activity by the sporting spirit of the athletic games. "They listened to their teachers with itching ears, not as men who wished to learn, but as partisans who sought occasion, either to applaud or to condemn."

2. "The Corinthian letter also made a high ethical contribution in the rules it sets forth for the Christian conscience. Meat offered to idols and then eaten became a serious stumbling block to many Corinthian Christians. Some rationalized that since the idol was a block of wood or stone, the meat was not actually affected. But Paul pointed out that 'Christian liberty must be willing to subject itself to the law of Love.' He recognized that a brother might be weak and would be adversely affected by eating meat offered to idols (1 Cor. 8:1–12). For the sake of the brother, Paul took the position that one should refrain from eating meat if it caused another brother to stumble (1 Cor. 8:13)." (See Matt. 22:37–39.)

3. "The exaltation of the cross of Christ is another outstanding feature of this Epistle. To the Apostle, human instrumentality was minimal. It was not what Paul or Apollos or Cephas did but what resulted from preaching Christ and him crucified (1 Cor. 1:18)." [12]

Ruins of a toilet facility at Corinth

Ruins of the Temple of Apollo at Corinth

Archaeological excavations at Corinth are extensive. This city, which once had 500,000 inhabitants, eventually crumbled in the dust. The best preserved part of Old Corinth is the Acrocorinth—the high city—a stony mountain about 1800 feet high whose summit is strewn with the remains of old temples and fortifications and is edged with a stone wall around its entire perimeter. A graphic description of the ruins of Corinth follows:

> More than 30 seasons of patient excavations of ancient Corinth by the American School of Classical Studies [located] in Athens have revealed much of the city known to Paul. Below the conspicuous Doric columns of the archaic temple of Apollo, already six centuries old in his day, and certainly seen by him, there spread the spacious Agora or marketplace—a rectangle bound by an amazing array of small shops shaded by impressive colonnades. The Stoa, largest in all Greece, ran 500 ft. along the south end of the Agora, and was elegantly colonnaded with Doric and Ionic columns. Many of the shops, with their storerooms and wells, from which various treasures and baubles have been excavated, had marble gutters and mosaics. Now visible, north of the Agora, was the 210 ft. long basilica, used for administrative purposes and law courts. The bema where Paul stood trial has been excavated. . . . It was a richly ornamented tribunal, in which the Roman Government sat. It . . . had three openings between massive piers. Between the piers were benches, where witnesses or prisoners waited to be heard. . . . From the NE corner of the Agora the stately Propylaea Gateway led down to the Lechaeum Road. . . . The "Straight Way" connected Corinth with her W. harbor . . . the lintel of a Jewish synagogue has been found. . . . The excavation at the Great Theatre—the Radio City of Corinth—revealed an inscription which refers to Erastus. . . . Might this be the "Erastus the city treasurer" whose greetings Paul included in his letter to the Romans (16:23) written from Corinth? . . . A short walk from ancient Corinth is the nearest ancient equivalent to a general hospital—the healing sanctuary of the Greek god Asklepios. Its dining room, with its sloping stone couches, low stone tables, and hearth where dishes were kept warm, has been excavated. "Ex Volo"—terra cotta "thank offerings," representing hands, legs, feet or organs healed or presented for healing, are now in the Corinth Museum.[13]

Second Epistle
to the
Corinthians
4269
Corinth
840, 4353

III. 2 CORINTHIANS

A. *The Name*

The Second Epistle to the Corinthians also derives its name from the Corinthian Church to whom it was addressed.

B. *Authorship and Date*

396   The author is Paul, the apostle, as indicated in the commentary on the First Corinthian letter. Most scholars are agreed

that this epistle was written by Paul from Macedonia, probably in Philippi, during his third missionary journey in about A.D. 57.

C. Background, Purpose, and Content

Paul had spent three years at Ephesus, where he wrote First Corinthians (A.D. 55). Soon after the tumult in Ephesus when Paul nearly lost his life (Acts 19), he went to Macedonia. While visiting the churches in the Philippi-Thessalonica area (A.D. 57), Paul wrote his second letter to the Corinthians. Somewhere in Macedonia Paul made contact with Titus, who had recently returned from Corinth with good news. Some of the previous problems had been resolved, but now new troubles began to develop. Most serious was the denial by a number of the Corinthians of Paul's apostleship. Had the criticism of the Corinthians been left unchallenged, Paul's authority and influence would have been greatly diminished. Paul immediately wrote the Second Corinthian letter in which he developed a defense of his apostleship. Paul sent this epistle to Corinth by Titus. A few days later Paul continued his journey to Corinth. He reminded the Corinthians that he had founded the church there and that he did have a right in its management.[14] In the introduction to the Second Corinthian letter, Paul once again shows great restraint in his admonition. He is most gracious and benevolent in his solution. Paul chooses to mingle his own sorrows, anxieties and shortcomings with those of the Corinthians. He uses the pronouns "we" and "us" frequently to show that he shares with them their problems.

"Out of much affliction and anguish of heart" he writes to them "with many tears" (2 Cor. 2:4). Wick Broomall describes this approach: "In spite of its ruggedness, this letter is as beautiful in its symmetry as a mountain flower—and it carries far more fragrance." [15]

Within the gentleness of his entreaty Paul gives the Corinthians an ultimatum that they must surrender totally to the authority of Christ's apostleship.[16] Paul subtly suggests that his apostleship is evidenced by the Corinthians being living epistles, "known and read of all men . . . written not with ink, but with the Spirit of the living God; not in tables of stone, but in fleshy tables of the heart" (3:2,3). In chapter 5 Paul assures the Corinthians of immortality: "if our earthly house of this tabernacle were dissolved, we have a building of God, an house not made with hands, eternal in the heavens" (5:1). Regarding readiness for death, Paul says, "Therefore we are always confident, knowing that, whilst we are at home in the body, we are absent from the Lord: . . . we are confident . . .

Macedonia
2222
Philippi
2756, 4405
Ephesus
1142, 4365

Titus
3641

Apostleship of Paul
202

Consecration
3508–3511

Immortality
2405, 2406

397

and willing rather to be absent from the body, and to be present with the Lord" (5:6–8).

Paul cautions the Corinthian Christians not to be "unequally yoked together with unbelievers" because believers and unbelievers have no communion or fellowship with each other (6:14; cf. Deut. 22:10). One frequently sees in Palestine a small donkey hitched to a plow with a large cow or ox, or a camel with a cow. It is evident that there could be little compatibility when a long-legged animal and one with short legs are yoked together. The spiritual analogy is clear.

Giving
2120, 4158

Paul acknowledges the benevolence of the believers in Macedonia and challenges the Corinthians to do likewise (8:1–22). In chapter 10 the apostle continues to discuss the matter of Christian giving, the use of spiritual weapons (10:4,5), and the spiritual discipline necessary in the Christian life (10:6–18).

In chapter 11 Paul affirms his apostleship and follows it with a review of his own sufferings (11:22–33). In the last two chapters Paul has visions of Paradise (12:1), discloses that he has a thorn in the flesh (12:7), and gives disciplinary warnings (13:1–4). He advises the Christians to examine themselves to see whether their conduct and attitude are consistent with the faith (13:5). In the final verses Paul expresses a heartfelt benediction of love for the Corinthians (13:11–14).

Paradise
2680
Discipline
497

21

The Shorter Epistles of Paul
(Galatians–Philemon)

I. GALATIANS

A. The Name

Epistle to the
Galatians
4270

The Book of Galatians derives its name from the people to whom it was addressed (Gal. 1:2). Galatia was a land-locked sub-division of Asia Minor in which the towns Paul visited were located. The city of Ankara, situated in the heart of the Galatian territory, is the modern capital of Turkey (Asia Minor).

B. Authorship and Date

There is little opposition to Pauline authorship for the Book of Galatians.[1] Its origin is confirmed by several considerations: the literary style, the doctrinal content, the historical background, and the analogies all point to Paul. Such ancient church writers as Clement of Rome, Polycarp, Justin Martyr, Irenaeus, and Tertullian affirm Pauline authorship. Both Marcion (A.D. 139) and the critical Tubingen scholars in Germany accept Paul as the author of Galatians.

The exact date of this book is not known. Scholars estimate that it was written between A.D. 55 and A.D. 60.

C. Background, Purpose, and Content

The question as to whether Paul evangelized the northern or the southern territory of Galatia has been a matter of some discussion. Since the epistle contains no reference to Paul's having been in the northern cities of Pessinus, Aneyra, and

399

Tavium, the area of travel must have been in the south where Pisidian Antioch, Iconium, Lystra, and Derbe are located. Paul visited these cities on all three of his missionary journeys.

Madeline Miller concludes that,

> the theory that Paul addressed the churches in the southern part of Galatia is supported by the following evidence: (1) Paul and Barnabas had visited the cities of Iconium, Lystra, Derbe and Pisidian Antioch, all in S. Galatia, and had founded churches there on the First Missionary Journey (Acts 13:4–14:28). (2) In these cities at this time there were Jews (Acts 13:14–51; 14:1; 16:1–3) who might have caused the situation reflected in the Epistle. (3) Familiar reference to Barnabas (Gal. 2:1,9,13) would have been pointless in a letter addressed to N. Galatia, where Barnabas was probably unknown.[2]

For a discussion of Paul's three missionary journeys in the Galatian territory see commentary on the Book of Acts, Ch. 19, see page 374ff.

In his letter to the Galatians, Paul discusses three major subjects: the authority of his apostleship, the false teaching of the Judaizers, and the doctrine of justification and sanctification by faith. A fourth division concerns the practical application of certain Christian principles.

The first two chapters of the letter deal chiefly with Paul's defense of his apostleship. Certain leaders in Galatia taught that before a Gentile could become a Christian he had to be circumcised and submit to ritualistic ordinances of Judaism, but Paul insisted that salvation was obtainable through faith alone (Gal. 2:16). To better promote their teachings, they sought to depreciate Paul's authority by raising questions concerning his apostleship (2:6–9). In answer to these complaints, Paul offered proof that the gospel he preached came by direct revelation from God (1:11,12). Paul also referred to his call (1:1,15); his call independent of the other apostles (1:15–24); his endorsement by the church (2:7–10), and his resistance to the teachings of the Judaizers, including his rebuke of Peter (2:5–14).

A second subject Paul discussed was the teachings of the Judaizers, i.e., salvation by works, the necessity of circumcision, and their effect upon the Galatians. In the introduction of his letter Paul stated the nature of the problem that prompted his discourse. After a brief greeting, he made a statement concerning the atonement, of which the Galatians had been partakers (1:4). He followed this affirmation almost immediately with words of reproof for the Galatians. Paul expressed surprise that they would "so soon" accept "another gospel: which is not another" gospel (1:6,7). Apparently the Galatians were too easily persuaded by the Jewish teachers who were insisting upon the observance of Mosaic law (3:1–22). Some Judaizers had gone so far as to reinstate the Jewish festivals and ceremonies as essential to Christian worship (4:8–11). Stating his argument in the form of a question, Paul shows the weakness of the position of the Galatians: "Does God give you his Spirit and work miracles among you because you observe the law, or because you believe what you heard?" (3:5, NIV), i.e., "or by the hearing of faith" (AV).

A prominent theme in the Book of Galatians is "justification by faith" without the works of the law, and in this regard the book is a companion to Romans and Hebrews. Each of these books includes the statement of faith made by the prophet Habakkuk (Hab. 2:4; cf. Rom. 1:17; Gal. 3:11; Heb. 10:38). In Galatians Paul clarified and defended his statement concerning faith, that justification is by faith alone (2:16); faith leads to a union with Christ and identification with the risen Christ (2:20,21); the justified are children of God by faith (3:26); the justified realize their sonship and liberty through faith (3:26–4:7).

Paul further supported his position of justification by faith by showing that Abraham and his seed were justified by faith (3:6–9). Paul pointed out that later the "law" was a means of bringing men to God. The messianic law did not prevent sin, but was to act as a schoolmaster, "a tutor" (NIV) "to bring us unto Christ, that we might be justified by faith . . . [and that all believers are] the children of God by faith in Christ Jesus" (3:24–26). Paul emphasized the unity of the faith when he wrote that "there is neither Jew nor Greek, there is neither bond nor free, there is neither male nor female: for ye are all one in Christ Jesus. And if ye be Christ's, then are ye Abraham's seed, and heirs according to the promise" (3:28,29).

George H. Findley writes that "The growth of the Christian consciousness has been traced from its germ in Abraham to its flower in the church of all nations. The Mosaic law formed a disciplinary interlude in the process, which has been all along a life of faith." [3]

Chapter 5 contains Paul's discussion of liberty through faith. The apostle explained that faith in Christ and the love of God frees the Christian from the "letter of the law—ordinances." Findley continues, "The ethical application is contained in the phrase of Romans 8:2, 'the law of the spirit of life in Christ Jesus.' (1) Love guards Christian liberty from license; it 'fulfills the whole law in a single word' (Gal. 5:13–15). (2) The Spirit, who imparts freedom, guides the free man's 'walk . . . Crucified with Christ' and 'living in the Spirit,' the Christian man keeps God's law without bondage under it (Gal. 5:16–26)." [4]

This formula of love was first expressed by Moses (Deut. 6:5,6; Lev. 19:18) and confirmed by Jesus and Paul (Matt. 22:36–40; Gal. 5:14).

Paul enumerated and amplified the consequences of the Spirit life in terms of "love, joy, peace, longsuffering, gentleness, goodness, faith" (Gal. 5:22). On the other hand, he identifies the works of the flesh with the conditions described in Romans 1:18–32 (cf. Gal. 5:19,20).

C. Fred Dickason notes that "Paul's purpose, then, is not to prove primarily that justification is by faith. His argument assumes this is true; and building upon the fact that justification has granted them perfect standing with God and full inheritance with Abraham, he seeks to establish that sanctification is in faith, apart from adherence to any part of Mosaic law (Gal. 2:19; 5:18). This is the contention of the whole letter as seen in the key exhortation (Gal. 5:1), the key question (3:3), and the significantly placed illustration of Peter's problem [discussed in] (2:11–21)." [5] Paul insists that "the Galatians must recognize that their salvation and early Christian experience were based on faith and not law." [6]

In the final chapter the apostle states that the duty of the believer toward the weak and depressed is to "bear . . . one another's burdens" (6:2). However, Paul makes a distinction between the burdens which can be shared [i.e., interest in the infirmities of others] (6:2) and the inner burdens which only the individual can bear (6:5).

Paul also presents an important rule in life, the law of input and return: "God is not mocked: for whatsoever a man soweth, that shall he also reap. For he that soweth to his flesh shall of the flesh reap corruption; but he that soweth to the Spirit shall of the Spirit reap life everlasting" (6:7,8).

In the final paragraph of chapter 6 Paul reveals that the objective of the Judaizers was their own self-glorification (6:12–16).

II. EPHESIANS

A. *The Name*

The Epistle to the Ephesians derives its name from the Ephesian church to whom it was addressed.

B. *Authorship and Date*

The Book of Ephesians has a traditional claim to Pauline authorship. Paul identified himself as the author of the book (1:1). The title was placed on the early manuscripts by the patristic fathers to preserve the integrity of the book. In addition, Paul claimed that he was both an apostle and a prisoner, a statement which is in agreement with Paul's life history (3:1). The literary style, terminology, and theology along with its historical references definitely indicate that the book is Pauline.[7] Church fathers, such as Clement of Rome, Ignatius, Polycarp, and Hippolytus, do not hesitate to credit Paul with the authorship. The internal and external evidence is so strong that there is no reasonable objection to Pauline authorship.[8]

The entire historical content suggests that Paul wrote the epistle while he was in prison, either in Caesarea or in Rome. The best judgment is that it was composed in Rome toward the end of Paul's imprisonment (A.D. 60–64). In the letter Paul tells the Ephesians that "Tychicus, a beloved brother and faithful minister in the Lord" was to be the messenger. The postscript states that it was written by him from Rome.

The Shorter
Epistles of
Paul

Caesarea
615, 4344

Rome
3095, 4408

C. Background, Purpose, and Content

Ephesus, the capital of the Roman Province in Asia Minor, was located on the west coast where the Cayster river enters the Aegean sea. The Great Temple of Diana, one of the Seven Wonders of the ancient world, made Ephesus the "Vatican City" of the religious world. This great temple has long been dismantled with parts of it on display in the renowned museums of the world, including the Louvre in Paris and the British Museum in London. Some of its massive pillars are standing in the St. Sophia Church in Istanbul, placed there by its leader Constantine. The site of this temple is now a swampy pit with only pieces of marble cherubs protruding from the ground. Historians say that Ephesus had a population of over 300,000; the 25,000-seat amphitheater supports this estimation.

Ephesus was a commercial and industrial center. Overland trade caravans delivered their cargoes to the port, a harbor for ships from all over the known world. Ephesus was the city in which the silversmiths manufactured shrines of the goddess Diana to be sent all over the heathen world. Diana was the mother goddess of the world; the name Diana is the Latinized form of the Greek name Artemis. She may be identified with the Phrygnan Cybele, the Cappadocean Ma, the Syrian Mylitta, the Phoenician Astarte, and the Assyrian-Babylonian Ishtar. Edgar J. Banks says,

Ephesus
1142, 4365
Diana
3940

False
Religions
2988–2996

403

She [Diana] lived in nature; she was everywhere, wherever there was life, the mother of all living things; all offerings of every possible nature were therefore acceptable to her, hence the vast wealth which poured into her Temple. Not only was she worshipped in her temple but in the minute shrines or "naoi" which were sometimes modeled after her temple. More frequently the shrines were exceedingly crude objects, either of silver, or stone or wood or clay. They were made at Ephesus by dependents of the temple, and carried by the pilgrims throughout the world.[9]

The economy of the area was directly linked to the idol industry. The opposition of the silversmiths to Paul's ministry was based on the decline of idol sales when people were converted to Christ. Banks gives this added insight:

> Though the shrines were sold as sacred dwelling places of the goddess, so that the pilgrims who carried them to their distant homes, or buried them in the graves with their dead, might be assured of her constant presence, their real purpose was to increase the temple revenues by their sale at a price which was many times their cost.[10]

The words "in Ephesus" do not occur in the Codex Sinaiticus and the Codex Vaticanus, which has led to speculation that the book was written to the churches in general and not specifically to the church in Ephesus. On the other hand some of the manuscripts such as "Aleph" and "B" include the heading "to Ephesians." The problem of accurately copying manuscripts by hand would make it easy to omit words or phrases. There is no strong reason for accepting the view that "in Ephesus" was not a part of the autograph when all the evidence is carefully evaluated. It is particularly significant that Paul mentions the designated church in almost all of his letters (1,2 Cor., Gal., Eph., Phil., Col., 1,2 Thess.). The evidence is strong that the book was for a particular church—most likely the one addressed—namely, the Ephesian.[11] A further reason for assuming that the book was sent to the Ephesians by Paul is his three-year ministry in Ephesus (Acts 20:31).

If Ephesus was a center for the "Mother Goddess," it was also a place where many people were exposed and converted to the gospel. The people were inclined toward religions; the very nature of heathendom engendered interest in all the gods.

Being religious, many people listened to Paul's preaching and were converted (Acts 19:18–20). In speaking of Ephesus, Luke states that "all they which dwell in Asia heard the word of the Lord Jesus, both Jews and Greeks" (Acts 19:10b).

Christ, the
Head of the
Church
735
Brotherly Love
2200–2202
Holiness
1596–1598

The general content of the Ephesian letter is similar to that of Colossians. Both letters were written about the same time and speak of Christ as the Head of the Church (Eph. 1:22; cf. Col. 1:18). In both epistles the people are warned against false teachers (Eph. 5:6; cf. Col. 2:8) and are encouraged to maintain an attitude of love and a state of holiness, both in heart and in conversation.

Paul reaches a high point of revelation when he shows that our Lord is the Head of the whole church and that all believers share a common seat with Christ (Eph. 2:6). Both groups are exhorted to live a life consistent with true holiness and the life and teachings of the Lord.

In the first three chapters of Ephesians, Paul tells the believers that they are in Christ; in the last three chapters the apostle tells them what to do because they are in Christ.[12] The book can be outlined with three words: sitting, walking, and standing. "By position, the believer is seated with Christ in the heavenlies (Eph. 2:6); his responsibility is to walk worthy of the calling wherewith he has been called (Eph. 4:1); and this walk is further seen as a warfare in which he is engaged against Satan and all his hosts and in which he is exhorted to stand against the wiles of the devil (Eph. 6:11)." [13]

Walk of Believers 3763–3765

Devil (Satan) 3148–3151

One of the purposes of the Ephesian book is to bring unity to the Jewish and Gentile Christians. It is a matter of record that enmity existed between Jew and Gentile. Hostility by the Jews toward the Christians reached its climax in the third quarter of the first century. In this book Paul pleads for a reconciliation and unification of the Jewish and Gentile Christians—not through compromise, but by fusing them together in the Body of Christ through divine love (4:3–6,11–13).

Unity Enjoined 3725

Body of Christ 726, 727

"The Church is 'in Christ'; it is His Body, and its members have 'put on' the new . . . life, which is 'Christ in them' (Eph. 2:11–22). Thus the corporate life of Christ is the Fulfiller of the purpose of God. Its ethical practice, down to details, is a working out of that purpose on the level of human experience." [14] Jew and Gentile alike are saved by the blood of Jesus Christ—the middle wall of partition is broken down (2:14), and the veil has been rent in twain, so all now come directly and personally to a common mercy seat. Paul describes this relationship: "For through him [Christ] we both have access by one Spirit unto the Father. Now therefore ye are no more strangers and foreigners, but fellowcitizens with the saints, and of the household of God; and are built upon the foundation of the apostles and prophets, Jesus Christ himself being the chief corner stone" (2:18–20).

Blood of Christ 679

Spiritual Foundation 3177–3179

The Book of Ephesians contains an exposition on predestination and election (1:3–12). Paul addresses his readers as the saints—the church, with whom he identifies himself by the use of the personal pronouns "we" and "us."

Predestination 2861

The predestination here discussed has a direct bearing on the saints—to those who are in Christ "chosen before the foundation of the world." It is the glorious church—the body of Christ—which is here predestined "to be holy and without blame" and to have "an inheritance" in Christ that the believer might "be holy and without blame before him in love" (1:4,11). As to election, God is "not willing that any should perish, but

Body of Christ 726
Election 1107
405

that all should come to repentance" (2 Peter 3:9). However, man has the power to reject God's will.

Some scholars raise the question whether the epistle refers to the visible or the invisible church. When the term church *(ekklesia)* is used in the Scripture it signifies those who are in Christ, the universal body of believers. The visible church consists of the members of local congregations, who should be true Christians. But this visible church is not to be confused with the modern ecumenical movement which sometimes emphasizes form along with liberal theology, without personal, "born again" experience. (See page 63ff. and page 125ff. for additional background information on the church.) The visible church also includes the counterfeit element of the church (see page 129ff., "the Counterfeit Covenant Community").

In the Book of Revelation the Ephesian church is listed as one of the seven churches of Asia Minor (Rev. 2:1–7). This church is commended for its patience and labors but warned of the danger of being self-sufficient and losing its "first love." (For additional information on this church, see page 470 on the Book of Revelation.) In Ephesians Paul gives a conclusive

Salvation by
Faith
1203

statement on salvation by faith as against works: "For by grace are ye saved through faith; and that not of yourselves: it is the gift of God: not of works, lest any man should boast" (2:8,9). "Salvation by works" would eliminate the need for the Savior's death on the cross.

Holiness
1596–1598

The Book of Ephesians is indeed a practical handbook for believers, setting forth facts on Christian maturity (4:13–32), holy living (5:1–15), Christian truths (5:16–23), sanctification (5:24–33), domestic duties (6:1–10), and the equipment Christians should use for warfare against spiritual wickedness (6:2–19). In his concluding statement Paul indicates he is "an ambassador in bonds" (prison) (6:20).

Christian
Warfare
358

III. PHILIPPIANS

A. The Name

Epistle to the
Philippians
4272
Philippi
2756, 4405

The Epistle to the Philippians derives its name from the church at Philippi (Phil. 1:1). The epistle was named after King Philip, the father of Alexander the Great. Julius Caesar planted a Roman colony in Philippi for retired Roman legionnaires. It became the chief city and capital of Northern Macedonia. The Greek word for Philippi means a "lover of horses."[15]

Journey Map
pp. 288–289

B. Authorship and Date

406

The letter to the Philippians was written by Paul after he founded the church on his second missionary journey. From

Ruins of a Byzantine church in Philippi

Ruins of another ancient church in Philippi

early times tradition has credited Paul with writing this book. He is recognized as the author by such church fathers as Ignatius, Clement of Rome, Polycarp, Irenaeus, Clement of Alexandria, Tertullian, and Marcion.[16] Authorship was never seriously opposed except by the liberal scholars. Ferdinand Christian Baur, professor at the Tubingen school in Germany, objected to Pauline authorship on unsubstantiated grounds. He said that the mention of bishops and deacons in the book was an anachronism, that the Clement referred to was one of a later date, that the letter misrepresented Paul's monetary standards, that the style was un-Pauline and that the reference to the incarnation was gnostic (Phil. 2:5–11).[17] Evaluation of these objections show them to be based purely on the premise of form criticism and not on biblical inspiration.

Bishops 755
Deacons 753

If the epistle was written toward the close of Paul's Roman imprisonment, it could be dated A.D. 60–64. If it was written from Ephesus, the date would be about A.D. 54.

C. Background, Purpose, and Content

The city of Philippi, a Roman colony, was located in the northern part of Macedonia, north of the port city of Neapolis. It was on the famous Roman road—the Via Ignatia, beginning at Dyrachion on the Adriatic Sea and terminating in Byzantium (modern Istanbul). Parts of the old Roman road are still visible by the side of the modern highway between Philippi and Neapolis (modern Kavalla). The archaeological excavations at Philippi are extensive. The work was begun by the French School of Athens in 1914. Philippi was a prosperous city with rich gold mines in the nearby mountains.

**Macedonia
2222**

**Arch. Philippi
4405**

In addition to being a Roman colony, Philippi was also a great religious and medical center. The shrine of Dionysus occupied a prominent position on nearby Mount Pangaeus.[18] As a Roman colony, it had few Jews—in fact not enough to have a formal synagogue. For the events leading to Paul's visit to Philippi refer to Acts 16.

**Synagogues
3521–3523**

When Paul and Silas came to Lystra they arranged to have Timothy assist them on their second missionary journey (Acts 16:1). While they were traveling in the Phrygian-Galatia area the Holy Spirit restrained Paul from conducting any meetings (Acts 16:6). The restriction was also exercised in Mysia and Bithynia. When Paul and Silas arrived in Troas they discovered the reason. They would have missed the vision of the "man of Macedonia" who gave the missionary call to the continent of Europe when he said, "Come over . . . and help us" (Acts 16:9).

**Journey Map
pp. 288–289**
Paul 2697
Silas 3288
Timothy 3628

408

Luke apparently was involved in what took place in Troas

because the pronouns "we" and "us" begin in Acts 16:9 and indicate that Luke joined the three men there. All four men, Paul, Silas, Luke, and Timothy sailed to Neapolis, the port city of Philippi. They continued overland, across the coastal range to Philippi where their first religious contact was on the Sabbath day with some women who were in a religious service. (For additional information on their visit to Philippi see page 406 on Acts.) Apparently Lydia, a seller of purple dye or cloth, was Paul's first convert (Acts 16:14,15).

The Shorter Epistles of Paul

When Paul healed a girl with "a spirit of divination," her owners became enraged and had Paul and Silas beaten and put into prison (Acts 16:16–24). During the night Paul and Silas prayed so fervently that God sent an earthquake, which shook the foundations and opened the prison doors (Acts 16:25,26). In the confusion, the jailer tried to commit suicide, but he was restrained by Paul; subsequently the jailer was converted (Acts 16:34). When the magistrates discovered that Paul and Silas were Roman citizens, they begged them to leave the city without delay, fearing that there would be repercussions from Rome for their illegal mistreatment of Roman citizens.

Divination
2226

Magistrates
2540–2544

Roman
Citizens
772

After a visit with Lydia and comforting the brethren, Paul, Silas, and Timothy departed for Thessalonica. Luke probably stayed in Philippi to oversee the church and perhaps also to practice medicine, as the pronouns "we" and "us" no longer appear in the text after the three departed (Acts 17:1ff.). Luke must have again joined Paul when he came through Philippi on his third missionary journey about six years later. At this point these plural pronouns are used again. The church in Philippi may have been founded on Paul's first visit there (Acts 16:12–40).

Lydia
2226

The Book of Philippians makes reference to Timothy's being with Paul. This statement is significant. It helps to tie the book in with the passage referring to Timothy in the Book of Acts (Phil. 1;1; cf. Acts 16:1). The book itself is a beautiful personal letter from Paul to the Philippians thanking them for the support they had lovingly given to him while he was in prison (Phil. 4:15–18).

It was Paul's policy, in order to avoid criticism, not to accept offerings for his own personal need. Paul supported himself with his tent-making trade (Acts 18:3). However, while in prison, he needed help from others.

Tent Making
262

The people in the church at Philippi were genuinely Christian. Perhaps it was the most devoted congregation among Paul's acquaintances. Their gifts were given in such a spirit of love that Paul could not refuse them.

Benevolence
2117, 2118

The immediate purpose for Paul writing the letter to the

Philippians was to acknowledge the arrival of Epaphroditus with their love offering. Soon after his arrival this messenger became seriously ill "nigh unto death" (Phil. 2:27), but God miraculously healed him. The situation gave Paul an opportunity to write a personal letter of gratitude to the church at Philippi, to be sent with Epaphroditus on his return. This letter also contained a warning against false teachers and dissension (Phil. 3).

D. Edmond Hiebert says:

> The letter was primarily inspired by friendship matters—Paul's outpouring of love for the church that always stood with him. He wrote to give them the anxiously awaited news about himself. . . . The epistle is distinctly a friendship letter. It is the spontaneous expression of Paul's strong esteem for the readers, wholly devoid of official stateliness. The tone is warmly personal and an undertone of deep joy runs through the whole. . . . Doctrinal formulations are at a minimum and where doctrinal points are touched they have a practical or polemical purpose.[19]

The Epistle to the Philippians expresses a remarkable example of tranquillity for a man who is in a Roman prison, momentarily waiting for a hearing before Nero and eventually his execution (Phil. 1:20–23; cf. Acts 28). Adam Clarke says:

> It is written in a very pleasing style; everywhere bearing evidence of that contented state of mind in which the apostle was, and of his great affection for the people. . . . [He] comforts them in their affliction for the Gospel, returns them thanks for their kindness to him, tells them of his state, and shows a great willingness to be a sacrifice for the faith he had preached to them: this is a Divine unction in this epistle which every serious reader will perceive.[20]

Paul expresses beautifully the spirit and meaning of Romans 8:28 when he says "that the things which happened unto me have fallen out rather unto the furtherance of the gospel. . . . And many of the brethren in the Lord, waxing confident by my bonds, are much more bold to speak the word without fear" (1:12,14; cf. 4:1–11). Paul's triumphant spirit in this time of crisis is remarkable. He gives them his formula for spiritual health (Phil. 4:8). Solomon once said, "As he [man] thinketh in his heart, so is he" (Prov. 23:7). Throughout the Scriptures the idea is developed that the quality of a man's thoughts affects his physical well being. (See Concordance in TCRB under "think" and "thinketh.")

Merrill C. Tenney gives an overview of this book:

> The theme of "the gospel" runs through Philippians like a current in the ocean. His relation with the church is "the fellowship in the gospel" (1:5). His preaching is "the confirmation of the gospel" (1:7). His career is the "progress of the gospel" (1:12). His conflicts are "the defense of the gospel" (1:17).

Ethical conduct is determined by the standards of the gospel (1:27), and the body of truth that Christians had is "the faith of the gospel" (1:27). The labors in which Paul and his associates are engaged are "the service of the gospel" (2:22), and he speaks of the women of Philippi "who labored with me in the gospel" (4:3) . . . In fact, so closely was his entire career bound with this subject that he called the beginning of his campaign in Macedonia and Achaia "the beginning of the gospel" (4:15). Paul used the term in several senses. It denoted his message about Christ, the content of the Christian faith, the sphere of Christian service, and the purpose of his whole career.[21]

The Shorter Epistles of Paul

Paul concluded his letter with exhortations such as these to maintain unity, to rejoice, to "think on . . . things" good, and with a salutation from "all the saints" to "every saint in Christ Jesus" (Phil. 4:2,4,8,22,21).

Exhortations
1182

IV. COLOSSIANS

Epistle to the Colossians
4273

A. *The Name*

The Epistle derives its name from the church to which it is addressed (Col. 1:2).

B. *Authorship and Date*

The Book of Colossians, one of the prison epistles, has been accorded Pauline authorship since the days of the church fathers. Paul identifies himself as the author (1:1). Evidence suggests that Paul wrote Colossians because about 25 percent of its content is the same as that in the Ephesian letter. The two churches, only a little over a hundred miles apart, apparently shared some of the same problems.

Colossae
4352

Ephesian Letter
4271

Some critics, including those at Tubingen,[22] object to Pauline authorship. They claim that the thought patterns do not conform to Romans, Corinthians, and Galatians. However, as each church had its own problems, the letters would be different. These critics also claim that the "Colossian heresy" (combining Judaistic teachings with gnostic elements) could not have developed in the first century so that the epistle must have been written in the second century by someone other than Paul. Evidence, however, points to Paul writing the letter shortly before his execution in Rome between A.D. 60 and 64.

Judaizers
1958

C. *Background, Purpose, and Content*

Colosse (or Colossae) is a city of Phrygia in the central part of Asia Minor, situated on the lower slopes of Mount Cadmus overlooking the Menderes river to the north. The city is near the great highway traversing the country from Ephesus via

Phrygia
2762

411

Istanbul to the Euphrates Valley. It is 13 miles east of Hierapolis (Holy City) and 10 miles from Laodicea.

Soon after the Epistle to the Colossians was written, an earthquake greatly damaged the city along with Laodicea (modern Danizli) and Hierapolis (modern Pamukkule). Chonos or Konos is the inhabited town near the Colossian ruins.[23] Evidence of earthquake damage remains in all these places, including broken marble columns and a ruined theater at Colosse; Laodicea is still mainly a huge mound where only the viaduct, an old basilica, and two amphitheaters are visible. In Hierapolis massive stones and pillars from the temples, baths, and the church lie strewn over a wide area. The great amphitheater is in relatively good condition. A deep fissure, called "plutonium," has erupted and still spews poisonous gas.

Special reference is made here to Laodicea and Hierapolis because they were on the same triangular circuit with Colosse, for whose churches Epaphras labored "fervently . . . in prayers" and for whom he had "great zeal" (Col. 4:12,13).

Theologians differ in opinion as to whether Paul founded the church, or even visited Colosse; nothing in Scripture is said on the subject. Logically and geographically there are several reasons for supporting the assumption that Paul visited Colosse and that he may even have founded the church.

1. Colosse was on the trade route between Mesopotamia and Ephesus. Paul traveled this route on his third missionary journey. Charles F. Pfeiffer and Howard F. Vos say, "The natural route for him [Paul] to have taken on that occasion was from Syria, through the Cilician Gates, then to Derbe, Lystra, Iconium, Antioch of Pisidia, Apamea, Colosse, Laodicea, and down the Menderes river to Ephesus." [24]

2. Paul spent three years in and around Ephesus. Colosse is only about 150 miles from Ephesus. Paul must have at least visited Colosse since he was so near.

3. Paul was in the Phrygian area twice. In this area where Colosse, Laodicea, and Hierapolis are located, he "went over all the country . . . , strengthening all the disciples" (Acts 18:23).

4. Paul's zeal and diligence were so great that all "Asia heard the word" (Acts 19:10).

5. Paul's close and intimate friend, Philemon, lived in Colosse. (See commentary on Philemon, page 431, for additional evidence that Paul was a visitor in Colosse.) It is likely that Paul visited him when he came through this area, especially since friendly Christian accommodations were not plentiful in this territory. Also, Philemon had a church in his house (Philem. 2). It is not probable that Paul would entrust to an assistant such an important matter as founding a church.

The New Testament

Laodicea 2050

Epaphras 1139

Journey Map pp. 290–291

Cilicia 763

Ephesus 1142, 4365

Philemon 4279

Calcium traces at the Hot Springs of Hierapolis (Col. 4:13)

Ruins of Grand Theatre at Hierapolis. Destruction caused by earthquakes (Col. 4:13)

The New
Testament
Tychicus
3715
Onesimus
2650

Among Paul's fellow-laborers at Colosse were Tychicus (Col. 4:18) and Onesimus (4:9). Apparently Aristarchus, Mark, Justus, Luke, and Demas were in prison with Paul or were assisting him in Rome (4:10,11,14). Later Paul wrote that "Demas hath forsaken me, having loved this present world" (2 Tim. 4:10). Archippus and Philemon seem to have been active workers in the Colossian church (Col. 4:17; Philem. 1).

A study of the Colossian letter suggests that Paul had something more than a second-hand knowledge of the situation in Colosse. Paul may have written the letter following a personal visit; the tone of the letter does not leave the impression that Paul was speaking to strangers (1:2,21–25). Its content suggests that he had more than indirect knowledge of the situation.

"The occasion of the epistle was . . . the information brought by Epaphras that the church in Colosse was subject to the assault of a body of Judaistic . . . [leaders] who where seeking to overthrow the faith of the Colossians and weaken their regard for St. Paul." This heresy is referred to in theological circles as "the Colossian heresy." [25] It was a peculiar, subtle heresy somewhat different from that in other areas (2:8–23). Gnosticism was indeed a present force in the time of the formation of the early Christian churches. Andrew K. Helmbold writes that Gnosticism "spread throughout the ancient Near East immediately before and after the time of Christ." [26] Conrad Henry Moehlman says that Adolph von Harnack "termed Christian Gnosticism, the 'acute Hellenization of Christianity'; Gnosticism is now regarded as a 'pre-Christian oriental mysticism.' " [27]

These false teachers were members of a system of metaphysical dualism which mediated through angelic beings for a redemption through knowledge or a "Gnosis." They believed that all religions were a manifestation of one hidden verity and that through knowledge men could find truth. It was not purely a "Gnosis" of the intellect—but rather an enlightment derived from a mystical experience through contact with angelic beings, along with an allegorical and mythical interpretation of many sacred writings. Through this strange exercise, spiritual enlightenment was supposedly to result in one's redemption from the world of sin and matter. [28]

This gnostic conception which regards matter as evil has no place in the Christian faith. The gnostic system was actually a syncretism (a mixture) of Greek, Oriental, Jewish, Anatolian, and Egyptian religions with heavy borrowings from Platonism and Stoicism (Col. 2:8,11,16,18). One must remember that in the early days of Christianity, when theological formulas had not yet been established, it would be easy for new believers out of heathendom to be deceived and confused, especially when these teachers taught their false doctrines as Christianity. Paul's refutation of this system is positive. He describes what Christ and the church is and does not deal negatively with the problem. Charles Harold Dodd presents a scholarly statement on how Paul refuted the "Colossian heresy":

> Paul presents and develops a new and more adequate statement of the position and dignity which Christian experience necessarily assigns to Christ . . . . The outcome of it is to set forth the person and work of Christ as having a cosmic significance. If Christ, known as Saviour, were but one among a host of unknowable Powers, the Christian would still be a stranger in the universe. If, however, what we find in Christ is the ultimate Meaning of the Universe, then the salvation he brings is absolute and final. This is the faith that Paul seeks to safeguard by identifying Christ with that divine Wisdom by which the world and all powers controlling it were brought into being, and through which at last, God will fulfill his power in it all . . . . Paul takes up the challenge of the "new thought," by placing his teachings about salvation in Christ upon a more philosophical basis. But in doing so he reasserts with remarkable force and clarity what had always been the core and center of his gospel. Christ died to reconcile men . . . to the will and purpose of God . . . . it is made plain . . . that this dying and rising again is an actual moral experience manifesting itself in character and conduct . . . . The Christian's way is above all, radically ethical, and the "emancipation" it brings is the one sure beginning of a free, progressive and positive morality for men individually and in society.[29]

Paul's approach is very practical: after explaining to the Colossians what he believed, he discussed Christian conduct (4:1–7). Instead of belittling the false teachings, he exalted Christ and the significance of his stature for the believers. As Savior, Jesus is to be their "all in all." Christ is "the head of the body, the church" (1:18,24). E. Earle Ellis says, "To establish the sole sufficiency of Jesus as Lord and Redeemer (in opposition to the gnostic substitution of redeeming disciplines and . . . mediating powers), Paul stresses both aspects [human and divine] of Christ's character. Important in this regard is the concept of the 'Body of Christ,' with which the Colossians undoubtedly were familiar (Col. 1:18–24); 2:17; 3:15)." [30]

Christian Conduct
808–812

Christ the Head
735

Body of Christ
726

V. 1 THESSALONIANS

A. *The Name*

First Epistle to the Thessalonians
4274

415

The First Epistle to the Christians at Thessalonica derives its name from the church to which it is addressed (1 Thess. 1:1). Tradition says that the city was named Thessalonica, after the daughter of Philip, the King of Macedonia, the father of Alexander the Great.[31]

B. Authorship and Date

The author of the First Thessalonian letter is Paul. He refers to himself by name twice (1:1; 2:18). This epistle is especially important because it is Paul's first letter and the earliest written Christian document dealing with the gospel message, earlier than any of the Four Gospels. The epistle was written from Corinth perhaps as early as A.D. 47, but no later than A.D. 53.[32] Pauline authorship is authenticated by the Muratorian Canon,* and such church fathers as Clement of Alexandria, Tertullian, and Polycarp.

C. Background, Purpose, and Content

Ancient records indicate that Thessalonica was founded in 315 B.C. by Cassander, King of Macedonia (354–287 B.C.). He challenged the sovereignty of Macedonia and captured Olympias, the mother of Alexander the Great, put her to death, and connected himself to the royal family by marrying Thessalonica, the half-sister of Alexander. In 306 B.C. he took the title of king; in 297 he was succeeded by his son Philip.[33]

After Thessalonica was made the capital, it grew to become the second largest city in that area; only Philippi, a hundred miles to the east, exceeded it. Because of its sheltered harbors, Thessalonica became a commercial and shipping center for the cargoes coming over the Great Highway, the Via Ignatis, from the Adriatic in the west to Byzantium in the east. Because of its position, Thessalonica had some of the same moral problems that characterized Corinth.

Paul founded the Christian church in Thessalonica on his second missionary journey. For a historical background of Paul's first visit, see Acts 17. After his arrival in Thessalonica from Philippi, Paul spent the following three Sabbath days reasoning with the Jews "out of the scriptures" to show that "Christ must needs have suffered, and risen again from the dead" and that Jesus was Christ (Acts 17:1–4). Some of the Jews responded favorably to the gospel appeal, but another segment of Jews rejected Paul's gospel message. With the assistance of a mob, they "set all the city on an uproar." When Jason, a Christian, befriended Paul and Silas, the Jews assaulted his house, hoping to take the missionaries. When the Jews failed to find Paul

Journey Map
pp. 288–289

Sabbath
3098–3101

Paul **2697**

Silas **3288**

---

* The Muratorian Canon was a list of the NT books, with the omission of the Books of James, Peter, and Hebrews, read in public worship in a church. It is evidently a translation from the Greek original and probably was used in the church in Rome about A.D. 200. It is named after an Italian scholar who found it in the Ambrosian Library at Milan. (Edgar G. Goodspeed in *Encyclopedia of Religion*, p. 511.)

Modern Thessalonica—city viewed from the wall

Another view of the modern city of Thessalonica

Jason **1847**
Timothy **3628**

Proselytes
2895, 2896

Gentile
Believers
4038

Vain
Philosophy
2759

Antioch
197

Paul's
Persecution
3482

and Silas, they "drew Jason and certain brethren" before the city officials, accusing them of treason. When Jason posted a bond, Paul and Silas were released. During the night the brethren sent Paul, Silas, and Timothy to Berea (Acts 17:5–10). The Jews in Berea were more open-minded, listened to Paul's message "and searched the scriptures" to determine whether his message was true (Acts 17:11). Adam Clarke says,

> Though the Jews, who were sojourners in this city, rejected the Gospel in general, yet a great multitude of the devout Greeks, i.e., such as were proselytes to Judaism, or the descendants of Jewish parents, born and naturalized in Greece, believed and associated with Paul and Silas, and not a few of the chief women of the city embraced the Christian faith. Acts XVII. 4.

> As the Jews found that, according to the doctrine of the Gospel, the Gentiles were called to enjoy the same privileges with themselves, without being obliged to submit to circumcision and other ordinances of the law, they persecuted that Gospel and those who proclaimed it: for, moved with indignation, they employed "certain lewd fellows of a baser sort"—the beasts of the people, "set the city on an uproar, assaulted the house of Jason," where the apostles lodged, "dragged him" and "certain of the brethren before the rulers" and charged them with seditious designs and treason against the Roman Emperor. The apostles escaped and got to Berea, where they began anew their important evangelical labors: thither the Jews of Thessalonica, pursuing them, raised a fresh tumult; so that the apostle, being counselled by the brethren, made his escape to Athens; Acts XVII 5–15.[34]

Timothy and Silas remained behind to direct the church (Acts 17:14,15) and then rejoined Paul in Athens. Before Paul left Corinth he sent Timothy back to Thessalonica (1 Thess. 3:1–3).

Upon arrival in Athens, Paul engaged the philosophers on the Areopagus (Mars Hill) in a theological discourse. He noted an altar with an inscription to "the unknown God" and told them that he represented the God who was unknown to them (Acts 17:23). From Athens Paul went to Corinth where Timothy and Silas met him (Acts 18:5). From Corinth Paul traveled to Antioch.

When Paul went to Macedonia on his third missionary journey, there is no reference to his journeying to Thessalonica. However, because of Paul's deep interest in the church, it is probable that he made at least a short visit.

In his epistle Paul commended the saints for the exemplary lives they were living under difficult circumstances (1 Thess. 1:1–10) and explained his early departure from Thessalonica because of Jewish hostility. He pointed out his motive for coming to them was to give and not to receive (2:1–14). Paul specifically charged the Jews with killing the Lord Jesus and their own prophets, and with preventing him from presenting the

Watch tower in wall around Thessalonica

Part of a Roman gate in downtown Thessalonica

gospel to the Gentiles (2:15,16; cf. Matt. 13:29–35). He told the church he would have returned to Thessalonica but that Satan prevented him (2:17–21).

Paul made it clear that tribulation was part of the cost of maintaining the Christian faith, that there would be continued suffering (3:4,5), and that the standard of the Christian life was one of holiness and love (4:4,5).

The good news from Thessalonica brought by Timothy made the apostle rejoice and he assured his readers that he would be praying for them day and night (3:6–13). In the fifth chapter Paul outlined the personal discipline which all Christians are to practice in their daily walk, using as an armor, faith, love, and hope for their spiritual warfare (5:8). In this letter Paul endeavored to clear up some of the misunderstandings about the Second Coming of Christ. These mistakes were twofold:

1. The saints neglected their daily work because they were expecting the Lord to return momentarily. Paul explained that no one knows the time or the season when the Lord will return, but he will return and when he does it will be suddenly. Paul amplified the importance of watching and being sober and encouraged them to comfort and edify each other (5:1–11).

2. Some had died between the time Paul had visited them and the writing of this letter. The present believers were concerned as to how the deceased saints could be a part of the glories of the kingdom which the returning Lord would establish.[35] Paul told the Thessalonians that when the Lord did return, he would bring with him the departed saints in their glorified bodies. Those who were still living would be "caught up together with them in the clouds, to meet the Lord in the air" (4:13–18; cf. 1 Cor. 15:12–58).

The second coming of Christ is mentioned in every chapter of both 1 and 2 Thessalonians (1 Thess. 1:10; 2:19; 3:13; 4:13–18; 5:1–7; 2 Thess. 1:7; 2:1–3; 3:5). Christianity has continued to prosper in Thessalonica since its inception there under Paul. It has about fifty active churches today, of which most are Greek Orthodox.[36]

VI. 2 THESSALONIANS

A. The Name

The Second Epistle to the Thessalonians derives its name from the church to which it is addressed (2 Thess. 1:1). (See Ch. 21, V for additional information on Thessalonians.)

B. Authorship and Date

420

Paul, the author of 2 Thessalonians, refers to himself by name (2 Thess. 1:1). The letter was probably written a few weeks or a few months after the first epistle. It may have been composed at Corinth as early as A.D. 47, but no later than A.D. 53.[37]

Pauline authorship is authenticated by the Muratorian Canon and such church fathers as Clement of Alexandria, Tertullian, and Polycarp.[38] (For Muratorian Canon see page 416.)

The Shorter
Epistles of
Paul

Corinth
840, 4353

C. Background, Purpose, and Content

The Second Epistle to the Thessalonians is a continuation and explanation of the First Epistle regarding Christ's second coming. The treatment on the Second Coming in this letter is somewhat different in emotional tone, but this in no way detracts from the book as a genuine Pauline Epistle. The subject of Christ's second coming was a relatively new concept for the early church members, and could be easily misunderstood. Up until now the church merely assumed Christ would return but had not had time to work out the mechanical details. Apparently Paul did not feel free to spend more time with the Thessalonians after his first visit; he had no choice but to discuss this misunderstanding in writing.

Christ's
Second
Coming
1344–1350

Paul informed the church at Thessalonica that the Day of the Lord was at hand, that the coming would be sudden, as a thief in the night (1 Thess. 5:2), and that the duty of the Christians was to expect it (1 Thess. 1:9,10). In the second epistle Paul added that the "Lord Jesus shall be revealed from heaven with his mighty angels, in flaming fire . . ." (2 Thess. 1:7,8).[39] Peter stated in 2 Peter 3:7,10 that the heavens and the earth are destined to be burned with "fire." [40]

Thessalonica
3610, 4420

In his second letter, Paul attempted to dispel the idea that the coming of the Lord was imminent. He indicated that before the Lord's return there would be a great apostasy, a falling away from the faith, and that the "man of sin [would] be revealed . . . ." It is generally assumed by the Christians that this "man of sin" is the Antichrist, who will claim that he is God (2 Thess. 2:3–6). Only when the Rapture takes place and the Holy Spirit is removed from the earth, will the Antichrist be revealed (2 Thess. 2:7–17).

Apostasy
1235

Antichrist
196

There has been controversy in the church from early times with regard to the Antichrist. The church fathers looked for a personal Antichrist in the fall of the Roman Empire. The Protestant Reformers looked upon the Pope as the Antichrist. Two thousand years have now passed and there are still differences of opinion. Many devout scholars believe that the Antichrist will be manifested before the Rapture. Others believe he will come after the Rapture. The Spirit of the Antichrist was already at work in Paul's day (2 Thess. 2:7). It is not wise to be dogmatic about the details regarding the Antichrist. We

*The New
Testament*

Prayer
2816–2839
Evil
Associations
276, 277, 290

can accept the fact of his coming, but we must let time determine the place and circumstance.[41]

In the last chapter, Paul deals with such practical things as
prayer (2 Thess. 3:1–4), patience (3:5), separation from evil associations (3:6–9), the evils of being idle busybodies (3:10,11),
and apostolic authority (3:12–15). He ends with a closing benediction (3:16–18). (See Commentary on First Thessalonians,
page 415ff.)

VII. 1 TIMOTHY

A. The Name

The First Epistle to Timothy derives its name from the person to whom it is addressed (1 Tim. 1:2; 2 Tim. 1:2). The name
Timothy appears eight times in the NT (2 Cor. 1:1; 1 Tim.
1:2,18; 6:20; 1 Tim. postscript; 2 Tim. 1:2; Philem. 1; Heb.
18:23). The name Timotheus appears nineteen times (Acts 16:1;
17:14,15; 18:5; 19:22; 20:4; Rom. 16:21; 1 Cor. 4:17; 16:10; 1
Cor. postscript; 2 Cor. 1:19; Phil. 1:1; 2:19; Col. 1:1; 1 Thess.
1:1; 3:2; 3:6; 2 Tim. 1:1; 2 Tim. postscript). *Timothy* is the Hebrew rendering of the greek *Timotheus*. It probably appears
in these two forms for the sake of both the Jews and the Greeks.

B. Authorship and Date

The superscription, "to Timothy," was placed at the head
of the First Book of Timothy by the patristic fathers at an
early date to preserve author identity. Such church fathers
as Clement I of Rome (A.D. 88–97), Polycarp (A.D. 69–156),

and Ignatius (A.D. 67–110) do not hesitate to credit Paul with
authorship. However, liberal critics have challenged this book,
as they have most NT books. They contend that the book was
written by "some unknown author who wrote in Paul's name
to promote certain doctrines." [42] Obviously this does violence
to the inspiration of the Bible and the integrity of the authors.
The three main critical objections are the following:

1. The Chronological Setting

Scholars of liberal persuasion insist that the pastoral letters,
of which 1 Timothy was the first, cannot be fitted into the
history of Paul's travels in Acts.

It is true that the content of the Pastoral Epistles cannot
be easily fitted into the record of Acts. Because the Scriptures
were not written as history but as religious documents, the
authors omit details (cf. John 21:25). Certain critics do not make

allowances for the two imprisonments and the events which occurred between. Jac J. Muller states that:

> The journeys and work of Paul mentioned in the Pastoral Epistles cannot be dated in the period covered by Acts but took place between his "first" and his "second" imprisonment to which II Timothy refers (1:8,16–17).
>
> That such was the case is borne out by the almost unanimous patristic testimony and tradition. Clemens Romanus, for instance, writing from Rome to Corinth (95 A.D.), asserts that Paul, after instructing the whole world (Roman Empire) in righteousness, "had gone to the extremity of the west (was that Spain? Compare with Romans 15:28) before martyrdom." The Canon of Muratori (170 A.D. alludes to "The Journey of Paul from Rome to Spain"; and Eusebius (beginning of the fourth century) clearly formulates the tradition as follows: "After defending himself successfully, it is currently reported that the Apostle again went forth to proclaim the Gospel, and afterward came to Rome a second time and was martyred by Nero." [43]

From this discussion it appears that the Pastoral Epistles belong to the period after A.D. 62 and before the apostle's martyrdom, probably A.D. 64–67.

2. The Ecclesiastical Complex

Some say that the Pastoral Epistles "reveal a more advanced church organization than we find in the rest of the New Testament and presumably too advanced for Paul's day . . . [based on the] mention of bishops or overseers, and elders or presbyters and deacons in what seems a firmly established church organization of a latter day." [44] However on his first missionary journey Paul ordained elders in every city (Acts 14:23); another reference indicates the presence of pastors and elders in every city (Acts 14:23); another reference indicates the presence of pastors and teachers at Ephesus (Eph. 4:11), while in Philippi bishops and deacons were active (Phil. 1:1). It was a very simple organization in which no sophisticated hierarchy was involved. [45]

Church Order 4012

In these early days the titles of church officials were not clearly defined. Some of them were interchangeable, e.g., bishop for presbyter (Titus 1:5–7).

Officers 753–755

3. The Linguistic Pecularities

Some critics claim that the language of these epistles to Timothy differs from that in Paul's other writings. But it seems plausible that Paul's style and vocabulary would change as he got older. Roy S. Nicholson quotes Ralph Earle as saying: "The difference in the vocabulary of Paul's earlier and later epistles is no greater 'than . . . [that] between some of the earlier and later works of Shakespeare or Milton.' Another [W. Graham Scroggie] has said that there are 'affinities between these and Paul's other letters . . . more than sufficient to override the objections which have been raised to their Pauline authorship.' " [46]

C. Background, Purpose, and Content

Timothy
3628

Lystra
2221, 4391
Derbe
2251, 4357
Eunice
1155

To identify Timothy, his history, and some characteristics, one may consult Acts 16 as well as almost any of the Pauline books. (See Section A under "Name" in this chapter.) Since the region of Lystra and Derbe was the home of Timothy, his mother Eunice, and his grandmother Lois, it seems certain that Timothy's family had contact with Paul on his first missionary journey. According to Scripture this family was a God-fearing one who looked forward to the coming of the Messiah (2 Tim. 1:5,6). Paul indicates that Timothy had been reared in the fear of God and in the Jewish religion as prophetically revealed in the OT Scriptures (2 Tim. 3:15–17).

When the apostle came to this area on his second journey, he found Timothy, a member of the church, so highly reputed and warmly recommended by the church in that place that Paul could take him to be his companion in his travels (Acts 16:1–3). Timothy had been taught in the Jewish faith, but, like gentile believers, he had not been circumcised. Since the head of the household had supreme authority, his Greek father had not permitted Timothy to undergo this Jewish initiation rite.

Circumcision
765–767

When Timothy joined Paul's missionary party, the apostle determined that Timothy should be circumcised, not for salvation "but because of the Jews who would neither have heard him nor the Apostle had this not been done. . . . The Gospel testimony they would not have received from Timothy, . . . a heathen; and they would have considered the Apostle in the same light. . . ." [47]

Timothy's call to be a minister seems to have been confirmed by several prophetic declarations relative to him (1 Tim. 1:18; 4:14). From this time on the name "Timothy" surfaces in most of Paul's epistles. Timothy became Paul's constant traveling companion and comforter. He refers to Timothy in these endearing words, "Unto Timothy, my own son" (1 Tim. 1:2); "To Timothy, my dearly beloved son" (2 Tim. 1:2); "Timotheus, who is my beloved son" (1 Cor. 4:17); and "Timotheus our brother" (Col. 1:1; 1 Thess. 3:2).

Ephesus
1142, 4365

424

Young Timothy had been appointed to oversee the work of the church in Ephesus (1 Tim. 1:3). Many problems developed in his parish, and Paul counseled his "beloved brother"

A perspective on the Marble Street of Ephesus and Celsus library, looking north

The ruins of a theatre at Laodicea

in prudent church decorum and practices. It is probable that Paul wrote his first letter to Timothy between his first and second imprisonments. It is not certain where Paul was when he wrote this book, but the postscript of 1 Timothy indicates Laodicea. To the very end Paul had hopes of visiting Timothy shortly (1 Tim. 3:14).

These Pastoral Epistles are important to the modern church because the problems discussed in them are still relevant to congregations today. The apostle expressed serious concern that the church should endure sound doctrines (1 Tim. 1:3,4,6–11; 4:7; 6:3–5). Adam Clarke says that four main errors were about to develop when Paul departed to Macedonia:

Good Doctrine
1029

1. Fables were invented by the Jewish doctors to recommend the observance of the law of Moses as necessary to salvation.
2. Uncertain genealogies, by which individuals endeavored to trace their descent from Abraham, in the persuasion that they would be saved, merely because they had Abraham for their father.
3. Intricate questions and strifes about some words in the law; perverse disputings of men of corrupt minds, who reckoned that which produced most gain to be the best kind of godliness.
4. Oppositions of knowledge, falsely so named.[48]

Fables
1200

Strife
3731–3734

Paul had a premonition that after he left Timothy in charge at Ephesus, serious problems would arise in the church. Paul said, "I know this, that after my departing shall grievous wolves enter in among you, not sparing the flock. Also of your own selves shall men arise, speaking perverse things, to draw away disciples after them" (Acts 20:29,30). There is also a personal note of tenderness, as a father writing his son, for to Paul Timothy was his spiritual son. Paul reinforces his plea for diligence by referring to his former experience as a blasphemer, but expresses thanks to Jesus Christ for the change, enabling him to be faithful and to enter the ministry (1 Tim. 1:12,13).

Enemies of the Church
3480–3484

In the second chapter he exhorts Timothy to fervent prayer (2:1) and again asserts his apostleship (1 Tim. 2:7). The irregularities of heathen women prompted the apostle to give some guidelines concerning modesty (2:9ff.). He dealt at length with the qualifications and requirements for bishops or "presbyters" (3:1–7). What he is saying about bishops applies equally to the membership at large. These same standards apply equally to deacons and elders (3:8ff.).

Prayer
2816–2841

Paul cautions the church to be consistent and to set a good example in daily living, pointing out the danger of hypocrisy (4:1–5). The faithful minister must be "nourished up in the words of faith and of good doctrine" so that he can distinguish between sound and unsound teachings (4:6–11). Paul reminds Timothy that even though he is young, he must not permit his youth to bring reproach upon the church, and exhorts him

Christlikeness
382

to "flee . . . youthful lusts" (2 Tim. 2:22) and to develop the gifts given him (1 Tim. 4:13,14).

The apostle indicated that poor widows are to be cared for by their immediate relatives (1 Tim. 5:3,4,8,16). He advised the younger widows to marry and bear children (5:14). Paul included advice on bishops and deacons; he then gave instruction for the elders to "rule well" and discreetly (5:17-20).

Widows
3873

In the final chapter Paul set forth rules for the servants who were an accepted part of most households (6:1,2). Paul again warned Timothy against false teachers (6:3-8) and about the peril of riches, pointing out that "the love of money is the root of all evil" (6:9,10; cf. 6:17-19); ministers were encouraged to "follow after righteousness, godliness, faith, love, patience, meekness" and to keep themselves unspotted from the world (6:11-14). The epistle concludes with a personal exhortation to Timothy for stewardship.

Servants
603, 604

Earthly Riches
2805-2809

Righteousness
3077-3085

VIII. 2 TIMOTHY

A. The Name

The Second Epistle to Timothy derives its name from the person to whom the epistle is addressed (2 Tim. 1:2). The name Timothy is the Hebrew for the Greek Timotheus. These two forms appear a total of 27 times in the NT. For a complete listing of these references see page 422.

Second Epistle to Timothy
4277
Timothy
3628

B. Authorship and Date

Paul is also the author of 2 Timothy which he wrote from Rome shortly before he was martyred. The epistle was his last known letter, written between A.D. 64-67, composed just a few months after 1 Timothy.

The objection of liberal scholars to 2 Timothy is the same as for 1 Timothy. For a study of these objections see page 422.

C. Background, Purpose, and Content

Paul must have written the second letter to Timothy soon after he was imprisoned the second time. The city had just been burned by Nero so that, presumably, Nero could realize his plans of building a new "eternal city" from the finest marble in the land.

Nero
614

Of the persecution described in 2 Timothy and 1 Peter Henry H. Halley writes:

427

this was "the persecution that brought Paul to his martyrdom, and according to some tradition, Peter also." He (Nero) knew that the

Christians did not burn Rome, but someone had to be made the scapegoat for the Emperor's crime. Here was a new and despised sect of people, mostly from humble walks of life, without prestige or influence, many of them slaves. Nero accused them of burning Rome and ordered their punishment. In and around Rome multitudes of Christians were arrested and put to death in the most cruel ways. They were crucified or tied in skins of animals and thrown into the arena to be worried to death by dogs for the entertainment of the people . . . they were thrown to the wild beasts or tied to stakes in Nero's garden.[49]

The bodies of the Christians were saturated with pitch and ignited to serve as torches to light Nero's gardens while he rode around naked in his chariot to indulge himself and gloat "over the dying agonies of his victims." [50]

During this difficult period Paul was probably apprehended in one of three places: Troas (2 Tim. 4:13), Corinth, or Miletus (2 Tim. 4:20) and brought back to Rome.[51] The charge for which Paul was arrested is not known. Some scholars think that Paul, as the leader of the Christians, may have been accused of instigating the burning of Rome.[52] Phygellus and Hermogenes (2 Tim. 1:15) as well as Demas (2 Tim. 4:10) had forsaken him. Paul had given his life for a cause that was being assailed by both persecution and apostasy. But in the face of all that darkness Paul expressed no regret or doubt. He was still confident that his cause would eventually triumph.

Persecution
1586, 1587,
3840, 3950
Martyrs
3487–3488
Martyrdom
3487

In the center of Rome is the ancient Mamertine prison with its two cells, one on top of the other, cut out of solid rock. The floor of the top compartment has in it a man-sized hole through which prisoners were lowered into the dungeon below. Tradition says that both Peter and Paul were imprisoned here. Today it is a tourist attraction. Not far away is the Colosseum where 45,000 pleasure-mad spectators once gathered to view the horrible torture and death which were inflicted upon innocent human beings for the sole pleasure of satisfying the spectators' blood-thirsty demands. Many Christians met their death here by gladiators or wild beasts. But today its galleries are empty, slowly decaying in the dust. Gone are the cries of the vanquished and the shouts of the crowds. The power of imperial Rome and its legions are only a faint memory. Towering over this ruin is a large cross symbolizing Christ's death and sacrifice for sin and the cause for which Paul and many others died. Today the church girdles the globe. Throughout the nations of the world, the gospel has penetrated, either by personal contact or through electronic devices. Believers who cannot read or write use tape recorders to give the Christian message.

Witnessing
3603–3605

According to the *Information Please Almanac,* the Christians in the world number 983,620,900. This is almost double the number of adherents to any other world religion. The Moslems hold second place and the Hindus third.[53] Some printing presses of the world are working overtime to provide Bibles. In some places the supply is not adequate to meet the demand. These developments certainly confirm Paul's belief that the cause of Christ would ultimately triumph.

Second Timothy indicates that one of Paul's sterling qualities was gratitude (1:1–4). In his old age he remembered his original contact with Timothy and Timothy's family in the Lystra community (1:5). Even as Paul came to the end of his life he encouraged Timothy to follow his steps, to be faithful in his ministry, and not to be ashamed of his old friend now in prison (1:8). Paul reminded Timothy that Jesus Christ gives sufficient grace which was provided before the world began (1:9,10).

Paul recalled how Onesiphorus befriended him in Rome, although some of Paul's friends had deserted him (1:15–18). He outlined for his beloved friend the works of a good soldier of the cross: to be strong to witness and teach, to endure hardships, and to receive from God understanding in all things (2:1–7). He told Timothy to "remember that Jesus Christ of the seed of David was raised from the dead" and that this fact was the basis for enduring all things for the sake of those who would yet be saved (2:8–14). Paul encouraged Timothy to study the Word, to avoid "profane and vain babblings" (arguments on religion) which only lead to more ungodliness (2:15–21,23–26). He advised Timothy to flee "youthful lusts" and to be actively involved in God's "righteousness, faith, charity, peace . . ." (2:22). Paul gave Timothy additional information on the apostasy which he described in his Thessalonian letters (3:1–9; cf. 2:3–17).

Timothy was to be comforted in his sufferings for Christ by reviewing Paul's own experiences. He recited for the young pastor his own longsufferings, persecutions, and afflictions (3:10–17). In the final chapter the apostle charged Timothy to "preach the word" and to be consistent and firm at all times as he reproved, rebuked, and exhorted the people in sound doctrine (4:1,2). Timothy was also alerted to the time when the people would not endure sound doctrine but would follow their own lusts (4:3–5). One wonders whether the modern trend to homosexual permissiveness in the churches is not one of the signs Paul was speaking about.

Paul had his house in order, he was ready for the executioner. He had no regrets because he had "fought a good fight" and had "kept the faith" (4:7). A crown in heaven was awaiting him. In these last moments Paul desired the company of his "faithful friend" and asked him to bring the coat he had left at Troas. He needed it in his cold, damp cell. Only Luke was with him to comfort him. Paul again urged his friends, Timothy

Prisons
2143

Onesiphorus
2651
False Friends
1330

Spiritual Fruit
1337

Lust
667

Preach
2087–2089

False Doctrine
1028

Troas
3965, 4422
429

and Mark, to come to him (4:6–13,21). All the others had either deserted him or had gone on mission assignments (4:10–12).

IX. Titus

A. The Name

The Epistle of Paul to Titus derives its name from the person to whom the letter is addressed (Titus 1:4). The name "Titus" appears several times in the NT (2 Cor. 2:13; 7:6,13,14; 8:6, 16,23; 12:18; Gal. 2:1,3; 2 Tim. 4:10; Titus 1:4; Titus in postscript).

B. Authorship and Date

The traditional view credits Paul with being the author of the Book of Titus, in which he identifies himself (1:1). The superscription also recognizes Paul as the author. As in 1 and 2 Timothy, ancient church fathers refer to Paul as the author (see commentary on 1 Timothy). The objections to Pauline authorship for Titus as well as the other two Pastoral Epistles, 1 and 2 Timothy, are given in the commentary on 1 Timothy. The letter was probably written about A.D. 63–67 between Paul's two imprisonments.

C. Background, Purpose, and Content

Titus was a frequent companion of Paul, as evidenced by the many references to him in the Pauline writings, but he is not mentioned in the Book of Acts, as were so many of Paul's other companions.[54] Since Titus, a Greek, was apparently converted directly from heathenism, he was not compelled to be circumcised (Gal. 2:3–5). Paul called Titus "Mine own son after the common faith" (Titus 1:4).

Titus was highly and deservedly esteemed by Paul (2 Cor. 2:13; 7:6,7,13,15; 8:16,23; 12:18).[55] When Paul, on Crete for only a short time, was unable to stay, he appointed Titus to supervise the affairs of the church on the island (Titus 1:5). Paul sailed to Judea about A.D. 63, taking Timothy with him. After a few months in Jerusalem Paul proceeded to Antioch, where he set out on his third missionary journey.

It is uncertain where Paul was when he wrote his letter to Titus. Some suggest Nicopolis, where Paul had planned to spend the winter, but others suggest that he wrote the epistle

in Corinth.[56] The postscript gives Nicopolis as the place. In the letter Paul expressed the hope that Titus could meet him

in Nicopolis (3:12). Whether Titus was able to accede to Paul's request is not known.

The book indicates that Paul gave Titus some general instructions concerning pastoral work. Apparently Titus had the responsibility of general oversight of the churches, including ordaining church officials and drawing up rules for general church conduct. Paul states that monogamy is the Christian standard for marriage (Titus 1:6) and that a bishop must be exemplary in all areas of life (1:7,8). False teachers seem to have been as prevalent here as in Ephesus, where Timothy labored. Paul commanded Titus to rebuke the false prophets "sharply" (1:10–16). Paul had advice for "the aged," the "young men," and the "servants," [57] all of whom were to be dedicated, temperate, chaste, and discreet. Titus is to set a "pattern of good work: in doctrine shewing uncorruptness, gravity, sincerity, sound speech, that cannot be condemned" (2:1–8).

The Shorter Epistles of Paul

Bishops
755

Virtues
564–573,
also **3874–3877**

Believers in Christ were to obey magistrates, to speak evil of no man, to be gentle (3:1,2). Paul reminded Titus that "we ourselves also were sometimes foolish, disobedient, deceived, serving divers lusts and pleasures, living in malice and envy, hateful, and hating one another" (3:3). This is a dark picture of their lives before they were committed to Christ. It is evident they were in a position to understand and empathize with those still without salvation.

Magistrates
2540–2544

Sensuality
667

Paul reviewed for Titus the change that has come to them after they accepted by faith "the kindness and love of God our Saviour" (3:4–8). He warned Titus against involvement with "foolish questions, and genealogies, and contentions, and strivings about the law" (3:9). If a man became a heretic, he was to be rejected after he refused the first and second admonition (3:10,11). Paul promised to send some evangelists to Titus in the persons of Artemas and Tychicus. Paul made reference to Zenas the lawyer and Apollos. Nothing is known about Zenas, but Apollos is well known among the missionaries under Paul (Acts 18:24; 1 Cor. 1:12; 3:5,6; 4:6). Apparently Paul was anxious for Titus to help these evangelists with their expenses (3:13).

Foolish
Questions
2933

Tychicus
3715

X. PHILEMON

A. *The Name*

The Epistle of Paul to Philemon derives its name from the person to whom the book is addressed (Philem. 1:1).

Epistle to
Philemon
4279

B. *Authorship and Date*

Pauline authorship is self-evident. The name Paul as author is referred to three times in this one-chapter book (Philem. 1,9,19). Robert G. Gromacki says, "He [Paul] identified himself

Paul
2697

431

twice as 'a prisoner of Jesus Christ' (1,9) and as 'the aged' (9); both of these appellatives would fit into Paul's life history at this time. Its similarity to Colossians (Philem. 1–2,23–24; cf. Col. 4:10–17) argues for a simultaneous writing from the same place by the same author." [58] Church fathers such as Tertullian, Origen, and Eusebius all attributed authorship of this book to Paul.[59] This epistle is judged to have been written between Paul's first and second imprisonment, somewhere between A.D. 63 and 67.

C. Background, Purpose, and Content

It is possible that Philemon was one of Paul's converts at Ephesus. He was probably a man of means as well as a man of hospitality. "Tradition makes Philemon the bishop of Colosse (*Apos. Const.,* vii,46) and the Greek Martyrology (Menae) . . . tells us that he, together with his wife and son and Onesimus were martyred by stoning before Androcles, the governor, in the days of Nero." [60]

In the address, it appears that Philemon was an active church member and that a Christian congregation met in his home in Colosse (v. 2). Scholars have assumed that Apphia was Philemon's wife and Archippus was his son (v. 2). The Colossian letter indicates that Archippus held an important office of some kind in Colosse (4:17), probably that of a presbyter or an evangelist. Paul recognizes him as a "fellow-soldier" of the faith (v. 2).

Paul expressed great spiritual affection for Philemon (vv. 2–9). Apparently, Onesimus, Philemon's personal slave, had appropriated some of his master's possessions and made his way to Rome to befriend Paul, who was in prison. After the slave Onesimus arrived in Rome, he was converted (v. 10). Then Paul wrote Philemon that he was sending Onesimus home to make things right, and he was now a brother in the Lord and no longer "just a slave."

A proper interpretation of the Book of Philemon might be as follows: A bond of friendship existed between Paul and Philemon, as described in the introductory verses (1–8). From the comments concerning the Colossians one gathers there are several reasons for assuming that Paul did visit Colosse. It is possible that Paul was a regular visitor in the home of Philemon and that while in his home, Paul befriended Onesimus, the slave who was probably treated in the customary manner and who apparently was hardly worth his room and board (v. 11). Paul may have made a special effort to show Christian love to Onesimus. At any rate, some motivation caused Onesimus to brave the dangers of traveling from Colosse to faraway Rome to be with his friend. The hazards were great. Often a runaway slave, when apprehended, was placed in the galley of a ship or was subjected to some other harsh employment. *The Shorter Epistles of Paul*

Onesimus was successful in evading the dangers enroute and arrived in Rome, where he sought out Paul. While there, he was converted (vv. 10,11). He was then a new creature in Christ and even his motivation for service changed. Paul appealed to Philemon to receive Onesimus back as a brother in the faith, as he would receive Paul himself should he come (v. 1).

There is evidence to suggest that Philemon was once a slave himself and that Paul bought his freedom. Paul reminded Philemon, "how thou owest unto me even thine own self besides" (v. 19). Could it be that Paul had bought Philemon's freedom and that he had established a tent-making partnership with his friend in Colosse? Paul asked Philemon to charge Onesimus' debts to his own account (vv. 18,19). Possibly Paul was saying: "When you figure our profits at the end of the year." The text could justify this interpretation without its doing theological violence.

Freedom
2134, 2135
Charitable
659

It is apparent that Paul was making plans to spend some time with Philemon soon (v. 22). In his closing remarks Paul sent greetings from his fellowprisoner, Epaphras, and his fellowlaborers Marcus, Aristarchus, Demas, and Lucas (vv. 23,24).

Modern-day Jews gathered at the Wailing Wall in Jerusalem

433

Special Epistles to Jewish Believers

I. HEBREWS

A. *The Name*

Epistle to the
Hebrews
4280

Timothy
3628

The Book of Hebrews derives its name from the traditional understanding that the book was written to the Hebrew Christians. The patristic postscript states: "Written to the Hebrews from Italy by Timothy." The name "Paul" was included in the superscription because of the judgment common among the early church fathers that the apostle wrote the book. However, there is no internal evidence to support this position.

B. *Authorship and Date*

The Book of Hebrews is devoid of any specific reference to authorship. Thomas Rees explains,

> For the purpose of tracing the history and interpreting the meaning of the book . . . the absence of a title or of any definite historical data, is [a] disadvantage. We are left to infer its historical context from a few fragments of uncertain tradition, and from such general references to historical conditions as the document itself contains. Where no date, name or well-known event is fixed, it becomes impossible to decide, among many possibilities, what known historical conditions, if any, are presupposed.[1]

The AV and the ERV retain the title: "The Epistle of Paul the Apostle to the Hebrews." Probably it was appended because of the conclusion that Paul was the best qualified to write the book.

434

Stephen S. Smalley says, "All of the existing manuscript copies of this Epistle include the title 'Pros hebraios' (to the Hebrews), which clearly belongs to a very early tradition, even if it is not original, since it is contained in some of the oldest manuscripts." [2] It is difficult to discover a historical clue in Hebrews because no biblical writers are mentioned by name, although the book contains frequent OT quotations.

Robert G. Gromacki observes that,

> Scholars have suggested several names as possibilities for the authorship of this book. Among them are Apollos, Barnabas, Luke, Priscilla, Silas, and of course, Paul. Generally the debate centers around Paul: Did he or did he not write the book? . . . Even the early church had problems over the authenticity of the book. The Eastern Church [Constantinople] accepted it as an original Pauline, canonical book, whereas the Western Church [Rome] denied its Pauline authorship [for some time] and excluded it from the canon, namely because of the uncertain authorship. [3]

All of the persons mentioned above have some qualifications for writing the Book of Hebrews. An analysis of these names provides the following conclusions:

1. Luke was a brilliant scholar with unusual research skill, but he was a Gentile and might not have possessed the intimate knowledge of Judaism which the book reflects.

Luke 2266

2. Silas was a constant companion of Paul, but there is no literary tradition to associate authorship with him.

Silas 3288

3. Barnabas was a Jew and a Levite with extensive Judaistic insights. He was an intimate friend and companion of Paul who was equally at home with the Jews and Gentiles. However, there is no literary history for Barnabas.

Barnabas 342

4. Apollos was well versed in the Scriptures and successful in his witness among the Jews. He was closely associated with Paul and was active in the ministry until the end of Paul's life (Titus 3:13). Nevertheless, tradition for making him the author is lacking.

Apollos 200, 201

5. Philip, the Evangelist, was appointed to supervise social services for the Greek widows. He preached the Savior, won many converts (Acts 8:4–8), and ministered to the Ethiopian eunuch (Acts 8:26–39). Philip entertained Paul on his last visit to Caesarea (Acts 21:8), but all of these activities do not constitute proof of his authorship of Hebrews.

Philip 2754

6. Prisca (Priscilla), the wife of Aquila, was highly esteemed by Paul (Acts 18:18,26; Rom. 16:3; 2 Tim. 4:19); there is no indication that she ever wrote a book.

Priscilla 208

7. Paul's credentials for writing Hebrews seem to have the greatest weight; however, many scholars question his authorship on the basis of style difference, content, and terminology. There is some validity in these objections, and the contenders

Paul 2697

435

do have unquestioned qualifications, but there is also some evidence for Pauline authorship.

Some of the reasons for favoring Pauline authorship include the following: The author was a prisoner; Paul was in prison many times (Heb. 10:34; cf. 2 Cor. 11:23). Numerous points of agreement in doctrine are recognizable between Hebrews and other acknowledged writings of Paul. Paul affirmed the preeminence of Christ (Heb. 1:1–3; cf. Col. 1:14–19) and the humiliation of Christ (Heb. 2:9–18; cf. Phil. 2:5–11).

The apostle referred to the wanderings of Israel as a warning for the Christians (Heb. 3:7–19; cf. 1 Cor. 10:1–11), and commented on the temporary character of the first covenant (Heb. 8:1–13; cf. 2 Cor. 3:6–18). He dwelt on the principle of faith as expressed in Habakkuk's prophecy, "The just shall live by his faith" (Hab. 2:4), and quoted it in Hebrews 10:38 (cf. Rom. 1:17 and Gal. 3:11). The writer of Hebrews was a close associate of Timothy; so the author could have been Paul (Heb. 13:23).

Paul made reference to himself as an apostle to the Gentiles (Rom. 11:13), but he usually ministered first in the local synagogue upon arrival in a new preaching place (Acts 13:14; 17:1,2,10,17; 18:4,8). Paul often visited the church in Jerusalem, showing deep concern for the Jews (Rom. 9:1–5; 10:1–4). His training under Gamaliel in Jerusalem was ample preparation for dealing with Jewish sacrificial and ritualistic complexities. Paul certainly demonstrated his knowledge of the OT and related it to NT theology in his sermon in the synagogue at Antioch (Acts 13:14–42).[4]

A noted scholar says of Hebrews: "The closing section bears a great resemblance to Pauline concerns. He requested prayer in his behalf (Heb. 13:18; cf. Eph. 6:18–20), desired a good conscience (Heb. 13:18; cf. Acts 24:16; 2 Tim. 1:3), identified the Father as the God of Peace (Heb. 13:20; cf. Rom. 15:33; Phil. 4:9; 1 Thess. 5:23), and pronounced a benediction of grace (Heb. 13:25; cf. Philem. 25)."[5] "One of the early fathers, Origen, is quoted as saying, 'Only God alone knows who wrote the Epistle.'"[6] This is probably the logical assumption for all scholars to make until new evidence is discovered.

Hebrews must have been written before the destruction of Jerusalem under Titus in A.D. 70. The content strongly suggests it was composed during severe Christian persecution, probably while Nero was the Emperor (A.D. 54–68).[7] (For information on the persecution under Nero see comments on 2 Timothy.)

C. Background, Purpose, and Content

436   The frequent references to the ritual and ordinances within Judaism suggest that the Book of Hebrews was addressed to

Jewish Christians. There is constant appeal to the OT, to illustrate that Christianity was the fulfillment of that which was spoken of by the OT prophets (Heb. 1:1,2; cf. Luke 24:25–27,44; Acts 3:21; Rom. 4:18). In the book there is no reference to gentile members being in the church. The author emphasizes that "their danger lay in a return, not so much to the law as to the ritual. These allusions best suit the Hebrew Christians of Palestine, and Jewish believers of the East." [8]

Special Epistles to Jewish Believers

Gentile Believers **4038**

The epistle seems to be addressed especially to the believers who were suffering persecution (Heb. 10:32) and to the faltering Christians who needed to make a complete commitment for inner strength to overcome temptation and to avoid apostasy. The writer speaks to the Christians as brothers in Christ (Heb. 3:1) and indicates that he had visited with them (Heb. 13:19). The people addressed in the epistle seem to have been believers for some time (Heb. 13:7), but apparently they were still "babes in Christ." When they should have been teaching, they needed to be taught. When they should have been taking the meat (of the word) they were still taking milk (Heb. 5:12–14). Their continued "spiritual infancy" along with the persecution made the danger of apostasy very great. There was the temptation to revert to the ritual of Judaism. To make the situation even more dangerous there were the false teachers with their syncretized heresies. One scholar says,

Persecution **3480**

The Word as Food **416**

Apostasy **1235**

> The writer of the Epistle to the Hebrews sees the danger of apostasy seriously threatening the community in question, and this causes him to direct his readers' minds to the finality of the Christian revelation: the cruciality of God's work in Christ (10:19), and the supremacy of the new priesthood and covenant (8:6), and of the new, once for all (ephapax) sacrifice (9:12). All the time he uses theological exposition as the basis for moral exhortation: he is concerned that the readers should "consider Him"—the Person, . . . (3:1), and the work (12:3) of the Lord Jesus Christ; and on this basis "advance toward maturity." [9]

Of the many subjects in the Book of Hebrews, at least five should have special attention:

1. God's Prior Revelation (1:1ff.)

The writer clearly shows that Christianity was not a new religion but a continuation of a religious system which had its beginning in Genesis. The God who spoke to the OT fathers and prophets had now spoken to the NT apostles through his Son Jesus Christ. The OT and NT are a unity—they both speak of a blood-bought salvation by the death of God's Son. In the OT the blood of bulls and goats prefigured the blood of the Lamb of God who did in fact take away the sins of the world.

Revelation **2495, 2498**

437

2. The Danger of Backsliding

Wallace Alcorn describes the danger of apostasy thus:

He [the writer] warns his readers of the inescapable consequences of neglecting salvation (2:1–3), about missing God's rest (3:7–19), about disqualification from the rest (4:1–11), of the impossibility of return from conscious apostasy (6:4–8), and of there being no provision for deliberate sin (10:26–31). Closely related to these are his exhortations: be alert, lest you drift away (2:1–4); be careful, lest you disbelieve (3:7–4:13); go on, lest you walk away (10:19–39); build up, lest you fall apart (12:12–29).[10]

3. Jesus Christ, the Great High Priest

In the OT the levitical high priest represented the people before God. Each year, on the Day of Atonement, he ceremonially received a sin offering from the people and transferred their sins to the scapegoat (see page 70). The high priest, under the law, was a type who foreshadowed the object. The writer of Hebrews presents Jesus Christ as the Great High Priest who now represents the saints and makes intercession for them before God (Heb. 7:25; cf. Isa. 53:12; Rom. 8:27,34).

4. The Unbelief of Israel and Apostasy

The writer of Hebrews uses Israel's apostasy as an object lesson to warn the Jewish Christians of the danger that their hearts might also cause them to miss their spiritual Canaan rest (4:11). The Israelites had the gospel preached to them, and they had a deliverance from the bondage of Egypt (cf. 1 Cor. 1:1–4), but they were in danger of missing the Promised Land. As the Israelites missed this rest, so the Jewish believers were now in danger of missing their spiritual Canaan—the experience of sanctification which comes from a complete commitment. One scholar describes this sanctification relationship in Hebrews thus:

Sanctification is described in terms highly peculiar to this epistle, and centers around a concept of perfection . . . the goal of God's rest, which is variously spoken of as arrival at one's destination, as a completion of one's own task, and as peace with God. The rest can be defined as perfect and eternal rest with God.[11]

5. Melchizedek

This ancient priest of Salem (Jerusalem) stands out in a shroud of mystery, both in the OT and NT. Greatly misunderstood by many people, he is mentioned twice in the OT, by the Hebrew form *Melchizedek* (Gen. 14:18; Ps. 110:4); he is referred to nine times in the NT by the Greek form *Melchisedec* and only in the Book of Hebrews (Heb. 5:6,10; 6:20; 7:1,10, 11,15,17,21).

There has been much theological speculation concerning Melchisedec. Some have suggested that he was an appearance of the preincarnate Son of God; others say that he was in some way identified with Christ. Any interpretation of this man should be governed strictly by what the Scriptures disclose; anything beyond that is pure speculation. In Genesis the writer clearly states that Melchizedek was the "king of Salem" and that "he was the priest of the most high God" (Gen. 14:18; cf. Heb. 7:2–4). He obviously was a high official in the religious hierarchy of that day because "Abraham recognized him as a priest of the True God and publicly testified to sharing the same or kindred faith by paying tithes to him who was representative of God Most High." [12]

The reference in the Psalms follows a Messianic prophecy: "Thou art a priest for ever after the order of Melchizedek" (Ps. 110:4). In the Hebrew reference it is stated he was "without father, without mother, without descent, having neither beginning of days, nor end of life; but made like unto the Son of God; abideth a priest continually" (Heb. 7:3).[13]

John Wesley gives a very reasonable explanation of these passages:

"Without father, without mother, without pedigree"—Recorded without any account of his descent from any ancestor or the priestly order. "Having neither beginning of days nor of life" . . . In all these respects, "Made like the Son of God"—who is really "without father," as to His human nature; "without mother," as to His divine; and in this also, "without pedigree"—Neither descended from any ancestors or the priestly order. "Remaineth a priest continually"— Nothing is recorded of the death or successor of Melchisedec. But Christ alone does really remain without death and without successor.[14]

"Keil and Delitzsch nicely summarize the ideas regarding the true identity of Melchizedek: 'We can see in him nothing more than one, perhaps the last, of the witnesses and confessors of the early revelation of God. Coming out into the light of history and the dark night of heathenism.' Herbert C. Leupold adds that 'we are compelled to regard this venerable king-priest as a worshipper and public adherent of the true religion of Yahweh as handed down from the sounder tradition of the times of the Flood.' " [15]

Christ's New Covenant is presented in chapter 8 (see pages 93–142 in this book). The First Covenant centered around the tabernacle and the Ten Commandments. They had served their purpose. The laws were now written on the tables of the heart (Heb. 8:10). The First Covenant was temporal; the Second Covenant replaced the First and was Eternal. The First Covenant was sealed with the blood of animals; Christ's Covenant was sealed with his own Blood (Heb. 10:29). It was a better covenant with better promises based on the immutability of God's Word (Heb. 6:18).[16]

**Tabernacle
3528**

An exposition on Christ and the True Tabernacle, made without hands, is presented in chapter 9. "The High Priest entered once a year; Christ entered once for all (Heb. 9:7,12). The High Priest obtained annual redemption; Christ obtained Eternal Redemption (Heb. 9:12). . . . The High Priest sacrifices cleansed the flesh; Christ's sacrifice cleanses the conscience (Heb. 9:13,14). The New Covenant is called 'The New Testament.' A Testament is a Will, a bequeathment to heirs, effective only after the death of the maker. The New Covenant is the Will which Christ made for His Heirs, which could not become effective till by His Death, He had atoned for their sins." [17]

**New Covenant
881**

**Sacrifice of
Christ
3366**

In chapter 10 the writer explains that there is no further need for sacrifice and that the death of Christ is sufficient to take care of every sin; God now forgives all those who confess their sins and put their trust in Christ. The author includes another warning against apostasy.

Hebrews 11 deals in a singular way with the OT heroes of faith. The writer defined faith as "the substance of things hoped for, the evidence of things not seen" (11:1). This is not too different from the understanding of the atomic structure of matter. Many of the visible things can be made invisible when the respective elements are separated from the substance, e.g., sodium and chloride are gases but when combined become salt; hydrogen and oxygen are invisible gases but in combination make water.

**Christ the
Mediator
3364**

**Sin Bearer
3362**

An important word in Hebrews is the term *better:* "the bringing in of a better hope" (7:19); "Jesus made a surety of a better testament" (7:22); "He is the mediator of a better covenant" (8:6); cf. "he is the mediator of the new testament" (9:15). Hebrews also includes the idea of "better" in the sense of "more enduring": (1) A better priest: "thou art a priest for ever" (7:17; cf. Ps. 110:4); "But this man, because he continueth ever, hath an unchangeable priesthood" (7:24); "he is able . . . to save them to the uttermost . . . seeing he ever liveth to make intercession for them" (7:25); "who [Jesus] needeth not daily . . . to offer up sacrifices . . . for this he did once, when he offered up himself" [better sacrifice] (7:27; cf. 10:11,12,14). (2) A better offering: "He offered up himself" (7:27); Christ . . . offered himself without spot" (9:14); "put away sin by the sacrifice of himself" (9:26).

440

The entire OT religion has its structure on the foundation

of faith. The great notables of faith mentioned in the eleventh chapter of Hebrews were children of God through faith. The book of Hebrews is a counterpart to the Book of Romans: both books major on justification by faith (Heb. 4:2,3; 9:19–33; 10:38; chapter 11; cf. Rom 1:17; 3:21,22,26–28; 5:1,2; 10:4–11).

II. JAMES

A. *The Name*

The name James is the English form of the Hebrew *Jacob* and is derived from the Greek word *Iacabos*. The Book of James is the first and the oldest of the seven General Epistles addressed to the Christian church at large.

Four men in the NT are named James:

1. James, the son of Zebedee, an apostle and the brother of the apostle John (Matt. 4:21; 10:2).
2. James, the son of Alphaeus, was also one of the apostles and styled "the less," probably because he was small in stature (Matt. 10:3; Mark 3:18).
3. James, the Lord's brother, was called "the just" (Matt. 13:55; Mark 6:3).
4. James, the brother of the apostle Judas (Luke 6:16; Acts 1:13).

B. *Authorship and Date*

It is commonly assumed that James, the brother of the Lord, was the author of the Book of James. Alexander Ross says that "the writer was a Jew, evidenced by the fact that he speaks of Abraham as 'our father' (James 2:21), he applies to a Christian place of worship the word 'synagogue' (James 2:2), he uses the Jewish word 'Gehenna' (James 3:6), and a specifically Jewish name for God in James 5:4." [18] Analysis shows that James, the brother of our Lord, is the only one to be seriously considered as the author. "The disciple of Jesus, James, the son of Alphaeus, seems to have been an obscure person; and James, the son of Zebedee, died early as a martyr in the year 44 (Acts 12)." [19] Estimates of the date for the epistle range from A.D. 45 to A.D. 60. It was probably written a few years before James' death.

C. *Background, Purpose, and Content*

When Jesus went to Nazareth, his work was hampered because of the people's unbelief. James and his brothers did not believe that Jesus was the Messiah; they probably contributed to his difficulties (John 7:5).

Those who take the position for Mary's perpetual virginity would say that James and his brothers were children of Joseph by a former marriage, which would make them step-brothers or half-brothers of Jesus.[20] However, this position is based merely on conjecture and finds no support in Scripture.

The "brothers" may not have attended the crucifixion because they may have been embarrassed by Jesus' claims to Messiahship. The fact that he was crucified as a "malefactor" may have further confirmed their doubts. Apparently, not until after Jesus was crucified and resurrected did James become a believer. Scripture states that the brothers may have been the first to receive the news of Jesus' resurrection (John 20:17). Later, Jesus appeared to James in person (1 Cor. 15:7). After Saul of Tarsus (Paul) was converted, he went to Jerusalem and stayed fifteen days with Peter; while there he met "James the Lord's brother" (Gal. 1:19). Following his conversion James became a zealous worker in the Christian movement. Shortly after Peter's miraculous deliverance from prison, James became the acknowledged leader of the Jerusalem church (Acts 15:13; 21:18). He was greatly esteemed by the other apostles; Paul regarded James, along with Cephas (Peter—see John 1:42) and John, as the pillars of the church (Gal. 2:9). The three of them are frequently mentioned, and they worked together as a team.

At the Council of Jerusalem, James took the lead in drafting the letter which was sent to the Gentiles (Acts 15:13–29).[21] James was very zealous for the cause of Christ. "It is said of him [that] he spent so much time on his knees in prayer that they became hard and calloused like a camel's knees." [22]

James gave his life as a martyr as did most of the other apostles. Josephus and Hegesippus, both historians in the Christian era, affirm James' martyrdom. In reporting on their statements, Henry H. Halley writes,

> Shortly after Jerusalem was destroyed by the Roman army [under Titus] in 70 A.D. . . . when Jews were, in large numbers, embracing Christianity, Ananus, the High Priest, and the scribes and Pharisees, in about the year 62 A.D. or 66 A.D. assembled the Sanhedrin, and commanded James, "the brother of Jesus who was called Christ," to proclaim from one of the galleries of the Temple that Jesus Was Not the Messiah. But instead, James cried out that Jesus was the Son of God and Judge of the World.
>   Then his enraged enemies hurled him to the ground, and stoned him, till a charitable fuller ended his sufferings with a club, while he was on his knees praying "Father, forgive them, they know not what they do." [23]

James was martyred in about A.D. 62–63.

The Book of James is addressed "to the twelve tribes which are scattered abroad" (James 1:1). This is understood to mean

---

Margin notes:

Brethren of Christ
544

Saul of Tarsus
2697

Background of Prisons
2143

Martyrs
3488

442

that it was addressed to the Christian churches at large (1:2). Similar to the OT book of Proverbs, the Book of James contains many short, pithy epigrams especially suited to the growing Christian church. Both the Books of Proverbs and James, as well as part of the Sermon on the Mount, are considered to be Wisdom Literature. The content suggests that it was written during a time of persecution, affliction, and suffering such as prevailed during Nero's reign of terror (1:3,4), probably A.D. 37–68.

Special Epistles to Jewish Believers

Proverbs
2904

In times of uncertainty James urged the Christians to "ask of God" for direction (1:5) in genuine faith (1:6–8). He recognized that Christian freedom can be dangerous for those who have been bound by a "letter of the law" legal code. The writer points out that the test of faith for the Christian comes in everyday life. He insisted that faith without works is dead (1:22–25; 2:26). James gave a simple definition for sin in 4:17. He also included directions concerning divine healing in 5:13–16.

Faith
1201–1213

Healing
1538, 1543, 4039

"James reminds us of the need for genuine Christian standards . . . in every area of life. It is . . . so easy for the world . . . to squeeze us into its own mold, to convince us that there are no absolutes, no black and white, only gray. The early Christians needed the letter—and so do we." [24]

It is apparent that there are many parallel statements between the message of James and the Sermon on the Mount. James may possibly have heard the sermon, and, if not, he probably talked to eyewitnesses (James 2:14–26, cf. Matt. 7:21–23; James 1:21, cf. Matt. 7:24–27; James 3:11,12, cf. Matt. 7:16–20; James 4:11,12, cf. Matt. 7:1; James 5:1–6, cf. Matt. 6:19–24; James 5:12, cf. Matt. 5:34–37).[25]

Sermon on the Mount
3237

As an overview, Alexander Ross gives this analysis of the book:

(1) Greeting (1:1); (2) trials from without (1:2–12), (3) trials from within (1:13–18), (4) hearing and doing (1:19–27), (5) respect of persons (2:1–13), (6) relation of faith and works (2:14), (7) sins of the tongue (3:1–12), (8) the false and the true wisdom (3:13–18), (9) mischief caused by strife and evil speaking (4:1–12), (10) the uncertainty and brevity of human life, leading us to humble dependence on the will of God (4:13–17), (11) the terrible doom that the rich oppressors of the church are to meet (5:1–6), (12) final exhortation to the Church to stand firm and to be forbearing in view of the coming of the Lord (5:7–12), (13) various activities of the Church— prayer, praise, visitation of the sick, confession of sins, and the restoration of backsliders (5:13–20).[26]

23

The Epistles of Peter

I. 1 PETER

A. The Name

The First Epistle of Peter derived its name from the initial verse, in which the writer identified himself as the author: "Peter, an apostle of Jesus Christ, to the strangers scattered throughout Pontus, Galatia, Cappadocia, Asia, and Bithynia."

B. Authorship and Date

From early times the First Epistle of Peter was acknowledged to have been the work of the apostle whose name it bears. By A.D. 200 the epistle had wide circulation in the Roman Empire and was considered to contain authoritative gospel information from an eyewitness.

Peter was diligent in recording and preserving the gospel account, including activities of the founding of the early church. His name appears 146 times in the four Gospels and 57 times in the Book of Acts.

Historical evidence for Peter's authorship is plentiful. Polycarp (A.D. 69–156), who was a disciple of John, made references to 1 Peter. Iraneus (A.D. 67–110) quoted from Peter's book frequently; Clement of Alexandria (A.D. 150–216) cited the apostle many times. The internal evidence for Peter's authorship is equally conclusive.

The basic teachings of the Gospels are contained in 1 Peter. Alan W. Stibbs observes that "The Gospel according to Mark was probably a writing of the typical content of Peter's preach-

444

ing; so 1 Peter may provide a Summary of Peter's customary teaching and exhortation." [1]

The writings also show familiarity with others of the epistles, especially James, Romans, and Ephesians, and the content of 1 Peter stands in close relationship with the Apostles' discourses in Acts.[2] The evidence for the authorship of Peter is overwhelming, although his close confidant and scribe, Silvanus, a Greek, may have added the excellent Greek style to Peter's original ideas, as suggested by the phrase, "By Silvanus" (1 Peter 5:12). From the evidence one might assume that this book was written shortly before or after Paul's martyrdom, probably about A.D. 63–64.

Martyrdom
3487

C. Background, Purpose, and Content

Simon Peter was a native of Bethsaida, a small fishing village on the northeast shore of Lake Galilee (John 1:44). He was in the fishing business with his father, Jonas, and his brother, Andrew (Matt. 16:17; John 1:40). Later he moved to Capernaum, where local archaeologists claim they have unearthed Peter's house, just south of the old synagogue, resting on the foundations where Jesus is said to have preached.

Bethsaida
411, 4340

Caparnaum
641, 4349

Simon Peter's brother, Andrew, accepted Jesus as the Messiah first and then introduced him to his brother (John 1:41–45). Jesus at once conferred upon Simon Peter the surname Cephas, meaning "rock" (John 1:42).

Andrew
140

It is uncertain whether Peter had a part in founding the church in Rome, or if he ever visited Rome. Some scholars believe that the church began in a synagogue congregation. Upon their return home, those who had been in Jerusalem at the time of Pentecost may have given witness to the effect of the Spirit upon the believers who had been assembled in the upper room when "they were all filled with the Holy Ghost" (Acts 2:4). In Acts the account states that "strangers of Rome, Jews and Proselytes" were present in Jerusalem (Acts 2:10b).

Day of
Pentecost
2722

Proselytes
2895, 2896

According to tradition, near the end of his life, Peter did go to Rome, either because of a summons from Nero or to aid the Christians suffering during the persecution under Nero. Tradition also indicates that Peter was imprisoned and finally executed at Rome in the Mamertine prison which bears his name. "The Quo Vadis Tradition [sic] has it that Peter . . . was crucified head downward, feeling unworthy to be crucified as the Lord was. This is only a tradition, and we do not know how much of historical fact it may contain." [3]

Persecution
3480–3484

See pages 428–429 on 2 Timothy for a statement about the Mamertine prison where Peter and Paul are alleged to have been confined and executed.

445

Call to Service
1790, 2082

John W. Davis states, "In common with the earliest followers of Jesus, Peter received three separate calls from his Master: first, to become His disciple (John 1:40 seq.) . . . secondly, to become His constant companion (Matt 4:19; Mark 1:17; Luke 5:10) and thirdly, to be His Apostle (Matt 10:2; Mark 3:14, 16; Luke 6:13–14)." [4]

Peter's activity in the early church is so varied that additional biographical information should be sought from other sources (including the endnotes for this chapter).

Church
726–762

The First Epistle of Peter is the second in a series of seven General Epistles written to comfort and strengthen the church at large, especially in Asia Minor.

First Peter is addressed to the "strangers scattered throughout Pontus, Galatia, Cappadocia, Asia, and Bithynia" (1:1), all provinces in Lesser Asia Minor. In speaking about the "strangers scattered," Stephen W. Payne explains, "The Greek may be rendered, 'to the foreign residents of the dispersion'; these were not strangers to Peter but temporary residents in the Provinces of Asia Minor." [5]

Persecution
3480, 3484
Nero
614

It had been Roman policy not to interfere with the Christian movement as long as it remained within Judaism, which enjoyed a *Religio Licita,* a religious group allowed by Rome. However, when Christians began to be conspicuous and developed their own identity, causing controversy with established Judaism, Rome began to take measures to restrict them. The persecution of the Christians under Nero, his burning of Rome, and Paul's martyrdom seemed to occur at about the time when Rome began to change from tolerance to hostility. Henry H. Halley says,

> Nero's persecution of Christians (A.D. 64–67) was very severe in and around Rome, but not generally over the Empire. However, the example of the Emperor in Rome encouraged the enemies of Christians everywhere to take advantage of the slightest pretext to persecute. . . . The Church was about 35 years old. It had suffered persecutions in various localities at the hands of local authorities. But now Imperial Rome, which hitherto had been indifferent . . . had accused the Church of a terrible crime and was undertaking to punish it. . . . The Epistle was born in the atmosphere of suffering shortly before Peter's own martyrdom, while exhorting Christians not to think it strange that they had to suffer, reminding them that Christ did His work by suffering. [6]

Babylon
329–331, 4334
446

The geographic origin of this epistle is uncertain. The reference to "the church that is at Babylon, elected together with you, saluteth you" (5:13) raises as many problems as it solves because three views of Babylon have developed. First, Babylon is a small town in Egypt, too small to be considered. Second, Babylon in Mesopotamia; but since it was almost deserted in NT times, it seems unlikely that Peter would have traveled to it. There is no indication in literature that Peter traveled to Babylon on the Euphrates. The third view is that Babylon is a symbolic name for wickednesses and abominations of every kind as indicated in Revelation 17:5; cf. Revelation 16:19; 18:2. Rome fitted well into this description of wickedness, and it is probable that the name Babylon was symbolically used to mean Rome. Some scholars have taken the position that intercommunications in the churches frequently employed symbolic language as a kind of code to prevent Roman authorities from identifying places where Christians were active.

Benjamin W. Robinson points out that "Babylon is mentioned repeatedly in Revelation (16:17–21; 17:5; 18:1–3) with reference to Rome. In all probability that is the meaning here. The reference then is to the Church at Rome. . . ." [7]

In 1 Peter, during those days of persecution and martyrdom, Peter kept the hope of the resurrection and an inheritance "reserved in heaven" ever before the people. He exhorted them to insure their salvation by resisting temptation to the end. Some, however, had taken the easy way out by renouncing the faith (John 6:66; 1 Tim. 1:20; 2 Peter 2:15; 3:17; 1 John 2:9). Peter encouraged the Christians by reminding them that the prophets in the OT suffered for their belief (1 Peter 1:10–12; cf. Dan. 3:19; James 5:10; Heb. 11:32–37). Throughout the book runs the idea that Christians were to prepare for impending persecution and martyrdom (1 Peter 1:13–14). In the midst of hardships, believers were to be holy in all manner of conversation and conduct (1:15–25).

Martyrdom
3487

Suffer
3474–3488

Peter uses a different figure in which he designates the believers as "lively stones" to be built into a "spiritual house." Christ is the "Chief Cornerstone," although he as the "living stone" is rejected by men but chosen of God [NIV]. Peter exhorted the believers to lay "aside all malice and guile and [deceit, NIV]" and "as babes in Christ desire the . . . milk of the Word, that ye may grow thereby" (1 Peter 2:1,2, NIV)

Holiness
1596–1598

In another comparison, the Christians are likened to a "royal priesthood" giving forth praises unto God (1 Peter 2:1–10). The believers are to "abstain from fleshly lusts" and to submit themselves "to every ordinance of man for the Lord's sake." They are to "love the brotherhood," to "fear God" and to "honor the king" or established authority (2:11–25). Peter instructs the wives to be modest, to be meek and of a quiet spirit (3:1–6). The husbands are to honor their wives as "the weaker vessel" (3:7). They are to sanctify the Lord in their hearts, to "love as brethren," and to be ready to give a reason for their faith at any time (3:8–15). Peter reminded them of an established principle: It is better to suffer for "well doing, than for evil doing" (3:15–22). They are to cease from sin and

Christians
382, 725

Brotherly Love
2200–2202

Fidelity
3871

447

The New
Testament

Good Works
3902–3905
Respect for
Aged
3974

follow their great Example—Christ (4:8–11). Suffering is to be taken for granted, and they are to rejoice because they are "partakers of Christ's sufferings" (4:12–19).

In the final chapter the elders are "to feed the flock" (5:1–4); the younger are to obey the elder and to be humble. All are to "be subject one to another," placing their care upon the Lord (5:5–9). In the last few verses Peter pronounces his words of blessing and benediction upon those who are persecuted (5:10,11). In closing, Peter mentions the letter is to be delivered by Silvanus (Silas).

II. 2 Peter

A. The Name

The Second Epistle of Peter derived its name from the first verse in the book, where Peter identified himself as the writer: "Simon Peter, a servant and an apostle of Jesus Christ . . ." (1:1).

B. Authorship and Date

The external evidence for assigning authorship of 2 Peter to the apostle is very scant, as compared to 1 Peter and some other NT books. Even such fathers of the third century as Origen and Eusebius expressed reservations for assigning authorship to Peter. Origen had doubts as to Peter being the author and Eusebius places the epistle among the disputed books. On the other hand, such fourth-century writers as Jerome, Athanasius, Augustine, and Ambrose were confident that Peter was the author. The famous church councils at Laodicea (A.D. 372) and Carthage (A.D. 392) affirmed Petrine authorship.[8] Merrill C. Tenney affirms the internal evidence favoring Peter as author:

> The writer claims at the outset to be "Simon Peter, a servant and an apostle of Jesus Christ" (1:1). He announces that the time has come for him to "put off this my tabernacle, even as our Lord Jesus Christ showed me" (1:14), a statement which accords with Jesus' prediction that Peter would die a violent death (John 21:18). He claims to have been present at the Transfiguration when . . . the divine voice said, "This is my beloved Son, in whom I am well pleased" (1:16–17); cf. Mark 9:5–7; Matt. 17:4–5) . . . . He identifies himself as one of the apostles of the Lord (3:2).[9]

Internal evidence for Peter's authorship of both epistles that bear his name is presented in 2 Peter 3:1: "This second epistle, beloved, I . . . write unto you. . . ." This verse also indicates that the group addressed in both books is the same.

448

Those critics who have questioned the authenticity of 2 Peter do so on the grounds that the writer's familiarity with the Pauline epistles, which, together with his reference to the authority of Paul's writings (2 Peter 3:15,16), is ". . . an indication that the NT canon had been well established by the time II Peter was written."[10]

According to this reasoning, the epistle would be too late to have been written by the apostle Peter. An answer to this objection may be that Peter did reach Rome and had fellowship with Paul, perhaps in prison. This visit could have provided opportunities to learn about Paul's epistles. As already discussed in the chapter on 1 Peter, tradition is strong for Peter's visit to Rome. Also mentioned, the old Mamertine prison bears the name of Peter and Paul. For information on Peter in Rome, see commentary on 1 Peter.

In regard to liberal criticism on 2 Peter, Henry H. Halley comments:

> Some modern critics regard it as a pseudonymous work of the late second century, written by some unknown person who assumed Peter's name, a hundred years after Peter's death. To the average mind this would be just plain, common forgery, an offense against civil and moral law and ordinary decency. The critics, however, over and over, aver that there is nothing at all unethical in this counterfeiting another's name.[11]

Although there had been hesitancy in admitting the Second Book of Peter into the NT Canon, the epistle was approved and became a part of the Scriptures. Those scholars who accept the superintendency of the Holy Spirit in matters of inspiration and canonization have no difficulty in accepting Peter's authorship for 2 Peter. It is thought that the epistle was written shortly before Peter was martyred in Rome—between A.D. 64 and 68.

C. Background, Purpose, and Content

The Second Epistle of Peter is addressed "to them that have obtained like precious faith with us through the righteousness of God and our Saviour Jesus Christ" (1:1). These people could have been any Christian group, but the internal evidence suggests that Peter is also speaking to the "strangers scattered" as mentioned in his first epistle (1:1).

In Peter's first letter, the danger to the believers was the ruthless persecution which the Roman Emperor Nero unleashed against them. At the time of the writing of 2 Peter, several years had passed and the political situation possibly had changed or the threatened persecution may not have

Divine
Inspiration
417, 1774

Strangers
3396, 3466

Persecution
3480

449

Greed
2133
Authority of
the Church
749
False
Teachers
2101

Morality-
Immorality
2403–2416

Gentile
Believers
4038
Synagogues
3521–3523

reached the provinces. Another danger jeopardizing the Christians was the perversion of the moral life of the church (2 Peter 2:2); greed (2:3); the despising of authority (2:10); boastfulness (2:18, and false liberty (2:19). In this letter Peter endeavored to avert the dangers of the teachings of the deceptive leaders.[12]

Shirley Jackson Case writes:

> The danger that loomed on the author's horizon was a threatened lowering of Christianity's [sic] Moral standards. As the new religion spread to the Gentile lands it had drawn into its membership persons whose ethical ideas were quite different from those cherished by its earlier adherents. . . . The moral life of the Greeks and Romans seemed frightfully low. As a rule Gentile converts lacked the discipline in virtuous living that had been furnished the Jews through attendance upon the services of the synagogue and study of the OT. . . . Even after the adoption of Christianity they were slow in making their conduct conform to the ethical requirements of the new religion.[13]

It is apparent that the writers of 2 Peter and Jude had some similarities. Second Peter 2:1–8 and 3:1–3 incorporate most of Jude 4–18 but omit the references in Jude 9 and 14 from the nonbiblical books of the Assumption of Moses and the Book of Enoch respectively.[14]

Merrill C. Tenney makes this observation:

Jude
1964

> The resemblance of II Peter 2 to the Epistle of Jude is so close that the literary relationship between the two books can hardly be accidental. One [author] must have known the work of the other. Although the brevity and compactness of Jude may be used as an argument for its priority, his [the author's] reference to "the apostles of our Lord Jesus Christ" (Jude 17) seems to imply that he was following the lead of some apostolic writer or writers. Since the author of II Peter claims to be an apostle (II Peter 1:1), it is more likely that Jude was stimulated to compose his epistle by Peter's missive than that a pseudonymous document was copied from Jude and published under Peter's name. The fact that II Peter predicts apostasy (2:1), whereas Jude announces that the declension has already begun (Jude 4) may indicate that II Peter belongs to an earlier stage in the history of the apostolic church.[15]

False
Teachers
2101

False Prophets
2100
Corrupt Priests
2102

450

There are two distinct differences between 2 Peter and Jude. Peter's statement about the false teachers is prophetic (2 Peter 2:1,2,3,12,13). Note the future tense "shall" in all the verses cited. The author uses the present tense in describing the character of the false prophets 2 Peter (2:17,18), but he puts their deceptive teachings in the future (2 Peter 2:13,14). Jude, on the other hand, makes reference to these corrupters as having already come among the people of God and doing their diabolical work (Jude 4,8).[16]

Four main subjects predominate in 2 Peter:

1. The Key Word *knowledge*

Second Peter contains a key word, *knowledge,* used seven times (1:2,3,5,6,8; 2:20; 3:18). The apostle is not writing of mere intellectual knowledge, but of the knowledge of God (3:18). This knowledge of Christ is a means of protection against heresy. Through this knowledge of God the Christian receives grace and peace that relate to life and godliness (1:2,3). Knowledge of Christ enables the believer to escape "the pollutions of the world"—the defilement of the flesh (2:20), and makes growth in grace possible (3:18; cf. James 4:4).

Divine
Knowledge
2031–2035
Heresy
1577

2. Infallibility of Scripture

Peter was committed to the belief that Scripture is God's infallible Word and to its integrity and trustworthiness. To Peter, all Scripture is divinely revealed ("God breathed"), but the reader of God's Word also needs God's assistance in the interpretation of it. He believed that, before a person can appropriate the promises of God, he must believe that "prophecy came not in old time by the will of man: but holy men of God spake as they were moved by the Holy Ghost" (1:21).

God's Word
417, 419, 427, 434, 436

Prophecy
Inspired
1774

3. False Prophets

In the second chapter Peter gives a description of the false teachers who will deceive the people (v. 1), whose shameful ways "many will follow" [NIV]. Peter speaks of them "as natural brute beasts . . . [who] speak evil of the things that they understand not. . . . Spots they are and blemishes, sporting themselves with their own deceivings . . . having eyes full of adultery, and that cannot cease from sin; beguiling unstable souls . . . they allure . . . the lusts of the flesh" (2:12–14,18).

False
Teachers
2101

4. The Second Coming of Christ

Peter was deeply disturbed over the doubt and uncertainty among early Christians concerning the imminent return of the Lord. This belief was based on such words of Jesus as Mark 9:1; 13; Luke 17:22–37. Belief in the Second Coming was also an article in the apostolic teaching (1 Thess. 4:15–17; 1 Cor. 7:29; 15:51,52; James 5:18; Phil. 4:5; 1 Peter 4:7). The early church interpreted these Scriptures to mean that the return of the Lord might be soon, even before the first generation of Christians had passed away.

As time passed and he did not return "hope began to give place to doubt, and doubt to impatience, and impatience even

Christ's
Second
Coming
1344–1350

451

to denial."[17] Peter predicted that the false prophets and scoffers would say, "Where is the promise of his coming?" (2 Peter 3:4). The apostle assures the people that God "the Lord is not slack concerning his promise" (2 Peter 3:4–9). Peter informed the people that God has a different time schedule than man, "that one day is with the Lord as a thousand years, and a thousand years as one day" (2 Peter 3:8). Peter reminded the people that the Lord will come suddenly, as "a thief in the night" (2 Peter 3:10; cf. 1 Thess. 5:2), and that his Coming will usher in a cataclysmic destruction of the worldly order. "The heavens shall pass away with a great noise, and the elements shall melt with fervent heat, the earth also and the works that are therein shall be burned up" (2 Peter 3:10).

The apostle emphasizes the importance of the people maintaining their readiness, that they are to "be diligent that ye may be found of him in peace, without spot, and blameless" (2 Peter 3:14). In other words, they were not to be merely concerned about the details of the Second Coming. They were to "work . . . while it is day"; the Second Coming would take care of itself in due time.

24

The Epistles of John and Jude

I. 1 JOHN

A. Name

The First Epistle of John derives its name from early tradition, when the patristic fathers added the caption of John to the manuscripts.

First Epistle of John
4284

B. Authorship and Date

No specific identification of an author appears in the three Epistles of John. However, early tradition points to John as the writer. Such church fathers as Polycarp, Papias, Iranaeus, Origen, Cyprian, and Eusebius were unanimous in attributing authorship to John the Apostle. The affirmation of Polycarp (A.D. 69–156) and Papias (A.D. 70–155) makes this claim of John being the author even more conclusive because they were pupils of John. Both men held the office of Bishop—Polycarp in Smyrna and Papias in Hierapolis. Both of these episcopal areas were within about a hundred miles of Ephesus.[1]

John the Beloved
392, 1902

The question naturally arises: What is the basis of this conclusion when internal evidence of authorship is lacking? Obviously the affirmation of Polycarp and Papias was based on their own association with John. Other traditions were also closely linked with the apostolic generation. Beyond these possible claims one may reach a satisfactory conclusion through analysis.

Eusebius shows that the author of 1 John and the Gospel of John was the same, mainly because of similar idioms, phrases, common themes, and theological agreements distinctive throughout these books.[2] In agreement with this conclusion, John Wesley says, "The great similitude, or rather sameness, both of spirit and expression which runs through St. John's Gospel and all his epistles, is clear evidence of their being written by the same person. In this epistle [1 John] he speaks not to any particular church but to all the Christians of that age; and in them to the whole Christian Church in all succeeding ages."[3]

Below, a set of comparative tables, by B. F. Westcott, shows notable parallels between the Gospel and the First Epistle of John:

1 John	Gospel of John	1 John	Gospel of John
1:2,3	3:11	3:16	10:15
1:4	16:24	3:22	8:29
2:11	12:35	3:23	13:34
2:14	5:38	4:6	8:47
3:5	8:46	4:16	6:69
3:8	8:14	5:9	5:32
3:13	15:18	5:20	17:3[4]
3:14	5:24		

Some scholars agree that 1 and 2 John have the same author because eight of the thirteen verses in the second book match those in the first book. There is also agreement that 2 and 3 John have a single author because they both begin with the designation "the elder": (2 John 1; 3 John 1).[5] Since the Gospel of John and 1 John have a common author, and all three of the John epistles have the same author, it seems possible to conclude that the four books were written by the same author. As an apostle wrote them and as John was the only living apostle when the books were written, it seems that John, the apostle, was the author of all four books. "First John was probably written as a circular letter from Ephesus about A.D. 85–95, to the believers of the Roman Province of Asia including the churches [addressed] in the Book of Revelation (1 John 2, 3)."[6] All of the other six churches of Asia Minor are within a radius of about 125 miles from Ephesus.

C. Background, Purpose, and Content

Although it contains no salutation, the First Epistle of John is called a letter. One of its unusual features among "NT books is that it does not contain a single proper name (except Our Lord's), or a single definition allusion, personal, historical, or geographical. It is a composition, however, which a person calling himself 'I' sends to certain other persons whom he calls 'you,' and is, in form at least, a letter."[7]

Elder
2078, 754

Apostles
2080–2082

Ephesus
1142, 4365

Letters
211

454

From tradition and conjecture, one concludes that John lived in Jerusalem, caring for the mother of Jesus until a few years before the fall of Jerusalem, A.D. 70. Between A.D. 65 and 70 John probably took Mary to Ephesus, the geographic and numerical center of the Christian community, where he labored among the churches until about A.D. 95, when he was exiled to the Isle of Patmos, about 60 miles southwest from the old harbor of Ephesus. At the time of his exile to Patmos, probably during the Domitianic persecution, John received his vision for the Book of Revelation. He returned to Ephesus in about A.D. 97 and died there at the turn of the century.[8] It is not known whether John actually wrote the Book of Revelation while on Patmos or after he returned to Ephesus.

The Epistle of John discusses the spiritual welfare of Christians, warning them of certain dangerous views concerning Christ and impressing upon the believers that faith in the Savior manifests itself in love.

By the time Christianity had been in existence for 60–70 years, it had spread throughout the Roman Empire. In this process the Christians had encountered popular philosophical ideas of that day. Some of the heresies in these systems, especially Gnosticism, penetrated the church bodies, causing confusion and apostasy. The gnostic *(know)* heresy, a combination of Oriental theology, Greek philosophy, and Christian doctrine, was the greatest rival of Christianity in its infancy. "Gnostics" are those who profess to have a deeper understanding or wisdom. The gnostics of the early Christian era were selective in their acceptance of the Christian doctrines. They claimed that all nature, intellectual and material, originated from the deity by successive manifestations, which they called Eons.

Henry H. Halley says,

> A form of Gnosticism which was disrupting the churches in John's day taught that there is in human nature an irreconcilable principle of Dualism: that the Spirit and Body are two separate entities: that Sin resided in the Flesh only: that the Spirit could have its raptures and the Body could do as it pleased: that lofty mental mystical Piety was entirely consistent with voluptuous sensual life. They denied the Incarnation, that God had in Christ actually become Flesh, and maintained that Christ was a Phantom, a man in appearance only. In Ephesus a man named Cerinthus was leader of this cult. . . . Throughout this Epistle it seems that John must have had these heretics in mind, in insisting that Jesus was the Actual, Material, Authentic Manifestation of God in the Flesh, and that Genuine Knowledge of God must result in Moral Transformation.[9]

The gnostic heresy could not be reconciled with Christianity. The gnostic philosophy of dualism: matter is evil, spirit is good; and the docetic interpretation of Christ: the union of Christ with the human Jesus was only apparent and was opposed to Christian doctrine. The gnostics could accept the deity of Jesus

The Epistles of John and Jude

John
392, 1902
Mary
2259

Ephesus
1142, 4365
Vision
508–511

Heresy
1577
Love
2200–2203

Vain
Philosophy
2759

Christ's
Doctrine
3558

455

but not the humanity. To some gnostics, Christ's office was to teach the knowledge or secrets of their system, pertaining to cosmic order. To them the heavenly Christ did not die on the cross, but separated himself from Jesus before death occurred. With this view the Incarnation was impossible, and the human nature of Jesus Christ was considered illusion.

Robert Law writes:

> It is with this docetic subversion of the truth of the incarnation that the "antichrists" are specially identified (2:22–23; 4:2–3), and against it that St. John directs with wholehearted fervor his central thesis—the complete, permanent, personal identification of the historical Jesus with the Divine Being who is the Word of Life (1:1), the Christ (4:2) and the Son of God (5:5): "Jesus is the Christ, come in the flesh.". . . To the Gnostic, knowledge was the sum of attainment. "They give no heed to love," says Ignatius, "caring not for the widow, the orphan or the afflicted, neither for those who are in bonds nor for those who are released from bonds, neither for the hungry nor the thirsty." That a religion which banished or neglected love should call itself Christian or claim affinity with Christianity excites St. John's latent indignation; against it he lifts up his supreme truth, God is love, with its immediate consequence that to be without love is to be without capacity for knowing God (4:7–8) . . . and the crucial test by which we may assure our self-accusing hearts that we are "of the truth" is love "not in word, neither with the tongue; but in deed and in truth." (3:18).[10]

John's answer then, to the gnostics, as noted above, contained the central message that "Jesus Christ is come in the flesh" (4:2b). The author further affirmed this position: "That which was from the beginning, which we have heard . . . have seen . . . have looked upon, and our hands have handled, of the Word of Life" (1:1).

By the time of John's writing some of those adhering to the false ideas of the gnostics had left the church to spread their teachings elsewhere (2:19). John identified and denounced

those who denied and opposed Jesus, as antichrists. "And every spirit that confesseth not that Jesus Christ is come in the flesh is not of God: and this is that spirit of antichrist" (4:3; see also

2:18). They were known as "many false prophets" (4:1b). Evidently some still remained within the church for John wrote "concerning them that seduce you" (2:26). Further, "Who is a liar but he that denieth that Jesus is the Christ? He is antichrist . . ." (2:22).

The writer urged his readers to "believe not every spirit," but to apply a test to distinguish the false from the true: ". . .

try the spirits whether they are of God" (4:1), "and every spirit that confesseth not that Jesus Christ is come in the flesh is not of God." The thought in 1 John 4:7–21 is to oppose the false views of those who deny Jesus to be the Christ. Because

of the confusion resulting from the teachings of the Gnostics, John emphasized that the Christian, the true believer, had a knowledge that came, not from speculation, as did that of the gnostics, but from a spiritual revelation (2:20). One of the serious problems of that day had to do with the question: Am I saved, and if so, how can I know? In this Epistle, John endeavors to show that the believers can have assurance—that they can know if they are saved. "The phrase 'we know' is used thirteen times to signify the certainty that is achieved through experience, or that is a part of normal spiritual consciousness (2:3,5,29; 3:14,16,19,24; 4:13,16; 5:15,18,19,20)." [11] The Gospel of John was written "that ye may know that ye have eternal life" (1 John 5:13).

John understood that to know God is to keep his commandments, to love God and man: "And this commandment have we from him, That he who loveth God love his brother also" (4:21); "and hereby we do know that we know him, if we keep his commandments" (2:3; cf. 4:7,8). Love does not originate with man; man loves God because "he first loved us" (4:19–21). Love, if genuine, comes from the heart and is directed toward man and God (3:18; cf. 4:7,8). John puts love in a proper focus; love of God and love of man are a unity; one cannot love God without loving man (5:2,3).

John saw clearly that "love is of God" and that it is the test of true discipleship (4:7,8,12,13,15). "We know that we have passed from death unto life, because we love the brethren" (3:14). God's love within a believer manifests itself not only in man's attitude but love may show itself in compassion for the needy. "If anyone has material possessions and sees his brother in need but has no pity on him, how can the love of God be in him?" (3:17, NIV).

The apostle cautioned the people that their love must not be directed toward "things that are in the world" (1 John 2:15–17). He pointed out that the antidote for fear is love, because "perfect love casteth out fear" (4:18). He declared that the true disciple must "walk in the light" (1:7), keep God's commandments (2:3), and "abide in him" (2:28). John affirmed that God cannot tolerate overt and willful sin because "sin is the transgression of the law" (3:4,5), and that "he that committeth sin is of the devil" (3:8–11; cf. John 8:44). Believers are exhorted to make proper discernment of "the spirits whether they are of God" (4:1,2,3).

II. 2 JOHN

A. *The Name*

The Second Epistle of John, like the First Epistle of John, also derives its name from early tradition, when the church fathers added the caption of John to the John manuscripts.

B. Authorship and Date

Many scholars are agreed that Second John was written by the apostle John, even though only limited evidence is available. Even in the fourth century, there were some who hesitated to ascribe authorship for this book to John. The manuscripts appeared to be only private letters. Even such scholars as James Moffatt (1870–1944) minimized the importance of both 1 and 2 John. Moffatt said, "We would not have suffered much loss if the second and third epistles of John had been excluded from the New Testament Canon." [12] "On the contrary, we would have suffered very serious spiritual loss if we had never read the subtle rebuke of 'advanced' thinkers in II John 9." [13]

However, in view of the difficulty in compiling canonical books and the lack of internal evidence for the author of the John epistles, "it is not surprising that these brief . . . [epistles] are among the NT writings over which there was a hard struggle for canonical recognition. One is probably, the other certainly, a private letter; and neither had an opportunity or a reason for circulating among the churches as did the other church epistles." [14]

Adam Clarke says:

> When first discovered, all the immediate vouchers were gone; and the Church of Christ, that was always on its guard and restrained by the Holy Spirit against imposture, and especially in relation to writings professing to be the work of Apostles, hesitated to receive them into the number of Canonical Scriptures till it was fully satisfied that they were Divinely inspired. Their extreme caution was of the uttermost consequence to the Christian faith: for had it been otherwise, had any measure of credulity prevailed, the church would have been inundated with spurious writings, and the genuine faith greatly corrupted, if not totally destroyed. The number of apocryphal gospels, acts of apostles and epistles, which were offered to the church in the earliest ages of Christianity is truly astounding.[15]

The Second Epistle of John was probably written from Ephesus between A.D. 85 and 95.

C. Background, Purpose, and Content

All but one of the original apostles had died. John, the sole survivor, may have moved from Jerusalem with Mary, the mother of Jesus, a few years before the Holy City was destroyed (A.D. 70). At the time John wrote his second epistle, he was probably the active supervisor of the churches in and around Ephesus. His opening words, "the elder," could have referred to his age, he being the last surviving companion of Jesus, and being a high church officer, an "elder" in the church.

Since early postapostolic times, scholars have been divided

as to the meaning of the expression, "the elect lady." Some
have understood the phrase to mean (1) that the letter was
addressed to an individual, or (2) addressed to a church group.
The thinking of the scholars is given below:

1. To an individual person

The "elect lady" in verse 1 may have been a prominent
woman in a neighboring church to whom John had ministered.
The letter, addressed to the lady (v. 1) speaks of her loyalty
to truth in verse 4. Verse 13 contains greetings to the lady
(kyria) and her children from the children of her sister.

Some scholars suggest that the Greek word *Kyria,* translated
"lady," should be taken as a proper name.[16]

2. To a church group

Another view is that the "elect lady" was used figuratively
to designate a church, and "the children," members of that
church. "This seems to be a legitimate position to take but
neither view can be categorically proved. Such scholars as William
Barclay, A. E. Brooke, Brooke Foss Westcott, and Amos
N. Wilder favor 'the Church' interpretation." [17] On the other
hand, Alexander Ross, D. D. Weadon, Albert Barnes, and John
Wesley think of the lady as an individual.[18]

Church the
Body of Christ
726

An analysis of 2 John indicates that the word *truth* is one
of the leading words, included five times in the first four verses:
(1) "I love in the truth" (v. 1), (2) "they that have known the
truth" (v. 1), (3) "for the truth's sake" (v. 2), (4) "in truth and
love" (v. 3), and (5) "walking in truth" (v. 4). This reference
to *truth* which implies that the Person Jesus is the Truth, is
in keeping with John's use of this word in the Gospel of John
in which Jesus says, "I am the way, the truth, and the life:
no man cometh unto the Father, but by me" (John 14:6).

Truth
3697, 3698

The word *love* as employed in 2 John is in agreement with
the writer's use of the word *love* 22 times in the Gospel of
John.

Love
2200–2203

John makes its clear that he is not writing a new commandment
(v. 5). He affirms Paul's statement that the faith "was
given us in Christ Jesus before the world began" (2 Tim. 1:9b;
Titus 1:2b), and agrees with Jude that the faith "was once delivered
unto the saints" (Jude 3). This faith was repeatedly identified
with the perfection of love referred to by the Master (Matt.
22:36–40).

Faith
1201

One of the serious dangers facing the church at this time
was the deceivers circulating among the congregations, who
denied the incarnation (2 John 7–9). John urged the believers

459

not to "receive" into their homes these false preachers (2 John 10). They were also warned against bidding these teachers "God speed" or giving encouragement to them, under the peril of identifying themselves with the evil ones (2 John 10,11).

Apparently John wrote this epistle at a time when his duties were strenuous. Even though he had "many things to write," he limited himself to thirteen short verses; he did express his hope that he would be able to visit this family soon and speak with them "face to face" (2 John 12,13). He concluded his letter by sending greetings from his host, or from the church as the case may be.

III. 3 JOHN

A. The Name

The Third Epistle of John also derives its name from early tradition when the patristic fathers added the caption of John to the John manuscripts.

B. Authorship and Date

The Third Epistle of John is closely associated with the second letter and can be considered as a Johannine Epistle. For a commentary on authorship see the discussions on 1 and 2 John. It is considered to have been written from Ephesus between A.D. 85 and 95.

C. Background, Purpose, and Content

The Third Epistle of John differs from John's other two epistles in at least one point. It is addressed to a particular person; in the book five other persons are identified.

In this letter John gave a description typical of many modern churches today. Gaius and Demetrius were faithful members in the church, but Diotrephes, who seems to have acted in a manner unbecoming to a Christian, opposed entertaining any of the missionaries. The epistle is addressed to Gaius, a common reference to a certain Gaius, a friend of Paul, who was dragged into the ampitheater during the riot at Ephesus (Acts 19:29). A man named Gaius, from Derbe in the Galatian area, accompanied Paul on his last journey of Asia (Acts 20:4). Paul makes mention of a third man by this name whom he baptized in Corinth (Rom. 16:23; 1 Cor. 1:14).[19] The Gaius at Ephesus (Acts 19:29) seems to be the one closest to John's area, but to name any one of the above would be speculation.

Paul
2697

Derbe
2221, 4357
Galatia
1382
Corinth
840, 4353
Ephesus
1142, 4365

460

The Gaius to whom this letter is addressed was apparently a church officer or the pastor of a church in or near Ephesus.

John commended Gaius for his faithful service in the church and for the hospitality he had rendered "the brethren, and to strangers" (3 John 5). John expressed joy over the faithful ministry of Gaius and mentioned that he "has no greater joy than to hear that my children walk in truth" (3 John 4). Because of the charitable treatment and financial help accorded the missionaries, they were able to continue their ministry without taking an offering from the Gentiles (3 John 7,8). *The Epistles of John and Jude*
Earthly joy
1940–1943

There were, however, difficulties existing in this congregation because of Diotrephes, who in a domineering manner tried to control the church. The name, Diotrephes, appears nowhere else in Scripture.

Apparently John had a desire to conduct a missionary conference in the church where Gaius was a member. John recounted, "I wrote unto the church: but Diotrephes, who loveth to have the preeminence among them, receiveth us not" (3 John 9). It is evident that this man not only opposed missionary activity but even resorted to casting "them out of the church" (3 John 10). Persecution
3480–3484

The third person to whom John addressed himself is Demetrius, a man of "good report of all men" (3 John 12). Only one other Demetrius is listed in the NT, and he was the silversmith in Ephesus who accused Paul of endangering the trade and bringing disrepute upon the goddess Diana (Acts 19:24ff.). It would be speculation to say that the man at Ephesus was converted and was then a faithful member in the church with Gaius. Since John's ministry was in and around Ephesus, it is at least a possibility, but the answer will have to remain conjecture. Silversmiths
255

In this epistle, as in the second letter, John says that he has "many things to write," but apparently church affairs prevent him from writing more than this short note. He is also hoping that he will "shortly see" Gaius and Demetrius (3 John 13,14).

As in both of the other Johannine epistles, the word *truth* is a leading word in 3 John: (1) "I love in the truth" (v. 1), (2) "testified of the truth" (v. 3), (3) "thou walkest in the truth" (v. 3), "fellowhelpers to the truth" (v. 8), and (4) "ye know that our record is true" (v. 12). Truth
3697, 3698

IV. JUDE

Epistle of Jude
4287

A. *The Name*

The General Epistle of Jude derives its name from the first verse in which Jude identifies himself as the author: "Jude, the servant of Jesus Christ, and brother of James, to them that are sanctified by God the Father, and preserved in Jesus Christ" (Jude 1). Jude
1964

461

The name *Jude* is the English form of the Greek *Judas (Iou-das)* and appears only in the Book of Jude. The Greek form *Judas* appears 33 times in the four Gospels and the Book of Acts.

B. Authorship and Date

The question of whether the writer of Jude was the brother of Jesus and whether he was an apostle has been the subject of scholarly debate since the time of the apostolic fathers.[20]

Apostles
2080–2082

The NT lists "two Judes: Judas, one of the twelve Apostles, Luke 6:16 . . . and Judas, the brother of Jesus, Matthew 13:55. The latter is commonly regarded as the writer of the Epistle." [21]

William C. Moorehead says, "Almost from the beginning of the Christian era, men, qualified to speak with authority on the question of genuineness and authenticity, endorsed it [Jude] as entitled to a place in the NT Scriptures." [22]

The church father, Origen, referred to Jude as an epistle with few lines "but full of powerful words of heavenly grace." Clement of Alexandria and Athanasius accepted it as a book written by Jude. The Muratorian Canon * includes Jude among the books of Scripture.[23]

Fallen Angels
147
Michael
2335

There are, however, a few critics who would assign authorship to Jude to "an unknown Jude or to pseudonymity and would place the date near the middle of the second century, but this appears quite unlikely." Objection to the authorship may have been based in part on Jude's reference to fallen angels and the archangel Michael in the book of Enoch. These quotations are from the pseudepigraphal books of The Assumption of Moses and The Book of Enoch. Such references do not mean that Jude approved these books in their entirety but that the passages he quoted contained remnants of truth (cf. Acts 17:28; Gal. 3:19; 2 Tim. 3:8; Titus 1:12ff.).[24]

Satan
3150, 3153,
3155

Jude's reference to the conflict between the archangel Michael and Satan over Moses' body (v. 9) is from the Assumption of Moses. For the historicity of this book scholars are dependent upon prior references to it by Origen (A.D. 185–254) and Clement of Alexander (A.D. 150–263). "There are several references to the Book [Enoch] up to the sixth century but thereafter it disappeared til [A. M.] Ceriani found a fragment of it which is published in the 'Acts Sacra Et Profana.' Vol I [at Milan in 1874]." [25]

This manuscript is full of scribal errors because of the copyists' ignorance of the Greek language. Many of the words are misinterpreted. The fragment did not contain the reference in Jude.

---

* For an explanation of the Muratorian Canon see Ch. 21, V, B.

Jude's reference to fallen angels (v. 6) is an allusion to a passage in Enoch (chs. 6–19). The only complete manuscripts of Enoch still extant are written in Ethiopic and copied from Greek originals.[26]

C. Background, Purpose, and Content

Even though the writer refers to himself as Jude [Judas], "the brother of James," because of modesty, "he refrains from calling himself directly the brother of our Lord. He remembered, may we not believe, that he had been too unworthy a brother to Jesus in the days of His flesh. Brother, though he is, he is content . . . to be his bond servant." [27] (For additional information on the brothers of the Lord, see page 441ff.

According to verse 3a Jude intended to write at length about the common salvation (Jude 3), but because of the crisis at hand, he shifted quickly to the perils of apostasy within the church and the need to "contend for the faith which was once delivered unto the saints" (v. 3b). Because of the rapid influx of members, not fully Christianized, the church body suffered internal turmoil. D. Russell Scott says, "There had crept into the church, people who were making the grace of God an excuse for licentiousness, defiant, without reverence, ignorant and sensual; they could not read the lessons of history that showed that upon all such, punishment must fall." [28]

Apostasy
1235
The Faith
1202

It is evident that there is a similarity between Jude and 2 Peter and this raises the question: Who copied from whom? However, it need not be that either one copied from the other. They could have been writing to the same people with the same problems, but at different times. Peter may have written before the fall of Jerusalem and Jude afterward. Both writers shared a common concern lest apostasy destroy the Christian heritage.[29] Jude courageously accepted the challenge to rebuke the church, but he did it adroitly and with understanding.

Peter
2746

Jude reveals some information not previously stated in Scripture: i.e., his reference to the fallen angels (v. 6) and Michael's contest with the devil (v. 9), not mentioned in the account of Moses' death and burial at Mount Nebo (cf. Deut. 34:5,6). The name *Michael* appears fifteen times in the Scriptures but only once in reference to Michael as an archangel, in Jude 9, and once as a leader of the angels in Revelation 12:7. It is possible that Daniel's reference to Michael alludes to this angel (10:13,21; 12:1). (For additional information on Angels, see page 83ff.)

Fallen Angels
147
Michael
2335

Archangel
211

The books in the pseudepigrapha, which also refer to these incidents, are generally considered to be fanciful and of inferior quality when compared with the canonical books, but Jude shows that there are some elements of truth, even in these nonbiblical books. "There were only five of the fathers between Adam and Enoch (1 Chron. 1:1). The first coming of Christ was revealed to Adam in Genesis 3:15; His second, glorious coming, to Enoch; and the 'seventh from Adam' foretold the things which will conclude the seventh age of the world." [30]

Jude must have had access to the sermon recorded in the Book of Enoch, of which he quoted only a small portion. Since Enoch was contemporary with Adam and Eve (v. 14) and the human family lived close together, it may be possible that Adam and Eve and their family heard the sermon of which this segment is a part. Jude went to the other side of the flood for his message and projected it beyond the flood to a future time (v. 23).

In respect to the Book(s) of Enoch, "After having been quoted in Jude and noticed by several of the Fathers, this work disappeared from the knowledge of the Christian Church." [31] In the eighteenth century, [James] Bruce, a British explorer, returned from Ethiopia with three copies of the Book of Enoch, written in Ethiopic. One copy each was placed in the Kinnard House, the Bodleian Library at Oxford, and the Royal Library in Paris. The book lay there unread until some years later when Sylvester de Sacy translated the first sixteen chapters, and Archbishop Laurence translated and published the entire work for the Bodleian Library. Later, additional copies were found at Magdala. A careful study shows that these Ethiopic copies were all translated from original Greek manuscripts. Some Greek fragments have been found at Giza, near Cairo, Egypt, the seat of the Coptic Church.[32]

Jude's information concerning the Book of Enoch, along with his insight into Old Testament history, indicates that he was well-read and a man of culture. "He is forcible and rhetorical, even though his usage of the Greek language suggests that he learnt Greek only late in life, gathering so large a vocabulary

that he became encumbered by it." [33]

Regardless of the state of apostasy, Jude approached their problem positively and urged the church to build themselves up in the holy faith and to pray in the Holy Ghost (v. 20).

They were to keep themselves "in the love of God" and to look "for the mercy of our Lord Jesus Christ unto eternal life" (v. 21). In the spirit of love, the writer confirmed that "some needed compassionate tenderness because they were close to the fire, some required cautious ministration lest their form of sin contaminate the believers." [34] In a beautiful benediction Jude suggests the Lord's ability to keep Christians "from falling" and to present them (the people of God) "faultless before the presence of his glory with exceeding joy" (v. 24).[35]

Dr. Hanke by the cave on Patmos where the apostle John report-
edly wrote the Revelation

Isle of Patmos—bay area

25

The Revelation of St. John the Divine

A. The Name

[margin]
Book of Revelation
4288
John the Beloved
392, 1902
Apocalyptic Portraits of Christ
4306[/margin]

The Book of Revelation derives its name from the first verse: "The Revelation of Jesus Christ . . . unto his servant John." The oldest form of the title was probably "Apocalypse of John"; the appended words, "the Divine," were added in about the fourth century.

The Latin background of the word *Revelation* is *revelatio* (from *revelare,* meaning "to reveal or explore that which was previously hidden"). The word *apocalypse* is the Greek title and is the first word in the Greek text—appearing as *Apokalypsis.*

B. Authorship and Date

[margin]
Inspiration of the Bible
417

Angel of the Lord
141[/margin]

The statement concerning the authorship of this book differs from that of any other book in the Bible. All scripture was given to the prophets and other writers by inspiration of the Holy Spirit (2 Tim. 3:16), but divine disclosure for the Book of Revelation was given by God the Father to Jesus Christ, his Son, who communicated the message to "his servant John" by "his angel" (Rev. 1:1). This John was assumed by the church to be the Apostle John. Wilbur M. Smith says, "As early as the first half of the second century, it was the conviction of the church that John was the author. Justin Martyr states that John, one of the apostles of Christ, wrote the book. Eusebius repeatedly assigned the book to John as did Tertullian." [1] The text itself mentions the name of John five times which adds

[margin]**466**[/margin]

strength to Johannine authorship. In style the language is similar to that of the Gospel of John.

The similarities between John's writings and Revelation are striking. Some of them are listed below:

Rev.	1:1	with John 18:37—Revelation of Jesus
	1:5	with 1 John 1:7—Jesus' blood
	1:9	with 1 John 5:10—Testimony, Witness
	2:17	with John 6:32—Manna, Bread
	3:8	with John 17:6; 1 John 2:5—Kept thy word
	3:21	1 John 2:13,14; 4:4; 5:5—Overcome
	19:13	John 1:1—Word was God
	22:8,10	John 4:23,24—Worship

The "Logos" (Word) appears only in the Gospel of John and in Revelation (19:13; cf. John 1:1). Merrill C. Tenney states that "there are a number of words and concepts, such as 'Word of God' [used] as a title of Christ, 'Witness,' the concept of the 'Lamb,' and some others that characterize both John and Revelation, and are common to no other writings of the New Testament." [2]

The Word as Christ **700**

Christ, a Witness **689**

Lamb of God **3365**

There is however, some disagreement among scholars concerning the question of the authorship of Revelation. Saint Dionysius, of Alexandria of the third century, asserted that John, the Apostle, did not write the Book of Revelation because: (1) author identification is given in Revelation but not in the Gospel, (2) the vocabulary, syntax, and certain theological concepts are different, and (3) the quality of grammar in Revelation is inferior to that in the fourth Gospel. But these objections cannot be sustained in considering the evidence presented supporting Johannine authorship. After all, "Truth . . . is not made or unmade by the literary form through which it is expressed: and in this case the Apocalypse differs from ordinary Jewish apocalyptic writings. . . . Although it possesses the usual characteristics of Apocalyptic literature . . . it is not pseudonymous. It was written to seven actual churches in seven well-known cities, and its emphasis on practical ethics is different from the general trend of apocalyptic words." [3]

Seven Churches **762**

The first sentence indicates that "God Himself . . . [gave] it through Jesus Christ, by an angel, to John, who wrote it down and sent the completed book to the Seven Churches (Rev. 1:1–4)." [4] The final affirmation is that the Holy Spirit approved the book for canonization. For a more complete discussion of apocalyptic literature see page 192, under Pseudepigrapha.

Holy Spirit Guides **1611**

C. Background, Purpose, and Content

The Book of Revelation has always been a difficult book to understand because its content is apocalyptic and its language,

467

in part, figurative and symbolic. However difficult, the book itself is commended to the reader for serious, prayerful study. "Blessed is he that readeth, and they that hear the words of this prophecy, and keep those things which are written therein" (1:3). Certain portions of Revelation are closely related to apocalyptic sections in the OT. Wilbur M. Smith writes,

> It is estimated that of 404 verses in this book [Revelation], 265 contain lines which embrace approximately 550 references to the Old Testament passages: there are 13 references to Genesis, 27 to Exodus, 79 to Isaiah, 53 to Daniel. . . . Many . . . agree . . . [that] the eschatology discourse of Jesus (Matt. 24:25; Mark 13; Luke 21) is . . . the key to the Apocalypse. This book is saturated with Old Testament prophecy, under the guidance of the word of Jesus, and the inspiration of God. It is the climax of the prophecy of the Old and New Testaments.[5]

For a further study of the apocalyptic parallels see:

Rev. 1:6, cf. Exod. 19:6; 1:7; Dan. 7:13; Zech. 12:10,12;
Rev. 1:14, cf. Dan. 7:9,13; 10:5;
Rev. 1:16, cf. Isa. 1:4; 49:2;
Rev. 1:17, cf. Isa. 46:6; 48:12;
Rev. 5:11, cf. Dan. 7:10;
Rev. 5:13, cf. Dan. 7:13,14;
Rev. 10:7, cf. Dan. 12:6,7;
Rev. 11:15, cf. Dan. 7:13,14;
Rev. 13:7, cf. Dan. 7:21,25.[6]

The Book of Daniel is frequently considered to be a companion book to Revelation. Many volumes have been written on the Book of Revelation which one may study privately. Space allocated for this study is limited to the less controversial chapters, especially such chapters as 1–3,21 and 22. For those who are new students of Revelation, the recommendation is to begin study with the devotional nature of the book in mind. The Holy Spirit will lead the reader into greater depths of truth.

As indicated in the discussion on the First Epistle of John, according to tradition, the apostle moved from Jerusalem to Ephesus sometime before the fall of Jerusalem. Later, because of his Christian faith he was exiled to the penal settlement on the island of Patmos in the Aegean sea about A.D. 95. There he remained until about A.D. 97. As understood from the text, John received his vision on the Isle but recorded the Revelation later, perhaps after his return from exile. At the time of writing, John used the past tense "was on the isle of Patmos for the word and the testimony of Jesus Christ" (1:9, NIV). Thus the internal evidence points to actual persecution during the time John wrote the book, probably under Domitian (A.D. 81–96), when attack on Christianity reached many areas in the Empire, especially in the year A.D. 95.

John's writings contain a message not only for the Christian's own time, but also for the future when the natural order of the universe will come to an end and Christ will set up his kingdom. Scholars have assumed that much of Revelation was written in figurative language so that the authorities could not understand what the Christians were doing. Three main methods of interpretation of Revelation have developed from the study of this book.

(1) The Preterist describes the events in the book as having been fulfilled. This view emphasizes the historical background and the ethical teachings of the book.

(2) The Futurist view suggests that Revelation, beginning with Chapter 4, is yet to be fulfilled at the end of time and that parts of the book refer to a period of apostasy (chs. 1–3). Chapters 4–22 describe future events including the Great Tribulation, the second coming of Christ, the Millennium, and the new kingdom under Christ.

(3) The Eclectic teaches that some things have been fulfilled, some things were being fulfilled, and still other events would be fulfilled at the end of the Age.

Furthermore, arising out of the prophetic positions were three aspects of the Millennium: (1) The postmillennial view presupposes that Christ will not return until the church has evangelized the world and has created a general state of peace. Christ will then come from heaven and occupy the throne of peace prepared for him by the church. (2) The amillennial view teaches that Christ could return any moment and immediately set up the Great Judgment seat to be followed by permanent heaven and hell. (3) The premillennial view postpones final judgment until Christ has reigned and ruled on earth with the saints for 1000 years. Near the end of this period the Great Seven-Year Tribulation is to take place, to be followed by the Final Judgment.[7] The premillennial view is generally accepted by many evangelical Christians. These three views of the Millennium raise three more questions: Will the Great Tribulation come (1) before, (2) during or (3) after the Second Coming when "the dead in Christ shall rise first . . . and we which . . . remain shall be caught up together with them in the clouds, to meet the Lord in the air: and so shall we ever be with the Lord" (1 Thess. 4:16,17)? This meeting in the air is frequently referred to as the "Rapture."

In the introduction to the seven churches, John gave an apocalyptic description of the second coming of Christ: "He cometh with clouds; and every eye shall see him, and they also which pierced him: and all kindreds of the earth shall wail because of him. Even so, Amen" (Rev. 1:7). Jesus Christ declared, "I am Alpha and Omega, the beginning and the ending, saith the Lord" (1:8). "What thou seest, write in a book, and send

The New
Testament

Body of Christ
726

See Journey
Map
p. 293

Ephesus
1142, 4365

Diana
3940

Mary Mother of
Jesus
2259

Ephesus
1142, 4365

it unto the seven churches which are in Asia; unto Ephesus, and unto Smyrna, and unto Pergamos, and unto Thyatira, and unto Sardis, and unto Philadelphia, and unto Laodicea" (1:11). The letters addressed to the seven churches in Asia are applicable to Christians in any age—the body of Christ, the church, as persons joined to Christ. As to church buildings, the places of Christian worship in this period were synagogues or churches in homes. The modern pilgrim is distressed to find no church ruins dating back to the first and second century; they are all dated from the third century onward (see page 63ff., "The Church" and page 125ff., "The Ekklesia in the New Testament").

1. The Church at Ephesus (Rev. 2:1–7)

a. *Location.* Ephesus was located about 50 miles south of Smyrna (modern Izmir), on the Aegean Sea near the mouth of the Cayster River, sometimes referred to by the natives as the "Little Menderes" river. The other six churches of Revelation were located to the north and the east within a radius of about 125 miles.

Ephesus was the capital city of Asia, a seaport town of about 300,000 population, where caravan routes from Europe and the Orient terminated. The dock facilities formerly had been located at the eastern edge of the city, at the foot of Arcadian Avenue, but silting action from the river, erosion in the mountains, and the "dust of the ages" have filled in the old harbor so that the waterfront is now several miles to the west. The modern seaport of Ephesus is now Kusadai, about 20 miles from where the ancient city stood.

b. *History.* About 1044 B.C. Greek settlers came to Ephesus; in 133 B.C. it became part of the Roman Empire. The city was known especially for the Temple of Artemis (Diana), in honor of the Anatolian fertility goddess, who was later Hellenized. Also, Ephesus was a banking center as well as a "city of refuge," where fugitives could find sanctuary in the Great Temple. When Christianity became dominant in Ephesus, another woman replaced Diana, namely the Virgin Mary.

Discovery of the shrine of the Virgin Mary on Mount Coressos came after Anna Emmerich, a nun in Germany, had a vision in 1890 about the home and the tomb of Mary in Ephesus, even though she had never been there. Two priests from Smyrna made a trip in 1891 and found the place on top of the mountain exactly as the nun had described it. Archaeologists, excavating in the area, determined that the ruin was a fourth-century house built over the ruins of a first-century structure. Greek Orthodox Christians in the area confirm the

Excavations at Ephesus

The Basilica of St. John at Ephesus. Built as a library by the
Roman Emperor Hadrian

traditional name, *Panaja Kapoulu*, meaning "The most of all." The present reconstructed house was built on the remains of the previous walls—now only 18–30 inches high.

The importance of Ephesus as a religious center is indicated by the number of church councils held here:

(a) The Council of A.D. 200 was convened by Polycrates, Bishop of Ephesus, to discuss the date of Easter.

(b) The Council of A.D. 401 gave its attention to restoring clerical discipline in Asia Minor.

(c) The Council of A.D. 431 was called by the Emperor Theodosius II and was presided over by Saint Cyril; 2000 bishops attended for the purpose of condemning the Gnostic heresy, Nestorianism, prevalent in Asia Minor.

(d) The most spectacular convention was the Robber Council of A.D. 449. Thea B. Van Halsema describes it thus:

> The Council was a rather rough affair in which one bishop died three days after being kicked in the stomach by another. It was called "Robber Council" because one group headed by Mennon of Ephesus and Cyril of Alexandria decided to begin the council before the arrival of the opposing groups led by bishops John of Antioch and Nestorius of Constantinople. The first group excommunicated Nestorius before his group arrived. The second group, upon arrival, met separately and excommunicated their opponents. . . . At issue was the question of Christ's incarnation. Nestorius said that Christ, being God, could not be born of a human mother and he stressed the separation of Christ's manhood and Godhead, so that Mary was to be regarded as mother of Christ—Christokos—but not of God—Theotokos.
>
> Cyril, though unscrupulous in his intrigues, defended the historic position that the two natures of Christ were united in one person, and that the Logos took human nature to himself in Mary's womb. This made her Theotokos, mother of God, opening the way for later Roman Church claims of Mary's sinlessness and bodily assumption, which in our day is leading toward a claim that Mary is co-mediatrix with the Son of God. Both Nestorius and Cyril had large followings. Cyril's group won out at the Ephesus council but the outlawed Nestorians established themselves strongly in Persia, Arabia and China. The ruins of the "double church" of Mary, where the council was held, lie beside the wall, west of the city site.[8]

(e) The Council of A.D. 476 declared the See of Ephesus to be independent of the Constantinopolitian Patriarchate.

c. *New Testament Ephesus.* Three references in the NT suggest the importance of the Ephesus church: the account in Acts 18:18–19:41, Paul's letter to the Ephesians, and the words of Jesus Christ himself in the Book of Revelation (2:1–7). These indicate the prominence of the Ephesian church. This group had once been a witnessing church; but at the time of the Revelation of Jesus the believers had left their "first love." Although Jesus recognized their "works," "labour," "patience," and perseverance (Rev. 2:2), he told them to "remember therefore from whence thou art fallen, and repent, and do the first works . . ." (Rev. 2:5), or else he would remove their candlestick. According to John Wesley the candlestick represented the faithful Christian believers in the church. Christ warned the church leaders that if they did not care for the flock it would be turned over to someone who would.[9]

Jesus acknowledged that the Ephesian believers were true and sound in their disfavor of the Nicolaitan heresy: a system of adulterous lewdness and sacrifices to idols which they condoned in the name of Christian liberty.[10] Those who overcome are to "eat of the tree of life which is in the midst of the paradise of God," which is generally understood to mean "the immortality of the soul and a final state of blessedness."[11]

d. *Archaeology.* The excavations at Ephesus are the most extensive of any in the Near-East. Each season Austrian archaeologists continue to uncover more of ancient Ephesus. Marble pillars and arches are visible for miles around. The famous library of Celsus, south of the Mazeus and Mithridates Gates, is under reconstruction; the façade can be seen from a great distance. This two-story library, built by Julius Aquilla, was named for his father, Celsus Poleneanus of Sardis, who was a Roman senator and Governor General of the province of Asia. (See page 403ff.)

2. The Church at Smyrna (Rev. 2:8–11)

a. *Location.* Smyrna (modern Izmir), located on the Bay of Smyrna facing the Aegean Sea toward the west, is situated about halfway between Pergamos to the north and Ephesus to the south, both about 50 miles distant. The crescent-shaped city drapes around the 525 ft. Mount Pagos, which was at one time the Acropolis of the city.[12]

b. *History.* Smyrna was founded as an Ionian Colony in about 1000 B.C. but was destroyed by the Lydians in 600 B.C..[13] In the third century it came under the control of a loosely knit group of Greeks who made an early association with imperial Rome. The city became a shipping center, with caravan routes from the north and the east terminating at its docks.

From early times Smyrna was a religious center. Pilgrims from all over Europe and the East traveled its streets. "In the year 23 A.D. a temple was built in honor of Tiberius and his mother, Julia, and the Golden Street connecting the temples of Zeus and Cybele is said to have been the best in any ancient city."[14]

Paul probably introduced Christianity in Smyrna during his extended ministry in nearby Ephesus. Ancient records in Izmire give this ecclesiastical sketch on Smyrna:

The Revelation of St. John the Divine

Repentance
2706–2710
Faithfulness
1228–1230

Immortality
2405, 2406
Archaeology at Ephesus
4365

See Colored Map No. 12 (25-D), see also pp. 292–293 Pergamos, see Map pp. 292–293

The ruins of the Agora at Smyrna

Water pipe between Hierapolis and Laodicea

In 105 A.D. a few years after St. John wrote the letter to the Christians at Smyrna, St. Ignatius, the third Bishop of Antioch passed through on his way to Rome, where he was thrown to the beasts in the Roman Colosseum. While waiting for a ship in Troy he [John] wrote the Smyrnaeans and commended them for their "immovable faith as if nailed to the cross of the Lord Jesus Christ." He also wrote to Polycarp, a disciple of John, who became Bishop of Smyrna and linked the apostolic period to the second-century church.

St. Iraenaeus served as an elder in the church of Smyrna. Later (249–251) Pionius the Presbyter and his companions suffered martyrdom in Smyrna.

But Smyrna was also a seat of paganism. Young men flocked to the colleges of Smyrna to learn the philosophies of paganism. In the fifth century, Attila the Hun conquered Smyrna. In 673 the city was occupied by the Arabs for a while but they were unable to take the citadel. The emperor, Leo the Wise (886–912), gave the church at Smyrna one of the major sees in the Byzantine Empire. In 1071 the Selcuk Turks defeated the Byzantine forces. During the later occupation in 1204–1261 several Byzantine emperors took refuge in the region of Smyrna. From the late 1300's until World War I, Turkey was under the dominion of the Ottoman Turks. During this Moslem control the church almost disappeared from the scene. Even today professing Christians in Smyrna are few.[15]

Edgar J. Banks says, "In Roman times Smyrna was considered the most brilliant city of Asia Minor, successfully rivaling Pergamos and Ephesus. Its streets were wide and paved. Its system of coinage . . . was from early times, and now about the city are coins of every period. The city was celebrated for its schools of science and medicine, and for its handsome buildings. Among them was Homerium, for Smyrna was one of several places which claimed to be the birth place of the poet." [16]

c. *New Testament Smyrna.* It seems probable that Smyrna was one of the cities which embraced Christianity at an early date because it already had a flourishing church in John's day. Paul may have stopped there on his third missionary journey.

Tradition indicates that many Jews in Smyrna accepted Jesus as the Messiah. Christ commended the church for its faith (Rev. 2:8,9). However some Jews did not accept Jesus as their Messiah. They based their hope on their practicing the Jewish ritual and upon being circumcised descendants of Abraham. The question of circumcision and of who were real Jews arose in the church at Rome. The New International Version puts the meaning of this matter in focus: "A man is not a Jew if he is only one outwardly, nor is circumcision merely outward and physical. No, a man is a Jew if he is one inwardly; and circumcision is circumcision of the heart, by the Spirit . . ." (Rom. 2:28,29, NIV). Jesus stated that the Jews who claimed to be Jews in spirit, but were not, were committing blasphemy and were of the synagogue of Satan (Rev. 2:9). (See pages 129, 133, 488 for further comments on the synagogue of Satan.)

Rejected Christ
2965
Spiritual Circumcision
766

Blasphemy
473, 474
475

It was in Smyrna where "Polycarp, the bishop of Smyrna, was martyred, though without sanction of the Roman government. Apparently the Jews of Smyrna were more antagonistic than were the Romans to the spread of Christianity, for even on Saturday, their sacred day, they brought wood for the fire in which Polycarp was burned. His grave is still shown in a cemetery there." [17] Jesus warned the believers that they would suffer severe tribulation for ten days and would be cast into prison by the devil himself (Rev. 1:10). Apparently the persecutions were to last only a short time. The reward for faithfulness was "a crown of life."

Tribulation
499
Persecution
3480–3483

According to the Greek philosopher, Apallonius of Tyana, the phrase, The "Crown of 'Smyrna' " referred to the appearance of Mount Pagos with the stately public buildings on its rounded top and the city spreading out and down its sloping sides. St. John, on the authority of God, promises the Christians a new crown. The earthly Smyrna wore a crown like that of the patron goddess. The Smyrnians "faithful unto death" would receive a celestial crown, "a crown of life" (Rev. 2:10).

d. *Archaeology.* Archaeological activity remains restricted in Smyrna because the modern city of Izmir grew up over the ruins before interest in the preservation of antiquities developed. However, archaeologists have made soundings in several parts of the city and unearthed the remains of NT Smyrna on the eastern rim of the city. They have excavated the Roman Agora in the center of the city and have located a theatre on the slopes of Mount Pagos, the ancient acropolis of Smyrna, with a seating capacity of 20,000 people.

3. The Church at Pergamos (Rev. 2:11–17)

Pergamos
2736, 4403
Journey Map
pp. 292–293

a. *Location.* The city of Pergamos (now Bergama) is situated in western Anatolia (Turkey) and located 50 miles north of Smyrna (Izmir) on the Caicus (Bakir) River, 15 miles above where it empties into the Aegean Sea. The city is built on three terraces with the 1000-foot high acropolis as its summit.

b. *History.* In historical records Pergamos also appears as Pergamon and Pergamum. The origin of Pergamos is unknown, but the city certainly predates the Greek period. Greek coins discovered here date back to the fifth century B.C.

Frederick C. Grant observes that independent political history of the city began when Lysimachus of Thrace, one of Alexander's bodyguards, deposited here a large part of his treasure of 9,000 gold talents. It was entrusted to Philetaerus, son of Attalus of Tios, who revolted in 283 B.C. and set himself up as a ruler in alliance with the Seleucids. Under Alexander's general the kingdom continued until 133 B.C. when the last

The Basilica of Serapis Temple at Pergamos. It later became
the church of St. John

A reconstructed model of the Temple of Zeus at Pergamos

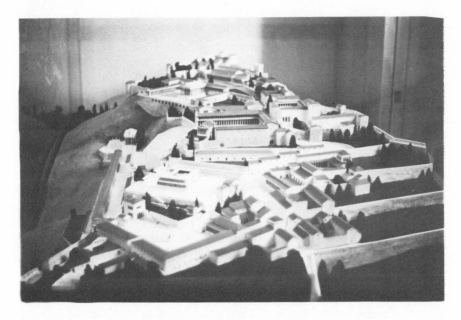

ruler, the childless Attalus III, bequeathed it to the Romans." [18] For a time Pergamos was the capital of Asia; however, in 6 B.C. Ephesus became the governor's official headquarters and place of residence. The Golden Age of Pergamos came under Eumenes II in about 190 B.C. During his reign the Menoun library was established.

c. *New Testament Pergamos.* The city of Pergamos was a thriving religious center from very early times. The acropolis, with its immense altar to Zeus, was the religious focal point of the city. Nearby stood the beautiful temple of Athena. In Roman times a temple to Augustus was also built on the acropolis—the crown of the city. Below was the shrine of Aesculapius, the god of medicine and healing. History does not record the origin of the Christian faith in Pergamos, but the church was probably founded by Paul, who was in the general area on his missionary journeys. Apparently the church became well established about 30 years later when John began his writing ministry in Ephesus, just 50 miles away. John's transmitting of the letter to the believers at Pergamos suggests that he had ministered in their midst.

In the middle of the second century A.D. Pergamos witnessed many martyrdoms. During the Decian persecution (249–251),

the martyrs included Carpus, bishop of Thyatira; Papylus, the deacon of Thyatira; Aga Thodoru; and a woman named Aga Thonida, who died, according to Eusebius, "after many glorious confessions." In 347 Eusebius became bishop of Pergamos. (See Rev. 2:13.)

Pergamos was the center of many theological debates. At the Robber Council of Ephesus in 449 (see section 1 "Church at Ephesus," this chapter). Eutropius of Pergamos accepted the Eutychian doctrines, which stated that Christ had only one nature, that of the incarnate Word. In the sixth century the city attracted an ever increasing number of Armenians. When in 716 the city fell to the Arabs, the town never recovered. Soon after 1211 the city came under the control of the Byzantine Empire (fifth and sixth centuries) of Nicaea. Early in the fourteenth century Pergamos fell under Turkish rule. By 1366 the Ottoman Turks seized control of the city and Christian influence began to decline. Churches were converted to mosques, including the Church of St. Sophia, in Constantinople (now Istanbul). When the Moslems converted the Church of St. Sophia into a mosque, they were confronted with the problem of what to do with the icons and mosaics depicting the saints, because to the Muslim all pictures are images or idols—not permitted in a mosque. They decided to paint over the beautiful mosaic pictures. Later when the church became a museum (as it now is), in the restoration process the use of paint remover brought the pictures back into view. The visitor can now see the beautiful artwork, typical of the period.

Of the seven churches St. John addressed, the two churches of Pergamos and Thyatira were treated with mingled praise and blame. In the opening sentence, he depicted Christ as having the two-edged sword (2:12). To the Romans the sword represented the power of life and death. In reference to Satan's throne (2:13), some scholars make an allusion to the great altar of Zeus, which was erected on a hill almost 1000 feet above the lower city. One of the sculptured walls featured a carved frieze 400 feet long, depicting the battle of the gods and the Titans (one of a family of giants born of Uranus and Gaea and rulers of the earth until they were overthrown by the Olympian gods).

Pergamos
2736, 4403
Thyatira
3621

Many years ago German archaeologists dismantled this beautiful altar and reassembled it in the Berlin Museum, now in communist East Berlin. This writer had to make several fruitless trips to examine this sculptured masterpiece before he could gain admission to the museum.

Despite the loyalty to Christ of some believers in the church at Pergamos, there were others holding to the heresy of Balaam, who caused Balak to induce the Israelites to "eat food sacrificed to idols and practice immorality" (2:14, RSV). The main message of Balaam is found in Numbers 22–24. According to Jewish tradition the religion of Balaam was associated with idolatry and temple prostitution. The doctrine of the Nicolaitans was both sensual and idolatrous.

Loyalty
2525

Christ admonished those who held the doctrine of the Nicolaitans to repent (2:15,16). However, the faithful Christians were promised a reward of "hidden manna." Each loyal believer would also receive a white stone and a new name to assure his immortality (2:17).[19] Little Christian witness is now evident in this once great Christian city.

d. *Archaeology.* Archaeological excavations in Pergamos are extensive and awe-inspiring. Many of the ancient buildings are now excavated or cleared of rubble and debris. The best known church discovered to date, the so-called Red Basilica, traditionally identified with St. John, stood on the ruins of a temple dedicated to the Egyptian god Serapis. Some materials from the temple were used in building the church. The walls and tower of the Red Basilica still stand. For centuries this church was a great Christian center. After repeated attempts by the Moslems to convert the Basilica to a mosque, they became discouraged. The minarets kept falling down so the Turks left the buildings in ruins and named it the Basilica Serapeion.

Arch.
Pergamos
4403

The library at the Aesculapion in Pergamos was once full of priceless parchments. Parchment was invented here. The visible remains of Pergamos give ample evidence of its once great splendor. The temple of Athena, the foundation of the Zeus altar, the gymnasiums, the baths, the art galleries are all there to see.

Most outstanding among the archaeological discoveries is the Aesculapion—the ancient medical center dedicated to Aesculapius, the Greek-Roman god of medicine. Pergamos was the medical center of that day. The healing art included both internal and external use of medicine, psychology, art, science, drama, music, hot and cold baths, and water cures. The remains of the uncovered medical center are quite extensive. Immediately outside the entrance is a monument, the symbol of the medical art, a serpent wrapped around a pole. The theater where drama was a part of the process for healing is one of the best preserved small amphitheaters in the world. The diagnostic rooms and treatment rooms now excavated may be viewed by the visitor. The psychological observation tunnel has an interesting feature. The holes in the ceiling enabled the healers to observe the patient secretly.

The Holy Spring, the Holy Passage, the temple of Athena, and the Temple of Serapis indicate that religion had an important part in the healing profession. The large gymnasium complex shows that exercise and gymnastics of all kinds were integral parts of making the body well and keeping it so.

4. The Church at Thyatira (Rev. 2:18–29)

a. *Location.* The city of Thyatira (now Akhisar) was located about 50 miles southeast of Pergamos on the caravan road to Sardis.

b. *History.* Historical information on Thyatira is relatively meager. In his *Letter to the Seven Churches*, William M. Ramsay, the noted historian, writes of the city, "Its history is a blank."

Thyatira was a border outpost, a buffer city between the border of Syria and Pergamos. The images and superscriptions on the coins found in the ruins indicate that the city-state often changed hands. The city was known both as Pelopia and Euhippa in 268 B.C. when Seleucus I (Alexander's general) colonized the area with Greek settlers and changed the name to Thyatira. In 189 B.C. it passed to Roman control. As a garrison outpost, the city had some disadvantages. It had no acropolis or fortification as did Ephesus, Pergamos, and Sardis. Being on the rolling plain, Thyatira was subject to frequent enemy attack. The defenders had to maintain their political integrity by sheer courage and bravery.

However, Thyatira's strategic location on a caravan route

made it a commercial center. In John's day, Thyatira had more trade guilds than any other city in Asia Minor. Inscriptions in the ruins mention workers in textiles, wool, leather, pottery, and bronze. Each group had its own guild, like the silversmiths in Ephesus.[20]

The city was especially noted for its dyeing industry. Lydia, Paul's first convert in Philippi, was "a seller of purple" from Thyatira (Acts 16:14). Purple was the color of kings and dignitaries. Purple dye, difficult to make and correspondingly expensive, may have been extracted from a certain kind of shellfish.[21] Ezekiel mentions the isles of Elishah and Syria as sources of purple (Ezek. 27:7,16; cf. Gen 10:4). Purple, as a distinctive color, is mentioned a number of times in the Bible (cf. Luke 16:19; Exod. 25:4; Judg. 8:26). Some scholars suggest that the dye was extracted from the madder root, growing in various select places in Asia.[22]

c. *New Testament Thyatira.* The beginning of Christianity in Thyatira is unknown, but it is quite likely that it was established by Paul or some of his associates. Paul had been martyred about 30 years before John wrote the letter to this church. Apparently the Thyatira church was a well-established congregation at that time. Few historians make reference to the city's pre-Christian religion. Harvey J. S. Blaney observes, "It contains no temple to the Roman emperor, but it did have a temple dedicated to Apollo, Tryimnaios and Artemis." [23]

The church at Thyatira was criticized because of its tolerance for false teachers. The members did have many good qualities such as "love," "service," "faith," "patience," and "zeal" (Rev. 2:19), but Christ rebuked them for permitting Jezebel, a prominent and influential woman, to teach their people that conduct had nothing to do with their faith. She may have taught that "worship was a mere form" and was irrelevant to their actions.

The influence of Jezebel was so great that the church adopted an attitude of tolerance (v. 20). She taught under the cloak of a prophetess and justified her conduct in the name of broad-mindedness (Rev. 2:20–23).[24] The prophetess, warned by God, had refused to repent. "Now her punishment is announced (v. 22). She is to be cast on a bed of suffering and with her those who, misled by her influence, had tried to combine Christianity with paganism: Those who were her spiritual progeny were to perish by the plague." [25]

Adam Clarke suggested that "this bad woman [Jezebel] was the wife of the bishop of the church, and his criminality in suffering [permitting] her was therefore the greater." He pointed out that some manuscripts read "thy wife, Jezebel" instead of "that woman Jezebel" (Rev. 2:20).[26] Henry H. Halley says that this false teacher "was called 'Jezebel' because, like

The Revelation of St. John the Divine

Silversmith's
255
Purple
2929, 2930

Thyatira
3621

False
Teachers
2101
Jezebel
1893

Prophetess
3868

Repentance
2706–2710

481

False
Teachers
2101

Idolatry
3928–3947
Revelry
3408

Thyatira
3621

Jezebel, the devilish wife of Ahab, who introduced the abominations of Astarte worship in Israel (1 Kings 16), she was introducing the same vile practices into the Christian Church." [27]

The trade guilds complicated the situation farther. In order to be employed it was necessary to belong to a guild, similar to modern day unions. "Eating food offered to idols" and licentious revelry were a part of the guild functions. "What was a Christian to do?" Both one's social and economic life depended on being a guild member.

When the English consul in Smyrna (now Izmir) visited the city of Thyatira in A.D. 1625, he found not more than ten Christians and the name of Thyatira was unknown. The consul reported seeing a small mosque which had been built on an old church foundation. Several times during the building operation, the minarets fell down, and consequently only a token mosque was built. George Wheeler explained that God brought judgment on the mosque because it was built upon the foundations of a church.

J. A. van Egmoat passed through Akhisar (Thyatira) in 1757 but makes no mention of a church. When Richard Chandler traveled the area in 1764, he found a Greek priest. In the eighteenth and nineteenth centuries, Greeks and Armenians settled in Akhisar. Chandler says, "the Greeks maintained one church—a wretchedly poor place below street level so that one had to walk down 5 steps to enter the church." In 1832 the Greeks built the cathedral of St. Nicholas. We are reminded that St. Nicholas—our Santa Claus—had his origin in Myra, Turkey, in the A.D. 300s; he was bishop of Myra. Tradition tells us that Nicholas went out at night and tossed bags of money into the homes of the poor people; subsequently he was called St. Nicholas.

Before World War I, 23,950 people lived in Akhisar (Thyatira): 11,000 Turks, 12,000 Greeks, 800 Armenians, and 150 Jews. In 1922 the Turkish troops occupied Akhisar (Thyatira). An estimated 7000 Christians were killed. There have been few Christians in Akhisar since that time. Today Akhisar is a thriving Turkish town. Its 1973 population was 48,000 with few traces of a Christian community. The church of St. Nicholas has been converted into a movie theater. In the inner court of the Grand Mosque, immediately to the east of the building, are the foundations of a large apse of an early Byzantine church. Local tradition has it that the mosque was built on the site of the church of St. Basil. [28]

d. *Archaeology.* The focal point in Thyatira (Akhisar) is a ruined ancient church, built on the foundations of an earlier one. A casual stroll up and down the streets of this city reveals antiquity evident everywhere. Much of the ancient marble carvings, many pillars and stones of the ancient city have become building material for the modern city. Capitals of columns are now horse troughs and well tops. Ancient marble columns support some roofs. Stones once in buildings are now used for paving streets.

5. The Church at Sardis (Rev. 3:1–6)

a. *Location.* The ancient city of Sardis (now Sart) was located about 35 miles southeast of Thyatira on the slopes of Mount Tmolus, 1500 feet high. It overlooked the Hermos river valley (now Gediz). The Pactolus river flowed along the western edge, which in ancient times provided a protective moat. On the eastern flank of the city was the acropolis fort.

Sardis
3147, 4410

b. *History.* In contrast to Thyatira, an abundance of historical information is available concerning Sardis. Its history was a rather bloody one. In 700 B.C. King Candaules was assassinated by his favorite palace guard, Gyges, over an incident involving the king's boast about the queen's beauty. Gyges became king, even though the citizens took up arms in the cause of their assassinated king despite the fact that the Delphic oracle spoke in Gyges' favor.

Thyatira
3621

In about 556 Croesus, the great king of Lydia, ushered in the Golden Age of Sardis. The wealth he gathered from his gold mines and trade with other countries made the name Croesus a synonym for fabulous wealth, and gave rise to the proverbial expression: "As rich as Croesus." He is said to have offered generous contributions for the rebuilding of the Artemisium in Ephesus and to the Greek oracular shrines, especially the one at Delphi, whom he frequently consulted for advice.[29]

The great wealth of the nation, along with its "impregnable" outer defense, fostered a false sense of security. The steep rocky fortress was unguarded; and while the soldiers slept at their posts, King Cyrus of Persia and his soldiers scaled the fortress walls and captured the city (546 B.C.). Herodotus describes the attack: "On the fourteenth day of the siege, Cyrus made a proclamation that he would give a reward to the man who should first mount the wall. After this he made an assault but without success. . . . One Hyroeades resolved to approach the citadel and attempt it at a place where no guards were ever set. On this side the rock was so precipitous, and the citadel so impregnable, that no fear was entertained of its being entered at this place. . . . He climbed the rock himself, and other Persians followed until a large number had mounted to the top; thus Sardis was taken." [30]

Sardis
3147, 4410

In 334 B.C., Sardis surrendered to Alexander the Great, but soon after his death Sardis became a part of the Seleucid King-

The theatre ruins at Pergamos

Ruins of the church at Sardis

dom. Rome gained control of Sardis in 190 B.C. at the battle of Magnesia.

In A.D. 17 a devastating earthquake destroyed the city, but it was soon rebuilt. "Sardis became an administrative center for Roman-Asia and when, in A.D. 26, the cities of the province contended for the honor of building the second temple for the Caesar-cult, the envoys spoke long and eloquently about the past glory of the place." [31]

c. *New Testament Sardis.* As with Thyatira, reliable information for the founding of Christianity in Sardis is lacking. It seems probable that Paul and his missionary associates should receive the credit. One may assume that the church of Sardis was founded in the middle of the first century. According to Menologion, Clement, a disciple of St. Paul (Phil. 4:3), was the first bishop of Sardis. As this city had flourished and then decayed, so the church there prospered and then declined. The letters of Sardis and Ephesus were strikingly similar though the spiritual degeneration was more severe at Sardis. Little is recorded about who the church officials were in Sardis during the first century, but documents show that Meliton was bishop of Sardis in the second century. He wrote the emperor Marchus Aurelius in defense of the Christians' faith. He is the first Christian theologian to provide a list of the OT canonical books.

Sardis was represented at the Council of Nicaea in 325 by Bishop Artemidorus (see page 198ff.). In 400 the Goths plundered Sardis. In 449 Florentius of Sardis sided with the Monophysite Alexandrian party at the infamous Robber Council of Ephesus (see Ch. 21, II on Ephesus). Sardis ranked sixth in the hierarchy of the Orthodox dioceses. By the seventh century it had 27 Suffragans (high subordinate church officials under a Metropolitan). Sardis became the center of numerous heretical controversies and political intrigues.

The Christian community deteriorated rapidly after the Turks occupied the city in the fourteenth century. In 1346 Sardis was still the See of the Metropolitan, but by 1369 the city did not have one high church official. The ecclesiastical affairs were transferred to Philadelphia.

In the first years of the fifteenth century Tamerlane occupied Sardis and massacred the population as he had in Ephesus, Magnesia, Pergamos, and Philadelphia (see section 6 of this chapter). Sardis became an abandoned city, but the nearby village of Sart struggled on.

The location of Sardis was never forgotten. In 1670 Jean-Baptiste Tavernier lodged in the park in Sart. He recognized three geographical landmarks familiar to ancient literature and realized he was in Sardis. He made few comments on what he saw. In 1671 Thomas Smith came to Sart and described it

The Revelation of St. John the Divine

Thyatira
3621

Philadelphia
2752

Sardis
3147, 4410

485

as a "beggarly and pitiful village." He alluded to a Christian church with several curious pillars of polished marble at the entrance which had been converted into a mosque. The few Christians who lived there had neither a church nor a priest. In 1698 Edmund Chishull reached the site; his account provides a clear description of the ruins of the great temple of Artemis. Sir Paul Lucas passed through Sardis in 1714, commenting only briefly on the vastness and beauty of the ruins and adding that the little village was called Sart.[32]

When Jesus addressed the Church at Sardis, it was living on its past glory. The believers were alive physically, but many of them were spiritually dead. The letter contains no commendations nor reproofs; it recognizes a faithful remnant, but these show a laxity and a carelessness to the encroaching dangers of heathen philosophies (Rev. 3:1).

William H. Ramsay the historian draws these conclusions: "It was a city whose history conspicuously and pre-eminently blazoned forth the uncertainty of human fortunes, the weakness of human strength and the shortness of the step which separates our confident might from the sudden and irreparable disaster. It was a city whose name was almost synonymous with pretentions unjustified, promises unfilled, appearance without reality, confidence which heralded ruin."[33]

The introductory exhortations in Revelation revolved around five strong words. They were: to be "watchful" (3:2), to be alert and to guard against the subtle encroachment of "the sin which doth so easily beset" (Heb. 12:1), to be "strengthened" (Rev. 3:2) by inner commitment, prayer, and supplications (Eph. 6:18), to "remember" (Rev. 3:3)—to be mindful not to trust in their own strength but to put on the spiritual weapons of war—"the whole armour of God" (Eph. 6:11–18), to "hold fast" (Rev. 3:3) the "profession of [their] faith" (Heb. 10:23) lest at any time they should let their first love slip away (Heb. 2:1b), and to "repent" (Rev. 3:3)—have a contrite heart and sorrow for their sins (Acts 22:16).

The promise to those who had remained faithful included white raiment and the retention of their names in the book of life (Rev. 3:4). Robert G. Gromacki says, "The believer-overcomer was promised a robe of divine righteousness, a guarantee of security and, a heavenly confession. Some identify this church with the Reformation period when individuals tried to strengthen the remaining good points of the Catholic Church."[34]

There was danger that history would repeat itself in a spiritual way. Prior civilizations had placed presumptuous confidence in their fortified walls (Babylon, Nineveh, Jerusalem): so now the church faced danger because of the people's over-confidence and their permissive attitude toward heathen sensuality.

d. *Archaeology*. Approaching Sardis, the capital of Lydia, one can see on the horizon massive marble pillars of the Cybel-Artemis temple. On the outer edge of the town flows the Pactolus river, a tributary of the Gediz.

6. The Church at Philadelphia (Rev. 3:7–13)

a. *Location*. The modern town of Alasehir stands on the ancient ruins of Philadelphia, the city of "brotherly love." It is situated on the Cogamus river at the base of Mount Tmolus, an ancient volcano, dubbed by the Turks as *Devitt*, meaning "ink wells." [35]

b. *History*. Philadelphia was one of the younger cities of Asia-Minor, founded by Attalus II Philadelphus, king of Pergamos. The king acquired the name Philadelphus because of his devotion to his brother, Eumenes—thus the descriptive phrase, "brotherly love." [36]

The city was an outpost of Greek culture, a show place for Hellenism, on the Roman Post Road, the commercial artery between Rome and the East. In A.D. 17 violent earthquakes almost completely destroyed the city. E. M. Blaiklock reports that "the historian, Tacitus, listed Philadelphia third among the cities of the province that were recipients of earthquake relief from the Roman senate." [37] To acknowledge this generous help, the Philadelphians renamed their city Neo-Caesarea after Tiberias. Sometimes Philadelphia was called "Little Athens" because of the beautiful temples and public buildings which graced its boulevards.[38]

The soil around Philadelphia, enriched by the volcanic residue of ages past, is well suited for certain crops. The area was and still is known for its excellent wine and raisin grapes. In the center of the town, and symbolizing the grape industry, stands a ten-foot monument in the form of a hanging cluster of grapes. A secondary industry is the manufacture of licorice, made from the roots of an Old World perennial plant used medically and in confections.

c. *New Testament Philadelphia*. The existence of a Christian church in Philadelphia is attested in Revelation 3:7, but it is not known who founded the church or under what circumstances. As was the case in most cities of Asia Minor, many Jews lived there and had a synagogue. Sometimes the church developed in local synagogues or in homes. The church may have been a result of the witness of the Jews who represented their synagogue at the Feast of Pentecost when the Holy Spirit filled the worshipers in the Upper Room. It is also possible

that Paul and his associates initiated a Christian movement
among the Jews.

Of the seven churches in Asia Minor, Philadelphia, the city
of "brotherly love," had the best Christian testimony. Christian
persecutions in this community were not pressed by the
heathen world but by the Jews who did not accept Jesus as
the Messiah, or by those Jews who had renounced the faith,
as defined in Romans 2:28,29.[39] These unregenerate Jews were
designated by Jesus as of the "synagogue of Satan" (Rev. 3:9).
(See page 129ff., "The Counterfeit Covenant Community.")

Many attacks were made against Philadelphia in the twelfth
century. The massive walled fortifications helped the city to
withstand assaults by the Turks and the Sultan of Rum. When

hostilities broke out between the Byzantine Empire and the
Sultanate of Iconium, the Byzantine Emperor, Manuel I. Co-
menus (1443), had to take refuge in Philadelphia. The city
remained a major center of feudal power even after Constantinople fell in 1204. Despite repeated attacks by the Turks, Philadelphia continued under Byzantine rule until the fourteenth
century, when the Ottoman Turks conquered all of Asia Minor.

Following the devastation of Asia Minor by Tamerlane in
the fifteenth century, most of the Christians fled to Venice.
The Patriarch of Constantinople then sent Severus to Venice

with the title of Metropolitan of Philadelphia.

In 1671 Thomas Smith visited Philadelphia and described
it as a "city of great strength and beauty, having three strong
walls toward the plain, a great part of the inner wall was standing though broken down in several places." Smith found that
the great church of St. John had become a dump for the offal
of slaughtered beasts by the decision of the Muslim Turks and
that they had converted other churches into mosques. He found

only four churches surviving. The roster of martyrs in Philadelphia carries the names of Demetrius and Hadji-George.

In 1785 Dr. James Griffiths reported seven or eight active
churches in Alasehir. In 1826 the Greek bishop informed Rev.
F. V. J. Arundell that the city had 3000 Turkish families and
300 Greek families. He reported that of the twenty-five
churches remaining only five were then in use. Arundell saw
the ruins of the church of St. John consisting of "a high stone
wall having the remains of a large arch on top." James Emerson
visited the city three years later; he returned with high praise
for the city "which still survives while her sister cities had
crumbled into decay." The number of Christians, estimated
between one and two thousand, were chiefly Turkish speaking.

Later travelers report seeing a portion of the wall believed
to have been built by the Ottoman-Turks with the bones of

the Christians who were massacred while they were worshiping
in a nearby church dedicated to St. John. In 1860 A. S. Noroff

listed the following five active churches: St. George, The Nativity of the Virgin, St. Theodore, St. Michael, and St. Marina.[40]

F. Bertram Clagg observes that,

> The Christianity of Philadelphia was of high character. This Missionary Church was neither vexed by heresy, nor shamed by heathen practices. Christ is described as "The Holy, par excellence," the true, the genuine Messiah, who has complete authority to admit or to exclude from the city of David. As the prophet (Isa. 45:14) anticipated the submission of the Gentiles to Israel, so the Philadelphians are bidden to anticipate that these Jews—who have belied their name and its privileges—will submit to the church, the true Israel of God.[41]

Even though the church of "brotherly love" was small and socially unrecognized, Christ encouraged and assured them that the children of God do not depend on worldly prestige. They were told that persecution would be their lot, but they were also assured that Christ would deliver them from temptation (3:10). All who were faithful to the end would receive a new name by which they would be identified in the "New Jerusalem" (3:12; cf. 21:1ff.).

d. *Archaeology.* One of the first objects of antiquity to be observed as one approaches Philadelphia is the remains of the ancient wall. It is broken here and there, but there is enough to show its original fortresslike structure. The effects of the repeated earthquakes are evident in the segmented wall around the city.

The ruins of the once great Christian basilica, built of red brick and still retaining some of the frescoes, are in Ismet Pash Street. Although the entrance to the ruins is locked, the keys are available at the Alasehir police station. The basilica is enclosed with a three-foot-high brick wall with a farm-type swinging gate at one end. When the police are not available, it is customary for visitors to climb over the wall. The enclosure is used as a stable for cattle. Inside are stumps of massive arches which once were part of a church building.

The Greek Orthodox Church has been active in Turkey for centuries, but with Turkish-Greek political hostility increasing, many of the Greek Orthodox Christians are moving to Greece. There are, however, still some active Christians in Philadelphia, but the number is uncertain. Based on American standards, the church exists at a very low level.

7. The Church at Laodicea (Rev. 3:14–22)

a. *Location.* The city of Laodicea was a thriving commercial center in the Lycos river valley at the juncture of three trade routes, of which the major one was the east-west highway. One of the spurs connected Laodicea with the Roman Post

Road at Philadelphia. Laodicea is about 15 miles west of Colosse, the same distance south of Hierapolis, and 125 miles east of Ephesus. The ancient mound is now called Eski Hissar, meaning "old castle," probably so-called because of the ancient ruins protruding out of the mound. The modern city of Denizli is located a few miles south of the old ruins.

b. *History.* Laodicea was one of those towns in the Neolithic period (following the Old Stone Age) characterized by new sources of food supply and the development of pottery and weaving. Historical references begin with the ancient name of Diaspolis and Rhoas. The Hellenistic ruler, Antiochus II (261–246 B.C.) rebuilt and renamed the city after his sister-wife, Laodice. Josephus says that his successor, Antiochus III (223–187 B.C.) brought in Jewish settlers to Laodicea from Syria and Babylon (Jos. Ant. XII, 147–149). Two other references indicate the presence of Jews in Laodicea. In his defense of Flocus, Cicero mentions that although the Jews of Asia were forbidden to send money to Jerusalem (pro Flacco, 28) they were guaranteed freedom of worship by the city magistrates (Jos. Ant. XIV, 241).

c. *New Testament Laodicea.* Evidence points quite definitely to Paul's involvement in establishing the church at Laodicea. It already had a Christian community when Paul wrote to the believers in Colosse (A.D. 60–64), which was only about 15 miles from Laodicea.

(Colossae)
Colosse
4352
Epaphras
1139

Laodicea
2050

In his letter Paul referred to Epaphras, who "hath a great zeal for you, and them that are in Laodicea, and them in Hierapolis" [15 miles from Laodicea] (Col. 4:12,13). Paul then referred to the "brethren which are in Laodicea, and Nymphas, and the church which is in his house" (Col. 4:14,15). Paul requested the Colossians to share their letter with "the church of the Laodiceans" and asked that "ye likewise read the epistle from Laodicea" (Col. 4:16). This, of course, raises the question: What was this letter to the Laodiceans mentioned by Paul, and who wrote it? Since John is communicating the Revelation message from Jesus Christ over 30 years after Paul wrote the Colossian letter, it must have been an epistle which Paul or some of his associates wrote the Laodiceans. Some scholars

suggest that this was actually the Ephesian letter. The reference to Laodicea in the epistle by Paul does show that there was a Christian community when he wrote the Colossian letter.

This gives credence to the possibility that the Laodicean Church was a result of witness or effort of those who had come from the Jewish community at the Feast of Pentecost in Jerusalem (about A.D. 33) when the Pentecostal outpouring prophesied by Joel was fulfilled (Joel 2:28–32; cf. Acts 2:16–21).

Both Laodicea, a commercial as well as an industrial city,

and the church were affluent. The gold in the river sands, along with its commercial enterprises, made Laodicea the banking center of Asia. Other industries included the minting of gold and silver coins and a textile center which produced and embroidered cloth shipped to many parts of the Near East. It was especially known for its carpets and blankets, made from the black sheep thriving there, its medical school, and a factory for making drugs, especially an eye medicine called "Perygian Powder" for a disease known as "Ophthalmia." These enterprises made Laodicea an industrial center and brought to it the typical immorality of a commercial city. Its abundant wealth tended to make the Laodiceans self-sufficent, exemplified by their rebuilding the city without help from Rome when an earthquake destroyed Laodicea in A.D. 60.

The Revelation of St. John the Divine

Laodicea
2050

The religious life of that part of the community embracing the worship of pagan gods revolved around the Temple of Zeus, where human beings were immortalized and the gods were "driven by human moods and passions, plotting against one another and taking sides in human conflicts." [42]

False Religion
2989

The wealth and worldly prestige led to an increased licentiousness and compromise on moral issues. Jesus' condemnation of the apostate church is direct and positive. What was true of the community was true of the church. F. Bertram Clegg gives this description of the church:

Wickedness
3065–3076

> There was money enough to support its enterprises: it was popular and well supported, for it did not set too high a standard of social and commercial life. Religious enthusiasm was characteristic of Phrygia, but Laodicea was a Greek city and was above that. The church adopted a spirit of accommodation and of broad toleration and was entirely self-satisfied. Proud of its prestige in the city, of its apostate tradition, of its generosity and wealth, it had "need of nothing (3:17) in its own eyes." [43]

False Pride
1724

The church was half-hearted, having a "one foot in heaven" attitude which was not accepted by either God or the selfish world. In his *Divine Comedy*, "Dante, at the gate of Hell, heard 'sighs with lamentations and loud moans.' Vergil explains that this was the fate of 'those who lived without . . . praise or blame,' Dante, Canto III . . . these Laodiceans, neutral souls, were driven forth from heaven and the depth of hell does not receive them." [44]

Of interest is the reference in Revelation to the lukewarmness of the Christians at Laodicea. They were neither "cold" nor "hot" but "lukewarm." Laodicea had no water supply of its own; so water was piped through a stone conduit from the hot springs in nearby Hierapolis (modern Pamukkale). By the time the water arrived in Laodicea it was indeed neither hot nor cold, merely lukewarm. Jesus knew about the hot springs

Laodicea
2050

491

at Hierapolis, which provided him with the imagery to describe the lack of spirituality and commitment of the Laodiceans (Rev. 3:15–16). (See page 411ff., "Colossians" and Appendix, page 513ff., a commentary on biblical archaeology.)

Using this analogy, Jesus rebuked the affluent and self-centered Laodiceans and counseled them to "buy of me gold tried in the fire." For those who would "repent," listen and "open the door" he would come in and "fellowship" with them. Sitting with Christ on his throne was to be their reward (Rev. 3:19,20).

The church at Laodicea suffered like the other churches of Asia Minor from the persecutions of the second and fourth centuries. In the latter part of the second century Sagaris, Bishop of Laodicea, was martyred and buried there. When

Artemon, the Presbyter of Laodicea, destroyed the images in the temples of Diana and Apollo, he was arrested and would have suffered martyrdom had not Sisinius healed the Roman centurion, Patricius, who then embraced the Christian faith.

Bishop Eugenius is credited with building a large and beautiful church in Laodicea during the reign of Constantine the Great. St. Sisinius, Bishop of Laodicea, states that the church was located five "stadia" outside the walls.

Laodicea had representation at the Council of Nicaea in 325, which condemned the Arians as heretics (see Ch. 13, II, A). (The Arians took the theological position that the Son is not of the same substance as the Father but was created as an agent for creating the world.) In 367 the fourth Synod was

held in Laodicea. It dealt with such matters as usury and the use of holy places by heretics. The Synod also ruled that priests should not perform marriages involving heretics, that the clergy should not enter taverns, and that beds should not be set up in churches. Other canons prohibited mixed bathing and marriages from taking place during Lent. Bishop Nunechius II of Laodicea participated in the "Robber Council" of Ephesus in 449. (See notes on the church at Ephesus for details.)

The city suffered intermittent defeats in the eleventh century and the early part of the twelfth. Late in the twelfth

century the Christians built a new city, also called Laodicea, on the site of modern Denizli, for it is described as being located at the foot of a lofty mountain, which would be true of Denizli, but not of the old Laodicea.

In 1190 the German emperor passed through Laodicea on his way to Jerusalem on the third crusade. After that time the city steadily declined. In the late seventeenth century Rev. Thomas Smith reported this of Laodicea: "It was inhabited only by wolves, jackals and foxes." In 1764 Richard Chandler

and his party were almost killed by robbers between Denizli and the ruins of Laodicea. The first ruin Chandler saw was the amphitheater, a hollow area about 1000 feet wide with many seats remaining. At its western end he identified the vaulted passage as a stable "designed for horses and chariots." He visited the odeum with its remaining seats, and beyond he saw some marble arches standing, the ruins of a gymnasium. No trace of churches or mosques was visible.

The nineteenth century travelers, James Emerson and Charles Fellows, made a similar report: "no wretched outcast dwells in the midst of it." [Laodicea] "has long been abandoned to the owl and the fox." [45]

d. *Archaeology.* The mound or tell of Laodicea is located only a few miles from the inhabited town of Denizli. The first ruins coming into view from the south are some segments of the massive stone arches of the aqueduct which once carried water from the hot springs in Hierapolis (Pamukkale) to Laodicea. On a more level area the aqueduct funnels into a stone waterpipe about three-feet square with a twelve-inch hole drilled through the center. These stones were joined together with cement to make a continuous conduit. Much of the material in the now dismantled water system was used in the construction of buildings.

The hot springs at Pamukkale are one of the principal tourist attractions of Western Turkey. Several large pools invite the visitors to enjoy the 95-degree water, which contains calcium, carbonate, sulphur, chlorine, and traces of sodium, iron, and magnesium. In the depths of the spring one can see columns and column capitals of ancient Hierapolis. (See par. 2, page 412, "Colossians.")

The mound rises about fifty feet above the terrain around it. Marble columns and stones of many shapes protrude from the surface. Local peasants sow and harvest wheat and barley on the mound in the area between the ruins. A cross carved in a stone identifies one excavated building as a former church.

Two amphitheaters, both reasonably well preserved, are visible in the mound. The remains of a stadium and a colonnade are also exposed to view. However, archaeological work is limited in Laodicea.

D. A Retrospective View of Revelation

After the prologue (1:1–20), which includes the vision of Christ (1:9–20), are the letters to the seven churches (chapters 2 and 3). A study of these messages has value today as they give a cross section of the various conditions of the church in every age. At the beginning of chapter 4 with the view of God's throne and the unusual symbols in a number of visions, the apocalyptic element becomes more evident (chs. 4–20).

Heaven
1356, 1547

The final vision of heaven (chs. 21, 22) has been a great comfort to believers throughout the ages.

These chapters have so engaged scholars that they have written numerous books about this subject even though there is no consensus concerning interpretation. However, serious students of the Bible find challenge and inspiration from a study of these passages as well as the entire book. In spite of both differences and difficulties of interpretation there are principles of truth that the true believer can comprehend if he asks for guidance of the Holy Spirit.

Holy Spirit
Guides
1611
Patmos
2695

The book contains the seven visions John had on the Isle of Patmos. George Tybout Purvis explains that "these visions are probably not to be understood as representing events which were to follow one another in history in the order of time, but as symbolical portraitures of certain religious truths or principles which were to be realized in the experience of the church. The whole is intended for comfort and warning of the church amid the conflicts of time and in preparation for the second coming of our Lord (1:7,8; 22:7,10,17,20)." [46]

Heavenly
Vision
511
Book of Life
526
Trumpets
2466, 2467

The seven visions may be summarized as follows:

(1) The vision of the glorified Christ and His church, followed by seven messages to the seven churches of Asia. . . .

(2) The vision of God, presiding over the destinies of the universe and adored by all creation, and the exalted but redeeming Lamb of God, who holds in His hand the sealed book. . . .

(3) The vision of the trumpets (VIII:2–XI:19). It opens with the vision of the angel offering the prayers of the saints to God (VIII:2–6). . . .

(4) The vision of the church under the figure of the woman, bringing forth the Christ against whom the dragon, or Satan, wages war (XII). . . .

(5) The vision of the vials, or bowls containing the last plagues, or judgments of God (XV, XVI). . . .

Christ the
Victor
372
Last Judgment
1351

(6) The vision of the harlot, city of Babylon (XVII), followed by the victory of Christ over her, ending in the last judgment (XVIII:1–XXII:7). [47]

The number seven has a peculiar place in Revelation. References in the book refer to: seven "churches" (1:4); "Spirits" (1:4); "golden candlesticks" (1:12); "stars" (1:16); "lamps" (4:5); "seals" (5:1); "horns" (5:6); "eyes" (5:6); "angels" (8:2); "trumpets" (8:2); "thunders" (10:3); "thousand" (11:13); "heads" (12:3); "crowns" (12:3); "last plagues" (15:1); "golden vials" (15:7); "mountains" (17:9); and "kings" (17:10).

In addition to the 400 instances in which the number "seven" occurs, the Scripture includes similar expressions: sevenfold, sevens, and seventeen. Henry H. Halley states that "used as often as it is, in the way it is, it must have some significance

494

over and above its numerical value. Symbolically it is thought to stand for completion, a unit of fullness, totality." [48]

Expositors agree that the presentation of the basic doctrines concerning God, Christ, Holy Spirit, sin, and redemption do not vary in Revelation essentially from those in other parts of Scripture:

God: Rev. 1:1 "The Revelation of Jesus Christ, which God gave"
His sovereignty: Rev. 17:14 "Lord of lords, and King of kings"
    Rev. 19:6 "God . . . reigneth"

Christ: Rev. 1:1 "The Revelation of Jesus Christ"
    Rev. 7:14b "they . . . have washed their robes, and made them white in the blood of the Lamb"
Holy Spirit: Rev. 2:7 ". . . let him hear what the Spirit saith unto the churches"

    Rev. 14:13 ". . . saith the Spirit"
    Rev. 22:17 ". . . the Spirit and the bride say, Come"
Sin: Rev. 22:3 "and there shall be no more curse"
Redemption: Rev. 7:14 "they . . . have washed their robes and made them white in the blood of the Lamb"
Heaven: Rev. 12:7 "war in heaven"
    Rev. 21:1 "I saw a new heaven"
Hell: Rev. 20:14 "death and hell were cast into the lake of fire"
Satan: Rev. 2:9d "synagogue of Satan"

    Rev. 20:1–3 Satan will be bound

Christology is evident; the Christ in Revelation is definitely equal with God (Rev. 1:4–17; 2:8; 5:12–14; 22:13).

There is also a striking similarity in the book to the teaching of Paul and Peter concerning redemption through the blood of Christ (1:5; 5:9; 7:14; 12:11; cf. Eph. 1:7; Col. 1:14; 1 Peter 3:18,19). Peter signified that the day of the Lord will come as a thief in the night (2 Peter 3:10a; cf. Rev. 3:3; 16:15). In the setting of the new order to come, at the last Judgment ". . . the earth and the heaven fled away . . ." (Rev. 20:11; 21:1). Peter had written a vivid prophetic description of this sudden (violent) cataclysmic event: ". . . the heavens shall pass away with a great noise, and the elements shall melt with fervent heat. . . . The heavens being on fire shall be dissolved . . ." (2 Peter 3:10,12). These details bear marked resemblance to the potential nuclear disaster generally feared in our day.

Some scholars suggest that the message in Revelation was entirely historical, that the believers of that period understood the message because they were familiar with the apocalyptic form of writing. The cryptic language is used to reveal to some believers, but to conceal from others. In an effort to interpret the meaning of Revelation, many have shown more enthusiasm than insight.[49] The Revelation of Jesus Christ indicates that God revealed himself to persons and groups in a way so that not only were their lives affected, but the destiny of others altered.

God intervened in the lives of (1) Adam and Eve (Gen. 3:9ff.), (2) Noah (Gen. 7:1ff.), (3) the Hebrews in Egypt and in their journey to Canaan (Exod. 1ff.), (4) the Judges (Judg. 1ff.), (5) Esther (Esther 1ff.), (6) Ezra and Nehemiah (Ezra 1ff.; Neh. 1ff.), (7) Mary (Matt. 1:20ff.), (8) the disciples in the Upper Room (Acts 1:13ff.).

His future coming will be a final invasion into the lives of men. The Book of Revelation deals with the second coming of the Lord Jesus Christ. This has been the blessed hope of the righteous since early times (see Enoch, Jude 14ff.; Dan. 7:9; Job 19:25). The twentieth chapter of Revelation contains information concerning events immediately preceding the Second Coming (cf. 1 Cor. 15:18–28,50–58; 1 Thess. 4:13–18; 5:1–7). The Book of Revelation was understood by the church to mean that the Second Coming was near, and in terms of God's time, it is always near. Because cataclysmic disaster is to usher in the kingdom of God, "John wrote to prepare his fellow Christians for these terrors, which he believed were already beginning, and to assure them that the outcome would be the triumph of Christ and His church. . . . His message . . . was not a message of doom but a call to courage and faith." [50]

A view of the "end of days" in chapter 20 describes the millennial reign of Christ when Satan will be bound and banished. Chapter 21 contains the vision of the "new heaven and a new earth" and a list of those people who will be excluded (v. 8). In the final chapter, John saw a "pure river of water of life," "the tree of life," and understood "there shall be no more curse" (vv. 1,2,3). The epilogue (vv. 6–21) emphasizes that Jesus will "come quickly" (translated by some as "suddenly"). The beautiful benediction concludes the book: "The grace of our Lord Jesus Christ be with you all." In Genesis, man's paradise is lost under a tree (Gen. 2:16ff.) and in the Last Book, Paradise is restored under "the tree of life" (Rev. 22:2).

Paradise
2680

Appendix 1

Thompson Chain-Reference Bible (TCRB)

I. INTRODUCTION

At last there is a Bible that the ordinary layman as well as the minister, teacher, and student can easily understand and use. It is the only work of its kind in the world, reliable, different, and better. This is the only Bible having marginal subjects alongside the references, without the use of letters, figures, or confusing signs in the Bible text. No longer does one need to waste time looking up mere references printed in a single column or beneath a verse.

With the Thompson Chain-Reference Bible, "blind" references become a thing of the past. The reference is always in the margin opposite the Scripture verse. The Text Cyclopedia number leads the reader into a limitless domain of Bible truth. Thus with the TCRB the use of a commentary becomes minimal. The Bible is its own best commentary when one is able to compare Scripture with Scripture.

Those who do or do not know the Bible well can benefit from the effort expended by the originator of the reference system in the TCRB. The General Index makes it possible to begin a study of the Bible on many different levels. Whether the area of interest is biographical, historical, philosophical, psychological, doctrinal, archaeological, or Christological, outlined data are all easily accessible.

The General Index is alphabetically arranged so that one may locate over 7,000 subjects as easily as one could if he were using a dictionary.

A. *Page 1 from the "General Index" of the TCRB* *See reproduction on following page.*

B. *The Analytical and the Chain-Reference Systems*

1. The Analytical System

This system consists of dividing the Word of God into different sections for study, as follows:

GENERAL INDEX

All *Numbers* refer to names, topics, charts, archaeology, etc., in The New Comprehensive Helps, except, in a few instances, where the word "page" precedes the number.

"*See*" used in the Index refers to a collateral subject.

Abbreviations:—ac., accor., according;—con., concerning;—Exa., Example;—Gen., General;—M., Marginal topic;—N. M., Not on margin;—C. N. M., Chain not complete on margin;—Phys., Physical; Prom., Promises;—Ref., References;—Spir., Spiritual.

In the Text Cyclopedia many topics do not appear in alphabetical order. Some subjects are subdivided and arranged under various appropriate headings. For example,—part of the sub-divisions of the topic *Marriage* appear under *Home*, the remainder under the letter "M."

The unity of the work is preserved by assembling all topics and their collateral subjects under complete alphabetical arrangement in the Index.

a. Analysis of Bible Books—Each of the sixty-six books of the Bible is thoroughly analyzed. In each case you are told the historical occasion, purpose, and key thought, with a synopsis of contents.

b. Analysis of Chapters—In the New Testament, the analysis extends to each chapter. Principal subjects contained in the chapter are printed in boldface type in the margin directly opposite.
c. Analysis of the Verses—Virtually every important verse has been analyzed by topics, which are printed in the margin opposite the corresponding ideas in the verse.
d. The Analysis of Characters—Prominent characters of both Testaments are analyzed, and a brief biography of each is given.
e. The Topical Analysis—Practical and spiritual topics are divided into subtopics in order that every aspect of the subject may be fully treated. Turn to page 21 of the TCRB Helps and note the amazing number of subtopics under the heading, "Christ's Divinity—Humanity."

2. The Chain System

This system, which is the counterpart of the Analytical System, assembles or harmonizes the scattered materials and presents a condensed view of the principal teachings of the Bible. The Synthetic Chains are grouped as follows:
a. The Topical Chains—Series of texts covering Bible teachings on a great number of varied subjects.
b. The Historical Chains—Series of references linked together, relating to ancient manners, customs, sects, and so on.
c. The Biographical Chains—Entirely separate from analysis of Bible Characters. These texts emphasize the main events in lives of Bible characters.
d. Chains Covering Modern Practical Subjects—"What are the teachings of the Bible concerning duties and customs of modern life?" Much light is thrown on this question by topics such as: Business Life, Dress, Pleasure-seekers, Gain through Loss, etc.
e. Chains Covering Ancient Sciences, Crafts, etc.—Bible teaching on subjects such as Law, Agriculture, and so on.

C. *Fifty-Seven Kinds of Helps in the TCRB*

1. Unique Chart Showing Origin and Growth of the English Bible. With this chart you will understand, as never before, the fascinating process of translating sacred writings. No. 4220.
2. The Outline Studies of Bible Periods. A clear comparison between biblical and secular history. No. 4222-b.
3. The Analysis of the Bible As a Whole. A general classification of the books of the Bible, with an instructive summary of each. No. 4222-a.
4. The Analysis of the Books of the Bible. Each of the sixty-six books of the Bible carefully analyzed, covering author, historical background, contents, themes, etc. Nos. 4223–4288.
5. Analysis of Each New Testament Chapter. In the New Testament, each chapter is thoroughly analyzed; principal subjects are printed in boldface type in the margin alongside the Bible text.
6. Analysis of Verses of Entire Bible. Nearly every Bible verse is

analyzed by topics. These are printed in a wide margin beside the verse.

7. The Numerical Chain-Reference System. The famed Numerical Chain-Reference system as used throughout the Bible facilitates and encourages Bible study.

8. Special Analysis of Important Bible Characters. A valuable and appreciated feature to the student and all Bible lovers. Nos. 4289–4300.

9. Contrast Between Old and New Testaments. This interesting chart compares principal dispensations of the two great divisions of the Bible. It is located between the Old and New Testaments.

10. The Topical Treasury. This feature suggests live new topics for Prayer Meetings, Women's Meetings, Missionary Meetings, Young People's Meetings, etc. No. 4312.

11. Special Bible Readings. Suggested readings for private devotions and public meetings include new and different subjects. Nos. 4130–4218.

12. Bible Harmonies. Harmonies of the lives of Moses and Paul. Complete outline of each life. Nos. 4307, 4309.

13. Special Portraits of Jesus. Portrayal of some special aspects of Christ's character and work. Nos. 4301–4306.

14. Chart of Messianic Stars. No. 4221.

15. Chart Showing Cause of Babylonian Captivity. Page 194 of the TCRB Helps.

16. Chart of Temple of Truth. Illustrating Sermon on the Mount. No. 4222.

17. Chart of Jesus' Hours on the Cross. Page 280 of the TCRB Helps.

18. The Christian Worker's Outfit. Especially valuable to Soul Winners. Gives Scripture texts to use with the unsaved, and other helpful data. No. 4313.

19. Prominent Bible Characters Classified. Listing of patriarchs, early Hebrew leaders, courageous reformers, etc., with the meaning of their names. Pages 239, 240 of the TCRB Helps.

20. Golden Chapters of the Bible. Seventy-four subjects such as Duty, Friendship, etc., with best chapter for each. No. 4311.

21. Complete General Index. A real index, listing over 7,000 topics, names, places. With this index you can find biblical information as easily and quickly as looking up a number in the telephone book. Immediately following Bible text.

22. Special Memory Verses. A careful selection from each book of the Bible. No. 4314.

23. Chart showing Seven Editions of Divine Law. No. 4219.

24. Graph of the Prodigal Son. No. 4310.

25. Bible Mnemonics. A unique system to aid in the memorization of Bible facts. No. 4315.

26. The Principles and Best Methods of Bible Study. Practical and worthwhile instruction as to how to get the most out of Bible study. Immediately preceding the Text Cyclopedia.

27. Pictorial Illustration of the River of Inspiration. Precedes Old Testament.

28. Bible Markings. Explaining the best methods of marking one's Bible. Page 303 of the TCRB Helps.

29. Revised Concordance. A Bible Concordance of 240 columns. Enlarged and reset with new type.

30. Atlas. Twelve colored maps with index for quickly locating places. Follows Concordance.

31. Topical Study of the Bible. Correlated Scriptures printed out in full under 2,467 topics and subtopics. Three times as many as in any other Bible.
32. Contrast Study of Great Truths of the Bible. Enables you to study the constructive and destructive forces of life, with Bible verses printed out in full under such subjects as Faith—Unbelief; Love—Hatred, etc. Listed alphabetically in Text Cyclopedia, pages 1–168 of the TCRB Helps.
33. Life Studies. These Life Studies include Business Life, Home Life, Devotional Life, the Surrendered Life, etc. Listed alphabetically in Text Cyclopedia, pages 1–168 of the TCRB Helps.
34. Bible Stories for Children. A list of fifty-six stories to be read from the Bible itself. No. 1672.
35. Miracles. Both Old and New Testament Miracles in chronological order. Nos. 2361–2374.
36. Parables. A listing of both Old and New Testament Parables, showing those given in one Gospel only; those in two; and those in three. Nos. 2678, 2679.
37. Titles and Names of Christ (No. 3632); of the Holy Spirit (No. 3634); of God the Father (No. 3633); and of Satan (No. 3638).
38. General Bible Prophecies. No. 2889.
39. A list of the Prophets of the Bible. No. 2066.
40. Chronological Lists of Judges of Israel and Kings of Israel and Judah. Nos. 1822–1824.
41. List of the Notable Women of the Bible. Page 240 of the TCRB Helps.
42. Mountains and Hills Referred to in the Bible. Listing the Scenes of Great Events. Nos. 2424–2447.
43. Dictionary Material. Found throughout the Text Cyclopedia.
44. Tables of Time, Money, Weights, and Measures. Nos. 3531–3542.
45. The Historical Bridge. A chart covering the interval between Old and New Testaments, together with a description of the books of the Apocrypha. Page 179 of the TCRB Helps.
46. Chart Giving the History of All Apostles. Page 241 of the TCRB Helps.
47. Harmony of the Gospels. Lists all events of Jesus' life in chronological order, and cites references on the different Gospels where the events are given; also contains references pertaining to the events recorded in the other books. Pages 269–272 of the TCRB Helps.
48. Calendar of the Christian Era. Page 245 of the TCRB Helps.
49. The Post-Resurrection Appearance of Jesus. An interesting feature, illustrated with reproductions of well-known paintings. Page 281 of the TCRB Helps.
50. Chart of the Seven Churches of Asia. As described by John. Page 282 of the TCRB Helps.
51. An Outline History of the Evangelistic and Missionary Work of the Early Church. Pages 294–295 of the TCRB Helps.
52. The Prophecies Concerning Jesus and Their Fulfillment. Arranged in chronological order with the principal references printed in full. Pages 246–249 of the TCRB Helps.
53. Map Showing Approximate Distances to Various Places from Jerusalem. Page 296 of the TCRB Helps.
54. Chart Showing the Interior Arrangement of the Temple of Jerusalem. Pages 306–307 of the TCRB Helps.
55. Special Illustrated Maps. This is a series of nineteen separate

501

Journey Maps, showing the journeys of Abraham, the children of Israel, Joshua, Gideon, Samuel, Saul, David, Solomon, Jesus, and Paul, and scenes in the life and ministry of Peter. See index on page 251 of TCRB Helps.

56. Places for Religious Worship, Hebrew Times, Seasons, Festivals, and Religious Officials. Nos. 4316–4318.

57. Archaeological Supplement. Over 100 accounts of discoveries made in Bible Lands. Pages 308–365 of the TCRB Helps.

II. Book, Chapter, and Expository Verse Analysis

The only way the Thompson Chain-Reference Bible can be fully appreciated is to get a copy and use it. If you are a teacher, see how much help it will be in the preparation of lessons. If you are a minister, you will be delighted with the many new insights it will reveal in sermon preparation. If you are a student or just a Bible lover, you will revel in the manner in which heretofore puzzling passages are made clear.

Among the many features that make this Bible worth many times its cost are the book and verse analysis throughout the Bible, and the analysis of the chapters in the New Testament. There are many books giving such analyses, but this is the only one in which no searching is required. All the information is directly keyed to the books, chapters, and verses. Following is an exact reproduction of a portion of the Gospel according to St. John. From this you will see how illuminating these helps really are.

A. Book Analysis

Each of the sixty-six books has been analyzed into outlined studies. The historical occasion of its composition, the purpose of the writer, the key thoughts, the more important teachings, and a synopsis of the contents are given. These are all assembled together as a section of the Comprehensive Helps and they are easily available by use of the numerical reference system at the beginning of each book throughout the Bible.

Now look at the first five topics in boldface type at the margin opposite the beginning of the chapter shown from the Book of St. John. They form a suggestive introduction to the book. The number at the left of "Writer" refers you to the Text Cyclopedia where a scriptural summary of his life is found. The next number, 4265, takes you to an exhaustive analysis of the entire book. The key verse tells why John wrote the book. The key thoughts unlock the deeper meaning of the book. The main theme gives a number which refers you to the Comprehensive Helps. For an actual reproduction of complete book analysis and further description, see the excerpt from the TCRB Helps on the Book of Genesis. See page 504.

B. Chapter Analysis

The chapter analysis is one of the features that has made the Thompson Chain-Reference Bible more workable than other Bibles. It is included right on the pages with the Scriptures throughout the New Testament and is of real help in quickly locating the portion of Scripture or text for which you are looking. It also presents an outline that tends to prevent missing any of the major points in teaching or studying.

(3) **The journey toward Jerusalem,** through Samaria and Perea; the ministry mainly in Perea, ch.9.51—ch.19.28.

(4) **The last days,** including the events of Passion Week and the crucifixion, ch.19.29—ch.23.55.

(5) **Events connected with the Resurrection** and the **Ascension,** ch.24.1–51.

4265—The Gospel of John

WRITER, The Apostle John, see Text Cyclo. No. 1902.

DATE uncertain. Probably late in the first century.

MAIN PURPOSE, To inspire faith in Jesus Christ as the Son of God.

KEY VERSE, ch.20.31.

DISTINCTIVE FEATURES.

(1) It is considered by many to be the **deepest** and **most spiritual book** in the Bible.

(2) In it **Christ** gives a more complete **revelation of himself, and of God,** than in either of the Synoptic Gospels.

　(a) Of his person and attributes. See the "I am's" of Christ, Bible Readings, No. 4166.

　(b) Of his Divinity, ch.1.1; 10.30–38; 12.45; 14.7–9; 16.15.

　(c) Of the work of the Holy Spirit. See 6's, 7's, 8's of the Holy Spirit, No. 4165.

　(d) Of his own divine commission. For example, in the fifth chapter he declares himself to be sent from God six times consecutively, in verses 23, 24, 30, 36, 37, 38.

　(e) Of the Fatherhood of God. Christ speaks of God as "The Father" over one hundred times.

　　God is the spiritual Father, ch.4.23; he is the life-giving Father, ch.5.21; the message is the Father's, ch.7.16; the Father is greater than all, ch. 10.29; the works are the Father's, ch. 14.10; God is the Indwelling Father, ch.14.23; the Eternal Father, ch.17.5; the Holy Father, ch.17.11; the Righteous Father, ch.17.25, etc.

(3) Perhaps the most notable of all the peculiarities of this gospel is the fact that **over one half of the space in the book is given to** the events of Christ's life, and his sayings during **his last days.**

(4) **Discourses** and **conversations** found only in John;—the talk with Nicodemus, ch.3.1–21; with the woman of Samaria, ch.4.1–26.

　　The discourse to the Jews at the Feast of Tabernacles, ch.7.14–39; 8.3–58; the parable of The Good Shepherd, ch.10.

　　The series of private instructions to the disciples, his comforting words and intercessory prayer, chs.14–17.

　　His meeting with the disciples at the Sea of Galilee, ch.21, etc.

(5) **John records eight miracles of Christ** (beside his own resurrection) **to prove his divinity.** Six of these are found only in this gospel:

The water made wine, ch.2.1–11; healing the nobleman's son, ch.4.46–54; healing the man at the pool, ch.5.1–9; the man born blind, ch.9.1–7; the raising of Lazarus, ch.11; the second draught of fishes, ch.21.1–6.

(6) **There are two great currents of thought** flowing through the book which it is profitable to follow—

　(a) Faith, ch.3.16–18; 5.24; 6.29,40; 7.38; 8.24; 10.37,38; 11.25–27; 12.46; 14.12.

　(b) Eternal life, ch.3.15,16,36; 4.14; 5.24; 6.27,51; 11.26; 12.50; 17.3; 20.31.

SYNOPSIS. The book may be divided into five parts;—

(1) **The Prologue.** The Eternal Word incarnate, ch.1.1–18.

(2) **The Manifestation of Christ's Divinity to** the world accompanied by a six-fold testimony. That of John the Baptist, the Holy Spirit, the disciples, Christ's mighty works, that of The Father, and the Scriptures, chs.1.19—12.50.

(3) **The Private Revelation** and instruction to the disciples, chs.13–17.

(4) **His Humiliation and Triumph over Death,** chs.18–20.

(5) **The Epilogue,** ch.21.1–23.

See also John's Portrait of Christ, No.4303.

—— The Tree of Christ's Life, No. 4308.

1902 **Writer,** Apostle John.
4265 **Analysis** of the book.
Key Verse, ch.20.31.
Key Thoughts,
"Faith" and
"Eternal Life."
Main Theme — see
Portraits of Christ's
Life, No. 4303.
Chap. 1, **The Divinity**
of Christ
700 Christ, "The Word."
709 Christ Eternal,
　　　　　[ch.8.58.
702 Christ Divine (2),
　　　　　[Ro.1.4.
709 Preëxistence of Christ.
　p.p.1 Jn.1.2.
680 Christ, Creator,
　　　　　[1 Co.8.6.
2152 Christ, the Life,
　　　　　[ch.5.26.
2168 Christ, the Light, v.9.
2175 Enlightenment.
2179 Spir. Darkness,
　　　　　[ch.3.19.
1010 Spir. Dullness.
Ministry of John the
Baptist, Is.40.3.
2074 God's Messengers.
1903 John the Baptist.
3855a Witnesses (2).

THE GOSPEL ACCORDI[

SAINT J(

CHAPTER 1

The divinity and incarnation of
Jesus Christ.

IN the beginning was the Word, and the Word was with God, and the Word was God.

2 The same was in the beginning with God.

3 All things were made by him; and without him was not any thing made that was made.

4 In him was life; and the life was the light of men.

5 And the light shineth in darkness; and the darkness comprehended it not.

6 ¶ There was a man sent from God, whose name *was* John.

7 The same came for a wit-

15 ¶ Jŏh
and cried
of whom
eth after;
me: for I
16 And
all we re
grace.
17 For t
Mō'şeş, b
came by
18 No m
any time
Son, whic
the Fath
him.
19 ¶ An,
of Jŏhn,
priests an
să-lĕm tc
thou?

Palestine among the Jews; the apostle Peter being the most prominent figure.

(1) **The Preparatory Events.**

　(a) The divine commission, ch.1.4–8.

　(b) The ascending Lord, ch.1.10,11.

　(c) The descending Spirit, ch.2.1–4.

　(d) The workers' equipment, ch.2.4; 4.31.

(2) **The Ministries.**

　(a) Of Peter at Pentecost, ch.2.14–40.

　　Peter's second sermon, ch.3.12–26.

　　Peter's address to the Sanhedrin, ch.4.5–12.

　(b) Of Stephen, ch.7.1–60.

　(c) Of Philip and Peter, ch.8.5–25.

　(d) Of Philip, ch.8.26–4).

Just think what a help it would be to have each book in the Old and New Testaments clearly and comprehensively analyzed, chapter by chapter. This analysis includes the authorship, the historical occasion which prompted the writing, the main theme, and other points of special interest. The intent of this analysis has been to strike the "keynote" of the book and open up its deeper spiritual meaning. An especially pleasing feature is the inclusion, wherever possible, of the more striking and dramatic passages in the book, under the heading,"Choice Selections." The specimen analysis reproduced on this page will clearly demonstrate the value of this feature.

4223—The Book of Genesis

AUTHOR, Moses (commonly accepted).

THE BOOK OF ORIGINS.

A record of the origin of,—Our Universe,—the Human Race,—Sin,—Redemption,—Family life,— Corruption of society,—The Nations,—the Different languages,—the Hebrew Race, &c.

The early chapters of the book have been continually under the fire of modern criticism.

But the facts they present, when rightly interpreted and understood, have never been disproved. It is not the purpose of the author of Genesis to give an elaborate account of the creation; only a single chapter is devoted to the subject; just a bare outline containing a few fundamental facts, while thirty-eight chapters are given to an account of the history of the chosen family.

MAIN THEME.

Man's sin, and the initial steps taken for his redemption by a divine covenant, made with a chosen race whose early history is here portrayed.

KEY WORD, Beginning.

FIRST MESSIANIC PROMISE, ch.3.15.

SYNOPSIS.

I. **The History of Creation.**
  (a) Of our Universe, ch.1.1–25.
  (b) Of Man, ch.1.26–31; 2.18–24.

II. **The Story of Primeval Man.**
  (a) The Temptation and Fall; the personality and character of the Tempter,—the penalty of sin, and the promise of a coming Redeemer, ch.3.
  (b) The story of Cain and Abel, ch.4.
  (c) The genealogy and death of the patriarchs, ch.5.
  (d) The events connected with the Flood, chs. 6,7,8.
  (e) The rainbow covenant and Noah's sin, ch.9.
  (f) The descendants of Noah, 10.
  (g) The confusion of tongues at Babel, ch.11.

III. **The History of the Chosen Family.**
  (1) **The Career of Abraham,** see Text Cyclo. Nos. 15, 4290.
    (a) His divine call, ch.12.
    (b) The story of Abraham and Lot, chs.13,14.
    (c) The divine revelations and promises to Abraham, particularly, the promise of a son, the possession of the Holy Land, and of a great posterity, chs. 15–17.

    (d) His intercession for the Cities of the Plain and their destruction, chs. 18,19.
    (e) His life at Gerar, and the fulfillment of the promise of a son in the birth of Isaac, chs. 20,21.
    (f) The test of his obedience by the divine command to offer up Isaac, ch.22.
    (g) His death, ch.25.8.
  (2) **The Career of Isaac,**
    (a) His birth, ch.21.3.
    (b) His marriage, ch.24.
    (c) The birth of his sons Jacob and Esau, ch. 25.20–26.
    (d) His later years, chs. 26,27.
    For other events connected with his life see Text Cyclo. No. 1802.
  (3) **The Career of Jacob,**
    (a) His craftiness in securing the birthright, ch.27.1–29.
    (b) His vision of the heavenly ladder, ch.28. 10–22.
    (c) Incidents connected with his marriage and life in Padan-aram, chs. 29–31.
    For further history of his life see Text Cyclo. No. 1837, also No. 4291.
  (4) **The Career of Esau** as related in Genesis, see Text Cyclo. No. 1149.
  (5) **The Career of Joseph,** the Later Years of Jacob, and the Descent of the Chosen Family into Egypt, chs. 37-50. See also "Joseph," Nos. 1917, 4292.

PROMINENT NAMES ASSOCIATED TOGETHER.

Adam and Eve,—Cain and Abel,— Abraham and Lot,—Isaac and Ishmael,— Esau and Jacob,—Joseph and his brethren.

FIVE GREAT SPIRITUAL CHARACTERS.
  (1) **Enoch,** the man who "walked with God," see Text Cyclo. No. 1135.
  (2) **Noah,** the Ark Builder, see Nos. 4289, 2597.
  (3) **Abraham,** the Father of the Faithful, see Nos. 4290, 15.
  (4) **Jacob,** the man whose life was transformed by prayer, see Nos. 4291, 1837.
  (5) **Joseph,** the son of Jacob, who rose from slavery to become the premier of Egypt, see Nos. 4292, 1917.

THE LESSON OF THE AGES. The Bible opens with Mankind ruined, Paradise Lost, ch.3.

The Plan of Salvation instituted, ch.3.15.

The Bible closes with the Promise Redeemed, Paradise Regained. See Rev. chs. 21,22.

That you may be able to know how stimulating this is, the following is the remainder of the analysis headings for the entire first chapter of the Gospel of St. John, along with the verse numbers opposite which they appear: verse 10, "Jesus Christ the Light of the World"; verse 15, "The Witness of John the Baptist"; verse 19, "John the Baptist's Answer to the Messengers of the Jews"; verse 22, "John the Baptist Announces His Office as Forerunner"; verse 28, "John the Baptist Baptizing"; verse 37, "John the Baptist's Disciples Follow Christ"; verse 40, "Andrew Brings Peter to Christ"; verse 43, "The Calling of Philip"; verse 45, "Philip Brings Nathanael to Christ"; verse 48, "Nathanael's Confession of Faith."

C. Verse Analysis

Every verse in the Bible that has any need to be analyzed has been treated in this way. It is necessary to the chain-reference system. It not only brings out the meaning of the verses but permits the continuation of the thought throughout the Bible. Just look at the wealth of thought and help there is opposite verses shown in the excerpt above. The fact that all such material is directly opposite the verse it refers to is of untold value for it gives you the helps on the Bible page where they are needed.

For further consideration on how the Expository Verse Analysis helps to bring out the hidden meaning of deep truths in Bible passages and at the same time ties in with the chain-reference system to give the greatest possible understanding and beauty to the Scriptures, note how it applies to Psalm 23.

This great song of the Shepherd King, as shown in the illustration from the text of the Thompson Chain-Reference Bible, contains six verses with twenty-four thought subjects, which with their complete

---

PSALM 23

3266 God's Sheep, Ps.74.1.
3264 Christ, Shepherd,
    [Is.40.11.
2905 Providence.
2906 Divine Supplies.
3011 Spir. Rest, Ps.55.6.
1306 Spir. Food.
1465 Guidance (1) ,Ps.25.9.
    Heb. *waters of rest.*
3025 Restoration (1).
1469 Divine Leader.
2688 Right Paths, Ps.25.10.
    p.p.Ps.31.3.
2160 Death of Right-
    [eous, Ps.116.15.
3246 Shadow of Death,
    [Ps.44.19.
1218 Confidence in God,
    [Ps.27.3.
1271 Divine Presence.
364 Divine Protection.
2907 Divine Preparation,
    [Ps.31.19.
1307 Spir. Feasts.
2640 Oil (3) , Ps.45.7.
1123 Spir. Fullness,
    [Mal.3.10.
2908 Superabundance,
    [Jl.2.24.
1438 God's Goodness.
2299 Mercy Promised.
3926 Love for God's
    [House, Ps.26.8.

David's confidence in God's grace.

A Psalm of Dā′vid.

THE LORD *is* my shepherd; I shall not want.

2 He maketh me to lie down in green pastures: he leadeth me beside the still waters.

3 He restoreth my soul: he leadeth me in the paths of righteousness for his name's sake.

4 Yea, though I walk through the valley of the shadow of death, I will fear no evil: for thou *art* with me; thy rod and thy staff they comfort me.

5 Thou preparest a table before me in the presence of mine enemies: thou anointest my head with oil; my cup runneth over.

6 Surely goodness and mercy shall follow me all the days of my life: and I will dwell in

505

reference chains embrace over 400 separate references. In the first verse, there are only nine words, yet four subjects appear in the margin. How did the author get four thoughts out of these nine words? If "The Lord is my shepherd," what am I? One of "God's Sheep." No sheep without a shepherd; hence, "Christ, Shepherd." "I shall not want." Why shall I not want? There must be a reason. Is it because of something I have done or merited? No, it is the "Providence" of God that is the source of "Divine Supplies."

It is the thought of a passage, its true spiritual meaning, and not just a subject index that is brought out in the expository verse topics. Under the old word system, much of the rich beauty and inner meaning of the Traveler's Psalm would never be brought out.

Opposite the second verse in Psalm 23, we find the subject "1465 Guidance (1), Ps. 25.9." The number 1465 is called the Pilot Reference and takes you to the Text Cyclopedia where the complete chain of reference on Guidance is given. The (1) refers to the first subtopic under this reference heading in the General Index of the TCRB. The forward reference is "Ps. 25.9" in this chain on Guidance. In Ps. 25:9, we find "The meek will he guide in judgment" with the forward reference to Ps. 32:8, and in this verse, we read "I will guide thee with mine eyes." The forward reference from Ps. 32:8 is to Ps. 48:14 which reads, "For this God . . . will be our guide even unto death."

The above three links of the chain on Guidance include judicial guidance, watchful guidance, and everlasting guidance, all of which are pretty exciting promises with God's backing even if there were no more. However, if we follow through on the chain we come to John 16:13 at the end. Here we read, "Howbeit when he, the Spirit of truth, is come, he will guide you into all truth." There is no further reference on "Guidance (1)," but where that ends, "Spirit Guides" begins, in other words, when God ceases to guide through the prophets, he sends his Holy Spirit to direct our way.

III. THE SPEEDY NUMERICAL REFERENCE SYSTEM IN THE TCRB

The Text Cyclopedia of the Thompson Chain-Reference Bible is superior to most books with "special" Bible helps. It contains about 200 pages of selected information, including comprehensive treatment of Topics, Doctrines, Places, Characters, Manners, Customs, Miracles, Parables, etc.

A. A Masterpiece of Condensation

In no other Bible can you find such unusual analysis and classification of material and so skillfully condensed as the material in the Text Cyclopedia. Not only is a new classification given to general information, but the teachings of the Bible on many new subjects are made available for ready reference. The subjects are arranged alphabetically, each one numbered so that you can readily find what you want. You have before you the progressive teaching of the ages, traced through the Bible from Genesis to Revelation, with the best verses relating to all important subjects. Nowhere can you find the teaching of the Bible on the master themes of life as perfectly assembled or so completely presented.

B. *Great Truths Taught by Contrast*

The great scriptural themes are correlated, and kindred subjects and their opposites are assembled under one contrasted heading, as: Abundance—Want; Association—Separation; Beauty—Disfigurement; Charitableness—Uncharitableness; Earnestness—Certainties; Stewardship—Ownership; Knowledge—Ignorance; Mind, Carnal—Spiritual, etc.

This new and exclusive arrangement gives you a complete view of all sides of a subject—shows you the positive and negative, the light and the dark side—on the same page with all the important Bible verses printed out in full for comparison.

It is but a step from the thought in any verse in the Bible to the Text Cyclopedia where the whole subject is developed and emphasized by contrast. An illustration of this feature "Earnestness—Indifference" follows.

**EARNESTNESS—
INDIFFERENCE**

1069—(A) **EARNESTNESS,**
Giving the Whole Heart to God (M. Whole Heart),
In Love,
De. 6.5. And thou shalt love the Lord thy God with all thine heart, and with all thy soul, and with all thy might. (De. 30.2)
In Obedience,
Ps. 119.2. Blessed *are* they that keep his testimonies, *and that* seek him with the whole heart. (Ps. 119.34)
In Trust,
Pr. 3.5. Trust in the Lord with all thine heart; and lean not unto thine own understanding.
In Prayer,
Je. 29.13. And ye shall seek me, and find *me*, when ye shall search for me with all your heart.
In Repentance,
Jl. 2.12. Therefore also now, saith the Lord, turn ye *even* to me with all your heart, and with fasting, and with weeping, and with mourning: (Mt. 22.37; Ac. 8.37)
See Consecration (1), (4), **3508, 3511;**
Undivided Service, **3898.**

IV. A GOLDMINE FOR THE SUNDAY SCHOOL LESSON

This work furnishes a great incentive to study and research. The reference system is so easy to use and the information brought to light is so fascinating that following the "Chains" on different subjects becomes a delightful game. Teachers who have felt that the usual lesson helps fall short of supplying connecting links between the Sunday school lesson and the other parts of the Scripture have their problems solved in the Thompson Chain-Reference Bible. There is no lesson to which this Bible will not add many points of interest.

This is the most rapid working Bible in the world. With the topical index and the comprehensive helps, you can find what you want instantly.

Teachers who have difficulty finding enough time for the preparation of the lesson find it indispensable.

For Instance: A teacher in front of her class, studying Acts 12, was asked which Herod was referred to. She did not know which, or where to find out. On the margin, this work says, "Herod Agrippa (1)." The Text Cyclopedia tells of four Herods and gives a character analysis of each containing more information than you would find after a long search in most libraries.

Sample Sunday School Lesson:
Topic: The Worried Housekeeper—Luke 10:38–42

We give this clipping from Luke 10 to illustrate the practical value of the Chain System of Bible Study as an aid to Sunday school workers.

With this work, teacher and scholar alike have an analysis of the thought of the lesson in the expository system. By consulting the margin of the clipping, you will see that there are twenty-four topics opposite the five verses of the lesson. Each topic contains a suggestive chain of thought for study at home or in the Sunday school class.

38 ¶ Now it came to pass, as they went, that he entered into a certain village: and a certain woman named Mär'thả received him into her house.

39 And she had a sister called Mā'rÿ, which also sat at Jē'ṣus' feet, and heard his word.

40 But Mär'thả was cumbered about much serving, and came to him, and said, Lord, dost thou not care that my sister hath left me to serve alone? bid her therefore that she help me.

41 And Jē'ṣus answered and said unto her, Mär'thả, Mär'thả, thou art careful and troubled about many things:

42 But one thing is needful: and Mā'rÿ hath chosen that good part, which shall not be taken away from her.

Christ at Martha's Home
404 Bethany, ch.24.50.
3399 Hospitality (2).
3867 Woman's Ministry.
3400 Christ a Guest, ch.14.1.
2261 Mary (c), Jn.11.1.
1721 At His Feet, Jn.11.32
2960 Spir. Receptivity,
    [Ac.2.41
4019 Deeper Life.
3885 Christ's Words.
2258 Martha, Jn.11.1.
3021 Worldly Care.
570 Industry (2).
831 Murmuring.
662 Fault-finding.
861 Discourtesy.
4152 Family Cares, ch.11.6
798 Christ Reproves.
3022 Care Forbidden,
    [ch.12.29
3008 Requirements.
4187 One Thing, Jn.9.25.
3874 Devout Women,
    [Ac.16.14
676 Wise Choice, He.11.25
791 Commendation.
3657 The Enduring.

The student and teacher, with this Bible in hand, have not only their Bible text, but also their lesson helps right before their eyes, and all in one book. The information needed to teach and study the lesson is not at home or in the library in the cumbersome form of many books.

To return to this simple lesson—look at the margin opposite the first line of verse 38 and you will find that here in boldface type is one of the topics of the Chapter Analysis, "Christ at Martha's Home." Right below it is the first topic in the Verse Analysis, "Bethany." This gives us the scene of the lesson.

Bethany was the home of Martha, Mary, and Lazarus. Preceding the word "Bethany" you will find the number 404. Referring to this number in the Text Cyclopedia, you will find a brief description of Bethany and the complete chain given; all the places where it is mentioned in the Scriptures are listed. The reference at right of "Bethany" tells where it is next mentioned.

Look at the margin of the clipping again and you will see that there are three other topics opposite verse 38. "Hospitality (2)," "Woman's Ministry," and "Christ a Guest." All of these have chains that present fruitful lines of study. Hospitality (2) suggests Martha's warm-hearted hospitality; but she was not the only one mentioned in the Scriptures who kept open house for the saints. The chain under this topic gives fourteen other notable examples of hospitality.

The chain on Woman's Ministry furnishes numerous instances of what women like Martha have done in various kinds of sympathetic service. The last topic opposite verse 38, Christ a Guest, suggests the social functions he attended.

The first reference opposite verse 39 is "Mary." Which Mary? There are six in the New Testament whose lives are given in the Text Cyclopedia. This is the Mary of Bethany, the woman immortalized by Christ.

We have only lightly touched on two verses of this sample lesson to show the abundance of material which this book places in the hands of teacher and student. You have probably already noted the interesting helps opposite the other verses of this lesson.

V. CHARACTER STUDY OF MEN AND WOMEN IN THE BIBLE

Why was Samuel termed "the upright Judge"? When was he dedicated to the Lord? What do you know of his early training and remarkable boyhood? What was his mother's birthday gift to Samuel each year? What were the accomplishments of his mature years? When and how did he become Judge of Israel? In what manner was he instrumental in saving his people from the Philistines? What can you tell of his declining years? Who were the two kings whom he anointed? When and how did he die?

These are just a few of the interesting points brought out by the Character Study of Samuel. Other character studies are equally interesting and worthwhile.

The biography of Noah, as given on the next page, is a good example of what you may expect from these character studies.

A. *Biographical Chains*

Interesting Bible Studies revolve around notable men and women:

1. Aaron

The first entry in the General Index is Aaron, the brother of Moses, who took a prominent part in Israel's deliverance from Egypt. Many moral and spiritual lessons may result from a study of Aaron's life. The numeral 1 after Aaron's name directs attention to the first entry in the Text Cyclopedia. Under subtopic (1) of numeral 1 are listed the general references to Aaron. By turning to the first reference, Exodus 4:14, one finds the first place in the Bible where Aaron is mentioned. This verse states that Aaron was eloquent of speech. He was a learned man, perhaps a graduate of an Egyptian school.

In the Bible text, the reference Exodus 5:20 follows Aaron's name in the margin and directs attention to the next place in the Scripture where his name appears. Here Aaron has joined Moses in an appeal to Pharaoh that he permit the people to leave Egypt. The reference after the name points to the next place in the Scripture where his name appears.

Exodus 6:20 contains something about Aaron's ancestry. The General Reference lists all the references in the Aaron chain, to the end, where Aaron dies.

By tracing a chain of references in the TCRB one cannot only read

Aaron
1
Moses
2420, 2421

Scriptures
3166
Pharaoh
2747, 2748

509

4289—Noah, the Ark Builder

HIS ORIGIN AND EARLY LIFE. Nothing is known of his early days. He first appears upon the scene when he was five hundred years old.

His great grandfather, Enoch, was a man of notable piety who, because of divine favor, escaped death by translation, Ge.5.22–24; He.11.5.

His grandfather, Methuselah, was the longest lived man, according to the record in Genesis, Ge.5.25–27. His father's name was Lamech, who was apparently a religious man, and gave his child a name that is thought to mean, "rest," Ge.5.29.

THE CONDITION OF SOCIETY IN HIS TIME. He lived in a desperately corrupt age, when men had become so universally depraved that the Lord had determined to destroy the race, Ge.6.1–7. In the midst of this moral darkness Noah's life was radiant with righteousness, Ge.6.8,9.

HIS DIVINE COMMISSION. The earth being filled with violence, it was divinely revealed to Noah that there was to be a great flood which would destroy man from off the face of the earth.

He was given a strange, and from a human standpoint, apparently impossible task to perform: to build an immense boat or vessel for the preserving of the lives of his own family, and certain numbers of the animal kingdom. The greatness of the task assigned to him has seldom been fully appreciated by men.

It must be remembered that he was surrounded by a mass of godless unbelievers, who would come to see his work, attracted by curiosity, and remain to scoff at him. He would become a laughingstock.

He must maintain his faith, and toil on year after year at a task which seemed to indicate that he had gone mad.

Considering his surroundings, the magnitude of the work he was called upon to perform, and the many years spent in hard labor, he stands among all the workers of the Bible unsurpassed, if not unequalled, in persistent faith.

The Ark

The dimensions of the ark are uncertain, depending upon the length of the ancient cubit.

We have accepted twenty-one inches as the standard length. For time consumed in building, compare Ge.5.32, with ch.7.6.

It would seem that Noah warned and exhorted the people while he was engaged in his work on the ark, 2 Pe.2.5.

LAST DAYS BEFORE THE FLOOD. The assembling of the animals and fowls and the entrance of Noah and his family into the ark, Ge.7.1–16.

The Lord closes the door of the ark, Ge.7.16.

EVENTS DURING AND AFTER THE FLOOD. The duration of the flood, Ge.7.24; recession of the waters, ch.8.3; the resting of the ark upon land, ch.8.4; the birds sent forth, ch.8.6–12; leaving the ark, ch.8.15–18.

Noah builds an altar, and offers a sacrifice, ch.8.20. He is honored by a divine covenant, ch.9.9–17. He plants a vineyard and yields to temptation, ch.9.21; his death, ch.9.28,29.

For other references to, see Text Cyclo. No. 2597.

---

the text but also get a context (setting). It is always of interest to learn what precedes and what follows a text. For meaningful Bible study one needs to consider the context. Someone has said, "A text without a context is a pretext." A "text only" study can lead to a legalistic interpretation of Scripture.

The following examination of random references affords a further grasp of the principles of the chain-reference system, starting with the index.

Abednego
3

2. Abednego

Abednego is the next choice. The Text Cyclopedia No. is 3. The first reference in the Text Cyclopedia section is Daniel 1:7. Before the name Abednego in the margin is the numeral 3, which is the Text Cyclopedia reference number. Since his name appears only six times in the Bible, the information on Abednego is somewhat limited. He is identified as one of the three Hebrew children delivered from the fiery furnace in Babylon. The first reference in the Bible to Abednego indicates that he was one of the four to whom favor was shown by the prince of Babylon. This same reference states that Daniel and the "three Hebrew children" were each given Babylonian names: Daniel became Belteshazzar; Hananiah became Shadrach; Mishael became Meshach; and Azariah received the name Abednego. The last general reference to this man is Daniel 3:30. After having gained favor with the authorities, following the fiery furnace incident, Abednego fades from the scene.

Arch. Babylon
4334

3. Abraham

The instructions in this guide omit Text Cyclopedia references 4–14 but do give attention to that illustrious figure, Abraham. Since he is a major character in the OT and is also mentioned in at least four NT books, the TCRB Helps has many references. Genesis 11:27 is the first place in the Bible where the name Abram (later, Abraham) appears. Here is given something about his ancestry. Terah was Abram's father and Haran and Nahor were his brothers. Genesis 17:1,5 states that Abram's name was not changed to Abraham until he was ninety years old. The name change came at a time when God made a special covenant with Abram. He was to be called Abraham, and from him a great nation would come. Exactly why his name was changed is not known. Some scholars suggest that the change to Abraham (Gen. 17:5) may indicate a greater position of responsibility. Certainly Abraham did receive a special commission to become the father of many nations.

The General References (or Chain-References) trace Abraham's name from the OT into the NT (Rom. 4:3; Gal. 3:6; Heb. 11:8; James 2:21). Thus Abraham is involved in NT theology. The TCRB Helps No. 4290 refers to a map showing briefly the journey of Abraham from Ur of the Chaldees to Canaan. Following this map is a biographical sketch or outline with Scripture references concerning Abraham's lifetime travels. In the last section of No. 4290 is a listing of the outstanding events and experiences of this great man of faith. Pages 252 and 253 of the TCRB Helps contain a chart with references to the place that Abraham visited on his journey from Haran to Canaan to Egypt. Each place visited in the journey has an identification number in chronological sequence. In the right margin and at the bottom is a short commentary with photographs illustrating how the number in the commentary is keyed to the chart.

4. David

TCRB Helps No. 919 yields a biographical sketch of David. Here again are the General References in the chain system. The first chain reference is Ruth 4:22, which is the initial reference to David. It is a statement of family origin. In the margin of Ruth 4:22 are the two TCRB Helps Nos. 919 and 4296, which give not only a biographical sketch but also an outline of what David did, with a list of the places he visited. With the use of these marginal notations it is always easy to find the basic reference charts of the person or subject to be studied. The Scripture reference 1 Samuel 16:13 is the next chronological reference where David's name is used. In the margin to the left of his name, the TCRB Helps Nos. 919 and 4296 are repeated. On pages 264–265 in the TCRB Helps there is a Journey Map with commentary on David's travels. The chronological number 1 starts in Bethlehem, where David lived and where his public ministry began. The commentary with illustrations helps to dramatize the events surrounding his life.

Of significance is David's ability as a musician. He is credited with writing more than half of the Psalms, which served as the hymnbook for Israel and the only hymnbook of the Christian church for 1500 years. Some Reformed and Presbyterian churches still use *The Psalter* exclusively as their hymnbook; see TCRB Helps No. 4241. The first-century Christians sang Psalms frequently (Eph. 5:19; Col. 3:16; James 5:13).

Thompson Chain-Reference Bible (TCRB)

Abraham
15, 4290,
pp. 252, 253
Terah
3597
Nahor
2510, 2511

David
919, 4296,
pp. 264, 265

Psalter
2462
511

5. Solomon

Solomon
3414,
pp. 266, 267

Under TCRB Helps No. 3414 is the name Solomon, where General References forming the chain-reference system are listed. This section is followed by a character sketch outline. Pages 266–267 in the TCRB Helps section include a Journey Map with commentary showing the principal events in the life of Solomon (1 Chron. 28:5; 2 Chron. 1–9).

6. Moses

Moses
2420, 2421

The General Reference and the first chain reference on Moses begin under TCRB Helps No. 2420 which is followed by a comparative study between Moses and Christ. Reference to Moses' rod is made in TCRB Helps No. 3092. Under No. 4307 a tree chart, with references placed on the roots and the branches, presents the early background of Moses. On pages 256–257 in the TCRB Helps is a Journey Map tracing the travels of Moses and of the Hebrew children from Goshen, in Egypt, to Mount Nebo, where he was permitted to view the Promised Land.

7. Gideon

Gideon
1414, 4294
pp. 260, 261

In the Index, Gideon appears under TCRB Helps No. 1414. The first link in the Gideon chain is Judges 6:11, followed by a list of character traits. No. 4294 in the TCRB Helps presents a more detailed study or outline on Gideon. On page 260 in the TCRB Helps, a Journey Map shows his travels.

8. Joshua

Joshua
1922
pp. 258, 259

The next character study is Joshua, who appears under No. 1922. The first reference in the chain is Exodus 17:9; the last one is 1 Kings 16:34. This set of references is followed by a list of personal characteristics. No. 4228 in the TCRB Helps presents a more detailed outline of the Book of Joshua. On pages 258–259 the Journey Map shows the area over which Joshua traveled, starting in Moab and ending with his death in Shechem.

9. Saul

Saul
3158,
pp. 262, 263

A record of Saul comes under No. 3158. The General References indicate that 1 Samuel 9:2 is the first chain entry. His characteristics are listed below the general references. Pages 262–263 present a Journey Map of Saul's travels.

The principles of study presented about these men apply to all the men and women listed in the Bible, although some biographical references are shorter than others. The General Index is always the place where a study of this nature begins. By using the General Index one can engage in a comprehensive study of any biblical topic. The preceding random selections from the Index serve to illustrate the principles of this method of study. After consideration of persons, for example, one could study places. The list includes the name and the TCRB Helps number. The reader may take it from there.

10. Prominent Women in the Bible

A list of prominent women from the Old and New Testaments and key index numbers and Scriptures can be found on page 240 of the TCRB Helps.

Thompson Chain-Reference Bible (TCRB)

Prominent Women p. 240

VI. PLACES IN THE BIBLE

1. Aijalon, No. 111
2. Alexandria, Nos. 114, 4325
3. Babylon, Nos. 329–331, 4334
4. Bethany, Nos. 404, 4336
5. Caesarea, Nos. 615, 4344

References to these and many more can be located in the Bible with the use of the General Index and the Text Cyclopedia of the TCRB.

VII. THINGS IN THE BIBLE

1. Altars, Nos. 120–123, 3948
2. Balm, No. 337
3. Books, No. 527
4. Chests, No. 674
5. Cisterns, No. 768

Begin with the alphabetical list in the General Index of the TCRB to study many other biblical objects.

VIII. DOCTRINES IN THE BIBLE

1. Baptism, Nos. 756–760
2. Confession, Nos. 813–818
3. Faith, Nos. 1201–1211
4. Heaven, Nos. 1356, 1547–1549, 2013
5. Hell, Nos. 1374–1375, 1558–1559
6. Regeneration, Nos. 835, 2154
7. Repentance, Nos. 2706–2710
8. Restitution, Nos. 3023–3024
9. Sin: there are over sixty aspects of sin. We list here only a few:
   (a) Against "The Spirit," No. 1608
   (b) Allurements of, No. 3351
   (c) Bondage of, No. 2139
   (d) Concealment of, No. 800
   (e) Confession of, Nos. 816–818
   (f) Conviction of, No. 1764

It is suggested that one thumb through the TCRB General Index and read each entry. He will be amazed to discover the comprehensive list of subjects the Bible discusses. Whether it is persons, mountains, lakes, seas, towns, valleys—they are all in the index. In a few minutes one can compile a massive amount of Bible information on any subject.

IX. BIBLICAL ARCHAEOLOGY

Archaeology **4320–4428** p. 309

A. *A Commentary on Biblical Archaeology*

G. Frederick Owen presents a scholarly analysis on the points of interest listed in the TCRB. Little could be added to improve these

Shown below is a portion of only one of more than 100 illustrated and fascinating accounts of discoveries in the Bible Lands from the "Archaeological Supplement" by Dr. G. Frederick Owen, renowned Archaeologist, professor and author. These concise, interesting and authoritative accounts covering the early findings on down to the present time, including the Dead Sea Scrolls, shed so much light on the Bible and Bible history. No other Bible offers such complete help on Archaeology and at the same time links it with the Bible text.

4346—CALAH, now called Nimrud, lies about twenty miles south of Nineveh, on the west bank of the Tigris river. According to Gen. 10:11, it was first built by Asshur: "And out of that land went forth Asshur, and builded Nineveh, and the city Rehoboth, and Calah."

Sir Henry Layard began exploring the mound in 1845 and found that the remains of the ancient city walls measured 7,000 by 5,500 feet. Within these walls he found the remains of the palaces of three kings: Ashur-nasir-pal (885–860 B.C.), Shalmaneser III (860–825), and Esarhaddon (680–669 B.C.), along with many wall sculptures. The most interesting of these sculptures was a series which record the victories of Tiglath-Pileser III, the "Pul" of II Kings 15:9. These figures show, in graphic style, the evacuation of a city, military operations connected with a siege, and the harsh treatment meted out to prisoners. They appear to have been removed from an older palace by King Esarhaddon and placed in his palace at Calah.

The statue of Nebo, the god of wisdom and writing, was excavated at Nimrud, and dates from the time of Adadnirari III (810–782 B.C.). Engraved on the statue is the following inscription: "Trust in Nebo; do not trust in any other god."

A relief from the palace of Tiglath-Pileser III shows four statues of gods being borne away from a conquered city on the shoulders of Assyrian soldiers.

The most important of all discoveries at Calah, however, was the "Black Obelisk" which had been set up by Shalmaneser III in the central building. It is a large, imposing monument of black marble, six feet, six inches high; and tapering at the top. It has twenty small bas-reliefs—five on each side—showing the officials from five different countries bringing tribute to the king. Above, below, and between the reliefs are 210 lines of cuneiform inscription which tell the story of the monarch's achievements in war and peace during the first thirty-one years of his reign. Among other individuals it mentions Hazael of Damascus and Jehu of Israel. On the

BRITISH MUSEI

An Assyrian Winged Bull from the palace gateway of King Ashur-nasir-pal in Calah (Nimrud).

articles. However, some general background information on an actual "dig" should be helpful. The countries of biblical interest include ancient Palestine, Egypt, Syria, Assyria and Babylon (now Iraq), Persia (now Iran), Asia Minor (now Turkey), Greece, and Italy, plus such islands in the Mediterranean as Cyprus, Crete, Rhodes, and Patmos.

The ideal archaeologist is a composite scientist with knowledge of many disciplines, who concerns himself with dead things as a means of learning something about the life and times of the ancients. He must be familiar with chemistry to be able to analyze ashes and decayed matter to determine the building materials which were used. He must be acquainted with anthropology to decide the age and sex of human skeletal remains. His knowledge of botany will help him to determine which kind of plant life existed in the vicinity of

514

the excavated "tell." He must know something about political science to be able to determine what kind of government and social order the people had. A knowledge of sociology, economics, and biology is helpful to properly evaluate the remnants from civilization being dug up. He must know the use of the many kinds of tools employed in his profession. The archaeologist must be able to determine why cities and civilizations disappeared. The Bible states that some cities disappeared because of divine judgment such as that which came upon Sodom (Gen. 19:24), Jericho (Josh. 6:20,21), Nineveh (Nah. 3:7), and Babylon (Isa. 13,14). Some destructions have come about through such phenomena as earthquakes, fires, pestilence, drought, floods, and famines. The archaeologist looks for causes.

Mound-shaped tells or hills usually mark the place of an ancient city, but no city name-signs remain. Sometimes the name can be determined by a study of geography, history, and other background information. Before the archaeologist can start digging, he must obtain permission from the government of the country in which the excavation is to take place.

Not least among the problems of a "dig" are finances. Money for ventures of this kind is not easily obtained. Moneyed men want quick dividends, which cannot be assured. Usually financing is done by educational institutions, archaeological societies, and museums. In addition, the selection of a staff is important. Digging in dry, hot, insectinfested areas calls for undivided dedication and commitment. A compatible staff is extremely important.

Before excavation can commence, a number of local laborers must be employed to do the hard work, the digging, and the hauling away of the excavated dirt. Permission from the owner of the land must be obtained and this frequently involves exorbitant sums of money. Local residents are often suspicious of foreigners who will pay money to dig up a "tomato patch." They suspect that the foreigner has come to dig up a "pot of gold" or some other treasure. Tools such as picks, shovels, rakes, hoes, and buckets made from old auto tires must be secured. Wheelbarrows are usually the standard vehicles for hauling large amounts of dirt; however, much of the dirt removed is by bucket brigades. In larger operations this work is accomplished by the laying of a narrow-gauge railroad track, over which small mine cars are pushed. Also the installation of field telephones is not unusual so that the head archaeologist can be in touch at all times with the several areas where excavation is going on.

When a skeleton, or some other artifact, is discovered, the workers resort to the use of small tools such as trowels, table knives, forks, spoons, brushes, and even toothpicks in order to preserve the exact posture of the object.

In the early days before archaeology became a science, mechanical equipment, such as scrapers, plows, and bulldozers, was used. This, of course, destroyed most of the archaeological evidence. A modern excavation starts with a survey of the area to mark out the boundaries of the dig. Men with spades and shovels begin a shallow trench, being continually on the alert for some object at the point of the spade. The photographer is always on hand to take pictures of the dig as it progresses. Whether the operation is tunneling, running a shaft, or digging down through the stratum, the original formation is destroyed with every shovelful of dirt.

Dating the find is important. This can frequently be done by examining the pottery, but pottery is easily broken. The archaeologist must

515

often determine the age of the pot by the kind of clay used and by the workmanship.

A more sophisticated type of dating is done with the carbon 14 process, a system developed by Dr. W. F. Libby of the Institute of Nuclear Studies at the University of Chicago. This device measures the amount of radioactive carbon remaining in the material tested. Dr. James R. Arnold produced a similar device called the "Atomic Clock" which is supposed to date material as much as 44,000 years old. Both systems have a margin-of-error factor of about 5 percent.

Archaeology has confirmed the historicity of the biblical record time and again. Likewise, excavation often presents evidence to support the credibility of the Scriptures. A personal example illustrates a point of interest in addition to those articles Dr. Owen has so brilliantly prepared.

After visiting most of the archaeological sites in the Near East, in over fifty visits, this writer discovered some water pipes at Laodicea which give credence and understanding to a scriptural statement. Laodicea is located in ancient Asia Minor which is now in Turkey. This mound extends nearly one mile in all directions yet has had very little archaeological attention. One of the most remarkable finds here is located on the outer edge of the city. Laodicea had no water supply of its own. Sometime during the Greek or Roman period, water pipes, three-foot square stones, hollowed out, were laid end to end across the valley to the hillside city of Hierapolis to the north, where hot springs provided an abundance of water. The visitor today still finds the hot water cascading over the calcified terraces into the valley below. By the time the once hot water reached Laodicea it was lukewarm or tepid.

Colosse, on the other hand, located about 15 miles from Laodicea, had its own cold water springs. The water at Hierapolis was hot and healing, but when it reached Laodicea by gravity flow it was neither hot, nor cold like the Colossian water. Jesus made reference to this lukewarm water to illustrate the insipid, lukewarm spiritual condition which prevailed in the church at Laodicea (Rev. 3:15,16). (Also cited ch. 21:IV and ch. 25:7, the church at Laodicea). In his letter to the Colossians, Paul writes of the spiritual zeal Epaphras had for the people at Hierapolis and Laodicea (Col. 4:12,13.) The modern town of Pamukkale has been built around the ruins of ancient Hierapolis.

B. Index to Archaeological Articles

Chorazin, No. 4351
Colossae, No. 4352
Corinth, No. 4353
Damascus, No. 4354
Dan, No. 4355
Dead Sea Scrolls, No. 4356
Derbe, No. 4357
Dibon, No. 4358
Dothan, No. 4359
Ecbatana, No. 4360
Edrei, No. 4361
Elam, No. 4362
En-Gedi, No. 4363
En-Rogel, No. 4364
Ephesus, No. 4365
Erech, No. 4366
Ezion-Geber, No. 4367
Gaza, No. 4368
Gerar, No. 4369
Gerizim, No. 4370
Gethsemane, No. 4371
Gezer, No. 4372
Gibeah, No. 4373
Gibeon, No. 4374
Gihon, No. 4375
Golgotha, No. 4347
Gomorrah, No. 4416
Hamath, No. 4376
Haran, No. 4377
Hazor, No. 4378
Jacob's Well, No. 4379
Jericho, No. 4380
Jerusalem, No. 4381
Joppa, No. 4382
Kadesh-Barnea, No. 4383
Khorsabad, No. 4384
Kidron, No. 4385
Kiriath-Sepher, No. 4386
Kish, No. 4387
Lachish, No. 4388
Lagash, No. 4389

Lydda, No. 4390
Lystra, No. 4391
Mareshah, No. 4392
Mari, No. 4393
Medeba, No. 4394
Megiddo, No. 4395
Memphis, No. 4396
Mizpah, No. 4397
Mount of Olives, No. 4402
Nazareth, No. 4398
Nebo, No. 4399
Nineveh, No. 4400
Nuzi, No. 4401
Olives, No. 4402
Pergamum, No. 4403
Petra, No. 4404
Philippi, No. 4405
Rabbath-Ammon, No. 4406
Ras Shamra, No. 4407
Rome, No. 4408
Samaria, No. 4409
Sardis, No. 4410
Shechem, No. 4411
Shiloh, No. 4412
Shushan, No. 4413
Sidon, No. 4414
Siloam, No. 4415
Sodom and Gomorrah, No. 4416
Taanach, No. 4417
Tadmor, No. 4418
Thebes, No. 4419
Thessalonica, No. 4420
Tirzah, No. 4421
Troas, No. 4422
Tyre, No. 4423
Ur, No. 4424
Zarephath, No. 4425
Zion, No. 4426
Zoan, No. 4427
Zorah, No. 4428

Thompson
Chain-
Reference
Bible (TCRB)

517

Appendix 2

The Concordance and Maps

I. CONCORDANCE AND CROSS REFERENCES

The TCRB Concordance is an integral part of the entire chain-reference system because "the main topics in the concordance are directly connected with the New Comprehensive Bible Helps by reference numbers. These numbers, in parentheses immediately following the main topics, refer to the paragraph or section in the New Comprehensive Bible Helps unless the number is preceded by p. or pp. indicating "page or pages" (TCRB).

In this way the Concordance can be used in conjunction with the General Index. If one needs a comprehensive view of a subject he has the double advantage of both systems; e.g., the Concordance lists the word *Christ* about 50 times while the General Index lists Christ under more than 170 correlated topics in the TCRB Helps. In this way one can gain an extensive knowledge of a subject from a scriptural point of view. By studying the instructions on page one of the Concordance, one can facilitate its use. For the sake of new students unfamiliar with the Bible or a concordance, the following observations are made.

A concordance is a book in which important words of the Bible, both OT and NT, are arranged alphabetically. Usually from five to eight words of a verse are printed, containing the word in question. As an example, one may remember two or more words, or perhaps all of a verse but not know where it is found in the Bible: "Man shall not live by bread alone." The key words are "man," "live," and "bread." By checking any of these words in the Concordance it is possible to locate the verse. Under "bread" is this phrase, "not live by bread only," the phrase is sufficient to show that it is the passage sought. This verse is usually associated with Christ, but the first reference is from the OT, Deuteronomy 8:3. The second one is Matthew 4:4. In checking this, one finds that Christ is quoting the passage from Deuteronomy 8:3. In fact, Christ often supported his teachings by quoting directly from the OT. Note that the Deuteronomy and the Matthew versions differ somewhat. The reason for this variance

518

is that the NT writers used and quoted from the Septuagint, the Greek version of the OT, and not from the ancient Hebrew text. There is a slight difference in terminology between the Hebrew and the Greek versions when they are translated into English. The Greek OT was used because it was the common language of that period.

In the Concordance under the word *call* are Nos. 1789–1793 from the TCRB Helps. A check of these references will show that the word *call* is used in several ways. Nos. 1789 and 1790 refer to methods used in Bible times to call men to service. In No. 1791 the passages listed illustrate the universal nature of the gospel call—it is to all men everywhere. No. 1792 points to instances of men who refused the call to discipleship. No. 1793 exemplifies a call to decision. These examples stem from the single word *call*. For additional information consult an edition of an unabridged concordance.

II. Maps and Map Index

The science of cartography is the key that opens up the world of geography, a Greek-derived word meaning "earth description." In the study of the TCRB maps, one may center his interest primarily upon the "earth description" of the lands where the Bible events unfolded. A study of the geography of the Bible lands makes a valuable contribution to the understanding of the Bible. There is an exact and wonderful agreement between the land and the Book. The plains, the mountains, the valleys, the rivers, the lakes, the cities, and the deserts are all part of the Scriptures, correctly named and correctly located. But this correspondence in the Bible goes much further. It gives minute and incidental details.

Lake Galilee is approximately 700 feet below sea level. When the Scripture refers to a storm, one would assume that it came sweeping across the terrain, but a passage in Luke 8:23 reads: "There came *down* a storm of wind on the lake." The word *down* is significant. This is the only way a storm could come to the lake—from above, because the lake rests in a bowl-shaped basin 700 feet below sea level with the surrounding mountains 1700 feet above sea level. The intense hot-air currents rising from the lake come into contact with the cold air from the perpetually snow-covered Mount Hermon, just to the northeast, and in a very short time a storm can come "down" upon the lake.

An excellent collection of maps concludes the section of study helps in the TCRB. An examination of these maps shows their unusual detail and clarity. Each name on the map is easily located by the use of the Index to the Scripture Atlas immediately preceding the maps. The index shows the map number and the cross lines of the place sought, e.g., in the index, Memphis is listed on Maps 2, 4, 8, and 12. Looking at the Map 2 reference one finds that the location is near the intersection of imaginary line 3 and imaginary line G. On Map 4 Memphis appears near the intersection of lines 3 and I. Sometimes the place, as in this case, may be removed from the point of intersection by an inch or so, but the place in question is always nearby. One may exercise his map skills by locating the position of each area he studies in the Bible text. Knowing where the places are in the Bible will add greatly to one's understanding of the Scriptures. Eventually there will come a mental impression of where each place is located in relationship to other places.

Appendix 2

Noah
2597, 4289
Shem
3262
Ham
1477
Japheth
1845

Ur
3738, 4424
Haran
1496, 1497

Hoshea
1705
Israel
1807–1829
Judah
1955, 1956
Babylon
329–331
Nebuchadnez-
zar 2573
Josiah 1923
Uzziah 3744
Hezekiah 1585
Jehoram
1863, 1864
Ahaz 103
Manasseh
2244, 2245
Zedekiah
3988, 3989
Arch.
Jerusalem
4381
Patriarchs
Antioch
197, 198,
4328
Flood 973
Abraham 15
Isaac 1802
Jacob 1837
Haran
1497, 4377

520

A. Map 1. The Ancient World—The Descendants of Noah

Map 1 shows the origin of the three basic races. The Bible plainly teaches that Noah's three sons, Shem, Ham, and Japheth, and their descendants are the progenitors of the inhabitants of three basic geographical areas: Shem and his descendants populated eastern and western Asia (Gen. 10:21,22). Ham and his sons established a society on the African continent (Gen. 10:6–20), and Japheth and his sons settled in Europe (Gen. 10:2–5). Most encyclopedias concur.

B. Map 2. Armenia with Assyria, Babylon, and Syria

The central part of Map 2 covers the so-called "cradle of civilization." According to the Bible, the human race originated in the area between the Tigris and Euphrates rivers. In about 2000 B.C. Abraham and his family emerged from Ur of the Chaldees area and migrated up the Tigris-Euphrates valley to Haran, located on one of the upper branches of the Euphrates River (7-C), and later down into Canaan, into Egypt, and finally back to the area around Hebron.

This region also includes Assyria, situated on the upper part of the Tigris River. In 722 B.C. the Assyrians conquered the Northern Kingdom (Israel) and took many of its inhabitants into captivity along with Hoshea, their idolatrous king. The Northern Kingdom's political structure was so completely disrupted that it never again regained its political identity. A number of Assyrians moved into the territory of Israel. Those Israelites who remained in the land began to intermarry with the heathen people, and from these intermarriages came the despised Samaritans. Over a hundred years later (587 B.C.) the Southern Kingdom, Judah, was taken captive into Babylon by Nebuchadnezzar, King of Babylon (2 Kings 25). Judah did have some godly kings, but gradually evil prevailed, and God imposed punishment upon them. They had been spared the judgment of God under such great kings as Josiah, Uzziah, and Hezekiah; but under such idolatrous kings as Jehoram, Ahaz, Manasseh, and finally Zedekiah the nation was attacked, destroyed, and most of the leading people were taken into captivity. See chart on page 194 in the TCRB Helps.

In the upper left of Map 2 is Asia Minor. This is now Turkey, where the early missionaries planted the seed of the NT church. After their break with unbelieving Judaism in Jerusalem, the climate for the Christ-Messiah movement in Jerusalem became uncomfortable. Consequently the church moved its official headquarters to Antioch, which was then in Syria, located a few miles inland on the north coast of Syria. The believers were first called Christians in Antioch (Acts 11:26). From here the early missionaries penetrated Asia Minor and southeastern Europe. For additional information consult the notes on Map 12.

C. Map 3. Canaan in the Age of the Patriarchs

The root meaning of the word *patriarch* suggests lineage or father of a line of people. Generally speaking, this word has three biblical connotations: (1) the early fathers of the human race, (2) the early fathers, from the flood to Abraham, and (3) the progenitors of the Israelites—Abraham, Isaac, Jacob, and the twelve sons of Jacob. See charts on pages 232, 252, and 253 and No. 4290 in the TCRB Helps. David is referred to as a patriarch in Acts 2:29. The maps indicate the area traversed by Abraham on his way from Haran to Egypt.

Nos. 15 and 4290 and pages 252 and 253 in the TCRB Helps offer information on Abraham, No. 1802 on Isaac, and Nos. 1837 and 4291 about Jacob. For a study of David refer to pages 264–265 and Nos. 919 and 4296 in the TCRB Helps. For the sons of Jacob see Genesis 29–50.

D. Map 4. The Sinai Peninsula with the Journeys of the Israelites from Egypt to the Promised Land

The Journey Map on pages 256–257 in the TCRB Helps brings into focus the area in which Joseph was enslaved after his brothers sold him to the Ishmaelites (Gen. 37:2–28), and they, in turn, sold him to Potiphar (Nos. 1917 and 4292). Later, Jacob and his sons moved to Goshen in the Nile Delta of Egypt. About 430 years later, when the families of Jacob's sons became slaves, Moses, the great lawgiver, led them out of Egypt to the border of the Promised Land.

Moses
2420–2422, 4307

Joseph
1917

Goshen
1439
Nile
2591

E. Map 5. Canaan as Divided among the Tribes

The tribes of Israel were a corporate political entity composed of related families. All of the groups acknowledged the oldest member of a family as the father or patriarch of the tribe with absolute authority in all matters, even life or death, civil or religious. The tribe was also communal in matters of flocks, wells, travel, and migration. Criminal acts of any kind were judged by the chief or by those to whom authority was delegated.

At the time of the Exodus into Egypt each son of Jacob had a sizeable number of descendants (Num. 1:21–43). Eventually an unfriendly Pharaoh (Exod. 1:8) came to the throne and oppressed the Hebrews. As Moses (referred to in the notes to Map 4) led the people from Egypt to Canaan, three Israelitish institutions were given to the tribes: the tabernacle, the priesthood, and the Law. A modern parallel would be the church, the minister, and the Bible. (See Journey Map on the Wilderness Journey, page 256.) Near Mount Nebo Moses died and Joshua was commissioned to succeed Moses and provide leadership for the entry into Canaan.

Pharaoh
2747, 2748
Moses
2420, 2421
Egypt
1100
Canaan
626–634

The map referred to shows how the land in Canaan was divided among the tribes. The division of the land was based on its quality and fertility. Generally speaking, if the land was more fertile, the plot was smaller and if less fertile it was larger. There were only eleven political subdivisions (counting Ephraim and Manasseh as the one for Joseph) because the tribe of Levi was designated as the priestly tribe, and its members were to be supported by the tithes and offerings from the other eleven. Ephraim and Manasseh, the two sons of Joseph and his Egyptian wife Asenath, were adopted by their aged grandfather Jacob (Gen. 48:5–14) and made fellow heirs with Joseph's other eleven brothers. Ephraim received the blessing customarily given to the eldest. In the dividing of Canaan, Ephraim and Manasseh each received choice parcels of land. Both Ephraim and Manasseh were considered as "half-tribes" and together they represented one patriarchal unit. This tribal unity continued until the death of Solomon, when the northern ten tribes separated themselves from Judah. They became a political entity under Jeroboam (933 B.C.). Judah, the Southern Kingdom, was ruled by Rehoboam, the son of Solomon (1 Kings 12:16–20).

The coastal map shows that a narrow strip of land was not taken but remained in the hands of the Philistines. God had commanded

Levites
2114
Priesthood
2863, 2864
Ephraim
1144–1147
Manasseh
2244, 2245
Joseph
1917
Jeroboam
1879, 1880
Rehoboam
2983
Philistines
2758

521

the tribes to take all of Canaan but by disobeying God at this point the Israelites suffered many difficulties at the hands of the Philistines.

F. Map 6. The Dominions of David and Solomon

David
919, 4296
pp. 264, 265
Solomon
pp. 266, 267
Saul
3158,
pp. 262, 263

Jerusalem
1881

Under the rule of David and his son Solomon, Israel attained its "golden age." David came to the palace as a humble shepherd boy to comfort King Saul (1 Sam. 9–31). In the course of time the sterling qualities of David won the esteem of the people, but this displeased Saul. The king became jealous and in fits of temper he made several attempts to kill David. Finally Saul committed suicide and David ascended the throne (1 Sam. 31:1–6). As a resourceful executive and a wise administrator, David united the divided tribes into one strong political entity with Jerusalem as its capital and the future site for the building of the temple.

G. Map 7. The Kingdoms of Judah and Israel

Solomon
3414, 4297,
pp. 266, 267
Idolatry
3948, 3949
Concubines
1665
Heathen
Temples
3949

Solomon's reign brought to a peak the "golden age" of Israel, but as his wealth and prestige grew, his devotion to God decreased. His great mistake was marriage to idolatrous women (cf. Deut. 17:17; 1 Kings 11:1). He, disregarding Israel's ideal of monogamy, had 700 wives and 300 concubines (1 Kings 11:3), many of whom were the idolatrous daughters of heathen rulers. They persuaded him to build heathen temples and altars by the side of God's Holy Temple. The apostasy of Solomon in his old age proves that no man is immune from sin and its consequences when he compromises with divine principles. Solomon's poor example for the nation may have contributed to the strife following his death.

H. Map 8. Assyria and the Adjacent Lands

For comments on this area see the notes on Map 2.

Jerusalem
**1393, 1881–
1885, 4381**

I. Map 9. The City of Jerusalem and Its Environs

The yellow map shows that Jerusalem was built on the top of a mountain range, drained by streams running both east and west. The western creeks or wadis emptied their waters into the Mediterranean Sea. The channels running eastward emptied into the Jordan River and the Dead Sea. Familiar Bible names in this region are clearly marked.

The pink map depicts the old walled city of Jerusalem, as it would appear from the air. It is still a city surrounded by a massive wall, much of it from Turkish times, A.D. 1517, built on older foundations. The central points of interest are the two mosques built on the large rectangular area of Mount Moriah. The central structure is usually called the Dome of the Rock; it was actually built by Abd el Melek Ibn Merwan. The object of the Omayyad founder, Sultan Merwan, was to make Jerusalem the center of pilgrimage worship rather than Mecca. Many of the materials for building were taken from the Byzantine churches destroyed by the Persians and the Islamic conquerors. An inscription on the inside of the Dome states that it was built in A.D. 691.

Moriah
2439

In the southern part of the Haram esh Sharif (noble enclosure—temple area) stands the Mosque of Aksa. Tradition says that it was built from the materials of Justinian's church. The Mosque has in it a beautiful pulpit dating back to the fifteenth century.

At the base of the west wall of the temple area is what the Gentiles call the wailing wall, because of the emotional expressions by the Orthodox Jews when praying for the restoration of the temple. The Jews now call it the Western Wall of Solomon's Temple.

The Concordance and Maps

Temple
3577–3581

J. Map 10. Palestine in the Time of Our Savior

Jesus' Journeys pp. 273–281

A glance at this map shows that the political subdivisions are much different from any so far examined. Greater Palestine was at that time under the dominion of Imperial Rome. The three northern territories, Galilee, Abilene, and Iturea-Trachonitis, are referred to in the NT as Tetrarchies, small territories reserved for lower eschelon princes whom Rome refused to dignify with the authority and rank of king. While Pontius Pilate was governor of Judea, Herod was tetrarch of Galilee; Philip, his brother, of Iturea and Trachonitis; and Lysanius of Abilene (Luke 3:1). The Palestine area was highly productive agriculturally. The Romans built cities with massive colonnaded buildings, many of which were in Decapolis, where the products of the land were gathered for shipment to Rome. Taxes were also freely collected in these cities. Archaeologists have excavated the towering columns and buildings which were once Gerasa (Jerash), a part of the Decapolis chain of ten cities, built in the wake of Alexander the Great's conquest. The architecture is typically Roman and comparable to the splendor of the buildings of ancient Rome.

Galilee
1384

Pilate
2763
Herod
1578
Philip
2755
Decapolis
950
Taxes
2529, 2530

Judea in Jesus' day was one of the main political subdivisions of western Palestine, as were Samaria and Galilee. Samaria, to the north, was separated by an imaginary line passing through the weak buffer territory, which was once the property of Benjamin. Judea and Samaria were rivals rather than friends. The Jews avoided Samaria because the Samaritans, former Israelites who had intermarried with the Assyrians and Babylonians (Map 2), were looked upon as being religiously and racially unclean (John 4:1–10). Because of their racial mixture, just to walk through Samaria placed a stigma upon the offender; consequently Jews traveling to Galilee usually went eastward across the Jordan River through Perea and thence over to Galilee.

Samaria
3133, 3134,
4409
Judea
1954
Assyrians
300
Babylon
329–331,
4334
Galilee
1384

The citizens of Judea were the descendants of Judah, one of the sons of Jacob; later the descendants of Judah became known as the Jews.

The orange section of this map represents Galilee-Peraea, the area ruled by Herod Antipas, the tetrarch. This is also the area in which Jesus lived (Nazareth) until his public ministry began. Much of Jesus' ministry was carried on in Galilee and Peraea. See Journey Maps on pages 273–278 in the TCRB Helps.

Jews
2723

The densely populated area contained over sixty cities, many of which were honored by a visit from Jesus. These included Bethsaida (Luke 9:10), Cana (John 2:1–11), Capernaum (Matt. 4:13; 8:5), Gadara (Luke 8:26), Nain (Luke 7:11), and Nazareth (Luke 2:39). Jesus was ministering in Peraea when the call came from Mary and Martha in behalf of their brother Lazarus (John 11:1ff.). Galilee, and especially Nazareth, was looked upon by political and religious circles as being on the outer edge of society. This is suggested by such gibes as "Shall Christ come out of Galilee?" (John 7:41), and "Can there any good thing come out of Nazareth?" (John 1:46). When Jerusalem was finally destroyed in A.D. 70, the homeless rabbinical school sought refuge in despised Galilee.

Bethsaida
411, 4340
Cana
624, 4348
Capernaum
241, 4349
Gadara
1380
Nazareth
2571, 4398

Iturea-Trachonitis, ruled by the tetrarch Philip, the brother of Herod, was a part of the northern region. Some of the Decapolis area overlaps this territory. The people were descendants of Jetur, one of the sons of Ishmael (Gen. 25:15; 1 Chron. 1:31). Some of the smaller subdivisions were Auranitis and Gaulanitis. The Golan Heights area, bordering Lake Galilee on the east, is named after Gaulanitis. Much of this area is mountainous and covered with volcanic rubble, but the land is fertile and productive. Grapes, figs, almonds, pomegranates, and garden vegetables are grown in large quantities for the needs of Amman and Damascus.

Abilene is the northernmost area, once ruled over by the tetrarch Lysanias, a contemporary of John the Baptist (Luke 3:1). Abilene straddles the Anti-Lebanon Mountains. Its western border is in the Beka valley near Heliopolis (Baalbeck), which was at one time a center for the worship of the nature deities, especially the sun god. Abel, according to tradition, is buried here; a tomb near some tall pillars and a cemetery bear his name. Apparently this little political subdivision of Abilene never gained much prominence.

K. Map 11. The Roman Empire in the Apostolic Age

This map shows the extent of the Roman Empire. During Roman rule the Mediterranean was referred to as the "middle of the earth" or "a Roman Inland Sea." One of the great achievements of Rome was the *Pax Romanas*, a term meaning "Roman Peace" (31 B.C.–A.D. 235). Although there was peace in general, absolute peace did not exist. However, in contrast to the periods of turmoil which preceded and followed, Roman rule seemed peaceful. Latin was the official language, but Greek was the vernacular which greatly helped the Christian missionary movement in the spread of the gospel. Fine Roman roads contributed to travel within the Empire; some of these roads are still in use today.

L. Map 12. Missionary Journeys and Last Voyage of Paul, the Apostle

For a number of years the Christ-Messiah movement had its headquarters in Jerusalem. However, when the relationship between those who believed in the Messiah and those who rejected him reached a stage of hostility, the headquarters for the Christ-Messiah group was moved to Syrian Antioch (now a part of Turkey). From there the missionaries penetrated the heathen world of Asia Minor and finally Europe. After his conversion in Damascus, Saul of Tarsus, who became Paul, eventually encountered such hostility from the Jews that he moved his residence to Antioch. Although the early missionary journeys are centered around Paul, he had many associates, whose names frequently appear in the Book of Acts of the Apostles and in Paul's Epistles. Among them are Luke, Barnabas, Timothy, Titus, Silas, Agabus, Lydia, the seller of purple, and Aquila and Priscilla. Paul's early journeys as an antagonist to the Christian cause and his conversion near Damascus are cited on page 286 in the TCRB Helps (Acts 9:3ff.). Paul's first missionary journey with Barnabas is presented on page 287 (Acts 13:1ff.), his second journey with Silas on pages 288–289 (Acts 15:40–18:22), and his third missionary journey on pages 290–291 (Acts 18:22–21:11). His final journey to Rome as a prisoner is charted on pages 292–293 in the TCRB Helps (Acts 23:31–28:16).

FOOTPRINTS OF JESUS IN THE YEAR OF POPULARITY (Jesus about 31 years of age)

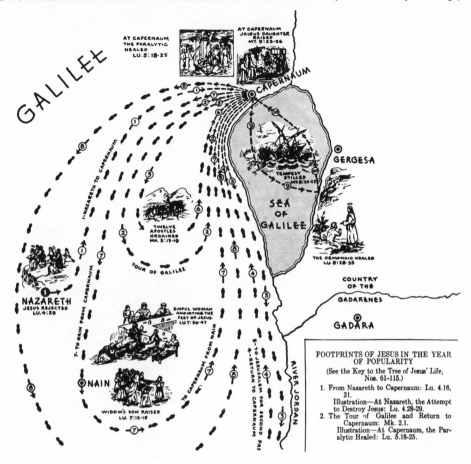

AT CAPERNAUM
THE PARALYTIC
HEALED
LU. 5: 18-25

AT CAPERNAUM
JAIRUS DAUGHTER
RAISED
MT. 9:23-26

GALILEE

CAPERNAUM

GERGESA

SEA OF GALILEE

TEMPEST
STILLED
MK. 4:47

THE DEMONIAC HEALED
LU. 8:28-35

TWELVE
APOSTLES
ORDAINED
MK. 3:13-19

TOUR OF GALILEE

NAZARETH
JESUS REJECTED
LU. 4:29

SINFUL WOMAN
ANOINTING THE
FEET OF JESUS.
LU.7: 36-47

COUNTRY
OF THE
GADARENES

GADARA

NAIN

WIDOW'S SON RAISED
LU. 7:12-15

I—NAZARETH TO CAPERNAUM

7—TO NAIN FROM CAPERNAUM

TO CAPERNAUM FROM NAIN

5—TO JERUSALEM FOR SECOND PAS

4—RETURN TO CAPERNAUM

RIVER JORDAN

FOOTPRINTS OF JESUS IN THE YEAR
OF POPULARITY
(See the Key to the Tree of Jesus' Life,
Nos. 61-115.)

1. From Nazareth to Capernaum: Lu. 4.16,
   31.
   Illustration—At Nazareth, the Attempt
   to Destroy Jesus: Lu. 4.28-29.
2. The Tour of Galilee and Return to
   Capernaum: Mk. 2.1.
   Illustration—At Capernaum, the Paralytic Healed: Lu. 5.18-25.

Pictured here is a portion of a full-page map, tracing Jesus' footprints in the Year of Popularity. See how clearly the story is told, with the aid of revealing illustrations.

This is only one of the nineteen illustrated Journey Maps included as an *extra feature* in the Fourth Improved Edition of the New Chain Reference Bible. Other maps include the Journeys of Jesus in His Early Life; the Year of Inauguration; the Year of Opposition; His Last Month and His Last Days;

Scenes in the Life and Ministry of Peter; the Journeys of Paul in Early Life; his First, Second and Third Missionary Journeys; his Voyage to Rome; and the Journeys of Abraham, the Children of Israel from Egypt to Canaan, Joshua, Gideon, Samuel, Saul, David and Solomon.

These are **separate** maps — not several crowded together on one page. And all are illustrated in the manner indicated above.

Notes

PART I

Chapter 1

1. Benjamin Breckenridge Warfield, "Inspiration," *ISBE*, III, 1473.
2. Frederick C. Grant, "Alexandrian Manuscript, or Codex Alexandrinus," *EA*, I, 374.
3. "Samaritan Pentateuch," *EA*, XXIV, 219; Norman L. Geisler, "Bible Manuscripts," *WBE*, I, 249.
4. William E. Nix, "Versions, Ancient and Medieval," *WBE*, II, 1776.
5. W. Russell Bowie, "History of the English Bible," *EA*, III, 671d.

Chapter 2

1. Madeleine S. Miller and J. Lane Miller, "Canon," *HBD*, p. 91.

Chapter 3

1. Henry H. Halley, "The Bible Is the Word of God," *HBH*, p. 26.
2. Rolston Holmes, "Revelation," *Twentieth Century Encyclopedia of Religious Knowledge* (Grand Rapids: Baker Book House, 1955), II, 971.
3. W. L. Walker, "Name," *ISBE*, IV, 2112.
4. Ibid.
5. James Orr, "The Bible," *ISBE*, I, 460.

Chapter 4

1. J. Harold Greenlee, "Texts and Manuscripts of the New Testament," *ZPEB*, V, 697ff.
2. Ibid., p. 708.
3. Donald Guthrie, "Canon of the New Testament," *ZPEB*, I, 743.
4. Madeleine S. Miller and J. Lane Miller, "Papyrus," *HBD*, p. 520–21.
5. Greenlee, p. 703.
6. Norman L. Geisler, "Bible Manuscripts," *WBE*, I, 248ff.
7. Ibid., p. 251.
8. Millar Burrows, *The Dead Sea Scrolls* (New York: Viking Press, 1955), p. 314.
9. Geisler, p. 252.

Chapter 5

1. W. T. Purkiser, *Exploring the Christian Faith* (Kansas City: Beacon Hill Press, 1966), p. 448; "Alexander Severius," *EA*, I, 367.

Chapter 6

1. Howard Vos, *Religion in a Changing World* (Chicago: Moody Press, 1959), p. 44.
2. G. Henry Waterman, "The Lord's Day," *ZPEB*, III, 962.
3. R. Allen Killen, "Sabbath Day's Journey," *WBE*, II, 1494.
4. Madeleine S. Miller and J. Lane Miller, "Festivals, Feasts and Fasts," *HBD*, p. 190; W. T. Purkiser, *Exploring the Old Testament* (Kansas City: Beacon Hill Press, 1967), p. 127.
5. Hobart E. Freeman, "Festivals," *WBE*, I, 605.

526

6. Wilhelm Moller, "Day of Atonement," *ISBE*, I, 324ff.
7. Miller and Miller, p. 52.
8. Freeman, pp. 501ff.

Chapter 7

1. Nathan J. Stone, *Names of God* (Chicago: Moody Press, 1944), pp. 10ff.
2. Ibid., p. 98.
3. Ibid.
4. James Orr, "Jesus," *ISBE*, III, 1627.
5. R. Allen Killen, "Names and Titles of God," *WBE*, I, 695.
6. Harold B. Kuhn, *God, His Names and Nature*, Fundamentals of the Faith (*Christianity Today*, 1014 Washington Blvd., Washington, D.C. 20005, n.d.), p. 13.
7. Stone, p. 151.
8. Ibid., p. 155.
9. Erich Sauer, *The Dawn of World Redemption* (Grand Rapids: Wm. B. Eerdmans Co., 1952), p. 156.
10. James A. Borland, *Christ in the Old Testament* (Chicago: Moody Press, 1978), p. 34.
11. Ibid., p. 10.
12. Ibid., p. 21.
13. Sauer, p. 156.
14. Thomas Rees, "God," *ISBE*, II, 1253.

Chapter 8

1. John D. Davis, "Priests," *DDB*, pp. 655ff.; Earl S. Kalland, "Priests and Priesthood," *WBE*, II, 1394.
2. Edward J. Young, "Prophets," *WBE*, II, 1412ff.
3. Madeleine S. Miller and J. Lane Miller, "Prophets," *HBD*, pp. 582ff.
4. John D. Davis, "Daniel," *DDB*, pp. 155ff.
5. Robert H. Gundry, *A Survey of the New Testament* (Grand Rapids: Zondervan Publishing House, 1978), p. 51.
6. W. T. Purkiser, *Exploring the Old Testament* (Kansas City: Beacon Hill Press, 1967), p. 61.
7. John D. Davis, "Elder," *DDB*, pp. 211ff.
8. John Rea, "Elder," *WBE*, I, 509.
9. Ibid.
10. Davis, "Elder," pp. 211ff.
11. Edwin Lueker, "Apostle," *WBE*, I, 116; "Apostle," *HBD*, p. 116.
12. Walter M. Dunnett, "Deacon," *WBE*, I, 430; "Deacon," *DDB*, p. 175.

Chapter 9

1. Gustave Oehler, *Theology of the Old Testament* (Grand Rapids: Zondervan Publishing House, 1883), p. 1.
2. For a definition of *demiurge* see Shirley Jackson Case, "Demiurge," *ER*, p. 222.
3. Oehler, p. 2.
4. Ibid., p. 30.
5. Grace Saxe, *Studies in Hebrews* (Chicago: Moody Press, n.d.), p. 49.
6. Erich Sauer, *The Dawn of World Redemption* (Grand Rapids: Wm. B. Eerdmans Co., 1952), p. 21.
7. Franz Julius Delitzsch, *The Old Testament History of Redemption* (Edinburgh: T. and T. Clark Publishers, 1881), p. 26.
8. Ibid., p. 27.
9. Sauer, p. 62.
10. Jasper Huffman, *The Messianic Hope in Both Testaments* (Butler, Ind.: The Higley Press, 1945), p. 75.
11. Ibid., p. 76.
12. John D. Davis, "Blood," *DDB*, p. 77.
13. Sauer, p. 63.
14. Walter Gellen Clippenter, "Blood," *ISBE*, I, 188.
15. Ibid.
16. Adam Clarke, "Genesis," *CBC*, I, 82.
17. Ibid., p. 77.
18. Delitzsch, p. 50.
19. Raissa Maritan, "Abraham and the Ascent of Conscience," *The Bridge*, ed. John M. Oesterreicher (New York: Pantheon Books, 1955), p. 35.
20. Huffman, p. 75.
21. Thomas Rees, "God," *ISBE*, II, 1253.
22. Oehler, p. 124.
23. Ibid., p. 508.
24. Wilhelm Pauck, "Atonement in Christianity," *ER*, p. 54.
25. Sauer, p. 21.
26. Adam Clarke, "Revelation," *CBC*, VI, 1019.
27. Sauer, p. 155.
28. Huffman, p. 29.
29. William Owen Carver, "Atonement," *ISBE*, I, 323.
30. Wilhelm Mohler, "Day of Atonement," *ISBE*, I, 326.
31. Ibid., p. 324.
32. Nathan Isaacs, "Passover," *ISBE*, IV, 2257.
33. Henry Riley Gummy, "Lord's Supper," *ISBE*, III, 1922.
34. John Nuelsen, "Regeneration," *ISBE*, IV, 2546.

35. Adam Clarke, "John," *CBC*, V, 532.
36. R. Allan Killen, "Baptism," *WBE*, I, 200.
37. Ibid., p. 194.
38. Nuelsen, p. 2547.
39. Ibid., p. 2548.
40. Ibid., p. 2544.
41. Grace Saxe, *Studies in Hebrews* (Chicago: Moody Press, n.d.), p. 1.

Chapter 10

1. Clarence T. Craig, "The Church of the New Testament," *The Universal Church of God's Design* (New York: Harper and Brothers, n.d.), p. 31.
2. Ibid., p. 32.
3. Ibid.
4. Ibid., p. 33.
5. Erich Sauer, *The Dawn of World Redemption* (Grand Rapids: Wm. B. Eerdmans Co., 1948), p. 21.
6. John Davis, "Church," *DDB*, p. 146.
7. A. R. Fausset, "Church," *Bible Encyclopedia and Dictionary* (Grand Rapids: Zondervan Publishing House, n.d.), p. 150.
8. Ibid., p. 23.
9. Erich Sauer, *The Triumph of the Crucified* (Grand Rapids: Wm. B. Eerdmans Co., 1952), p. 22.
10. J. C. Lambert, "Church," *ISBE*, I, 651.
11. Sauer, *Triumph of the Crucified*, p. 32.
12. F. F. Bruce, "The Acts of the Apostles," *NBC*, ed. F. Davison (Grand Rapids: Wm. B. Eerdmans Co., 1953), p. 913.
13. Craig, p. 32.
14. Adam Clarke, "Romans," *CBC*, VI, 40.
15. John Wesley, *Wesley's Explanatory Notes on the New Testament* (London: Epworth Press, 1966), pp. 435, 520.
16. Gustave Frederick Oehler, *Theology of the Old Testament* (Grand Rapids: Zondervan Publishing House, 1950), p. 159.
17. Charles S. Browden, "Religious Humanism," *ER*, p. 349.
18. Sauer, *Dawn of World Redemption*, p. 52.
19. Fausset, p. 130.
20. Andri Dupont-Sommer, *The Jewish Sect of Qumran and the Essenes* (New York: Macmillan Co., 1955), V, 134ff.
21. Millar Burrows, *The Dead Sea Scrolls* (New York: The Viking Press, 1955), p. 245.
22. J. E. H. Thompson, "The Essenes," *ISBE*, II, 997ff.
23. William G. Morehead, "Priesthood," *ISBE*, IV, 2444.
24. Adam Clarke, "Matthew," *CBC*, V, 110.
25. Dupont-Sommer, p. 134.
26. Fausset, p. 131.
27. Ibid., p. 130.
28. Père de Vaux, "Dead Sea Jewels," *Time Magazine* (September 5, 1955), 33–34.
29. Frank M. Cross, "The American Schools of Oriental Research in Jerusalem," *Time Magazine* (September 5, 1955), 34.
30. Thompson, I, 163.
31. Morton Scott Enslin, "Therapeutae," *ER*, p. 784.
32. Thompson, II, 998.
33. Ibid.
34. Cross, p. 34.

Chapter 11

1. A. M. Hodgkin, *Christ in All the Scriptures* (London: Pickering and Ingals, 1907), p. 20.
2. Ibid.
3. Grace Saxe, *Studies in Hebrews* (Chicago: Moody Press, n.d.), p. 45.
4. Ibid., p. 44.
5. Ibid.
6. Charles Slemming, *Made According to Pattern* (London: Marshall, Morgan and Scott, n.d.), p. 61.
7. Iris McCord, *The Tabernacle* (Chicago: Moody Press, n.d.), p. 30.
8. Ibid., p. 34.
9. A. B. Simpson, *Christ in the Tabernacle* (Harrisburg: Christian Publications, Inc., n.d.), p. 70.
10. W. S. Hottel, *Typical Truth in the Tabernacle* (Cleveland: Union Gospel Press, n.d.), p. 180.
11. Slemming, p. 87.
12. Simpson, p. 98.
13. Slemming, p. 94.
14. Simpson, p. 106.
15. Hottel, p. 199.
16. Ibid., p. 161.
17. Slemming, p. 109.
18. Ibid., p. 96.
19. John D. Davis, "Day of Atonement," *DDB*, p. 65.
20. McCord, p. 59.
21. Simpson, pp. 118ff.
22. McCord, p. 61.

Chapter 12

1. Madeleine S. Miller and J. Lane Miller, "Medes," *HBD*, p. 431.
2. Howard Clark Kee, Franklin W. Young, and Karlfried Froehlich, *Understanding the New Testament* (Englewood Cliffs, N.J.: Prentice-Hall, 1973), p. 34.
3. Ibid., p. 43.
4. Ibid.
5. "Judaeo Philo," *EA*, XXI, 766.
6. William Whiston, *Josephus' Complete Works* (Grand Rapids: Kregel Publications, 1963), Wars, II, VIII, 14; Antiquities, XIII. X. 6.
7. Ibid., XIII. 10. 6; Louis Goldberg, "Sadducees," *WBE*, II, 1500.
8. Millar Burrows, *The Dead Sea Scrolls* (New York: The Viking Press, 1955), p. 327.
9. Ibid., p. 329.
10. Ibid., p. 328.
11. Theodore Gaster, *The Dead Sea Scriptures* (New York: Doubleday and Co., 1956), p. 5; Père de Vaux, "Dead Sea Jewels," *Time Magazine* (September 5, 1955), p. 34.
12. Gaster, pp. 10ff.
13. Herman Hausheer, "Peter Waldo and Waldenses," *ER*, p. 817.
14. Gaster, pp. 12ff.
15. Alvin B. Rogers, *The Land of Jesus* (Minneapolis: Augsburg Publishing House, 1974), p. 8.
16. C. S. Lewis, *Reflection on the Psalms* (New York: Harcourt Brace and Co., 1958), p. 120.
17. Martin J. Wyngaarden, "Psalms in the Christian Liturgy," *ISBE*, IV, 2494A.
18. John R. Sampey, "Book of Psalms," *ISBE*, IV, 2494.
19. The Book of Psalms was the hymn book of the Christian church for the first 1500 years of its history. The Psalms are still used exclusively by several Christian groups, including certain Presbyterian and Reformed denominations. A hymnal containing all of the Psalms in metrical form, set to familiar tunes, is currently published by Wm. B. Eerdmans Co., in Grand Rapids, Michigan, under the title *The Psalter*. It is available through any book store. The Christian use of the Psalter is irrefutable proof that the Book of Psalms has extensive Christological content. The Psalms reveal what Jesus meant when he said, "All things must be fulfilled, which were written in the law of Moses, and in the prophets, and in the psalms, concerning me" (Luke 24:44).
20. *The Methodist Hymnal* (New York: The Methodist Book Concern, 1939).
    No. 5, Daniel Ben Judah, "The God of Abraham Praise"
    No. 85, James Montgomery, "Hail to the Lord's Anointed"
    No. 150, William J. Irons, "Sing with All the Sons of Glory"
    No. 193, John M. Neale, "Art Thou Weary, Art Thou Troubled"
    No. 199, John Chennick, "Jesus My All, to Heaven Is Gone"
    No. 390, Percy Dearmer, "Book of Books, Our People's Strength . . . Poets, Prophets, Scholars, Saints"
    No. 488, Thomas Hastings, "Hail to the Brightness . . ."
    No. 543, William P. Merrill, "Not Alone for Mighty Empire"
21. Fenton John Anthony Hort, *The Ecclesia* (London: Macmillan Co., 1828–1892), p. 1.
22. Ibid., p. 8.
23. H. L. Drumwright, Jr., "Diaspora," *ZPEB*, I, 120.
24. Robert Pfeiffer, "The Apocrypha," *EA*, III, 650.

Chapter 13

1. Robert H. Gundry, *A Survey of the New Testament* (Grand Rapids: Zondervan Publishing House, 1970), p. 65.
2. Jack P. Lewis, "Apocrypha," *WBE*, I, 111; T. Witton Davies, "Apocrypha," *ISBE*, I, 178ff.; Adam Fyfe Findlay, "Apocryphal Acts," *ISBE*, I, 183; John Hutchinson, "Apocryphal Gospels," *ISBE*, I, 195; R. K. Harrison, "Apocrypha," *ZPEB*, I, 205ff.; Robert McL. Wilson, "Apocryphal New Testament," *ZPEB*, I, 210; Ward W. Gasque, "Pseude-Gospel of Matthew," *ZPEB*, IV, 950ff.; Solomon J. Schepps (Foreword) "The First Gospel of the Infancy of Jesus" in *The Lost Books of the Bible* (New York: Bell Publishing Co., 1979 Ed.), pp. 38–54.
3. Gundry, p. 84; Ward W. Gasque, "Pseudepigrapha," *ZPEB*, IV, 949ff.
4. "Tyrannus Rufinus," *EA*, XXIII, 755.
5. Henry Wheeler, *The Apostles Creed* (New York: Eaton and Main, 1912), p. 13.
6. Ibid.
7. Ibid., p. 21; see also Solomon J. Schepps (Foreword), "The Apostles' Creed," in *The Lost Books of the Bible* (New York: Bell Publishing Co., 1979 Ed.), p. 91.
8. W. T. Purkiser, *Exploring the Christian Faith* (Kansas City: Beacon Hill Press, 1966), p. 88.
9. Ibid.
10. R. Allen Killen, "Pelagianism," *WBE*, II, 1303.
11. Purkiser, p. 89.
12. "Creeds and Confessions," *EA*, VIII, 174ff.
13. "Henry Gerhard Appenzeller," *EA*, II, 81; "Horace Grant Underwood," *EA*, XXVII, 275.
14. Herbert Welch, "The Story of the Creed," *The Christian Advocate* (August 1, 1946), p. 973.
15. Ibid.
16. Nolan B. Harmon, "The Apostles Creed Says it Best," *The Christian Advocate* (August 22, 1968), pp. 11–12.

Chapter 14

1. Karl S. Sabiers, *The Virgin Birth* (Los Angeles: Robertson Publishing Co., 1943), p. 58.
2. J. Gresham Machen, *The Virgin Birth of Christ* (New York: Harper and Brothers, 1930), pp. 29ff.
3. Adam Clarke, "Isaiah," *CBC*, IV, 56.

PART II

Chapter 15

1. Elmer B. Smick, "Pentateuch," *WBE*, I, 675.
2. George H. Livingston, "General Introduction to the Pentateuch," *TWBC*, I, 4.
3. Smick, 675.
4. W. T. Purkiser, *Exploring the Old Testament* (Kansas City: Beacon Hill Press, 1967), p. 67.
5. Charles Darwin, *The Autobiography of Charles Darwin, 1809–1882*, ed. Nora Barlow (New York: W. W. Norton and Co., 1958), pp. 85–87. Omissions are restored in this edition. The editor, who also added an appendix and notes, is Darwin's granddaughter.
6. Ibid.
7. Laird Harris, "The Bible and Cosmology," *Bulletin of the Evangelical Theological Society* (March 1962), p. 11.
8. James D. Bales, "The Relevance of Scriptural Interpretation," *The Bulletin of the Evangelical Theological Society* (December 1961), p. 127.
9. Howard A. Hanke, *The Validity of the Virgin Birth* (Grand Rapids: Zondervan Publishing House, 1963), pp. 78ff.
10. Herbert C. Leupold, "Genesis," *ZPEB*, I, 678.
11. Ibid., p. 680.
12. R. Laird Harris, "Genesis," *WBE*, I, 665.
13. Lee Haines, "Genesis," *TWBC* I, 65.
14. Harris, "Genesis," p. 668.
15. Henry H. Halley, "Genesis," *HBH*, p. 60.
16. John Rea, "The Book of Exodus," *WBC*, I, 566.
17. Allan A. MacRae, "The Book of Exodus," *ZPEB*, II, 437.
18. Robert H. Pfeiffer, *Introduction to the Old Testament* (New York: Harper and Brothers, 1941), p. 188.
19. Bruce K. Waltke, "Leviticus," *ZPEB*, III, 915.
20. Robert O. Coleman, "Leviticus," *WBC*, p. 87.
21. Thomas Whitelaw, "Book of Numbers," *ISBE*, IV, 2169.
22. Howard A. Hanke, "The Book of Deuteronomy," *TWBC*, vol. I, part I, 471.

Chapter 16

1. John Rea, "Joshua," *ZPEB*, III, 698.
2. Ibid.
3. Charles R. Wilson, "Joshua," *TWBC*, vol. I, part I, 11.
4. Adam Clarke, "The Book of Judges," *CBC*, II, 99.
5. F. F. Bruce, "The Book of Judges," *NBC*, p. 237.
6. Charles R. Wilson, "The Book of Judges," *TWBC*, vol. I, part II, 64.
7. Clarke, "Book of Judges," p. 98.
8. Madeleine S. Miller and J. Lane Miller, "The Book of Ruth," *HBD*, p. 630.
9. Adam Clarke, "The Book of Ruth," *CBC*, II, 190.
10. Arthur E. Cundall, "The Book of Ruth," *ZPEB*, V, 176ff.
11. Herbert W. Wolf, "Samuel 1 and 2," *ZPEB*, V, 256.
12. Elmer B. Smick, "Books of Samuel," *WBE*, II, 1515.
13. Charles R. Wilson, "The First Book of Samuel," *WBC*, vol. I, part II, 138.
14. Ibid.
15. Samuel J. Schultz, "Books of Kings," *ZPEB*, III, 812.
16. "1 and 2 Kings," *EHB*, p. 251.
17. Schultz, p. 812.
18. Adam Clarke, "The Two Books of Chronicles," *CBC*, II, 572.
19. Ibid.
20. Ibid., p. 573.
21. Ibid., p. 574.
22. J. Barton Payne, "The Books of Chronicles," *WBE*, I, 338.
23. Henry H. Halley, "Ezra," *HBH*, p. 218.
24. Charles R. Wilson, "The Book of Ezra," *TWBC*, II, 435.
25. Adam Clarke, "The Book of Ezra," *CBC*, II, 716.
26. Ibid.
27. Halley, "Ezra," p. 218.
28. Henry H. Halley, "Nehemiah," *HBH*, p. 220.
29. Ibid.
30. Ibid.
31. Charles R. Wilson, "The Book of Nehemiah," *WBC*, vol. I, part II, 436.
32. Robert B. Demsey, "Book of Esther," *WBE*, I, 549.
33. Henry H. Halley, "Esther," *HBH*, p. 222.
34. Demsey, p. 549.
35. Charles R. Wilson, "The Book of Esther," *TWBC*, vol. I, part II, 483.
36. Demsey, p. 551.

Chapter 17

1. Stephen Barabas, "The Book of Job," *ZPEB*, III, 600.
2. M. G. K., "Job," *WBE*, I, 931.
3. Madeleine S. Miller and J. Lane Miller, "The Book of Job," *HBD*, p. 337.
4. Henry H. Halley, "Job," *HBH*, p. 225.
5. Adam Clarke, "The Book of Job," *CBC*, III, 6–7.
6. Halley, "Job," p. 225.

7. Ibid.
8. John D. Davis, "The Book of Job," *DDB*, p. 722.
9. Henry H. Halley, "Psalms," *HBH*, pp. 230ff.
10. William Smith, "The Book of Psalms," *SBD*, p. 551.
11. Ralph L. Smith, "Book of Psalms," *WBE*, II, 1425.
12. J. Barton Payne, "The Book of Psalms," *ZPEB*, IV, 936ff.
13. Ibid., p. 937.
14. Halley, "Psalms," p. 239.
15. Payne, p. 939.
16. W. T. Purkiser, *Exploring the Old Testament* (Kansas City: Beacon Hill Press, 1967), p. 221.
17. Payne, pp. 939–40.
18. "Christ in the Psalms," *EHB*, p. 329.
19. W. O. E. Oesterley, "Proverbs," *TSB*, II, 614.
20. Purkiser, *Exploring the Old Testament*, p. 239.
21. W. T. Purkiser, *Know Your Old Testament* (Kansas City: Beacon Hill Press, 1947), p. 141.
22. Dennis Kinlaw, "The Book of Ecclesiastes," *TWBC*.
23. Henry H. Halley, "Ecclesiastes," *HBH*, p. 255.
24. John Richard Sampey, "Song of Songs," *ISBE*, V, 2833.
25. N. H. Snaith, "Solomon and the Rose of Sharon: A Springtime Idyll," *TSB*, II, 646.
26. Ibid.
27. John D. Davis, "The Song of Songs," *DDB*, p. 777.

Chapter 18

1. George L. Robinson, "Isaiah," *ISBE*, III, 1504.
2. Robert H. Pfeiffer, *Introduction to the Old Testament* (New York: Harper and Brothers, 1941), pp. 453ff.
3. R. Laird Harris, "Isaiah," *ZPEB*, III, 313–21.
4. Allan A. MacRae, "Prophets and Prophecy," *ZPEB*, IV, 879.
5. Henry H. Halley, "Isaiah," *HBH*, p. 262.
6. Robinson, "Isaiah," pp. 1495ff.
7. Halley, "Isaiah," p. 263.
8. G. Frederick Owen, "4356, Dead Sea Scrolls," *TCRB*, p. 327.
9. Robinson, "Isaiah," p. 1505.
10. Adam Clarke, "Jeremiah," *CBC*, IV, 249.
11. Henry H. Halley, "Jeremiah," *HBH*, p. 284.
12. Samuel J. Schultz, "Jeremiah the Prophet," *ZPEB*, III, 435.
13. Halley, "Jeremiah," p. 282.
14. D. D. Deere, "The Book of Jeremiah," *WBE*, I, 899.
15. Bruce K. Waltke, "The Book of Lamentations," *ZPEB*, III, 863.
16. Adam Clarke, "The Lamentations of Jeremiah," *CBC*, IV, 398.
17. Wilhelm Moeler, "Ezekiel," *ISBE*, XIX, 445.
18. Henry H. Halley, "Ezekiel," *HBH*, p. 298.
19. Lewis L. Orlin, "Tyre," *TWBE*, XIX, 445.
20. Halley, "Ezekiel," p. 303.
21. Edward J. Young, *The Prophecies of Daniel* (Grand Rapids: Wm. B. Eerdmans Co., 1955), p. 318.
22. A. H. McDonald, "Porphyrius," *TME*, p. 931.
23. Gleason L. Archer, Jr., trans., *Jerome's Commentary on Daniel* (Grand Rapids: Baker Book House, 1958), pp. 15–16.
24. Clyde J. Hurst, "Book of Daniel," *WBE*, I, 422.
25. Bert Harold Hall, "The Book of Daniel," *TWBC*, III, 503.
26. William Smith, "The Book of Daniel," *SBD*, p. 130.
27. Henry H. Halley, "Genesis," *HBH*, p. 86.
28. Ibid., p. 308.
29. W. T. Purkiser, *Exploring the Old Testament* (Kansas City: Beacon Hill Press, 1967), pp. 377–78.
30. Henry H. Halley, "Hosea," *HBH*, p. 324.
31. John Davis, "Jezebel," in *DDB*, p. 414.
32. Halley, "Hosea," p. 325.
33. P. D. F., "Book of Hosea," *WBE*, I, 814.
34. MacRae, "Prophets and Prophecy," p. 879.
35. John D. Davis, "Joel," *DDB*, pp. 419–20.
36. James Robertson, "Joel," *ISBE*, III, 1688ff.
37. "Joel," *EHB*, p. 442.
38. Henry H. Halley, "Amos," *HBH*, p. 329.
39. Ibid., p. 330.
40. Adam Clarke, "Amos," *CBC*, IV, 691.
41. John Richard Sampey, "Obadiah," *ISBE*, IV, 2173.
42. G. Herbert Livingston, "Obadiah," *WBC*, p. 839.
43. Pfeiffer, *Introduction to the Old Testament*, p. 587.
44. G. Herbert Livingston, "Jonah," *WBC*, p. 844.
45. Henry H. Halley, "Jonah," *HBH*, p. 333.
46. Wallace A. Alcorn, "Book of Jonah," *WBE*, I, 845.
47. Ibid.
48. M. Rowton, "Nineveh," *EA*, XV, 368.
49. Livingstone, p. 844.
50. Ibid.
51. Andrew K. Helmbold, "Micah," *ZPEB*, V, 215.
52. "Micah," *EHB*, p. 449.
53. Claude A. Ries, "The Book of Micah," *TWBC*, III, 677.
54. Henry H. Halley, "Micah," *HBH*, p. 337.

531

55. Ibid.
56. Frederick Carl Eiselen, "The Book of Nahum," *ISBE*, IV, 2100.
57. William C. Graham, "Nahum," *ABC*, p. 799.
58. Henry H. Halley, "Nahum," *HBH*, p. 340; Joseph F. Free, *Archaeology and Bible History* (Wheaton: Van Kampen Press, 1950), p. 28.
59. Claude A. Ries, "The Book of Habakkuk," *TWBC*, III, 711.
60. Henry H. Halley, "Habakkuk," *HBH*, p. 342.
61. MacRae, "Prophets and Prophecy," p. 879.
62. Howard A. Hanke, "Zephaniah," *WBC*, p. 883.
63. Frederick Carl Eiselen, "Book of Zephaniah," *ISBE*, V, 3145.
64. Madeleine S. Miller and J. Lane Miller, ed., "Zephaniah," *HBD*, p. 838.
65. Eiselen, p. 3145.
66. Ibid.
67. Henry H. Halley, "Zephaniah," *HBH*, p. 343.
68. R. K. Harrison, "Haggai," *ZPEB*, III, 11.
69. Charles L. Feinberg, "Haggai," *WBC*, p. 895.
70. George L. Robinson, "Book of Zechariah," *ISBE*, V, 3136.
71. Ibid.
72. John D. Davis, "Zechariah," *DDB*, p. 878.
73. Henry H. Halley, "Zechariah," *HBH*, p. 346.
74. Ibid., p. 347.
75. R. K. Harrison, "Book of Zechariah," *ZPEB*, V, 1045–46.
76. Halley, "Zechariah," p. 349.
77. J. Kenneth Grider, "The Book of Zechariah," *TWBC*, III, 757.
78. Burton L. Goddard, "Malachi," *WBC*, p. 913.
79. Hobart E. Freeman, "Malachi," *WBE*, II, 1071.
80. "Malachi," *EHB*, p. 459.
81. Henry H. Halley, "Malachi," *HBH*, p. 353.

PART III

Chapter 19

1. Clark H. Pinnock, "Gospels," *ZPEB*, II, 788.
2. James Iverach, "The Synoptic Gospels," *ISBE*, II, 1281.
3. Robert McL. Wilson, "Gospel of Matthew," *ZPEB*, IV, 122.
4. Howard Clark Kee, Franklin W. Young, and Karlfried Froehlich, *Understanding the New Testament* (Englewood Cliffs, N.J.: Prentice-Hall, 1973), p. 315.
5. George Henry Schodde, "The Gospel of Matthew," *ISBE*, III, 380.
6. Wilson, p. 136.
7. Henry H. Halley, "Matthew," *HBH*, p. 380.
8. *Exploring New Testament Backgrounds*, A Special Survey of the New Testament Books (Washington, D.C.: Christianity Today, n.d.), p. 7.
9. Robert H. Gundry, *A Survey of the New Testament* (Grand Rapids: Zondervan Publishing House, 1970), pp. 86ff.
10. Canon R. J. Campbell, "Mark," *TSB*, III, 1052.
11. Ralph Earl, "The Gospel According to Mark," *TWBC*, IV, 131.
12. Henry H. Halley, "Mark," *HBH*, pp. 418ff.
13. Adam Clarke, "St. Mark," *CBC*, V, 287.
14. Donald W. Burdeck, "Mark," *WBE*, II, 1078.
15. Gundry, pp. 68ff.
16. Weldon O. Klopfenstein, "Gospel of Mark," *ZPEB*, IV, 80–81.
17. J. Newton Davies, "Mark," *ABC*, p. 998.
18. A. T. Robertson, "The Evangelist Luke" and "The Gospel of Luke," *ISBE*, III, 1935.
19. Robert G. Gromacki, *New Testament Survey* (Grand Rapids: Baker Book House, 1974), pp. 110ff.
20. Adam Clarke, "St. Luke," *CBC*, V, 352.
21. Henry H. Halley, "Luke," *HBH*, p. 444.
22. Henry H. Halley, "John," *HBH*, p. 485.
23. Ibid.
24. Everett F. Harrison, "The Gospel of John," *WBC*, p. 1118.
25. Gromacki, p. 130.
26. Halley, "John," p. 484.
27. George A. Turner, "The Gospel of John," *ZPEB*, III, 673.
28. William Smith, "Salome," *SBD*, p. 595.
29. Conrad Henry Muehlman, "Gnosticism," *ER*, p. 301.
30. Ibid., p. 300.
31. Paul H. Halsel, "Logos," *ER*, p. 449.
32. Ibid.
33. George A. Turner, "Logos," *ZPEB*, p. 953.
34. Halsel, p. 449.
35. Adam Clarke, "The Acts of the Apostles," *CBC*, V, 679.
36. A. T. Robinson, "The Acts of the Apostles," *ISBE*, I, 39.
37. Joseph S. Exell, "The Acts of the Apostles," *The Pulpit Commentary* (New York: Anson D. F. Randolph & Co., n.d.), I, iv.
38. Exell, p. ix.
39. Ibid.
40. Ibid.
41. Ibid., x.
42. Ibid.

43. Charles W. Carter, "The Acts of the Apostles," *TWBC*, IV, 489.
44. Merrill C. Tenney, "The Book of Acts," *WBE*, I, 22.
45. F. F. Bruce, "The Acts of the Apostles," *Exploring New Testament Backgrounds* (Washington, D.C.: *Christianity Today*, n.d.).
46. Exell, p. iii.

Chapter 20

1. Handley Dunelm, "Epistle to the Romans," *ISBE*, IV, 2614.
2. Joseph S. Exell, "The Epistle of Paul to the Romans," *The Pulpit Commentary* (New York: Anson D. F. Randolph & Co., n.d.), I, iff.
3. "Romans," *EHB*, p. 588.
4. John Wesley, "Romans," *Explanatory Notes upon the New Testament* (Napierville, Ill.: Alec R. Allenson, 1966), p. 515.
5. Dunelm, pp. 2616ff.
6. R. Dykes Shaw, "First Epistle of the Corinthians," *ISBE*, II, 711.
7. John Wesley, "1 Corinthians," *Explanatory Notes upon the New Testament* (Naperville, Ill.: Alec R. Allenson, 1966), p. 584.
8. S. Lewis Johnson, "The First Epistle to the Corinthians," *WBC*, p. 1228; Shaw, p. 713.
9. John D. Davis, "Corinth," *DBD*, p. 152; Joseph Edward Harry, "Corinth," *ISBE*, II, 711.
10. Shaw, p. 714.
11. Ibid.
12. Ibid., p. 715.
13. Madeleine S. Miller and J. Lane Miller, "Corinth," *HBD*, p. 113.
14. Henry H. Halley, "II Corinthians," *HBH*, p. 552.
15. Wick Broomall, "The Second Epistle to the Corinthians," *WBC*, p. 1261.
16. Ibid.

Chapter 21

1. Lorman M. Peterson, "Epistle to Galatians," *ZPEB*, II, 627.
2. Madeleine S. Miller and J. Lane Miller, "The Epistle of Paul the Apostle to the Galatians," *HBD*, p. 211.
3. George G. Findley, "Epistle to the Galatians," *ISBE*, II, 1157.
4. Ibid.
5. C. Fred Dickason, "Epistle to the Galatians," *WBE*, I, 648.
6. Ibid.
7. Robert G. Gromacki, *New Testament Survey* (Grand Rapids: Baker Book House, 1974), p. 241.
8. Charles Smith Lewis, "Epistle to the Ephesians," *ISBE*, II, 956.
9. Edgar J. Banks, "Diana," *ISBE*, II, 843.
10. Ibid.
11. Alfred Martin, "The Epistle to the Ephesians," *WBC*, p. 1301.
12. Ibid.
13. Ibid.
14. Charles Harold Dodd, "Ephesians," *ABC*, p. 1223.
15. Gromacki, p. 256.
16. Ibid.
17. James Alex Robinson, "Philippians," *ABC*, p. 1238.
18. Ibid., p. 1239; "Philippians," *EBH*, p. 1973.
19. D. Edmond Hiebert, "Letter to the Philippians," *ZPEB*, IV, 766.
20. Adam Clarke, "The Epistle of Paul the Apostle to the Philippians," *CBC*, VI, 488.
21. Merrill C. Tenney, "Philippians," *Exploring New Testament Backgrounds* (Washington, D.C.: Christianity Today, n.d.).
22. Charles Smith Lewis, "Epistle to the Colossians," *ISBE*, II, 617.
23. Edward M. Blaiklock, "Colosse," *ZPEB*, I, 914; Adam Clarke, "The Epistle of Paul the Apostle to the Colossians," *CBC*, VI, 510.
24. Charles F. Pfeiffer and Howard F. Voss, "Other Pauline Cities," *The Wycliff Historical Geography of the Bible Lands* (Chicago: Moody Press, 1967), p. 376.
25. Lewis, "Colossians," p. 677.
26. Andrew R. Helmbold, "Gnosticism," *WBE*, I, 687; E. Earle Ellis, "The Epistle to the Colossians," *WBC*, p. 1334.
27. Conrad Henry Moehlman, "Gnosticism," *EBH*, p. 300.
28. Ellis, p. 1333.
29. Charles Harold Dodd, "Colosians," *ABC*, pp. 1250ff.
30. Ellis, p. 1334.
31. Adam Clarke, "The First Epistle of Paul the Apostle to the Thessalonians," *CBC*, VI, 537.
32. Rolin Hough Walker, "The First Epistle of Paul to the Thessalonians," *ISBE*, V, 2966.
33. "Cassander," *EA*, V, 706.
34. Clarke, "Thessalonians," p. 537.
35. John D. Davis, "Epistles to the Thessalonians," *DDB*, p. 817.
36. Clarke, "Thessalonians," p. 537.
37. Rollin Hough Walker, "The Second Epistle of Paul to the Thessalonians," *ISBE*, V, 2966.
38. John D. Davis, "The Second Epistle to the Thessalonians," *DDB*, p. 818.
39. Henry H. Halley, "II Thessalonians," *HBH*, p. 578.
40. Ibid.
41. Ibid.
42. Henry H. Halley, "I Timothy," *HBH*, p. 580.
43. Jac J. Muller, "I Timothy," *Exploring New Testament Backgrounds* (Washington, D.C.: Christianity Today, n.d.), p. 39.
44. Ibid.

45. Ibid.
46. Roy S. Nicholson, "I Timothy," *TWBC*, V, 567.
47. Adam Clarke, "The Epistle of Paul the Apostle to Timothy," *CBC*, VI, 580.
48. Ibid.
49. Henry H. Halley, "II Timothy," *HBH*, p. 584.
50. Ibid.
51. John Rutherford, "The Pastoral Epistles," *ISBE*, IV, 2260.
52. Robert G. Gromacki, "Second Timothy," *New Testament Survey* (Grand Rapids: Baker Book House, 1974), p. 302.
53. Adelaide L. Lewis, "Religion," *Information Please Almanac* (New York: Information Please Publishing Co., 1979), p. 430.
54. Walter W. Wessel, "Titus," *Exploring New Testament Backgrounds* (Washington, D.C.: Christianity Today, n.d.), p. 43.
55. Adam Clarke, "The Epistle of Paul the Apostle to Titus," *CBC*, VI, 642.
56. Wessel, p. 43.
57. Henry H. Halley, "Titus," *HBH*, pp. 588ff.
58. Robert G. Gromacki, "Philemon," *New Testament Survey* (Grand Rapids: Baker Book House, 1974), p. 314.
59. John Rutherford, "Philemon," *ISBE*, IV, 2367.
60. Ibid., p. 2366.

Chapter 22

1. Thomas Rees, "Epistle to the Hebrews," *ISBE*, II, 1355.
2. Stephen J. Smalley, "Hebrews," *Exploring New Testament Backgrounds* (Washington, D.C.: Christianity Today, n.d.), p. 49.
3. Robert G. Gromacki, *New Testament Survey* (Grand Rapids: Baker Book House, 1947), p. 319.
4. Ibid., p. 321.
5. Ibid.
6. Smalley, p. 49.
7. "Hebrews," *EBH*, p. 626.
8. John B. Davis, "Epistle to the Hebrews," *DDB*, p. 309.
9. Smalley, p. 49.
10. Wallace A. Alcorn, "Epistle to the Hebrews," *WBE*, I, 775.
11. Ibid., p. 776.
12. James D. Borland, *Christ in the Old Testament* (Chicago: Moody Press, 1978), pp. 164ff.
13. Davis, p. 511.
14. John Wesley, "Hebrews," *Explanatory Notes upon the New Testament* (Naperville, Ill.: Alec R. Allenson Inc., 1960), p. 827.
15. Borland, p. 171–72.
16. Henry H. Halley, "Hebrews," *HBH*, p. 598.
17. Ibid.
18. Alexander Ross, "The Epistle of James," *Exploring New Testament Backgrounds* (Washington, D.C.: Christianity Today, n.d.), p. 51.
19. Ibid.
20. Merrill C. Tenney, *New Testament Survey* (Grand Rapids: Wm. B. Eerdmans Col., 1953), p. 262.
21. Doremus Almy Hays, "Epistle of James," *ISBE*, III, 1567.
22. Henry H. Halley, "James," *HBH*, p. 602.
23. Ibid., p. 602.
24. "James," *EHB*, p. 633.
25. Gromacki, p. 340.
26. Ross, p. 52.

Chapter 23

1. Alan M. Stibbs, "I Peter," *Exploring New Testament Backgrounds* (Washington, D.C.: Christianity Today, n.d.), p. 53.
2. William G. Moorehead, "The First Epistle of Peter," *ISBE*, IV, 2352.
3. Henry H. Halley, "I Peter," *HBH*, p. 606.
4. John D. Davis, "Peter," *DDB*, pp. 624ff.
5. Stephen W. Payne, "The First Epistle of Peter," *WBC*, p. 1444.
6. Halley, "I Peter," p. 607.
7. Benjamin W. Robinson, "First Peter," *ABC*, p. 1344.
8. Robert G. Gromacki, *New Testament Survey* (Grand Rapids: Baker Book House, 1974), p. 359.
9. Merrill C. Tenney, "II Peter," *Exploring New Testament Backgrounds* (Washington, D.C.: Christianity Today, n.d.), p. 55.
10. Stephen W. Payne, "The Second Epistle of Peter," *WBC*, p. 1453.
11. Henry H. Halley, "II Peter," *HBH*, p. 610.
12. Merrill C. Tenney, "The Second Epistle of Peter," *WBE*, II, 1321.
13. Shirley Jackson Case, "Second Peter," *ABC*, p. 1345.
14. Madeleine S. Miller and J. Lane Miller, "The Second Epistle of Peter," *HBD*, p. 544.
15. Tenney, "Second Epistle of Peter," p. 1321.
16. William G. Moorehead, "The Second Epistle of Peter," *ISBE*, IV, 2356.
17. D. Russell Scott, "Second Peter," *TSB*, IV, 1539ff.

Chapter 24

1. Henry H. Halley, "1 John," *HBH*, p. 614.
2. Huber L. Drumwright, Jr., "The Epistles of John," *ZPEB*, III, 650.

3. John Wesley, "I John," *Explanatory Notes upon the New Testament* (Naperville, Ill: Alec R. Allenson, 1966), p. 902.
4. Drumwright, p. 650.
5. Alexander Ross, "The Johannine Epistles," *Exploring New Testament Backgrounds* (Washington, D.C.: Christianity Today, n.d.), p. 57.
6. Robert G. Gromacki, *New Testament Survey* (Grand Rapids: Baker Book House, 1974), p. 370.
7. Robert Law, "The First Epistle of John," *ISBE*, III, 1711.
8. Drumwright, p. 469.
9. Halley, "I John," p. 614.
10. Law, "First Epistle of John," p. 1713.
11. Merrill C. Tenney, "First John," *New Testament Survey* (Grand Rapids: Wm. B. Eerdmans Co., 1953), p. 370.
12. Ross, p. 56.
13. Ibid., p. 58.
14. Robert Law, "The Epistles of John," *ISBE*, III, 1718.
15. Adam Clarke, "The Second Epistle of John," *CBC*, V, 934.
16. John Wesley, "The Second Epistle of St. John," *Explanatory Notes upon the New Testament* (Naperville, Ill.: Alec R. Allenson, 1966), p. 921; Drumwright, p. 656.
17. Leo G. Cox, "Second John," *TWBC*, VI, 315.
18. Ibid.
19. Drumwright, p. 657.
20. Adam Clarke, "The Epistle General of Jude," *CBC*, VI, 944ff.
21. Henry H. Halley, "Jude," *HBH*, p. 620.
22. William C. Moorehead, Jr., "The Epistle of Jude," *ISBE*, III, 1768.
23. Ibid.
24. S. Maxwell Coder, "Epistle of Jude," *WBE*, I, 968.
25. J. E. H. Thompson, "Apocalyptic Literature," *ISBE*, I, 169.
26. Ibid.
27. D. Russell Scott, "Jude," *TSB*, IV, 1545.
28. R. Ruane Thompson, "Jude," *TWBC*, VI, 386.
29. Coder, p. 968.
30. John Wesley, "The Epistle General of St. Jude," *Explanatory Notes upon the New Testament* (Naperville, Ill.: Alec R. Allenson, 1966), p. 929.
31. Thompson, p. 164.
32. Ibid.
33. Scott, p. 1549.
34. Coder, p. 969.
35. Ibid.

Chapter 25

1. Wilbur M. Smith, "Revelation," *WBC*, p. 1493.
2. Merrill C. Tenney, "Revelation," *Exploring New Testament Backgrounds* (Washington, D.C.: Christianity Today, n.d.), p. 61.
3. Ibid.
4. Henry H. Halley, "Revelation," *HBH*, p. 622.
5. W. M. Smith, p. 1495.
6. Ibid.; Merrill C. Tenney, *Interpreting Revelation* (Grand Rapids: Wm. B. Eerdmans Co., 1957), pp. 101ff.
7. Halley, p. 623; Robert G. Gromacki, *New Testament Survey* (Grand Rapids: Baker Book House, 1974), pp. 393ff.
8. Thea B. van Halsema, *Safari for Seven* (Grand Rapids: Baker Book House, 1967), p. 100.
9. John Wesley, "Revelation," *Explanatory Notes upon the New Testament* (Naperville, Ill.: Alec R. Allenson, 1966), p. 944.
10. Ibid.
11. Adam Clarke, "Revelation," *CBC*, VI, 977.
12. Howard F. Voss, "Revelation," *WBE*, II, 1601.
13. Harvey J. S. Blaney, "Revelation," *TWBC*, VI, 430.
14. Edgar J. Banks, "Smyrna," *ISBE*, IV, 2319.
15. Based on research data obtained at Smyrna and the Department of Antiquities in Izmir.
16. Banks, "Smyrna," p. 2819.
17. Ibid., p. 2818.
18. Frederick C. Grant, "Pergamum," *EA*, XXI, 582.
19. Based on research data obtained at Pergamum and the Department of Antiquities at Izmir.
20. Edward M. Blaiklock, "Thyatira," *ZPEB*, V, 743.
21. Madeleine S. Miller and J. Lane Miller, "Thyatira," *HBD*, p. 594; John D. Davis, "Thyatira," *DBD*, p. 672.
22. Edgar J. Banks, "Thyatira," *ISBE*, IV, 2977.
23. Blaney, p. 434.
24. E. Bertram Clagg, "Revelation," *ABC*, p. 1374.
25. Ibid.
26. Clarke, p. 980.
27. Halley, p. 638.
28. Based on research data obtained at Thyatira and the Department of Antiquitiest Izmir.
29. Editors, *EA*, 1957, VIII, 219ff.
30. Edward M. Blaiklock, "Sardis," *ZPEB*, V, 278.
31. Ibid.
32. Based on research data obtained in Sart and at the Department of Antiquities at Izmir.
33. William H. Ramsey, *The Letters to the Seven Churches*, 4th ed. (London: Hodder and Stoughton, 1895), p. 85.

34. Robert G. Gromacki, "Revelation," *New Testament Survey* (Grand Rapids: Baker Book House, 1974), pp. 402ff.
35. Robert J. Banks, "Philadelphia," *ISBE*, IV, 2366.
36. Edward M. Blaiklock. "Philadelphia," *ZPEB*, IV, 755.
37. Ibid.
38. Charles Lewis Smith, "Philadelphia," *ISBE*, IV, 2366.
39. Blaney, p. 439.
40. Based on research data obtained at Philadelphia and the Department of Antiquities at Izmir.
41. Clagg, p. 1375.
42. Robert H. Pfeiffer, "Greek Religion," *ER*, p. 311.
43. Clagg, p. 1376.
44. Ibid.
45. Based on research data obtained in Laodicea and the Department of Antiquities at Izmir.
46. George Tybout Purvis, "Revelation," *DBD*, p. 687.
47. Ibid.
48. Halley, p. 627.
49. Miller and Miller, p. 615.
50. Ibid.

Bibliography

Adams, J. McKee. *Ancient Records and the Bible*. Nashville: Broadman Press, 1946.
_____. *Biblical Backgrounds*. Rev. ed. Nashville: Broadman Press, 1938.
Aharoni, Yohanan. *The Land of the Bible: A Historical Geography*. Translated by A. F. Rainey. London: Burns & Oates, 1967.
Aharoni, Yohanan, and Avi-Yonah, Michael. *The Macmillan Bible Atlas*. Prepared by Carta, Jerusalem. New York: Macmillan Co., 1968.
Albright, William F. *Archaeology and the Religion of Israel*, 2nd ed. Baltimore: Johns Hopkins Press, 1946.
_____. *The Archaeology of Palestine*. Rev. ed. Baltimore: Penguin Books, 1961.
_____. *From the Stone Age to Christianity*. Baltimore: Johns Hopkins Press, 1940.
Allenby, E. H. H. *The Advance of the Egyptian Expeditionary Force, July, 1917 to October, 1918*. London: His Majesty's Stationery Office, 1919.
Amiran, David H. K.; Elster, Joseph; Gilead, Mordeha; Rosenan, Naftali; Kadmon, Naftali; and Paran, Uzi, eds. *Atlas of Israel*. Jerusalem: Survey of Israel, Ministry of Labour; Amsterdam: Elsevier Publishing Co., 1970.
Anati, Emmanuel. *Palestine Before the Hebrews: A History from the Earliest Arrival of Man to the Conquest of Canaan*. New York: Alfred A. Knopf, 1963.
Anderson, Bernhard W. *Rediscovering the Bible*. New York: Association Press, 1951.
_____. *Understanding the Old Testament*. 2nd ed. Englewood Cliffs, N.J.: Prentice-Hall, 1966.
Anderson, George W. *A Critical Introduction to the Old Testament*. London: Gerald Duckworth & Co., 1959.
Angus, S. *The Environment of Early Christianity*. New York: Charles Scribner's Sons, 1920.
Archer, John Clark. *Faiths Men Live By*. New York: Thomas Nelson and Sons, 1934.
Arminius, James. *The Writings of Arminius*. Edited by James Nichols and W. R. Bagnall. Reprint. Grand Rapids, Mich.: Baker Book House, 1956.
Ashbed, C. R., ed. *Jerusalem*. London: John Murray, 1920, 1924.
Auerbach, Joseph, *The Bible and Modern Life*. New York: Harper and Brothers, 1914.
Aulen, Gustaf. *Christus Victor*. Translated by A. G. Hebert. New York: Macmillan Co., 1931.
Avi-Yonah, Michael. *The Holy Land*. Grand Rapids: Baker Book House, 1966.
Baab, Otto J. *The Theology of the Old Testament*. New York: Abingdon-Cokesbury, 1949.
Bacher, Wilhelm. "Synagogue." In *Jewish Encyclopaedia*. New York: Funk and Wagnalls, 1912, XI, 619–628.
Baikie, James. *The English Bible and Its Story*. London: Seeley, Service and Co., Ltd., 1928.
Bailey, Cyril, ed. *The Legacy of Rome*. Oxford: Clarendon Press, 1924.
Baillie, Donald M. *The Theology of the Sacraments*. New York: Charles Scribner's Sons, 1957.
Baillie, John. *The Idea of Revelation in Recent Thought*. New York: Columbia University Press, 1956.
Bainton, Roland H. *Here I Stand: A Life of Martin Luther*. New York: Abingdon-Cokesbury, 1950.
Bales, James D. "The Relevance of Scriptural Interpretation to Scientific Thought." *Bulletin of the Evangelical Theology Society*, Dec. 1961.
Baly, Denis. *The Geography of the Bible: A Study in Historical Geography*. New York: Harper & Row, 1957.
Baly, Denis, and Tushingham, A. D. *Atlas of the Biblical World*. New York: World Publishing Co., 1971.
Banks, Edgar J. *The Bible and the Spade*. New York: Association Press, 1913.
Barbour, Clarence A. *The Bible in the World of Today*. New York: Association Press, 1911.
Barnes, Albert. *Barnes' Notes on the New Testament*. Grand Rapids: Baker Book House, 1949–50.
Baron, Salo Untermeyer. *A Social and Religious History of the Jews*. 2nd ed., rev. 2 vols. New York: Columbia University Press, 1952.

Bibliography

Barth, Karl. *The Doctrine of the Word of God. Prolegomena to Church Dogmatics.* Vol. I, Part I. Translated by G. T. Thompson. New York: Charles Scribner's Sons, 1936.

Bartlet, James Vernon. *The Apostolic Age* in *Ten Epochs of Church History.* Vol. I. New York: Charles Scribner's Sons, 1900.

Barton, George A., *Archaeology and the Bible.* 7th ed. Philadelphia: American Sunday School Union, 1937.

Batten, Samuel Z. *The Social Task of Christianity.* New York: Fleming H. Revell, 1911.

Battenfield, James R. "An Exegetical Study of the YHWH Mal'ak in the Old Testament." Postgraduate seminar paper, January 1971, Grace Theological Seminary, Winona Lake, Ind.

Bavinck, Hermann. *Our Reasonable Faith.* Grand Rapids, Mich.: Wm. B. Eerdmans Co., 1956.

Baxter, J. Sidlow. *Explore the Book.* 6 vols. Grand Rapids: Zondervan Publishing House, 1960.

Beach, Waldo, and Niebuhr, Reinhold, eds. *Christian Ethics.* New York: Ronald Press Co., 1955.

Beavan, Albert W. *The Local Church.* New York: Abingdon-Cokesbury, 1937.

Bentzen, Aage. *Introduction to the Old Testament.* Reprint (2 vols. in 1). Copenhagen: G.E.C. Gad, 1952.

Berkhof, Louis. *The History of Christian Doctrines.* Grand Rapids, Mich.: Wm. B. Eerdmans Co., 1949.

———. *The Kingdom of God.* Grand Rapids, Mich.: Wm. B. Eerdmans Co., 1951.

———. *Systematic Theology.* 4th ed., rev. Grand Rapids, Mich.: Wm. B. Eerdmans Co., 1949.

Berkouwer, G. C. *Faith and Sanctification.* Grand Rapids, Mich.: Wm. B. Eerdmans Co., 1952.

———. *The Person of Christ.* Grand Rapids, Mich.: Wm. B. Eerdmans Co., 1954.

Bewer, Julius. *The Literature of the Old Testament.* Revised by Emil G. Kraeling. 3rd ed. New York: Columbia University Press, 1962.

Biederwolf, William Edward. *The Visible God: or The Nature of Christ, A Study in Theophany.* Reading, Pa.: Boyer, n.d.

Birch, W. Grayson. *Veritas and The Virgin or The Son of God and the Children of Joseph and Mary.* Berne, Ind.: Berne Witness, Inc., 1960.

Blaikie, William G., and Matthews, Charles D. *A Manual of Bible History.* Rev. New York: Ronald Press Co., 1940.

Blaiklock, E. M. *The Archaeology of the New Testament.* Grand Rapids: Zondervan Publishing House, 1970.

———. *Out of the Earth.* Rev. ed. Grand Rapids, Mich.: Wm. B. Eerdmans Co., 1961.

———. *The Zondervan Pictorial Bible Atlas.* Grand Rapids, Mich.: Zondervan Publishing House, 1969.

Blair, J. Allen. *Living Faithfully.* Neptune, N.J.: Loizeaux Bros., 1961.

Boak, A. E. R. *A History of Rome to 565 A.D.* New York: Macmillan Co., 1921.

Bogardus, Emory S. *Fundamentals of Social Psychology.* New York: The Century Co., 1924.

Booth, Henry K. *The World of Jesus.* New York: Charles Scribner's Sons, 1933.

Boslooper, Thomas. *The Virgin Birth.* Philadelphia: Westminster Press, 1962.

Boulanger, Robert. *Hatchette World Guides: The Middle East, Lebanon, Syria, Jordan, Iraq, Iran.* Translated by J. S. Hardman. Paris: Hatchette, 1966.

Bowne, Borden Parker. *Metaphysics.* Rev. ed. Boston: Boston Univerity Press, 1898.

———. *Theory of Thought and Knowledge.* New York: American Book Co., 1897.

Boyer, James L. *Chart of the Period Between the Testaments.* Winona Lake, Ind.: Bible Charts, n.d.

———. *New Testament Chronological Chart.* Winona Lake, Ind.: Bible Charts, n.d.

Braden, Charles S. "Anglo-Israel." In *Twentieth Century Encyclopedia of Religious Knowledge.* Grand Rapids, Mich.: Baker Book House, 1955, I, 44.

Breasted, James H. *A History of Egypt.* 2nd ed., rev. New York: Charles Scribner's Sons, 1945.

Brew, William Thomas. "A Study of the Process of Revelation in the Pentateuch." Th.M. thesis, Dallas Theological Seminary, 1963.

Bright, John. *Early Israel in Recent History Writing.* London: S.C.M. Press, 1956.

———. *A History of Israel.* Philadelphia: Westminster Press, 1959.

———. *The Kingdom of God.* New York: Abingdon-Cokesbury, 1953.

Brightman, Edgar Sheffield. *Moral Laws.* New York: Abingdon Press, 1933.

———. *Person and Reality.* New York: Ronald Press Co., 1958.

———. *A Philosophy of Religion.* New York: Prentice-Hall, 1940.

———. *Religious Values.* New York: Abingdon Press, 1925.

Brockett, Henry E. *Scriptural Freedom from Sin.* Kansas City, Mo.: Beacon Hill Press, 1941.

Brown, Charles Ewing. *The Meaning of Salvation.* Anderson, Ind.: The Warner Press, 1944.

———. *The Meaning of Sanctification.* Anderson, Ind.: The Warner Press, 1945.

———. *The Reign of Christ.* Anderson, Ind.: Gospel Trumpet Co., 1950.

Brown, Francis; Driver, Samuel Rolles; and Briggs, Charles A. *A Hebrew and English Lexicon of the Old Testament.* Oxford: Clarendon Press, 1907.

Brown, William Adams. *Christian Theology in Outline.* New York: Charles Scribner's Sons, 1906.

Bruce, F. F. *The Books and the Parchments.* Old Tappan, N.J.: Fleming H. Revell, 1953.

———. *The Spreading Flame: The Rise and Progress of Christianity.* Grand Rapids, Mich.: Wm. B. Eerdmans Co., 1953.

Bruce, W. S., *The Wisdom Literature of the Old Testament.* London: James Clark and Co., 1904.

Brunner, Emil. *The Christian Doctrine of God: Dogmatics.* Vol. I. Philadelphia: Westminster Press, 1950.

———. *The Divine Imperative.* Translated by Olive Wyon. Philadelphia: Westminster Press, 1947.

———. *Eternal Hope.* Translated by Harold Knight. Philadelphia: Westminster Press, 1954.

———. *The Scandal of Christianity.* Philadelphia: Westminster Press, 1951.

Buck, Harry M. *People of the Lord.* New York: Macmillan Co., 1965.

Buis, Harry. *The Doctrine of Eternal Punishment.* Philadelphia: Presbyterian and Reformed Publishing Co., 1957.

Bullock, William Thomas. "Melchizedek." In *Dr. William Smith's Dictionary of the Bible.* Edited and revised by Horatio B. Hackett. 4 vols. Reprint. Grand Rapids: Baker, 1971.

Bultmann, Rudolf. *Theology of the New Testament.* New York: Charles Scribner's Sons, 2 vols., 1951, 1955.

Burrows, Millar. *The Dead Sea Scrolls.* New York: Viking Press, 1955.

———. *An Outline of Biblical Theology.* Philadelphia: Westminster Press, 1946.

_____. *What Mean These Stones?* New Haven, Conn.: American Schools of Oriental Research, 1941.

Burtner, Robert W., and Chiles, Robert E. *A Compend of Wesley's Theology.* New York: Abingdon Press, 1954.

Burton, Ernest D. *The Records and Letters of the Apostolic Age.* New York: Charles Scribner's Sons, 1923.

Busch, Fritz-Otto. *The Five Herods.* Translated by E. W. Dickes. London: Robert Hale, Ltd., 1958.

Bush, George. *Notes, Critical and Practical on the Book of Exodus.* 2 vols. New York: Newman, 1844.

Buttrick, George A. *Prayer.* New York: Abingdon-Cokesbury, 1942.

Caiger, S. L. *Bible and Spade.* Oxford: Oxford University Press, 1936.

Calloway, T. W. *Christ in the Old Testament.* New York: Loizeaux Bros., 1950.

Calvin, John. *Institutes of the Christian Religion.* Translated by Henry Beveridge. 2 vols. Grand Rapids, Mich.: Wm. B. Eerdmans Co., 1953.

_____. *Calvin's New Testament Commentaries.* Edited by T. F. Torrance and D. W. Torrance. 12 vols. Grand Rapids: Wm. B. Eerdmans Co., 1960.

Cannon, William. *The Theology of John Wesley.* New York: Abingdon-Cokesbury, 1946.

_____. *The Redeemer: The Work and Person of Jesus Christ.* New York: Abingdon-Cokesbury, 1951.

Carmichael, P. H. *Understanding the Books of the Old Testament.* Richmond, Va.: John Knox Press, 1950.

Carter, Charles W., ed. *The Wesleyan Bible Commentary.* 6 vols. Grand Rapids: Wm. B. Eerdmans Co., 1965–69.

Carter, John Franklin. *A Layman's Harmony of the Gospels.* Nashville, Tenn.: Broadman Press, 1961.

Cartledge, Samuel A. *A Conservative Introduction to the Old Testament.* 2nd ed. Athens, Ga.: University of Georgia Press, 1944.

Casola, Pietro (1427–1507). *Canon P. Casola's Pilgrimage to Jerusalem.* Translated by M. M. Newett. Manchester, Eng.: University Press, 1907.

Cawood, John. *Let's Know the Bible.* Old Tappan, N.J.: Fleming H. Revell, 1971.

Ceram, C. W. *The March of Archaeology.* New York: Alfred A. Knopf, 1970.

Chadwick, Samuel. *The Gospel of the Cross.* Kansas City, Mo.: Beacon Hill Press, 1949.

Chafer, Lewis Sperry. *Systematic Theology.* 8 vols. Dallas, Tex.: Dallas Seminary Press, 1947.

Charlier, C. *The Christian Approach to the Bible.* Translated by H. J. Richards and B. Peters. Westminster: Newman, 1958.

Cheney, Johnston M., and Ellisen, Stanley A. *The Life of Christ in Stereo.* Portland: Western Baptist Seminary Press, 1969.

Cherbonnier, Edmund LaB. *Hardness of Heart.* Garden City, N.Y.: Doubleday and Co., 1955.

Churchill, Randolph S., and Churchill, Winston S. *The Six Day War.* Boston: Houghton Mifflin Co., 1967.

Clark, Elmer T. *The Small Sects in America.* New York: Abingdon-Cokesbury, 1949.

Clark, Neville. *An Approach to the Theology of the Sacraments.* Chicago: Alec R. Allenson, 1956.

Clarke, Adam, ed. *Clarke's Bible Concordance.* Grand Rapids: Baker Book House, 1968.

Clarke, William Newton. *An Outline of Christian Theology.* New York: Charles Scribner's Sons, 1898.

Collett, Sidney. *All About the Bible.* 3rd ed. Chicago: Christian Witness Co., n.d.

Conner, C. R., and Kitchener, H. H. *The Survey of Western Palestine.* 8 vols. London: Palestine Exploratory Fund, 1883.

Cook, Thomas C. *New Testament Holiness.* London: Epworth Press, 1952.

Cooke, Richard J. *Did Paul Know of the Virgin Birth?* New York: Macmillan Co., 1926.

Cooper, David L. *Messiah: His Nature and Person.* Los Angeles: David L. Cooper, 1933.

Coppens, J. *The Old Testament and the Critics.* Translated by E. A. Ryan, S.J., and E. W. Tribbe, S.J. Paterson, N.J.: Guild Press, 1942.

Corlett, Lewis T. *Holiness in Practical Living.* Kansas City, Mo.: Beacon Hill Press, 1948.

_____. *Holiness, the Harmonizing Experience.* Kansas City, Mo.: Beacon Hill Press, 1951.

Couch, Herbert N., and Geer, Russell M. *Classical Civilization: Rome.* Edited by Russell M. Geer. 2nd ed. New York: Prentice-Hall, 1950.

Couriet, A. *La Prise De Jerusalem Par Les Perses en 614 A.D.* Orleans, 1896.

Cowan, Henry. *Landmarks of Church History to the Reformation.* Rev. ed. New York: Fleming H. Revell, n.d.

Craig, Clarence T. "The Church of the New Testament." In *The Universal Church in God's Design.* New York: Harper and Brothers, 1948.

Crain, Orville E. *The Credibility of the Virgin Birth.* New York: Abingdon Press, 1925.

Cross, Frank Moore, Jr. *The Ancient Library of Qumran and Modern Biblical Studies.* Garden City, N.Y.: Doubleday & Co., 1958.

Cunliffe-Jones, H. *The Authority of the Biblical Revelation.* Boston: Pilgrim Press, 1948.

Curtis, Olin A. *The Christian Faith.* New York: Methodist Book Concern, 1903; Grand Rapids, Mich.: Kregel Book Store, reprint, 1956.

Daiches, David. *The King James Version of the English Bible.* Chicago: University of Chicago Press, 1941.

Dalman, Gustaf. *Sacred Sites and Ways: Studies in the Topography of the Gospels.* Translated by Paul P. Levertoff. London: Society for Promotion of Christian Knowledge; New York: Macmillan Co., 1935.

Daniel-Rops, Henry. *Sacred History.* New York: Longmans, Green and Co., 1949.

Daugherty, John J. "The One God." In *The Bridge.* Edited by John M. Oesterreicher. New York: Pantheon Books, 1955.

David, M., and Van Groningen, B. A. *Papyrological Primer.* 2nd ed. Leyden: E. J. Brill, 1946.

Davidson, A. B. *The Theology of the Old Testament.* Edinburgh: T. and T. Clarke, 1904.

Davidson, Robert F. *The Old Testament.* London: Hodder and Stoughton, 1964.

Davies, D. R. *Secular Illusion or Christian Realism.* London: Latimer House, 1942.

Davis, Jerome. *Contemporary Social Movements.* New York: The Century Co., 1930.

Davis, John D. *Davis Dictionary of the Bible.* Grand Rapids, Mich.: Baker Book House, 1972.

Davison, W. T. *The Praises of Israel.* London: Charles H. Kelly, 1902.

_____. *The Wisdom Literature of the Old Testament.* London: Charles H. Kelly, 1894.

Deal, William S. *Baker's Pictorial Introduction to the Bible.* Grand Rapids, Mich.: Baker Book House, 1967.

Bibliography

Deane, William J. *David, His Life and Times.* Men of the Bible. New York: Fleming H. Revell, n.d.
———. *Samuel and Saul: Their Lives and Times.* Men of the Bible. New York: Fleming H. Revell, n.d.
Dearden, Robert R., Jr. *The Guiding Light on the Great Highway.* Philadelphia: John C. Winston Co., 1929.
De Joinville, Lord John, comp. *Chronicles of the Crusades: Contemporary Narratives of the Crusade of Richard Coeur de Lion, by Richard of Devizes and Geoffrey de Vinsauf, and of the Crusade of Saint Louis.* London: Bell and Daldy, 1870.
Demaray, Donald E. *Basic Beliefs: An Introductory Guide to Christian Theology.* Grand Rapids, Mich.: Baker Book House, 1958.
Denney, James. *The Atonement and the Modern Mind.* New York: A. C. Armstrong and Son, 1903.
———. *The Christian Doctrine of Reconciliation.* New York: George H. Doran Co., 1918.
DeVaux, Roland, et al. "Method in the Study of Early Hebrew History." In *The Bible in Modern Scholarship.* Edited by J. Philip Hyatt. Nashville: Abingdon Press, 1965.
Dewey, John. *Democracy and Education.* New York: Macmillan Co., 1939.
DeWolf, L. Harold. *A Theology of the Living Church.* New York: Harper and Brothers, 1953.
Dinsmore, C. A. *The English Bible as Literature.* New York: Houghton Mifflin Co., 1931.
Dodd, C. H. *According to the Scripture.* New York: Charles Scribner's Sons, 1953.
———. *The Bible Today.* New York: Macmillan Co., 1947.
———. *The Epistle of Paul to the Romans: Moffatt New Testament Commentary.* New York: Charles Scribner's Sons, 1932.
———. *The Parables of the Kingdom.* London: Nisbet and Co., 1936.
Donovan, Robert J. *Israel's Fight for Survival: Six Days in June.* New York: The New American Library; London: The New English Library, A Signet Book, 1967.
Douglas, J. D., ed. *The New Bible Dictionary.* Grand Rapids, Mich.: Wm. B. Eerdmans Co., 1962.
Driver, S. R. *Introduction to the Literature of the Old Testament.* Rev. ed. New York: Charles Scribner's Sons, 1913.
Duckworth, H. T. F. "The Roman Provincial System." In *Beginnings of Christianity,* Part I, Vol. I, pp. 171–207. Edited by F. J. Foakes-Jackson and Kirsopp Lake. London: Macmillan & Co., Ltd., 1920.
Dummelow, J. R., ed. *A Commentary on the Holy Bible.* London: Macmillan Company, 1909.
Dunnett, Walter. *Outline of New Testament Survey.* Chicago: Moody Press, 1963.
Dupont-Sommer, A. *The Jewish Sect of Qumran and the Essenes.* New York: Macmillan Co., 1955.
Eason, J. Lawrence. *The New Bible Survey.* Grand Rapids: Zondervan Publishing House, 1963.
Easton, W. Burton, Jr. *Basic Christian Beliefs.* Philadelphia: Westminster Press, 1957.
Edersheim, Alfred. *The Bible History: Old Testament.* Grand Rapids: Wm. B. Eerdmans Co., 1949.
Edwards, Douglas. *The Virgin Birth in History and Faith.* London: Faber and Faber, Ltd., 1941.
Ehrlich, Ernst Ludwig. *A Concise History of Israel.* Translated by James Barr. London: Darton, Longman and Todd, 1962.
———. *Man in the Old Testament.* Studies in Biblical Theology, no. 4. Translated by K. and R. Gregor Smith. London: S.C.M. Press, 1956.
Eichrodt, Walther. *Theology of the Old Testament.* Vol. 1. Translated by J. A. Baker. Philadelphia: Westminster Press, 1961.
Eiselen, F. C., ed. *Abingdon Bible Commentary.* New York: Abingdon Press, 1929.
Eissfeldt, Otto. *The Old Testament: An Introduction.* Translated by Peter R. Ackroyd. New York: Harper & Row, 1965.
Ellis, Peter F. *The Men and the Message of the Old Testament.* Collegeville, Minn.: The Liturgical Press, 1962.
Ellison, H. L. *Jesus and the Pharisees.* Edited by Jakob Jocz. London: The Victoria Institute, 1953.
Ellwood, Charles. *The Reconstruction of Religion.* New York: Macmillan Co., 1922.
Ellyson, E. P. *Ye Must.* Marshalltown, Iowa: Christian Messenger Publishing Co., 1904.
Erdman, Charles R. *An Exposition of the New Testament.* 17 vols. Philadelphia: Westminster Press, 1948.
Eusebius. *The Ecclesiastical History.* 2 vols. Translated by J. E. L. Oulton. London: William Heinemann; New York: G. P. Putnam's Sons, 1932.
Everett, Walter G. *Moral Values.* New York: Henry Holt and Co., 1918.
Farrar, F. W. *The Life of Lives.* Cleveland: F. M. Barton, 1900.
———. *Solomon, His Life and Times.* New York: Fleming H. Revell, 1895.
Ferm, Vergilius. *Living Schools of Religion.* Ames, Iowa: Littlefield, Adams and Co., 1956 (originally published as *Religion in the Twentieth Century.* New York: The Philosophical Library, 1948).
Ferrar, William J. *The Uncanonical Jewish Books.* London: Society for Promoting Christian Knowledge, 1925.
Ferre, Nels F. S. *The Christian Understanding of God.* New York: Harper and Brothers, 1951.
———. *Evil and the Christian Faith.* New York: Harper and Brothers, 1947.
———. *Strengthening the Spiritual Life.* New York: Harper and Brothers, 1951.
Field, Benjamin. *The Student's Handbook of Christian Theology.* New York: Eaton and Mains, n.d.
Filson, Floyd V. *The New Testament Against Its Environment.* Chicago: Henry Regnery Co., 1950.
———. *One Lord, One Faith.* Philadelphia: Westminster Press, 1943.
Finegan, Jack. *Light from the Ancient Past.* 2nd ed. Princeton, N.J.: Princeton University Press, 1960.
Finkelstein, Louis, ed. *The Jews, Their History, Culture, and Religion.* New York: Harper and Brothers, 1949.
———. *The Pharisees.* 2 vols. Philadelphia: The Jewish Publication Society of America, 1938.
Fisher, George Park. *History of Christian Doctrine.* New York: Charles Scribner's Sons, 1911.
Fison, J. E. *The Christian Hope.* London: Longmans, Green and Co., 1954.
Flanders, H. K.; Crapps, R. W.; and Smith, D. A. *People of the Covenant: An Introduction to the Old Testament.* New York: Ronald Press Co., 1963.
Flew, R. N. *Jesus and His Church.* London: The Epworth Press, 1943.
Flewelling, Ralph Tyler. *Personalism and the Problems of Philosophy.* New York: The Methodist Book Concern, 1915.
———. *The Things That Matter Most.* New York: The Ronald Press Co., 1946.

540

Fodor, Eugene, and Foder, William, eds. *Fodor's Modern Guides: Israel 1967–68*. New York: David McKay Co., 1967.

Ford, Jack. *What the Holiness People Believe*. Birkenhead, Cheshire: Emmanuel Bible College, n.d.

Forster, Arnold. *Report from Israel*. New York: Anti-Defamation League of B'nai B'rith, n.d.

Forsyth, Peter Taylor. *The Person and Place of Jesus Christ*. London: Independent Press, 1951.

———. *Positive Preaching and the Modern Mind*. New York: George H. Doran Co., 1907.

Francisco, Clyde T. *Introducing the Old Testament*. Nashville: Broadman Press, 1950.

Free, Joseph. *Archaeology and Bible History*. Wheaton, Ill.: Scripture Press, 1956.

Free, Joseph P. *Archaeology and Bible History*. Wheaton, Ill.: Van Kampen Press, 1950.

Freedman, David Noel, and Greenfield, Jonas C., eds. *New Directions in Biblical Archaeology*. Garden City, N.Y.: Doubleday, 1969.

Freeman, John D. *More than Money*. Nashville: Sunday School Board of the Southern Baptist Convention, 1935.

Friedlander, L. *Roman Life and Manners Under the Early Empire*. 4 vols. Authorized translation of the 7th enlarged and revised edition of the *Sittengeschichte Roms* by L. A. Magnus. 2nd ed. New York: Dutton, n.d.

Fulcher of Chartres. *A History of the Expedition to Jerusalem, 1095–1127*. Translated by Frances Rita Ryan (Sisters of Saint Joseph). Edited by Harold S. Fink. Knoxville: University of Tennessee Press, 1969.

Fuller, R. H. *The Mission and Achievement of Jesus*. London: S.C.M. Press, 1953.

Gaebelein, Arno C. *The Annotated Bible*. Neptune, N.J.: Loizeaux Bros., 1970.

Gaebelein, Frank. *Exploring the Bible*. Reprint; Wheaton, Ill.: Van Kampen Press, 1950.

Garstang, John. *Joshua, Judges*. London: Constable and Co., 1931.

Gaster, Theodore H. *The Dead Sea Scriptures*. New York: Doubleday and Company, Inc., 1956.

Geikie, Cunningham. *Hours with the Bible*. New York: John B. Alden, n.d.

Gelin, Albert. *The Key Concepts of the Old Testament*. New York: Sheed and Ward, 1955.

———. *The Religion of Israel*, Twentieth Century Encyclopedia of Catholicism, J. R. Foster, tr. New York: Hawthorne Books, 1959.

Genung, John F., *The Epic of the Inner Life*. New York: Houghton Mifflin Co., 1891.

Glueck, Nelson. *The Other Side of the Jordan*. New Haven, Conn.: American Schools of Oriental Research, 1940.

———. *Rivers in the Desert: A History of the Negeb*. New York: Farrar, Straus, and Cudahy, 1959.

Godet, Frederick C. *Commentary on the Epistle to the Romans*. Translated by A. Cusin, revised by T. W. Chambers. Grand Rapids, Mich.: Zondervan Publishing House, reprint, 1956.

Goodspeed, C. "The Angel of Jehovah." *Bibliotheca Sacra* 36 (1879): 593–615.

Gordon, Alex R. *Early Traditions of Genesis*. Edinburgh: Clark, 1907.

———. *Poets of the Old Testament*. New York: Hodder and Stoughton, 1912.

Gordis, Robert, *Koheleth, The Man and His World*. New York: Jewish Theological Seminary of America, 1951.

Gordon, Cyrus H. *Introduction to Old Testament Times*. Ventnor, New Jer.: Ventnor Publishers, Inc., 1953.

Gore, Charles. *Dissertation on the Incarnation*. London: John Murray and Co., 1907.

———. *The Holy Spirit and the Church*. New York: Charles Scribner's Sons, 1924.

———. *The Incarnation of the Son of God*. New York: Charles Scribner's Sons, 1891.

Gould, J. Glenn. *The Precious Blood of Christ*. Kansas City, Mo.: Beacon Hill Press, 1959.

Gottwald, Norman, *A Light to the Nations*. New York: Harper and Row, 1959.

Graetz, H. *Popular History of the Jews*. Translated by Rabbi A. B. Rhine. Six volumes. Fifth Edition. New York: Hebrew Publishing Co., 1937. See vol. II, pp. 1–232.

Grant, Elihu, ed., *Haverford Symposium on Archaeology and the Bible*. New Haven: American Schools of Oriental Research, 1938.

Grant, F. W. *The Numerical Bible*. Neptune, N.J.: Loizeaux Bros., 1944–53.

Grant, Frederick C. *Introduction to New Testament Thought*. New York: Abingdon-Cokesbury Press, 1950.

Grant, Michael. *The Climax of Rome*. London: Weidenfeld & Nicolson, 1968.

Gray, Albert F. *Christian Theology*. Anderson, Ind.: The Warner Press, 1944.

Gray, James M. *Synthetic Bible Studies*. Old Tappan, N.J.: Fleming H. Revell, 1923.

Gray, John. *Archaeology and the Old Testament World*. New York: Thomas Nelson and Sons, 1962.

———. *A History of Jerusalem*. London: Robert Hale, 1969.

Greathouse, William M. *The Fullness of the Spirit*. Kansas City, Mo.: Nazarene Publishing House, 1958.

Green, Thomas Sheldon. *A Greek-English Lexicon to the New Testament*. New York: Macmillan Co., 1890.

Greenleaf, Simon. *The Testimony of the Evangelists*. Grand Rapids: Baker Book House, 1965.

Greenway, Leonard. *Basic Questions About the Bible*. Grand Rapids, Mich.: Zondervan Publishing House, 1948.

Gregory, Caspar R. *Canon and Text of the New Testament* in *International Theological Library*. New York: Charles Scribner's Sons, 1907.

Griffith-Thomas, W. H. *The Holy Spirit of God*. Grand Rapids, Mich.: Wm. B. Eerdmans Co., 1955.

Grimes, Howard. *The Church Redemptive*. New York: Abingdon Press, 1958.

Grollenberg, L. H., comp. *Nelson's Atlas of the Bible*. New York: Thomas Nelson and Sons, 1956.

Groves, John A. *A Greek and English Dictionary*. Philadelphia: J. B. Lippincott and Co., 1861.

Grutzmacher, Richard H. *The Virgin Birth*. New York: Eaton and Mains, 1907.

Guthrie, D., et al. *The New Bible Commentary: Revised*. Grand Rapids: Wm. B. Eerdmans Co., 1970.

———. *New Testament Introduction*. Downers Grove, Ill.: Inter-Varsity Press, 1961.

Hadjiantoniou, George A. *New Testament Introduction*. Chicago: Moody Press, 1957.

Halderman, I. M. "Does It Make Any Difference? or The Question of the Virgin Birth." *Book Bulletin*. Malverne, N.Y.: The Christian Evidence League.

Halley, Henry H. *Halley's Bible Handbook*. Grand Rapids: Zondervan Publishing House, 1964.

Halverson, Marvin, and Cohen, Arthur A., eds. *A Handbook of Christian Theology*. New York: Meridian Books, Inc., 1958.

Hamilton, Floyd E. *The Basis of Christian Faith*. 3rd ed., rev. New York: Harper and Brothers, 1946.

Bibliography

Hamlin, Howard H. *From Here to Maturity*. Kansas City, Mo.: Beacon Hill Press, 1955.
Hanke, Howard A. *Christ and the Church in the Old Testament*. Grand Rapids, Mich.: Zondervan Publishing House, 1957.
———. *From Eden to Eternity*. Grand Rapids, Mich.: Wm. B. Eerdmans Co., 1960.
———. "The Origin and Development of the Baal Religion." Th.D. dissertation, Iliff School of Theology, Denver, Colo., 1949.
———. *The Tabernacle in the Wilderness*. Grand Rapids, Mich.: Wm. B. Eerdmans Co., 1952.
———. *The Virgin Birth of Christ*. Grand Rapids, Mich.: Wm. B. Eerdmans Co., 1953.
Harkness, Georgia. *Christian Ethics*. New York: Abingdon Press, 1957.
Harper, Robert F. *The Code of Hammurabi*. Chicago: The University of Chicago Press, 1904.
Harrelson, Walter. *From Fertility Cult to Worship*. Garden City, N.Y.: Doubleday Anchor Books, 1970.
———. *Interpreting the Old Testament*. New York: Holt, Rinehart and Winston, 1964.
Harrington, John B. *Essentials in Christian Faith*. New York: Harper and Brothers, 1958.
Harris, Laird. "The Bible and Cosmology." *Bulletin of the Evangelical Theological Society*. March, 1962.
Harrison, Everett F., ed. *Baker's Dictionary of Theology*. Grand Rapids, Mich.: Baker Book House, 1960.
———. *Introduction to the New Testament*. Grand Rapids, Mich.: Wm. B. Eerdmans Co., 1964.
Harrison, R. K. *The Archaeology of the Old Testament*. London: The English Universities Press, 1963.
———. *Old Testament Times*. Grand Rapids, Mich.: Wm. B. Eerdmans Co., 1970.
Hastings, James, ed. *Prayer*. Great Christian Doctrines. New York: Charles Scribner's Sons, 1915.
Hazelton, Roger. *On Proving God*. A Handbook in Christian Conversation. New York: Harper and Brothers, 1952.
———. *Renewing the Mind*. New York: Macmillan Co., 1949.
Hedenquist, Gote. *The Church and the Jewish People*. London: Edinburgh House Press, 1954.
Hedley, George. *The Christian Heritage in America*. New York: Macmillan Co., 1946.
Heidt, William George. *Angelology of the Old Testament: A Study in Biblical Theology*. Washington, D.C.: Catholic University of America, 1949.
Heinisch, Paul. *Theology of the Old Testament*. Collegeville, Minn.: The Liturgical Press, 1950.
Henry, Carl F. H., ed. *The Biblical Expositor*. Vol. 3. Philadelphia: A. J. Holman Co., 1960.
———. *Christian Personal Ethics*. Grand Rapids, Mich.: Wm. B. Eerdmans Co., 1957.
Hessert, Paul. *Introduction to Christianity*. Englewood Cliffs, N.J.: Prentice-Hall, 1958.
Hiebert D. Edmond. *Introduction to the Non-Pauline Epistles*. Chicago: Moody Press, 1962.
———. *Introduction to the Pauline Epistles*. Chicago: Moody Press, 1954.
Hills, A. M. *Fundamental Christian Theology*. 2 vols. Pasadena, Calif.: Pasadena College, 1931. Abridged edition, C. J. Kinne, 1932.
Hindson, Edward E. *The Philistines and the Old Testament*. Grand Rapids, Mich.: Baker Book House, 1971.
Hoade, Eugene. *Guide to the Holy Land*. 4th ed., rev. Jerusalem: Franciscan Press, 1962.
Hocking, William Ernest. *The Meaning of God in Human Experience*. New Haven: Yale University Press, 1912.
Hodge, A. A. *The Atonement*. Grand Rapids, Mich.: Wm. B. Eerdmans Co., 1953.
Hodge, Charles. *Systematic Theology*. 3 vols. New York: Charles Scribner's Sons, 1893.
Hodges, J. W. *Christ's Kingdom and Coming*. Grand Rapids, Mich.: Wm. B. Eerdmans Co., 1957.
Hodgkin, A. M. *Christ in All the Scriptures*. London: Pickering and Inglis, Ltd., 1943.
Hort, Fenton. *The Christian Ecclesia*. New York: Macmillan Co., 1898.
Horton, Walter Marshall. *Christian Theology: An Ecumenical Approach*. New York: Harper and Brothers, 1955.
Howley, G. C. G.; Bruce, F. F.; and Ellison, H. L., eds. *A New Testament Commentary*. Grand Rapids, Mich.: Zondervan Publishing House, 1969.
Huffman, J. A. *The Meaning of Things*. Winona Lake, Ind.: The Standard Press, 1953.
———. *Voices from Rocks and Dust Heaps of Bible Lands*. Rev. Marion, Ind.: The Standard Press, 1943.
Hunter, Archibald M. *Introducing New Testament Theology*. Philadelphia: Westminster Press, 1957.
———. *The Message of the New Testament*. Philadelphia: Westminster Press, 1944.
———. *The Work and Words of Jesus*. London: S. C. M. Press, 1950.
Hyatt, J. Philip, ed. *The Bible in Modern Scholarship*. Nashville: Abingdon Press, 1965.
Hyde, Walter Woodburn. *Paganism to Christianity in the Roman Empire*. Philadelphia: University of Pennsylvania Press, 1946.
Hyde, William DeWitt. *The Five Great Philosophies of Life*. New York: Macmillan Co., 1923.
Ironside, H. A. *In the Heavenlies*. Neptune, N.J.: Loizeaux Bros., 1937.
Irwin, W. A. *The Old Testament: Keystone of Human Culture*. New York: Henry Schuman, 1952.
Jacob, Edmond. *Theology of the Old Testament*. Translated by A. W. Heathcote and P. J. Allcock. New York: Harper and Brothers, 1958.
Jastrow, Morris. *The Song of Songs*. Philadelphia: J. B. Lippincott and Co., 1921.
Jauncey, James H. *Science Returns to God*. Grand Rapids, Mich.: Zondervan Publishing House, 1961.
Jeans, Sir James. *This Mysterious Universe*. Rev. New York: Macmillan Co., 1937.
Jenkins, Daniel. *The Strangeness of the Church*. Garden City: Doubleday and Co., 1955.
Jensen, Joseph, O.S.B. *God's Word to Israel*. Boston: Allyn and Bacon, 1968.
Jeremias, Joachim. *Jerusalem in the Time of Jesus*. Translated by F. H. Cave and C. H. Cave. London: S.C.M. Press, 1962, 1967.
Jessop, T. E., et al. *The Christian Understanding of Man*. London: George Allen and Unwin Ltd., 1938.
Jirku, Anton. *The World of the Bible*. Translated by Ann E. Kepp. London: Weidenfeld and Nicholson, 1967.
Johns, C. N. *Palestine of the Crusades*. Jaffa: 1938.
Johnson, Aubrey. *The Vitality of the Individual in the Thought of Ancient Israel*. Cardiff: University of Wales Press, 1949.
Johnson, Paul E. *Psychology of Religion*. New York: Abingdon-Cokesbury, 1945.
Join-Lambert, Michael. *Jerusalem*. Translated by Charlotte Haldane. London: Elek Books, 1958.

542

Jones, E. Stanley. *Christ and Human Suffering*. New York: Abingdon Press, 1933.

Josephus. *Josephus: Complete Works*. Translated by William Whiston. Grand Rapids, Mich.: Kregel Publications, 1964.

Jurji, Edward J., ed. *The Great Religions of the Modern World*. Princeton, N.J.: Princeton University Press, 1946.

Kantonen, T. A. *The Christian Hope*. Philadelphia: Muhlenberg Press, 1954.

Kaufmann, Yehezkel. *The Religion of Israel*. Translated by Moshe Greenberg. Chicago: University of Chicago Press, 1960.

Kautzsch, Emil Friedrich. "Theophany." In *The New Schaff-Herzog Encyclopedia of Religious Knowledge*. Edited by S. M. Jackson. 13 vols. Grand Rapids, Mich.: Baker Book House, 1957.

Kay, James. *The Nature of Christian Worship*. New York: Philosophical Library, 1954.

Keil, Carl Frederick, and Delitzsch, Franz. *The Pentateuch*. Vols. 1–3. Translated by James Martin. *Biblical Commentary on the Old Testament*. Grand Rapids, Mich.: Wm. B. Eerdmans Co., n.d.

Kelchner, John Wesley. *A Description of Solomon's Temple and the Tabernacle in the Wilderness*. New York: A. J. Holman, 1925.

Kelly, Howard A. *A Scientific Man and the Bible*. Philadelphia: The Sunday School Times Co., 1925.

Kennedy, Gerald. *God's Good News*. New York: Harper and Brothers, 1955.

Kennedy, H. A. A. *St. Paul and the Mystery Religions*. London: Hodder & Stoughton, 1913.

Kent, Charles Foster. *A History of the Jewish People During the Babylonian, Persian, and Greek Periods*. 5th ed. New York: Charles Scribner's Sons, 1902.

_____. *The Kings and Prophets of Israel and Judah*. New York: Charles Scribner's Sons, 1913.

Kent, Homer A., Jr. *Jerusalem to Rome*. Grand Rapids, Mich.: Baker Book House, 1972.

Kenyon, Kathleen M. *Archaeology in the Holy Land*. New York: Praeger, Publishers, 1960.

_____. *Jerusalem: Excavating 3000 Years of History*. New York: McGraw-Hill Book Co.; London: Thames & Hudson, 1967.

Kenyon, Sir Frederic. *Our Bible and the Ancient Manuscripts*. 4th ed. New York: Harper and Brothers, 1939.

Kepler, Thomas S., ed. *The Fellowship of the Saints*. New York: Abingdon-Cokesbury, 1948.

Kerr, Hugh Thompson, Jr., ed. *A Compend of the Institutes of the Christian Religion by John Calvin*. Philadelphia: Presbyterian Board of Christian Education, 1939.

Kerr, John H. *A Harmony of the Gospels*. Old Tappan, N.J.: Fleming H. Revell, 1903.

Kierkegaard, Soren. *Works of Love*. Translated by David and Lillian Swenson. Princeton, N.J.: Princeton University Press, 1946.

King, Albion R. *The Problem of Evil*. New York: Ronald Press Co., 1952.

Kirk, Thomas. *Solomon: His Life and Works*. Edinburgh: Andrew Elliot, 1915.

Kitchen, J. Howard. *Holy Fields: An Introduction to the Historical Geography of the Holy Land*. Grand Rapids, Mich.: Wm. B. Eerdmans Co., 1955.

Kittel, Gerhard, ed. *Theological Dictionary of the New Testament*. Translated by Geoffrey W. Bromiley, 9 vols. Grand Rapids, Mich.: Wm. B. Eerdmans Co., 1964–74.

Knight, George A. F. *A Christian Theology of the Old Testament*. London: S.C.M. Press, 1959.

Knopf, Carl S. *The Old Testament Speaks*. New York: Thomas Nelson and Sons, 1934.

Knott, Laura A. *Student's History of the Hebrews*. New York: Abingdon Press, 1922.

Knudson, Albert C. *The Principles of Christian Ethics*. New York: Abingdon-Cokesbury, 1943.

_____. *The Religious Teaching of the Old Testament*. New York: Abingdon-Cokesbury, 1918.

Köhler, Ludwig. *Old Testament Theology*. Translated by A. S. Todd. Philadelphia: Westminster Press, 1957.

Kollek, Teddy, and Pearlman, Moshe. *Jerusalem: A History of Forty Centuries*. New York: Random House, 1968.

Kopp, Clemens. *The Holy Places of the Gospels*. New York: Herder & Herder, 1963.

Kraeling, Emil G. *The Old Testament Since the Reformation*. New York: Harper and Row, 1955.

_____, ed. *Rand McNally Historical Atlas of the Holy Land*. Chicago: Rand McNally & Co., 1959.

Kuhl, Curt. *The Old Testament: Its Origins and Composition*. Translated by C. T. M. Herriott. Richmond: John Knox Press, 1961.

Kunkel, Fritz. *In Search of Maturity*. New York: Charles Scribner's Sons, 1946.

Kuntz, John Kenneth. *The Self-Revelation of God*. Philadelphia: Westminster Press, 1967.

Kurtz, Johann Heinrich. *History of the Old Covenant*. Translated by Alfred Edersheim and James Martin. 3 vols. Clark's Foreign Theological Library. 3d ser. Edinburgh: Clark, 1859.

Ladd, G. H. *Crucial Questions About the Kingdom of God*. Grand Rapids, Mich.: Wm. B. Eerdmans Co., 1952.

Lake, Kirsopp. *The Text of the New Testament*. 6th ed. Revised by Silva New, A. B. London: Rivingtons, 1933.

Landau, Eli. *Jerusalem the Eternal: The Paratroopers' Battle for the City of David*. Translated by R. Lev. Edited by Murray Roston. Tel-Aviv: Otpaz, 1968.

Lange, John Peter. "Genesis." Translated by Tayler Lewis and A. Gosman. In *Commentary on the Holy Scriptures*. Vol. 1. Edited by Philip Schaff. 12 vols. Grand Rapids, Mich.: Zondervan, 1960.

Larue, Gerald A. *Old Testament Life and Literature*. Boston: Allyn and Bacon, Inc., 1968.

Latimer, Elizabeth W. *Judea from Syrus to Titus 537 B.C.–70 A.D.* Chicago: A. C. McClurg & Co., 1899.

Latourette, Kenneth Scott. *A History of Christianity*. New York: Harper and Brothers, 1953.

Laurin, Roy L. *John: Life Eternal*. Chicago: Moody Press, 1972.

Lawrence, T. E. *Crusader Castles*. London: Golden Cockerel Press, 1936.

Lawson, John. *The Biblical Theology of Saint Irenaeus*. London: Epworth Press, 1948.

Leavell, Roland Q. *Evangelism*. Nashville: Broadman Press, 1951.

Leighton, J. A. *Man and the Cosmos*. New York: D. Appleton and Co., 1922.

Lenski, R. C. H. *Interpretation of the New Testament*. 12 vols. Minneapolis: Augsburg Publishing House, 1933–46.

Levie, Jean, S.J. *The Bible, Word of God in Words of Men*. New York: Kenedy, 1961.

Levison, Nahum. *The Jewish Background of Christianity*. Edinburgh: T. & T. Clark, 1932.

Lewis, C. S. *The Case for Christianity*. New York: Macmillan Co., 1944.

_____. *The Great Divorce*. New York: Macmillan Co., 1946.

_____. *Miracles*. New York: Macmillan Co., 1947.

543

Bibliography

Lewis, Edwin. *The Creator and the Adversary.* New York: Abingdon-Cokesbury, 1948.
———. *A Manual of Christian Beliefs.* New York: Charles Scribner's Sons, 1927.
———. *A Philosophy of the Christian Revelation.* New York: Harper and Brothers, 1940.
Liddell, Henry George, and Scott, Robert. *A Greek-English Lexicon.* Oxford: Oxford University Press, 1940.
Liddon, Henry Parry. *The Divinity of Our Lord and Savior Jesus Christ.* 18th ed. London: Longmans & Green, 1897.
Lloyd-Jones, D. Martyn. *God's Way of Reconciliation.* Grand Rapids, Mich.: Baker Book House, 1972.
Lockyer, Herbert. *All the Prayers of the Bible.* Grand Rapids, Mich.: Zondervan Publishing House, 1959.
Louvish, Misha, ed. *Facts About Israel, 1970.* Jerusalem: Keter Books, 1970.
Luck, G. Coleman. *The Bible Book by Book.* Chicago: Moody Press, 1955.
McClain, Alva J. *Romans: The Gospel of God's Grace.* Edited by Herman A. Hoyt. Chicago: Moody Press, 1973.
McCown, C. C. *The Ladder of Progress in Palestine.* New York: Harper and Brothers, 1943.
MacDonald, William Graham. "Christology and 'The Angel of the Lord.'" In *Current Issues in Biblical and Patristic Interpretation.* Edited by Gerald F. Hawthorne. Grand Rapids, Mich.: Wm. B. Eerdmans Co., 1975.
McFayden, John E. *The Wisdom Books.* London: James Clarke and Co., n.d.
McGiffert, A. C. *A History of Christian Thought.* 2 vols. New York: Charles Scribner's Sons, 1932.
McGregor, G. H. C. *Jew and Greek: Tutors unto Christ. The Jewish and Hellenistic Background of the New Testament.* New York: Charles Scribner's Sons, 1936.
McKibben, Frank M. *Christian Education Through the Church.* New York: Abingdon-Cokesbury, 1947.
McKenzie, John L. *The Two-Edged Sword.* Milwaukee: Bruce Publishing Co., 1960.
Machen, J. Gresham. *The Origin of Paul's Religion.* Grand Rapids, Mich.: Wm. B. Eerdmans Co., 1947.
———. *The Virgin Birth of Christ.* New York: Harper and Brothers, 1930.
Macintosh, Robert. *Historic Theories of the Atonement.* London: Hodder and Stoughton, 1920.
Maclaren, Alexander. *Expositions of Holy Scripture.* 11 vols. Grand Rapids, Mich.: Wm. B. Eerdmans Co., 1944.
Manley, G. T. *The New Bible Handbook.* Chicago: The Inter-Varsity Christian Fellowship, 1949.
Marsh, Frank Burr. *The Reign of Tiberius.* Oxford: University Press, 1931.
Marston, Leslie R. *From Chaos to Character.* Winona Lake, Ind.: Light and Life Press, 1944.
Martin, Ralph P. *Mark: Evangelist and Theologian.* Grand Rapids, Mich.: Zondervan Publishing House, 1973.
Matson, G. Olaf. *The Palestinian Guide, Including Trans-Jordan.* Jerusalem: Joshua Simon, 1946.
Matthews, C. E. *Every Christian's Job.* Nashville: Broadman Press, 1955.
Mattingly, Harold. *Roman Imperial Civilization.* London: Edwin Arnold Ltd., 1957.
Mazzolani, L. S. *The Idea of the City in Roman Thought (from walled city to spiritual commonwealth).* Translated by S. O'Donnell. Toronto: Hollis & Carter, 1967, 1970.
Meistermann, P. Barnabe. *Guide de Terre Sainte.* Paris: Editions Franciscaines; Librarie Letouzey & Ané, 1936.
Mendenhall, George E. "Biblical History in Transition." In *The Bible and the Ancient Near East.* Edited by G. Ernest Wright. New York: Doubleday Anchor Books, 1965.
———. *Law and Covenant in Israel and the Ancient Near East.* Pittsburgh: Biblical Colloquium, 1955.
Metzger, Bruce M. *An Introduction to the Apocrypha.* New York: Oxford University Press, 1957.
Meysels, Theodor F. *Israeli in Your Pocket.* Tel Aviv: Ben-Dor Israel Publishing Co., 1956.
Michaud, Joseph Francis. *History of the Crusades.* Translated by W. Robson. New York: Redfield, 1853.
Miley, John. *The Atonement in Christ.* New York: Phillips and Hunt, 1879.
Miller, Dorothy Ruth. *A Handbook of Ancient History in Bible Light.* New York: Fleming H. Revell, 1937.
Miller, H. S. *General Biblical Introduction.* 2nd ed. Houghton, N.Y.: The Word-bearer Press, 1940.
Miller, H. V. *The Sin Problem.* Kansas City, Mo.: Nazarene Publishing House, 1947.
———. *When He Is Come.* Kansas City, Mo.: Nazarene Publishing House, 1941.
Miller, M. S. and J. L., eds. *Harper's Bible Dictionary.* New York: Harper and Brothers, 1952.
Miller, Park Hays. *How to Study and Use the Bible.* Boston: W. A. Wilde Co., 1949.
Mills, Sanford C. *A Hebrew Christian Looks at Romans.* Grand Rapids, Mich.: Zondervan Publishing House, 1968.
Minear, Paul S. *The Eyes of Faith.* Philadelphia: Westminster Press, 1946.
Mitchell, T. Crichton. *Mr. Wesley.* Kansas City, Mo.: Beacon Hill Press, 1957.
Moore, Elinor A. *The Ancient Churches of Jerusalem: The Evidence of the Pilgrims.* London: Constable, 1961.
Moore, George Foot. *Judaism.* 2 vols. Cambridge: Harvard University Press, 1927.
Morgan, G. Campbell. *The Analyzed Bible.* Old Tappan, N.J.: Fleming H. Revell, 1971.
———. *Hosea, the Heart and Holiness of God.* New York: Fleming H. Revell, 1934.
———. *Living Messages of the Books of the Bible.* New York: Fleming H. Revell, 1912.
Morgenstern, Julian. *The Fire upon the Altar.* Chicago: Quadrangle Books, 19₃3.
Moriarty, Frederick L. *Introducing the Old Testament.* Milwaukee: Bruce Publishing Co., 1960.
Morris, Leon. *The Apostolic Preaching of the Cross.* London: Tyndale Press, 1955.
———. *The Epistles of Paul to the Thessalonians.* The Tyndale New Testament Commentaries. Grand Rapids, Mich.: Wm. B. Eerdmans Co., 1957.
Mott, John R. *The Larger Evangelism.* New York: Abingdon-Cokesbury, 1944.
Mould, Elmer K. *Essentials of Bible History.* Rev. New York: Ronald Press Co., 1951.
Moule, H. C. G. *Veni Creator.* London: Hodder and Stoughton, 1895.
Moulton, James H. *A Grammar of New Testament Greek.* Vol. I: *Prolegomena.* 3rd ed. Edinburgh: T. & T. Clark, 1908.
Moulton, James Hope, and Milligan, George. *The Vocabulary of the Greek Testament.* Grand Rapids, Mich.: Wm. B. Eerdmans Co., 1952.
Mowinckel, Sigmund. *He That Cometh.* Translated by G. W. Anderson. New York: Abingdon Press, 1956.
Mozley, J. K. *The Doctrine of the Atonement.* New York: Charles Scribner's Sons, 1916.

544

Muilenburg, James. "The History of the Religion of Israel." In *The Interpreter's Bible*. Vol. I. New York: Abingdon Press, 1952.
_____. *The Way of Israel*. New York: Harper and Row, 1961.
Muir, James C. *His Truth Endureth*. Philadelphia: National Publishing Co., 1937.
Nash, Arnold S., ed. *Protestant Thought in the Twentieth Century*. New York: Macmillan Co., 1951.
Nease, Orval J. *Heroes of Temptation*. Kansas City, Mo.: Beacon Hill Press, 1950.
Needler, Winifred. *Palestine Ancient and Modern*. Toronto: Royal Ontario Museum of Archaeology, 1949.
Neil, William. *Harper's Bible Commentary*. New York: Harper & Row, 1963.
Nelson, Lawrence E. *Our Roving Bible*. New York: Abingdon-Cokesbury, 1945.
Neve, J. L. *A History of Christian Thought*. 2 vols. Philadelphia: Muhlenberg Press, 1946.
Nevius, Warren N. *The Old Testament: Its Story and Religious Message*. Philadelphia: The Westminster Press, 1942.
Newman, Murray. *The People of the Covenant*. New York, 1962.
Newton, A. P., ed. *Travel and Travellers in the Middle Ages*. London: 1930; Freeport, N.Y.: Brooklyn Libraries Press, 1967.
Nicholson, Ernest W. "The Interpretation of Exodus XXIV 9–11." *Vetus Testamentum* 24 (1974): 77–97.
Nicoll, W. Robertson, *The Expositor's Greek Testament*. Grand Rapids, Mich.: Wm. B. Eerdmans Co., 1961.
Niebuhr, Reinhold. *Beyond Tragedy*. New York: Charles Scribner's Sons, 1948.
_____. *The Nature and Destiny of Man*. 2 vols. New York: Charles Scribner's Sons, 1943.
Niles, Daniel T. *The Preacher's Task and the Stone of Stumbling*. New York: Harper and Brothers, 1958.
Noth, Martin. *The History of Israel*. Translated by S. Godman. Revised by P. R. Ackroyd. 2nd ed. New York: Harper & Row, 1960.
Nygren, Anders. *Agape and Eros*. Translated by Philip S. Watson. Philadelphia: Westminster Press, 1953.
Oehler, Gustav. *Theology of the Old Testament*. Grand Rapids, Mich.: Zondervan Publishing House, 1950.
Oesterley, W. O. E. *A History of Israel*. Vol. II: *From the Fall of Jerusalem to the Bar-Kokhba Revolt, A.D. 135*. Oxford: Clarendon Press, 1939.
_____. *An Introduction to the Books of the Apocrypha*. New York: Macmillan Co., 1935.
Oldenbourg, Zoe. *The Crusades*. Translated by Anne Carter. London: Weidenfeld and Nicolson, 1966.
Oman, W. W. C. *A History of the Art of War in the Middle Ages*. 2nd ed., rev. 2 vols. London, 1934.
Orchard, B.; Sutcliffe, E. F.; and Russell, R., eds. *A Catholic Commentary on Holy Scripture*. Edinburgh: Thomas Nelson and Sons, 1953.
Orlinsky, Harry M. *Ancient Israel*. Ithaca, N.Y.: Cornell University Press, 1964.
Orni, Efriam, and Efrat, Elisha. *Geography of Israel*. Jerusalem: Israel Program for Scientific Translations, 1964.
Orr, James. *International Standard Bible Encyclopedia*. 5 vols. Grand Rapids, Mich.: Wm. B. Eerdmans Co., 1939.
_____. *The Virgin Birth of Christ*. New York: Charles Scribner's Sons, 1907.
Ottley, R. L. *A Short History of the Hebrews to the Roman Period*. New York: Macmillan Co., 1940.
Otto, Rudolf. *The Kingdom of God and the Son of Man*. Grand Rapids, Mich.: Zondervan Publishing House, 1938.
_____. *The Idea of the Holy*. Translated by J. W. Harvey. London: Oxford University Press, 1957.
Owen, G. Frederick. *Abraham to Allenby*. 2nd ed. Grand Rapids, Mich.: Wm. B. Eerdmans Co., 1941.
Parker, DeWitt H. *The Principles of Aesthetics*. New York: Appleton-Century-Crofts, 1920.
Parkes, James. *A History of Palestine from 135 A.D. to Modern Times*. New York: Oxford University Press, 1949.
Paxson, Ruth. *Wealth, Walk, and Warfare of the Christian*. Old Tappan, N.J.: Fleming H. Revell, 1939.
Peake's Commentary on the Bible. Rev. ed. Edited by M. Black and H. H. Rowley. New York: Thomas Nelson and Sons, 1962.
Pearlman, Moshe, and Yannai, Yaacov. *Historical Sites in Israel*. New York: Vanguard Press, 1964.
Perowne, J. J. S. *The Book of Psalms*. 7th ed., rev. Boston: Bradley and Woodruff, n.d.
Perowne, Stewart. *Jerusalem–Bethlehem*. South Brunswick, N.Y.: A. S. Barnes Co., 1965.
_____. *The Life and Times of Herod the Great*. London: Hodder & Stoughton, 1956.
Peters, John. *Christian Perfection and American Methodism*. New York: Abingdon Press, 1956.
Pfeiffer, Charles F. *Baker's Bible Atlas*. Grand Rapids: Baker Book House, 1961.
_____. *The Biblical World*. Grand Rapids, Mich.: Baker Book House, 1972.
_____, ed. *The Biblical World: A Dictionary of Biblical Archaeology*. Grand Rapids, Mich.: Baker Book House, 1966.
_____, and Vos, Howard F. *The Wycliffe Historical Geography of the Holy Lands*. Chicago: Moody Press, 1967.
Power, A. D. *The Proverbs of Solomon*. New York: Longmans, Green and Co., 1949.
Price, Ira M. *The Ancestry of Our English Bible*. 2nd ed., rev. New York: Harper and Brothers, 1949.
_____. *The Dramatic Story of Old Testament History*. 4th ed. New York: Fleming H. Revell, 1945.
_____. *The Monuments and the Old Testament*. 17th ed. Philadelphia: The Judson Press, 1946.
_____. *A Syllabus of Old Testament History*. 8th ed. New York: Fleming H. Revell, 1912.
Pritchard, James B., ed. *The Ancient Near East: An Anthology of Texts and Pictures*. Princeton: Princeton University Press; London: Oxford University Press, 1958.
_____. *Archaeology and the Old Testament*. Princeton, N.J.: Princeton University Press, 1958.
Purkiser, W. T. *Conflicting Concepts of Holiness*. Kansas City, Mo.: Beacon Hill Press, 1953.
Qualben, Lars Pederson. *A History of the Christian Church*. Rev. New York: Thomas Nelson and Sons, 1936.
Rad, Gerhard, von. *Old Testament Theology*. Vol. I: *The Theology of Israel's Historical Traditions*. Translated by D. M. G. Stalker. Vol. II: *The Theology of Israel's Prophetic Traditions*. New York: Harper & Row, 1962, 1965.

Bibliography

Ralston, Thomas N. *The Elements of Divinity.* Nashville: Publishing House of the M.E. Church, South, 1919.

Ramm, Bernard. *The Christian View of Science and Scripture.* Grand Rapids, Mich.: Wm. B. Eerdmans Co., 1954.

Ramsay, W. M. *The Church in the Roman Empire Before* A.D. 170. New York and London: G. P. Putnam's Sons, n.d.

Ramsey, Paul. *Basic Christian Ethics.* New York: Charles Scribner's Sons, 1950.

Rappoport, A. S. *The Pslams.* London: The Centenary Press, 1935.

Rashdall, Hastings. *The Idea of Atonement in Christian Theology.* London: Macmillan Co., 1920.

Rauschenbusch, Walter. *Christianity and the Social Crisis.* New York: Macmillan Co., 1920.

———. *A Gospel for the Social Awakening.* New York: Association Press, 1950.

———. *The Social Principles of Jesus.* New York: Association Press, 1916.

Raven, John H. *Old Testament Introduction, General and Special.* New York: Fleming H. Revell, 1910.

Read, David H. C. *The Christian Faith.* London: English Universities Press, 1955.

Redford, M. E. *The Rise of the Church of the Nazarene.* Kansas City, Mo.: Nazarene Publishing House, 1948.

Rees, Paul S. *Stir Up the Gift.* Grand Rapids, Mich.: Zondervan Publishing House, 1952.

Reid, J. K. S. *The Authority of Scripture.* London: Methuen and Co., 1957.

Renckens, Henry. *The Religion of Israel.* Translated by N. B. Smith. New York: Sheed and Ward, 1966.

Reno, Cora. *Evolution: Fact or Theory?* Chicago: The Moody Press, 1953.

Rice, John M. *The Old Testament in the Life of Today.* New York: Macmillan Co., 1920.

Richardson, Alan, ed. *Theological Word Book of the Bible.* London: S.C.M. Press, 1950; New York: Macmillan Co., 1955.

Richardson, Cyril C. *The Church Through the Centuries.* New York: Charles Scribner's Sons, 1938.

Riggs, James Stevenson. *A History of the Jewish People During the Maccabean and Roman Periods.* New York: Charles Scribner's Sons, 1908.

Ringenberg, Loyal R. *The Word of God in History.* Butler, Ind.: The Higley Press, 1953.

Ringgren, Helmer. *Israelite Religion.* Philadelphia: Fortress Press, 1966.

———. *The Messiah in the Old Testament.* Studies in Biblical Theology, no. 18. Chicago: Alec R. Allenson, 1956.

Robertson, A. T. *The Pharisees and Jesus.* New York: Charles Scribner's Sons, 1920.

Robinson, Edward. *Biblical Researches in Palestine and in the Adjacent Regions.* Boston: Crocker and Brewster, 1868.

———. *Later Biblical Researches in Palestine and in the Adjacent Regions.* Boston: Crocker and Brewster, 1856.

Robinson, H. Wheeler, *The History of Israel,* Studies in Theology, no. 42. London: Duckworth Press, 1957.

———. *The Old Testament, Its Making and Meaning.* Nashville: Cokesbury Press, 1932.

———. *The Religious Ideas of the Old Testament.* New York: Charles Scribner's Sons, 1913.

Robinson, Theodore. *The Poetry of the Old Testament.* London: Duckworth, 1947.

Rogers, A. K. *A Student's History of Philosophy.* 3rd ed. New York: Macmillan Co., 1932.

Romanoff, Paul. *Onomasticon of Palestine.* New York: American Academy of Jewish Research, 1937.

Roop, Hervin U. *Christian Ethics.* New York: Fleming H. Revell, 1926.

Rowley, Harold H. *The Biblical Doctrine of Election.* London: Lutterworth Press, 1950.

———. *The Faith of Israel.* Philadelphia: Westminster Press, 1956.

———, ed. *The Old Testament and Modern Study.* New York: Oxford University Press, 1951.

———. *The Rediscovery of the Old Testament.* London: James Clarke and Co., 1945.

———. *The Unity of the Bible.* Philadelphia: Westminster Press, 1953.

———. *Worship in Ancient Israel: Its Forms and Meaning.* Philadelphia: Fortress Press, 1967.

Rose, Herbert J. *Ancient Roman Religion.* London: Hutchinson's University Library, n.d.

Rosenau, William. *Jewish Ceremonial Institutions and Customs.* New York: Bloch Publishing Co., 1929.

Rostovtzeff, M. *A History of the Ancient World.* Vol. II: *Rome.* Translated by J. D. Duff. Oxford: Clarendon Press, 1928.

———. *The Social and Economic History of the Hellenistic World.* 3 vols. Oxford: Clarendon Press, 1941.

Roth, Cecil. *The Casale Pilgrim.* London: Soncino Press, 1919.

Rowley, Harold H. "Israel, History of" In *Interpreter's Dictionary of the Bible.* New York: Abingdon Press, 1962, vol. II, pp. 750–765.

———. *From Joseph to Joshua.* London: Oxford University Press, 1950.

———. *From Moses to Qumran: Studies in the Old Testament.* London: Lutterworth Press, 1963.

———. *The Rediscovery of the Old Testament.* Philadelphia: Westminster Press, 1946.

———. *The Zadokite Fragments and the Dead Sea Scrolls.* Oxford: Basil Blackwell, 1952.

Runciman, Steven. *A History of the Crusades.* Cambridge: University Press, 1951.

Sachar, Abram Leon. *A History of the Jews.* 2nd ed., rev. New York: Alfred A. Knopf, 1940.

Salmon, Edward T. *A History of the Roman World from 30* B.C. *to* A.D. 138. New York: Macmillan Company, 1944.

Salmon, F. J. *Palestine of the Crusades.* Jaffa, 1937.

Sampey, John R. *The Heart of the Old Testament.* Rev. Nashville: Broadman Press, 1922.

———. *Syllabus for Old Testament Study.* New York: George H. Doran Co., 1924.

Sanday, William. *Sacred Sites of the Gospels.* Oxford: Oxford University Press, 1903.

Sandmel, Samuel. *Herod: Profile of a Tyrant.* Philadelphia: J. B. Lippincott Co., 1967.

Sangster, W. E. *The Path to Perfection.* New York: Abingdon-Cokesbury, 1943.

Sauer, Erich. *The Dawn of World Redemption.* Grand Rapids, Mich.: Wm. B. Eerdmans Co., 1952.

———. *From Eternity to Eternity.* Grand Rapids, Mich.: Wm. B. Eerdmans Co., 1954.

———. *The Triumph of the Crucified.* Grand Rapids, Mich.: Wm. B. Eerdmans Co., 1952.

Sawtelle, Henry A. "The Angel of Jehovah." *Bibliotheca Sacra and Biblical Expositor* 16 (1859): 805–35.

Sayce, A. H. *Babylonians and Assyrians, Life and Customs.* New York: Charles Scribner's Sons, 1909.

———. *Fresh Light from Ancient Monuments.* New York: Fleming H. Revell, 1895.

Scholer, David M. *A Basic Bibliographic Guide for New Testament Exegesis.* Grand Rapids, Mich.: Wm. B. Eerdmans Co., 1973.

Schroeder, Fredrick W. *Preaching the Word with Authority.* Philadelphia: Westminster Press, 1954.

Shubert, Kurt. *The Dead Sea Community: Its Origin and Teachings.* Translated by J. W. Doberstein. London: Adam & Charles Black, 1959.

Schweitzer, Albert. *The Quest of the Historical Jesus.* New York: Macmillan Co., 1922.

Scroggie, W. Graham. *A Guide to the Gospels.* London: Pickering and Inglis, 1948.

_____. *Know Your Bible.* 2 vols. London: Pickering & Inglis, 1940.

_____. *The Unfolding Drama of Redemption.* Grand Rapids, Mich.: Zondervan Publishing House, 1970.

Segal, J. B. *Edessa: The Blessed City.* Oxford: Clarendon Press, 1970.

Serao, Matilda. *In the Company of Jesus.* Translated by Richard Davey. London: Thomas Nelson and Sons, n.d.

Sheldon, Henry Clay. *History of Christian Doctrine.* 2 vols. New York: Harper, 1886.

Shelton, O. L. *The Church Functioning Effectively.* St. Louis: Christian Board of Publication, 1946.

Shepard, J. W. *The Life and Letters of St. Paul.* Grand Rapids, Mich.: Wm. B. Eerdmans Co., 1950.

_____. *Basic Introduction to the New Testament.* Grand Rapids, Mich.: Wm. B. Eerdmans Co., 1964.

Shield Bible Study Series. 18 vols. Grand Rapids, Mich.: Baker Book House, 1957—.

Simons, J. *Jerusalem in the Old Testament.* Leiden: E. J. Brill, 1952.

Simpson, John E. *Faithful Also in Much.* New York: Fleming H. Revell, 1948.

Skeel, C. A. J. *Travel in the First Century.* Cambridge: University Press, 1901.

Souter, Alexander. *The Text and Canon of the New Testament.* New York: Charles Scribner's Sons, 1923.

Smail, R. *Crusading Warfare, 1097 and 1193.* Cambridge: University Press, 1956.

Smart, W. A. *Still the Bible Speaks.* New York: Abingdon-Cokesbury, 1948.

Smith, C. Ryder. *The Bible Doctrine of Man.* London: Epworth Press, 1951.

_____. *The Bible Doctrine of Sin.* London: Epworth Press, 1953.

Smith, David. *The Days of His Flesh.* New York: George H. Doran Co., n.d.

Smith, George Adam. *The Historical Geography of the Holy Land.* 15th ed. New York: A. C. Armstrong & Son, 1909.

_____. *Jerusalem: The Topography, Economics and History from the Earliest Times to A.D. 70.* 2 vols. New York: A. C. Armstrong & Son, 1908.

Smith, George D., ed. *The Teaching of the Catholic Church.* 2 vols. New York: Macmillan Co., 1955.

Smith, Hannah Whitall. *The Christian's Secret of a Happy Life.* Rev. Boston: The Christian Witness Company, 1885.

Smith, Henry P. *Old Testament History.* New York: Charles Scribner's Sons, 1915.

Smith, Timothy L. *Revivalism and Social Reform.* New York: Abingdon Press, 1957.

Smith, Wilbur M. *Profitable Bible Study.* Boston: W. A. Wilde Co., 1939.

Smith, William. *Old Testament History.* New York: American Book Company, n.d.

Smyth, J. Patterson. *How to Read the Bible.* New York: James Pott and Co., 1925.

Snaith, Norman H. *The Distinctive Ideas of the Old Testament.* Philadelphia: Westminster Press, 1946.

_____. *The Jews from Cyrus to Herod.* New York: Abingdon Press, 1956.

Speer, Robert E. *The Finality of Jesus Christ.* New York: Fleming H. Revell, 1933.

Spence, H. D. M., and Exell, Joseph S. *The Pulpit Commentary.* 8 vols. Grand Rapids, Mich.: Wm. B. Eerdmans Co., 1959.

Sperry, Willard L. *Religion in America.* New York: Macmillan Co., 1947.

Spurrier, William A. *Guide to the Christian Faith.* New York: Charles Scribner's Sons, 1952.

Stanton, V. H. "New Testament Canon." In Hastings' *Dictionary of the Bible,* III, 529b–542b. New York: Charles Scribner's Sons, 1902.

Stearns, O. S. *Introduction to the Books of the Old Testament.* New York: Silver, Burdett and Co., 1892.

Stevenson, William B. *The Poem of Job.* London: Oxford University Press, 1947.

Stewart, James S. *A Faith in Proclaim.* New York: Charles Scribner's Sons, 1953.

_____. *The Life and Teaching of Jesus Christ.* New York: Abingdon Press, n.d.

_____. *A Man in Christ.* New York: Harper and Brothers, n.d.

Stinson, Ernest C. *The Temple of King Solomon.* No publisher given, 1934.

Stoffel, E. L. *His Kingdom Is Forever.* Richmond: John Knox Press, 1956.

Stone, John Timothy. *Winning Men.* New York: Fleming H. Revell, 1940.

Stott, John R. W. *Basic Christianity.* Grand Rapids, Mich.: Wm. B. Eerdmans Co., 1958.

Strong, James. *Exhaustive Concordance of the Bible.* New York: Abingdon Press, 1890.

Stuart, Moses. *A Commentary on the Epistle to the Hebrews.* Edited by R. D. C. Robbins. 4th ed. Andover: Draper, 1864.

Stump, Joseph. *The Christian Faith: A System of Dogmatics.* Philadelphia: The Muhlenberg Press, 1942.

Sweet, William Warren. *Revivalism in America.* New York: Charles Scribner's Sons, 1944.

Sykes, Percy H. *A Brief History of King Solomon's Reign.* Philadelphia: Hiram Abibb, 1929.

Tarn, W. W. *Alexander the Great.* Vol. I: *Narrative.* Cambridge: University Press, 1948.

Tasker, R. V. G. *The Old Testament in the New Testament.* Grand Rapids, Mich.: Wm. B. Eerdmans Co., 1954.

Taylor, Richard S. *A Right Conception of Sin.* Kansas City, Mo.: Beacon Hill Press, 1945.

Taylor, Vincent. *The Atonement in New Testament Teaching.* London: Epworth Press, 1941.

_____. *The Gospel According to St. Mark.* London: Macmillan Company, 1953.

_____. *The Person of Christ in New Testament Teaching.* New York: Macmillan Co., 1958.

Taylor, William M. *David, King of Israel.* New York: Harper and Brothers, 1874.

Temple, William. *Foundations.* London: Macmillan and Co., 1912.

_____. *Nature, Man, and God.* London: Macmillan and Co., 1934.

Tenney, Merrill C. *New Testament Survey.* Grand Rapids, Mich.: Wm. B. Eerdmans Co., 1961.

_____. *New Testament Times.* Grand Rapids, Mich.: Wm. B. Eerdmans Co., 1965.

_____, ed. *The Zondervan Pictorial Bible Dictionary.* Grand Rapids, Mich.: Zondervan Publishing House, 1963.

Terrien, Samuel. "History of the Interpretation of the Bible; Modern Period," *Interpreter's Bible,* vol. I. New York: Abingdon Press, 1952, pp. 127–141.

Bibliography ———. *The Psalms and Their Meaning for Today.* New York: Bobbs-Merrill Co., 1952.

Thelen, Mary F. *Man as Sinner.* New York: King's Crown Press, 1946.

Thiessen, Henry C. *Introduction to the New Testament.* Grand Rapids, Mich.: Wm. B. Eerdmans Co., 1943.

Thomas, D. Winton, ed. *Archaeology and Old Testament Study.* Oxford: Clarendon Press, 1967.

Thompson, Edward. *Crusaders Coast.* London: Ernest Benn, 1929.

Thompson, J. A. *The Bible and Archaeology.* Grand Rapids, Mich.: Wm. B. Eerdmans Co., 1962.

Thomson, William M. *Central Palestine and Phoenicia.* The Land and the Book, vol. 2. Hartford, Conn.: S. S. Scranton Co., 1908.

Tillett, Wilbur F. *Personal Salvation.* Nashville: Cooksbury Press, 1930.

Titus, Harold H. *Ethics for Today.* New York: American Book Co., 1947.

Torrey, Reuben A. *The Person and Work of the Holy Spirit.* New York: Fleming H. Revell, 1910.

Toynbee, Arnold, ed. *The Crucible of Christianity: Judaism, Hellenism and the Historical Background to the Christian Faith.* London: Thames and Hudson, 1969.

Tristram, H. B. *The Land of Israel: A Journal of Travels in Palestine.* London: Society for Promoting Christian Knowledge, 1865.

Trueblood, D. Elton. *The Logic of Belief.* New York: Harper and Brothers, 1942.

———. *Philosophy of Religion.* New York: Harper and Brothers, 1957.

———. *The Trustworthiness of Religious Experience.* London: George Allen and Unwin, 1939.

Trueblood, D. Elton, and Trueblood, Pauline. *The Recovery of Family Life.* New York: Harper and Brothers, 1953.

Tsanoff, R. A. *The Moral Ideals of Our Civilization.* New York: E. P. Dutton and Co., 1942.

———. *Ethics.* Rev. New York: Harper and Brothers, 1955.

Tucker, T. G. *Life in the Roman World of Nero and St. Paul.* New York: Macmillan Company, 1924.

Turner, George A. *Historical Geography of the Holy Land.* Grand Rapids, Mich.: Baker Book House, 1973.

———. *The More Excellent Way.* Winona Lake, Ind.: Light and Life Press, 1952.

Turnowsky, W., ed. *Tour Guide to Israel.* Tel Aviv: Litour, 1952.

Turretin, Francis. *The Atonement.* New York: Board of Publication of the Reformed Protestant Dutch Church, 1859.

Uhlhorn, Gerhard. *The Conflict of Christianity and Heathenism.* Edited and translated by Egbert C. Smyth and C. J. H. Ropes. Rev. New York: Charles Scribner's Sons, 1901.

———. *Archaeology and the New Testament.* Grand Rapids, Mich.: Zondervan Publishing House, 1964.

Unger, Merrill F. *Archaeology and the Old Testament.* Grand Rapids: Zondervan Publishing House, 1954.

———. *Introductory Guide to the Old Testament.* Grand Rapids, Mich.: Zondervan Publishing House, 1951.

———. *Unger's Bible Dictionary.* Chicago: Moody Press, 1957.

———. *Unger's Bible Handbook.* Chicago: Moody Press, 1966.

Van Diest, John W. "A Study of the Theophanies of the Old Testament." Th.M. thesis, Dallas Theological Seminary, 1966.

Vilnay, Zev. *The Guide to Israel.* Jerusalem: Ahiever, 1968.

———. *The New Israel Atlas: Bible to Present Day.* Jerusalem: Israel University Press, 1968.

Vincent, L. H. *Jerusalem de L'Ancien Testament: Recherches d'Archeologie et d'Histoire.* Paris: Librarie Lecoffre, 1954.

Vincent, Marvin R. *Word Studies in the New Testament.* 4 vols. Grand Rapids, Mich.: Wm. B. Eerdmans Co., 1957.

Vine, W. E. *Expository Dictionary of New Testament Words.* 4 vols. London: Oliphants, Ltd., 1939–41.

———. *An Expository Dictionary of New Testament Words.* Old Tappan, N.J.: Fleming H. Revell, 1956.

Von Allmen, J.-J., ed. *A Companion to the Bible.* New York: The Oxford Press, 1958.

———. *Biblical Theology.* Grand Rapids, Mich.: Wm. B. Eerdmans Co., 1954.

Vos, Geerhardus. *The Teaching of Jesus Concerning the Kingdom of God and His Church.* New York: American Tract Society, 1903.

Vos, Howard F. *Beginnings in the New Testament.* Chicago: Moody Press, 1973.

———. *Religions in a Changing World.* Chicago: Moody Press, 1959.

Vriezen, Thomas. *An Outline of Old Testament Theology.* Translated by S. Neuijen. Oxford: Basil Blackwell, 1958.

———. Walvoord, John F. *Jesus Christ Our Lord.* Chicago: Moody, 1969.

———, ed. *Inspiration and Interpretation.* Grand Rapids, Mich.: Wm. B. Eerdmans Co., 1957.

Warren, C., and Conder, C. R. *Survey of Western Palestine and Jerusalem.* London: Palestine Exploration Fund, 1884.

Waterman, Leroy. *The Song of Songs.* Ann Arbor: University of Michigan Press, 1948.

Watson, George D. *Spiritual Feasts.* Cincinnati: Revivalist Office, 1904.

Watson, J. B., ed. *The Church.* London: Pickering and Inglis, Ltd., 1949.

Weatherhead, Leslie D. *The Will of God.* New York: Abingdon-Cokesbury, 1944.

Welch, Claude. *In This Name.* New York: Charles Scribner's Sons, 1952.

Wesley, John. *Explanatory Notes upon the New Testament.* London: The Epworth Press, 1950.

———. *The Plain Account of Christian Perfection.* Boston: The Christian Witness Co., n.d.

———. *Sermons.* 2 vols. New York: Lane and Scott, 1852.

———. *Works.* 14 vols. Kansas City, Mo.: Nazarene Publishing House, 1958.

Wesley, John, et al. *New Testament Commentary.* Grand Rapids, Mich.: Baker Book House, 1972.

Westcott, B. F. *General Survey of the History of the Canon of the New Testament.* 7th ed. London: Macmillan & Co., 1896.

Westermann, Claus, ed., *Essays on Old Testament Hermeneutics.* Translated and edited by James Luther Mays. Richmond, Va.: John Knox Press, 1963.

Whale, J. S. *Christian Doctrine.* New York: Macmillan Co., 1945.

White, Stephen S. *Essential Christian Beliefs.* Kansas City, Mo.: Beacon Hill Press, n.d.

Whitehead, John. *The Life of the Rev. John Wesley, M. A.* New York: The United States Book Company, n.d.

Whitesell, Faris D. *Basic New Testament Evangelism.* Grand Rapids, Mich.: Zondervan Publishing House, 1959.

Wieand, Albert Cassel. *A New Harmony of the Gospels.* Grand Rapids, Mich.: Wm. B. Eerdmans Co., 1953.

Wiener, Harold M. "The Rama of Samuel." *Journal of the Palestine Oriental Society,* 1927.

Wiley, H. Orton. *Christian Theology.* 3 vols. Kansas City, Mo.: Beacon Hill Press, 1940.

_____ and Culbertson, Paul T. *Introduction to Christian Theology.* Kansas City, Mo.: Nazarene Publishing House, 1945.

Wilkes, A. Paget. *The Dynamic of Redemption.* Kansas City, Mo.: Beacon Hill Press, 1946.

Willett, Herbert L. *Our Bible: Its Origin, Character, and Value.* Chicago: The Christian Century Press, 1917.

William, Archbishop of Tyre. *A History of Deeds Beyond the Sea,* vol. 2. Translated by E. A. Babcock and A. C. Krey. New York: Columbia University Press, 1943.

Williams, Daniel Day. *God's Grace and Man's Hope.* New York: Harper and Brothers, 1949.

Williams, George. *The Student's Commentary on the Holy Scriptures.* Grand Rapids, Mich.: Kregal Publications, 1971.

Williams, R. T. *Temptation: A Neglected Theme.* Kansas City, Mo.: Nazarene Publishing House, 1920.

Williams, Walter G. *Archaeology in Biblical Research.* New York: Abingdon Press, 1965.

Wilson, Edmund. *The Scrolls from the Dead Sea.* New York: Oxford University Press, 1955.

Wilson, Capt. Warren. *The Recovery of Jerusalem: A Narrative of Exploration and Discovery in the City and the Holy Land.* Edited by Walter Morrison. New York: D. Appleton & Co., 1871.

Winchester, Olive M., and Price, Ross E. *Crisis Experiences in the Greek New Testament.* Kansas City, Mo.: Beacon Hill Press, 1953.

Wiseman, Donald J. *Illustrations from Biblical Archaeology.* Grand Rapids, Mich.: Wm. B. Eerdmans Co., 1958.

Wittek, P. *The Rise of the Ottoman Empire.* London, 1938.

Wood, J. A. *Perfect Love.* Chicago: Christian Witness Co., 1905.

Wood, Nathan R. *The Secret of the Universe.* Grand Rapids, Mich.: Wm. B. Eerdmans Co., 1936.

Wright, G. Ernest, ed. *The Bible and the Ancient Near East.* Garden City, N.Y.: Doubleday and Co., 1961.

_____. *Biblical Archaeology.* 2nd ed. Philadelphia: Westminster Press, 1962.

_____. *The Challenge of Israel's Faith.* Chicago: The University of Chicago Press, 1944.

_____. *God Who Acts,* Studies in Biblical Theology, no. 8. London: S.C.M. Press, 1952.

_____. *The Old Testament Against Its Environment,* Studies in Biblical Theology, no. 2. London: S.C.M. Press, 1950.

_____. *The Old Testament and Theology.* New York: Harper & Row, 1969.

Wright, G. Ernest, and Filson, Floyd Vivian, eds. *The Westminster Historical Atlas to the Bible.* Philadelphia: Westminster Press, 1945.

Wright, G. Ernest, and Freedman, D. N., eds. *The Biblical Archaeologist Reader.* Garden City, N.Y.: Doubleday Anchor Books, 1961.

Wright, Sara Margaret. *A Brief Survey of the Bible.* Neptune, N.J.: Loizeaux Bros., 1958.

Wright, Thomas, ed. *Early Travels in Palestine.* New York: KTAV Publishing House, 1948, 1968.

Wuest, Kenneth S. *Word Studies in the Greek New Testament.* 4 vols. Grand Rapids, Mich.: Wm. B. Eerdmans Co., 1966.

Yates, Kyle M. *Preaching from the Prophets.* New York: Harper and Brothers, 1942.

_____. *Preaching from the Psalms.* New York: Harper and Brothers, 1948.

_____. *Studies in Psalms.* Nashville: Broadman Press, 1953.

Yohn, David Waite. *The Christian Reader's Guide to the New Testament.* Grand Rapids, Mich.: Wm. B. Eerdmans Co., 1973.

Young, Edward J. *An Introduction to the Old Testament.* Grand Rapids, Mich.: Wm. B. Eerdmans Co., 1949.

_____. *The Study of Old Testament Theology Today.* Westwood, N.J.: Fleming H. Revell, 1959.

Young, Kimball. *Personality and the Problems of Adjustment.* New York: F. S. Crofts and Co., 1940.

Young, Robert. *Analytical Concordance to the Bible.* Grand Rapids, Mich.: Wm. B. Eerdmans Co., 1955.

Young, Warren C. *A Christian Approach to Philosophy.* Wheaton, Ill.: Van Kampen Press, 1954.

Zahn, Theodor. *Introduction to the New Testament.* 3 vols. Grand Rapids, Mich.: Kregel Publications, 1953.

Zenos, Andrew C. *Compendium of Church History.* Philadelphia: Presbyterian Board of Publication, 1896.

Zwemer, Samuel M. *The Moslem Doctrine of God.* New York: Young People's Missionary Movement, 1905.

549

Subject Index

Author Index

561

Scripture Index